# Minnesota Legal Research Guide
## Second Edition

# Minnesota Legal Research Guide
## Second Edition

*by*

### John Tessner
*Head of Public Services*
*Hamline University Law Library*

### Brenda Wolfe
*Director*
*Industrial Relations Center Reference Room*
*Carlson School of Management*
*University of Minnesota*

### George R. Jackson
*Reference Librarian*
*University of Minnesota Law Library*

William S. Hein & Co., Inc.
Buffalo, New York
2002

*Library of Congress Cataloging-In-Publication Data*

Tessner, John.
    Minnesota legal research guide / by John Tessner, Brenda Wolfe, George R. Jackson—2nd ed.
    p. cm.
    Rev. ed. of: Minnesota legal research guide / by Arlette M. Soderberg and Barbara L. Golden. 1985.
    Includes bibliographical references and index.
    ISBN 1-57588-696-0 (cloth : alk. paper)
    1. Legal research—Minnesota. I. Wolfe, Brenda. II. Jackson, George R. III. Soderberg, Arlette M. Minnesota legal research guide. IV. Title.
KFM5475 .S63 2001
340'.07'20776—dc21

2001039470

Copyright © 2002 William S. Hein & Co., Inc.
All rights reserved.

Printed in the United States of America

This volume is printed on acid-free paper by
William S. Hein & Co., Inc.

# DEDICATION

To my Ma and Dad
R.I.P.


To J.T.
a.k.a. Mr. Know-It-All
a.k.a. Mr. Library

# Table of Contents

| | |
|---|---|
| About the Authors | xxi |
| Introduction | xxiii |
| **Chapter One. Historical Beginnings and the Minnesota Constitution** | 1 |
| § 110. Under Foreign Jurisdiction | 1 |
| § 111. French Sovereignty | 2 |
| § 112. English Sovereignty | 3 |
| § 120. United States Sovereignty | 4 |
| § 121. Minnesota Territory | 5 |
| § 122. Minnesota Statehood | 5 |
| § 130. The Minnesota Constitution | 6 |
| § 131. Constitutional Convention of 1857 | 6 |
| § 132. Constitutional Reform | 7 |
| § 132.1. Minnesota Constitutional Commission, 1947–1948 | 7 |
| § 132.2. Minnesota Constitutional Study Commission, 1971–1973 | 7 |
| § 133. Restructured Constitution of 1974 | 8 |
| § 134. Procedures for Changing the Constitution | 9 |
| § 134.1. Convention | 9 |
| § 134.2. Amendments | 9 |
| § 135. Sources Containing Constitutional Documents | 10 |
| § 136. Sources of Constitutional Interpretation | 11 |
| **Chapter Two. Legislation** | 13 |
| § 210. Legislative Offices that Serve the Public | 13 |
| § 220. Legislature | 15 |
| § 221. Sessions | 15 |
| § 222. Members | 16 |
| § 223. Apportionment | 16 |
| § 224. Committees | 17 |
| § 225. Rules | 18 |
| § 226. Commissions and Offices that Aid the Legislature | 18 |
| § 226.1. Attorney General | 19 |
| § 226.2. Commission on Uniform State Laws | 19 |
| § 226.3. Legislative Reference Library | 19 |

§ 226.4. Minnesota Historical Society  20
§ 226.5. Revisor of Statutes  20
**§ 230. Enactment of Legislation**  **21**
§ 231. Drafting  21
§ 232. Introduction of the Bill  22
§ 233. Reading  23
§ 234. Committee Hearings  23
§ 235. Calendars  24
§ 236. Conference Committees  24
§ 237. Action by the Governor  25
§ 238. Effective Dates  25
§ 239. Resolutions  25
**§ 240. Legislative History**  **26**
§ 241. Sources of Legislative History  26
§ 241.1. Journals  26
§ 241.2. Committee Books  29
§ 241.3. Tape Recordings  30
§ 241.4. Locating Bills  30
§ 241.41. Bills Introduced During a Current Legislative Session  31
§ 241.42. Bills Introduced During Prior Legislative Sessions  32
§ 241.5. Legislative Research  33
§ 242. Use of Legislative History to Determine Legislative Intent  34
§ 243. Commercial Publishers of Legislative Materials  35
§ 243.1. Phillips Legislative Service  35
§ 243.2. Minnesota Government Report  35
§ 243.3. St. Paul Legal Ledger  36
§ 243.4. Politics in Minnesota  36
§ 243.5. Checks and Balances—Minnesota  36
§ 243.6. Minnesota E-Democracy Political Desktop  37
§ 243.7. Lexis Publishing  37
§ 243.8. Westlaw  38
§ 243.9. Other Sources  39
**§ 250. Session Laws**  **40**
§ 251. Contents of Official Session Laws  41
§ 252. General and Special Laws  41
§ 253. Indexes and Tables  42
§ 254. Minnesota Session Law Service  43
§ 255. LEXIS-NEXIS Minnesota Advance Legislative Service  43
§ 256. Curative Acts  44

## Table of Contents

| | |
|---|---|
| § 260. Statutes | 45 |
|   § 261. Compilations, Revisions, Codes | 45 |
|     § 261.1. Compilations | 45 |
|     § 261.2. Revisions | 45 |
|     § 261.3. Codes | 46 |
|   § 262. Minnesota Statutes | 46 |
|     § 262.1. Arrangement | 47 |
|     § 262.2. Research Aids | 47 |
|     § 262.3. Features | 48 |
|     § 262.4. Index and Supplementation | 49 |
|     § 262.5. Minnesota Statutes on the Web | 49 |
|     § 262.6. Minnesota Statutes—Subscription Services | 49 |
|   § 263. Minnesota Statutes Annotated | 49 |
|     § 263.1. Arrangement | 50 |
|     § 263.2. Research Aids | 50 |
|     § 263.3. Special Features | 50 |
|     § 263.4. Tables and Index | 52 |
|     § 263.5. Supplementation | 52 |
|   § 264. Statutory Construction | 52 |
| **§ 270. Other Sources of Law** | **53** |
|   § 271. Interstate Compacts and Reciprocal Statutes | 53 |
|   § 272. Uniform State Laws | 54 |
|   § 273. Local Lawmaking Bodies | 54 |
|   § 274. Initiative and Referendum | 57 |
|   § 275. Compilations of State Statutes on One Subject | 57 |
|     § 275.1. Sources Providing Text or Digest of Laws | 58 |
|     § 275.2. Sources Providing Statutory Citations | 59 |
|     § 275.3. Bibliographic Sources | 60 |
|     § 275.4. Other Sources | 61 |
| **Chapter Three. Executive and Administrative Law** | **63** |
| **§ 310. Constitutional Officers** | **63** |
|   § 311. Governor | 64 |
|   § 312. Secretary of State | 64 |
|   § 313. Attorney General | 65 |
|     § 313.1. Responsibilities | 65 |
|     § 313.2. Opinions | 66 |
|       § 313.21. Hardcopy Availability of Opinions | 66 |
|       § 313.22. Electronic Availability of Opinions | 67 |
|       § 313.23. Research Aids | 67 |
| **§ 320. Administrative Agencies** | **68** |
|   § 321. Administrative Rules | 69 |
|     § 321.1. State Register (Weekly, July 1976 to date) | 71 |
|     § 321.2. Minnesota Compiled Rules | 71 |

§ 321.21. Rules before 1970   71
§ 321.22. Rules from 1970 to 1976   72
§ 321.23. Rules from 1976 to 1977   72
§ 321.24. Rules from 1977 to 1982   72
§ 321.25. Rules from 1982 to 1983   72
§ 321.26. Rules after 1983   73
§ 321.3. Updating Agency Rules   74
§ 321.4. Compilations of State Regulations on One Subject   74
§ 322. Office of Administrative Hearings (OAH)   75
§ 323. Agency Decisions   75
**§ 330. Administrative Courts**   **76**
§ 331. Tax Court   76
§ 332. Workers' Compensation Court of Appeals   77
**§ 340. Public Access and Privacy Rights**   **77**
**§ 350. State and Local Documents**   **78**

**Chapter Four. Judiciary**   **83**

**§ 410. Minnesota Courts**   **83**
§ 411. Judges and Juries   84
§ 411.1. Judges   84
§ 411.2. Juries   84
§ 411.21. Grand Jury   84
§ 411.22. Petit Jury   85
§ 412. Minnesota State Courts   87
§ 412.1. Supreme Court   87
§ 412.11. Supreme Court Jurisdiction and Powers   87
§ 412.12. Supreme Court Justices   88
§ 412.13. Personnel that Aid the Supreme Court   89
§ 412.14. Supreme Court Procedures   90
§ 412.2. Court of Appeals   91
§ 412.21. Court of Appeals Jurisdiction   91
§ 412.22. Court of Appeals Judges   91
§ 412.23. Personnel that Aid the Court of Appeals   91
§ 412.24. Court of Appeals Procedures   92
§ 412.3. District Court   93
§ 412.31. District Court Jurisdiction   93
§ 412.32. District Court Judges   93
§ 412.33. Personnel that Aid the District Court   94
§ 412.34. District Court Procedures and Records   95
§ 412.4. County Courts   95
§ 412.5. Justice and Municipal Courts   96
§ 412.6. Conciliation Courts   97
§ 412.7. Court System in Hennepin and Ramsey Counties   98

### Table of Contents

|   |   |
|---|---|
| § 412.71. District Courts in Hennepin and Ramsey Counties | 98 |
| § 412.72. Municipal Courts in Hennepin and Ramsey Counties | 98 |
| § 412.73. Conciliation Courts in Hennepin and Ramsey Counties | 99 |
| § 412.74. Housing Courts in Hennepin and Ramsey Counties | 99 |
| § 413. Court Unification | 99 |
| § 414. Federal Courts in Minnesota | 100 |
| **§ 420. Reports of Cases** | **101** |
| § 421. Minnesota Appellate Courts | 101 |
| § 421.1. Minnesota Reports | 102 |
| § 421.2. Northwestern Reporter | 103 |
| § 421.3. Minnesota Reporter | 104 |
| § 421.4. Current Opinions | 104 |
| § 422. Minnesota Trial Courts | 105 |
| § 423. Federal Courts | 106 |
| **§ 430. Records and Briefs** | **107** |
| § 431. Briefs | 107 |
| § 432. Record or Appendix | 107 |
| § 433. Indexes | 108 |
| § 434. Briefs on Microfiche | 108 |
| § 435. Law Library Holdings | 109 |
| § 435.1. Records and Briefs in Cases Decided by Minnesota Appellate Courts | 109 |
| § 435.2. Records and Briefs in Cases Decided by Minnesota Trial Courts | 110 |
| § 435.3. Records and Briefs in Cases Decided by the U.S. Supreme Court | 111 |
| § 435.4. Records and Briefs in Cases Decided by Federal Courts in Minnesota | 111 |
| § 435.41. Eighth Circuit Court of Appeals | 111 |
| § 435.42. U.S. District Court | 111 |
| **§ 440. Rules of Court** | **112** |
| § 441. Court Rulemaking Procedures | 113 |
| § 442. Professional Rules for Attorneys and Judges | 114 |
| § 443. Sources of Court Rules | 114 |
| § 444. Jury Instruction Guides | 115 |
| § 445. Minnesota Sentencing Guidelines | 116 |
| **§ 450. Alternative Dispute Resolution** | **116** |

| | |
|---|---|
| § 460. Judicial Boards and Organizations | 118 |
| § 461. Conferences | 118 |
| § 462. Professional Boards | 118 |
| § 462.1. Board on Judicial Standards | 118 |
| § 462.2. State Board of Law Examiners | 119 |
| § 462.3. Lawyers Professional Responsibility Board | 119 |
| § 462.4. State Board of Legal Certification | 120 |
| § 462.5. Client Security Board | 121 |
| § 463. Continuing Education | 121 |
| § 463.1. Board of Continuing Legal Education | 121 |
| § 463.2. Continuing Education for State Court Personnel | 122 |
| **Chapter Five. Finding Aids and Secondary Sources** | **123** |
| § 510. Digests | 124 |
| § 511. Dunnell Minnesota Digest: Fourth Edition: An Encyclopedia of Minnesota Law | 124 |
| § 512. West's Minnesota Digest 2d | 125 |
| § 513. West's Minnesota Digest 2d Law Finder | 125 |
| § 514. West's North Western Digest 2d | 126 |
| § 515. Martindale-Hubbell Law Digest | 126 |
| § 520. Citators in General | 127 |
| § 521. Shepard's Citations in General | 127 |
| § 522. Shepard's Minnesota Citations | 128 |
| § 523. Shepard's North Western Reporter Citations: A Compilation of Citations to All Cases Reported in the North Western Reporter | 129 |
| § 524. Shepard's Minnesota Citations and North Western Reporter Citations Compared | 129 |
| § 525. West's KeyCite® | 129 |
| § 526. Shepard's Online | 130 |
| § 530. Quick-Reference Tools | 130 |
| § 531. Citation of Legal Authority | 130 |
| § 532. Tables of Cases | 132 |
| § 533. Popular Name Tables | 132 |
| § 534. Parallel Citations | 133 |
| § 535. Words and Phrases | 134 |
| § 536. Directories | 135 |
| § 536.1. General Sources | 135 |
| § 536.2. Judiciary | 136 |
| § 536.3. Lawyers | 138 |
| § 536.4. Government Personnel | 141 |
| § 537. Historical Works | 143 |

## Table of Contents

| | |
|---|---|
| **§ 540. Secondary Sources** | **147** |
| § 541. Restatements | 148 |
| § 541.1. Access Tools and Special Features | 148 |
| § 541.2. Minnesota Annotations to the Restatement | 149 |
| § 542. Encyclopedias | 150 |
| § 543. Form Books | 151 |
| § 544. Annotations | 154 |
| § 545. Reports of the Judiciary and Attorney General | 154 |
| § 545.1. Selected Reports to the Supreme Court | 155 |
| § 545.2. Selected Minnesota Attorney General Reports | 159 |
| § 546. Treatises and Practice Manuals | 163 |
| § 546.1. Continuing Legal Education Publications | 164 |
| § 546.2. Selected Treatises and Practice Manuals | 165 |
| § 546.3. Popular Works | 177 |
| § 546.4. Jury Instruction Guides | 180 |
| § 546.5. Jury Verdicts, Valuation Handbooks, Etc. | 182 |
| § 546.6. Judicial Bench Books | 183 |
| § 546.7. Handbooks, Manuals, Etc. | 184 |
| § 546.8. Statistics | 186 |
| **§ 550. Legal Periodicals** | **188** |
| § 551. Research Aids | 189 |
| § 552. Major Legal Indexes | 190 |
| § 553. Other Periodical Indexes Useful to the Legal Researcher | 191 |
| § 554. Minnesota Legal Periodicals | 192 |
| § 554.1. Minnesota Legal Periodical Indexes | 192 |
| § 554.2. Law Reviews | 193 |
| § 554.3. Bar Journals | 195 |
| § 554.4. Representative Special Interest Publications or Newsletters | 197 |
| § 554.5. Periodicals That Have Ceased Publication | 201 |
| § 554.6. Legal Newspapers | 205 |
| **§ 560. Materials in Special Formats** | **207** |
| § 561. Loose-Leaf Services | 207 |
| § 562. Legal Newsletters | 207 |
| § 563. Microforms | 207 |
| § 564. CD-ROM | 208 |
| § 565. Videotapes and Audiotapes | 208 |
| § 566. Computer-Assisted Research | 208 |
| § 567. Internet Sources | 210 |

| | |
|---|---|
| **Chapter Six. Institutions and Organizations** | **213** |
| § 610. Libraries | 213 |
| § 611. Law Libraries | 214 |
| § 612. Private Law Libraries | 214 |
| § 613. Academic Law Libraries | 214 |
| § 613.1. Hamline University School of Law Library | 215 |
| § 613.2. University of Minnesota Law Library | 215 |
| § 613.3. University of Saint Thomas, School of Law Library | 215 |
| § 613.4. William Mitchell College of Law, Warren E. Burger Library | 215 |
| § 614. Government Law Libraries | 216 |
| § 614.1. Minnesota State Law Library | 216 |
| § 614.2. Federal Court Libraries | 216 |
| § 614.21. Eighth Circuit Library. Minneapolis | 217 |
| § 614.22. Eighth Circuit Library, St. Paul | 217 |
| § 615. Federal Document Depository Libraries in Minnesota | 217 |
| § 615.1. Government Publications Library | 217 |
| § 616. Minnesota State Document Depository Libraries | 217 |
| § 617. County Law Libraries | 218 |
| § 617.1. Anoka County Law Library | 220 |
| § 617.2. Dakota County Law Library | 220 |
| § 617.3. Hennepin County Law Library | 220 |
| § 617.4. Ramsey County Law Library | 220 |
| § 617.5. Saint Louis County Law Library | 220 |
| § 617.6. Scott County Law Library | 220 |
| § 617.7. Stearns County Law Library | 220 |
| § 617.8. Washington County Law Library | 220 |
| § 618. Non-Law Libraries | 221 |
| § 618.1. James J. Hill Reference Library | 222 |
| § 618.2. League of Minnesota Cities | 222 |
| § 618.3. Association of Minnesota Counties | 223 |
| § 618.4. Legislative Reference Library | 223 |
| § 618.5. Minnesota Historical Society | 223 |
| § 618.6. Metropolitan Council | 224 |
| § 618.7. University of Minnesota Human Rights Library | 224 |
| § 619. Library Organizations | 224 |
| § 619.1. Minnesota Association of Law Libraries (MALL) | 225 |
| § 619.2. Capitol Area Library Consortium (CALCO) | 226 |
| § 619.3. Special Libraries Association (SLA) | 226 |
| § 619.4. American Society for Information Science (ASIS) | 226 |
| § 619.5. Metropolitan Library Service Agency (MELSA) | 227 |
| § 619.6. Metronet | 227 |
| § 619.7. Minnesota Library Association (MLA) | 227 |

## Table of Contents

| | |
|---|---|
| **§ 620. Library School Programs** | **227** |
| § 621. College of Saint Catherine | 228 |
| § 622. University of North Texas (UNT) | 228 |
| § 623. University of Wisconsin–Milwaukee (UWM) | 228 |
| **§ 630. Law Schools** | **229** |
| § 631. Hamline University School of Law | 229 |
| § 631.1. Dispute Resolution Institute | 230 |
| § 631.2. The Dred & Harriet Scott Institute for International Human Rights | 230 |
| § 631.3. Annual Law, Religion, and Ethics Symposium | 231 |
| § 632. University of Minnesota Law School | 231 |
| § 632.1. Institute on Criminal Justice | 231 |
| § 632.2. Human Rights Center | 232 |
| § 632.3. Institute on Race & Poverty | 232 |
| § 633. University of Saint Thomas, School of Law | 232 |
| § 634. William Mitchell College of Law | 233 |
| § 634.1. Center for Conflict Management/Americord® | 233 |
| § 634.2. Center for Health Law & Policy | 233 |
| § 634.3. Center for Professional Programming | 234 |
| § 635. Alternative Dispute Resolution | 234 |
| § 635.1. American Arbitration Association (AAA)—Minnesota Regional Office | 235 |
| § 635.2. Hamline University's Dispute Resolution Institute | 235 |
| § 635.3. Center for Conflict Management/Americord® | 235 |
| **§ 640. Bar Associations** | **236** |
| § 641. Minnesota State Bar Association | 236 |
| § 642. Hennepin County Bar Association | 236 |
| § 643. Ramsey County Bar Association | 237 |
| § 644. Bar Associations in Greater Minnesota | 237 |
| § 645. Special Interest Bar Associations in Minnesota | 237 |
| **§ 650. Legislatively and Judicially Sanctioned Agencies** | **238** |
| § 650.1. Board of Pardons | 239 |
| § 650.2. Board of Judicial Standards | 239 |
| § 650.3. Client Security Board | 239 |
| § 650.4. Commission on Judicial Selection | 240 |
| § 650.5. Continuing Education for State Court Personnel | 240 |
| § 650.6. Court Information Office | 240 |
| § 650.7. Lawyers Professional Responsibility Board | 240 |
| § 650.8. Lawyers Trust Account Board | 241 |
| § 650.9. Minnesota Sentencing Guidelines Commission | 241 |
| § 650.10. Office of the State Court Administrator | 241 |
| § 650.11. Office of Administrative Hearings | 241 |
| § 650.12. State Board of Continuing Legal Education | 242 |
| § 650.13. State Board of Law Examiners | 242 |

| | |
|---|---|
| § 650.14. State Board of Legal Certification | 243 |
| § 650.15. State Board of Public Defense | 243 |
| § 650.16. State Public Defender | 243 |
| § 650.17. Tax Court | 243 |
| § 650.18. Workers' Compensation Court of Appeals | 243 |
| **§ 660. Continuing Legal Education (CLE)** | **244** |
| § 661. Advanced Legal Education | 244 |
| § 662. Minnesota Continuing Legal Education | 244 |
| § 663. Minnesota Institute of Legal Education | 245 |
| § 664. Professional Education Systems, Inc. | 245 |
| § 665. Law School Programs | 245 |
| § 666. Other Organizations | 245 |
| **§ 670. Legal Assistance** | **245** |
| § 671. Public Defenders | 247 |
| § 671.1. Federal Public Defender | 247 |
| § 671.2. State Public Defender | 247 |
| § 671.3. The Legal Advocacy Project | 248 |
| § 671.4. Public Defense Corporations | 248 |
| § 671.5. Legal Assistance to Minnesota Prisoners | 248 |
| § 671.6. Law Library Service to Prisoners Project | 249 |
| § 672. United States Attorney for the District of Minnesota | 249 |
| § 673. County Attorneys | 250 |
| § 674. Attorney General | 250 |
| § 674.1. Consumer Division | 251 |
| § 674.2. Human Rights Division | 251 |
| § 675. Legal Aid | 251 |
| § 675.1. Minnesota Legal Services Coalition (MLSC) | 252 |
| § 675.2. Minnesota Legal Services Coalition State Support Center | 256 |
| § 676. Law School Clinics | 256 |
| § 676.1. Hamline University School of Law | 257 |
| § 676.2. William Mitchell College of Law | 257 |
| § 676.3. University of Minnesota Law School, Practical Skills Programs | 258 |
| § 676.4. University Student Legal Service | 258 |
| § 677. Public Education and Referral Services | 259 |
| § 678. Pro Bono Programs | 260 |
| § 678.1. Minnesota Justice Foundation | 260 |
| **§ 680. Support Personnel** | **261** |
| § 681. Legal Administrators | 261 |
| § 681.1. Association of Legal Administrators | 262 |
| § 681.2. Minnesota Legal Administrators Association | 262 |

## Table of Contents

| | |
|---|---|
| § 682. Legal Secretaries | 262 |
|     § 682.1. National Association of Legal Secretaries (NALS) Resource Center | 262 |
|     § 682.2. National Association of Legal Secretaries— Twin Cities Chapter | 263 |
| § 683. Legal Assistants | 263 |
|     § 683.1. National Association of Legal Assistants | 263 |
|     § 683.2. American Association for Paralegal Education | 264 |
|     § 683.3. Minnesota Paralegal Association | 264 |
|     § 683.4. Two-Year Programs | 265 |
|         § 683.41. Inver Hills Community College, Paralegal Program | 265 |
|         § 683.42. Itasca Community College | 265 |
|         § 683.43. North Hennepin Community College, Paralegal Program | 265 |
|         § 683.44. Proprietary Programs | 266 |
|     § 683.5. Four-Year Programs | 266 |
|         § 683.51. Hamline University, College of Liberal Arts, Legal Studies Department | 266 |
|         § 683.52. Moorhead State University, Paralegal Program, Center for Business | 266 |
|         § 683.53. Winona State University, Paralegal Program | 266 |
|     § 683.6. Post-Baccalaureate Programs | 267 |
|         § 683.61. Hamline University, Post-Baccalaureate Paralegal Program | 267 |
|         § 683.62. Minnesota Paralegal Institute, Post-Baccalaureate Certificate Program | 267 |
|     § 683.7. Legal Studies | 268 |
| § 684. Law Clerks | 268 |
| § 685. Court Reporters | 268 |
| **Appendix A. Constitutional Documents** | **271** |
| **Appendix B. Amendments to the Minnesota Constitution Proposed to the Voters Since 1858** | **273** |
| **Appendix C. Checklist of Session Laws** | **289** |
| **Appendix D. Statutory Compilations, Revisions, and Codes** | **297** |
|     I. Compilations, Revisions, and Codes | 297 |
|     II. Legal Research Checklist | 316 |
| **Appendix E. Reports of the Attorney General** | **319** |
| **Appendix F. Numerical Index to the Selected Opinions of the Minnesota Attorney General 1933–1968** | **329** |

| | |
|---|---|
| **Appendix G. Minnesota Guidelines for Legal Reference Service** | **383** |
|   **Guidelines for Legal Reference Service** | **383** |
|     In General | 383 |
|     In-House Reference | 384 |
|     Telephone Reference | 385 |
|   **Attachment 1. Sample Warnings** | **387** |
|   **Attachment 2. Minnesota State Law Library** | |
|     **Suggested Referrals** | **389** |
|     Sources | 389 |
|     Agencies/Organizations | 389 |
|       African Americans | 389 |
|       Aged | 389 |
|     Agriculture | 390 |
|     AIDS-HIV-ARC | 390 |
|     Consumers | 390 |
|     Crime Victims | 390 |
|     Criminal | 391 |
|     Disabled | 391 |
|     Divorce | 391 |
|     Gays and Lesbians | 392 |
|     Human Rights | 392 |
|     Landlord/Tenant | 392 |
|     Lawyers Referral | 392 |
|     Legal Assistance | 393 |
|     Migrants | 393 |
|     Municipal Law | 394 |
|     Native Americans | 394 |
|     Prisoners | 394 |
|     Research and Writing | 394 |
|     Southeast Asians | 394 |
|     Spanish-Speaking | 394 |
|     Taxes | 395 |
|     Special Collections in Law Libraries | 395 |
|       Hamline University Law Library | 395 |
|       Hennepin County Law Library | 395 |
|       Minnesota State Law Library | 395 |
|       Ramsey County Law Library | 395 |
|       University of Minnesota Law Library | 395 |
|       William Mitchell College of Law Library | 395 |
|   **Attachment 3. Legal Services Memorandum** | **396** |
| **Appendix H. Selected Legal Research Texts** | **399** |
| **Appendix I. Minnesota Supreme Court Justices 1858–1999** | **401** |

Table of Contents xix

| | |
|---|---|
| Appendix J. Federal Depository Libraries in Minnesota | 427 |
| Appendix K. Minnesota Abbreviations | 431 |
| Appendix L. Directory of Local Pro Bono Programs | 435 |
|     Statewide | 435 |
|     Multi-County | 435 |
|     Anoka County | 435 |
|     Blue Earth County | 436 |
|     Clay County | 436 |
|     Crow Wing County | 436 |
|     Dakota County | 436 |
|     Freeborn County | 436 |
|     Hennepin County | 437 |
|     Isanti County | 437 |
|     Itasca County | 437 |
|     Nobles County | 438 |
|     Olmsted County | 438 |
|     Pine County | 438 |
|     Ramsey County | 438 |
|     Scott County | 438 |
|     Saint Louis County | 439 |
|     Stearns County | 439 |
|     Washington County | 439 |
|     Winona County | 439 |
| Appendix M. Minnesota State Document Depository Libraries | 441 |
| Appendix N. District Bar Associations | 443 |
| Appendix O. Capitol Area Library Consortium Directory | 449 |
| Index | 455 |

# ABOUT THE AUTHORS

John Tessner is a graduate of Gonzaga University School of Law. He received his Master of Arts in Library Science from the University of Wisconsin–Milwaukee and a bachelor's degree in education from the University of Wisconsin–Oshkosh. Prior to his appointment as Head of Public Services at Hamline University School of Law Library in Saint Paul, Minnesota, he was catalog librarian at the University of Arkansas at Little Rock.

Brenda Wolfe currently is the Director of the Industrial Relations Center Reference Room at the University of Minnesota. Prior to her present position she was the Reference/Electronic Resources Librarian at Hamline University School of Law Library. She holds a B.A. from the University of Minnesota, a J.D. from William Mitchell College of Law in Saint Paul, and a M.L.I.S. from Rosary College in River Forest, Illinois.

George Jackson is a graduate of the University of Pennsylvania, the University of Pittsburgh School of Library Science, and the University of Pittsburgh School of Law. He has held positions at the Montana State Law Library, the Ohio State University Law School Library, and the University of Minnesota Law School Library. His present position includes duties as reference librarian, advanced legal research instructor, and documents librarian.

# Introduction

Since 1984, those needing assistance with Minnesota legal research have been able to use the valuable first edition of the *Minnesota Legal Research Guide* authored by Arlette Soderberg and Barbara Golden. Countless researchers have benefitted from their hard work in creating the first comprehensive Minnesota guide. We continue their tradition of providing citations and instructions for retrieving primary and secondary sources concerning all Minnesota governmental branches, as well as hard-to-find information, in one volume.

We have provided both paper and electronic resources in this second edition. Even though the ephemeral nature of the Internet can result in rapidly outdated website citations, we still included relevant sites. We attempted to choose those government and company websites that we knew could be accessed even if, in the future, some URLs may change.

To enable the reader to derive the most information from the citation, we used both the *Chicago Manual of Style* and *The Bluebook: A Uniform System of Citation,* as our citation guides.

While revising and updating this edition, we not only conferred with each other, we also contacted numerous Minnesota libraries for research assistance. We were met with a collegial and professional response to our requests. We sincerely express our appreciation for any and all help we received.

# CHAPTER ONE
# Historical Beginnings and the Minnesota Constitution

Chapters one through four deal with primary sources of law. "Primary source of law" refers to materials such as constitutions, legislation, court decisions, court rules, and administrative regulations that emanate from authoritative organs of the state. A primary source of law has mandatory effect; it is the law itself. This chapter traces the legal development of Minnesota from a territory to a state and concludes with a discussion of its most basic legal document, the Minnesota Constitution.

## Chapter Contents

§ 110. Under Foreign Jurisdiction
§ 120. United States Sovereignty
§ 130. The Minnesota Constitution

## § 110. UNDER FOREIGN JURISDICTION[1]

§ 111. French Sovereignty
§ 112. English Sovereignty

The area that was to become Minnesota has been under the jurisdiction of four different sovereign powers: England, France, Spain, and the United States. As early as the seventeenth century, European explorers journeyed into the heart of the North American continent, enticed by rumors of a great inland river that would provide passage to the Pacific Ocean. Parts of what later was to become Minnesota were claimed by French and English explorers for their respective sovereigns. Additionally, the colony of Virginia had rather extensive

---

1. Major sources for this section are 1 W. FOLWELL, A HISTORY OF MINNESOTA (1922); W. LOSS, MINNESOTA, A BICENTENNIAL HISTORY (1977); Robert J. Sheran & Timothy J. Boland, *The Law, Courts, and Lawyers in the Frontier Days of Minnesota: An Informal Legal History of the Years 1835 to 1865*, 2 WM. MITCHELL L. REV. 1 (1976).

claims to the "western lands" under its Charter of 1609 from James I (1603–1625), that granted Virginia the lands extending from "sea to sea, west and northwest."[2] Of course, the land already was inhabited by the Sioux, sometimes called the Dakota, and the Chippewa who also were known as the Ojibway.[3]

## § 111. French Sovereignty

At a picturesque ceremony in 1671 at Sault Ste. Marie, in what was to become Michigan, the French claimed Lakes Huron and Superior, as well as undiscovered lands bounded by the northern, western, and southern seas. The title and claim was as good as that of any other European country, and included nearly nine-tenths of North America. By that time, the French reportedly had set foot in Minnesota, the first Europeans to do so.[4] French expeditions had reached Minnesota in 1654 and 1660, although the accuracy of the former date is questioned by some.

The French continued their exploration of the territory along the Mississippi and the northern shore of Lake Superior throughout the late seventeenth century and into the middle of the eighteenth century. Their activity in the region resulted in nothing more permanent than trading posts, forts, and missions, all of which had disappeared by the middle of the eighteenth century. Independent French fur traders, the voyageurs, continued to ply the waters of northern Minnesota for another century, until the late 1800s.

In 1763, at the end of the Seven Years' War between France and England (called the French and Indian War in the United States), France ceded her territory east of the Mississippi (Minnesota East) to

---

2. CHARTERS OF THE BRITISH COLONIES IN AMERICA 84 (1776).
3. The Sioux were driven to the western plains by the Chippewa, the most decisive battle occurring near Mule Lacs Lake in 1743. Many treaties were made to acquire land from these tribes during the middle of the nineteenth century. The texts of Indian treaties can be found in 7 Stat. (Treaties Between the United States and the Indian Tribes 1778–1842), and in 2 CHARLES J. KAPPLER, INDIAN AFFAIRS (1904) (5 Laws and Treaties Doc. No. 319, 58th Cong., 2d Sess. (1904)). A large collection of prints of many individual treaties and other compilations of Indian treaties are available at the University of Minnesota Law Library.
4. Other reports indicate that the Vikings traveled to Minnesota in 1362, evidenced by the Runestone found near Kensington. *See generally,* ROLF M. NILSESTUEN, THE KENSINGTON RUNESTONE VINDICATED (1994). For more information on the debate concerning the validity of the Kensington Runestone, check your local library.

**Chapter One. Historical Beginnings and the Minnesota Constitution**　　　　3

England under the Treaty of Paris.[5] To prevent the loss of all of Louisiana to the English, France had, in 1762, secretly conveyed its territory west of the Mississippi (Minnesota West) to its ally Spain. In 1800, Spain retroactively ceded the Louisiana Territory west of the Mississippi to France. The United States, fearful that Napoleon would deploy a large French army on North American soil, offered to purchase New Orleans and the two Floridas from France for two million dollars. Napoleon, desperately in need of funds for his continental campaigns, offered instead to sell the whole Louisiana Territory, which the United States ultimately purchased in 1803 for the sum of fifteen million dollars.[6]

### § 112. English Sovereignty

In 1611, forty years before French explorers reached Minnesota, English explorers had discovered Hudson Bay. They claimed the bay, all tributary waters, and all adjacent lands for Great Britain. The English claim, therefore, included the Red River Valley of northwestern Minnesota because the waters of the Red River ultimately empty into Hudson Bay. In 1763, when the British acquired Minnesota East from the French, British outposts for the fur trade were established in Minnesota by the Northwest Company. The first Minnesota outpost of the company was located at Grand Portage.

The British relinquished their claim to Minnesota East under a treaty of peace between England and the United States, entered into on September 3, 1783.[7] Even then, however, England held its posts and forbade the Americans to explore or trade. Jay's Treaty in 1794[8] provided for the withdrawal of British garrisons by June 1, 1796, but the

---

5. *Definitive Treaty of Peace between Great Britain, France and Spain, Feb. 10, 1763*, reprinted in 1 BRITISH AND FOREIGN STATE PAPERS 422 (1841) (extract); I GEORGE CHALMERS, A COLLECTION OF TREATIES BETWEEN GREAT BRITAIN AND OTHER POWERS 467 (1790).
6. Treaty Between the United States of America and the French Republic, Apr. 30, 1803, 8 Stat. 200 (1867).
7. Definitive Treaty of Peace between the United States of America and His Britannic Majesty, Sept. 3, 1783, U.S.-Gr. Brit., 8 Stat. 80, *reprinted in* MINN. STAT. ANN. § 29 (West 1976).
8. Treaty of Amity, Commerce and Navigation, Nov. 19, 1794, U.S.-Gr. Brit., 8 Stat. 116.

Northwest Company continued to operate in the territory for another twenty years.

The Minnesota portion of the Red River Valley was acquired by the United States at the Treaty of Ghent,[9] which concluded the War of 1812. The international boundary on the north was set at the forty-ninth parallel, with the exception of the northwest angle, which extends into Lake of the Woods. The northwest angle was created because of the belief, prevalent at the conclusion of the 1783 treaty between the United States and Great Britain, that the Mississippi River originated in Lake of the Woods.

## § 120. UNITED STATES SOVEREIGNTY

§ 121. Minnesota Territory
§ 122. Minnesota Statehood

As noted above, the United States acquired rights (subject to the rights of the Indians) to Minnesota East in 1783 and to Minnesota West in 1803. Before the U.S. Constitution was adopted, the Congress of the Confederation passed the Northwest Ordinance of 1787.[10] This created a government for the Northwest Territory that extended from the colonies to the Mississippi River. The Ordinance provided for a territorial governor; a secretary to preserve the acts, laws, and public records; three judges with common law jurisdiction; and a general assembly consisting of the governor, a legislative council, and a house of representatives. The Ordinance also provided for civil and religious liberty, the writ of habeas corpus, trial by jury, adoption of the common law of England, proportionate representation and taxation, bail, eminent domain, encouragement of education, rights of Indians, and free use of navigable waters. Additionally, it prohibited cruel and unusual punishment and slavery.[11]

Minnesota East at different times came under the jurisdiction of the territories of Ohio, Indiana, Illinois, Michigan, and Wisconsin.

---

9. Treaty of Peace and Amity, Dec. 24, 1814, U.S.-Gr. Brit., 8 Stat. 218.
10. Northwest Ordinance of 1787, July 13, 1787, Rev. Stat. 13 (2d ed. 1878), *reprinted in* 1 MINN. STAT. at xxxiii (1998); 1 MINN. STAT. ANN. § 39 (West 1976).
11. A list of session laws and of statutes passed by the government of the Northwest Territory may be found in MEIRA. PIMSLEUR, PIMSLEUR'S CHECKLISTS OF BASIC AMERICAN LEGAL PUBLICATIONS (Marcia Zubrow ed., 1992).

# Chapter One. Historical Beginnings and the Minnesota Constitution

Minnesota West, to which the Northwest Ordinance did not apply, came under the jurisdiction of the territories of Louisiana, Missouri, and Iowa. At times, parts of what was to become Minnesota were not under the jurisdiction of any territory.[12]

## § 121. Minnesota Territory

In 1849, Congress passed the Organic Act, establishing a government for the Territory of Minnesota.[13] This act, similar to the organic acts of other territories, provided for a governor, a secretary, a chief justice and two associate justices of a supreme court, an attorney, and a marshal, all to be appointed by the President of the United States. Provision was made for probate judges and justices of the peace to be appointed by the territorial governor. An elective legislative assembly was prescribed consisting of a council of nine members and a house of representatives of eighteen members. Free white male residents aged twenty-one and older were entitled to vote. The labors of the first legislature were lightened because, until altered, modified, or repealed, the laws in force in the territory of Wisconsin were to continue operation in Minnesota.

## § 122. Minnesota Statehood

There is some uncertainty as to when Minnesota became a state. The state's Enabling Act, passed by Congress on February 26, 1857, provided that the inhabitants of the territory that was to become the State of Minnesota were "authorized to form for themselves a Constitution and State Government . . . and to come into the Union on an equal footing with the original States, according to the federal constitution."[14] It is not known whether this provision meant that statehood

---

12. BENCH & BAR OF MINNESOTA, A HISTORICAL AND BIOGRAPHICAL SKETCH 4 (1901).
13. An Act to Establish the Territorial Government of Minnesota, ch. 121, 9 Stat. 403 (Mar. 3, 1849), *reprinted in* 1 MINN. STAT. at xxxvii (1998), 1 MINN. STAT. ANN. § 51 (West 1976) (Organic Act).
14. An Act to Authorize the People of the Territory of Minnesota to Form a Constitution and State Government, preparatory to their Admission in the Union on an Equal Footing with the original States, ch. 60, II Stat. 166 (Feb. 26, 1857), *reprinted in* 1 MINN. STAT. at xliii (1998), 1 MINN. STAT. ANN. § 61 (West 1976) (Enabling Act).

began upon passage of the Enabling Act or upon passage by Congress of the Act of Admission.[15] Nevertheless, the legislature convened in December 1857 and enacted laws during the period between the passage of the Enabling Act and the Act of Admission. The laws enacted at this legislative session subsequently were adopted by the state and have not been questioned judicially.

## § 130. THE MINNESOTA CONSTITUTION[16]

- § 131. Constitutional Convention of 1857
- § 132. Constitutional Reform
- § 133. Restructured Constitution of 1974
- § 134. Procedures for Changing the Constitution
- § 135. Sources Containing Constitutional Documents
- § 136. Sources of Constitutional Interpretation

### § 131. Constitutional Convention of 1857

Minnesota's Constitutional Convention, which assembled in St. Paul on July 13, 1857, the seventieth anniversary of the passage of the Northwest Ordinance of 1787, was marred by bitterness and division. Feelings were so intense that the Republicans and Democrats met in separate rooms and drafted different constitutions. Finally, after national party leaders had counseled them to stop acting like "border ruffians," the leadership of both parties met and appointed a bipartisan committee. This compromise committee fashioned a constitution from the partially finished drafts of the two parties, and this document was accepted with almost no discussion. Some delegates still refused to inscribe their names on a document signed by members of the other party, so two copies hastily were drawn up—one signed by the Democrats, the other by the Republicans. There are more than 300 differences in spelling, punctuation, and wording between these two documents.[17] The courts never have been faced with the issue of which

---

15. An Act for the Admission of the State of Minnesota into the Union, ch. 31, II Stat. 285 (May 11, 1858), *reprinted in* 1 MINN. STAT. at xlv (1998), 1 MINN. STAT. ANN. § 67 (West 1976) (Act of Admission).
16. Appendix A lists historical constitutional documents.
17. For a list of these differences, *see* WILLIAM ANDERSON, A HISTORY OF THE CONSTITUTION OF MINNESOTA 270 (1921).

# Chapter One. Historical Beginnings and the Minnesota Constitution

document was definitive, so Minnesota is unique in having had two official constitutions simultaneously.

## § 132. Constitutional Reform

§ 132.1. Minnesota Constitutional Commission, 1947–1948
§ 132.2. Minnesota Constitutional Study Commission, 1971–1973

### § 132.1. Minnesota Constitutional Commission, 1947–1948

In 1947, the Minnesota legislature, perceiving a need for reform, created the Minnesota Constitutional Commission to study the constitution.[18] In its 1948 *Report*, the commission recommended major changes in the constitution, including the addition of six new sections. Although the calling of a constitutional convention never passed the legislature, many of the commission's recommendations were adopted during the following decade through the efforts of reform groups and aroused citizen interest.[19]

### § 132.2. Minnesota Constitutional Study Commission, 1971–1973

In 1971, answering a renewed movement for reform, the legislature created the Minnesota Constitutional Study Commission to study the constitution and make recommendations for its revision.[20] The commission recommended that major changes in the constitution be made through phased amendment revision. Foremost among its recommendations was a proposal to revise the format of the constitution so that future amendments could be properly phrased and placed in an orderly, well-structured, and clearly written framework.

The commission recommended that the structure and form of the original constitution be changed to delete obsolete and inconsequential language, correct grammar and stylistic defects, and reorganize constitutional provisions to produce a more coherent and readable document,

---

18. Act creating an interim commission to make a study of the Constitution, ch. 614, 1947 Minn. Laws 1111.
19. G. Theodore Mitau, *Constitutional Change by Amendment: Recommendations of the Minnesota Constitutional Commission in Ten Years' Perspective*, 44 MINN. L. REV. 461 (1960).
20. Establishing Constitutional Study Commission, ch. 806(3), 1971 Minn. Laws 1539, 1541.

all without making any consequential change in the meaning or interpretation of the present constitution.[21] The commission drafted a restructured constitution and urged the legislature to approve it and submit it to the electorate at the 1974 general election.

### § 133. Restructured Constitution of 1974

The restructured constitution drafted by the Constitutional Study Commission was introduced in the 1974 legislative session as S.F. No. 1713. After a few changes were made in the wording of the commission's draft, the legislature approved it. The first of the bill's three sections contained the text of the proposed restructured constitution.

The proposal was submitted to the public at the 1974 general election, where it was ratified by the required majority of all those voting in the election.[22] Thus, the entire constitution was amended at one time by one amendment, and that amendment became the new, or restructured, constitution. At the same election, the commission's recommendation for easing the amendatory process was defeated. A majority voting on the question favored the change but this was less than the required majority of the electors voting at the election.

The new constitution reduced the number of articles from twenty-one to fourteen and the number of words from 15,864 to 10,297.[23] The restructured constitution did not alter the meaning of the 1857 Constitution. If questioned, the original document remains the final authority. Thus, to determine whether the restructured constitution has consequentially altered any provision of the old constitution, reference should be made to the Constitution of 1857 as amended.

---

21. MINNESOTA CONSTITUTIONAL STUDY COMMISSION, FINAL REPORT 14 (1973) [hereinafter MINN. CONST. STUDY COMM'N, FINAL REPORT].
22. Act proposing an amendment to the Minnesota Constitution, ch. 409, 1974 Minn. Laws 787; Proclamation of adoption of Constitutional Amendments, 1975 Minn. Laws ix.
23. MINN. CONST. STUDY COMM'N, FINAL REPORT, *supra* note 21.

# § 134. Procedures for Changing the Constitution

§ 134.1. Convention
§ 134.2. Amendments

Article IX of the Minnesota Constitution provides for two methods of changing the Constitution: convention and amendment.

## § 134.1. Convention

Calling a constitutional convention is a difficult process requiring that two-thirds of the members of each house in the legislature submit the question of constitutional revision to the electors. Then, a majority of *all* the electors voting at the election (not just on the question) must vote for the convention. Following the convention, "[i]f three-fifths of all the electors voting on the question vote to ratify the revision, it becomes a new constitution of the State of Minnesota."[24]

Only once has the question of a convention gone to the electors. In 1896, a majority voting on the question said yes to a convention, but this was not the required majority of *all* the voters at the election; thus, no convention was called.

## § 134.2. Amendments[25]

A proposed amendment must be introduced in the legislature as a bill and approved by a majority of the legislature. The legislature uses the same method for considering amendments as it uses for considering bills. If a majority approves a proposed amendment, it is submitted to the public at the following general election.

Originally, Minnesota had a very simple process for ratifying constitutional amendments. Known as the "Great Compromise" of the 1857 convention, a simple constitutional amendatory process allowed the Compromise Committee essentially to adopt the Democratic version as the final constitution. The Republicans believed that they soon would gain a political majority and then easily could amend the constitution to conform to their views. Approval by a majority of those voting on the amendment was all that was necessary to secure passage. In 1898, the amendatory process was changed to require approval by

---

24. MINN. CONST. art. IX, § 3.
25. For a list of all constitutional amendments proposed since 1857, *see* Appendix B.

a majority of all persons voting in an election, not just those voting on the proposed amendment.[26] This change remains in effect today.

Amendments to the Minnesota Constitution are incorporated directly into the body of the text, with the superseded provision then deleted. Copies of amendments proposed and approved by the legislature are printed in *Laws of Minnesota* under their chapter number. They are listed under "Constitutional Amendments" in the index. Proclamations of the adoption of an amendment currently are printed in the first volume of *Laws of Minnesota* published subsequent to approval of the amendment by the people. The proclamation does not reprint the amendment. To find the text, therefore, one must refer back to the session in which the legislature approved the amendment. Check the table of contents to locate these.

### § 135. Sources Containing Constitutional Documents

The following chart indicates where copies of the Minnesota Constitution and other documents discussed in this chapter can be found.

|  | Current Statutes[27] | Session Laws | Legislative Manual | Constitutions of the United States[28] |
|---|---|---|---|---|
| Northwest Ordinance of 1787 | X |  | X |  |
| Organic Act of Minnesota (1849) | X |  | X |  |
| Enabling Act | X |  | X |  |
| Act of Admission to the Union | X |  | X |  |
| Constitution of 1857 | X[29] |  | X[30] |  |

---

26. *See* 1899 Minn. Laws at iv (amending MINN. CONST. of 1857, art. XIV, § 1).
27. Official *Minnesota Statutes* (1984) and *Minnesota Statutes Annotated*.
28. CONSTITUTIONS OF THE UNITED STATES: NATIONAL AND STATE (1974) 7 vols., loose-leaf, Oceana for Columbia University Legislative Drafting Fund).
29. The 1857 Constitution is included in *Minnesota Statutes Annotated* and editions of *Minnesota Statutes* before 1976. A disposition table, showing where articles and sections of the 1857 Constitution appears in the restructured constitution is provided in 1 MINN. STAT. ANN. at ix (1976).
30. The 1857 Constitution with amendments can be found in the 1973–1974 *Minnesota Legislative Manual*.

# Chapter One. Historical Beginnings and the Minnesota Constitution

|  | Current Statutes[27] | Session Laws | Legislative Manual | Constitutions of the United States[28] |
|---|---|---|---|---|
| Restructured Constitution of 1974 | X |  | X | X |
| Proposed Amendments to the Constitution |  | X | X[31] |  |
| Amendments to the Constitution | X |  | X | X |

The Minnesota Constitution, adopted October 13, 1857, generally revised November 5, 1974, further amended November 1974, 1980, 1982, 1984, 1988, 1990, 1996, and 1998 is available on the Web at <http://www.house.leg.state.mn.us/cco/rules/mncon/preamble.htm>.

The Minnesota Constitution is available online via LEXIS in the Minnesota library-Minnesota Constitution file (MINN; MNCNST) or the Constitutional Law library-Minnesota Constitution file (CONLAW; MNCNST), or online via Westlaw in Minnesota Statutes Annotated database (MN-ST-ANN) and Minnesota Statutes database (MN-ST).

## § 136. Sources of Constitutional Interpretation

Law review articles and cases discussing particular articles and sections of the constitution are two resources for interpretation of the Minnesota Constitution. Article citations can be found in *Minnesota Statutes Annotated* following the constitutional article and section. Another source is *Shepard's Minnesota Citations*, which refers to legal authority concerning the 1857 and 1974 versions of the Minnesota Constitutions. *Shepard's Minnesota Citations* includes citations to selected law reviews, journals, *American Law Reports (ALR)*, federal and Minnesota case law, and Minnesota Session Laws. A search in *Index to Legal Periodicals (ILP), Legal Resource Index (LRI)*, or *Criminal Justice Abstracts* (*CJA*) also helps researchers to find articles in this area. *Shepard's* is available online by subscription or credit card via LEXIS. *Minnesota Statutes Annotated* is available online via Westlaw. *ILP, LRI,*

---

31. This source includes only a brief description of the proposed amendments.

and *CJA* are available online by subscription or via Westlaw. *ILP* and *LRI* are available via LEXIS.

A number of books and series, or portions of books and series, have been written concerning the history and interpretation of the Minnesota Constitution. Often these books contain bibliographies that cite articles, cases, and other books. Following is a selected list of treatises that, at least in part, discuss the distinctive features and history of the Minnesota Constitution.

Anderson, William & Albert J. Loeb, *A History of the Constitution of Minnesota* (University of Minnesota 1921).

Bjornson, Val, *The History of Minnesota* (Lewis Historical Pub. Co. 1969).

Blegen, Theodore C., *Minnesota: A History of the State* (University of Minnesota Press 1975).

Christianson, Theodore, *Minnesota: The Land of Sky Tinted Waters: A History of the State and Its People* (American Historical Society 1935).

Folwell, William Watts, *A History of Minnesota* (Minnesota Historical Society 1956).

Friesen, Jennifer, *State Constitutional Law: Litigating Individual Rights, Claims, and Defenses* (M. Bender 1992).

Hubbard, L. F. & R. I. Holcombe, 3 *Minnesota in Three Centuries*, 1655–1908, 29 (Publishing Society of Minnesota 1908).

Kumm, Harold F., *The Constitution of Minnesota Annotated* (University of Minnesota 1924).

Morrison, Mary Jane, *A Minnesota State Constitution: A Reference Guide* (Greenwood Press, projected publication date 2001).

Neill, Edward D., *The History of Minnesota: From the Earliest French Explorations to the Present Time* (J.B. Lippincott 1858).

Sturm, Albert Lee, *A Bibliography on State Constitutions and Constitutional Revision, 1945–1975* (Citizens Conference on State Legislatures 1975).

Swinder, William F., 5 *Sources and Documents of United States Constitutions* 283 (Oceana Publications 1976).

# CHAPTER TWO
# Legislation

Article IV of the Minnesota Constitution vests the state's legislative power in the House of Representatives and Senate. Local governments also have the power to enact law. This chapter describes the legislative process in Minnesota, the procedures for tracing legislative history, and the sources in which Minnesota's laws may be found.

## Chapter Contents

§ 210. Legislative Offices that Serve the Public
§ 220. Legislature
§ 230. Enactment of Legislation
§ 240. Legislative History
§ 250. Session Laws
§ 260. Statutes
§ 270. Other Sources of Law

## § 210. LEGISLATIVE OFFICES THAT SERVE THE PUBLIC

Listed below are the names, addresses, and phone numbers of offices that assist the public in obtaining legislative information. References are made to these offices throughout the chapter. For general information, call or write:

House Information Office
175 State Office Building
St. Paul, MN 55155
phone 651-296-2146
House of Representatives Web address
http://www.hours.leg.state.mn.us

Senate Public Information
Room B-29, State Capitol
St. Paul, MN 55155
phone 651-296-0504
Minnesota Senate Web address
<http://www.senate.leg.state.mn.us>

To track legislative progress of bills, contact:

House Index
Room 211, State Capitol
St. Paul, MN 55155
phone 651-296-6646

Senate Index
Room 231, State Capitol
St. Paul, MN 55155
phone 651-296-2887

Minnesota legislation and bill tracking Web address
<http://www.leg.state.mn.us/leg/legis.htm>

The journals of the House and Senate are the official record of daily activity during session. Recorded votes are included in the journals. A journal of the daily proceedings in each house is printed and given to each member at the beginning of the next day's session. After it has been publicly read and corrected, a copy, kept by the secretary and chief clerk, is certified by the secretary or clerk to the printer who prints the corrected permanent journal.[32] The bound paper versions of the House and Senate journals include topical, author, file number, and popular names indexes (*see* § 241.1). To obtain copies of *Journals*, bills, and laws, contact:

Office of the Chief Clerk
  of the House
Room 211, State Capitol
St. Paul, MN 55155
phone 651-296-2314

Office of the Secretary
  of the Senate
Room 231, State Capitol
St. Paul, MN 55155
phone 651-296-2343

The Minnesota Journal of the House, from 1994 forward, can be accessed by date or searched by keyword at <http://www.house.leg.state.mn.us/cco/journals/journl.htm>. The Minnesota Journal of the Senate, from 1996 forward, can be accessed by date or searched by keyword at <http://www.senate.leg.state.mn.us/journals/index.htm>. For current committee schedules, call:

House Public Information
Hotline: 651-296-9283

Senate Public Information
Hotline: 651-296-8088

Committee information is available on the Web at <http://www.senate.leg.state.mn.us/committee/>.

---

32. MINN. STAT. § 3.17 (1998).

# § 220. LEGISLATURE

§ 221. Sessions
§ 222. Members
§ 223. Apportionment
§ 224. Committees
§ 225. Rules
§ 226. Commissions and Offices that Aid the Legislature

## § 221. Sessions

Under the flexible session constitutional amendment of 1972, the legislature meets during each biennium (a two-year period) for a total term not to exceed 120 legislative days. The regular session is convened in each odd-numbered year on the first Tuesday after the first Monday in January. The legislature may meet in each year of a biennium, it may not meet in regular session after the first Monday following the third Saturday in May of any year. The adjournment between the session of the first year and the second year of the biennium is temporary because the biennium is considered as one continuous session.[33] The governor is authorized to call the legislature into a special or extra session at any time, but he does not have the power to limit the length or scope of that session.

The Minnesota Senate and House of Representatives provides unedited coverage of their floor sessions and selected committee hearings. This coverage is available on several broadcast television stations and on many cable television systems in various areas of the state. This coverage consists of live and recorded programs from the Senate and House. Live coverage of both the Senate and House television programming is available to the public over the Public Internet and to government organizations over the State's Intranet. This programming consists of live coverage produced by Senate Media Services and by House Television Services.[34]

---

33. State v. Hoppe, 298 Minn. 386, 215 N.W.2d 797, 803 (1974).
34. <http://www.house.leg.state.mn.us/htv/htvserv.htm>.

### § 222. Members

Minnesota is divided into sixty-seven Senate districts, each of which elects one senator. Then each Senate district is divided in two to form the 134 House districts, each of which elects one representative. Therefore, membership of the legislature presently consists of sixty-seven senators and 134 representatives.[35] Senators are elected to four-year terms and representatives are elected to two-year terms. Legislators must be qualified voters and residents of the state for one year and of the district from which they are elected for six months preceding the election.[36] Since 1974, members have been nominated and elected with party designation.

The Senate elects a president as presiding officer[37] and the House elects a speaker. These officers alternate annually as chair of the Legislative Coordinating Commission.[38] For directories of members of the legislature, see § 536.4, *infra*. Biographical information is available in the *Minnesota Legislative Manual*. Numerous other brochures published by the legislature and by other organizations as well as local newspapers provide additional information about members. On the Web, member information for the Senate is at <http://www.senate.leg.state.mn.us/members/index.htm>. Member information for the house is at: <http://www.house.leg.state.mn.us/hinfo/hmem.htm>.

### § 223. Apportionment

All legislative (House and Senate) districts must be apportioned by population.[39] The legislature is authorized to prescribe the boundaries of legislative districts at the first session of the legislature after each

---

35. MINN. STAT. § 2.031, subd. 1 (1998).
36. MINN. CONST. 1974, art. IV, § 6.
37. Until a 1972 constitutional amendment gave the Senate the power to choose its own presiding officer, the lieutenant governor presided over the Senate.
38. The Legislative Coordinating Commission coordinates the legislative activities of the Senate and the House of Representatives, supervises the Office of the Revisor of Statutes and the Legislative Reference Library, and reviews the budget requests of certain statutory commissions. MINN. STAT. § 3.303, subds. 1, 3 (1998); MINN. STAT. 3.304, subd. 1 (1998).
39. MINN. CONST. art. IV, § 2.

## Chapter Two. Legislation

U.S. census.[40] Legislative district maps can be found in the *Minnesota Legislative Manual* and the various legislative reporting services at the time of reapportionment. The Geographic Information Systems (GIS) Office provides the legislature with timely, accurate spatial data (usually in the form of maps) and is the repository of statewide boundary information for legislative use. The office maintains a map library of spatial databases, provided by the Census Bureau and several Minnesota State agencies. These databases can be integrated with many sources of information to produce maps and tables of pertinent information for legislators and legislative staff. For district maps, visit the legislative maps Web page at <http://www.commissions.leg.state.mn.us/gis/html/gismaps.html>. Paper copies of congressional district boundaries; legislative district boundaries; and county, city, and township boundaries maps may be ordered from the Secretary of State's office with a form available on the Web at <http://www.sos.state.mn.us/election/maporder.pdf>. A booklet of maps may be purchased from the Minnesota State Documents Center (*see* § 350, *infra*). Local newspapers publish maps preceding elections.

### § 224. Committees[41]

Most legislative work is done by committees. The number of committees varies in each legislative body from session to session. The Speaker of the House and the Senate Committee on Committees name members to standing committees, which may hold over from year to year. Committees study proposed legislation in their fields, hold hearings, and listen to testimony; they may amend a bill, recommend it for passage, refer it to another committee, or table it. Some committees meet between legislative sessions to study specific problems. Subcommittees and special committees may be appointed to study specific topics or bills. Further information on committees and their meeting schedules may be obtained from many of the sources cited in § 240, *infra*.

---

40. MINN. CONST. art IV, § 3.
41. Minn. House Rules 6.01–6.50 (2000); Minn. Senate Rules 57–61 (1999–2000).

Additional information about committees is contained in §§ 234–236, *infra*. The Senate Committee Web address is <http://www.senate.leg.state.mn.us/committee/>. The House Committee Web address is <http://www.house.leg.state.mn.us/comm/commemlist.asp>.

### § 225. Rules

The legislature conducts its business under rules prescribed in the constitution and statutes. Additionally, each body formulates its own rules each session.[42] These rules can be found in the Legislative Directory, Legislative Manual, inside the front cover of the Daily Journal binders, and in the Journal when reported out by the Committee on Rules and Administration. Copies of the Senate rules are also available in the Senate Information Office, Room 231, State Capitol. The Senate rules also are printed as a separate document upon adoption by the Senate and are available on the Senate website at <http://www.senate.leg.state.mn.us/general/index.htm>. Additionally, the House publishes its rules on the House website at <http://www.house.leg.state.mn.us/cco/rules/permrule/permrule.htm>. The joint Senate/House rules are also available on the Web at <http://www.house.leg.state.mn.us/cco/rules/jtrule/jtrule.htm>.

### § 226. Commissions and Offices that Aid the Legislature

§ 226.1. Attorney General
§ 226.2. Commission on Uniform State Laws
§ 226.3. Legislative Reference Library
§ 226.4. Minnesota Historical Society
§ 226.5. Revisor of Statutes

The *Minnesota Legislative Manual* and the *Minnesota Guidebook to State Agency Services* available on the Web at <http://www.comm.media.state.mn.us/BOOKSTORE/guidebook.asp> provide information on the various offices and commissions that serve the legislature. Minnesota's state government searchable website <http://www.state.mn.us> also has information related to legislative offices and commissions. Legislative commissions are composed

---

42. MINN. CONST. art. iv, § 7.

# Chapter Two. Legislation

exclusively of members of the Senate and the House.[43] These commissions generally focus on a specific problem. For Web access to joint departments, commissions, and task forces, see the links listed at <http://www.leg.state.mn.us/leg/depts.htm>. Noted here are those offices and commissions that issue or control publications and documents used in legal research.

### § 226.1. Attorney General[44]

The attorney general is the legal advisor to the legislature and its committees. For a more detailed description of the attorney general's responsibilities and publications, see § 313, *infra*.

### § 226.2. Commission on Uniform State Laws

This commission participates in the National Conference of Commissioners on Uniform State Laws and cooperates in the consideration and drafting of uniform acts.[45] One commissioner is the Revisor of Statutes or the Revisor's designated assistant.[46]

### § 226.3. Legislative Reference Library[47]

This library was established in 1969 to provide legislators with research facilities and assistance. The library's collection is governed by the current and future interests of the legislature. It maintains an extensive clipping file of newspaper articles and a large selection of magazines and newsletters. A list of periodical holdings with a description of the titles and indexes by issuing agency and subject is available at the library and on the Web at <http://www.library.leg.state.mn.us/lrl/mndocs/mnper.htm>. In 1974, it became the designated depository of all state documents and is responsible for bibliographic access.[48] For a discussion of state documents, see § 350, *infra*.

The library's on-line catalog (PALS) is available on the Web at <http://www.pals.msus.edu/webpals/home.html>. WebPals is a

---

43. MINN. STAT. § 3.305 (1998).
44. Web address <http://www.ag.state.mn.us/default.htm> (last visited Jan. 21, 2002).
45. MINN. STAT. § 3.252(5) (1998).
46. *Id.* § 3.251.
47. 645 State Office Building, St. Paul, MN 55155; phone 651-296-8338; Web address <http://www.library.leg.state.mn.us/lrl/lrl.htm> (last visited Nov. 4, 2001).
48. MINN. STAT. § 3.302, subd. 3 (1998).

gateway that provides internet access to the Minnesota State Colleges and Universities Statewide Automated Library System (MnSCU/PALS). MnSCU/PALS is a consortium of more than 125 libraries and branches with a common philosophy of resource sharing. Select "Legislative Reference Library" from the library catalog pull-down menu to retrieve holdings information for the Legislative Reference Library collection.

Available to the public at the Legislative Reference Library, are tape recordings of the House and Senate floor proceedings and committee debates from eight years ago to the present. The Minnesota Historical Society Library houses the tape recordings covering the previous eight-year period. Pursuant to the agreement of the legislature and the Legislative Reference Library, all tapes transferred from the originating body, prior to this sixteen-year period, are destroyed.

### § 226.4. Minnesota Historical Society[49]

When any department, agency, or official of the state, issues for public distribution, any book, document, map, pamphlet, or report, copies are delivered to the Minnesota Historical Society.[150] In addition to the tape recorded floor proceedings and committee debates, legislative materials available at the Minnesota Historical Society Library include the historical collection of legislative journals, both manuscript and published copies, committee minutes, miscellaneous committee records, bills, legislative manuals, statutes, and session laws (*see* § 241.3 and § 618.5, *infra*).

### § 226.5. Revisor of Statutes[51]

The revisor's office maintains a drafting department. Upon request of the governor, members of the legislature, departments or agencies of the state, or committees or commissions created by the legislature or appointed by the governor to study or revise laws, the revisor drafts or assists in the drafting of bills, resolutions, and amendments.[52] The revisor's staff provides drafting service to legislators, heads of

---

49. 345 Kellogg Blvd. West, St. Paul, MN 55102; phone 651-296-6126; Web address <http://www.mnhs.org> (last visited Nov. 4, 2001).
50. MINN. STAT. § 15.18 (1998).
51. 700 State Office Building, St. Paul, MN 55155; phone 612-296-2868.
52. MINN. STAT. § 3C.03, subd. 2 (1998).

**Chapter Two. Legislation**

executive agencies, and the governor. Its bill drafting guide is a clear and excellent source for legislators, agency officials, and citizens. The guide, *Minnesota Revisor's Manual with Styles and Forms*,[53] is available in print and on the Web at <http://www.revisor.leg.state.mn.us/bill_drafting_manual/Cover-TOC.htm>.

The revisor compiles the session laws and statutes and prepares their indexes and tables. The revisor also is charged with publishing the permanent agency rules, maintaining an agency rules drafting department, and preparing and publishing an agency rules drafting guide *Minnesota Rules Drafting Manual*,[54] which is available in print and on the Web at <http://www.revisor.leg.state.mn.us/arule/Cover1.htm>.[55]

## § 230. Enactment of Legislation

§ 231. Drafting
§ 232. Introduction of the Bill
§ 233. Reading
§ 234. Committee Hearings
§ 235. Calendars
§ 236. Conference Committees
§ 237. Action by the Governor
§ 238. Effective Dates
§ 239. Resolutions

### § 231. Drafting

The first step in the enactment of legislation is the formulation of a proposal. Anyone can propose an idea for a bill—an individual, a consumer group, corporation, professional association, governmental unit, the governor—but ideas usually come from members of the legislature. Proposals must be drafted, or put into proper legal form, before they can be introduced in the House or Senate. The revisor of statutes drafts bills, but only at the request of legislators, the governor's office, other constitutional offices, or other governmental agencies.[56]

---

53. Office of the Revisor of Statutes 1997.
54. *Id.*
55. Minn. Stat. § 14.07, subd. 1(1), (2); § 14.47, subd. 1 (1998).
56. Minn. Stat. § 3C.03, subd. 2 (1998).

## Illustration 1. How a Bill Becomes a Law[57]

```
House or Senate
  Proposal &         First           Committee
  Bill Drafting  →   Reading    →    Action      →  Trapped
  (§ 231)            (§ 233)         (§ 234)

              Third                          Second
  Defeated ←  Reading &   ←  Lay-over   ←    Reading
              Passage                        (§ 235)

  Trapped     Bill to
  or          Senate      →  Passage
  Defeated    or
              House                           (§ 237)
                                              Governor
                                                              BILL
                            Conference                        BECOMES
              Trapped       Committee                         LAW
              or            (§ 236)                           (§ 250)
              Defeated                        Veto
                                              Override

                                              Vetoed
```

## § 232. Introduction of the Bill[58]

After a proposal is drafted it must be introduced in the legislature. Only a legislator named the "chief author," may introduce a bill. The bill's chief author may find other members of his or her house to co-author the bill and a member of the other house to introduce it there as a companion bill. Legislative rules limit the total number of "authors." There can be up to thirty-five co-authors from the House and five from the Senate,[59] and their names also appear on the bill. The chief author plays an important role in handling the bill. The author determines when to request a committee hearing, when it will be considered in the

---

57. References are to section numbers in this book.
58. Minn. Senate Rule 32 (1999–2000); Minn. House Rule 1.12 (2000).
59. Minn. Senate Rule 32 (1999-2000); Minn. House Rule 1.12 (2000).

**Chapter Two. Legislation**

Committee of the Whole and submitted for a final vote, and whether to move either to concur in amendments attached to the bill by the other house or to request a conference committee. No action is taken on a bill unless the chief author is present.

After obtaining co-authors, the chief author submits the bill to the secretary of the senate or to the chief clerk's office in the House for the assignment of its file number. This number indicates the bill's chronological order of introduction. Bills are printed upon introduction and then reproduced; they are printed and paginated when they are reported out of committee. Each time the bill is amended, a new engrossment (copy) is made.

### § 233. Reading[60]

For a bill to become a law, it must receive three readings (on three separate days) in each body. A "reading" is the presentation of a bill before either body when the bill title is read. The bill is given its first reading when introduced (before it is referred to a committee), its second reading when reported out of committee, and its third reading prior to final passage.

### § 234. Committee Hearings[61]

No further action is taken on a bill after its introduction and first reading until the chief author requests a committee hearing, at which time a date for the hearing is set and interested persons are notified. At the hearing, the chief author explains the bill and presents expert testimony if he or she thinks it will aid the bill's passage. Proponents and opponents state their views. After testimony is heard and debate is completed, the committee may defeat the bill by vote or by ignoring it, or it may recommend that the bill be reported to the entire House or Senate in its original form or with amendments. A committee also may refer a bill to another committee. All committee meetings are open to the public.

---

60. MINN. CONST. art. IV, § 19; Minn. Senate Rules 34, 35, 36 (2000); Minn. House Rules 1.04, 1.10, 1.11, 1.13, 1.15 (1999–2000).
61. Minn. Senate Rules 35, 36, 49, 65 (2000); Minn. House Rules 1.11, 1.13, 1.15, 6.24, 6.30 (1999–2000)

After acting on a bill, the committee sends a report to the House or Senate stating its actions and recommendations. Committee reports usually are very brief and non-explanatory. Committee recommendations of bills generally are adopted by the House and Senate without discussion. This enables a bill that has received favorable committee action to be brought before the full body.

### § 235. Calendars[62]

After adoption of the committee report, the bill is given its second reading. If floor debate is expected or desired, bills are placed on the Calendar of General Orders. If the reported bill is noncontroversial, it is placed on the Consent Calendar. Bills placed on the Calendar of General Orders are considered by the Committee of the Whole (i.e., by the entire Senate or the entire House). Rules at this time are less formal than at other times during the daily session. Discussion and amendment may occur. The chief author explains the purpose of the bill and offers amendments that will improve the quality of the bill or enhance its chances of gaining approval. If a simple majority approves, the bill is placed on the "Calendar," a list of bills previously on General Orders that are ready for final approval. There the bill is given its third reading and summarizing arguments are presented. At this time, no amendments may be offered without the unanimous consent of the body. Legislators then vote on the bill for the final time, unless the other house amends it.

### § 236. Conference Committees[63]

After a bill has passed the Senate or the House it is sent to the other body for consideration. If the other body amends the bill, then the body that originally passed the bill either can adopt the amendment and pass (or defeat) the bill as amended, or it can request that a conference committee be appointed to resolve differences between the two houses. If the differences are resolved, the committee makes its report to each body. When the conference committee's report (printed in the *Journals*) is adopted, the bill as amended by the committee is

---

62. Minn. Senate Rule 45 (2000); Minn. House Rule 1.30 (1999–2000).
63. Minn. Senate Rule 49 (2000); Minn. House Rule 1.15 (1999–2000).

**Chapter Two. Legislation**                                                25

resubmitted for approval in both houses. These bills cannot be amended on the floor.

### § 237. Action by the Governor[64]

When a bill has been approved by both houses, a correct copy, called the "enrolled bill," is sent to the governor for approval or veto. A two-thirds vote in favor of the bill from each body of the legislature is required to override a veto. If, while the legislature is in session, the governor does not sign or veto a bill within three days after receiving it, the bill becomes law without his signature. The governor may "pocket veto" a bill after the legislature has adjourned. A pocket veto results when a bill passed during the last three days of a biennial session is not signed and filed by the governor within fourteen days after final adjournment. When a bill becomes a law, it is given a chapter number and printed as a slip law (*see* § 250, *infra*). Chapter numbers are assigned chronologically during each biennium in order of passage.

### § 238. Effective Dates[65]

All general laws become effective August 1, unless otherwise provided. An act containing an appropriation takes effect at the start of the state's fiscal year, July 1.

### § 239. Resolutions[66]

Simple House and Senate resolutions are internal matters and concern the operation of those chambers. They are adopted only by the body that introduces them. Concurrent resolutions concern both bodies and each must adopt them. Procedures for adopting resolutions are not as formal as those required for enacting laws and do not require the governor's signature; if money is appropriated, a roll call is required. Resolutions are printed in the House and Senate *Journals* if adopted.

Memorial resolutions, which are given a House or Senate file number, are addressed to the U.S. government. They normally require the same procedures that are followed for the passage of a bill, including

---

64. MINN. CONST. art IV, §§ 23, 24.
65. MINN. STAT. § 645.02 (1998).
66. Minn. Senate Rule 53 (2000); Minn. House Rule 4.02 (1999–2000).

the governor's signature. If approved, they are given resolution numbers and are printed following the laws in *Laws of Minnesota*.

## § 240. LEGISLATIVE HISTORY

§ 241. Sources of Legislative History
§ 242. Use of Legislative History to Determine Legislative Intent
§ 243. Commercial Publishers of Legislative Materials

Tracing Minnesota legislative history (i.e., the background and events leading up to enactment of a law) can be difficult. First, the amount of material available is limited. Second, the material is relatively inaccessible. Physically, much of the material is on audio tape that is neither well-indexed nor complete. Also, accessibility is hampered by the location of the materials. Third, the use of some items for the purpose of discerning legislative intent may be prohibited.

### § 241. Sources of Legislative History

§ 241.1. Journals
§ 241.2. Committee Books
§ 241.3. Tape Recordings
§ 241.4. Locating Bills
§ 241.5. Legislative Research

### § 241.1. Journals[67]

For every session, each body of the legislature publishes its multi-volume *Journal*. The *Journals* provide chronological information on the actions taken on all bills, such as bill introductions, readings, and approvals. They also contain the names of the legislators, committee assignments, meeting schedules, and votes on bills and amendments. They do not provide any interpretative discussion or debates on the bills.

Indexing of the *Journals* is different from most other materials, but has been quite consistent. Access to the *Journals* is by bill number,

---

67. A list of Minnesota *Journals*, with dates and pagination, from 1849 to 1937, is published in CHECKLIST OF LEGISLATIVE JOURNALS OF THE STATES OF THE UNITED STATES OF AMERICA 108–11 (Grace E. Macdonald (comp.) for the National Ass'n State Libraries, Oxford Press 1938) (William S. Hein & Co., Inc., reprint 1980).

## Chapter Two. Legislation 27

referred to as the "file number." For bills enacted into law, this number can be found in the *Laws of Minnesota*. Using the file number, researchers should consult the index volume of the *Journal* for page references to specific actions. When researching the history of a bill by its file number, the index volumes of both *Journals* should be consulted. When tracing a bill by its Senate file number, for example, researchers must use both the *Journal of the Senate* and its index and the *Journal of the House of Representatives* and its index of "Bills of the Senate" for actions on Senate bills in the House.

The *Journals* also include indexes by title, author, topic, chapter, and companion bill number. A miscellaneous index lists organizations, committees, executive addresses, and other information.

For up-to-date *Journal* information on bills currently before the legislature, call either the Senate Index Office or the House Index Office. Both Index Offices provide access by author, subject, and file number. The Senate Index Department is located in Room 110 of the Capitol. The Senate Index provides information on the content, status, and progress of bills during legislative sessions and later compiles the Index to the Senate Journal. Information via computer terminals is available in the Senate Information Office in Room 231 of the Capitol, or by calling 651-296-2887 or 651-296-0504.

The Index Department of the Chief Clerk's Office of the House of Representatives in Room 211 of the Capitol, records all official House action on legislation from the Journal of the House. Its staff also prepares descriptions of all bills and prepares various indexes. This data is entered on the Minnesota Legislative Bill Tracking website <http://www.leg.state.mn.us/leg/legis.htm>. For bill status inquiries, selected reports, and information on training and use of the House Index Information system, contact the House Index at 651-296-6646.

Daily issues of the *Journals* usually are distributed on the day after legislative action has occurred and are available upon request from the Office of the Secretary of the Senate or the Office of the Chief Clerk of the House. Bound volumes of the *Journals* are published at the end of a session. These *Journals* are available in most large public and law libraries. Senate daily journals are available on the Web at <http://www.senate.leg.state.mn.us/journals/index.htm>. House daily journals are available on the Web at <http://www.house.leg.state.mn.us/cco/journals/journl.htm>.

## Illustration 2. Page from Journal of the Senate

INDEX** 7345
** (From *Journal of the Senate* 1983-84)
BILLS OF THE SENATE—Continued.

| S. F. No. | TITLE | First Reading and Reference | Second Reading | Other Proceedings | Third Reading | Subsequent Proceedings | Returned from House | Approved | Chapter |
|---|---|---|---|---|---|---|---|---|---|
| 509 | A bill for an act relating to retirement; highway patrol; restating the definition of average monthly salary; amending Minnesota Statutes 1982, section 352B.08, subdivision 2. | 304 | 940 | 927 (11624) | 995 | | | | |
| 510 | A bill for an act relating to housing; prohibiting certain rent control ordinances in cities, counties, and towns; proposing new law coded in Minnesota Statutes, chapter 471. | 304 | 1584 | 1278 1555 | 1282 2917a | 2920 | 4460 | 3808 | Veto 4452 4459 | |
| 511 | A bill for an act relating to low-level radioactive waste; entering the Midwest Interstate Low-Level Radioactive Waste Compact; assessing certain low-level radioactive waste generators; providing for enforcement of the compact; providing for civil and criminal penalties; creating an advisory committee; appropriating money; proposing new law coded in Minnesota Statutes, chapter 116C. | 305 | 2742 | 486a 991a 2883 | 740a 2738 | 2883 2983 | 2983 | 2982 | 4453 | 353 |

## Illustration 3. Page from Journal of the House

| 530 | INDEX** **(From *Journal of the House* 1983-84) NUMERICAL INDEX OF SENATE BILLS—Continued |||||||||
|---|---|---|---|---|---|---|---|---|---|
| Number | AUTHORS<br>At Time of Adjournment<br>TITLE<br>At Time of First Reading In House | Received from Senate | First Reading and Reference | Second Reading | Other Proceedings || Third Reading and Passage | Subsequent Proceedings | General Laws Chapter & Year |
| 510 | Wegscheid, Storm, Vega<br>A bill for an act relating to housing; prohibiting certain rent control ordinances in cities, counties, and towns; proposing new law coded in Minnesota Statutes, chapter 471. | 4284 | 4284 | 4423 | 4284<br>4350s<br>5352a<br>5355 | 4350<br>5090<br>5354 | 5357 | | |
| 511 | Pehler, Merriam, Benson, Luther, Davis<br>A bill for an act relating to low-level radioactive waste; entering the Midwest Interstate Low-Level Radioactive Waste Compact; assessing certain low-level radioactive waste generators; providing for enforcement of the compact; providing for civil and criminal penalties; appropriating money; proposing new law coded in Minnesota Statutes, chapter 116C. | 4169 | 4170 | 4255 | 4170<br>4255a | | 4216s | 4275 | 6235 | 353<br>1983 |

### § 241.2. Committee Books

Each committee maintains a committee book. These books, written or typed by the committee's secretary, provide summarized minutes of committee proceedings, a record of formal actions, names of witnesses, the text of written testimony, the authors and text of amendments, roll calls, and subcommittee actions. The content and arrangement of these committee books vary from committee to committee. Infrequently they are quite detailed, containing supplemental materials and occasionally a report; most, however, merely are records of committee actions taken, with no explanations or justifications.

Only one copy of each committee book exists. During the current legislative session, they are kept in the Office of the Chief Clerk of the House or the Office of the Secretary of the Senate. The Minnesota Historical Society Library, State Archives, houses the committee books. Not all minutes for these committees have survived. The House committee books begin in 1919 and the Senate committee books begin in 1911. The records of both House and Senate judiciary committees begin in 1883. There is a scattering of House and Senate minutes for the years prior to 1919 and 1911.[68]

### § 241.3. Tape Recordings[69]

Pursuant to Senate and House rules, floor proceedings must be tape recorded and delivered to the Minnesota Legislative Reference Library.[70] The tape recording of Senate floor actions and committee proceedings began in 1971, and House tapes began in 1973. An agreement between the legislature and the Legislative Reference Library mandates that all tapes transferred from the originating body be destroyed after sixteen years. The Minnesota Legislative Reference Library houses the tape recordings from eight years ago to the present. The Minnesota Historical Society Library houses the tape recordings covering the previous eight-year period. The date of a floor proceeding is needed to locate a tape recording, and these dates can be determined from the *Journals*. To locate taped committee hearings for a specific bill, the name of the committee and the date of the hearing is needed. The committee minutes provide that date. Use the Legislature Inventory Notebook to locate the Senate or House tapes. Both floor and committee debates are available only on tape, no written transcripts of the proceedings are made. The Minnesota Historical Society provides tape duplication services for a fee.

### § 241.4. Locating Bills

§ 241.41. Bills Introduced During a Current Legislative Session
§ 241.42. Bills Introduced During Prior Legislative Sessions

A thorough legislative history requires reviewing all actions on a bill in both bodies as well as researching other bills pertaining to the same subject. To accomplish this, a researcher should look at each engrossment.

---

68. Minnesota Historical Society <http://www.mnhs.org/library/tips/legislative/step3.html> (last visited Nov. 4, 2001).
69. Minnesota Historical Society <http://www.mnhs.org/library/tips/legislative/step4.html> (last visited Nov. 4, 2001).
70. Minn. Senate Rule 65 (1999–2000); Minn. House Rule 2.15 (2000).

### § 241.41. Bills Introduced During a Current Legislative Session

Copies of individual bills may be obtained at no cost from the Office of the chief clerk of the house or the secretary of the senate. Information on bills introduced during a current legislative session may be obtained from the following sources.

1. On the Web at <http://www.library.leg.state.mn.us/leg/legis.htm>. The full-text of bills, House and Senate bill introductions, bill summaries, unofficial engrossments, and conference committee reports are available.
2. House Index and Senate Index. The Index offices compile the indexes to the bound volumes of the *Journals*. During legislative sessions, they provide legislators and the public with up-to-the minute information on the status of bills, including bill numbers, their titles, summaries of contents, authors, references made to a bill in the *Journals,* etc. The personnel of each Index office monitor daily floor sessions and provide information on legislative organization, committee appointments, reports, resolutions, and votes. Both House and Senate Index files are online. For up-to-date *Journal* information on bills currently before the legislature call either the Senate Index or the House Index. The Senate Index Department is located in Room 110 of the Capitol. The Senate Index provides information on the content, status, and progress of bills during legislative sessions and later compiles the *Index to the Senate Journal*. Information via computer terminal is available in the Senate Information Office in room 231 of the Capitol, or by calling 651-296-2887 or 651-296-0504.

   The Index Department of the Chief Clerk's Office of the House of Representatives (in room 211 of the Capitol), records all official House action on legislation from the House *Journal*. Its staff also prepares descriptions of all bills and prepares various indexes. The data is entered on the Minnesota Legislative Bill Tracking website at <http://www.leg.state.mn.us/leg/legis.htm>. For bill status inquiries, select reports, and information on training and use of the House Index Information system, contact the *House Index* at 651-296-6646.
3. Daily *Journals* (*see* § 241.1, *supra*).
4. Newsletters and brochures issued by the Public Information Offices are available free of charge. For example, the House issues *The Session Weekly* and the Senate publishes *Senate Briefly,* both of

which provide committee schedules, summaries of bills filed, and information about other legislative activities.
5. Newspapers and commercial publishers (*see* § 243, *supra*).
6. Public and special interest groups that opposed or supported the bill.

### § 241.42. Bills Introduced During Prior Legislative Sessions

§ 241.421. Bills Enacted into Law that Are Coded
§ 241.422. Bills Enacted into Law that Are Not Coded
§ 241.423. Bills Not Enacted into Law

Selected unofficial bill engrossments are available on the Web at <http://www.revisor.leg.state.mn.us/forms/getccrue.shtml>. Engrossed laws from the archives of the Secretary of State's Office are housed at the Minnesota Historical Society Library. The set of the engrossed laws consists of the final signed copies of House files, Senate files, chapter files, and resolutions from 1858 forward, but this set is not complete. The Minnesota Legislative Reference Library houses bill engrossments from 1957 forward.

### § 241.421. Bills Enacted into Law that Are Coded

Information on bills enacted during prior legislative sessions and codified in *Minnesota Statutes* may be obtained by following these procedures:

1. Ascertain the session law citation(s) provided after the text of each section of *Minnesota Statutes* or *Minnesota Statutes Annotated.*[71] This citation provides the year of the bill's enactment and its chapter and section number. Thus, the session law citation for section 525.921 of the *Minnesota Statutes* is "1969 c 79 s 1." This signifies that this section was enacted at the 1969 legislative session as chapter 79, section 1, and may be located in the 1969 *Laws of Minnesota*.

---

71. *Minnesota Statutes* references to *Minnesota Revised Laws* 1905 are in brackets and those to *Mason's Minnesota Statutes* 1927 are in parentheses. Those compilations must be consulted for citations to the session laws from which the individual sections printed there were derived. *Minnesota Statutes Annotated,* under the history notes, cites all former session laws and compilations. It also publishes pertinent sections that reflect the amendatory changes.

**Chapter Two. Legislation**　　　　　　　　　　　　　　　　　　　　33

2. Check the appropriate volume of *Laws of Minnesota* for the bill's file number, which is noted after the chapter number. Thus, chapter 79 of the 1969 *Laws of Minnesota* was Senate File No. 448.
3. Check the indexes in the *Journals* (*see* § 241.1, *supra*) of the appropriate year to find pages on which actions on the bill are reported. For a thorough legislative history, check the subject index as well as file number index to follow the birth and death of similar bills.
4. For a summary of action in the committee, search the minutes of the committee to which the bill was sent (*see* § 241.2, *supra*). The name of this committee is obtained from the *Journals* by checking the "Bills" section of the index under the heading "First Reading and Reference."
5. Check any existing tape recordings (*see* § 241.3, *supra*).
6. Check newspapers for background information. The bill's chief author and those public or special interest groups that lobbied for or against the legislation are other good sources for supplementary information. Personal papers of legislators are another source that may be helpful.

### § 241.422. Bills Enacted into Law that Are Not Coded

Table 1 in the *Minnesota Statutes* Tables and Index volume lists uncoded local special laws enacted since 1849. If the researcher knows the year of the bill's enactment, then he or she can check the appropriate volume of *Laws of Minnesota*. Having obtained the session law citation, the researcher may follow the procedures outlined in steps 2 through 6 of § 243.421, *supra*.

### § 241.423. Bills Not Enacted into Law

If a researcher does not know the file number of the unenacted bill, then the subject indexes in the *Journals* must be searched. Once the file number is found, the researcher may follow the procedures listed in § 243.421, *infra*.

### § 241.5. Legislative Research

The Legislative Research Committee,[72] a joint committee that existed from 1947 to 1969, prepared more than 100 reports that gave advance consideration to problems expected to confront upcoming legislatures.

---

72. Act of April 10, 1947, ch. 306, 1947 Minn. Laws 489 (repealed 1969).

These studies might be helpful in conducting research on the legislative history of actions taken during that period. To find these reports, check the holdings of individual libraries.

Since 1969, the Legislative Reference Library has provided access to reports that may be pertinent for legislative history. Some internal reports not generally distributed may be obtained from committee members or their staffs (*see* § 226.3, *supra*).

### § 242. Use of Legislative History to Determine Legislative Intent

Minnesota's interpretation and construction statute[73] is similar to that found in most jurisdictions. Section 645.16 of *Minnesota Statutes* provides that when there is ambiguity in the words of a law, the law should be construed to effectuate legislative intent. Eight suggestions are listed for determining intent including "the contemporaneous legislative history." Although the items of "contemporaneous legislative history" are not specified, they would seem to include the committee books and the tape recordings as well as the *Journals*. The courts of Minnesota have allowed these materials to be used on the issue of legislative intent.[74]

The Minnesota legislature, however, has said otherwise. Both the House and the Senate, in their rules for the production and preservation of the tapes and committee books, have explicitly prohibited the use of these materials for the determination of legislative intent: "It is the intention that testimony and discussion preserved under this rule not be admissible in any court or administrative proceeding on an issue of legislative intent."[75] "Discussion preserved under this rule is not intended to be admissible in a court or administrative proceeding on an issue of legislative intent."[76] The reason for this prohibition is the assertion that no one legislator, or even a group of legislators, can speak for the entire body and statements of individual legislators should only be regarded as their own opinions. Thus far, both the reasoning and the rules have been ignored by the courts.

---

73. MINN. STAT. §§ 645.001–645.51 (1998).
74. *See, e.g.*, Haage v. Steies, 555 N.W.2d 7, 9 (Minn. Ct. App. 1996).
75. Minn. Senate Rule 65 (1999–2000). *See* § 225, *supra*.
76. Minn. House Rule 2.15 (2000). *See* § 225, *supra*.

## § 243. Commercial Publishers of Legislative Materials

§ 243.1. Phillips Legislative Service
§ 243.2. Minnesota Government Report
§ 243.3. St. Paul Legal Ledger
§ 243.4. Politics in Minnesota
§ 243.5. Checks and Balances—Minnesota
§ 243.6. Minnesota E-Democracy Political Desktop
§ 243.7. LEXIS-NEXIS
§ 243.8. Westlaw
§ 243.9. Other Sources

### § 243.1. Phillips Legislative Service[77]

Phillips provides a variety of services and subscriptions. The basic subscription includes a list of members of the legislature and committee and subcommittee assignments; a list of bills by file number, names of their authors, the committees to which they are assigned, companion bill numbers, and brief summaries of the contents; and a brief summary of laws by chapter number, including file number and date signed by the governor. Also available are daily *Journals,* complete texts of first bill engrossments (companion bills are not provided), and complete texts of laws.

*Phillips' Legislative Interim Reporter,* issued weekly when the legislature is not in session, provides information on committee and subcommittee hearing schedules, committee appointments, and summaries of committee hearings. Neither the session nor interim service is indexed. During the legislative session, Phillips' subscribers may access an online computerized bill tracking service that can be searched by subject, statute, author, bill number, and initial committee referral.

### § 243.2. Minnesota Government Report[78]

The *Minnesota Government Report,* formerly called *Capitol Reporter,* is a newsletter published twice weekly about state government activities. It provides information on the governor's activities and appointments; legislative highlights; administrative actions; notices of meetings, governmental announcements, news shorts; and syllabi of selected

---

77. 969 Rice St., St. Paul, MN 55117; phone 651-487-0809.
78. P.O. Box 441, Willernie, MN 55090; phone 651-426-6339.

appellate court decisions and orders, and information on administrative rules hearings.

### § 243.3. St. Paul Legal Ledger[79]

The *St. Paul Legal Ledger* is a twice-weekly newspaper published on Mondays and Thursdays. It is dedicated to providing year-round coverage of the Minnesota legislative process and public policy issues. It features regular articles by Republican and Democratic leaders and a policy briefing section.

### § 243.4. Politics in Minnesota[80]

*Politics in Minnesota* is a newsletter that bills itself as an insiders' look at Minnesota politics. It provides political and public affairs analysis and tracks people in public affairs including lobbyists, elected officials, and consultants. It is published twenty-two times a year.

### § 243.5. Checks and Balances—Minnesota[81]

The Checks and Balances site is divided into several parts. Of note are the following sections: The "Issues" section covers Minnesota political issues such as the legislative agenda, the economy, and property taxes. "Bookmarks" reviews books of interest to Minnesotans concerned with politics. The "Other Articles" section features reprinted political articles by Checks and Balances staff and contributors. "External Opinions" is a forum on matters of political, economic, and social concern. Links to other sites of a political nature are also included. The proclaimed intent of the site is to challenge the political frontier. Its focus is to apply positive, practical, and pragmatic approaches to political questions that recognize the importance of the swing voter in Minnesota. Checks and Balances seeks to open the eyes of party people, elected officials, and those concerned with the future of Minnesota.

---

79. 332 Minnesota St., Suite W-122, St. Paul, Minnesota 55101; phone 651-222-0059; Web address <http://www.legal-ledger.com/index.htm> (last visited Nov. 4, 2001).
80. 500 Robert Street North, #238, St. Paul, MN 55101-2246; phone 651-293-0949; Web address <http://www.politicsinminnesota.com/> (last visited Nov. 4, 2001).
81. Web address <http://checksandbalances.com/MN/> (last visited Nov. 4, 2001).

## § 243.6. Minnesota E-Democracy Political Desktop[82]

E-Democracy is a non-partisan citizen-based project whose mission is to improve participation in democracy in Minnesota through the use of information networks. Minnesota political, public policy, and news sources are linked at one convenient site.

## § 243.7. Lexis Publishing[83]

The LEXIS-NEXIS full-text database is accessible via the Web at <http://www.lexis.com>. LEXIS is a subscription service, but non-subscribers can make credit card transactions via the Web.

This service provides access to numerous Minnesota legislative databases. The Minnesota Advance Legislative Service (MNALS) file contains the full-text of all laws enacted during a legislative session. It is a cumulative collection of laws enacted since the 1989 Regular Session. The file is updated continuously throughout the legislative session when information is received from the State of Minnesota.

The Minnesota Bill Tracking and Full-Text Bills (MNBILL) file contains Minnesota bill tracking and bill text from the current session.

The Minnesota Bill Tracking Reports (MNTRCK) file contains a summary and legislative chronology of all pending Minnesota legislation in the current legislative session. Note that changes made to bills during the legislative process are not reflected in the synopsis section of the bill tracking report. Consequently, the full-text of the bill should be consulted and reviewed for any changes to the language of the bill. This file covers the current session's legislative activity and is updated within forty-eight hours of publication by Information for Public Affairs Incorporated.[84]

The Minnesota Full-Text Bills (MNTEXT) file contains the full-text of bill pending in the Minnesota legislature. Changes to the full-text of the bill are not incorporated into the digest portion of the full-text. Therefore, review the entire text of the bill for any changes. The file is updated within two weeks of publication by Information for Public Affairs, Incorporated.[85]

---

82. Web address <http://www.e-democracy.org/links/> (last visited Nov. 4, 2001).
83. 9443 Springboro Pike, P.O. Box 933, Dayton, OH 45401; phone 800-543-6862.
84. Information for Public Affairs, Incorporated (IPA), 2101 K Street, Sacramento, CA 95816; phone 916-444-0840.
85. Id.

The Minnesota Statutes and Advance Legislative Service Materials (MNCODE) file contains Minnesota statutes and constitution produced from material provided by the Minnesota Revisor of Statutes and the Advance Legislative Service. Materials include only those documents that have been enacted since the code was last updated. The code and constitution are updated annually. The Advance Legislative Service is updated continuously throughout the legislative session.

The Minnesota Statutes Archive (MNARCH) file is a statutes archive with coverage beginning in the 1991 legislative session. Once a user enters the MNARCH file, a choice of years is displayed for the year(s) of the code a researcher wishes to search. The Minnesota Statutes contains all laws of a general and permanent nature enacted by the Minnesota legislature plus the Minnesota state constitution.

### § 243.8. Westlaw[86]

Westlaw is a subscription service that offers numerous Minnesota legislative databases. The Westlaw full-text database is accessible via the Web at <http://www.westlaw.com>. Westlaw software also is available and can be downloaded from its website.

The Minnesota Legislative Service (MN-LEGIS) contains documents, chapters, and resolutions passed by the legislature in the current or most recent session. The Minnesota Historical Legislative Service (MN-LEGIS-OLD) currently covers the years 1988 to 1999.

Minnesota Bill Tracking-Full Text (MN-BILLTXT) contains the full text of all available bills introduced and amended and enacted versions from the current session. It also contains a legislative session status calendar providing information about session status, adjournment dates, and action deadlines. This database is provided through an agreement between West and Information for Public Affairs, Inc.

Minnesota Bill Tracking (MN-BILLTRK) contains summaries and status information concerning current Minnesota legislation. Bills are tracked from their introduction throughout the legislative process. This database also contains a legislative session status calendar.

Minnesota Bill Tracking-Summaries and Full-Text Combined (MN-BILLS) combines MN-BILLTRK with MN-BILLTXT. MN-BILLS, MN-BILLTRK, and MN-BILLTXT are produced from

---

86. West Group, 620 Opperman Dr., P.O. Box 64779, St. Paul, MN 55164-0779; phone 800-937-8529.

**Chapter Two. Legislation**

electronic data transmissions provided by State Net, a service of Information for Public Affairs, Inc.[87]

Westlaw also provides access to the full-text of Minnesota Statutes and the West publication, *Minnesota Statutes Annotated*. Currently, Westlaw provides access to the statutes and the annotated statutes from 1991 forward.

### § 243.9. Other Sources

Legal newspapers (*see* § 554.6, *infra*) and local major newspapers issue periodic reports on the status of legislation. These reports may include information on the bill itself (file number and content) and the action taken on it. News coverage of major legislative issues often is extensive. Public libraries might have indexes to local daily newspapers and to periodicals. The Legislative Reference Library (*see* § 618.4, *infra*) has an extensive clipping file of Minnesota newspapers. Additionally, news periodicals and the publications of public and special interest groups often provide background information on legislation.

The Minnesota Library Information Network, MNLINK, is an Internet-based virtual library providing no-cost access to multiple information resources. It currently offers free access to the full-text of the *Minneapolis Star Tribune* from 1986 to the present.[88] Another Internet source for a collection of links to newspaper sites around the country, including Minnesota, is Newspapers Online at <http://www.newspapers.com>.

---

87. *Id.*
88. <http://www.mnlink.org>.

## § 250. Session Laws[89]

§ 251. Contents of Official Session Laws
§ 252. General and Special Laws
§ 253. Indexes and Tables
§ 254. Minnesota Session Law Service
§ 255. LEXIS-NEXIS Minnesota Advance Legislative Service
§ 256. Curative Acts

Session laws are the individual acts passed by the legislature during each of its sessions (*see* § 221, *supra*). Each act or resolution passed at a session is issued as a "slip law" after it has been approved by the governor and filed with the secretary of state. Copies of slip laws may be obtained from the Office of the Chief Clerk of the House, the Office of the Secretary of the Senate, and the Minnesota State Documents Center (*see* § 350, *infra*). Some libraries maintain files of slip laws. Commercial publishers (*see* § 243, *supra*) may supply slip laws by subscription.

Slip laws are reproduced in bound volumes, the *Laws of Minnesota*, in the order of their enactment as signified by the chapter number assigned on the date of approval.[90] Thus, the citation "1977 Minn. Laws ch. 7" indicates that the bill was the seventh act signed into law during the 1977 session.

Available on the Web is the consolidated Table 1 from 1945 to 2000, which allows researchers to search for uncoded session law sections and subdivisions that have been amended, repealed, or the subject of other action from the 1945 regular session through the 2000 regular session. These session law sections are compiled annually into Table 1, one of several tables found at the end of *Laws of Minnesota*. The Minnesota Session Law Service lists the most recent amendments and new and repealed statutes in its Table 1. The session laws from 1994 forward are also available on the Web at <http://www.leg.state.mn.us/leg/statutes.htm>.

---

89. A checklist of Minnesota session laws is contained in Appendix C.
90. Since 1977–78, chapters of the session laws have been numbered consecutively through the biennium, instead of each year. This chapter number of the session laws has no relationship to the chapter numbers of *Minnesota Statutes*. For a discussion of the meaning of chapter numbers in *Minnesota Statutes*, *see* § 262.1, *infra*.

## § 251. Contents of Official Session Laws

Note that the title *Laws of Minnesota* is used for all official publications of session laws that have had various titles throughout the years. Each session law is printed in *Laws of Minnesota* exactly as enacted. The contents of each act include the chapter number, Senate or House file (bill) number, title, date of approval, and the text. If the law amends an existing statute, additions to that statute are underscored and deletions are crossed out. Unless a different date is specified in the act, appropriations acts take effect at the beginning of the first day of July following their enactment; other acts take effect on the following August first.[91]

## § 252. General and Special Laws

Session laws are all the laws passed by the legislature. General laws, those that affect the community at large, are later incorporated into *Minnesota Statutes*.[92] Not all laws become statutes. Special laws usually are found only in the session laws. Special laws include proposed constitutional amendments, and local, appropriation, private, temporary, and curative acts.[93] These laws do not apply on a general level. Appropriations are applicable for a two-year period, and laws that are codified in the statutes are permanent.

In published volumes of session laws, "General Laws" and "Special Laws" were physically separated from 1857 until 1893, sometimes published in one volume and sometimes in two. An 1881 constitutional amendment forbade the passage of "special or private" laws on eleven different subjects. This did not seem to discourage their enactment, so an additional amendment that extended and strengthened the prior amendment was added in 1892.[94] Therefore, since 1893, there have been no separate volumes of special laws. Many acts continued to be passed, however, which by judicial interpretation actually were

---

91. MINN. STAT. § 645.02 (1998).
92. The *Laws of Minnesota* and *Minnesota Statutes* are distributed to various public officials and libraries throughout the state according to MINN. STAT. § 3C.12(2) (1998).
93. Special laws should be distinguished from special sessions of the legislature. In either a regular or special session, the legislature may pass both general and special laws.
94. These amendments added sections 33 and 34 to article IV of the Minnesota Constitution of 1857. The sections now appear as article XII, sections 1 and 2 of the Minnesota Constitution of 1974.

special in nature. These laws did not name a specific local area or entity but, rather, listed criteria that made the law applicable only to one entity or area.[95] In 1958, a constitutional amendment was passed allowing for special legislation relating to local government under specific conditions. Usually the legislation becomes effective only after approval by the local unit named in the law.[96]

There now is a complete cumulative index to local laws. Table I in the 1998 *Minnesota Statutes* Tables and Index volume lists local special acts since 1849 alphabetically by local governmental unit with citations to the session laws. Table I does not indicate whether local approval was granted. This information is found in Table 4 in *Laws of Minnesota* in a volume published in the year the law was enacted or within two years of enactment. The dates of the local approval and filing appear in the table. If a special law provides for approval by more than one local governmental unit, the approval and filing dates are listed after the name of each unit. If local approval is not required, that fact is indicated.

Prior to the publication of the 1984 *Minnesota Statutes,* the most complete index to special laws was the *Index Digest to All the Laws of the State of Minnesota General and Special Including the Joint Resolutions and Memorials to Congress* (1894), by John F. Kelly. It still may be necessary to consult this index for information on private laws passed before 1894 (*see* Appendix D).

## § 253. Indexes and Tables

Early indexes to the session laws are incomplete, inconsistent, and difficult to use. Terms and entries for the same topic sometimes varied from year to year. Indexes to more recent volumes, however, are systematic and quite complete.

---

95. *See, e.g.,* Hamlin v. Ladd, 217 Minn. 249, 252, 14 N.W.2d 396, 398 (1944); Millet v. City of Hastings, 179 Minn. 358, 229 N.W. 346 (1930). *See generally* Anderson, *Special Legislation in Minnesota,* 7 MINN. L. REV. 133, 187 (1923); Dawley, *Special Legislation and Municipal Home Rule in Minnesota: Recent Developments,* 16 MINN. L. REV. 659 (1932). For a brief discussion of the relationship between the reduction in the number of special laws passed by the legislature to the increase in the powers of local government units, see § 273, *infra.*
96. MINN. CONST. art. XII, § 2, MINN. STAT. §§ 645.021–645.024 (1998).

## Chapter Two. Legislation

The names of the officers and members of the legislature are listed at the beginning of each volume. Tables vary from year to year. Generally, the following tables are appended:

- Session laws that have been amended or repealed
- Sections of *Minnesota Statutes* that have been amended, repealed, or newly enacted[97]
- Special laws
- Senate and House files enacted

### § 254. Minnesota Session Law Service

West's *Minnesota Session Law Service* is published in pamphlet form periodically during the legislative session. The lag time between enactment of the law and publication is three to six weeks. A list of legislators with their addresses and committee assignments is supplied in the first pamphlet. Each issue includes an explanation of the general effective dates of the laws; the convening and adjournment dates of the session; an alphabetical listing of the laws; a cumulative table of sections of *Minnesota Statutes Annotated* affected by the laws; a cumulative table of laws identifying sections of *Minnesota Statutes Annotated* affected thereby or identifying laws as special laws; a cumulative table of file numbers and the corresponding chapter or resolution number; a cumulative table of state court rule changes; and a descriptive word index.

The *Minnesota Session Law Service* also is available on Westlaw in the MN-LEGIS database. Web access is available at: <http://www.westlaw.com>.

### § 255. LEXIS-NEXIS Minnesota Advance Legislative Service[98]

The online Minnesota Advance Legislative Service (MNALS) file contains the full-text of all laws enacted during a legislative session. It is a cumulative collection of laws enacted since the 1989 Regular

---

97. The Revisor of Statutes provides a table of uncoded session laws that have been amended, repealed, or the subject of other action on the Web at <http://www.revisor.leg.state.mn.us/forms/ltab1.shtml>.
98. Web address <http://www.lexis.com>.

Session. The file is updated continuously throughout the legislative session when information is received from the State of Minnesota.

## § 256. Curative Acts

A curative act is a form of retrospective legislation to validate legal proceedings that would otherwise be void because of defects or irregularities. It operates to accomplish a result that the parties intended, but failed, to accomplish. The majority of curative acts passed by the legislature deal with title to real estate. For example, a curative act might validate a mortgage foreclosure sale in which there was a procedural defect. The following sources provide information on curative acts.

*Minnesota Statutes Annotated,* ch. 647, "Minnesota Curative Acts 1849–1947" (updated by pocket parts).

This chapter is not included in *Minnesota Statutes.* Included are explanations, cross references, alphabetical and chronological indexes, and judicial constructions.

*Minnesota Standards for Title Examination* (Minneapolis: Minnesota State Bar Ass'n, Sec. Real Property Law) (updated annually) (loose-leaf).

This volume provides a table listing curative acts passed since 1931 that are pertinent to the examination of real property titles.

*Stalland's Minnesota Curative Acts Affecting Title to Real Estate,* Knute D. Stalland (St. Paul, MN: Mason Publishing Co. 1930).

This book was designed to aid those examining title to real estate by furnishing a quick guide to acts that cured defects that had been the subject of dispute in actions, such as those to quiet title. The table of contents is divided into two topics: specific defects and county. Material under each of the topics is arranged in alphabetical order. *Mason's Minnesota Statutes,* volume 3, appendix 5, page 1779, and volume 4, appendix 5, page 1020, extend this list of curative acts to 1944 (*see* Appendix D).

## § 260. Statutes

§ 261. Compilations, Revisions, Codes
§ 262. Minnesota Statutes
§ 263. Minnesota Statutes Annotated
§ 264. Statutory Construction

### § 261. Compilations, Revisions, Codes[99]

§ 261.1. Compilations
§ 261.2. Revisions
§ 261.3. Codes

An arrangement of statutes may be characterized as a compilation, a revision, or a code.[100]

### § 261.1. Compilations

A compilation is a rearrangement by subject matter of current laws of general application without change in the language or substance of the laws as originally enacted.[101] In Minnesota, compilations have been prepared by individuals, by commissions officially authorized by the legislature, and by private publishers without official authorization.

If a disparity between a law printed in a compilation and a session law is found, the text of the session law will control. Sometimes legislatures by statute create various forms of presumption in favor of compilations.[102] The compilations then are presumed to be correct until a disparity is established.

### § 261.2. Revisions

A revision is similar to a compilation in that it is a rearrangement by subject matter of the current statutes of general application. A revision

---

99. A list of all official compilations, revisions, and codes, as well as major unofficial compilations that have been published in Minnesota is included in Appendix D. Not included are compilations of selected statutes published for individual subjects. These may be issued by state agencies, interested organizations, or commercial publishers such as Code Systems, Inc. of St. Paul.
100. *See generally,* J. Franklin Wheeler & Thomas B. Wheeler, *Statute Revision: Its Nature. Purpose and Method,* 16 TULANE L. REV. 165 (1942).
101. *See generally id.* at 168.
102. *See, e.g.,* MINN. STAT. § 3.C.13 (1998).

differs from a compilation in that the language of a law as originally enacted may be changed to clarify ambiguities, reduce verbiage, or eliminate conflict between laws.

The legislature authorizes an individual or commission to prepare a revision. After the revisors have completed their work, the proposed revision is submitted to the legislature, where it is introduced as a bill and considered and passed according to procedures used in enacting other legislation. If a proposed revision is enacted, it theoretically becomes the law, and its authority supersedes the authority of the session laws from which it was derived. Legislatures often limit the authority of a revision by stipulating that its provisions are to be construed as a continuation of the session law, not as a new enactment.[103] If this is done, it is necessary to examine the original session law to interpret a revised statute accurately.[104]

### § 261.3. Codes

A code is a systematic rearrangement of the statutory and non-statutory law in a particular field. Codification is the process of putting into statutory form the rules of law annunciated in cases, treatises, or statutes. Codification changes the form and may change the substance of the law. The Criminal Code of 1963 and the Probate Code of 1975 are examples of Minnesota codes.

### § 262. Minnesota Statutes

§ 262.1. Arrangement
§ 262.2. Research Aids
§ 262.3. Features
§ 262.4. Index and Supplementation
§ 262.5. Minnesota Statutes on the Web
§ 262.6. Minnesota Statutes—Subscription Services

---

103. *See, e.g., id.* § 3C.07.
104. *See, e.g.,* Vlasak v. Vlasak, 204 Minn. 331, 283 N.W. 489 (1939); case comment, *Statutes—Construction—Revisions—Age of Majority of Females in Minnesota*, 23 MINN. L. REV. 851 (1939); Becklin v. Becklin, 99 Minn. 307, 312, 109 N.W. 243, 245 (1906); In Re Haskvitz, 104 F. Supp. 173, 182–83 (D. Minn. 1952).

## § 262.1. Arrangement

The general session laws in force at the time of compilation are arranged by subject and compiled into *Minnesota Statutes*. This set is prepared by the Office of the Revisor of Statutes and is the official statutes for Minnesota. Proposed constitutional amendments and local, special, appropriation, private, temporary, or curative laws generally are not included.[105] A few temporary and local laws have been included because of public interest in them.

*Minnesota Statutes* is divided into six major parts:

- Part I Public Rights, ch. 1–494
- Part II Private Rights, ch. 500–523
- Part III Estates of Decedents; Guardianships, ch. 524–529
- Part IV Redress of Civil Injuries, ch. 540–606
- Part V Crimes, Criminals, ch. 609–643
- Part VI Statutes; Construction and Publication, ch. 645

These parts are divided further into titles and subtitles to clarify their organization. Parts, titles, and subtitles are not used in references or citations; chapters and sections are the units of classification. The chapter numbers of *Minnesota Statutes* bear no relation to the chapter numbers of the *Laws of Minnesota*. Statute chapters are intended to divide laws into logical subject divisions.

In a citation to *Minnesota Statutes* the chapter number precedes the decimal point; the section of the chapter follows it. A citation refers to this complete number as the "section." Because *Minnesota Statutes* uses a decimal numbering system, the mathematical value rather than the length of the number after the decimal point determines the position of a section within a chapter. Consequently, section 124.185 appears in *Minnesota Statutes* before section 124.19.

## § 262.2. Research Aids

At the beginning of each section of the statutes, immediately following the section number, there is a word or phrase in boldface capital letters. This word or phrase, called a headnote, is intended to be a

---

105. *See* the description of Curative Acts (§ 255, *supra*) and their index in MINN. STAT. ANN. § 647. *See also* § 252, *supra*.

catch-word or phrase to indicate the contents of the statute. Except in the case of the Uniform Commercial Code the headnote is not a part of the law. Subdivisions of some sections also have headnotes.

Under each section there is a boldface entry entitled "History" followed by an italicized note. The note shows the publication history of each section beginning with *Revised Laws* 1905. For laws originally enacted in 1905 or later, the history note cites the session law that originally enacted the section and any session law that amended it. References to the session laws are in chronological order. Following the session law references, some history sections include a number in parentheses. This number refers to the location of the section in *Mason's Minnesota Statutes 1927* and its supplements. The following is a typical history note: History: RLs 4602; 1961 c 660 s 1 (9768). This note means that the law originated as section 4602 of Revised Laws 1905.[106] In 1961, it was amended by chapter 660, section 1, of the 1961 *Laws of Minnesota*. This law appeared as section 9768 in *Mason's Minnesota Statutes 1927*.

Throughout *Minnesota Statutes,* editor's notes may appear where special information about a chapter, section, or subdivision will aid the reader's understanding. Notes usually call a reader's attention to a delayed effective date, delayed repeal of a section, or conflicting amendments to a section or subdivision.

### § 262.3. Features

There is an excellent "User's Guide" within the Preface in volume 1 of *Minnesota Statutes*. Volume 1 also includes copies of the following documents relating to the government of the state: the Northwest Ordinance of 1787, the Organic Act of Minnesota—Act to Establish the Territorial Government of Minnesota, the Act Authorizing a State Government, the Act of Admission into the Union, and the Constitution of the State of Minnesota. It also contains the Constitution of the United States, the University Charter, and the law adopting the compiled laws and statutes of Minnesota (*see* Appendix D).

Volume 11 contains the following tables: a list of local special acts since 1849; acts not previously included and published for the first time in *Minnesota Statutes*; table converting to a statute number the

---

106. Use *Revised Laws* 1905 to locate prior history of the section.

**Chapter Two. Legislation** 49

session law citation of an act published in the current edition of *Minnesota Statutes* for the first time; organization and structure of the state government; an internal cross-reference table designating where a section is referred to in another part of the statutes, and a table of statutory authorities for administrative rules.[107]

### § 262.4. Index and Supplementation

The index is published in volumes 12 to 14. Topics are broad with many subdivisions. Most constitutional topics are indexed under the entry "Constitution of Minnesota." The entry "Popular Names of Acts" is helpful for finding citations to acts with popular names, for example the Administrative Procedures Act or the Open Meeting Law. The entry "Limitation of Actions" refers to the various statutes that place a time limit on specific procedures.

The set now is republished completely every two years. Obsolete or repealed laws are deleted and new laws or amendments are inserted. Since 1983, interim supplementation is in pocket-part format.

### § 262.5. Minnesota Statutes on the Web[108]

The current edition of *Minnesota Statutes* is available on the Web and can be searched using the table of contents, and by key words or phrases, retrieval of a section, or an entire chapter.

### § 262.6. Minnesota Statutes—Subscription Services[109]

The unannotated version of Minnesota statutes may be searched in the Westlaw database MN-ST or the LEXIS file MNCODE.

## § 263. Minnesota Statutes Annotated

　　§ 263.1. Arrangement
　　§ 263.2. Research Aids
　　§ 263.3. Special Features

---

107. The table of statutory authorities for administrative rules first appeared in the 1984 edition of *Minnesota Statutes*.
108. Web address <http://www.leg.state.mn.us/leg/statutes.htm> (last visited Nov. 4, 2001).
109. Westlaw Web address <http://www.westlaw.com>, Lexis Web address <http://lexis.com>.

§ 263.4. Tables and Index
§ 263.5. Supplementation

### § 263.1. Arrangement

*Minnesota Statutes Annotated* is an unofficial compilation published by West from 1946 to date. The language, order, and arrangement of *Minnesota Statutes* is retained. Additionally, *Minnesota Statutes Annotated* provides annotations offering quick access to case law and other authority.

### § 263.2. Research Aids

*Minnesota Statutes Annotated* provides the following features after sections when applicable.

- ▶ Publication history with excerpts from amendments showing changes
- ▶ Closely related constitutional provisions
- ▶ Cross references to other statutes
- ▶ Administrative code references
- ▶ References to West's digest system Key Numbers and to *Corpus Juris Secundum*
- ▶ Revisor's code comments
- ▶ Digests and citations of reported cases decided by Minnesota courts as well as federal courts and the courts of other states that have construed or interpreted Minnesota law
- ▶ Digests and citations of Minnesota Attorney General opinions and opinions by the State Ethical Practices Board
- ▶ Citations of periodical commentaries
- ▶ Disposition tables for revised topics, providing cross references from old to new section numbers
- ▶ Tables preceding each uniform act that Minnesota has passed, citing other adopting jurisdictions
- ▶ Westlaw topic numbers

### § 263.3. Special Features

Some administrative material is included following the relevant statute, for example Workers' Compensation Practice and Procedure,

# Chapter Two. Legislation 51

chapter 176 appendix,[110] and sentencing guidelines, chapter 244 appendix, or in a special pamphlet. Administrative code references to related Minnesota agency rules follow the text of the statute.

The following special features are included in individual volumes of *Minnesota Statutes Annotated.*

- ▶ Volumes 1–2: Historical documents. The major portion of the two volumes consists of the original Constitution of Minnesota (both Republican and Democratic documents), historical notes on territorial existence, statehood, and the Restructured Constitution, completely annotated.
- ▶ Volume 21A: Disposition Table of M.S.A. and Uniform Acts and the Uniform Commercial Code. The table lists comparative M.S.A. sections with citations to various relevant uniform acts and the Uniform Commercial Code.
- ▶ Volumes 24–25: Minnesota Cities—Home Rule and Statutory and Population Table of Minnesota Cities.
- ▶ Volume 42: This volume contains express repeals by *Revised Laws* 1905 (chapter 646) and by *General Statutes* 1866 (chapter 646 app.). Curative acts, 1849–1947(1949 to date in pocket parts) are indexed alphabetically and chronologically (*see* § 255, *supra*). Curative Acts Judicial Construction (chapter 647).
- ▶ Volumes 48–52: *Court Rules.* These volumes provide the text of rules governing practice and procedure in Minnesota state and federal courts with annotations.

Historical and informational articles by distinguished authorities are published as special features in some volumes.

- ▶ *Comments on the Restructured Constitution of 1974,* vol. 1, p. 129 (1976)
- ▶ *Territorial Existence and Constitutional Statehood of Minnesota,* Judge Julius Haycraft, vol. 1, p. 145 (1976)
- ▶ *Report to the Senate By Advisory Task Force on Corporation Law,* Bert Black, vol. 20, p. x (1985)

---

110. This material currently is found in a 1985 Special Pamphlet entitled "Rules Governing Workers' Compensation Practice and Procedure."

- *The Minnesota Code Comments Origin and Revision,* Stanley Kinyon, vol. 21A, p. vii (1966)
- *An Overview of the Rules of Criminal Procedure,* George Scott, vol. 49, p. vii (1979)

There also reporters notes to the criminal, corporation, non-profit corporations, professional firms, and partnership acts.

### § 263.4. Tables and Index

- Volume 43–43A *Tables.* These tables provide information on where session laws, year by year, and sections of former compilations may be located in the current statutes. A table of Minnesota population by county, mortality tables, annuity tables, United States life tables, and interest tables also are included. Volume 43A is the cumulative supplement and is updated by pocket part.
- Volume 44–47 *Index.* The index, although much more comprehensive, is similar in format to the index in *Minnesota Statutes* (*see* § 262.4, *supra*). Some *Minnesota Statutes Annotated* volumes contain separate, more detailed, indexes. These are not updated by the volume's pocket part.

### § 263.5. Supplementation

The set is kept current by cumulative annual pocket parts. Interim supplementary pamphlets update the annotations and reprint older laws that may have been reclassified or modified by the revisor or laws changed due to printing errors. Copies of newly enacted laws are not included. Such laws may be found in the *Minnesota Session Law Service.* The *Minnesota Session Law Service* final issue of each legislative session contains a cumulative table of new, amended, and repealed statutes.

Separate pamphlets may be published when comprehensive acts are passed (e.g., Business Corporation Act). Bound volumes are revised and reprinted when extensive new legislation or adjudication warrants. Major law libraries often retain copies of the obsolete volumes.

### § 264. Statutory Construction

Minnesota statutes are interpreted in accordance with the statutory construction statutes, Minn. Stat. §§ 645.01–645.49 (1998 and Supp. 1999) and judicial opinions. In the interpretation of a statute, the court may be guided by the following presumptions as outlined in Minn. Stat. § 645.17 (1998).

1. The legislature does not intend a result that is absurd, impossible of execution, or unreasonable;
2. The legislature intends the entire statute to be effective and certain;
3. The legislature does not intend to violate the constitution of the United States or of this state;
4. When a court of last resort has construed the language of a law, the legislature in subsequent laws on the same subject matter intends the same construction to be placed upon such language; and
5. The legislature intends to favor the public interest as against any private interest.

The rule of law is that a penal statute should be sufficiently explicit to enable one of common knowledge to ascertain what conduct is prohibited thereby.[111]

## § 270. OTHER SOURCES OF LAW

§ 271. Interstate Compacts and Reciprocal Statutes
§ 272. Uniform State Laws
§ 273. Local Lawmaking Bodies
§ 274. Initiative and Referendum
§ 275. Compilation of State Statutes on One Subject

### § 271. Interstate Compacts[112] and Reciprocal Statutes

A compact is an agreement or contract between states. The texts of compacts are published in state codes and, because they require congressional consent, they also are published in the *United States Statutes at Large*. Minnesota interstate compacts are listed under the entry "Interstate Compacts" in the index to *Minnesota Statutes* and "Compacts" in the index to *Minnesota Statutes Annotated*.

A comprehensive list of state compacts can be found in *Interstate Compacts & Agencies* (1998) published periodically (under varying titles)

---

111. State v. Johnson, 282 Minn. 153, 158–59, 163 N.W.2d 750, 753–54 (1968) (citations omitted).
112. *See generally,* F. ZIMMERMAN, THE LAW AND USE OF INTERSTATE COMPACTS (1961).

by the Council of State Governments. A biennial publication by the same publisher, *The Book of the States* (*see* § 275.4, *infra*), discusses new developments with respect to compacts.

Reciprocal statutes give citizens of another state certain rights and privileges in Minnesota if that state has granted mutual rights to Minnesota citizens. These laws are referenced under the term "Reciprocity" in the index to *Minnesota Statutes* and "Reciprocal" in the index to *Minnesota Statutes Annotated*.

### § 272. Uniform State Laws

Uniform laws are acts or codes formulated for the purpose of promoting uniformity among states on subjects where such uniformity is desirable. A number of different organizations draft such material. Two major organizations are the American Law Institute[113] and the National Conference of Commissioners on Uniform State Laws.[114] The latter organization has drafted and recommended more than 120 uniform acts for adoption by the states. The members of Minnesota's Commission on Uniform State Laws represent the state in the National Conference. The list of Minnesota uniform and model acts adopted is available on the Web at <http://www.nccusl.org/uniformact_state/minnesota.htm>.

Statutory citations to Minnesota uniform acts may be located in the indexes to *Minnesota Statutes* and *Minnesota Statutes Annotated* under the entry "Uniform Laws" (see § 275.1, *infra*).

### § 273. Local Lawmaking Bodies

Cities, villages and boroughs are termed cities.[115] Counties are legal entities organized as subordinate agencies of state government.[116] At

---

113. The American Law Institute (ALI) Web address is <http://www.ali.org>.
114. The National Conference of Commissioners on Uniform State Laws (NCCUSL) in conjunction with the University of Pennsylvania Law School, makes uniform and model acts drafts available for reading online or for downloading at <http://www.law.upenn.edu/bll/ulc/ulc.htm> (last visited Nov. 4, 2001). The NCCUSL Web address is <http://www.nccusl.org/> (last visited Nov. 4, 2001).
115. MINN. STAT. §412.016 (1998). *See generally* 32, 33 DUNNELL'S MINN. DIGEST, *Municipal Corporations* §§1.00–12.10 (4th ed. 1991, Supp. 2000).
116. *See generally* 10 DUNNELL'S MINN. DIGEST *Counties* §§ 1.00–7.09 (4th ed. 1991, Supp. 2000).

**Chapter Two. Legislation** 55

common law, state legislatures had absolute power over municipalities in the absence of express constitutional limitation. Gradually, constitutional provisions that granted municipalities power over certain matters were adopted.[117] Changes in the Minnesota Constitution over the years have increased local independence in two ways. First, the legislature's power to enact special legislation has been circumscribed (*see* § 252, *supra*), and second, municipalities have been authorized to exercise some power without prior legislative sanction.[118] In enacting ordinances (laws), municipalities must act in pursuance of the power derived from their charters.[119] Many municipalities and counties publish their ordinances in a code. State law requires that city and county ordinances be deposited with their local county law library.[120] Researchers may obtain information about a current code or ordinance from the office of the city clerk.[121] The Minnesota State Law Library provides links to Minnesota city ordinances available on the Web.[122] Hennepin County[123] and Ramsey County[124] also post their county ordinances on the Web.

*Shepard's Minnesota Citations*[125] includes sections on municipal charters and municipal ordinances. Each of these sections is arranged alphabetically by city and then by topic (e.g., buildings, fire

---

117. The term used to describe the distribution of power between state and local government is "home rule." For a discussion of home rule, *see* Terrance Sandalow, *Limits of Municipal Power Under Home Rule: A Rule for the Courts,* 48 MINN. L. REV. 643 (1964); Michelle Timmons, Judy Grant, Teri Popp & Heidi Wesby, *County Home Rule Comes to Minnesota,* 19 Wm. Mitchell L. Rev. 811 (1993).
118. MINN. CONST. art. XII, § 4.
119. MINN. STAT. § 412.191, subd. 4 (2000) provides the procedures to be used for adoption or amendment of charters.
120. MINN. STAT. §§ 375.52, 415.021 (2000).
121. The League of Minnesota Cities (145 University Ave. West, St. Paul, MN 55103; phone 651-281-1200) maintains a collection of charters for home-rule cities and the codified ordinances for many of the cities of the state. The collection is maintained primarily for the cities that belong to the association. Sample ordinances and research memoranda on specific subjects (e.g., licensing, zoning) are available on a limited basis. Some research memoranda are available on the Web at <http://www.lmnc.org/library/libindex.cfm#res> (last visited Nov. 4, 2001). Ordinances generally are published in local legal newspapers (*see* § 546, *infra*).
122. Web address <http://www.state.mn.us/courts/library/mnlr.html#ord>.
123. Web address <http://www.co.hennepin.mn.us/ords/words.html>.
124. Web address <http://www.co.ramsey.mn.us/cm/About/Charter/index.asp> (last visited Nov. 4, 2001).
125. Shepard's/McGraw-Hill, 1995– .

regulation). Citations of cases, selected attorney general opinions, and periodical articles that have discussed a topic, ordinance, or charter are listed. Detailed topical indexes are provided for both the section on charters and that on ordinances.

*Shepard's Ordinance Law Annotations*[126] is a comprehensive multi-volume digest of American cases that have interpreted or construed ordinances of cities and counties throughout the United States. It provides access by fact situation (e.g., air pollution, gasoline business) rather than by general legal concept (e.g., constitutional law, contracts). Its aim is to collect all legal matter regarding the topic under a single heading. A general index is located in the last volume. The last two volumes of the set consist of a table of cases arranged alphabetically by state, then by city within each state. The section number of the topic discussed is provided after each case in the table of cases to direct the researcher to the topical discussion.

Townships have authority over zoning and planning, public works, parks, cemeteries, hospitals, elections, tax levies, township roads, and other matters.[127] Statutory city government formation, officers, council, taxation, utilities, and parks is outlined in Minn. Stat. §§ 412.01–412.901 (1998 and Supp. 1999). Each of Minnesota's eighty-seven counties has authority to plan and to zone; to establish housing and redevelopment authorities; to direct the assessments; and to administer state functions dealing with welfare, elections, tax levies, highways, vital statistics, and other matters enumerated by statute.[128] Information on counties is available from the Association of Minnesota Counties (AMC). The AMC is a voluntary statewide organization that assists the state's eighty-seven counties in providing effective county governance to the people of Minnesota. It provides educational programs, training, research and communications for county officials.[129] Some regional organizations or districts also have the authority to enact ordinances or issue regulations. These bodies promote intergovernmental cooperation, provide services, and

---

126. Shepard's/McGraw-Hill, 1969– .
127. MINN. STAT. §§ 365.01–368.85 (1998 & Supp. 1999).
128. *See id.* §§ 370.01–403.14 (2000).
129. 125 Charles Ave., St. Paul, MN 55103; phone 651-224-3344; Web address <http://www.mncounties.org/> (last visited Nov. 4, 2001).

ensure coordination in planning. Examples are the Metropolitan Council, school districts, and local development corporations.[130]

## § 274. Initiative and Referendum

Initiative is the process by which a small percentage of voters may propose legislation and compel officials to submit the proposed legislation to the voters. Referendum is the process by which a small percentage of voters may delay the effective date of legislation and compel officials to submit it to the voters for approval or rejection.[131]

All states, including Minnesota, require that constitutional amendments be submitted by the legislature to a referendum for ratification or rejection by the electorate. Many states also have provided for voter initiative and referendum in enacting laws. An attempt to amend the Minnesota Constitution to provide for voter initiative and referendum failed in 1981.[132] Article XII, section 4, of the Minnesota Constitution allows for voter initiative in regard to charter amendments. Municipalities are granted the power of initiative, referendum, and recall in city ordinances.[133]

## § 275. Compilations of State Statutes on One Subject

§ 275.1. Sources Providing Text or Digest of Laws
§ 275.2. Sources Providing Statutory Citations
§ 275.3. Bibliographic Sources
§ 275.4. Other Sources

At times, a researcher might wish to compare Minnesota law on one topic with the law of other jurisdictions on the same topic, or to find all states that have laws on a particular subject. Unfortunately, there is no comprehensive subject list of all state laws. All the state statutes

---

130. MINN. STAT. § 473.122–473.249, chs. 122–123, 472–472A (1984).
131. St. Paul Citizens for Human Rights v. City Council of the City of St. Paul, 289 N.W.2d 402, 404, n. 2 (Minn. 1979) (citing Fordham & Prendergast, *The Initiative and Referendum at the Municipal Level in Ohio*, 20 U. CIN. L. REV.; 5 MCQUILLAN, MUNICIPAL CORPORATIONS (3d ed. 1969 rev. vol.) §§ 16.52, 16.53).
132. 1980 Minn. Laws ch. 587, art. 1, §§ 3–30 included the initiative and Referendum Implementation Act. This act was contingent upon ratification of the amendment and was repealed by 1981 Minn. Laws, 1st Spec. Sess., ch. 4, art. I, § 187 (the act also may be found as chapter 3B of *Minnesota Statutes* 1980).
133. MINN. STAT. § 410.20 (1998).

appear full-text in LEXIS and Westlaw and are available, at no cost, on the Web at numerous comprehensive legal research sites. Additionally, the following paper sources may provide assistance when making comparisons. Note that researchers always should check the statutes of each state for currentness.

This is a selective listing. The two *Subject Compilations of State Laws* (*see* § 275.3, *infra*) are highly recommended for their excellent introductory guides on comparative state statutory and regulatory research. Readers are referred to them for further ideas on where to research state law by subject.

### § 275.1. Sources Providing Text or Digest of Laws

*Martindale-Hubbell Law Directory* (Summit, NJ: Martindale-Hubbell. 2000).

Two volumes in the Martindale-Hubbell set contain digests of laws summarizing statutory law in each of the United States, District of Columbia, Puerto Rico, and the Virgin Islands. It is arranged alphabetically by state and therein alphabetically by topics and subheadings. Important uniform laws are printed in their entirety. This publication is available online through LEXIS in the MARHUB library, MHDIG file.

*Shepard's Lawyer's Reference Manual* (Colorado Springs, CO: Shepard's/McGraw-Hill 1983) (no longer published; last annual supplement 1988).

This volume includes summaries and comparisons of both federal and state statutory provisions on a wide variety of legal subjects ranging from abortion to wills. The summaries have code references presented in tabular form.

*State Legislative Report* (Denver, CO: National Conference of State Legislatures 1975–2000, irregular).

Published twelve to eighteen times per year, each issue of this series, is distinctively titled with a statutory issue. A summary of each state's current legislation may be included.

Suggested State Legislation (Lexington, KY: Council of State Governments 1941–1999).

This series compiles draft legislation from state statutes on topics of current interest and importance to the states. Most are based on existing state statutes and provide citations thereto.

## Chapter Two. Legislation

*Uniform Laws Annotated* (St. Paul, MN: West Publishing Co. various pub. dates) (annual pocket parts).
This set includes tables of statutory citations for adopting jurisdictions preceding the complete text of the uniform law. Annotations include specific variations by state and case summaries. Uniform Laws are available online through Westlaw and LEXIS.

Loose-leaf services often reprint, digest, or provide statutory citations of state laws for the particular subject field they cover (*see* § 551, *infra*). Many looseleaf services are now available online via LEXIS and Westlaw. Check the database directories of these services for the most current information.

Continuing legal education organizations often provide legislative updates in seminars in various subject areas. Check the local law library's collection for these materials.

Many comprehensive legal sites on the Web offer the full-text of the current version of all state statutes. The subscription services, LEXIS and Westlaw, have the full-text of all state statutes available electronically. Additionally, both services enable researchers to search the text of all state statutes simultaneously.

### § 275.2. Sources Providing Statutory Citations

*American Jurisprudence Pleading and Practice Forms Annotated* (San Francisco: Bancroft-Whitney Co. 1983– ) (annual pocket parts).
State statutory citations are listed for many topics. This publication is available online through LEXIS and Westlaw.

*American Law Reports* (A.L.R.) series (Rochester, NY: Lawyers Cooperative Publishing Co.) (annual supplements).
These sources often cite, or give lists of, state laws on a topic covered by the annotations. This publication is available online through LEXIS and Westlaw.

*National Survey of State Laws,* Richard A. Leiter (ed.) (Detroit: Gale 1993).
Presented in chart format, this book shows comparisons of current state laws, with statutory citations, on forty-two legal topics. It is divided into eight general topics sections. Within each section, subtopics are arranged alphabetically.

*Shepard's Acts and Cases by Popular Names, Federal and State* (Colorado Springs: Shepard's/McGraw Hill 1999) (annual supplement).

This publication provides citation information for statutes and cases that commonly are referred to by popular name.

*State Law Index* (Washington DC: Government Printing Office (1925–48).

This multi-volume set covers the permanent and general enactments of all the state and territorial legislatures, offering citations for the session laws of the states. It is in alphabetical order by subject. Volumes 1–5 (1925/26–1933/34) include digests of important state legislation, important statutory changes, and important changes in state laws relating to administrative organization and personnel. Beginning with 1938, digests on selected subjects were published separately as numbers of the series *State Law Digest Report*.

Periodical articles and treatises often provide state statutory citations for the topics discussed.

### § 275.3. Bibliographic Sources

*(A) Bibliography of Bibliographies of Legal Material*, M. Howell (New Jersey Appellate Printing Co., Inc. 1969; 1969–1971 supplement).

This source contains a substantial list of books and periodical articles that contain bibliographies, arranged by topic. Many of these may be useful in finding citations of statutes.

*Government Publications and Their Use*, Lawrence F. Schmeckebier & Roy B. Eastin (2d rev. ed., Washington, DC: The Brookings Institution 1969).

The chapter entitled "Compilations in Specific Fields" contains more than 180 entries arranged by subject and organized by issuing federal government agencies.

*Statutes Compared*, Jon S. Schultz (1st rev. ed. Buffalo, NY: William S. Hein & Co., Inc. 1992).

This volume indexes selected sources, primarily looseleaf services, which include comparative tables of American state and Canadian provincial statutes by topic.

*(The) Statutes of the Forty-Eight States, by Subject: An Annotated Bibliography*, J. Jacobstein, 48 L. Lib. J. 40 (1955).

Although an early source of statutory compilation, this title still may be useful for some topics.

## Chapter Two. Legislation

*Subject Compilations of State Laws: Research Guide and Annotated Bibliography,* L. Foster & C. Boast (Greenwood Press 1981), updated by C. Nyberg & C. Boast, 75 L. Lib. J. 121 (1982).

*Subject Compilations of State Laws 1979–1999: Research Guide and Annotated Bibliography,* Charyl Rae Nyberg (Twin Falls, Idaho: Carol Boast & Charyl Rae Nyberg 2000).

These books attempt to list all subject compilations of statutory sources published in books and periodical articles since 1960. The books are complementary and should be used together. The first title presents a thorough introduction to research techniques for comparing the laws of the states. The following titles update this guide and provide a similar analysis for preparing subject compilations of state regulations.

Searching in *Criminal Justice Abstracts, Index to Legal Periodicals,* or *Legal Resource Index* reveals comparative studies published in law reviews and journals. Generally, these studies are for a single purpose and never are updated, but can be a fruitful source of information.

Searching for treatises addressing comparative state laws may be done in library catalogs. Another approach is to search Indexmaster[134] a subscription-based electronic service. This database includes the indexes and tables of contents from thousands of legal treatises.

### § 275.4. Other Sources

*American Jurisprudence 2d Desk Book* (Rochester, NY: Lawyers Cooperative Publishing Co. 1992) (occasional pocket parts).
 This volume provides tables of provisions of selected state statutes (e.g., marriage and divorce laws).

*Backgrounder,* Council of State Governments (1982–90).
 This series addresses three or four subjects each month. The format consists of an introductory overview, selected resources, occasionally tables with state profiles concerning the topic, and statutory citations sometimes included in footnotes.

*Book of the States* (Lexington, KY: Council of State Governments) (biennial 2000).
 This volume provides tables of provisions of selected state statutes.

---

134. Web address <http://www.indexmaster.com>.

*CIS Index* and *CIS Abstracts* (Washington, DC: Congressional Information Service, Inc.) (monthly with quarterly, annual, and multi-year cumulations).

CIS generally is considered to be the most comprehensive index to the publications of the U.S. Congress. In this set the index heading "State laws" is used to bring together all compilations after April 1979. At times, compilations of state laws will be featured in reports. The detailed abstracts are very helpful in determining the usefulness of a particular publication. CIS also is available electronically via the subscription service, Congressional Universe.[135]

*Encyclopedia of Associations* (Detroit: Gale Research Co.) (annual 1999).

This directory gives subject access to special-interest associations, primarily non-profit American membership organizations of national scope, that might publish helpful information.

*The Lawyer's Almanac,* 4th ed. (Clifton, NJ: Law & Business, Inc. 1985).

This volume includes a number of charts and tables listing and comparing common statutes and codes within the states.

*Monthly Catalog of U.S. Government Publications* (U.S. Government Printing Office).

This source indexes publications of the federal government that publishes many summaries or bibliographies of state laws. One approach to research is to look under "state" in the index. This publication is available online through the Westlaw database GPO-CTLG.

Studies by state legislative councils and legislative reference or research groups may list statutes of other states. Also, an agency with enforcement responsibility may maintain information on similar laws in other states. To locate relevant agencies, check the sources discussed in § 536.4, *infra*.

---

135. For information on this commission contact the Revisor of Statutes (*see* § 226.5, *infra*) who is a statutory member. Web address <http://www.lexis-nexis.com/congcomp>.

# CHAPTER THREE
# Executive and Administrative Law

The executive officers and the agencies of the executive branch implement and administer laws enacted and programs created by the Minnesota legislature.[136]

## Chapter Contents

§ 310. Constitutional Officers
§ 320. Administrative Agencies
§ 330. Administrative Courts
§ 340. Public Access and Privacy Rights
§ 350. State and Local Documents

## § 310. CONSTITUTIONAL OFFICERS

§ 311. Governor
§ 312. Secretary of State
§ 313. Attorney General

Article V of the Minnesota Constitution establishes a five-member executive branch.[137] The constitutional officers are the governor, lieutenant governor, secretary of state, auditor, and attorney general. Each officer is nominated with political party designation and is elected on a statewide ballot for a four-year term. Together these officers constitute the Executive Council of the State.[138]

The powers, functions, responsibilities, and services of these officers are set out in the Constitution, *Minnesota Statutes, Minnesota Legislative Manual, Minnesota Guidebook to State Agency Services,* and other publications. Noted here are those officers that issue or control publications and documents used for legal research.

---

136. Authority: MINN. CONST. art. V; MINN. STAT. §§ 4–14.
137. In the 1998 general election, the office of state treasurer was abolished, effective as of the first Monday in January 2003. 1998 Minn. Laws 387, ch. 387, § 1.
138. MINN. STAT. § 9.011 (1998).

## § 311. Governor[139]

As chief executive officer of the state,[140] the major duties of the governor are to oversee government operations, make sure that laws are faithfully executed,[141] and take the lead in shaping public policy by proposing legislation.

The governors' addresses to the legislature, bills approved, and veto messages are published in the House or Senate *Journals*. Executive orders currently are printed in the *State Register*. Prior to the first issue of the *State Register* on July 1, 1976, they were not generally published. Early records are preserved by the Minnesota Historical Society. Gubernatorial proclamations with respect to constitutional amendments and special sessions of the legislature are found in the session laws. The budget proposed by the governor and other special reports and studies prepared by his or her office are published separately. The budget and other executive documents also are available on the governor's homepage at <http://www.mainserver.state.mn.us/governor/bonding.html>.

A law enacted in 1971 gave the governor authority to delegate some of her or his powers, duties, responsibilities, and functions (except for those imposed by the Constitution) to the lieutenant governor by filing a written order with the secretary of state.[142]

## § 312. Secretary of State[143]

The secretary of state, among many duties and responsibilities, maintains official state records, administers elections and oaths, approves articles of incorporation, regulates businesses, and administers state filings under the Uniform Commercial Code. As keeper of the Minnesota Seal, the secretary of state certifies the authenticity of the executive documents of the governor and legislative acts. Documents are open for public inspection. The secretary of state prepares and

---

139. 130 State Capitol, 75 Constitution Ave., St. Paul, MN 55155; phone 651-296-3391; Web address <http://www.mainserver.state.mn.us/governor/>.
140. MINN. CONST. art. V.
141. MINN. STAT. §§ 4.01–4.47 (1998).
142. *Id.* § 404(2).
143. 180 State Office Building, 100 Constitution Ave., St. Paul, MN 55155; phone 651-296-2803; Web address <http://www.sos.state.mn.us/>.

## Chapter Three. Executive and Administrative Law

publishes biennially the *Minnesota Legislative Manual,* also called the "Blue Book" (*see* § 526.2, *infra*).[144]

The secretary of state database offers online, fee-based, dial-up access to business records, UCC filings, and legal newspapers at <http://www.sos.state.mn.us/olacc.html>.

### § 313. Attorney General[145]

§ 313.1. Responsibilities
§ 313.2. Opinions

#### § 313.1. Responsibilities[146]

The attorney general is the chief legal officer and advisor of the state.[147] He or she appears for the state in all cases in which it is directly interested.[148] The attorney general's office has approximately twenty divisions organized along both functional and geographic lines. Some divisions serve one particular state department or agency; other divisions serve all the state departments or agencies that are housed in one particular state office building. Several divisions offer direct assistance to the public.

The Office of the Attorney General occasionally publishes compilations of selected laws, actions, and opinions in specific areas such as antitrust, education, consumer protection, assistance and relief programs, and elections. The Consumer Division publishes a wide range of educational and informational brochures and publications.

---

144. MINN. CONST. art. V; MINN. STAT. §§ 5.01–5.26 (1998).
145. 102 State Capitol (main office), St. Paul, MN 55155; phone 651-296-6196; Web address <http://www.ag.state.mn.us/home/mainhi.shtml>.
146. *See generally* MINN. STAT. §§ 8.01–8.35 (1998).
147. MINN. CONST. art. V.
148. MINN. STAT. § 8.06 (1998).

## § 313.2. Opinions[149]

§ 313.21. Hardcopy Availability of Opinions
§ 313.22. Electronic Availability of Opinions
§ 313.23. Research Aids

The attorney general's opinions generally do not have the force or effect of law.[150] They are advisory, persuasive, and may have influence on the courts.

### § 313.21. Hardcopy Availability of Opinions

Individual opinions are available from the Office of the Attorney General.[151] Beginning in 1968, Minnesota Attorney General opinions have been published monthly in the *Minnesota Legal Register*.[152] Copies or summaries of opinions also can be found in selected legal newspapers (*see* § 554.6, *infra*).

Opinions also are available on microfiche (1858 to date) from Minnesota's Bookstore (*see* § 350, *infra*). The complete set was first published in 1978 and included all opinions issued through 1977. The opinions were filmed in the order that they were found in the files of the Office of the Attorney General—by subject classification number, not chronological order. Since 1978, fiche have been issued or refilmed annually to incorporate new or revised opinions. William S. Hein & Co., Inc.[153] publishes the attorney general opinions of all states on microfiche including Minnesota opinions from 1968 to date.

Hardbound attorney general biennial reports issued between 1893 (1894 *Report*) and 1960 contained selected opinions arranged

---

149. This discussion concerns only formal opinions. Letter, memorandum, or informal opinions are issued by the office on an individual basis. They are neither classified nor intended to be used as precedent by other parties.
150. On all school matters and in some matters relating to the Commissioner of Revenue, attorney general opinions are decisive until decided otherwise by the courts. MINN. STAT. §§ 8.07, 120A.10, 270.09 (1998). *See* MINNESOTA REVISOR'S MANUAL WITH STYLE AND FORMS § 2.7(d) at 30 (1984).
151. The University of Minnesota Law Library has mimeographed copies of opinions issued since 1950, arranged in chronological order and bound, as do other libraries.
152. 1414 Soo Line Building, Minneapolis, MN 55402; phone 612-332-0726. Individual issues are headed *Minnesota Legal Register (Attorney General Opinions Issue)*. The binder title is *Opinions of the Attorney General*.
153. 1285 Main St., Buffalo, NY 14209; phone 800-828-7571.

## Chapter Three. Executive and Administrative Law

alphabetically by topic and numbered consecutively.[154] In the 1934 *Report*, the subject classification numbering scheme was introduced for internal office filing purposes. The number assigned was printed at the end of each opinion. The Oceana Group[155] supplies the biennial reports on microfilm. Compilations of selected opinions were published for the years 1858–1865, 1858–1883, and 1960–1968.

### § 313.22. Electronic Availability of Opinions

Opinions are available on both Westlaw and LEXIS with coverage beginning in 1977. West Group provides coverage of opinions from 1977 on its *Minnesota Reporter* CD-ROM with PREMISE software. *LEXIS Law Publishing on Disc—Minnesota, Dunnell's Edition* is a Folio®-based CD-ROM that also includes opinions since 1977. The official attorney general website offers electronic coverage of opinions beginning in 1993 at <http://www.ag.state.mn.us/library/index.htm>.

### § 313.23. Research Aids

*Minnesota Statutes Annotated* contains digests of opinions following those statutes that have been interpreted or discussed by an opinion, citing either the classification numbers assigned by the attorney general (since 1934) and the date the opinion was issued (e.g., Op. Atty. Gen., 373-B-17-D, June 24, 1941), or the number assigned to an opinion that was published in a biennial report (e.g., Op. Atty. Gen. 1928, No. 295, p. 276).

The Office of the Attorney General maintains the only complete list of subject classification numbers. Because numbers are assigned by the attorney writing the opinion, inconsistencies exist. The Minnesota Attorney General Library offers researchers assistance in locating relevant classification numbers for a subject.[156]

The *Numerical Index to the Selected Opinions of the Minnesota Attorney General 1933–1969*,[157] provides a cross-reference table from the subject classification numbers assigned by the attorney general to the numbers

---

154. *See* Appendix E for a list of Minnesota Attorney General *Reports*. The *Reports* from 1934 to 1960 were widely distributed to law libraries throughout Minnesota.
155. 75 Main St., Dobbs Ferry, NY 10522; phone 914-693-5956.
156. Phone 651-296-8152.
157. Compiled by Barbara L. Golden (Hennepin County Law Library Aug. 1976). *See* Appendix F for an edited version of this title.

assigned to the selected opinions in the bound biennial reports, the 1960–1968 compilation, and volumes 1 and 2 of *Minnesota Legal Register*. Thus, the researcher who has obtained the attorney general's classification number for an opinion may use this index to obtain the number of the opinion in other sources, if it is one of the selected opinions reprinted. If the opinion being sought has the number and page cite, the researcher will find that opinion most easily by using the hardbound volumes of the *Biennial Report of the Attorney General to the Governor of the State of Minnesota*, bearing a spine title of *Report of the Attorney General, Minnesota*.

Subject indexes are available in each volume of the biennial reports of the attorney general and annually in the *Minnesota Legal Register*. A subject index for 1894 to 1902 was compiled by the public examiner. A cumulative subject index published by the Minnesota County Attorneys' Association covered opinions issued from 1910 to 1930, with pocket-part updating to 1938.

*Shepard's Minnesota Citations* includes attorney general opinions from 1902 through 1960, both citing and cited by cases, statutes, and constitutions. The citations provide references only to the selected opinions published in the biennial reports.

After 1970, all attorney general opinions have been published in the *Minnesota Legal Register* in three-ring binders with the spine title *State of Minnesota, Opinions of the Attorney General*. To find opinions dated after 1970, go directly to these three-ring binders. After 1993, Internet availability is an alternative. Since then, opinions have been published on the attorney general's website at <http://www.ag.state.mn.us/library/index.htm>.

## § 320. ADMINISTRATIVE AGENCIES

§ 321. Administrative Rules
§ 322. Office of Administrative Hearings
§ 323. Agency Decisions

Administrative agencies are those instruments of the sovereign state, other than courts or legislative bodies, that administer governmental functions. Administrative agencies affect the public in a number of ways, for example rule-making, investigating, prosecuting, negotiating, and settling disputes.

## Chapter Three. Executive and Administrative Law

Excluding local government agencies, there are more than 100 state administrative agencies in Minnesota, many of which are subdivided into additional divisions and sections. Information on state departments and agencies is published in the following selected sources, all of which provide citations to the enabling legislation for each agency.

- *Minnesota Guidebook to State Agency Services*
- *Minnesota Legislative Manual*
- *Minnesota Statutes,* volume 11, Table III (1998)

Links to Internet websites for Minnesota Government Branches, Agencies, Offices, and other Publicly Supported Institutions are available at <http://www.state.mn.us/govtoffice/index.html#10>.

### § 321. Administrative Rules[158]

§ 321.1. State Register
§ 321.2. Minnesota Compiled Rules
§ 321.3. Updating Agency Rules
§ 321.4. Compilations of State Regulations on One Subject

State legislatures delegate the authority to promulgate rules to administrative bodies (usually agencies in the executive branch). For this reason, these rules also are referred to as delegated legislation. They generally have the force of law unless suspended by the legislature or overruled by the courts.

Many states have passed the Model Administrative Procedure Act drafted by the American Bar Association and originally adopted by the National Conference of Commissioners on Uniform State Laws (NCCUSL) in 1946. Minnesota has not adopted the uniform act, but instead enacted an administrative procedure act in 1945, making

---

158. The federal government uses the terms "rules" and "regulations" interchangeably. Other jurisdictions often use the term "regulations." Minnesota law refers to administrative promulgations only as "rules."

substantial changes in 1957, 1975,[159] the early 1980s, and again in 1995.[160] Administrative procedure acts control the formal administrative process.

The Minnesota Administrative Procedure Act (APA)[161] provides for an Office of Administrative Hearings and requires that agency rules and regulations be published. Section 14.02, subdivision 2, of *Minnesota Statutes* defines state agencies, and section 14.03, subdivision 1, lists agencies to which the APA does not apply. With the exception of these exempt agencies, state agencies are required to submit their rules, proposed rules, notices, and orders, in a form approved by the Revisor of Statutes,[162] to the Office of the State Register for publication. They also are required to utilize the services of the Office of Administrative Hearings (OAH).

Rule-making authority is limited to areas specifically granted by statute.[163] In almost all cases, the agency must make an affirmative presentation of facts establishing the need for, and reasonableness of, the rule at a public hearing conducted by the Office of Administrative Hearings. Any person may petition (as prescribed by statute) an agency requesting adoption, suspension, amendment, or repeal of a rule.[164] The agency must respond within sixty days.

The rules of an exempt agency should be obtained from the agency itself, although they may be published in unofficial sources such as *Minnesota Statutes Annotated* (*see* § 263.3, *supra*) or loose-leaf services.

---

159. *See* A STAFF REPORT TO THE HOUSE AND SENATE GOVERNMENTAL OPERATIONS COMMITTEES ON THE MINNESOTA ADMINISTRATIVE PROCEDURES ACT AND ITS CURRENT APPLICATION, SUBMITTED BY JAMES R. NOBLES, HOUSE RESEARCH, AND THOMAS TRIPLETT, SENATE COUNSEL, TO THE OFFICE OF LEGISLATIVE RESEARCH OF THE MINNESOTA LEGISLATURE (1975).
160. George A. Beck, *Minnesota Administrative Procedure* (Weekend Publications 1998).
161. MINN. STAT. §§ 14.001–14.70 (1998).
162. To aid drafters, the Office of the Revisor of Statutes periodically (albeit irregularly) publishes *Rulemaking in Minnesota* by Paul M. Marinac, most recently in 1997.
163. MINN. STAT. § 14.05, subd. 1 (1998).
164. *Id.* § 14.09.

## § 321.1. State Register[165] (Weekly, July 1976 to date)

With the exception of those of exempt agencies, regulations must be published in the *State Register* to be effective. The *State Register* also publishes governors' executive orders, proposed rules, final rules, state contracts, and official notices. During the late 1980s and early 1990s, the *State Register* published advance notice of cases scheduled for hearing before the Supreme Court, including a summary of issues involved. Research aids include a table of "MCAR Amendments and Additions," "Minnesota Rules Amendments and Additions," and an annual index.

## § 321.2. Minnesota Compiled Rules

§ 321.21. Rules before 1970
§ 321.22. Rules from 1970 to 1976
§ 321.23. Rules from 1976 to 1977
§ 321.24. Rules from 1977 to 1982
§ 321.25. Rules from 1982 to 1983
§ 321.26. Rules after 1983

It is very difficult to determine the permutations in the text of a rule over the years. Until recently, there have been no bound sets, and because rules frequently were reprinted by agencies, much of the historical record is lost. There are two possible sources for historical information and they may not yield positive results. First, the agency itself may have back editions of its own rules. Second, most (but not all) rules had to be filed with the secretary of state to be effective; therefore, the files at the secretary of state's office may yield prior copies of rules.

### § 321.21. Rules before 1970

Compilations generally were nonexistent unless published by the individual agency. Format varied widely. Some were indexed, but most were not. Some libraries have collected the individual publications into a file or bound set, but no official compiled set of all rules exists.

---

165. The *State Register* is distributed to various libraries throughout the state according to MINN. STAT. § 14.46(4) (1998).

### § 321.22. Rules from 1970 to 1976

The commissioner of administration issued an eleven-volume loose-leaf set entitled *Minnesota State Regulations*. The set was a collection of regulations previously published by individual agencies. There was no general index.

### § 321.23. Rules from 1976 to 1977

The title of the publication was changed to *Manual of State Agency Rules*. This was the only change.

### § 321.24. Rules from 1977 to 1982

During this period the commissioner of administration issued the *Minnesota Code of Agency Rules* (MCAR). This set consisted of fifteen loose-leaf binders with tab dividers separating the rules of each agency. It really was a collection of the individual agency publications. A common numbering system was introduced but many rules never were renumbered. There was no index; a table of contents provided general access to the set, and some agencies provided individual indexes. The set was updated quarterly. Publication was terminated July 1, 1982.

### § 321.25. Rules from 1982 to 1983

Chapter 615 of the 1980 *Laws of Minnesota* mandated comprehensive changes in the publication of agency rules. Responsibility for publication transferred to the revisor of statutes with the intention of making agency rules as accessible as the statutes. The authority of the commissioner of administration to publish MCAR expired July 1, 1982.

In 1982, MCAR was reprinted by the revisor of statutes in seventy pamphlets, arranged by agency. The *Minnesota Code of Agency Rules Reprint* was a one-time publication used to fill the gap between the end of MCAR and the beginning of *Minnesota Rules*. It contains all the rules in effect on September 15, 1982. The MCAR numbering was not changed but an attempt was made to include all rules in force free from filing errors. Thus, the *Reprint* includes more rules than previously had been published.

Chapter Three. Executive and Administrative Law 73

### § 321.26. Rules after 1983

*Minnesota Rules* 1983 was the first edition of the recompiled agency rules under the direction of the revisor of statutes.[166] This bound multi-volume set is produced and updated in a manner similar to the process used for *Minnesota Statutes*. Whereas *Minnesota Statutes* is published in even-numbered years with odd-numbered year pocket-part supplements, *Minnesota Rules* is published in odd-numbered years with even-numbered year pocket-part supplements. Proposed and adopted emergency (formerly called temporary) rules generally are not published in *Minnesota Rules* because of the short-term nature of their legal effectiveness (they do appear in the *State Register*). All current agency rules adopted as of July 31, 1983, were collected, arranged, and renumbered into a uniform, comprehensive decimal numbering scheme. The numbering scheme is based on an alphabetical arrangement by agency name. Editorial notes and statutory authority citations were added. The rules generally are grouped under the state agency that administers them. Some agencies have one chapter; others have many. The revisor included an excellent "User's Guide" in volume 1.

Each agency must adopt rules in a form prescribed by the revisor of statutes. The revisor's standards include provisions for incorporating texts by reference into the rules (i.e., a citation is provided), but the text is not reprinted.[167] Typically, "incorporations" are uniform codes, standards, or professional handbooks. One stipulation is that the material being incorporated is conveniently available to the public. A list of the publications or documents that the revisor has approved is conveniently available and the location is published in the Incorporation by Reference Table in volume 6. Since 1982, the State Law Library has served as a depository for materials incorporated but not otherwise "conveniently available."

The final volume of *Minnesota Rules* contains a comprehensive subject index to agency rules. The index is an alphabetical arrangement of agency names and main subject headings. The subject headings are derived from terms used in the rules, concepts associated with the rules, or common usage. Cross references are provided generously.

---

166. *Minnesota Rules* is distributed to various libraries throughout the state according to MINN. STAT. § 14.47(8) (1998).
167. MINN. STAT. § 14.07, subd. 4 (1998).

Pocket parts update the set in even-numbered years. Between supplements, new or amended rules are published in the *State Register*.

### § 321.3. Updating Agency Rules

To update *Minnesota Rules* 1983 between the publication of pocket parts, use the "Minnesota Rules Amendments and Additions" table in the *State Register*. This table is cumulated on a quarterly basis.[168]

### § 321.4. Compilations of State Regulations on One Subject

As with statutes (*see* § 275, *supra*), there is no single source in which to search the regulatory law of all agencies in every state. The task is further complicated by the fact that some states still do not publish their agency regulations, and the quality and accessability of the published codes vary widely. In recent years, several more states have begun publishing administrative codes and registers. Readers may consult several publications to learn which states publish administrative codes and registers,[169] as well as which codes and registers are available via the Internet.[170] Minnesota researchers are fortunate in that the University of Minnesota Law Library is one of a small number of U.S. law libraries to maintain a collection of published state administrative codes and registers. The reader is referred to *Subject Compilations of State Laws* (published periodically) for another excellent guide relevant to multi-jurisdictional regulatory (as well as statutory) research.

---

168. The *State Register* also includes a table entitled "MCAR Amendments and Additions." The *Minnesota Rules* table was not introduced until March 19, 1984. This makes it necessary to convert the citation of *Minnesota Rules* back to an MCAR citation to check on possible changes between July 1983 and March 1984. Volume 6 of *Minnesota Rules* 1983 includes tables cross referencing MCAR and *Minnesota Rules* citations. Before the publication of the *State Register*, there was no systematic method for updating rules.
169. Since 1979, the National Association of Secretaries of States periodically has published *Administrative Codes and Registers; State and Federal Survey. See also, BNA's Directory of State Administrative Codes and Registers: A State-By-State Listing*, 2d ed. (1995).
170. Internet access to administrative codes and registers is available from the National Association of Secretaries of State, Administrative Codes and Registers Section at <http://www.nass.org/acr/index.htm>.

## Chapter Three. Executive and Administrative Law 75

### § 322. Office of Administrative Hearings (OAH)[171]

This office was created in 1975 to preside over the hearings required by the Administrative Procedure Act (APA). Hearings are held when a state agency proposes new or amended rules, or when contested cases arise (i.e., when a person has a right to a hearing under the Constitution, statutes, or agency rules). Rules of the Office are published in chapter 1400 of the *Minnesota Rules*. Reports and orders of the hearing examiner are available for review at the Office and in the Legislative Reference Library. Since 1993, they also are available in the searchable OAH ALJ Report Database at <http://search.state.mn.us/oah/>. The Legislative Reference Library catalogs the hearings and lists them in the *LRL Checklist of Minnesota Government Publications*. The catalog for the Legislative Reference Library is available at <http://www.pals.msus.edu/webpals/home.html>. Transcripts of hearings may be purchased from the Office. All hearings are open to the public.

The Office also conducts all hearings under the Minnesota Workers' Compensation Law. Final orders issued by the compensation judges can be appealed to the Workers' Compensation Court of Appeals. Copies of orders may be purchased from the office. Workers' compensation decisions have been published since 1975.[172] Since January of 1999, these opinions also are available at <http://www.workerscomp.state.mn.us/>.

*Administrative Law Reports* is a monthly newsletter summarizing decisions issued by the Office of Administrative Hearings. Volume one, number one, was dated September 1984.

### § 323. Agency Decisions

An agency decision usually may be procured from the issuing agency, the Office of Administrative Hearings, or from the Minnesota State Documents Center (*see* § 350, *infra*). Some loose-leaf services include state agency decisions. Annual reports of agencies sometimes contain

---

171. 100 Washington Square, Suite 1700, Minneapolis, MN 55401; phone 612-341-7600; Web address <http://www.oah.state.mn.us/>. MINN. STAT. §§ 14.48–14.56 (1998).
172. WORKERS' COMPENSATION DECISIONS/RENDERED BY THE STATE SUPREME COURT AND THE WORKERS' COMPENSATION BOARD OF MINNESOTA (St. Paul, MN: The Board 1975– ).

selected opinions or digests of opinions, e.g., early reports of the Minnesota Railroad and Warehouse Commission include decisions, and the *Minnesota State Claims Commission Report* includes summaries of claims, listing the claimant, nature of claim, and amount allowed. Administrative construction or interpretation of a statute is not binding on the courts, but the decision does carry weight if it is long standing.[173]

## § 330. ADMINISTRATIVE COURTS

§ 331. Tax Court
§ 332. Workers' Compensation Court of Appeals

### § 331. Tax Court[174]

The Tax Court (formerly the Board of Tax Appeals) is an independent agency of the executive branch of the state government created to review questions of law and fact regarding taxes, fees, and assessments appealed by a taxpayer from a decision of the commissioner of revenue. The Minnesota Supreme Court hears appeals from the Tax Court. Rules are found in the appendix to chapter 271 of *Minnesota Statutes Annotated* and in chapter 8600 of *Minnesota Rules*.

Since 1985, Tax Court decisions have been published in *Minnesota Legal Register, Tax Court Decisions Issue*. Previously, they appeared in the *State Register*. Slip decisions since 1991 are available from the Tax Court website at <http://www.taxcourt.state.mn.us/pubsrch.asp>. They also are available from Minnesota's Bookstore (*see* § 350, *infra*) and are published commercially by legal newspapers (*see* § 554.6, *infra*). Commerce Clearing House and Prentice-Hall publish opinions in their respective Minnesota tax court loose-leaf reporters.

---

173. Mattson v. Flynn, 216 Minn. 354, 13 N.W.2d 11 (1944).
174. MINN. STAT. §§ 271.01–271.21 (1998). Minnesota Judicial Center, Suite 245, 25 Constitution Ave., St. Paul, MN 55155; phone 651-296-2806; Web address <http://www.taxcourt.state.mn.us/>.

## § 332. Workers' Compensation Court of Appeals[175]

The Workers' Compensation Court of Appeals is constituted as an independent agency in the executive branch, exercising appellate jurisdiction in all matters under the Workers' Compensation Law. Decisions may be appealed directly to the Supreme Court. Rules are found in the appendix to chapters 175–176 of *Minnesota Statutes Annotated* and in chapter 9800 of *Minnesota Rules*. A subscription to *Workers' Compensation Decisions* (selected opinions) is available from Minnesota's Bookstore (*see* § 350, *infra*). Cumulative indexes to this set also are available.[176] The court's website contains its opinions dating back to the beginning of 1999.

## § 340. PUBLIC ACCESS AND PRIVACY RIGHTS

The Minnesota Government Data Practices Act[177] balances the rights of public access to government information and the individual's privacy rights pertaining to specific data supplied to the government. It provides that public records be made available to any person, and that copies be furnished upon request. Restrictions related to private or confidential data are legislated.

The Act also requires that notice be given to subjects whenever an agency collects private or confidential data.[178] The required notice must inform the individual about the nature of and purpose for collecting the data and the consequences of refusing to supply the data. This provision of the Act is popularly known as the "Tennessean Warning" after the senate author of the original Data Privacy Act.[179] Failure to

---

175. *Id.* §§ 175A.01–175A.10. 405 Judicial Center, 25 Constitution Ave., St. Paul, MN 55155; phone 651-296-6526; Web address <http://www.workerscomp.state.mn.us/>.
176. *Workmen's Compensation Decisions Cumulative Index*, vols. 1–22 (1923–1963) prepared by the Division. *Workmen's Compensation Decisions Cumulative Index*, vols. 23–26 (1963–1972) prepared by Minnesota Continuing Legal Education (Minnesota Practice Manual 58). *Workers' Compensation Decisions Cumulative Index*, vols. 26–34 (1971–1982) prepared by Minnesota Continuing Legal Education. Minnesota Continuing Legal Education issues index supplements semiannually.
177. MINN. STAT. §§ 13.01–13.99 (1998).
178. *Id.* § 13.04, subd. 2.
179. Gemberling & Weissman, *Data Privacy: Everything You Wanted to Know About the Minnesota Government Data Practices Act—From "A" to "Z,"* 8 WM. MITCHELL L. REV. 573, 586 (1982).

provide the Tennessean Warning bars use or dissemination of the information[180] and may incur civil damages.[181]

The Public Information Policy Analysis Division (PIPA)[182] of the Department of Administration helps government agencies and the public to understand, implement, and enforce rights under the Act. PIPA answers questions, issues advisory opinions, provides educational and consultative services, reviews compliance policies and procedures, consults on legal questions, and acts as a resource on legislation for information policy matters.[183] Government units or individuals seeking resolution of disputes relating to the Government Data Practice Act and other statutes may request an advisory opinion from the Commissioner of Administration[184] by writing to the commissioner c/o Information Policy Analysis Division, 305A Centennial Office Building, 658 Cedar Street, St. Paul, MN 55155, phone 651-296-6733. Such advisory opinions dating back to 1993 are available on the division's website.[185]

## § 350. STATE AND LOCAL DOCUMENTS

From 1860 to 1924, agency reports were compiled annually in bound volumes entitled *Minnesota Executive Documents*. This set is available at the State Law Library and the Minnesota Historical Society, which also holds the microfiche edition *Minnesota Executive Documents, 1860–1924*.[186] Retrospective bibliographic access to state publications is provided in checklists covering the years 1849 through 1950, compiled by Esther Jerabek and published by the Minnesota Historical Society. In chronological order these are:

- *A Bibliography of Minnesota Territorial Documents* (1936)
- *Check List of Minnesota State Documents 1858–1923* (1972)

---

180. MINN. STAT. § 13.05, subd. 4 (1988).
181. *Id.* § 13.08.
182. Room 320 Centennial Office Building, 658 Cedar St., St. Paul, MN 55155; phone 651-296-6733.
183. MINNESOTA GUIDEBOOK TO STATE AGENCY SERVICES 1996–99, 10 (Dep't Admin. ed. 1996).
184. MINN. STAT. § 13.072 (1998).
185. *Admin. Minnesota* at <http://northstar.state.mn.us/ebranch/admin/ipo/pipa/> (last visited May 29, 2001).
186. Brookhaven Press 1975.

## Chapter Three. Executive and Administrative Law

- *Check List of Minnesota Public Documents* (monthly, then quarterly, from July 1923, through Oct.-Dec. 1940)
- *Check List of Minnesota Public Documents Issued from 1941 through 1950* (1952)

Most of the documents listed are available in the Historical Society's library (established in 1849). A few documents may be found at the State Law Library or the University of Minnesota. Some are retained by individual state agencies such as the departments of natural resources and health.

The University of Minnesota (general library) was designated as the first and only depository library for state documents in 1905. Minn. Stat. § 15.18 (1998) was added in 1947 to designate the Historical Society and the State Library as additional depositories. In 1963, the statute was amended to include public libraries of cities of the first class[187] and libraries of state colleges (now universities). Currently, thirty-eight college, university, and public libraries throughout the state are designated to receive state documents.[188]

Minn. Stat. § 3.302 (1998) established the Legislative Reference Library (LRL) as a depository for documents published by the state.[189] The statute defines a document as: "Any publication issued by the state, constitutional officers, commissions, councils, bureaus, research centers, societies, task forces, including advisory task forces, or other agencies supported by state funds, or any publication prepared for the state by private individuals or organizations and issued in print. . . ." Minn. Stat. § 15.18 (1998) pertains to state depository libraries and defines a document as "any book, document, journal, map, pamphlet or report issued for public distribution by any department, agency or official of the state."

The publications of Minnesota state government agencies are an integral part of the Minnesota Legislative Reference Library's

---

187. MINN. STAT. § 410.01 (1998).
188. Community college libraries and the James J. Hill Reference Library were added to the list by undocumented agreement. For a thorough discussion and explanation of the depository system, consult *Minnesota State Documents: A Guide for Depository Libraries*, prepared by an ad hoc committee of the Government Documents Round Table, Minnesota Library Association, and published by the Office of Library Development and Services, Minnesota Department of Education, in 1984.
189. MINN. STAT. § 3.302 (1998).

collection which is searchable through its catalog.[190] The library has a comprehensive collection of Minnesota state documents, including consultants' reports, published since 1974.

Since 1981, depository libraries have received microfiche copies of most documents issued by the executive, judicial, and legislative branches of Minnesota state government.[191] State documents also may be available publicly through Minnesota's Bookstore[192] which, in partnership with the Legislative Reference library, also handles the distribution of state agency publications to depository libraries pursuant to Minn. Stat. § 15.18 (1998).

In addition to access to the documents provided by the library's catalog, there are several library publications designed to make the state documents more accessible:

- *Minnesota Resources*[193] (selected list of current Minnesota documents)
- *Minnesota State Agency Periodicals*[194]
- *Minnesota State Documents Lists* ("Docs on Fiche")[195]

The depository system applies only to documents produced for the public or the legislature. Internal publications or those meant for limited distribution still must be obtained from the issuing agency. These include policy and procedural manuals, which may be the most important documentary sources for legal research. For example, the Minnesota Department of Human Services and the Minnesota Department of Corrections publish a variety of program, administrative, and procedural manuals.

---

190. The Legislative Reference Library's catalog is available at <http://www.pals.msus.edu/webpals/home.html>.
191. Minnesota Legislative Reference Library, *Minnesota State Documents; About Minnesota State Documents and the State Document Depository System* at <http://www.leg.state.mn.us/lrl/mndocs/mndocs.htm> (last modified Aug. 31, 1999).
192. Minnesota's Bookstore, 117 University Ave., Rm. 110A, St. Paul, MN 55155; phone: (800) 657-3757 (toll-free), (651) 297-3000 (local).
193. Minnesota Legislative Reference Library, *Minnesota Resources; A Selected List of Current Minnesota Documents*, at <http://www.leg.state.mn.us/lrl/resource/mnres.htm> (last modified Aug. 24, 2000).
194. Minnesota Legislative Reference Library, *Minnesota State Agency Periodicals*, at <http://www.leg.state.mn.us/lrl/magsnews.htm> (last visited Jan. 21, 2002).
195. Minnesota Legislative Reference Library, *Minnesota State Document Lists Docs on Fiche*, at <http://www.leg.state.mn.us/lrl/mndocs/docs.htm> (last modified July 12, 2000).

## Chapter Three. Executive and Administrative Law 81

City and county documents issued for public distribution should be deposited in libraries according to Minn. Stat. § 471.68 (1998). Major cities may establish separate offices or libraries to collect local documents and assist government personnel and the public in their use.[196]

---

196. Two helpful sources are the Minneapolis Municipal Information Library, Room 300, City Hall, 305 South Fifth St., Minneapolis, MN 55415, phone 612-673-3029; and the St. Paul Council Investigation and Research Library, 310 City Hall, St. Paul, MN 55102, phone 651-266-8560.

# CHAPTER FOUR
# Judiciary

Article VI of the Minnesota Constitution vests the judicial power in a Supreme Court, a Court of Appeals, a District Court, and such other inferior courts as the legislature may establish. This chapter describes the courts of Minnesota and their practices.[197]

## Chapter Contents

§ 410. Minnesota Courts
§ 420. Reports of Cases
§ 430. Records and Briefs
§ 440. Rules of Court
§ 450. Alternative Dispute Resolution
§ 460. Judicial Boards and Organizations
§ 470. Judicial Websites

## § 410. MINNESOTA COURTS

§ 411. Judges and Juries
§ 412. Minnesota State Courts
§ 413. Court Unification
§ 414. Federal Courts in Minnesota

---

197. For information on the Minnesota court system, contact the Office of the State Court Administrator (*see* § 412.131, *infra*). This office assists the court in carrying out its responsibility for the administration of all courts in the state. The *Second Annual Report* (1965) is recommended for a historical overview of Minnesota courts. For a good overview of the current court structure, see MINNESOTA GUIDEBOOK TO STATE AGENCY SERVICES 1996–99 (Dept. Administration 1996) at 367, or *Finding Your Way Around the Court System at* <http://www.courts.state.mn.us/mncourts.htm> (last visited May 30, 2001); *Minnesota Supreme Court* at <http://www.courts.state.mn.us/supreme%20court.htm> (last visited Oct. 15, 2001).

## § 411. Judges and Juries

§ 411.1. Judges
§ 411.2. Juries

### § 411.1. Judges

All state judges and justices are elected on a non-partisan ballot to a six-year term.[198] Vacancies are filled by gubernatorial appointment according to the provisions of Minn. Stat. § 480B.01 (1998) with the appointee serving until the expiration of the term to which he or she was appointed. Minn. Stat. § 480B.01 (1998) also establishes a commission on judicial selection to advise the governor.[199] All judges must be learned in the law[200] (*see also* §§ 412.12, 412.22, 412.32, *infra*).

Federal judges are appointed by the president with the advice and consent of the U.S. Senate. They hold office for life (*see also* § 414, *infra*). Directories of judges are listed in § 536.2.

### § 411.2. Juries[201]

§ 411.21. Grand Jury[202]
§ 411.22. Petit Jury[203]

There are two kinds of juries in Minnesota: the grand jury and the petit jury. Procedures used in selecting jurors may vary. Generally, they are chosen at random from lists of qualified voters.[204]

### § 411.21. Grand Jury

A grand jury is a body of persons returned at stated periods from the citizens of a county or counties chosen by lot and sworn to inquire as to public offenses committed or triable in the county or counties.[205] If, after presentation of evidence, it determines that a public offense has been

---

198. MINN. CONST. art. VI, § 8.
199. Commission on Judicial Selection, Office of the Governor, 130 State Capitol, St. Paul, MN 55155; phone 651-296-0019.
200. MINN. CONST. art. VI, § 5.
201. *See, e.g.,* MINN. STAT. §§ 593.19–593.51, 628.41, 628.48, 628.54 *et. seq.* (1998).
202. *See, e.g.,* MINN. R. CRIM. P. 18.01.
203. *See, e.g.,* MINN. GEN. R. PRAC. 802.
204. *But see* State v. Dilliard, 279 Minn. 414, 157 N.W.2d 75 (1968).
205. MINN. STAT. § 628.41 (1998).

committed, and that there is reasonable ground for believing that a particular individual has committed the offense, the grand jury returns an indictment. For certain criminal proceedings, a grand jury is required by statute to return an indictment before the prosecutor may proceed. The grand jury also inquires into the condition of persons imprisoned in the county on a criminal charge and not indicted; into the condition and management of the public prisons in the county; and into willful and corrupt misconduct of all public officers in the county.[206]

Twenty-three persons serve as grand jurors, and at least sixteen members must be present for the grand jury to conduct proceedings.[207] The length of the term of service may vary from four months to a year or more.

### § 411.22. Petit Jury

A petit jury is a body of persons impaneled and sworn as a trial jury to determine a question or issue of fact in a civil or criminal proceeding.[208] In certain criminal actions, unless the defendant consents to a jury of six, the petit jury must consist of twelve persons. In all other actions, a petit jury consists of six persons.

---

206. MINN. STAT. § 628.61 (1998).
207. *See id.* § 628.41; MINN. R. CRIM. P. 18.03.
208. MINN. R. GEN. PRAC. 802.

## Illustration 4. How the Minnesota Court System is Structured

| |
|---|
| **MINNESOTA SUPREME COURT** |
| *Appeals From*<br>Court of Appeals<br>Trial court decisions if Supreme Court chooses to bypass the Court of Appeals<br>Tax Court Appeals<br>Workers' Compensation Court of Appeals<br>*Original Actions*<br>First-degree murder convictions<br>Writs of prohibition[209]<br>Writs of habeas corpus[210]<br>Writs of mandamus[211]<br>Legislative election contests |
| ↑ |
| **MINNESOTA COURT OF APPEALS** |
| *Appeals From*<br>All trial court decisions, except first-degree murder convictions<br>Decisions of Commissioner of Economic Security<br>Administrative agency decisions, except Tax Court & Workers' Compensation<br>*Original Actions*<br>Writs of mandamus or prohibition which order a trial judge or public official to perform a specified act, such as permitting media coverage of a hearing |
| ↑ |
| **Minnesota Trial Courts** |
| *Original Actions*<br>Civil Actions<br>Criminal Actions<br>Family<br>Juvenile<br>Probate<br>Violations of city ordinances<br>*Appeals From*<br>Conciliation Court<br>(Conciliation Division: Civil disputes up to $7,500) |

---

209. A writ of prohibition asks that a governmental body or official be prevented from doing something that might cause harm.
210. A writ of habeas corpus is a complaint alleging that someone has been confined unlawfully and is asking for release.
211. A writ of mandamus asks that a governmental body or official be commanded to perform a specific act.

# Chapter Four. Judiciary

## § 412. Minnesota State Courts[212]

§ 412.1. Supreme Court
§ 412.2. Court of Appeals
§ 412.3. District Court
§ 412.4. County Courts
§ 412.5. Justice and Municipal Courts
§ 412.6. Conciliation Courts
§ 412.7. Court System in Hennepin and Ramsey Counties

## § 412.1. Supreme Court[213]

§ 412.11. Supreme Court Jurisdiction and Powers
§ 412.12. Supreme Court Justices
§ 412.13. Personnel that Aid the Supreme Court
§ 412.14. Supreme Court Procedures

### § 412.11. Supreme Court Jurisdiction and Powers

The Supreme Court is the highest judicial tribunal of Minnesota. It has original jurisdiction in such remedial cases as are prescribed by law, and appellate jurisdiction in all cases. Trial by jury in the Supreme Court is forbidden by the Constitution. With the establishment of the Court of Appeals, the Supreme Court has jurisdiction as the first appellate court in appeals from the Minnesota Tax Court,[214] the Workers' Compensation Court of Appeals,[215] and defendants convicted of first-degree murder. In a case of appeal from first-degree murder, the Supreme Court also may hear other matters decided during the same trial. The Supreme Court also has jurisdiction over legislative election contests and may issue writs of mandamus, prohibition, and habeas corpus.

The Supreme Court may grant further review of any decision of the Court of Appeals upon the petition of any party. Section 480A.10 of *Minnesota Statutes* lists certain factors to consider before deciding to review a decision:

1. An important question of first impression;
2. A statute has been held to be unconstitutional;

---

212. References to appellate courts refer to the Supreme Court and the Court of Appeals. All other courts are described as trial courts.
213. *See, e.g.*, MINN. CONST. art VI, § 2; MINN. STAT. §§ 480.01–480.30 (1998).
214. MINN. STAT. § 271.10 (1998).
215. *Id.* § 176.471.

3. Direct conflict with applicable precedent; and
4. Lower courts so far have departed from the accepted and usual course of justice as to call for an exercise of the court's supervisory powers.

The Supreme Court must issue a decision as to whether it will grant review within sixty days of the filing of the petition.[216]

Upon petition of any party, the statute also allows the Supreme Court to grant accelerated review of any case pending in the Court of Appeals if "the case is of such imperative public importance as to justify the deviation from normal appellate processes and to require immediate settlement in the supreme court."[217] On its own motion or upon certification of the Court of Appeals, the Supreme Court also may grant accelerated review of a case if factors (1), (2), or (4) listed above exist.[218] The court also regulates pleading, practice, and procedure in civil actions by promulgating rules of court (*see* § 440, *infra*).[219]

### § 412.12. Supreme Court Justices

Whereas the Constitution provides for one chief justice and from six to eight associate justices,[220] the court currently consists of one chief justice and six associate justices. All of the justices hear appeals and write opinions. The court temporarily may assign a judge to act as a justice of the Supreme Court or judge of the Court of Appeals to alleviate the imbalance of case loads.

The chief justice supervises and coordinates the work of the courts of the state. He or she exercises general supervisory powers over their financial affairs and administrative operations, supervises programs of continuing education for judicial personnel, and serves as the chief representative of the court system for the public. The chief justice also has power to assign judges to sit on courts in districts other than their own when convenience and necessity require it.[221]

---

216. *Id.* § 480A.10, subd.1.
217. *Id.* § 480A.10, subd. 2.
218. *Id.*
219. *Id.* § 480.051.
220. MINN. CONST. art. VI, § 2.
221. MINN. STAT. § 2.724 (1998).

## § 412.13. Personnel that Aid the Supreme Court
### § 412.131. State Court Administrator
### § 412.132. State Librarian

### § 412.131. State Court Administrator[222]

The state court administrator is appointed by the Supreme Court and assists the court in carrying out its responsibility for the administration of all courts in the state. Included within the scope of these administrative responsibilities are budget, facilities management, legislation, caseflow management, personnel, continuing education, operations research, records management, information systems, planning, and research.[223]

The Administrative Services Division provides technical support in the areas of budget, personnel, space management, and education. Continuing Education for State Court Personnel is an office that conducts orientation and instruction courses and training for judges, court administrators, deputies, district administrators, probate registrars, court reporters, bailiffs, and state court administration staff. It also administers the mandatory judicial education requirement and the family mediation training certification requirement.

The Information Systems Office has two primary functions: the improvement of the accuracy, efficiency, accessibility, security, and standardization of court record-keeping, and the collection of timely and accurate information on the operations of the court system. It also operates the State Judicial Information System (SJIS) that provides a comprehensive, online record-keeping system for the trial and appellate courts of the state. Planning is the division responsible for general legal and operational research concerning administration issues. The Research division statistically analyzes caseloads and researches and evaluates programs and operations of the courts in the state. The Judicial Advisory Service provides a centralized law clerk service to trial court judges. The staff conducts research and prepares written memoranda for use in their opinions.

---

222. Supreme Court of Minnesota, 25 Constitution Ave., St. Paul, MN 55155; phone 651-296-2474; fax 651-297-5636. This office formerly was called the Office of Administrative Assistant to the Supreme Court.
223. MINNESOTA GUIDEBOOK TO STATE AGENCY SERVICES 1996–99, 365 (Dept. Administration 1996) [hereinafter MINN. GUIDEBOOK].

### § 412.132. State Librarian

The librarian administers the State (law) Library, which is under the supervision of the justices of the Supreme Court.[224] For further information on the State Library, see § 614.1, *infra*.

### § 412.14. Supreme Court Procedures

The Supreme Court has one court term each year beginning in September and continuing through May, often going into June. During the summer, the court conducts hearings that do not require oral argument.[225]

The appellate courts may direct the parties or their attorneys to appear before a justice, judge, or other person designated by the appellate courts for a pre-hearing conference to consider settlement, simplification of the issues, and other matters that may aid in the disposition of the proceedings. If a settlement cannot be reached, the pre-hearing judge makes an order reciting the agreement by the parties and limiting the issues.[226]

Cases scheduled for oral argument in the Supreme Court are heard and decided by the court en banc (the entire court). Cases submitted on briefs may be considered by a non-oral panel of three or more members of the court assigned by the chief justice. The disposition proposed by the panel is circulated to the full court for review.[227] Oral argument is allowed subject to the exceptions listed in rule 134.01 of the Minnesota Rules of Civil Appellate Procedure.

---

224. MINN. STAT. § 480.09 (1998).
225. MINN. GUIDEBOOK, *supra* note 223, at 365.
226. MINN. R. CIV. APP. P. 133.01.
227. MINN. R. CIV. APP. P. 135.

# Chapter Four. Judiciary

## § 412.2. Court of Appeals[228]

§ 412.21. Court of Appeals Jurisdiction
§ 412.22. Court of Appeals Judges
§ 412.23. Personnel that Aid the Court of Appeals
§ 412.24. Court of Appeals Procedures

In the November 1982 state general election, voters approved amending the Constitution to provide for a Court of Appeals.[229] The court began taking filings on August 1, 1983.

### § 412.21. Court of Appeals Jurisdiction

The Court of Appeals has jurisdiction over appeals from all trial courts except Conciliation Court and individuals convicted of first-degree murder. The court also hears appeals from the commissioner of economic security and various administrative agencies.[230]

### § 412.22. Court of Appeals Judges

The 1982 constitutional amendment created a single Court of Appeals to which the governor appointed twelve judges. The court reached its full complement on April 1, 1984. Each Minnesota federal congressional district has a designated seat on the Court of Appeals bench. Judges not representing a congressional district serve at-large.

The governor designates one of the judges of the Court of Appeals to be chief judge for a term of three years. He or she may be reappointed. The chief judge, subject to the authority of the chief justice of the Supreme Court, exercises general administrative authority over the Court of Appeals, assigns judges to serve on panels of the court, and designates the places at which the panels will hear arguments.[231]

### § 412.23. Personnel that Aid the Court of Appeals

The clerk of the appellate courts serves as clerk of the Supreme Court and the Court of Appeals. The state court administrator directs the

---

228. *See* MINN. CONST. art. VI; MINN. STAT. §§ 480A.01–480A.11 (1998).
229. 1982 Minn. Laws ch. 501, § 2.
230. MINN. GUIDEBOOK, *supra* note 223, at 365.
231. MINN. STAT. § 480A.03 (1998).

district administrators and clerks of court in providing facilities and support services for the Court of Appeals.[232]

### § 412.24. Court of Appeals Procedures

Procedures are governed by the Minnesota Rules of Civil Appellate Procedure as adopted by the Supreme Court (*see* § 440, *infra*).[233] A panel of at least three judges decides each case with the decision of the majority being the decision of the court.[234]

Oral arguments in appeals from trial courts in Hennepin or Ramsey counties are heard by Court of Appeals sessions in those counties. Appeals from trial courts in all other counties are heard at a session of the Court of Appeals in the judicial district in which the county is located. Upon the joint request of the parties and with the approval of the court, an argument may be heard in a location other than that provided by the rules.[235]

The enabling statute provides that a case must be decided within ninety days after oral argument or after the final submission of briefs or memoranda by the parties, whichever is later. The chief justice or the chief judge may waive the ninety-day limitation for any proceeding before the Court of Appeals if good cause is shown. In every case, the decision of the court, including any written opinion containing a summary of the case and a statement of the reasons for it, is made available.[236]

---

232. *Id.* § 480A.04.
233. *Id.* § 480A.11.
234. *Id.* § 480A.08, subd. 1.
235. MINN. R. CIV. APP. P. 134.09, subd. 2 (1998).
236. MINN. STAT. § 480A.08, subd. 3 (1998).

# Chapter Four. Judiciary

## § 412.3. District Court[237]

§ 412.31. District Court Jurisdiction
§ 412.32. District Court Judges
§ 412.33. Personnel that Aid the District Court
§ 412.34. District Court Procedures and Records

### § 412.31. District Court Jurisdiction[238]

The Minnesota District Court currently is divided into ten judicial districts with the territory of each district prescribed by law.[239] The Supreme Court has the authority to alter the number of districts and their boundaries.[240] The District Court has original jurisdiction in all civil and criminal cases and appellate jurisdiction as prescribed by law.

The court system in the second (Ramsey County) and the fourth (Hennepin County) judicial districts is different from that of the other districts and is discussed separately (*see* § 412.7, *infra*).

### § 412.32. District Court Judges

The Minnesota Constitution provides for two or more district judges in each judicial district.[241] Resident judges of the district and county courts in each of the judicial districts meet and elect from among their number a chief judge and an assistant judge who each serve for two-year terms. Subject to the authority of the chief justice of the Supreme Court, the chief judge of each judicial district exercises general administrative authority over the courts in the district. He or she assigns judges to serve on any of the courts in the district and convenes conferences of all judges to consider administrative matters. The chief judges of all judicial districts meet semiannually to consider problems relating to judicial business and administration.[242]

---

237. *See* MINN. CONST. art. VI; MINN. STAT. §§ 484.01–484.76 (1998).
238. Maps of judicial districts are available at *Welcome to the Minnesota State Court System at* <http://www.courts.state.mn.us/home/default.asp> (last visited May 30, 2001), and MINN. GUIDEBOOK, *supra* note 223, at 364.
239. MINN. STAT. § 2.722, subd. 1 (1998).
240. *Id.* § 2.722, subd. 2.
241. MINN. CONST. art. 6, § 4.
242. MINN. STAT. § 484.69 (1998).

### § 412.33. Personnel that Aid the District Court

§ 412.331. Referees
§ 412.332. District Administrators
§ 412.333. Court Administrators (Clerks of Court)

### § 412.331. Referees[243]

The chief judge of the judicial district may appoint one or more persons learned in the law to act as referees. No referee may hear a contested trial, hearing, motion, or petition if a party or the attorney for a party objects in writing to the assignment of a referee. All referees are subject to the administrative authority and assignment power of the chief judge. The recommended findings and orders of a referee become the findings and orders of the court when confirmed by a judge.

### § 412.332. District Administrators[244]

District administrators are appointed by the chief judge in each judicial district, with the advice of the judges of the district and subject to the approval of the Supreme Court. The district administrator assists the chief judge in the performance of his or her administrative duties, manages the administrative affairs of the courts of the judicial district, supervises clerks of court, and complies with the requests of the state court administrator for statistical or other information relating to the courts of the judicial district.

### § 412.333. Court Administrators[245] (Clerks of Court)

A clerk is appointed for each county by a majority of District Court judges within the district after consultation with the County Court judges affected. The clerk of District Court also serves as the clerk of County Court.[246] In 1985 the legislature enacted chapter 273 which provides that clerks of District Court shall be known as court administrators.[247] The clerk keeps civil and criminal indexes, registers of actions, judgment dockets, and judgment books.

---

243. *See id.* § 484.70.
244. *See id.* § 484.68.
245. *See id.* §§ 485.01–485.27.
246. *Id.* § 487.10(1).
247. *Id.* § 485.01.

## § 412.34. District Court Procedures and Records[248]

Court rules (*see* § 440, *infra*) prescribe the procedures for District Court. Minnesota's *Rules of Public Access to Records of the Judicial Branch* apply to the records of all judicial branch courts (i.e., not the Tax or Worker's Compensation courts, which are in the executive branch) and court administrators.[249] Judicial branch records generally are open to the public for inspection and copying during regular business hours. Rules 4, 5, and 6 set out exemptions pertaining to specific case records (employee records, work product, correspondence, security records, copyrighted material, competitive bidding records, and vital statistics). Rules 7 and 8 contain procedures for requesting access to inspect or copy records. Rule 9 governs appeals from denial of access to records.

## § 412.4. County Courts[250]

Article VI, section 1, of the Minnesota Constitution authorizes the legislature to establish courts with jurisdiction inferior to that of the District Court. The legislature enacted the County Court Act establishing the county court system, effective July 1, 1972. The purpose of the Act was to replace the fragmented lower court system with one court having broad jurisdiction in each county. The County Court Act effectively eliminated the part-time judge. When counties elect to combine, or when the population of a county is not large enough to justify having a full-time judge, multi-county districts are permitted. The Supreme Court also may combine two or more County Court districts into a single district. Hennepin and Ramsey counties were excluded from the County Court Act, but in all other counties (except St. Louis, although this exception subsequently was removed), the 1972 legislation merged municipal and probate courts into the county court system. Hennepin and Ramsey counties are discussed in § 412.7, *infra*.

County courts are divided into a probate division, a family division, and a civil and criminal division that includes a conciliation court, and

---

248. For detailed historical information on all types of records, retention schedules, and sample records, see M. LAZARUS, A REPORT ON RECORDS OF THE MINNESOTA DISTRICT AND COUNTY COURTS 2d ed. (Minnesota Historical Society 1979). For more current information on court records and the Total Court Information System, see SUE K. DOSAL, TCIS ON-LINE ACCESS PILOT PROJECT: REPORT TO THE LEGISLATURE (1992).
249. MINN. STAT. ch. 13, app. (1998).
250. *See id.* §§ 487.01–487.40.

that may establish within the civil and criminal division a traffic and ordinance violations bureau.

The jurisdiction of the probate division includes cases and proceedings relating to the administration of the estates of deceased persons, persons under guardianship, proceedings for the administration of trust estates, and cases relating to the management of the property of persons who have disappeared. The jurisdiction of the Family Court division includes actions arising under the Juvenile Court Act and matters affecting family relationships such as divorce, annulment, civil commitment, and support obligations.[251]

Civil jurisdiction includes actions where the amount in controversy does not exceed $15,000.00, except for causes involving title to real estate.[252] Criminal jurisdiction includes gross misdemeanors, misdemeanors, petty misdemeanors, and ordinance or charter violations.[253] The court also has the power to conduct preliminary hearings. The right to a jury trial is guaranteed in actions where conviction could result in imprisonment.[254]

The County Court has exclusive original jurisdiction in some cases and concurrent jurisdiction with the District Court in others. In some instances, cases may be transferred from the district to the county (or from the county to the district) court. Parties may appeal the decisions of the County Court to the Court of Appeals. Where the jurisdiction of the County Court is concurrent with that of the District Court, the Rules of Civil Procedure of the District Court apply.

### § 412.5. Justice and Municipal Courts

All justice courts (popularly known as justices of the peace) have been abolished.[255] Only Hennepin and Ramsey counties have municipal courts (*see* § 412.72, *infra*).[256]

---

251. *Id.* § 487.27.
252. *Id.* § 487.15.
253. *Id.* § 487.18.
254. *Id.* § 487.25, subd. 6.
255. *Id.* § 488A.113 (abolishing justice courts in Hennepin and Ramsey counties); *id.* § 487.35 (abolishing the remaining justice courts).
256. 1977 Minn. Laws, ch. 432, § 49 (repealing the Municipal Court Act).

# Chapter Four. Judiciary

### § 412.6. Conciliation Courts[257]

Conciliation courts, popularly known as small claims courts, are established by the district court in each county.[258] Jurisdiction is limited to civil claims where the amount in controversy does not exceed $7,500.00, or $4,000.00 if the claim involves a consumer credit transaction. The territorial jurisdiction of the court is coextensive with the county in which it is established.[259] Judges of the District Court serve as judges of Conciliation Court, and District Court administrators serve as Conciliation Court administrators.[260] Procedures are simple and informal, lawyers are deemed unnecessary, and matters are to be settled quickly. Jury trials are not allowed. Proceedings must not be reported.[261] Appeals may be taken by removal to the District Court for a trial de novo and are governed by rules promulgated by the Supreme Court.[262] Decisions of the District Court on removal from a Conciliation Court determination on the merits may be appealed to the Court of Appeals.[263] The Supreme Court is authorized to prescribe uniform forms for use in all conciliation courts of the state (*see* § 440, *infra*).

Information on conciliation courts may be obtained from the conciliation court administrator or from a number of websites.[264] Under supervision of Conciliation Court judges, court administrators have a statutory duty to explain to litigants the procedures and functions of the conciliation court and assist them in filling out all forms and pleadings. The law further requires them to assist successful litigants in preparing "the forms necessary to obtain satisfaction of a final judgment."[265]

---

257. MINN. STAT. §§ 491A.01–491A.03 (1998).
258. *Id.* § 491A.01, subd. 1.
259. *Id.* § 491A.01, subd. 2.
260. *Id.* § 491A.03.
261. *Id.* § 491A.02, subd. 1.
262. *Id.* § 491A.02, subd. 6.
263. *Id.* § 491A.02, subd. 8.
264. Minnesota Legal Services Coalition publishes a fact sheet titled *Conciliation Court, available at* <http://www.mnlegalservices.org/publications/fact_sheets/d1.html> (visited Jan. 24, 2002). The Fourth Judicial District Court (Hennepin County) publishes *Conciliation Court, available at* http://www.co.hennepin.mn.us/courts/ConcCtccmain.htm> (last visited May 30, 2001). For the second judicial district, see Ramsey County Courts—Conciliation Court *at* <http://www.courts.state.mn.us/districts/second/ramsey_conciliation.htm> (last visited May 30, 2001).
265. MINN. STAT. § 491A.02, subd. 2 (1998).

## § 412.7. Court System in Hennepin and Ramsey Counties

§ 412.71. District Courts in Hennepin and Ramsey Counties
§ 412.72. Municipal Courts in Hennepin and Ramsey Counties
§ 412.73. Conciliation Courts in Hennepin and Ramsey Counties
§ 412.74. Housing Courts in Hennepin and Ramsey Counties

Both Hennepin and Ramsey Counties have district, municipal, conciliation, and housing courts.

### § 412.71. District Courts in Hennepin[266] and Ramsey[267] Counties[268]

In addition to the jurisdiction exercised by other district courts, the district courts of Hennepin County and Ramsey County have jurisdiction over probate, juvenile, and family court matters. In both counties, one or more judges are assigned duty to each of these divisions for a specified period of time during which the judge handles these matters exclusively.

Resident judges of the courts in Hennepin and Ramsey counties meet and elect from among their number a chief judge and an assistant chief judge, whose duties are the same as those of the chief judges of other districts (*see* § 412.32, *supra*).

### § 412.72. Municipal Courts in Hennepin and Ramsey Counties[269]

The jurisdiction of the municipal courts of Hennepin County and Ramsey County is essentially coextensive with the territories of those counties. Municipal courts have jurisdiction in both civil and criminal matters. Jury trials are permitted and are a matter of right where a conviction could result in imprisonment. In civil disputes, excepting cases involving title to real estate, the court may try actions where the amount in controversy does not exceed $15,000.00. In criminal actions, it may hear cases involving misdemeanors, gross

---

266. *See* Fourth Judicial District Court, State of Minnesota *at* <http://www.co.hennepin.mn.us/courts/court.htm> (last visited May 30, 2001).
267. *See* Minnesota Second District Courts Home Page *at* <http://www.courts.state.mn.us/districts/second/default.htm> (last visited May 30, 2001).
268. *See* MINN. STAT. § 260.021, §§ 484.01–484.76 (1998).
269. *See id.* §§ 488A.01–488A.287 (1998).

## Chapter Four. Judiciary

misdemeanors, ordinances, charter provisions, and some felonies. Appeals may be taken to the Court of Appeals.

Misdemeanor violations bureaus have been organized under the supervision of the court administrator in both counties. These bureaus operate in accordance with the rules of criminal procedure[270] and perform duties relating to misdemeanors violations.

### § 412.73. Conciliation Courts in Hennepin and Ramsey Counties[271]

In the second (Ramsey) and fourth (Hennepin) judicial districts, a majority of the judges of the district may appoint referees in conciliation court. For a general discussion of conciliation courts, see § 412.6, *supra*.

### § 412.74. Housing Courts in Hennepin[272] and Ramsey[273] Counties[274]

In 1989, the legislature created housing courts in Hennepin and Ramsey counties as specialty courts to provide an accessible and efficient forum for litigants with landlord and tenant disputes. Rules for these housing courts are in Title VII of the General Rules of Practice for the District Courts.[275]

## § 413. Court Unification[276]

1982 legislation provided for a voluntary merger of all the trial courts within a judicial district into one general trial court called the District Court. Except in the second, third, fourth, and seventh districts, this reorganization took effect one year following certification to the secretary of state of intention to reorganize the trial courts by a majority of the district, county, and municipal judges of the judicial district.[277]

---

270. MINN. R. CRIM. P. 23.
271. *See* MINN. STAT. §§ 491A.01–491A.03 (1998).
272. *See Fourth Judicial District Court, State of Minnesota, Housing Court*, at <http://www.co.hennepin.mn.us/courts/Housing/hcmain.htm> (last visited May 30, 2001).
273. *See Ramsey County Courts—Housing Court*, at <http://www.courts.state.mn.us/districts/second/ramsey_housing.htm> (last visited May 30, 2001).
274. *See* MINN. STAT. §§ 484.013, 504B.001–504B.471 (1998).
275. MINN. GEN. R. PRAC. §§ 601–612.
276. *See* MINN. STAT. § 487.191 (1998).
277. Unification has occurred in the third, seventh, ninth, and tenth judicial districts.

### § 414. Federal Courts in Minnesota

Article III of the U.S. Constitution fixes the scope of the judicial power of the federal government. It gives Congress the power to establish courts inferior to the U.S. Supreme Court. Congress has established federal courts of appeal, federal district courts, and other courts. The jurisdiction of the federal courts is defined by the U.S. Constitution and by statute. To determine whether a federal court has the authority to exercise jurisdiction over a case or controversy, it is necessary to examine the federal statutes and court rules.

Minnesota is included within the jurisdiction of the Eighth Circuit Court of Appeals[278] which maintains a branch office in St. Paul. Minnesota constitutes one federal judicial district[279] with district clerks' offices in Duluth, Minneapolis, and St. Paul. Bankruptcy court is a unit of the U.S. district court with bankruptcy clerks' offices in Duluth, Fergus Falls, Minneapolis, and St. Paul.[280]

Magistrates serve to relieve judges of some judicial work.[281] They are nominated by a majority of U.S. district court judges and approved by the Administrative Office of the U.S. Courts. They may hear any civil case upon the consent of the parties. Jurisdiction is limited to pretrial hearings and motions. Magistrates also may hear and pass sentence in petty misdemeanor cases.

---

278. *See Welcome to the United States Court of Appeals, at* <http://www.ca8.uscourts.gov/index.html> (last modified Apr. 4, 2000).
279. *See U.S. District Court District of Minnesota, at* <http://www.mnd.uscourts.gov/> (last visited May 30, 2001).
280. *United States Bankruptcy Court, District of Minnesota, at* <http://www.mnb.uscourts.gov/> (last visited May 30, 2001).
281. For a historical listing of magistrates serving in Minnesota, see *The First 100 Years* (Minneapolis, MN: Minnesota State Bar Ass'n 1983).

## § 420. Reports of Cases

§ 421. Minnesota Appellate Courts
§ 422. Minnesota Trial Courts
§ 423. Federal Courts

### § 421. Minnesota Appellate Courts[282]

§ 421.1. Minnesota Reports
§ 421.2. Northwestern Reporter
§ 421.3. Minnesota Reporter
§ 421.4. Current Opinions

Opinions of the Minnesota Supreme Court were published in *Minnesota Reports* (Minn.) from the first reported territorial cases through volume 312 (1977) when publication ceased; in *Northwestern Reporter* (N.W. and N.W.2d) series from 26 Minn. (1879) to date; and in *Minnesota Reporter* from 256 N.W.2d (1978) to date.[283] Note that cases from the end of *Minnesota Reports* (1977) to the first volume of *Minnesota Reporter* (1978) are published only in N.W.2d (representing a period of a few months).

Opinions of the Minnesota Court of Appeals, since its establishment in 1983, have been published in both *Minnesota Reporter* and *Northwestern Reporter 2d*. Not every appellate court decision is published. Court rules provide for decisions in civil cases without written opinions. These decisions are not officially published and cannot be cited as precedent by non-parties.[284] All appellate court decisions are kept on file with the clerk of the appellate courts.

Westlaw and LEXIS services both contain Minnesota Supreme Court cases dating from 1851 and Minnesota Court of Appeals cases dating from 1983 (the court's inception). The state court system's

---

282. *See* MINN. STAT. §§ 480.11–480.12 (1998).
283. Minnesota Supreme Court cases also have been published in discontinued titles. *Minnesota Supreme Court Decisions* was published weekly during the court year by the Court Publishing Company, Robbinsdale, MN. The first issue was dated October 15, 1938, and only seventeen issues were published. *Minnesota Law Reports* was published by Mason Publishing Co. (semi-monthly). Eleven issues appeared between October 15, 1982 and April 1983. *See also* notes accompanying § 421.2, *infra*.
284. MINN. R. CIV. APP. P. 136.01. The appellate courts will prepare short descriptions of the cases known as "summary decisions." *See also* MINN. STAT. § 480A.08 (1998); MINN. STAT. SPEC. R. PRAC. APP. CT. R. 4.

website is the official source for current opinions.[285] The website's archive contains Supreme Court opinions and orders dating from May 1996; Court of Appeals published opinions dating from May 1996; and Court of Appeals unpublished and order opinions also dating from May 1996.[286]

### § 421.1. Minnesota Reports

In addition to the Supreme Court opinions, the official *Minnesota Reports* included court rules, amendments to court rules, names of attorneys recently admitted to practice in the state, memorials to Supreme Court justices recently deceased,[287] lists of judges of the Supreme Court and district court, a table of cases, and a topical index. For each case, a parallel citation to *Northwestern Reporter* series, the date of decision, and Supreme Court file number are provided. The court writes concise summary statements of the points of law decided in the case.[288] These statements, or headnotes, are placed after the date and case number, and are followed by a statement of the procedural posture and facts of the case written by the court reporter.

Volume one of *Minnesota Reports* is supposed to include "all cases decided by the Supreme Court of Minnesota, from the organization of the Territory [1849] until its admission into the Union in 1858." Unfortunately, records were lost or destroyed by a fire at the Capitol in July 1857. The first cases reported date from the court's second term in 1851, which was the first term to have an official reporter appointed. Cases from this term and those terms reported by the second reporter survived the fire intact. The extent of the loss of later case files cannot be determined.

Until the middle of the nineteenth century, it was common for law reports to be named after the reporter who prepared them for publica-

---

285. *Welcome to the Minnesota State Court System* at <http://www.courts.state.mn.us/home/default.asp> (last visited May 30, 2001).
286. *Opinions of the Minnesota State Appellate Courts Archive* at <http://www.lawlibrary.state.mn.us/archive/> (last visited Jan. 22, 2002).
287. When the preceding material was included in a volume, reference was made at the bottom of the spine.
288. The contents of these "headnotes" are not the same as the content of West's Key Number headnotes. West published the court's statements under the title "Syllabus by the Court" and places them after the Key Number headnotes written by West editors.

**Chapter Four. Judiciary**

tion. Known as nominatives, the multiplicity of personal name titles caused so much confusion that the practice was abandoned and the name of the jurisdiction became the integral part of the series title. Minnesota never had nominative reporters per se. The first two preparers of reports did have their reports published as part of the *Collated Statutes of the Territory of Minnesota,* 1853 (*see* Appendix D) under the titles of Hollingshead's Reports and Atwater's Reports. These reports were reprinted along with all subsequent cases starting with volume 1 of *Minnesota Reports.* Then, in 1877, because an insufficient number of the first twenty original volumes of *Minnesota Reports* was printed, James Gilfillan, a former chief justice of the Minnesota Supreme Court, republished them as *Gilfillan's Reports* (*Gil.*). These are not exact reprints of the original reports; Justice Gilfillan deleted some material and added other information. Differences exist in the addition of briefs, in headnotes, punctuation, paragraphing, and page numbering, but Justice Gilfillan did give the citation to the original volume at the beginning of each case. Pages, however, are not starred[289] except in volume one.

### § 421.2. Northwestern Reporter[290]

*Northwestern Reporter,* published by West, was an unofficial reporter until designated the official reporter in 1978.[291] It contains appellate opinions of the courts of Iowa, Michigan, Nebraska, North Dakota, South

---

289. A "starred page" is a page in a republished volume with a notation or asterisk showing precisely where each page in the original volume begins.
290. *The Syllabi* and the *North Western Reporter* were predecessors of *Northwestern Reporter* and of the complete National Reporter System. *The Syllabi* was a legal newspaper published by West in 1876–77. It contained the syllabus of Minnesota Supreme Court opinions, and the more important decisions of the Minnesota District Court and U.S. federal courts in Minnesota. The *Northwestern Reporter,* issued by West periodically, published the appellate and lower federal court decisions of Minnesota and Wisconsin in four volumes (bound in two) from April 1877 through April 1879. The current *Northwestern Reporter* series began in 1879, with *Northwestern Reporter 2d* (second series) beginning in 1942.
291. The court order filed June 9, 1978 stated:

> IT IS HEREBY ORDERED that the *Northwestern Reports* [sic], beginning with the May 1977 Minnesota Supreme Court cases reported in 254 N.W.2d, et seq., is adopted by the Supreme Court of Minnesota as the official publication of the opinions and decisions of the Court, and that publication of the *Minnesota Reports* shall cease with Volume 312.

Dakota, and Wisconsin in addition to Minnesota. West editors add headnotes that summarize each point of law discussed in an opinion; a Key Number then is assigned to that headnote. A Key Number digest is included in the back of each hardbound volume, and in the front of the advance sheets. A table of cases and tables of statutes, rules, and laws construed by the court in reported cases also are provided.

### § 421.3. Minnesota Reporter

*Minnesota Reporter,* published by West, reprints pages of the *Northwestern Reporter 2d* that cover Minnesota cases. They bear the same volume and page number as the *Northwestern Reporter 2d* and include tables and indexes.

The *Minnesota Reporter on Premise* is a two-disc CD-ROM publication containing Supreme Court decisions from 1942 to date; Court of Appeals reported decisions from 1983 to date; Court of Appeals unpublished decisions from 1987 to date; Tax Court unpublished decisions 1965 to date; slip opinions; and Minnesota attorney general opinions from 1977 to date.

*LEXIS® Publishing Law on Disc—Minnesota, Dunnell's Edition* is a Folio®-based two-disc CD-ROM publication containing Supreme Court decisions since 1898; Court of Appeals decisions since 1983; selected unpublished Court of Appeals decisions; opinions of the attorney general since 1977; and selected other primary and secondary legal materials for Minnesota.

### § 421.4. Current Opinions

Since March 15, 1999, individual opinions have been published electronically at the courts' website, according to its opinion release policy.[292] Opinions are published in *Northwestern Reporter 2d* advance sheets about two to six weeks after issuance unless held back by the court.[293] LEXIS and Westlaw also are reliable sources for current opinions as they are released by the courts.

---

292. *See Notice of Change in the Release of Appellate Opinions,* at <http://www.courts.state.mn.us/opinions/relpolicy.html> (last visited May 30, 2001).
293. If a losing party has moved for reargument, and if the court has granted that motion, the opinion is withheld from publication. The opinion is available for inspection, but is of limited precedential value.

## § 422. Minnesota Trial Courts

Opinions of Minnesota district, county, and municipal courts are not published. Conclusions of law, findings of fact, and the order for judgment are filed by the judge for each case under the name of the parties to the action and may be examined in the office of the clerk of those courts. A few District Court opinions are published in some loose-leaf services.[294] At various times, *Hennepin Lawyer* has printed digests of "significant" District Court opinions. Local newspapers generally cover court proceedings.

Since 1982, the Minnesota Trial Lawyers Association[295] has published *Minnesota Case Reports* that summarizes the outcome of cases submitted by its membership. The intent of this publication is to provide an index to verdicts and settlements. *Finance & Commerce,* a legal newspaper, also publishes information about settlements and verdicts on a selective basis. Another source for information on local jury verdicts is *Personal Injury Valuation Handbooks* published by Jury Verdict Research, Inc. This set predicts national verdict trends based upon past verdicts, and includes a pamphlet discussing the local variations for areas within Minnesota. A monthly newsletter that summarizes cases and their verdicts nationwide is available separately.[296]

A court reporter is appointed by a judge to act as his or her secretary for judicial duties. The reporter makes a complete stenographic record of all testimony and all proceedings before the judge.[297] The stenographic report generally is filed with the clerk of court. A transcript (readable record) of the trial rarely is made if there is no appeal, but a transcript must be furnished to any person upon payment of a fee, and sentencing transcripts always are made a part of the District Court file. Electronic recording equipment may be used to record court proceedings in lieu of a court reporter except for felony

---

294. *See, e.g.,* Reserve Mining Co. v. Minnesota Pollution Control Agency, No. 05011, 2 ENV'T REP. (BNA) 1135 (D. Minn. Dec. 15, 1970).
295. 706 Second Ave. South, 140 Baker Building, Minneapolis, MN 55402; phone 612-375-1707.
296. Some other national sources for verdict information are *ATLA Law Reporter, CCH Products Liability Reports, Negligence and Compensation Cases Annotated,* and *Verdicts & Settlements.*
297. MINN. STAT. §§ 486.01–486.10 (1998).

and gross misdemeanor offenses, District Court jury trials, contested District Court trials, and fact-finding hearings.[298]

### § 423. Federal Courts

Federal district court opinions for all states were published in *Federal Reporter* until October 1932; since then they have been published in *Federal Supplement*. Federal court of appeals cases are published in the *Federal Reporter* series. All of these sets are published by West. *U.S. Law Week, General Law Section,* published by the Bureau of National Affairs, prints summaries of significant federal district and appellate court opinions less than one month after their release. Current opinions are available from the courts' websites, which can be found among the links available at The Federal Judiciary Homepage.[299]

Not every federal district court or court of appeals decision is published. Federal judges have the discretion not to publish their decisions. They are encouraged to publish only those opinions having theoretical or precedential value. Some circuits publish lists indicating the disposition of unpublished cases in the *Federal Reporter 2d*. Federal district court orders and opinions are kept on file by docket number in the office of each district clerk of court. A table of cases is available. Records are open to the public.

Computerized legal databases include published and some unpublished decisions of federal courts. Some "unpublished" federal district and court of appeals opinions are published in loose-leaf services.

---

298. *Id.* § 484.72.
299. *Court Links, at* <http://www.uscourts.gov/links.html> (last visited May 30, 2001).

Chapter Four. Judiciary

## § 430. RECORDS AND BRIEFS

§ 431. Briefs
§ 432. Record or Appendix
§ 433. Indexes
§ 434. Briefs on Microfiche
§ 435. Law Library Holdings

### § 431. Briefs

Briefs are submitted to trial and appellate courts in support of the positions taken by the parties. The term "brief" has a number of meanings. It can refer not only to that which is written to aid the lawyer in organizing and presenting his case, but also to the material that is submitted to the court. Briefs ultimately seek to persuade the judge of the soundness of the writer's position.

The format that a brief must follow (organization, quality and size of paper, etc.) is governed by rules of court.[300] Because individual judges have discretion to impose additional requirements on the form of briefs, it is advisable to check with their offices or to examine previously submitted briefs for additional requirements.

### § 432. Record or Appendix

The "record"[301] consists of a trial transcript or partial trial transcript, prepared by the court reporter, and includes the complaint, answer, motions, and orders. It accompanies the brief to the appellate court.

Beginning in 1968, the Supreme Court no longer required transmittal of the record.[302] Minnesota Civil Appellate Procedure Rule 130 states that the "record shall not be printed." Instead, the appellant prepares and files an "appendix" to his brief that contains specified portions of the record (i.e., relevant pleadings, motions, orders, etc.). A party may prepare and file a supplemental record containing any relevant portion of the record not contained in the appendix. Within

---

300. *See, e.g.,* MINN. R. CIV. APP. P. 128.
301. This formerly was known as the "paperbook."
302. The Minnesota State Law Library bound the records along with the briefs until about 1964. Since 1964, records received by the library have been separately shelved at the Supreme Court Library, arranged by docket number. The library receives the transcript when two copies are filed.

ten days after the due date for filing the appellant's brief, the trial court administrator transmits the record to the clerk of the appellate court.

### § 433. Indexes

Some indexes to records or briefs for cases concerned with specific topics have been prepared. For an index to briefs of criminal appeals cases from 1968 to 1971, see Minnesota, Office of the Attorney General, *Legal Memoranda and Appellate Brief Bank Index*. Approach is by topical analysis, by alphabetical word index, and by defendant. File numbers and citations to *Northwestern Reporter 2d* are provided. Legal memoranda on criminal cases also are available in the attorney general's office.

For an index to transcripts of cases between 1947 and 1958 that involved medical testimony, see *Minnesota Trial Transcript, Medical Index* (Paulik & Brown eds., 1959).

### § 434. Briefs on Microfiche

In the past, copies of appellate briefs were distributed to various law libraries around the state after the justices disposed of the case. Libraries receiving copies were the State Law Library, University of Minnesota Law School Library, William Mitchell College of Law Library, Hamline University School of Law Library, and the following county law libraries: Brown, Chippewa, Clay, Freeborn, Hennepin, Mower, Otter Tail, Ramsey, St. Louis, Stearns, Steel, and Winona. These collections were incomplete with significant gaps and deteriorating volumes. Shortages of space, cost of storage, and other factors were developing into serious problems. Because all the libraries had to face this situation, the directors of the Minneapolis/St. Paul area law libraries met to search for a solution. The result was the implementation of a microfiche program in late 1981 under the supervision of the State Law Library.

The microfiche edition begins with the Minnesota cases in volume 300 of *Northwestern Reporter 2d* (1980). Briefs are arranged by citation in the order that they appear in the N.W.2d advance sheets. State Law Library staff prepare the briefs for filming as soon as an advance sheet volume has been completed. One copy then is bound for the circulating depository collection at the Supreme Court branch of the State Law Library. Copies of the microfiche are distributed to subscribing libraries.

# Chapter Four. Judiciary

The Minnesota State Law Library now is the official depository for Minnesota appellate briefs in hard copy after disposition by the courts. Briefs for cases not published in *Northwestern Reporter 2d* are discarded. These would include cases that have been settled, dismissed, or otherwise summarily disposed. On August 1, 1983, the Clerk of the Appellate Courts discontinued distributing briefs to other libraries.

## § 435. Law Library Holdings

§ 435.1. Records and Briefs in Cases Decided by Minnesota Appellate Courts
§ 435.2. Records and Briefs in Cases Decided by Minnesota Trial Courts
§ 435.3. Records and Briefs in Cases Decided by the U.S. Supreme Court
§ 435.4. Records and Briefs in Cases Decided by Federal Courts in Minnesota

## § 435.1. Records and Briefs in Cases Decided by Minnesota Appellate Courts

All six metropolitan-area law libraries subscribe to the microfiche edition, which is filmed in the order of the *Northwestern Reporter 2d* case citation. Their holdings in hard copy are listed below. There may be gaps in the hard copy collections. Storage and arrangement vary from library to library. Call first to facilitate access.

Briefs generally were arranged by either calendar number or case citation. Calendar numbers for cases through 1902 may be found in the alphabetical table of cases at the end of the *Law Book Catalogue of the Minnesota State Library* (1903). Between volumes 61 (1895) and 138 (1917), calendar numbers are found in parentheses after the file number at the beginning of each case in *Minnesota Reports*. The University of Minnesota Law Library uses additional methods of arrangement that are listed below its entry.

### University of Minnesota Law Library

Holdings: October term 1887–1983 (hard copy); 300 N.W.2d (1980) to date (microfiche).

*Arrangement*

Oct. 1887 to Oct. 1911, briefs arranged by calendar number.
119 Minn. (1912) to 240 Minn. (1954), briefs arranged alphabetically by case name.

241 Minn. (1954) to 312 Minn. (1977), briefs arranged by case citation of *Minnesota Reports*.

After v. 312 of *Minnesota Reports* (1977) to 1983, briefs arranged and bound by docket number.

**Minnesota State Law Library**

Holdings: 1864 to date (hard copy); 300 N.W.2d (1980) to date (microfiche).

**Hamline University School of Law Library**

Holdings: Apr. 1881–1981 (hard copy); 300 N.W.2d (1980) to date (microfiche).

**William Mitchell College of Law Library**

Holdings: 282 Minn. (1968) to 1983 (hard copy); 300 N.W.2d (1980) to date (microfiche).

**Hennepin County Law Library**

Holdings: 21 Minn. (1874) to 1983 (hard copy); 300 N.W.2d (1980) to date (microfiche).

**Ramsey County Law Library**

Holdings: 230 Minn. (1950) to 1983 (hard copy); 300 N.W.2d (1980) to date (microfiche).

**Other County Law Libraries**

The following out-of-state libraries received briefs from the Minnesota Supreme Court until August 1, 1983: Brown, Chippewa, Clay, Freeborn, Mower, Otter Tail, St. Louis, Stearns, Steele, and Winona. They should be consulted for their holdings. Freeborn, Otter Tail, and Stearns counties subscribe to the microfiche edition.

### § 435.2. Records and Briefs in Cases Decided by Minnesota Trial Courts

Records and briefs, if prepared, are not distributed. Briefs, if submitted to the court, are in the district court file. To view these files, researchers must visit the relevant county courthouse.

Chapter Four. Judiciary

### § 435.3. Records and Briefs in Cases Decided by the U.S. Supreme Court[303]

**University of Minnesota Law Library**

Holdings: 1832–1896 (microfilm); 1896–1906 (microfiche); 1905 to date (hard copy with gaps); 1974/75 term to date (microfiche) (these are received about six weeks after argument).

**Hamline University School of Law Library**

Holdings: 1940 to date (microfiche).

**William Mitchell College of Law Library**

Holdings: 1939 to date (microfiche).

### § 435.4. Records and Briefs in Cases Decided by Federal Courts in Minnesota

§ 435.41. Eighth Circuit Court of Appeals
§ 435.42. U.S. District Court

#### § 435.41. Eighth Circuit Court of Appeals

The Eighth Circuit Court of Appeals has reduced the number of briefs that must be submitted. The University of Iowa is the only library currently receiving briefs and records. The court determines which briefs and records will be deposited. Files may be examined and copied in the clerk's office in St. Louis at the expense of the user, although recent filings may be available locally at the federal courthouse.

**University of Minnesota Law Library**

Holdings: 1890s–1960; 1968–1973 (hard copy with gaps).

**University of Iowa Law Library**[304]

Holdings: 1893 to date (hard copy with gaps).

#### § 435.42. U.S. District Court

Records and briefs are not published, but are located in the court's files.

---

303. Arrangement and storage of briefs vary from library to library. To facilitate access, call the library before visiting.
304. Iowa City, IA 52242; phone 319-335-9002.

## § 440. Rules of Court[305]

§ 441. Court Rulemaking Procedures
§ 442. Professional Rules for Attorneys and Judges
§ 443. Sources of Court Rules
§ 444. Jury Instruction Guides
§ 445. Minnesota Sentencing Guidelines

The Minnesota Supreme Court has the power to regulate the pleadings, practice, procedure, and forms in criminal and civil actions in all courts of the state. In promulgating rules, the courts cannot abridge or modify substantive rights, and the legislature has reserved the right to modify or repeal any rule.

Court rules enable courts to conduct their business efficiently, and also serve to inform disputants of the manner of proceeding. Rules have been promulgated to govern general areas such as civil, criminal, and appellate procedure. Court rules for civil cases govern such areas as commencement of the action, pleadings, discovery, and remedies. Rules for criminal cases deal with such areas as issuance of warrants and pretrial hearings. In addition to prescribing procedures to be followed in the various phases of an action, rules also prescribe the form of the numerous papers that must be filed (e.g., motions and briefs). Rules also may concern specific topics such as commitment[306] and arbitration[307] proceedings.

Minnesota Rules of Civil Procedure, Minnesota Rules of Civil Appellate Procedure, and Minnesota Rules of Evidence substantially conform to the federal rules.[308] Federal interpretation of a rule therefore may be consulted when Minnesota courts have not yet construed a rule.

---

305. *See* MINN. STAT. §§ 480.051–480.0595 (1998).
306. Minnesota Supreme Court Order C4-94-1646 dated November 10, 1999 adopted the Special Rules of Procedure Governing Proceedings Under the 1997 Minnesota Commitment and Treatment Act, effective January 1, 2000. *See* MINN. STAT. §§ 253B.01–253B.23, App. B. for these rules.
307. Arbitration Procedure; Rules of Court, MINN. STAT. § 65B.525 (1998).
308. Deviations occur because of the differences in the structure of the federal and state court systems and because the form of some Minnesota rules may be shaped by state statutory requirements. *See, e.g.,* tables of comparable rules of appellate procedure and civil procedure in the obsolete 27A *Minnesota Statutes Annotated* (1968), pages 5 and 357, respectively.

## § 441. Court Rulemaking Procedures

Procedures for adoption of rules are delineated by statute. Additionally, the Supreme Court has adopted rule-making procedures to follow due process and ensure public access.[309] These procedures are patterned after those followed by administrative agencies and include prior publication, comment period, open hearings, and use of committees. An advisory committee consisting of attorneys and judges assists the Supreme Court in proposing and considering rules.[310] Before any rule is adopted, the Supreme Court is required to distribute copies of the proposed rules to the bench and bar for comments.[311] Suggestions are to be seriously considered by the court. The Supreme Court edition of *Finance and Commerce* and the *Saint Paul Legal Ledger* are designated as the media for official publication of notices from the Supreme Court.[312] Proposed and new rules also usually are published in *Bench and Bar of Minnesota*, other bar association publications, other legal newspapers, *Northwestern Reporter 2d* advance sheets, and West's *Minnesota Session Law Service*. Rules are open to public inspection in the Office of the Clerk of the Appellate Courts. The Minnesota State Bar Association Court Rules Committee reviews and suggests modifications to proposed rules and amendments to rules. Formal hearings on existing or proposed rules may be requested by Court of Appeals judges, the District Court Judges Association, the Minnesota County Court Judges Association, or the Municipal Court Judges Association.

Judges of lower courts may adopt additional rules governing their procedures if those rules do not conflict with the rules promulgated by the Supreme Court.[313] Each of the ten judicial districts has adopted special district court rules.

Each set of rules is adopted and numbered separately by its judicial promulgating body. Thus, there is no consistent numbering system throughout the rules. Most of the major sets of rules have indexes following the text.

---

309. A copy of the Supreme Court order dated December 19, 1974 governing adoption of rules is published at 9 MINN. STAT. at xvi (1984).
310. MINN. STAT. § 480.052 (1998).
311. *Id.* § 480.054.
312. SUP. CT. R., Notice of Promulgation Filing and Record (Dec. 19, 1974).
313. *See, e.g.,* MINN. STAT. § 480A.11 (1998) (Court of Appeals), MINN. STAT. § 487.23(2) (1998) (county courts).

### § 442. Professional Rules for Attorneys and Judges

The *Minnesota Civil Trialbook*[314] is a declaration of practical policies and procedures to be followed in the civil trials in all the trial courts of Minnesota. Its purpose is the standardization of practices and procedures throughout the state.

Professional rules usually are promulgated by the Supreme Court. The topics and areas they address include professional conduct and responsibility, Lawyer's Professional Responsibility Board opinions, admission to the bar, student practice, attorney registration, continuing legal education, the Lawyer's Trust Account Board, the State Board of Legal Certification (internal rules), the Client Security Board, the Board of Judicial Standards, and the Code of Judicial Conduct. Also included are character and fitness standards, the Plan for the Minnesota State Board of Legal Certification, the Code of Professional Responsibility for Interpreters in the Minnesota State Court System, and grounds for judicial recall.

### § 443. Sources of Court Rules

Following are the major sources providing copies of the rules of Minnesota courts.

- *Minnesota Statutes,* court rules volume. Until 1992, the preface to this volume included an excellent introduction to court rulemaking and practical research strategy.
- *Minnesota Statutes Annotated,* volumes 48–52. Annotations include advisory committee and editorial notes, law review citations, and digests of decisions. Set also includes Minnesota federal court rules.
- *Minnesota Rules of Court.* Desk Copy. Annual pamphlet published by West. The 2000 edition is published in two volumes with one for state court rules and the other for federal court rules in Minnesota.
- *Minnesota Practice Series* (West Group). Volumes 1, 1A, 2, and 2A comprise *Civil Rules, Annotated,* David F. Herr & Roger S. Haydock. Volume 3 is *Appellate Rules, Annotated,* Eric J. Magnuson & David F. Herr. Volume 3A contains *General Rules of Practice, Annotated,* David F. Herr.

---

314. MINN. STAT., General Rules of Practice for the District Courts, tit. II, pt. H (adopted Sept. 5, 1991, eff. Jan. 1, 1992).

# Chapter Four. Judiciary

The following selected sources provide rules of Minnesota federal courts.

- *United States Code; United States Code Annotated; United States Code Service*
- *United States Supreme Court Digest, Lawyer's Edition,* vols. 17–19
- *United States Supreme Court Digest,* West, vols. 16 & 17
- *Federal Local Court Rules,* Callaghan and Co., provides the practice rules promulgated by each individual federal circuit and district court
- *Federal Procedure Rules Service,* Lawyers Co-operative, publishes the general federal rules in one volume and local federal circuit and district court rules in separate volumes divided by circuit
- *Minnesota Rules of Court; Federal* (West Group 2000– ) publishes rules for federal courts in Minnesota

Practice manuals also often reprint and discuss court rules (*see* § 546, *infra*).

## § 444. Jury Instruction Guides

Before deliberation by the jury, the judge gives instructions to define the issues, explain burden of proof, and provide guidelines for finding facts on disputed evidence, and generally instructs the jury on the law to be applied to the facts.

Minnesota is one of many states using "pattern" jury instructions, i.e., standard or uniform instructions to be used in typical cases. Pattern jury instructions are prepared by panels of trial judges and other representatives of the bar. In Minnesota, they are prepared by the Minnesota District Judges Association and its advisory committees.[315]

Jury instruction guides are published privately and indexed by West in its *Minnesota Practice* series. Volumes 4 and 4A contain *Minnesota Jury Instruction Guides: Civil,* 4th ed. (West Group 1999), and volumes 10 and 10A contain *Minnesota Jury Instruction Guides: Criminal,* 4th ed. (West Group 1999). Both titles are accompanied by computer diskettes that include the jury instruction guides (JIGs).

It is stressed that the published instructions are intended to be a guide and may be changed for a particular trial. Thus, many judges

---

315. Minnesota District Judges Association, 73 Spruce St., Mahtomedi, MN 55115; phone 651-426-1746

and attorneys utilize additional sources in search of an effective jury instruction. These sources include previous instructions found in court records or briefs, JIGS from other states, federal jury instructions,[316] statutes or regulations, and other secondary sources.

### § 445. Minnesota Sentencing Guidelines[317]

To reduce disparity in sentencing practices, Minnesota introduced a system of determinate sentencing. In 1978, the Minnesota Sentencing Guidelines Commission[318] was established to promulgate advisory guidelines for the district courts. The commission consists of eleven members drawn from the courts, public defender offices, county attorney offices, the corrections department, police departments, and the public.

The commission monitors, modifies, and evaluates the effectiveness of the guidelines at least annually. The commission also conducts research and recommends to the legislature improvements in sentencing and other criminal procedures.

Deviations from the guidelines must be accompanied by written reasons. Appeals may be taken to the Court of Appeals. Persons convicted and sentenced prior to May 1, 1980 may file a petition for re-sentencing.[319] The sentencing guidelines may be found in most of the Minnesota sources listed under § 443, *supra* (*see also* § 263.3, *supra*).

## § 450. ALTERNATIVE DISPUTE RESOLUTION[320]

The Division of Conciliation, established in 1939[321] under the Minnesota Labor Relations Act, was created to facilitate a stable working relationship between employers and employees. In 1969, the division

---

316. *See, e.g.,* EDWARD J. DEVITT ET AL., FEDERAL JURY PRACTICE AND INSTRUCTIONS (5th ed. 2000). Edward J. Devitt is a Senior Judge for the U.S. District Court in St. Paul.
317. *See* MINN. STAT. §§ 244.01–244.24 (1998).
318. University National Bank Building, 200 University Ave. West, Suite 205, St. Paul, MN 55103; phone 651-296-0144.
319. MINN. STAT. § 590.01, subd. 3 (1998).
320. *See,* Wolf & Weissman, *Alternative Dispute Resolution,* 42 BENCH & B. MINN., July 1985, at 23.
321. MINN. STAT. §§ 179.02–.05 (1998). 1380 Energy Lane, Suite Two, St. Paul, MN 55108-5253; phone 651-649-5421.

## Chapter Four. Judiciary

was renamed the Bureau of Mediation Services (BMS).[322] The bureau certifies representative bargaining units, maintains a list of arbitrators, and employs staff to serve as mediators. Since July of 1983, the bureau has published *Arbitration Award Summaries* on a monthly basis. The BMS administers programs in mediation, representation, arbitrator referral, labor-management cooperation, labor relations training, and the Office of Dispute Resolution.[323]

Minnesota has been a leader in establishing non-judicial methods of resolving problems. Another good example is the Minnesota News Council,[324] organized in 1971, which provides a public forum for complaints against the news media.[325] In 1984, the legislature passed several acts sanctioning and reinforcing those methods providing effective alternative means to the traditional civil case processing in the courts.

The Minnesota Civil Mediation Act[326] allows third parties to mediate civil disputes under contract principles. Minn. Stat. § 484.73 (1998) allows a majority of the judges in a judicial district to establish a system of mandatory, non-binding arbitration of civil matters and to promulgate rules subject to Supreme Court approval.

The state court administrator administers the community dispute resolution program according to guidelines developed by the state court administrator to provide community groups with a comprehensive policy manual covering everything from facilitator training to session mechanics. The guidelines ensure that participation in dispute resolution is voluntary and that the program meets the specific criteria to receive certification for court referrals. A listing of alternative dispute resolution programs can be found in the *Bench & Bar of Minnesota* directory issue (*see* § 536.3, *infra*).

---

322. For information about the Bureau of Mediation Services, see <http://www.bms.state.mn.us/about.html> (last visited May 30, 2001).
323. 340 Centennial Building, 658 Cedar St., St. Paul, MN 55155; phone 651-296-2633, fax: 651-282-6396.
324. *Minnesota News Council*, at <http://www.mtn.org/~newscncl/> (last visited May 30, 2001) . Offices are at: 12 S. Sixth St., Suite 1122, Minneapolis, MN 55402; phone 612-341-9357, fax 612-341-9358.
325. *See* Cullen & Betzold, *Between the Media and the Bar*, 42 BENCH & B. MINN., Feb. 1985, at 11, 13.
326. MINN. STAT. §§ 572.31–572.40 (1998).

## § 460. JUDICIAL BOARDS AND ORGANIZATIONS

§ 461. Conferences
§ 462. Professional Boards
§ 463. Continuing Education

A number of boards and organizations have been created to consider and oversee the business of the judiciary and to improve the judicial system and administration of justice.

### § 461. Conferences

Various groups of judges and support personnel meet periodically to discuss matters of mutual concern. For example, the Conference of Judges meets annually to consider matters relating to judicial business, the improvement of the judicial system, and the administration of justice. The conference consists of all the judges of courts of record in Minnesota.[327]

### § 462. Professional Boards

§ 462.1. Board on Judicial Standards
§ 462.2. State Board of Law Examiners
§ 462.3. Lawyers Professional Responsibility Board
§ 462.4. State Board of Legal Certification
§ 462.5. Client Security Board

#### § 462.1. Board on Judicial Standards[328]

This board, established in 1971, serves as the disciplinary body for state judges. The board investigates complaints against judges and determines if a judge has violated the Code of Judicial Conduct. The board may recommend to the Supreme Court that it suspend or remove any judge, judicial officer, or referee convicted of a felony or of any crime involving moral turpitude. It also may recommend the

---

327. MINN. STAT. § 480.18 (1998).
328. *See* MINN. STAT. §§ 490.15–490.18 (1998); Minnesota Code of Judicial Conduct. 2025 Centre Pointe Blvd., Suite 420, Mendota Heights, MN 55120; phone 651-296-3999, fax 651-688-1865; Web address <http://northstar.state.mn.us/ebranch/judstnds/> (last visited May 30, 2001).

# Chapter Four. Judiciary

retirement of a judge who is disabled or unable to perform his or her duties effectively.

The board consists of one judge of the Court of Appeals, three trial court judges, two lawyers who have practiced law in the state for ten years, and four citizens who are not judges, retired judges, or lawyers. Members are appointed by the governor with the advice and consent of the Senate. Terms are for four years, and no one may serve more than two terms.

## § 462.2. State Board of Law Examiners[329]

Twice a year, the board examines applicants for admission to the practice of law in Minnesota. The qualifications with which applicants must comply are promulgated by the Supreme Court. The board also maintains a record of persons admitted to the practice of law. *From Diploma to License: A Guide to Minnesota Bar Admission for Law Graduates Published by the Minnesota Board of Law Examiners* is published by the board.[330]

The board is appointed by the Supreme Court and consists of two public members and seven attorneys at law, who serve for three-year terms and until their successor qualifies.

## § 462.3. Lawyers Professional Responsibility Board[331]

The board issues opinions on questions of professional conduct,[332] considers complaints of professional misconduct, administers private warnings, and in more serious matters, petitions the Supreme Court for disciplinary proceedings against attorneys. Private warnings issued by the board are not published and are not open for public inspection. Opinions of the Supreme Court with respect to disciplinary actions are

---

329. *See* MINN. STAT. § 481.01; Rules for Admission to the Bar. 25 Constitution Ave., Suite 110, St. Paul, MN 55155-6102; phone 651-297-1800, fax 651-296-5866; Web address <http://www.ble.state.mn.us/>.
330. *Available at* <http://www.ble.state.mn.us/from_diploma_to_license.htm> (last visited May 30, 2001).
331. Lawyers Prof. Resp. R. 4. The board first was established in 1971 as the State Board of Professional Responsibility. 25 Constitution Ave., Suite 105, St. Paul, MN 55155-1500; phone 651-296-3952, toll-free 1-800-657-3601, fax 651-297-5801; Web address <http://www.courts.state.mn.us/lprb/>.
332. *See Opinions of the Lawyers Professional Responsibility Board: Index*, at <http://www.courts.state.mn.us/lprb/opinions.html> (last visited May 30, 2001).

matters of public record and are published as described in § 420, *supra*. A list of disbarred and currently suspended lawyers is published by the board.[333]

The board consists of a chairman and twenty-three members, of whom fourteen are lawyers and nine are non-lawyers. Terms are for three years with a maximum of two terms. A director is appointed by the Supreme Court and serves at its pleasure.

### § 462.4. State Board of Legal Certification[334]

The Board of Legal Certification regulates the certification of lawyers as specialists by certifying agencies, so that public access to appropriate legal services may be enhanced. The board defines certain areas of legal practice that are subject to specialty designation; approves appropriate agencies as qualified to certify lawyers as specialists in a particular field of law; adopts standards that must be met by certifying agencies in certifying lawyers as specialists; reviews and evaluates the programs of certifying agencies to assure compliance with this specialization program; denies, suspends, or revokes the approval of a certifying agency upon the board's determination that the agency has failed to comply with the standards established by the rules of the board; keeps appropriate records of lawyers certified as specialists by agencies approved under the rules; and reports to the Lawyers Professional Responsibility board any lawyers who have violated the provisions of the rules. The board is made up of twelve members, nine lawyers licensed in the State of Minnesota and three public members, who are appointed by the Supreme Court. Three of the lawyer members are nominated by the Minnesota State Bar Association. Lawyer members are representatives of the various fields of legal practice, including general practice.

---

333. *See Minnesota Disbarred and Currently Suspended Lawyers*, at <http://www.courts.state.mn.us/lprb/dbintro.html> (last visited May 30, 2001).
334. Supreme Court of Minnesota, Board of Legal Certification, 25 Constitution Ave., Suite 110, St. Paul, MN 55155-6102; phone 651-297-1857, fax 651-296-5866; Web address <http://www.courts.state.mn.us/blcert/index.html>.

## § 462.5. Client Security Board[335]

The Minnesota Client Security Board compensates victims of lawyer theft. It consists of five attorneys and two non-attorneys appointed by the Supreme Court. The board meets approximately every other month to consider claims, does not charge claimants to file a claim, and has a maximum payment of $100,000 per claim, but no limit per attorney. This board uses the administrative services of the Office of Lawyers Professional Responsibility to receive, investigate, and handle claims filed with the Client Security Fund. The director is appointed by the Supreme Court and serves at its pleasure. Upon request, the board will send out a claim form that must be used in filing a claim.

## § 463. Continuing Education

§ 463.1. Board of Continuing Legal Education
§ 463.2. Continuing Education for State Court Personnel

### § 463.1. Board of Continuing Legal Education[336]

Licensed attorneys in Minnesota are required to continue their legal education throughout their careers. The mandatory continuing legal education requirement was established by the Minnesota Supreme Court which has the power to regulate the practice of law in Minnesota. The regulations are contained in the *Rules of the Minnesota Supreme Court* and *Rules of the Minnesota Board for Continuing Legal Education of Members of the Bar*. The rules establish a State Board of Continuing Legal Education to administer the mandatory CLE system. The board consists of twelve volunteer members appointed by the court, plus a chair. The board employs a permanent salaried staff to handle day-to-day administration. The staff consists of an executive director and executive assistant (whose time is shared with other Supreme Court duties), and two staff members who handle CLE matters full time.

---

335. Minnesota Client Security Board, 25 Constitution Ave., Suite 105, St. Paul, MN 55155-1500; phone 651-296-3952, toll-free 1-800-657-3601, fax 651-297-5801; Web address <http://www.courts.state.mn.us/csb/csb.html>.
336. 25 Constitution Ave., Suite 110, St. Paul, MN 55155; phone 651-297-7100, fax 651-296-5866; Web address <http://mbcle.state.mn.us/>.

Created in 1975, the board consists of twelve members and a chairperson. Three members of the board are non-lawyers, one is a district judge, and the others are attorneys. All serve terms of three years (not to exceed two terms) except for the chair, who serves at the pleasure of the Supreme Court.

The board has general supervisory authority over the administration of the Supreme Court's rules on continuing legal education.[337] The rules require attorneys to complete forty-five hours of approved course work over a three-year period. The board accredits courses and programs that satisfy the educational requirements of the rules,[338] and it reports instances of non-compliance to the Supreme Court.

### § 463.2. Continuing Education for State Court Personnel[339]

Established in 1973, this office administers the Minnesota Supreme Court's mandatory judicial education requirement and the court support personnel education requirement. Orientation and training programs are conducted for judges, court administrators, clerks of court, court reporters, and other personnel.

---

337. *See Rules of the Minnesota Board of Continuing Legal Education*, at <http://mbcle.state.mn.us/clerules_7_0.htm> (last visited May 30, 2001).
338. A list of approved courses is available from the board's office. This list is published periodically in *Bench & Bar of Minnesota. See, e.g., CLE Approved Courses*, 40 BENCH & B. MINN., July 1983, at 25. Publications distributed with courses organized for the continuing legal education of the Minnesota bar are available in many law libraries.
339. 140 Minnesota Judicial Center, St. Paul, MN 55155; phone 651-297-7590.

# CHAPTER FIVE
# Finding Aids and Secondary Sources

## Chapter Contents

§ 510. Digests
§ 520. Shepard's Citators
§ 530. Quick-Reference Tools
§ 540. Secondary Sources
§ 550. Legal Periodicals
§ 560. Materials in Special Formats

This chapter discusses various finding aids and secondary sources for legal research. Many of those listed are specific to Minnesota law. The reader is referred to Appendix H for a selected list of legal research texts that provide information on general reference tools.

"Secondary source of law" refers to materials that have persuasive rather than mandatory effect. Secondary sources of law such as restatements, treatises, and periodical articles generally attempt to explain or summarize the law or influence its development. They aid researchers in finding primary authorities.

Another category of legal materials can be designated as "finding aids." These materials exist as locators or indexes to primary or secondary sources. They also may aid in determining whether particular legal authority still is valid.

## § 510. DIGESTS

§ 511. Dunnell Minnesota Digest
§ 512. Minnesota Digest
§ 513. West's Minnesota Digest 2d Law Finder
§ 514. North Western Digest[340]
§ 515. Martindale-Hubbell Law Digest

Digests are indexes to case law. They provide "subject access" to cases as well as tables listing cases by name. They provide access to cases that discuss the point of law that interests the researcher. Digests give concise summaries of points of law decided in cases. These summaries, also referred to as "digests," are arranged by subject matter under a classification scheme.

A number of case digests have been published for Minnesota in the past century. Many are not current and are out of print. Minnesota cases are digested in state digests and West's decennial, federal, and regional digests. Two current Minnesota state digests include all cases decided by Minnesota appellate courts and all published Minnesota cases decided by federal courts.

### § 511. Dunnell Minnesota Digest: Fourth Edition: An Encyclopedia of Minnesota Law[341]

This digest is similar in style to a legal encyclopedia and might be called an encyclopedic digest (*see* § 542, *infra*). The set is divided into numerous legal topics arranged alphabetically with some cross references. Minnesota law on each topic is summarized in textual format and footnoted with case or statutory authority. The set is supplemented by annual pocket parts and semiannual pamphlets. Volumes are split and revised as needed. There is a comprehensive index that directs the user to the proper digest topic. The table of cases and defendant-plaintiff table of cases also have digest topics with each citation.

---

340. Although most dictionaries spell "northwestern" as a single word, the publisher, West Group, has spelled it both ways, sometimes as two words and sometimes a single word.
341. Charlottesville, VA: Lexis Law Publishing 1989– .

Chapter Five. Finding Aids and Secondary Sources                125

## § 512. West's Minnesota Digest 2d[342]

The second edition replaces the original *Minnesota Digest*. It covers all cases, both federal and state, since 1851. Similar to other West publications, this digest is divided into more than 400 legal topics alphabetically arranged with each topic further divided or classified into fixed subtopics designated by "Key Numbers." A "Key Number" is assigned by West editors to each point of law discussed in reported cases. Each point is summarized and the summary is printed under its appropriate Key Number in the relevant digest(s).

The set is comprised of several components, a Table of Cases and a Defendant-Plaintiff Table of Cases. The tables of cases also have digest topics with each citation. Words and Phrases refers to words and phrases that Minnesota courts have interpreted or defined. A Descriptive Word Index provides access to the digest topics and its many Key Numbers. The index contains entries on five elements: parties, places and things, basis of action or issue, defenses, and relief sought.

The set is updated by annual pocket parts and a semiannual cumulative supplementary pamphlet. It can be further supplemented by using the Key Number digests in each volume and advance sheet of West reporters or the online service, Westlaw.

To update the digest for the most recent cases, one needs to check the supplementary pamphlet for the last *North Western Reporter* volume digested. Then proceed to the digest portion of the subsequently published *North Western Reporter* volume and *North Western Reporter* advance sheets.

## § 513. West's Minnesota Digest 2d Law Finder[343]

Not a digest but a finding aid based on the digest, this is an attempt to bring together topical references found in *Minnesota Statutes Annotated, Minnesota Digest,* Minnesota practice series, *United States Code Annotated, Corpus Juris Secundum,* federal publications, key number publications, texts, and treatises.

---

342. St. Paul, MN: West Group, Inc. 1988– . West Publishing Company, now West Group, Inc., was acquired by the Thomson Legal Publishing Co. in 1996.
343. St. Paul, MN: West Group, Inc. 1988– , 1 v. (annual).

### § 514. West's North Western Digest 2d[344]

In addition to the titles listed in sections 511 and 512 above, Minnesota appellate cases are digested in the *North Western Digest* and *North Western Digest 2d* that also include the other jurisdictions covered by *North Western Reporter* series.[345] The organization and features are substantially the same as in *Minnesota Digest*. *North Western Digest* includes cases through 1932. *North Western Digest 2d* begins with cases decided in 1933 and continues to date. It is updated by annual pocket parts and semiannual non-cumulative supplemental pamphlets. The Descriptive Word Index and Table of Cases[346] volumes for both time periods are included in *North Western Digest 2d*.

To update the *Digest* for the most recent cases, researchers must check the supplementary pamphlet for the last *North Western Reporter* volume digested, and then proceed to the digest portion of the subsequently published *North Western Reporter* volume and *North Western Reporter* advance sheets.

### § 515. Martindale-Hubbell Law Digest[347]

Strictly speaking, the *Law Digest* segment of *Martindale-Hubbell* is not a case-finding aid such as *North Western Digest* or *Minnesota Digest*. Instead it provides summaries of the statutory law of each U.S. state, Canadian province, and more than seventy-five countries. The summaries are written by practitioners and scholars from each jurisdiction. Each jurisdictional summary covers more than 170 legal topics. Additionally the *Law Digest* is available in the *Martindale-Hubbell* library

---

344. St. Paul, MN: West Group, Inc. 1970– .
345. The other jurisdictions are Iowa, Michigan, Nebraska, North Dakota, South Dakota, and Wisconsin.
346. When West published *North Western Digest 2d* (bound in red), it did not recompile the Table of Cases volumes. It did republish them in the red bindings for aesthetic purposes. Therefore, the two Table of Cases volumes (A–L; M–Z) may be bound in blue (labeled *North Western Digest)* or red (labeled *North Western Digest 2d*). There also is an eight-volume bound cumulative supplement Table of Cases labeled *North Western Digest 2d*. Therefore, to locate a decision by name, two sources must be checked. In chronological order these are the two Table of Cases volumes (either bound in red or blue), the red-bound cumulative supplements, and pocket parts and supplements.
347. Summit Hill, NJ: Martindale-Hubbell, Inc. (annual).

## Chapter Five. Finding Aids and Secondary Sources 127

though LEXIS-NEXIS and on the World Wide Web at <http://www.martindale.com>.

## § 520. CITATORS IN GENERAL

§ 521. Shepard's Citations in General
§ 522. Shepard's Minnesota Citations
§ 523. Shepard's Northwestern Citations
§ 524. Shepard's Minnesota and Northwestern Citators Compared
§ 525. West's KeyCite®
§ 526. Shepard's Online

Citators link primary materials together. Citators link a specific statute to cases that have discussed it as well as give a brief legislative history of its origin, amendments, and repeals. Citators also link a specific case to subsequent cases that have in some form or in some way mentioned the cited case. Citators not only link subsequent cases but also ordinances, court rules, and constitutional provisions to subsequent legal activity.

### § 521. Shepard's Citations in General

*Shepard's Citations* provide the history of a case (whether it has been affirmed, dismissed, modified, or reversed on appeal) and its treatment by other courts (whether later cases have criticized, distinguished, explained, followed, questioned, or overruled it). Parallel citations to official reports and unofficial reporters are given.

Statute citators provide information on the status of statutes, on session laws that are not included in the statutes, and on provisions of constitutions. They also provide information on whether a law or constitutional provision has been cited or interpreted by a court, and whether it has been upheld, voided, or changed in some other manner.

Citations of other authorities discussing the cases or statutes also are included. To make the best use of the citators, it is advisable to read the introductory explanations that are printed in each volume because the coverage varies from title to title. Additionally, Shepard's has its own unique way of abbreviating sources for the most compressed form of citation. Always check the prefatory pages for information about abbreviations and their meanings.[348]

Access is entirely by citation. It is essential to begin the search with the citator covering the first appearance of the case or statute and then to follow it through all later supplements. The researcher should find the latest supplement and carefully note the complete list of volumes and supplements in each unit on the cover of the latest supplement. This is listed under "What Your Library Should Contain."

An online tutorial on "how to Shepardize" is available at <http://helpcite.shepards.com/howtoshep/howframe.htm>.

### § 522. Shepard's Minnesota Citations[349]

*Shepard's Minnesota Citations* includes Minnesota cases reported in *Gilfillan Reports; Minnesota Reports; Opinions of the Attorney General of Minnesota, 1902–1960; North Western Reporter* series; Constitutions; codes; statutes; session laws; rules of evidence; court rules; jury instructions; acts and ordinances; in the various federal reports as well as to major law school periodicals that have cited the case; the *Minnesota Law Review*; and the *William Mitchell Law Review*. It also includes citations in *American Law Reports* series. It does not list cases from reports of other states.

*Shepard's Minnesota Citations* also has a case name index that lists alphabetically all cases with their official citation and unofficial citation as well as indication of court and year of decision. Both plaintiffs and defendants are listed.

---

348. A printed pamphlet entitled *How to Shepardize, Your Guide to Legal Research Using Shepard's Citations in Print, CD-ROM and On-Line* is available at no cost. Call Shepard's Customer Service at 800-899-6000 or visit their website <http://www.shepards.com>. Shepard's/McGraw-Hill. P.O. Box 1235, Colorado Springs, CO 80901-1235.

349. 1995 ed., Colorado Springs: Shepards/McGraw-Hill, 3 v. plus supplementation.

## § 523. Shepard's North Western Reporter Citations: A Compilation of Citations to All Cases Reported in the North Western Reporter[350]

"A compilation of citations to all cases reported in the *Northwestern Reporter.*" The citations, that include affirmances, reversals, and the dismissals by the highest state courts and by the U.S. Supreme Court, appear in West's regional reports, West's specialty reports, such as *Federal Rules Decisions, Federal Claims Reporter, Bankruptcy Reporter,* and *Military Justice Reporter,* as well as *U.S. Supreme Court Reports, Lawyers' Edition, West Supreme Court Reporter,* and the *U.S. Reports* as well as the *American Bar Association Journal* and in the annotations of *U.S. Supreme Court Reports, Lawyers' Edition* and the *American Law Reports.*[351]

## § 524. Shepard's Minnesota Citations and North Western Reporter Citations Compared

Material contained in *Shepard's North Western Reporter Citations* does not completely overlap the material contained in *Shepard's Minnesota Citations.* To some extent, these citators complement each other.

*Shepard's North Western Reporter Citations* includes citing cases from the complete West National Reporter System, Lawyers Cooperative *American Law Reports* series, *American Law Reports Federal,* and *United States Supreme Court Reports, Lawyers' edition* series, but does not list attorney general opinions or law review articles citing the cases.

Individual state Shepard's volumes include local citing references, such as federal courts within the jurisdiction, the state attorney general, and law reviews within the jurisdiction, while the regional Shepard's provide citations to all published decisions that have cited the case.

## § 525. West's KeyCite®

KeyCite is a comprehensive online citation service provided by Westlaw. It is accessible by citation only. KeyCite provides case validation and subsequent citations to the case are listed as well as case

---

350. 5th ed., Colorado Springs, CO: Shepard's/McGraw-Hill 1993. 2 v. in 10.
351. Description from title page.

history, if available. KeyCite is available as a service on Westlaw and as a "stand-alone" service available through Web access.

### § 526. Shepard's Online

*Shepard's North Western Reporter Citations* as well as *Shepard's Minnesota Citations* are available on CD-ROM as well as direct online access through the World Wide Web. LEXIS-NEXIS provides *Shepard's Citations* as part of its subscription.

## § 530. QUICK-REFERENCE TOOLS

- § 531. Citation of Legal Authority
- § 532. Tables of Cases
- § 533. Popular Name Tables
- § 534. Parallel Citations
- § 535. Words and Phrases
- § 536. Directories
- § 537. Historical Works

Quick-reference tools are those materials that provide easily found information in a format that is easy to use. Information usually is organized in alphabetical or numerical order and is brief in nature.

### § 531. Citation of Legal Authority

The most commonly used citation forms are listed in *The Bluebook: A Uniform System of Citation*.[352] This is a joint effort by the law review editors of the *Columbia Law Review,* the *Harvard Law Review,* the *University of Pennsylvania Law Review,* and the *Yale Law Journal.* The *Bluebook* generally is followed in law review writing.

*Citation Manual,* Minnesota Supreme Court (St. Paul, MN: Minnesota Supreme Court 1979).
> The *Citation Manual* concerns only case citation. Often, suggested citation forms are included in the first few pages of a particular source. Also, some texts use their own method of citing that generally is explained in the prefatory pages. The courts of Minnesota have not officially

---

352. 17th ed., Cambridge, MA: Harvard Law Review Ass'n 2000.

## Chapter Five. Finding Aids and Secondary Sources 131

sanctioned any particular citation style or manual. Most practicing attorneys follow the *Bluebook* rules.

*Minnesota Revisor's Manual with Styles and Forms* (St. Paul, MN: Office of the Revisor of Statutes 1997 ed.) <http://www.revisor.leg.state.mn.us/bill_drafting_manual/Cover-TOC.htm>.
This manual is used by the revisor's office, and is a result of a legislative mandate.[353] The manual has several purposes:

> The manual serves several functions. First, it is used by the revisor's office as a text to teach new drafters general methods of drafting legislative bills and the specialties of drafting for the Minnesota legislature. Second, the manual is a ready reference for those who are familiar with Minnesota bill drafting. A wide variety of cases, laws, rules, and principles available in other publications have been collected here. Third, the manual serves as a guide to drafting as a part of the legislative process.[354]

Universal case citation is a recent development in the citation of legal authorities. The American Association of Law Libraries has advocated a "vendor-neutral" style of case citation and has developed a manual.[355] While neighboring states have adopted this idea, Minnesota has not.[356]

*ALWD Citation Manual: A Professional System of Citation*, Association of Legal Writing Directors & Darby Dickerson (Gaithersburg, MD: Aspen Law and Business 2000) <http://www.alwd.org>. Includes index.
The Association of Legal Writing Directors[357] has created a citation manual because the legal community "need[s] a citation manual that is easy to use, easy to teach from and easy to learn from."[358] Time will tell if this manual will supplant *The Bluebook*.

---

353. MINN. STAT. § 3C.03, subd. 4.
354. MINNESOTA REVISOR'S MANUAL WITH STYLES AND FORMS § 1.2 (Functions of Manual).
355. COMMITTEE ON CITATION FORMATS, AMERICAN ASSOCIATION OF LAW LIBRARIES, AALL UNIVERSAL CITATION GUIDE (Madison: State Bar of Wisconsin 1999). Includes bibliographical references.
356. States that have adopted or allow uniform citation are: Arizona, Colorado, Louisiana, Maine, Mississippi, Montana, New Mexico, North Dakota, Oklahoma, South Dakota, and Wisconsin.
357. Information available at <http://www.alwd.org> (last visited June 1, 2001).
358. ALWD CITATION MANUAL: A PROFESSIONAL SYSTEM OF CITATION at xxiii (2000).

*(The) University of Chicago Manual of Legal Citation,* University of Chicago Law Review and the University of Chicago Legal Forum (Rochester, NY: Lawyers Co-operative Pub. Co.; San Francisco: Bancroft-Whitney Co.; Dayton, Ohio: Mead Data Central, Inc. 1989). 63 p. Includes index. Although this work has not gained the wide-spread use or recognition of *The Bluebook,* it is an alternative. Its most remarkable characteristic is its encouragement of using common sense in legal citation.

### § 532. Tables of Cases

There are several resources that a researcher can use to find a case name and its accompanying citation. *West's Minnesota Digest 2d* has a table of cases and a Defendant-Plaintiff Table. *Dunnell Minnesota Digest* has a table of cases and a reverse table of cases.[359] *Shepard's Minnesota Citations* also has a table of cases. *West's North Western Digest 2d* has a table of cases, but no reverse table. Although most treatises also include tables of cases cited, this method of finding a case citation is haphazard.

Case citations also can be found by using online services such as Westlaw[360] and LEXIS-NEXIS. One can specifically search by field or segment. On Westlaw that is the "title" field and on LEXIS-NEXIS it is the "name" segment.

### § 533. Popular Name Tables

Popular name tables generally refer to legislative acts or laws that have become known by a catch word (e.g., the "Volstead Act"[361]). Popular names, however, also can refer to a case that has entered popular usage by that name, for example the "Lindbergh[362] Kidnaping Case."

---

359. Reverse tables of cases are tables arranged by the name of the defendant.
360. Citations also may be obtained by calling West, Searchers Department, 651-228-2668. West requests that persons with more than five citations inquire by letter specifying any deadline they may have.
361. The Volstead Act gets its name from Minnesota Representative Andrew John Volstead (1860–1947) who authored the bill that brought about prohibition in the United States.
362. What became known as the Lindbergh Law is a result of the kidnaping and murder of Charles A. Lindbergh Jr. in 1932. Five years earlier, in 1927, Lindbergh Sr. had made the first solo flight across the Atlantic Ocean. He had spent his youth in Little Falls, Minnesota.

**Chapter Five. Finding Aids and Secondary Sources** 133

*Shepard's Acts and Cases by Popular Names—Federal and State,* 5th ed. (Colorado Springs: Shepard's/McGraw-Hill 1999) 3 v.
This work cumulates popular names for all states as well as federal acts. Its separate case section is the only systematic access to cases by popular name.

At times, a law or case will become known by a descriptive, unofficial, or "popular" name. Laws can be located in the *Minnesota Statutes* index under the heading "Popular Names, Acts by." *Minnesota Statutes Annotated* also cites them under a special "Popular Name Table" at the end of the index. *Shepard's Minnesota Citations* has a table of Minnesota Acts by Popular Names or Short Titles with references to statutory cites.

Popular names for federal legislative materials also may be found in the *United States Code* in volume 50 and its supplement; *United States Code Annotated* in the last volume of the index; and *United States Code Service* in the supplemental volume at the end of the set.

## § 534. Parallel Citations

Parallel citations are citations to the same case in different sources. The standard tool for locating parallel cites is the appropriate Shepard's volume.

*Shepard's Minnesota Citations* uses parallel citation from *Minnesota Reports* to *North Western Reporter* and vice versa. *Shepard's Northwestern Citations* cites the appropriate state reports.

The *National Reporter Blue Book* published by West Group is a multi-volume set of tables that convert the official volume and page of a state reporter to its corresponding National Reporter System citation. Although Minnesota discontinued publishing its official court reports in 1977, the *National Reporter Blue Book* is useful in finding cases when the only reference is to the *Minnesota Reports* citation and the only available reporter is the *North Western Reporter.* Because of its late publication schedule, *Minnesota Reports,* from v. 247 (1956) to v. 312 (1977), included parallel citations to *North Western Reporter* series.

The *Minnesota Blue and White Book*[363] was published by West from 1944 to 1977. This tool gives cross-reference citations from *Minnesota*

---

363. St. Paul, MN: West Publishing 1944, 1v. (various pagings).

*Reports* to the *North Western Reporter* series in the blue section, and from the *North Western Reporter* series to *Minnesota Reports* in the white section. It was updated by printed strips that were glued to blank pages. The book was sold as part of the reporter or digest subscription and now is out of print.

Tables of cases that accompany West's digests and Dunnell Minnesota Digest list both official and unofficial citations.

## § 535. Words and Phrases

The first choice for finding legal definitions is a law dictionary.[364] Many of the definitions listed refer to authoritative text such as treatises, cases, or statutes.

Several sources provide judicial interpretations of words and phrases, or citations to such interpretations. *West's Minnesota Digest 2d* includes a "Words and Phrases" volume. It provides an alphabetical list of words, with citations to cases that have definitions in them. The semiannual supplements to the digest also provides a table of words and phrases.

*Minnesota Reporter, North Western Reporter* series, *Federal Reporter* series, and *Federal Supplement* series provide "words and phrases" sections in the front of each volume that cite the interpretations provided by the cases therein. *Minnesota Reports* had no such section.

*Words and Phrases*, published by West Group, is the national compilation of state and federal "judicially interpreted" words and phrases. The set covers cases from 1658 to date and consists of ninety volumes supplemented annually by pocket parts or other cumulative pamphlets.

Statutory definitions can be located by looking under the heading "Words and Phrases" in the index to *Minnesota Statutes Annotated*. In 1982, *Minnesota Statutes* added the heading "Definitions" to the index to list words and phrases defined by the statutes. This listing includes only definitions found in newly enacted laws since 1981 and re-indexed sections.

---

364. There are many law dictionaries by various publishers. Probably the most well-known is *Black's Law Dictionary* (Bryan A. Garner ed., St. Paul, MN: West Group, 7th ed. 1999).

## Chapter Five. Finding Aids and Secondary Sources

### § 536. Directories

§ 536.1. General Sources
§ 536.2. Judiciary
§ 536.3. Lawyers
§ 536.4. Government Personnel

### § 536.1. General Sources

Finding names, addresses, and phone numbers of lawyers, judges, and government officials is relatively easy. General reference sources such as telephone books, city directories, government directories, directory issues of various publications, and rosters of professional associations may contain the information sought.

Finding biographical information may be somewhat more difficult because, in an effort to maintain their privacy, many government officials and judges release little information.

*Minnesota Biographical Dictionary* (2d ed. St. Clair Shores, MI: Somerset Publishers 2000) xv, 385 p.
Lists people of all times and all places who have been important to the history and life of the state. Helpful for those needing specific biographical information of people related to Minnesota.

*Who's Who in American Law* (New Providence, NJ: Marquis Who's Who, Inc., millennium ed. 2000–2001) 1 v.
*Who's Who* may be helpful in finding biographical information about the Minnesota legal community. The Field of Practice Index and Professional Index is arranged geographically.

Biographical information about faculty members of Minnesota law schools can be found in the *AALS Directory of Law Teachers*.[365] Although the main body is alphabetically arranged biographies, at the beginning of this work there is a list containing each member law school and the names of its faculty and some staff.

Pamphlets and other publications with directory information often are available from courts, state agencies, and professional associations.

---

365. Prepared by the Association of American Law Schools (St. Paul, MN: West Pub. Co.; Westbury, NY: Foundation Press 1988– ) 1 v. annual.

## § 536.2. Judiciary[366]

*Almanac of the Federal Judiciary* (Chicago, IL: LawLetters 1984– ) (annual updates) 2 v. (loose-leaf).

One volume lists U.S. district court judges profiles and evaluations and the other deals with the U.S. appellate court judges.[367] Staff information also is listed.

*American Bench* (Sacramento, CA: Forrester and Long, Inc. 10th ed. 1999–2000) (irregular) 1 v.

This is the most comprehensive source for biographical information on judges. Descriptive information on each federal and state court is arranged geographically. Judicial district maps are included. An alphabetical name index provides access to the biographies.

*Biographical Sketches of Justices of the Minnesota Supreme Court from Territorial Days to 1990* (St. Paul, MN: West Publishing Co. 1990).

The title is self-explanatory. Biographies of justices are arranged in historical sequence. A version was published in *North Western Reporter 2d* advance sheet, volume 357, number 3 (Dec. 25, 1984).

*Directory, United States District Court for the District of Minnesota* (Minneapolis, MN: Office, U.S. District Court Clerk) (triennial) 1 v.

Biographies of judges, magistrates, and bankruptcy judges. Court information, fees, and maps.

*Directory of Minnesota Judges 1998*, Prepared by Minnesota District Judges Association (St. Paul, MN: West Publishing Co. 1998).

"Printed as a public service by West Publishing Company."

*Finance and Commerce Legal Directory*[368] (Minneapolis, MN: Finance and Commerce, Inc. 1998– ) (irregular) 1 v. (loose-leaf).

A good deal of information for lawyers including miscellaneous reference, government, courts, judges, counties, fees, federal and states office and courts, citations, law enforcement, corrections, and online services.

---

366. Sources included here are particularly pertinent to Minnesota. Many sources provide information about federal judges that would include some Minnesota judges. *See also* § 536.3, *infra*.
367. The Eighth Circuit Court of Appeals is comprised of Arkansas, Iowa, Minnesota, Missouri, Nebraska, North Dakota, and South Dakota.
368. Formerly *Bachman Legal Directory*.

## Chapter Five. Finding Aids and Secondary Sources 137

*Judges of the United States,*[369] 2d ed. (Bicentennial Committee of the Judicial Conference of the United States, Washington, DC: Government Printing Office 1983) 1 v.

A particularly good source for biographical information, especially brief biographies of past judges.

*Judicial Profiles Desk Book,* Hennepin County Bar Association (Minneapolis, MN: Hennepin County Bar Ass'n 1996– ) 1 v. (loose-leaf).

Directory information, biographical sketches, and some portraits.

*Judicial Yellow Book: Who's Who in Federal and State Courts* (New York: Leadership Directories, Inc. 1995– ) (semiannual) 1 v.

Contents are judges and staff of federal courts at all levels including courts of limited jurisdiction and the territories. Directory information regarding the Administrative Office of the United States and the Federal Judicial Center as well as United States Sentencing Commission. Biographical information of all state appellate courts is included. Includes a law school index and name index.

*Minnesota Attorney's/Paralegal's/Secretary's Handbook* (Minneapolis, MN: Mariposa Publishing 1994– ) (annual with interim supplementation) 1 v. (loose-leaf).

This source provides names and addresses of Minnesota judges and county officials. Also included are sections on filing fees, miscellaneous forms, mileage tables, and zip code information.

*Minnesota e-Direct* <http://www.minndir.net>.

A Web-based product providing legal, business, and information professionals with automated access to law-related information. It provides information about federal and state legal, judicial, legislative, government, library, business, and professional resources. There are hyperlinks to state and federal Internet sites, as well as access to e-mail addresses (when available). *Minnesota e-Direct* is updated on a continuing basis. Complete reviews and updates of entire sections are performed on a quarterly basis.

*Minnesota Judicial Directory* (St. Paul, MN: Klara Media LLC 1998– ) (annual) 1 v. (loose-leaf).

This loose-leaf publication contains comprehensive biographies of federal and state judges currently serving in Minnesota. A partial list of

---

369. The previous edition was published in 1978 as part of the United States bicentennial celebration.

areas covered in each biography is staff, education, employment background, military service, academic positions, published materials, lectures, award and honors, and notable decisions.

*Minnesota Legal Directory* (Dallas, TX: Legal Directories Publishing Co., Inc. 1982– ) (annual) 1 v. <http://www.legaldirectories.com/>.
This directory lists federal and state officials, judges, attorneys, and law-related services. Its best feature is an alphabetical list of attorneys practicing in Minnesota.

*Minnesota Legislative Manual*[370] (St. Paul, MN: Secretary of State, Election Division 1967/68– ) (biennial) 1 v.
The chapter on the judicial branch lists the appellate court judges, and has photographs and brief biographical information. Each of the Minnesota Judicial District courts in Minnesota is listed with very brief biographical information listed for each judge. Administrative agencies closely associated with the justice system also are listed with brief descriptions of their duties. The manual includes legislative and executive officials with some biographies and other pertinent state information. An abridged edition is available for students.

*Minnesota Reports, Minnesota Reporter,* and *North Western Reporter* series (St. Paul, MN: West Group) (irregular).
Names of appellate judges with locations of their chambers are included in the prefatory material of each bound volume.

### § 536.3. Lawyers[371]

Many associations, organizations, and societies print membership directories, but so do commercial publishers. Periodically, district bar associations issue membership directories. Both the Hennepin County and Ramsey County Bar Associations have published pictorial registers. Special-interest bar associations often publish directories of their members, however they are not always regularly printed.

---

370. MINN. STAT. § 5.08(2) (1997) mandates distribution of the *Manual.* Remaining copies are available to the public at no charge.
371. *See also* § 536.2, *supra.* Although it may be desirable to know something about the ability of a lawyer, no adequate rating system for lawyers has been devised. Certain directories, such as *Martindale-Hubbell,* list ratings but they are incomplete and subjective. The Minnesota Supreme Court keeps a record of admissions to the bar and of lawyers currently in good standing.

### Chapter Five. Finding Aids and Secondary Sources

*2000 Pictorial Membership Directory,* Hennepin County Bar Association (Minneapolis, MN: Minnesota Law Center 2000) 368, 56 p.

The latest in pictorial registers for Hennepin County lawyers.

*Bench & Bar of Minnesota* (Minneapolis, MN: Minnesota State Bar Ass'n) (annual directory issue).

This official membership directory contains both an alphabetical and a geographical listing of lawyers. It also includes information on the bar association structure and organization and on bar-related agencies. Additionally, judges and court support personnel are listed for all courts in Minnesota (*see* § 554.3, *infra*). For a list of Minnesota lawyers who have been disbarred or are otherwise suspended, see the Minnesota Lawyers Professional Responsibility Board website at <http://www.courts.state.mn.us/lprb/list.html>.

*The Blue Pages. Minnesota. Directory of Lawyers Practicing in the Areas of: Criminal Defense, DWI/DUI Defense, Traffic Violations* (Minneapolis: Blue Pages, Inc. 1997– ) 1 v.

This is a resource for arrestees. The attorney listings are free or advertisements may be purchased.

*Business Guide Book to Law & Leading Attorneys* (Minneapolis: American Research Corp. 1994/1996– ) (biannual) 1 v.

Contains biographies of Minnesota attorneys who are recommended by their peers in a survey. Also has a description of Minnesota's legal system and basics of law; descriptions of various areas of business law; and indexes.

*Directory of Minnesota Law Firms on the Web* (Pritchard Law Web).

This website is a compilation of Minnesota law firm sites. There are alphabetical and geographic indexes. Available at <http://www.priweb.com/mnlawfirms.htm>.

*Guide to Leading American Attorneys. Minnesota: Profiles of the Minnesota Members of the Network of Leading American Attorneys* (Minneapolis, MN: Leading American Attorneys, 1998– ) v. ports.; (annual).

Profiles of leading American attorneys practicing law in Minnesota. Practice areas included are divorce and family law; estate, tax, and real estate law; and employment, consumer, and personal injury law. Inclusion in this directory is by peer review.

*Martindale-Hubbell Law Directory* (New Providence, NJ: Martindale Hubbell, Inc.) (annual).

For more than 100 years *Martindale-Hubbell* has been the most widely used directory of lawyers. It provides a geographical roster containing the names and addresses of lawyers from every state; a selected list of lawyers in foreign countries; and a biographical section containing information on law firms, lawyers associated with the firms, and representative lists of clients. The last volume provides digests of the laws of states and foreign governments, information on the American Bar Association, and information on special services for lawyers. *Martindale-Hubbell* is available through LEXIS-NEXIS and on the Web at <http://www.martindale.com>.

*Membership Directory,* Minnesota American Indian Bar Association (Minneapolis: MAIBA, 1992– ) 1 v.

This is a directory of the Minnesota American Indian Bar Association (MAIBA), a non-profit organization of American Indian attorneys and law students and non-Indian attorneys and law students who are interested in Indian law, as well as the American Indians who serve as advocates, prosecutors, or judicial officers in tribal courts. The membership directory is available online at <http://www.maiba.org/directory01.html>.

*Minnattorney.com*

This "Internet Home of Minnesota's Legal Professionals," is an online directory of legal summaries, resources, job listings, an attorney directory, and support services. It can be accessed at <http://www.minnattorney.com/>.

*Minnesota Divorce & Family Lawyers & Law,* 1998–99 ed. (Minneapolis: American Research Corporation 1998) 1 v.

Contains summaries of the law and profiles of leading American attorneys practicing in divorce, adoption, and family law in Minnesota.

*Minnesota Legal Directory* (Dallas: Legal Directories Publishing Company, Inc. 1982/83– ) (annual).

Lists federal and state officials, judges, attorneys, and law-related services. Has an alphabetical list of all Minnesota attorneys. Available at <http://www.legaldirectories.com/>.

## Chapter Five. Finding Aids and Secondary Sources 141

*MWL: Minnesota Women Lawyers. Membership Directory* (Minneapolis: The Association) (annual).
Arranged alphabetically and includes lists of members by city and area of practice. Available at <http://www.mwlawyers.org/>.

*Sullivan's Law Directory for the State of Minnesota* (Bloomington, MN: Law Bulletin Publishing Co. 2000– ) 1 v.
A directory of Minnesota lawyers and law firms. Includes both federal and Minnesota court rules and a roster of Minnesota State officials and employees.

*West Legal Directory.*
An online directory, this provides profiles of more than 1,000,000 lawyers and law firms, in addition to profiles of international counsel, corporate counsel, and U.S. government attorneys. It is available on the Web at <http://www.lawoffice.com/direct/direct.asp>.

### § 536.4. Government Personnel

*Directory of Minnesota City Officials*[372] (St. Paul, MN: League of Minnesota Cities 1985– ) (annual) 1 v.
A comprehensive listing of Minnesota cities. County, population, type of city, and city hall telephone numbers and addresses are provided. Names of elected and appointed officials also are included.

*Handbook to Minnesota State Government* (Minnesota, Department of Administration, Communications, Media Division, St. Paul, MN: State of Minnesota 2000) 1 v.
Describes the State of Minnesota administrative agencies and executive departments.

*Minnesota County Attorney Directory* (St. Paul, MN: Minnesota County Attorneys' Ass'n) 1 v.
The MCAA is an independent, voluntary organization of county attorneys in the State of Minnesota. *Minnesota County Attorney Directory* is available online at <http://www.safenet.org/mcaa/mcaa.html>. The site has an alphabetical list and a list by county.

---

372. Prior title was *Directory of Minnesota Municipal Officials* and that was preceded by *Directory of Minnesota City & Village Officials.*

*Minnesota County Directory* (St. Paul, MN: Ass'n of Minnesota Counties 2000) 1 v.

A directory of county government in Minnesota. Includes county officials and employees.

*Minnesota Elected Officials. . . . compiled by . . . Secretary of State* (St. Paul, MN: Office of the Secretary of State, Elections Division 1977– ) 1 v.

A directory of state, congressional, legislative, judicial, and county officials and employees.

*Minnesota Guidebook to State Agency Services* (St. Paul, MN: Department of Administration, State Register and Public Documents Division 1996/99 ed.) (biennial) 1 v.

The *Guidebook* provides descriptions of judicial and state agencies listing addresses and phone numbers, organizational structure, and key personnel. This is perhaps the most valuable guide to Minnesota government. Available at <http://www.comm.media.state.mn.us/bookstore/intro.pdf>.

*Minnesota Legislative Manual* (St. Paul, MN: Secretary of State, Election Division) (biennial) 1 v.

The title has changed several times during the last 150 years. Since 1967/1968, it has been called the *Minnesota Legislative Manual*. This is a very useful reference work. Biographical information about the current members of the legislature and the executive branch and judicial branch with other pertinent state information. A "student edition" also is available.

*Minnesota Session Law Service* (St. Paul, MN: West Group). First issue of each legislative session.

This issue lists names and addresses of legislative members with committee assignments.

*Minnesota Statutes* (St. Paul, MN: Office of the Revisor of Statutes) (biennial).

Volume 11, Table III, p. 757 is a table illustrating the organization and structure of state government.

*Municipal Yellow Book. Who's Who in the Leading City and County Governments and Local Authorities* (New York: Leadership Directories, Inc. 1991– ) (semiannual) 1 v.

Lists cities of Duluth, St. Paul, and Minneapolis, and Ramsey and Hennepin counties.

## Chapter Five. Finding Aids and Secondary Sources 143

*Official Directory of the Minnesota Legislature*[373] (St. Paul, MN: Minnesota House Information Office and Office of the Secretary of the Senate) (biennial) 1 v.

This directory lists addresses, brief biographical information, and committee assignments, and includes pictures of legislators. An online directory is available at <http://www.leg.state.mn.us/leg/legdir.htm>.

*Qwest Dex White Pages.*

The government "blue" pages section lists city, county, state, and federal agencies along with addresses and phone numbers.

*State of Minnesota Telephone Directory* (St. Paul, MN: Department of Administration, State Register and Public Documents Division) (biennial) 1 v. Available at <http://www.state.mn.us>. This directory has an alphabetical name index, classified section, quick reference, and greater Minnesota directory and a list of department acronyms.

*State Yellow Book. Who's Who in the Executive and Legislative Branches of the 50 State Governments* (New York: Leadership Directories, Inc.) (semiannual) 1 v.

Arranged by executive branch and legislative branch, with state profiles and an alphabetical list of personnel.

### § 537. Historical Works

*150 Years of Justice: Fence Rails, Riot, Bad Marriages and More* (compiled for the 150th anniversary of the Dakota County Courts by the Dakota County Historical Society [S.l.: s.n.; 1999]) (various pagings)1 v.

A history of the legal community in Dakota County, Minnesota.

*Beginning a Judicial Tradition: Formative Years of the Minnesota Court of Appeals,* Peter J. Popovich (St. Paul, MN: State Court Administrators Office 1987) 1 v.

This report examines the restructured appellate court system in general and reviews the statistical evidence to gauge the effectiveness of the new court.

---

373. The Minnesota House of Representatives directory is available online at <http://www.house.leg.state.mn.us/hinfo/mem.htm>. The Senate directory is located at <http://www.leg.state.mn.us/leg/sendir.htm>.

*Bench and Bar of Minnesota, a Historical and Biographical Sketch* (Publisher unknown 1901) 1 v.
Contains a history of the bar association, the state, the courts, and the law schools, followed by biographies and pictures of lawyers and judges. There is an alphabetical index to the biographies.

*Biographical Sketches of Justices of the Minnesota Supreme Court and Judges of the Minnesota Court of Appeals from Territorial Days to 1990* (St. Paul, MN: West Pub. Co. 1990) 1 v.
Brief biographies of Minnesota appellate judges.

*(The) First 100 Years. . . .* (Minneapolis, MN: Minnesota State Bar Ass'n 1983) 1 v.
This "chronicle of judges, lawyers and legal events of the past 100 years" was a centennial project of the association. State and federal judiciary are presented in tables of succession. The remainder of the book is arranged alphabetically by county with a legal and architectural history of their courthouses and personal reminiscences. Numerous photographs are included.

*For the Record: 150 Years of Law and Lawyers in Minnesota. An Illustrated History* (Minneapolis, MN: Minnesota State Bar Ass'n 1999) 1 v.
Well illustrated with narrative describing the private and public legal community in Minnesota.

*History of the Bench and Bar of Minnesota,* Hiram F. Stevens (Minneapolis, MN: Legal Publishing & Engraving Co. 1904) 2 v.
This title includes a history of the state, the bar, the courts, famous cases, and law schools, and has biographies of members of the bar with some portraits.

*(A) History of the Office of the Attorney General, State of Minnesota* (St. Paul, MN: Minnesota Att'y General's Office 1997) 1 v.
A brief history of the AG's office with biographies and portraits.

*History of the United States District Court for the District of Minnesota,* Kenneth Owens (St. Paul, MN: West Publishing 1989) 1 v.
Examines eight cases that illustrate the role the court has played in addressing and resolving dynamic constitutional issues of significance to Minnesotans and to all Americans. It also provides brief biographies of those judges who have served on the court.

## Chapter Five. Finding Aids and Secondary Sources 145

*In Pursuit of Excellence: A History of the University of Minnesota Law School,* Robert A. Stein (St. Paul, MN: Mason Division, Butterworth Legal Publishers 1980).
Covers the period of 1888 to 1979. Arranged according to each dean's tenure. Epilogue, tables, notes, index, and photographs are included.

*(The) Law, Courts, and Lawyers in the Frontier Days of Minnesota: An Informal Legal History of the Years 1835 to 1865,* Robert J. Sheran & Timothy J. Baland (St. Paul, MN: William Mitchell College of Law 1976) 1 v.
A brief history of legal and judicial administration in early Minnesota. Includes bibliographic references.

*Minnesota Congressmen, Legislators, and Other Elected Officials: An Alphabetical Checklist, 1894–1971,* W. F. Toensing (St. Paul, MN: Minnesota Historical Society 1971).
Contains entries arranged in alphabetical order by surname, followed by years of birth and death if known, county and post office address, office to that elected, and term of service. All appointed officials have been omitted as have district court judges. Indexes by position and county are included.

*Minnesota Justices Series* (Minnesota State Law Library).
Currently, this is a series of twelve titles edited, written, and compiled by the staff of the Minnesota State Law Library in Saint Paul. Each title deals with the professional, public, and judicial career of a Minnesota State Supreme Court justice who recently has retired. Most are single volumes with portraits, tables, and bibliographies. Titles in the series and dates of publication are:

- *The Professional Career of Fallon Kelly: 1933–1980* (1981; Minnesota Justices Series; no. 1)
- *The Professional Career of Robert J. Sheran* (1982; Minnesota Justices Series; no. 2)
- *The Professional Career of Walter F. Rogosheske* (1984; Minnesota Justices Series; no. 3)
- *The Professional, Public and Judicial Career of C. Donald Peterson* (1987; Minnesota Justices Series; no. 4)
- *The Judicial Career of James C. Otis* (1987; Minnesota Justices Series; no. 5)
- *The Civic and Judicial Career of George M. Scott* (1989; Minnesota Justices Series; no. 6)

- *Stepping Stones and the Judicial Career of Douglas K. Amdahl* (1992; Minnesota Justices Series; no. 7)
- *The Judicial Career of Glenn E. Kelley* (1993; Minnesota Justices Series; no. 8)
- *The Political, Professional and Judicial Career of Lawrence R. Yetka* (1996; Minnesota Justices Series; no. 9)
- *The Judicial Career of Peter S. Popovich* (1998; Minnesota Justices Series; no. 10)
- *The Judicial Career of John E. Simonett* (1998; Minnesota Justices Series; no. 11)
- *The Social Justice, Legal and Judicial Career of Rosalie Erwin Wahl* (2000; Minnesota Justices Series; no. 12)

*Minnesota State Law Library 150th Anniversary Event, November 5, 1999,* produced by Dave Carlson for the State Law Library (St. Paul, MN: Minnesota State Law Library 1999) 1 videocassette (VHS) (1:38): sd., col.; ½ in.

Entertainment, tributes, and featured speaker at the Minnesota State Law Library 150th anniversary celebration.

*(A) Search for Place: The History of the Minnesota Judicial Center,* Roland C. Amundson (St. Paul, MN: Minnesota Court of Appeals 1995) 1 v.

The history of the supreme court and its quest to establish a judicial center. Includes notes and bibliographic references as well as photographs and sketches.

*William Mitchell College of Law: Opportunity, Leadership and Service,* produced by Visual Reality, Inc.; executive producer, Christine DeMoss; writer-director, Joe Lovitt (St. Paul, MN: William Mitchell College of Law 1999) 1 videocassette (21:30 min.): sd., b&w; ½ in.

Narrated by Hy Berman, this is a film celebrating the law school's first century.

*With Satisfaction and Honor: William Mitchell College of Law, 1900–2000,* Douglas R. Heidenreich (St. Paul, MN: William Mitchell College of Law 1999) 1 v.

Celebrating a century of legal education in Minnesota.

Several Minnesota law firms upon occasion have published their histories to mark anniversaries.

*60th Anniversary: 1938–1998,* Robins, Kaplan, Miller & Ciresi, L.L.P. [S.l.: Robins, Kaplan, Miller & Ciresi 1998]

*Oppenheimer Wolff & Donnelly: Brussels, Chicago, Minneapolis, New York, St. Paul, Washington, D.C.* ([Minneapolis, MN: The Firm, between 1985 and 1990]) 16 p.
The law firm and its partners in Saint Paul and Minneapolis.

*(The) View From the 17th Floor: Oppenheimer Wolff & Donnelly and Its 111-Year history,* Virginia L. Martin (reprinted from *Ramsey County History,* vol. 32, no. 1 (spring 1997)) 21 p.
History of the Minnesota law firm with particular attention to William H. Oppenheimer, Benno Wolff, and Stanislaus Dillon Donnelly.

## § 540. SECONDARY SOURCES[374]

§ 541. Restatements
§ 542. Encyclopedias
§ 543. Form Books
§ 544. Annotations
§ 545. Treatises and Practice Manuals
§ 546. Legal Periodicals
§ 547. Legal Newspapers

Secondary sources offer analysis and commentary upon the law. Secondary sources run from scholarly treatises to the practical guides used by legal practitioners.

---

374. The term "secondary sources" as opposed to "primary sources" which is the law in its pure form of constitutions, statutes, regulations, and cases.

## § 541. Restatements[375]

§ 541.1. Access Tools and Special Features
§ 541.2. Minnesota Annotations

The *Restatements of the Law*, prepared by the American Law Institute (A.L.I.), are codified arrangements or interpretations of principles of common law. *Restatements* consist of statements of legal principles, comments on those principles, and illustrations of how the principles are applied to specific factual situations.

As laws change, as new developments in the law occur, or as the position of the A.L.I. on a particular subject changes, revisions are made to the *Restatements*. Before adoption of a proposed revision, the Institute prepares preliminary and temporary drafts and circulates them to its members, together with statements supporting and opposing the proposed revision. All the *Restatements* have been succeeded by a second edition and in some cases a third edition is being published.

### § 541.1. Access Tools and Special Features

A permanent general index to the *Restatements*, *Restatement of the Law: Permanent General Index, Covering Agency, Conflict of Laws, Contracts, Judgments, Property, Restitution, Security, Torts, Trusts*[376] was published in 1946 that covered all first series *Restatements*. This index superseded the temporary general index published in 1941. Since then an index has been provided for each new *Restatement*.

Most *Restatements* include appendix volumes. The appendix contains reporters' notes, citations to court decisions, cross references to the West Key Number system, and annotations to the *American Law Reports* series.

---

375. For general information on the process of preparing the *Restatements, see* Goodrich, *Story of the American Law Institute,* 1951 Wash. U. L.Q. 283, GOODRICH & WOLKIN, THE STORY OF THE AMERICAN LAW INSTITUTE (St. Paul, MN: ALI Publishers 1961). The American Law Institute also has prepared studies on federal law and model acts that state legislatures may consider, follow, or adopt. A comprehensive bibliography of the *Restatements* is printed in 3 PIMSLEUR'S CHECKLISTS OF BASIC AMERICAN LEGAL PUBLICATIONS § 5 (Marcia S. Zubrow ed., 1991). Many law libraries have most of the items listed in this bibliography.
376. St. Paul, MN: American Law Institute Publishers, 1946; 1 v.

## Chapter Five. Finding Aids and Secondary Sources 149

*Restatement in the Courts*,[377] permanent ed., American Law Institute (St. Paul, MN: American Law Institute Publishers 1945).

This work cites all federal and state appellate court cases in which a *Restatement* was quoted. Bound supplements were issued from 1946 to 1976. Beginning in 1977, court references to the *Restatement* were issued in pocket parts and other supplements to each of the specific subject segments of the Restatement, i.e., Contracts, Torts, Agency, etc. Besides these pocket parts and other supplements which are issued annually, the American Law Institute publishes an "Interim Case Citations" pamphlet every six months that lists those cases which have cited the *Restatement*.

*Shepard's Restatement of the Law Citations: A Compilation of Citations to the American Law Institute's Restatement of the Law* (Colorado Springs, CO: Shepard's Citations, Inc. 1976– ).

This volume lists citations to cases and law review articles (indicating annotations, comments, and illustrations) that have cited the *Restatements*. It continues the section on the *Restatements* formerly found in Shepard's state citators.

### § 541.2. Minnesota Annotations to the Restatement

State annotations, although published some years ago, provide a guide to the positions taken on the *Restatements* by the highest courts of the states. State annotations to *Restatements* were prepared for most states, including Minnesota, under the auspices of local bar associations and were published by the American Law Institute. Minnesota annotations were prepared for the following *Restatements*.

*Restatement of the Law of Conflict of Laws: As Adopted and Promulgated by the American Law Institute: Containing Minnesota Annotations*, prepared by H. L. McClintock; under the auspices of the Minnesota State Bar Association (St. Paul, MN: American Law Institute Publishers 1935) 1 v.

*Restatement of the Law of Contracts: As Adopted and Promulgated by the American Law Institute: Containing Minnesota Annotations*, prepared by Harvey Hoshour & Ralph H. Dwan under the auspices of the Minnesota State Bar Association (St. Paul, MN: American Law Institute Publishers 1934) 2 v. in 1.

---

377. *See* William Draper Lewis, *History of the American Law Institute and the First Restatement of the Law. "How We Did It" in* RESTATEMENT IN THE COURTS, perm. ed. (St. Paul, MN: American Law Institute Publishers 1945), at 1–23.

*Minnesota Annotations to the Restatement of the Law of Property: As Adopted and Promulgated by the American Law Institute,* prepared by R. G. Patton & Carroll G. Patton; under the auspices of the Minnesota State Bar Association (St. Paul, MN: American Law Institute Publishers 1938) 2 v. in 1.

*Minnesota Annotations to the Restatement of the Law of Restitution: As Adopted and Promulgated by the American Law Institute,* prepared by Edward G. Jennings; under the auspices of the Minnesota State Bar Association (St. Paul, MN: American Law Institute Publishers 1941) 1 v.

## § 542. Encyclopedias

*Corpus Juris Secundum* (St. Paul, MN: West Publishing Co. 1936– ), and *American Jurisprudence: A Modern Comprehensive Text Statement of American Law, State and Federal,* 2d ed., completely revised and rewritten in the light of modern authorities and developments, by the editorial staff of the publisher (Rochester, NY: Lawyers Co-operative Pub. Co. 1977– ).

Each of these sources is kept up to date by cumulative annual pocket parts, replacement volumes, and additional numbered and lettered volumes covering new supplements. Now published by West Group, both are legal encyclopedias that summarize the law under broad topics from a national perspective. References to Minnesota case law are provided in both encyclopedias. *American Jurisprudence 2d* is available on Westlaw and LEXIS-NEXIS.

*Dunnell Minnesota Digest* (Charlottesville, VA: Lexis Law Publishing 1989– ) (*see* § 511, *supra*).

This is subtitled "an encyclopedia of Minnesota law" and functions as such by providing access to information not easily located in the primary sources. For example, locating all the statutes on expunging criminal records in *Minnesota Statutes* or *Minnesota Statutes Annotated* is difficult because the term "expungement" does not appear as a distinct index entry. *Dunnell Minnesota Digest* indexes this term under the heading "Criminal Records" and refers to the section entitled "Expungement of Criminal Records" that discusses the topic and cites to cases and several statutes. *Dunnells* is available on CD-ROM.

# Chapter Five. Finding Aids and Secondary Sources

*West's Encyclopedia of American Law*[378] (St. Paul, MN: West Group 1998) 12 v.

Not strictly a Minnesota legal research tool, this set is written for the lay reader. Besides coverage of numerous topics, a list of abbreviations, bibliography, table of case cited, name index, and subject index, there is a "Milestones in the Law" section that analyzes five landmark U.S. Supreme Court cases. It is a starting point for many questions students and laypeople may have. It is illustrated with photographs, drawings, charts, and graphs.

## § 543. Form Books

Forms are instruments designed to enable practitioners to draft papers or documents quickly, efficiently, and with some degree of uniformity. Procedural forms[379] are those designed to assist the lawyer in preparing papers, such as briefs or motions, for submission to a court. The form and content of papers that must be filed often are prescribed by statute or court rule, and will be published in the statutes or with the rules of court. Substantive forms, also called legal forms,[380] are those designed to assist the lawyer in preparing papers and documents, such as wills or leases, for the business or personal affairs of clients. The form and content of these papers also may be prescribed by statute and published in the statutes.

Forms on specific subjects may be found in treatises and in manuals prepared in conjunction with continuing legal education courses (*see* § 546.1, *infra*). Because many Minnesota court rules are patterned after federal rules, many of the forms provided in general form books and federal treatises can be adapted.[381] General substantive form books,

---

378. The predecessor title is *Guide to American Law* first published by West in 1983.
379. Compilations of federal procedural forms are published by various companies. They often are found in law libraries at the call number KF8863.
380. *West's Legal Forms* and *American Jurisprudence Legal Forms 2d* compile general forms in multi-volume sets. The call number for general form books is KF170.
381. MINN R. CRIM. PROC. states that

> No attempt is made to furnish a complete manual of forms. For all complaints charging a misdemeanor offense the prosecuting attorney, judge, judicial officer or clerk of court authorized to issue process shall use the appropriate form as set forth in the following criminal forms or *a form substantially in compliance with these forms*. The other forms provided herein *are not mandatory*, but shall be accepted by the court if offered by any party or counsel for their designated purpose

(emphasis added).

organized by legal topic, may provide forms for use in different states. Some have statutory and case law annotations.

The Court Rules volume of *Minnesota Statutes* has selected criminal forms in the section on criminal procedure. There are more forms in the General Rules of Practice section.

*Minnesota Legal Forms* series is published by Lexis Law Publishers as an eleven-volume ringbound set, updated annually. This set covers both procedural and substantive topics. The individual titles are listed below. Computer diskettes are included with each volume.

- *Bankruptcy*, by Michael C. Wagner & Cass S. Weil
- *Commercial Real Estate*, by John Michael Miller
- *Creditors' Remedies*, by Thomas F. Miller
- *Criminal Law*, by Rick E. Mattox
- *Family Law*, by Daniels W. McLean
- *Law Office Systems*, by Robert L. Newell
- *Personal Injury*, by Gary Stoneking
- *Probate*, by James D. Bates & Jeffery M. Hucek
- *Residential Real Estate*, by Kathleen M. Roer
- *Workers' Compensation*, by Michael T. Peck

*Civil Practice Forms/Forms on Disk*, Roger S. Haydock, David F. Herr & Sonja Dunnwald Peterson (St. Paul, MN: West Pub. Co. 1995) 2 v. and 2 computer disks (3½ in.)

Part of the Minnesota practice series; vols. 15 and 16 specifically focus on forms that correspond to civil rules 1–70. Other volumes of the series also have forms interspersed within the text.

*Minnesota Civil Practice*, 3d ed., Douglas McFarland & William Keppel (Charlottesville, VA: Lexis Law Publishing 1999) 4 v.

Numerous forms may be found throughout this set. The forms index is located in volume 4.

*Pirsig on Minnesota Pleading*, 5th ed., Maynard E. Pirsig (Charlottesville, VA: Lexis Law Publishing 1991) 2 v. (pocket -part supplementation).

More fully described in section § 546.2, *infra*. These two volumes have many procedural forms.

## Chapter Five. Finding Aids and Secondary Sources 153

*Practitioner's Guide to Minnesota Personal Injury Forms,* 3d ed., Robert J. Hauer Jr. (ed.) (Minneapolis, MN: Minnesota Trial Lawyers Ass'n 1994) 1 v. (various pagings).
Forms for initial interview, settlement, trial documents, releases, statutes of limitation, and wrongful death, and minor settlement forms.

*Secretary's Guide,* Jean Stewart Longfellow.
This is a supplement to *Minnesota Legal Forms,* providing checklists for document preparation and filing information.

Minnesota Continuing Legal Education materials often have forms. (*see* § 547.1, *infra*) Choosing a subject keyword search in an electronic catalog and using the terms "Minnesota" and "forms" often will retrieve various MCLE offerings that have forms in them.

Various sets of legal forms are published by major legal publishing companies. These general forms often can be tailored to the needs of the client and the jurisdiction.

*American Jurisprudence Legal Forms 2d* (Rochester, NY: Lawyers Co-operative Pub. Co.; San Francisco, CA: Bancroft-Whitney Co. 1971– ) (kept up to date by pocket parts).
Practice-oriented forms for legal and business transactions, exhaustively annotated, and keyed to the substantive law, integrating legal and form-drafting principles with statutes, tax notes, tables, checklists, and checkpoints. Includes unnumbered general index volumes and separately numbered federal tax guide to legal forms volumes (in binders). Kept up to date by pocket parts and revised volumes. These also are available on Westlaw and LEXIS-NEXIS.

*American Jurisprudence Pleading and Practice Forms Annotated* (San Francisco, CA: Bancroft-Whitney Co. 1956– ) (pocket-part updating).
Not the same as the *American Jurisprudence Legal Forms,* these form books deal with the initiation, preparation, and disposition of legal matters brought to court.

*West's Federal Forms* (St. Paul, MN: West Pub. Co. 1969– ).
Includes various editions of some volumes. Includes unnumbered General Index and table of statutes and court rules volume. Kept up to date by supplements, replacement volumes, pocket parts, and interim pamphlets.

*West's Legal Forms,* 3d ed. (St. Paul, MN: West Pub. Co. 1996– ) (kept up to date by pocket parts).
Emphasis on forms for business enterprises and corporations. These also are available on Westlaw and LEXIS-NEXIS.

### § 544. Annotations

*American Law Reports,* now in a fifth series, refers to Minnesota cases and statutes at the start of each annotation in its "Jurisdictional Table of Cited Statutes and Cases." This table is organized alphabetically by state and includes references to statutes, rules, regulations, and constitutional provisions bearing on the subject of the annotation. The last index volume has a table of state statutes and constitutions organized alphabetically by state. References to Minnesota statutes and constitutional provisions are referenced to ALR volume and pages. *American Law Reports* is available on both Westlaw and LEXIS-NEXIS.

### § 545. Reports of the Judiciary and Attorney General

§ 545.1. Selected Reports to the Supreme Court
§ 545.2. Selected Attorney General Reports

The Minnesota justice system from time to time requests that advisory committees, or other task forces, be formed to investigate a particular issue or problem affecting the administration of the legal system. In some instances, the legislature will direct the court to respond to a particular issue or problem. The following is a selected list of reports written by these committees in the past twenty years.

The Minnesota Attorney General publishes various guides and pamphlets for the citizens of Minnesota such as consumer fraud, lemon laws, telephone solicitations, charitable solicitation, etc. The AG's office also publishes various reports at the request of the legislature regarding current issues such as hate crimes, safe schools, etc., and also writes various manuals, handbooks, and guides for attorneys regarding procedural issues.

## Chapter Five. Finding Aids and Secondary Sources

### § 545.1. Selected Reports to the Supreme Court

Works are listed alphabetically by title.

*Advisory Committee on Civil Procedure. Report,* Minnesota, Supreme Court (St. Paul, MN: The Minnesota Supreme Court 1984) 50 leaves.

Discusses the recommendations for the revision of the rules of civil procedure in Minnesota.

*Advisory Committee on Judicial Growth and Enrichment. Final Report,* Minnesota (St. Paul, MN: The Committee 1995) 11 leaves.

Addresses the issue of continuing education for the Minnesota judiciary.

*Advisory Committee on the Minnesota Rules of Juvenile Procedure. Final Report,* Minnesota, Supreme Court (St. Paul, MN: The Committee 1995) 1 v.

Covers the issues of reform of the juvenile court system in Minnesota and how juvenile justice is administered.

*Advisory Task Force on the Civil Commitment System. Final Report,* Minnesota, Supreme Court (St. Paul, MN: Research and Planning Office, State Court Administration, Minnesota Supreme Court 1996) 1 v.

Mandated by 1994 Minn. Laws, ch. 636, art. 8, § 18, subd. 4, this report summarizes and recommends changes in the civil procedure regarding capacity, disability, conservatorships, and other mental health laws in Minnesota.

*Advisory Task Force on the Guardian Ad Litem System: Final Report,* Minnesota, Supreme Court (St. Paul, MN: Minnesota Supreme Court, Office of Research and Planning 1996) 1 v. (various pagings).

Background, deliberations and recommendations, and proposed rules of procedure regarding guardians ad litem.

*Advisory Task Force on the Juvenile System: Final Report,* Minnesota, Supreme Court (St. Paul, MN: Research and Planning Office, State Court Administration, Minnesota Supreme Court 1994) 1 v.

Addresses the issues of juvenile justice administration and juvenile delinquency in Minnesota.

*Advisory Task Force on Visitation and Child Support Enforcement. Final Report,* Minnesota, Supreme Court (St. Paul, MN: Minnesota Supreme Court, State Court Administration, Office of Research and Planning 1997) 1 v.

Addresses the issues of visitation rights, child support, parent and child relations, and custody of children.

*Civil Commitment in Minnesota. Final Report,* Minnesota, Supreme Court Study Commission on the Mentally Disabled in the Courts (St. Paul, MN: The Commission 1979) 1 v. (various pagings).

Addresses the issues of capacity, disability, commitment, detention, and insanity in the Minnesota justice system.

*Committee on the Role of Judges in Pro Bono Activity. Report,* Minnesota, Supreme Court (St. Paul, MN: The Committee 1994) 5 leaves.

This report addresses the issue of the role of Minnesota judiciary in pro bono activities.

*Court Consolidation Study Commission. Final Report,* Minnesota, Judicial Planning Committee, Prepared by Janet Marshall (St. Paul, MN: Judicial Planning Committee 1984) 19 leaves.

A result of a legislative mandate 1983 Minn. Laws, Ch. 359, § 150, subd. 3, regarding the reform of the court system in Minnesota.

*Criminal Courts Study Commission. Final Report,* Minnesota, Supreme Court (St. Paul, MN: Criminal Courts Study Commission [1990]) 1 v. (various pagings).

Addresses the issue of the administration of criminal justice and criminal courts in Minnesota.

*Expedited Child Support Process: Interim Evaluation Report,* Minnesota Supreme Court (St. Paul, MN: State Court Administrator's Office, Court Services Division 2001). 15, [10] leaves.

Mandated by the 1999 Minn. Laws Chap. 196 Art. 1 Sec. 10, this report was performed in consultation with the Department of Human Services on the topic of child support laws in Minnesota.

*Final Report,* Minnesota Supreme Court, Parental Cooperation Task Force (Saint Paul, MN: Minnesota Supreme Court, State Court Administration, Court Services Division 2000) 49 leaves.

This report deals with the role of mediation and the divorce and custody of children.

*Final Report,* Minnesota Supreme Court, Task Force on Court Appointed Civil Counsel (St. Paul, MN: Minnesota Supreme Court, 2001) 54 leaves.

Deal with the right to counsel as it applies to civil cases and legal assistance to the poor in Minnesota.

## Chapter Five. Finding Aids and Secondary Sources 157

*Foster Care and Adoption Task Force. Final Report,* Minnesota, Supreme Court (St. Paul, MN: Minnesota Supreme Court, State Court Administration, Office of Research and Planning [1997]) 1 v. (various pagings).
Addresses the issue of foster home care and adoption law and legislation in Minnesota.

*Guidelines for Minnesota Court Facilities. Final Report,* Minnesota, Judicial Planning Committee (St. Paul, MN: The Committee 1979) 1 v.
A summary of recommendations and standards for courthouses in Minnesota.

*Juvenile Representation Study Committee. Report,* Minnesota, Supreme Court (St. Paul, MN: The Committee 1990) 1 v.
Mandated by 1989 Minn. Laws, ch. 335, art. 3, § 43, this report addresses the right to counsel and legal assistance to juvenile delinquents in Minnesota courts.

*Parental Cooperation Task Force. Final Report,* Minnesota, Supreme Court (St. Paul, MN: Minnesota Supreme Court, State Court Administration, Court Services Division [2000]) 49 leaves.
Covers the issues of communication in divorce mediation, custody of children, divorce and mediation, and the law of separation in Minnesota.

*Report of the Advisory Committee to Review Lawyer Discipline in Minnesota and Evaluate the Recommendations of the American Bar Association,* Minnesota, Supreme Court (St. Paul, MN: The Committee 1994) 1 v. (various pagings).
Addresses the issue of legal ethics and the discipline of lawyers in light of the ABA report on ethics in the legal profession.

*Report on Juror Compensation Issues,* Minnesota Juror Compensation Workgroup (St. Paul, MN: Court Services Division, State Court Administration [1999]) 1 v. (various pagings).
Mandated by 1999 Minn. Laws, ch. 71, § 1, this report relied also on the knowledge of the conference of chief judges in regard to jury duty and jury fees in Minnesota.

*Report on the Minnesota Court Interpreter Program Fees,* Minnesota, Supreme Court, Minnesota Court Interpreter Program (St. Paul, MN: Minnesota Court Interpreter Program, Supreme Court of Minnesota [2000]) [2] leaves and letter of transmittal.

Mandated by 1999 Minn. Laws, ch. 216, art. 6, § 15, this report deals with financing of training and staffing for language interpreters in the Minnesota courts.

*Report on the Use of Para-Judicial Personnel in the Minnesota Courts,* Minnesota, Judicial Planning Committee (St. Paul, MN: Minnesota Supreme Court 1980) 39 leaves.

Deals with the employment of paralegals in the Minnesota court system.

*Report to the Minnesota Legislature on the Development of the New Minnesota Court Information System* (St. Paul, MN: Minnesota Supreme Court, Information Technology Division 2001) 14 leaves.

Mandated by 2000 Minn. Laws ch. 311, art. 5, § 5, subd. 2, this report deals the present status and the development of information storage and retrieval systems in the Minnesota court system.

*(A) Report to the Minnesota Supreme Court: The Impact of Rule 114 on Civil Litigation Practice in Minnesota,* Bobbi McAdoo ([S.l.]: Minnesota Supreme Court Office of Continuing Legal Education 1997) 1 v. (various pagings).

This report details the impact and effect of dispute resolution and mediation in Minnesota.

*Special Court Reporter Certification Fact Finding Committee, Final Report,* Minnesota, Supreme Court (St. Paul, MN: State of Minnesota, Supreme Court 1993) 1 v. (unpaged).

Addresses the issue of court reporters and their role in the Minnesota courts.

*Task Force for Gender Fairness in the Courts. Final Report,* Minnesota, Supreme Court (St. Paul, MN: Task Force for Gender Fairness in the Courts 1989) 1 v. (various pagings).

Mandated by 1987 Minn. Laws, ch. 404, § 3, subd. 2, this report addresses how judges, officials, and employees of the courts address the issues of spousal maintenance, property division, child support, custody, domestic violence, sexual assault, sexual harassment, and sex discrimination in the administration of criminal justice in Minnesota.

# Chapter Five. Finding Aids and Secondary Sources 159

*Task Force on Alternative Dispute Resolution. Final Report.* Minnesota, Supreme Court (St. Paul, MN: Task Force on Alternative Dispute Resolution 1989) 1 v.
Addresses the issue of dispute resolution and its role in the courts in Minnesota.

*Task Force on Financing of the Trial Courts. Final Report,* Minnesota, Supreme Court (St. Paul, MN: [The Task Force?] 1990) 1 v.
Mandated by 1989 Minn. Laws, ch. 335, art. 3, § 43, this report addresses the financial cost of administering the Minnesota court system.

*Task Force on Racial Bias in the Judicial System. Final Report,* Minnesota, Supreme Court (St. Paul, MN: The Court 1993) 1 v. (various pagings).
Addresses the issues of racial discrimination and attitudes of judges may have on the denial of justice in Minnesota.

*Task Force on Recommendation on Conciliation Court Rules. Final Report,* Minnesota, Supreme Court (St. Paul, MN: State of Minnesota, Supreme Court [1993]) 1 v. (various pagings).
Addresses the issue of civil procedure in small claims courts in Minnesota.

*U.S. Commission on Civil Rights. State Advisory Committee Reports. Minnesota* (Washington, DC: U.S. Commission on Civil Rights 1998).
Focus is on affirmative action. July 1998 summary of a community forum held on affirmative action in Minneapolis. Participants at this forum included individuals with diverse opinions on the subject from business, religious and academic communities. Additionally, minority communities and constituencies contributed to the discussion.

### § 545.2. Selected Minnesota Attorney General Reports

Aside from the opinions,[382] some reports are written by the staff of the Minnesota Attorney General's office. Other reports are mandated by the legislature, or requested by the governor; others are on-going at regular intervals, and some are the result of special task forces created by the legislature. Below is a selected list from the past ten years.

---

382. Minnesota Attorney General opinions from 1993 to date are available online at <http://www.ag.state.mn.us/library/index.htm>.

Consumer pamphlets are not included. There are several reports that are issued on an annual or biennial basis.

*Annual Expenditure Report, Fiscal Year.* . . . (St. Paul, MN: State of Minnesota, Office of Attorney General).
Mandated by 1994 Minn. Laws, ch. 636, art. 10, subd. 4.

*Antitrust Annual Report* (St. Paul, MN: State of Minnesota, Office of Attorney General 1979–80– ).
Mandated by the legislature, this report deals with the antitrust investigations and projections of the Minnesota AG's office.

*Attorney General's Task Force on Food Safety: Final Report* (St. Paul, MN: Attorney General's Task Force on Food Safety 1990) 13, 102 p.
Deals with investigations into the food industry and trade as it pertains to public health issues for the Minnesota consumer. Includes bibliographical references.

*Biennial Report* (St. Paul, MN: State of Minnesota, Office of the Attorney General 1981–82– ).
This is a continuation of the *Selected opinions of the Attorney General* which included a report of the AG's activities for a two-year period.

*Biennial Report of the Attorney General of Minnesota for the Two Years, Ending.* . . . (St. Paul, MN: The Pioneer Press Co., [1939] v. –1938) 24 cm.
Continued by *Report of the Attorney General to the Governor, State of Minnesota.*

*Funding Legal Services: A Report to the Legislature* (St. Paul, MN: State of Minnesota, Office of the Attorney General, Task Force for Funding Legal Services 1994) 45 leaves.
This report deals with the responsibility of the state to fund legal services to indigent persons.

*(The) Hofstede Committee Report: Juvenile Prostitution in Minnesota* (St. Paul, MN: State of Minnesota, Office of the Attorney General, 1999) 22, [8] p. Includes bibliographical references.
A report on teenage prostitution in Minnesota.

## Chapter Five. Finding Aids and Secondary Sources 161

*(The) Landfill Cleanup Insurance Recovery Project: 1997 Progress Report to the Legislature,* Michelle Beeman & Thomas Newman (St. Paul, MN: State of Minnesota, Office of the Attorney General: Minnesota Pollution Control Agency [1998]) 1 v. (various pagings).

Mandated by 1996 Minn. Laws, ch. 370, § 6, this is a study of pollution liability insurances and a review of the law of sanitary landfills and recommendations for future legislation in Minnesota.

*Medical Malpractice Reform and Healthcare Costs: Final Report* (St. Paul, MN: State of Minnesota, Office of the Attorney General 1996) 20 p.

A review of the medical malpractice and its impact on health care cost and the insurance industry in Minnesota.

*OSHA Staffing: A Report to the Legislature* (St. Paul, MN: State of Minnesota, Office of the Attorney General 1992) 1 v. (various pagings)

This report deals with the adequacy of staff and budget to inspect Minnesota work sites.

*Opinions of the Attorneys General of the State of Minnesota* (St. Paul, MN: West Publishing Co., Jan. 1, 1884– ).

Report dated Jan. 1, 1884 covers the period from the organization of the state in 1858 to 1884. Continued by Minnesota, Attorney General, *Biennial Report of the Attorney General of Minnesota, for the Two Years Ending....*

*Report of the Attorney General to the Governor, State of Minnesota* ([S.l.: s.n., v.; 1939/1940– ).

Title may vary. Continued by Minnesota, Attorney General, *Selected Opinions of the Attorney General....*

*Report of the Attorney General's Arson Task Force* (St. Paul, MN: Office of Minnesota Attorney General [1997]) 1 v. (various pagings).

Report of a fifteen-month study aimed at reducing arson by a nineteen-member group of fire investigators, police, prosecutors, legislators, and others.

*Report Pursuant to Minnesota Statutes Sections 8.08 and 8.15, Subdivision 4 . . . Fiscal Year. . . .* (St. Paul, MN: State of Minnesota, Office of the Attorney General 1996– ).

Biennial report to the governor of all actions and proceedings in which the AG has appeared for the state along with a tabulation of expenses incurred, fines, penalties and tables showing offenses reported to the AG by county attorneys.

Other reports are specific to particular topics or mandates of the legislature. Note that titles often are indicative of the content of the report.

*Report to the Legislature from the Task Force for Funding Legal Services,* Minnesota, Attorney General, Task Force for Funding Legal Services (St. Paul, MN: State of Minnesota, Office of the Attorney General, Task Force for Funding Legal Services [1999]) 3, [8] leaves.

Mandated by 1998 Minn. Laws, ch. 366, § 3, regarding the role of government attorneys in Minnesota state government. Deals with funding legal services, both criminal and civil, in Minnesota.

*Report to the Legislature on the Status of Indian Gambling in Minnesota,* submitted by Governor Arne H. Carlson, Attorney General Hubert H. Humphrey III, Tribal-State Compact Negotiating Committee (St. Paul, MN: The Governor [1991]) 1 v. (various pagings).

A report on Indian gambling in Minnesota which discusses the benefits to the various tribes involved in the gaming industry as well as the problems gambling is creating for the Indians such as graft and corruption.

*(A) Report to the Minnesota Legislature Concerning Interscholastic Athletic Equity in Minnesota High Schools,* Robert A. Dildine (St. Paul, MN: State of Minnesota, Office of the Attorney General 1992) 1 v. (various pagings).

This report deals with gender issues in sports and athletic programs in Minnesota secondary education.

*Report to the Minnesota Legislature Regarding the Formation and Activities of the Minnesota Criminal Gang Oversight Council and the Minnesota Gang Strike Force,* David Steinkamp (St. Paul, MN: State of Minnesota, Office of the Attorney General 1998) 6 leaves.

This report deals with the Minnesota Criminal Gang Oversight Council and Minnesota Gang Strike Force and their role in relationship to gangs in Minnesota.

## Chapter Five. Finding Aids and Secondary Sources

*Report to the Senate Committees on Environment and Natural Resources, and Crime Prevention and the House Committees on the Environment and Natural Resources, and Judiciary* (St. Paul, MN: State of Minnesota, Office of the Attorney General 1994) 1, [9] leaves.
A report on the role of the Minnesota Pollution Control Agency in relation to Minnesota environmental law and policy. Special focus on the criminal provisions and liability for environmental damages.

*Safe Schools: Secondary Survey Compilation Report 1994–2000* (St. Paul, Mn: Office of the Minnesota Attorney General 2000) 42 p. Includes illustrations.
A report on preventing school violence and the role of school discipline in Minnesota schools.

*Selected Opinions of the Attorney General . . . State of Minnesota* [S.l.: s.n., v.) 28 cm.
Continued by Minnesota, Attorney General, *Biennial Report.*

*State Government Attorneys: An Attorney General Report to the Legislature,* Minnesota, Attorney General (St. Paul, MN: State of Minnesota, Office of the Attorney General 1990) 19 leaves.
Mandated by 1989 Minn. Laws, ch. 335, art. 1, § 12, subd. 7, ¶ 4, this report deals with the role of government attorneys in Minnesota.

*Status Report: Joint Executive Legislative Task Force on the Availability and Funding for Legal Services* (St. Paul, MN: State of Minnesota, Office of the Attorney General [1998]) [4] leaves.
Mandated by 1998 Minn. Laws, ch. 366, § 3. Follow-up to the 1994 report.

### § 546. Treatises and Practice Manuals

§ 546.1. Continuing Legal Education Publications
§ 546.2. Selected Treatises and Practice Manuals
§ 546.3. Popular Works
§ 546.4. Jury Instruction Guides
§ 546.5. Jury Verdicts, Valuation Handbooks, Etc.
§ 546.6. Judicial Bench Books

§ 546.7. Handbooks, Manuals, Etc.
§ 546.8. Statistics

A legal treatise is a volume (or volumes) written by one or more authors and concerning a specific legal subject. A treatise usually provides more exhaustive coverage of a topic than a legal encyclopedia or a periodical article. Treatises may serve as an introduction to a subject, as the definitive treatment of a subject, or as a guide to practitioners.

Practice manuals are similar to treatises but contain less editorial commentary. They generally provide step-by-step procedures for practitioners.

### § 546.1. Continuing Legal Education Publications

In November 1975, Minnesota became the first state with a mandatory continuing legal education (CLE) requirement. The State Board of Continuing Legal Education[383] approves courses for credit. These courses usually are accompanied by substantive treatises or practical manuals. More than 1,500 manuals have been published in connection with these MCLE courses. Many traditional topics are presented annually, e.g., corporation law, family law, probate and trust law, labor law, and tax law. Additionally, MCLE publications often provide the first source of information on developing areas of law. Lists of MCLE approved courses are published periodically in *Bench & Bar of Minnesota*. The following Minnesota organizations,[384] created to offer CLE courses, are primary sources of course materials.

- ▶ Minnesota Continuing Legal Education. A Division of the Minnesota State Bar Association; 40 North Milton Street, St. Paul, MN 55104-7027; phone 651-227-8266; Web address <http://www.minncle.org>.
- ▶ Minnesota Institute of Legal Education. Suite 202, 1313 5th Street SE, Minneapolis, MN 55414-4504; phone 612-379-1128; Web address <http://www.mile.org>.

---

383. See *Rules of Minnesota Board of Continuing Legal Education*. 15 MINN. STAT. "Court Rules," § 1202. *See also* <http://mbcle.state.mn.us/clerules_7_0.htm> (last visited Jan. 22, 2002).
384. Advanced Legal Education at Hamline University School of Law sponsored more than 350 seminars and workshops. It was disbanded in 1991.

# Chapter Five. Finding Aids and Secondary Sources

Most of the major law libraries collect CLE publications. Generally, CLE materials in libraries are cataloged and classified by subject. Few libraries place CLE materials in one particular area of the library. Instead, the CLE item will be classified and fall within the Library of Congress classification scheme. Hence a subject search of the library's catalog is the best way to locate CLE items.

## § 546.2. Selected Treatises and Practice Manuals

The following list of treatises and practice materials clearly is not exhaustive. Out-of-print materials have been included because many libraries keep them. The works are arranged alphabetically by title.

*Advising Minnesota Corporations & Other Business Organizations,* Richard Saliterman et al. (Charlottesville, VA: Michie 1995– ) 4 v.

Covers all issues concerning business from start-up to dissolution. Includes internal issues such as governance but also external forces that affect the business, such as legislation.

*Civil Commitment in Minnesota,* 2d ed., Eric S. Janus (St. Paul, MN: Butterworth Legal Publishers, ceased publication) 1 v. (loose-leaf).

This manual, written by the chair of the committee that drafted the special commitment rules, is a guide to the commitment process from admission through discharge or review. Numerous forms are included.

*Criminal Procedure from Police Detention to Final Disposition: Under the United States Constitution and Minnesota Law,* C. Paul Jones (St. Paul, MN: William Mitchell College Law Forum Publications 1981) 2 v.

As indicated by the title, this work by the Minnesota Public Defender (*see* §§ 650.14, 671.1, *infra*) sets forth the step-by-step processing of a criminal case. Interpretation of criminal procedure by the U.S. Supreme Court and the Minnesota Supreme Court is emphasized.

*Debtors' and Creditors' Rights and Remedies* (St. Paul, MN: Minnesota Continuing Legal Education 1992) 1 v. (various pagings).

This text discusses the topics of judgments, execution and discovery, receiverships, composition agreements and assignments for the benefits of creditors, replevin and claim and delivery, attachment, mechanics liens, contractors' surety bonds, statutory liens, fraudulent transfers, bulk transfers, and remedies of a secured creditor under Uniform Commercial Code Article 9.

*Desk Manual: Checklists, Worksheets and Forms,* prepared by Forms and Worksheets Committee, Minnesota State Bar Association (St. Paul, MN: Minnesota Continuing Legal Education 1979– ) 1 v. (loose-leaf).

This publication explains, step by step, the major legal transactions a Minnesota lawyer is likely to face. Each chapter provides checklists, worksheets, forms, and practice tips for handling the most common legal problems. Twelve major areas of Minnesota law are covered: business organizations, credits and collections, workers' compensation, civil trial preparation, secured transactions, real estate, family law, estate planning, personal injury, misdemeanors, professional responsibility, and general matters.

*Drafting Wills and Trust Agreements,* 5th ed. (St. Paul, MN: Minnesota Continuing Legal Education 1999– ) 1 v. (loose-leaf), forms.

Includes essentials of estate planning; basic will; contingent/disclaimer trust will; maritalized family trust will; spouse's contingent pour-over will; maritalized revocable trust; pour-over will to maritalized trust; revocable trust for single person; pour-over will to revocable trust; health care directive; minor's trust under IRC 2503(c); annual exclusion (Crummey) trusts; antenuptial agreement; powers of attorney; designation of guardian; disclaimer; revocable trust with disclaimer; qualified domestic trust will (QDOT); miscellaneous documents.

*(The) Drinking Driver in Minnesota: Criminal and Civil Issues,* 3d ed., Frederic Bruno (Charlottesville, VA: Michie, 2000– ) 1 v. (loose-leaf). Includes index.

Written for the practicing attorney, this volume contains substantive and procedural material on the legal aspects of prosecuting and defending a drinking and driving case. It provides practical and technical information on chemical testing and the medical aspects of alcohol consumption including a chapter on "treatment for the alcoholic." Features include forms and questions for voir dire, direct, and cross examination.

*(An) Employer's Guide to Employment Law Issues in Minnesota,* Minnesota Small Business Assistance Office, Lindquist & Vennum (St. Paul, MN: Minnesota Department of Trade and Economic Development 1990– ) 1 v. (annual).

Covers labor and employment law in Minnesota. Includes bibliographical references.

## Chapter Five. Finding Aids and Secondary Sources

*Employment in Minnesota: A Guide to Employment Practices and Regulations,* 3d ed., Maynard. G. Sautter (Charlottesville, VA: Lexis Law Publishing 1997) 1 v. (loose-leaf) (annual supplementation).

This clearly written guide is intended for the small business. It provides a comprehensive overview of the laws that govern working conditions and the employer-employee relationship.

*Mason's Dunnell on Minnesota Probate Law,* 3d ed. (St. Paul, MN: Butterworth Legal Publishers 1969–70) 3 v. (pocket-part supplementation).

Although this work was superseded in part by *Stein on Probate,* and is outdated to some extent by the enactment of the Uniform Probate Code, some sections still are useful, e.g., the chapters on wills. Because the text consists of summaries of court decisions with footnoted citations to case law and statutes, it also may be used as a digest to probate case law.

*Mason's Minnesota Motor Vehicle Law,* 3d ed. (St. Paul, MN: Mason Publishing Co. 1975) 3 v.

This work, although dated, is the only comprehensive treatment of Minnesota motor vehicle law. Its format is similar to that of *Dunnell Minnesota Digest.* There is an appendix of pleading forms suggested by *Pirsig on Minnesota Pleading.* Although a commentary on no-fault insurance is included, more recent texts should be used for this information.

*Minnesota Administrative Practice and Procedure,* William J. Keppel & Dayton Gilbert (St. Paul, MN: Advanced Legal Education, Hamline University School of Law 1982) 1 v.

The preface states that the book is a summary answering the most frequently encountered questions and referring to other sources for more complete information. This well-written treatise is a fairly current overview of a subject experiencing great change and development.

*Minnesota Adoption Law and Practice with Forms and Statutes,* Amy M. Silberberg (Charlottesville, VA: Michie 1999) 1 v.

Suitable for judges, lawyers, social workers, or adoption agency workers. Reflects the 1994 change in the Minnesota statute regarding adoption. Includes index.

*Minnesota Civil Commitment and Treatment Act Training Seminar: Training Materials,* prepared by members of the staff of the Office of the Minnesota Attorney General; presented by the Office of the Attorney General and Hamline University School of Law (produced with the assistance of HUSL with funds provided by the Office of the Ombudsman for Mental Health and Mental Retardation [S.l.: s.n. 1998]) 1 v. (various pagings), forms, samples.

Overview of civil commitment in Minnesota. Topics include advance directives, early intervention, hold orders, sample pre-commitment and recommitment forms, reports, neuroleptic medication procedures, provisional discharge, alternatives to commitment, and advocacy.

*Minnesota Civil Practice,* 3d ed., Douglas D. McFarland & William J. Keppel (Charlottesville, VA: Lexis Legal Publishing 1999) 4 v. (annual pocket-part supplementation).

This work is a comprehensive treatment of civil procedure, including sample forms. The textual statements are supported by footnoted citations to case law and statutes, legal periodicals, and treatises. Volume 4 includes an index to rules discussed and to forms discussed, and a subject index for all four volumes.

*Minnesota Collections,* Allen J. Zlimen (West Pub. Co. 1980– ) 1 v. (annual updates) (loose-leaf).

This volume is written for lawyers and their secretaries or legal assistants. It provides an overview of the law citing statutes and cases, detailed checklists of procedures, and forms. Also included are references to relevant articles found in other publications.

*Minnesota Condemnation Law,* Robert J. Lindall, John M. LeFebre & Mary G. Dobbins (Lexis Law Publishing 1992) 1 v. (loose-leaf) forms.

Contains practice tips; forms; and analysis of the history of eminent domain, its limitations, purpose, and power; as well as the proceedings.

*Minnesota Corporation Law & Practice,* John H. Matheson & Philip S. Garon (Englewood Cliffs, NJ: Prentice Hall Law & Business 1992) 1 v. (various pagings).

National corporation law series. Includes index.

*Minnesota Corporations Practice Manual,* Bert Black (Lexis Law Pub. 1993) 1 v. (loose-leaf).

Analysis of a Minnesota corporation's life from inception to dissolution. Includes forms.

## Chapter Five. Finding Aids and Secondary Sources

*Minnesota Crimes and Defenses,* James W. Forbess (ed.) (St. Paul, MN: Butterworth Legal Publishers 1991–1993) 3 v. (loose-leaf).
This practice guide covers the topic of Minnesota criminal law and procedure, and actions and defenses. Includes index.

*Minnesota Crimes, Vehicles and Related Statutes* (Gould Publications) (annual).
The complete, up-to-date Minnesota criminal and motor vehicle laws; plus related statutes with all legislative changes in text on CD-ROM.

*Minnesota Criminal Law Series* (Butterworth).
A series of six titles.

- *Criminal Appeals: Effective Practice and Procedure,* Michael F. Cromett & Gregory A. Gaut (Minnesota Criminal Law Series; St. Paul, MN: Butterworth Legal Publishers 1984–1992) 1 v. (loose-leaf). Includes bibliographical references and index. This is a practitioner's guide to the title topic and includes sample forms.
- *Criminal Evidence: Constitutional, Statutory & Rules Limitations,* Richard S. Frase (Minnesota Criminal Law Series; St. Paul, MN: Butterworth Legal Publishers 1985–1992) 1 v. (loose-leaf). Includes bibliographical references and index. Covers in detail the rules of criminal evidence, the exclusionary rule, search and seizure, and other aspects of criminal procedure in Minnesota.
- *Felony Sentencing in Minnesota,* C. Peter Erlinder & John M. Stuart (Minnesota Criminal Law Series; St. Paul, MN: Butterworth Legal Publishers 1985–1992) 1 v. (loose-leaf). Includes bibliographical references and index.
- *(The) Juvenile Court Handbook: A Practitioner's Guide to Juvenile Court Practice in Minnesota,* Wright S. Walling (Minnesota Criminal Law Series; St. Paul, MN: Butterworth Legal Publishers 1984–1992) 1 v. (loose-leaf). Includes bibliographical references and index.
- *Minnesota Criminal Jury Trial Handbook,* Carol Grant with contributions by Diane M. Wiley (Minnesota Criminal Law Series; St. Paul, MN: Butterworth Legal Publishers 1988–1992) 1 v. (loose-leaf). Includes index.
- *Minnesota Criminal Pretrial Practice & Procedure,* Mark W. Peterson, Mark D. Nyvold & Jerod H. Peterson (Minnesota Criminal Law Series; St. Paul, MN: Butterworth 1986– ) 1 v. (loose-leaf), forms. Includes bibliographical references and index.

*Minnesota Cause of Action Manual*, 2d ed., Shawn M. Bartsh (ed.) (Minneapolis, MN: Minnesota Trial Lawyers Ass'n 1990) 1 v. (various pagings), forms.
Analysis of various causes of action and their defenses in Minnesota.

*Minnesota Criminal and Traffic Law Manual, 2000–2001 Edition,* Publisher's Editorial Staff (Charlottesville, VA: Michie 2000) 1323 p. (softbound).
Compiles Minnesota statutes dealing with criminal and traffic offenses.

*Minnesota Data Privacy Opinions Reporter* (St. Paul, MN: American Law Books, first issue 1998) (semiannual), 1 v. (loose-leaf).
Reports of the opinions of the Minnesota Commissioner of Administration regarding the Minnesota Government Data Practices Act.

*Minnesota Dissolution of Marriage,* William Haugh Jr. (Rochester, NY: Lawyers Co-operative Pub. Co. 1979– ) 1 v. (loose-leaf) (annual supplementation).
Practice systems library series. Includes index. Contains analysis of matrimonial actions and divorce in Minnesota with forms.

*Minnesota Environmental Law Handbook,* 2d ed., the attorneys of Dorsey & Whitney, William J. Keppel & Steven M. Christenson (eds.) Rebecca A. Comstock et al. contributors (Rockville, MD: Government Institutes 1994) xvi, 360 p. State Environmental Law Handbook Series.
Includes bibliographical references and index. Overview of Minnesota environmental regulation. Contains descriptions of state and local agencies with responsibility for environmental programs including air, water, wetlands, Superfund administration hazardous waste, etc.

*Minnesota Evidence Courtroom Manual,* Glen Weissenberger (Anderson Publishing 1998) 400 p.
Provides analysis, commentary, and answers for applying the rules of evidence arising in trials and hearings.

*Minnesota Evidence Trialbook,* Bertrand Portinsky (Charlottesville, VA: Lexis Law Publishing 1987) 1 v. (loose-leaf) (annual supplementation).
Provides access to rules of evidence that apply to the courtroom and the taking of depositions.

## Chapter Five. Finding Aids and Secondary Sources 171

*Minnesota Evidentiary Foundations,* Roger C. Park, Bertrand Portinsky, Martin J. Costello & Edward J. Imwinkelried (Charlottesville, VA: Lexis Law Publishing 1996) (annual supplementation).
Demonstrations on how to lay the foundation for the admission of evidence and conduct questioning in both civil and criminal cases.

*Minnesota Family Law Digest,* Marybeth Dorn (ed.) (St. Paul, MN: Mason Pub. Co. 1983– ) 1 v. (loose-leaf).
Includes index.

*Minnesota Family Law Practice Manual,* 3d ed., Neil B. Davidson (St. Paul, MN: Butterworth 2000– ) 2 v. (loose-leaf), forms.
Outlines the procedural and substantive guidance on the full range of issues that arise in family law practice including domestic relations, parent and child law, and support. Statutes, rules, and forms needed to handle divorce and other family law matters in Minnesota courts.

*Minnesota Family Law Primer,* Lawyer's 2d ed., Robert E. Oliphant (St. Paul, MN: Creative Legal Communications, Inc. 1990– ) 1 v. (loose-leaf).
Covers primarily marriage and divorce topics but also includes discussions on adoption, antenuptial agreements, determining parental rights, paternity, and domestic abuse.

*Minnesota Insurance Law,* Clarance E. Hagglund, Britton D. Weimer & Andrew F. Whitman (Minneapolis, MN: Common Law 1995) 1 v.
Includes index.

*Minnesota Legal Systems, Probate,* Mark D. Helland (Rochester, NY: Lawyers Co-operative 1979– ) 1 v. (loose-leaf) (annual supplementation).
Overview of statutes and practice of probate in Minnesota. Details the proceedings, administration, and taxation of estates. Includes letters, forms, local court rules, and probate definitions. Includes bibliographical references and index.

*Minnesota Limitations Manual: Abstracts of Time Limitations from Minnesota Statutes and Rules of Court,* 3d ed. (Charlottesville, VA: Michie 2000– ) 1 v. (loose-leaf) (annual supplementation).
Includes all time limitations, both civil and criminal, of concern to the practicing attorney. A detailed subject index is included. The reader also is referred to "Minnesota Statutes of Limitations" in 1978 *Hamline Law Review* issue I, for additional information.

*Minnesota Liquor Liability Law,* Lindsay G. Arthur Jr., Colby B. Lund, et al. (Minneapolis, MN: Minnesota Institute of Legal Education 1994) 207 p., forms. Includes bibliography.

Provides an historical background of the Minnesota Dram Shop Act as well as elements of proof under the act and common issues involving the Dram Shop Act.

*Minnesota Mechanics Liens Practice Manual,* James. E. Snoxell (Charlottesville, VA: Lexis Law Publishing 1991).

A practical analysis of Minn. Stat. 514, with forms and practice tips.

*Minnesota Medical Malpractice,* John F. Eisberg (Charlottesville, VA: Lexis Law Pub. 1990– ) 1 v. (loose-leaf), forms. Includes bibliographical references and index.

Details the trial of a medical malpractice suit in Minnesota.

*Minnesota Misdemeanors and Moving Traffic Violations,* 3d ed., Martin J. Costello, Richard S. Frase & Stephen M. Simon (Charlottesville VA: Michie 1999) 2 v. (loose-leaf) (semiannual supplementation).

These volumes provide practitioners with coverage of pretrial, trial, and appellate practice for offenses ranging from enhanced gross misdemeanors to traffic violations. Includes information on criminal procedure and the substantive law of misdemeanors and moving traffic violations. Textual statements are supported by citations to federal and state case law and state statutes.

*Minnesota No-Fault Automobile Insurance,* 2d ed., Michael K. Steenson (Charlottesville, VA: Lexis Law Publishing 2000) 2 v. (loose-leaf).

This book, by a professor of tort law specializing in this field, reflects the importance of the legislative history of the act and provides a comprehensive overview and analysis of policy and cases. A checklist of issues with citations to statutes and case law is included.

*Minnesota Nonprofit Corporations: A Corporate and Tax Guide,* John S. Hibbs (St. Paul, MN: Minnesota Continuing Legal Education 1979) (annual pocket parts).

This guide is a one-volume compilation of corporate, tax, and other law applicable to the organization, operation, and dissolution of a nonprofit corporation in Minnesota.

## Chapter Five. Finding Aids and Secondary Sources

*Minnesota Objections at Trial,* Ann D. Montgomery, Myron H. Bright & Ronald L. Carlson (Charlottesville, VA: Lexis Law Publishing 1992) 1 v.
In a pocket-sized format, this guide is designed for use as a quick finder for state and federal objections.

*Minnesota Partnership Practice,* Minnesota State Bar Association, Continuing Legal Education (St. Paul, MN: Minnesota Continuing Legal Education 1992) 1 v. (various pagings).
This book is designed to assist Minnesota attorneys in drafting effective partnership agreements and to provide guidance on handling partnership litigation, dissolution, and taxation. It also includes an appendix of sample clauses and forms.

*Minnesota Practice* (St. Paul, MN: West Group) (pocket-part supplementation.
This multi-volume set has annotations to court rules, jury instruction guides, and other matters of concern to the practicing attorney. Volumes are published and authored separately.

- Volumes 1, 1A, 2, 2A, *Civil Rules Annotated,* 3d ed., David F. Herr & Roger S. Haydock (1998).[385]
- Volume 3, *Appellate Rules Annotated,* 3d ed., Eric J. Magnuson & David F. Herr (1996).
- Volume 3A, *General Rules of Practice Annotated,* David F. Herr (West Group 1992– ).
- Volumes 4, 4A, *Jury Instruction Guides, Civil* (CIVJIG), 4th ed., Minnesota District Judges Association Committee on Jury Instruction Guides, Michael K. Steenson & Peter B. Knapp, Reporters (1999). *See also* § 546.4, *infra.*
- Volumes 5, 5A, 6, 6A, *Methods of Practice,* 3d ed., Steven J. Kirsch and a group of Minnesota practice experts (1998).
- Volumes 7–9, *Criminal Law and Procedure,* Henry W. McCarr (1976).
- Volumes 10, 10A, *Minnesota Jury Instruction Guides, Criminal* (CRIMJIG), 4th ed., Minnesota District Judges Association Committee on Criminal Jury Instruction Guides, Stephen Forestell, Interim Reporter (1999). *See also* § 546.4, *infra.*
- Volume 11, *Evidence,* 2d ed., Peter N. Thompson (1992).

---

385. Predecessors to this set are: O. Aaron Youngquist & Benjamin J. Blacik, *Minnesota Rules Practice* (1953); James L. Hetland Jr. & Oscar C. Adamson II, *Rules of Civil Procedure Annotated* (1970).

- Volume 11A, *Courtroom Handbook of Minnesota Evidence,* Peter N. Thompson & David F. Herr (2000).
- Volumes 12–13, *Juvenile Law and Practice,* Robert Scott & John O. Sonsteng (1997).
- Volume 14, *Family Law,* 2d ed., Martin L. Swaden & Linda A. Olup (St. Paul, MN: West Pub. Co. 2000), xxix, 864 p.; forms; 27 cm.
- Volume 15, *Civil Practice Forms,* Roger S. Haydock (1995).
- Volume 17, *Employment Law and Practice,* Stephen F. Befort (1995).
- Volume 17A, *Minnesota Employment Laws* (2000).
- Volume 18, *Corporation Law and Practice,* John H. Matheson (1996).
- Volume 20, *Business Law Deskbook,* John H. Matheson (1998).
- Volume 21, *Administrative Practice and Procedure,* William J. Keppel (1998).

*Minnesota Public Sector Labor Law,* Stephen D. Gordon et al. (St. Paul, MN: Mason Publishing Co. 1983) 1 v.

Covers Minnesota collective labor agreements, collective bargaining procedure, and employee-management relations in Minnesota government. It also provides a detailed analysis of administrative agency decisions and policies, court decisions, and attorney generals' opinions. It also predicts future trends based upon this historical analysis, private sector law, and cases from other states. Includes bibliographical references.

*Minnesota Real Estate,* Gordon W. Shumaker & Clinton R. McLagan (Rochester, NY: Lawyers Co-operative Pub. Co. 1981– ) 1 v. (loose-leaf). Practice systems library series.

Provides the information a Minnesota lawyer needs to schedule, complete, and document routine real estate transactions. Contains forms and letters. Annual supplementation.

*Minnesota Residential Real Estate,* James. D. Olson (ed.) (Charlottesville, VA: Lexis Law Publishing 1991) 2 v. (loose-leaf).

Covers all aspects of realty law from purchase to closing. Includes the areas of property interest, title, conveyancing, types of residences, brokers, landlord/tenant, mortgages, foreclosure, contract for deed, and restrictions on use. Includes forms. Semiannual supplementation.

## Chapter Five. Finding Aids and Secondary Sources

*Minnesota Real Estate Law Practice Manual,* Neil B. Davidson [sr. ed.] [Steven C. Pedersen, editor-in-chief] (St. Paul, MN: Butterworth Legal Publishers 1985–1990) 1 v. (loose-leaf).

Written for the Minnesota practitioner, this manual outlines real property law in Minnesota. Includes forms.

*Minnesota Standards for Title Examination* (Minneapolis, MN: Minnesota State Bar Ass'n, Section of Real Property Law 1947) 1 v. (loose-leaf) (with supplementation when standards are revised or issued).

This volume is a compilation of the standards used in examining title to real property in Minnesota. These standards, approved by the Minnesota State Bar Association, are designed to distinguish between those defects that impair marketability of title and those that are inconsequential. A table listing curative acts passed since 1931 that are pertinent to the examination of real property titles also is provided (*see also* § 255, *supra*).

*Minnesota State Rules of Evidence with Objections,* Anthony J. Bocchino, David A. Sonenshein & John O Sonsteng (National Institute of Trial Advocacy 1994).

Pocket-sized *Minnesota Rules of Evidence with Objections* has practice tips, key phrases, interpretations, and thumb indexing for quick reference.

*Minnesota Tax Appeals,* Earl B. Gustafson, original material on Minnesota Tax Court and legal research provided by Eileen Knabe (Charlottesville, VA: Lexis Law Pub. 1989) 1 v. (loose-leaf).

Includes procedures on lodging tax protests and appeals in Minnesota as wells as techniques and methods of researching tax law in Minnesota. Includes forms and index.

*Minnesota Tax Reporter: State and Local, All Taxes, All Taxables* (Chicago, IL: Commerce Clearing House 1958– ) 2 v. (loose-leaf).

Covers statutes and cases and analysis of income, property, excise, and city taxes, as well as new matters in Minnesota tax law. Includes forms. Kept up to date by current reports.

*Minnesota Unemployment Insurance Guide,* Clarence A. Anderson (St. Paul, MN: Mason Publishing Co. 1984).

This brief guide provides a thorough analysis of unemployment law in Minnesota including the appeal process. A supplement reprints the relevant statutes.

*Minnesota Uniform Commercial Code Deskbook,* Uniform Commercial Code Committee of the Corporation, Banking and Business Law Section of the Minnesota State Bar Association (St. Paul, MN: Minnesota CLE Press 1983, 1984– ) 2 v. (loose-leaf) (annual supplements). Includes bibliography and index.

This *Deskbook,* designed to provide a quick and accurate guide to the UCC in Minnesota, is intended to replace the 1966 *Deskbook.* It includes an outline and official comments of the UCC, the text of the Minnesota UCC with deviations noted, and related statutes and regulations. New in the *Deskbook* is a section on the federal bankruptcy code and an outline of various Minnesota usury laws.

*Minnesota Wills & Estate Planning,* Susan L. Neumeyer & Joyce M. James (eds.) (Charlottesville, VA: Lexis Law Publishing 1993) 1 v. (loose-leaf).

Prepared for the general practitioner who does not have particular expertise in estate planning.

*Municipal Codes of Minnesota: A Working Bibliography,* Ted Kruse (Chicago, IL: CPL Bibliographies 1985) 20 p. CPL bibliography series; no. 163.

Although out of date, this text remains a good source for finding bibliographic data regarding municipal ordinances in Minnesota.

*Pirsig on Minnesota Pleading,* 5th ed., Maynard E. Pirsig (Charlottesville, VA: Lexis Law Publishing 1991) 2 v.

Contains information of practical value for the practitioner. Describes the factors that the lawyer must consider in drafting the pleadings for a lawsuit and includes sample forms. Textual statements are supported by case law and statutory citations. Pocket-part supplementation.

*Practitioner's Guide to Minnesota No-Fault Act,* 2d ed., James R. Schwebel & Diane C. Hanson (Minneapolis, MN: Minnesota Trial Lawyers Ass'n 1983).

Discusses the special issues involved in Minnesota motor vehicle insurance law stemming from this act and its implications for attorneys.

*State and Local Taxes, Minnesota* (New York: Research Institute of America, Inc. 1993– ) 1 v. (loose-leaf).

Covers Minnesota law and legislation regarding taxation in general as well as local taxation and taxation of corporations.

### Chapter Five. Finding Aids and Secondary Sources

*Stein on Probate, Administration of Decedents' Estates Under the Uniform Probate Code as Enacted in Minnesota,* 3d ed., Robert Stein (Charlottesville, VA: Lexis Law Publishing 1995) 2 v. (loose-leaf) (updated irregularly).

A practical reference about Minnesota probate law, this book describes the actions required and choices available in all phases of the administration of a decedent's estate. Includes more than 400 pages of probate forms.

*(The) Student Lawyer: A Guide to Minnesota's Legal System,* 4th reprint ed., Minnesota State Bar Association & Joseph L. Daly et al. (St. Paul, MN: West Publishing Co. 1986) 217 p., ill.

Topics include consumer law, alcohol, tobacco and drugs; civil law; parents and children; school issues; lifestyles; dissolution of marriage; criminal and juvenile justice.

*(The) Student Lawyer: High School Handbook of Minnesota Law,* 3d ed., Joseph L. Daly et al. (St. Paul, MN: West Publishing Co. 1986) 1 v.

A brief but comprehensive text covering questions asked frequently by non-lawyers. Especially useful for speaking to students or community groups.

*Trial Handbook for Minnesota Lawyers,* Ronald I. Meshbesher (Rochester, NY: Lawyers Cooperative Publishing 1992) 1 v.

Trial guide designed to be used at trial. Focuses on procedural and substantive aspects of trial with analysis of recent federal and Minnesota cases, statutes, and rules. Supplemented with annual pocket parts.

*Usury Laws in Minnesota,* Mary K. McLaughlin (St. Paul, MN: Butterworth Legal Publishers 1984) 1 v. (loose-leaf).

A brief but comprehensive overview of usury law. Liberal references to primary sources are included.

#### § 546.3. Popular Works

The term "popular works" generally applies to legal materials designed for the layman. The following titles fall into that category.

*Dealing with Debt: A Guide to the Rights and Responsibilities of Debtors in Minnesota,* 3d ed. (St. Paul, MN: Minnesota Legal Services Coalition 2001) 45 p., ill., forms.

This work by several Minnesota legal services organizations gives basic information about consumer debt.

*Divorce in Minnesota for Non-Lawyers: A Guide to the Legal System,* new & rev. ed. Judith A. Mart (Anaheim, CA: Divorce Seminars & Information 2000) 91 p. Includes bibliographic references.

This is a revised edition of an earlier work dealing with the steps for filing for divorce in Minnesota.

*Getting a Divorce: A Basic Guide to Minnesota Law,* 9th ed. (St. Paul, MN: Minnesota Legal Services Coalition 2000) 45 p.

This publication is the work of several Minnesota legal services organizations. It offers basic information regarding marriage dissolution.

*Getting Protection from Abuse and Harassment: A Guide for Obtaining Court Orders,* 1st ed., Maria K. Pastoor, Liz Richards & Margaret A. Penn (St. Paul, MN: Minnesota Legal Services Coalition 1995) 42 p., forms.

A discussion for the victims of family violence; law, legislation, and the legal status and laws pertaining to victims of abuse and harassment in Minnesota.

*Guide to Public Assistance Programs: People's Rights and the Law,* 10th ed. (St. Paul, MN: Minnesota Legal Services Coalition with Minnesota Board on Aging 1994) 1 v.

Deals with public welfare law in Minnesota. "Prepared by the Minnesota Legal Services Coalition, with assistance from Southern Minnesota Regional Legal Services and Legal Services of Northwest Minnesota."—*Preface*

*How to File for Divorce in Minnesota: With Forms,* Thomas Tuft (Naperville, IL: Sphinx Pub. 2001) 282 p., forms, Legal Survival Guide Series.

A self-help manual that discusses the basics of the legal system; selection of a lawyers; case evaluation; procedures; summary dissolution; uncontested divorces; contested divorces; and court hearings.

*How to Form a Corporation, LLC or Partnership in Minnesota,* W. Dean Brown (Consumer Publishing Corporation 1999) 139 p.

This title guides the layman in forming a Minnesota corporation or other business enterprise.

*How to Form a Simple Corporation in Minnesota,* Donna-Marie Boulay & Mark Warda (SourceBooks, Clearwater, FL: Sphinx Pub. 1996) 138 p., forms. Take the Law into Your Own Hands Series; Self-help Law Kit Series.

Sections on securities law, non-profit corporations, Internet sites, sales tax, county and local use taxes, and licenses and permits.

**Chapter Five. Finding Aids and Secondary Sources** 179

*How to Form Your Own Minnesota Corporation Before the Inc. Dries: A Step by Step Guide with Forms,* Phillip Williams (Oak Park, IL: P. Gaines Company 1996) 138 p. Small business incorporation series; v. 7
This is basic guide on Minnesota corporation law and the process for incorporating a small business for the layman.

*How to Incorporate & Start a Business in Minnesota,* J. W. Dicks (Holbrook, MA: Adams Media Corp. 1998) 283 p., forms.
For the layman. Provides information for deciding what form a business will take along with raising capital, employment law, contracts, leases, credit, insurance, taxes, etc.

*How to Make a Minnesota Will,* Mark Warda & Elizabeth Wolf (Clearwater, FL: Sphinx Pub. 1996) 94 p., forms. Take the Law into Your Own Hands Series; Self-help Law Kit Series.
Gives Minnesota residents a basic understanding of the laws regarding wills, joint property and other types of ownership of property as they affect estate planning.

*How to Start a Business in Minnesota* by Julianne E. Ortman, Raymond C. Ortman & Mark Warda (Clearwater, FL: Sphinx Pub. 1996) 136 p.: forms. Take the Law into Your Own Hands Self-help Law Kit Series.
Part of the series dealing with business law and business enterprises in Minnesota.

*If You Lose Your Job . . . : Your Rights and Responsibilities,* 8th ed. (St. Paul, MN: Minnesota Legal Services Coalition 1995) 42 p.
A compilation of laws, rights, and services for the unemployed in Minnesota. Compiled by a group of legal service organizations and the Minnesota Department of Employment Security.

*Knowing Your Rights : a Guide to Minnesota's Senior Citizens' Legal Rights,* 10th ed. (St. Paul, MN: Minnesota Legal Services Coalition 1994) 84 p.
A legal guide for the elderly regarding their legal status, rights and responsibilities.

*Minnesota Divorce Law,* Robert W. Garrity (Minneapolis: Wellington Pub. Co. [1972]) 1 v.
Discussion of Minnesota divorce law and legislation.

*(The) Minnesota Divorce Revolution: A Plain English Explanation of Minnesota Divorce Law,* 2d ed., Jeanette A. Frederickson, Cort C. Holten & Jeffrey D. Bores (Minneapolis, MN: Regency Press 1995) 1 v.
Includes bibliographical references and forms.

*(A) Practical Guide to Successful Estate Planning: Iowa, Minnesota, North Dakota, South Dakota, Wisconsin,* Mark P. Alvig & Thomas M. Petracek (Specialty Press Publishers & Wholesalers, Inc. 1999) vii, 147p. The User Friendly Financial Series.
An overview of the law dealing with estates and the distribution of assets.

*Tenants' Rights & Responsibilities in Public Housing,* 4th ed. (St. Paul, MN: Minnesota Legal Services Coalition [1995]) 30 p.
A guide for residents of public housing, by a group of legal assistance organizations. Forms are included.

*Tenants Rights Handbook: Rights and Responsibilities for Tenants and Landlords in Minnesota,* [4th ed.] (joint project of: the Minnesota Public Interest Research Group, the Minnesota Tenants Union, and the St. Paul Tenants Union [Minneapolis, MN]: MPIRG, MTU, and SPTU 1991) 84 p., forms. Includes index.
A handbook for residential renters and landlords in Minnesota.

*Tenants' Rights in Minnesota,* 7th ed. (St. Paul, MN: Minnesota Legal Services Coalition 1994) 1 v.
Deals with landlords, tenant law, rental housing, etc. Prepared by the Minnesota Legal Services Coalition and the Southern Minnesota Regional Legal Services. Revised in 1995.

### § 546.4. Jury Instruction Guides

The rules governing juries are found in the court rules for civil procedure and criminal procedure (*see also* § 444, *supra*). The general rules of practice found in the court rules volume of the *Minnesota Statutes.* Additionally, the legislature has passed various statutes dealing with juries, courts, jury trials, trials, venire, and verdicts.

The "Civil JIGs" were first published in 1962.[386] They are published under the aegis of the Minnesota District Judges' Association. The CIVJIG committee is made up of about twenty trial judges who

---

386. Succeeding editions were published in 1974 and 1986, with the latest being 1999.

## Chapter Five. Finding Aids and Secondary Sources

draft the rules assisted by reporters. The practicing bar contributes to the revision of the CIVJIGS through the Civil Litigation Section of the Minnesota State Bar Association. Now in a fourth edition, the civil jury instructions are part of the Minnesota Practice series published by West Group.

*Minnesota Jury Instruction Guides: Civil* (CIVJIG), prepared by the Minnesota District Judges Association, Committee on Jury Instruction Guides (St. Paul, MN: West Group 1999) 2 v., forms; 1 computer diskette (3½ in.) v. 4, 4A Minnesota Practice series.

The instructions for criminal juries also are prepared by the Minnesota District Judges Association, Committee on Criminal Jury Instruction Guides (with the aid of a reporter). The committee is made up of thirteen district court judges. The CRIMJIGs are divided into three parts: general instructions to the jury, general principles of criminal law, and specific crimes. Previous editions were published in 1977, 1985, and 1990.

*Minnesota Jury Instruction Guides, Criminal* (CRIMJIG), prepared by the Minnesota District Judges Association, Committee on Criminal Jury Instruction Guides (St. Paul, MN: West Group 1999) 2 v., forms; 2 computer diskettes (3½ in.). v. 10, 10A Minnesota Practice series.

Another set of jury instructions deals with misdemeanors. It is not clear as to whether these JIGs have been superseded by the succeeding CRIMJIGs.

*Minnesota Jury Instruction Guides, Misdemeanor and Gross Misdemeanor* (MJIG), prepared by Sheryl Ramstad Hvass & H. Peter Albrecht (St. Paul, MN: West Pub. Co. 1986).

This title has been discontinued and misdemeanor jury instructions are now incorporated in the CRIMJIG volume.

*Manual of Model Criminal Jury Instructions for the District Courts of the U.S. Eighth Circuit*, 1996 ed., Committee on Model Criminal Jury Instructions within the Eighth Circuit (St. Paul, MN: West Publishing 1996) 1 v.

Minnesota is in the eighth circuit. These instructions were prepared to help judges communicate more effectively with juries. The manual is meant to provide judges and lawyers with models of clear, brief, and simple instructions calculated to maximize juror comprehension.

*Manual of Model Civil Jury Instructions for the District Courts of the Eighth Circuit*, 1999 ed., Committee on Model Jury Instructions (St. Paul, MN: West Publishing 1999) 1 v.

Provides judges and lawyers with models of clear, brief and simple instructions calculated to maximize juror comprehension.

### § 546.5. Jury Verdicts, Valuation Handbooks, Etc.

Damages awarded by juries are an important part of personal injury practice and other tort practice. Finding information about the amount of these awards sometimes are difficult to find. Several publications are issued for lawyers in Minnesota.

*Minnesota Case Reports* ([St. Paul], MN: Minnesota Trial Lawyers Ass'n 1981– ) 20 v. (loose-leaf).

Loose-leaf service issued as a supplement to *Minnesota Trial Lawyer*. Includes a complete set of all cases ever published in *Minnesota Trial Lawyer* (1975– ), and replaces the case reports section previously published in that magazine.

*Minnesota Damages Awards: Personal Injury & Intentional Torts: Analysis of Specific Dollar Awards by Type of Injury or Action* (Rochester, NY: Lawyers Cooperative Pub. 1993– ) 1 v., forms.

Provides a quick and easy means of researching Minnesota decisions for adequacy or excessiveness of damages in a number of key categories. There are separate chapters summarizing and analyzing punitive damages and under what circumstances punitive damages are allowed in medical malpractice suits and cases involving voluntary intoxication.

*Minnesota Lawyer* (Minneapolis, MN: Finance and Commerce, Inc. 1997– ) v. 1, no. 1 (Sept. 5, 1997).

Published weekly each Friday during the terms of the court, this newspaper prints full-text decisions by the Supreme Court and Court of Appeals including all criminal and civil decisions, tax court, and Office of Administrative Hearings decisions.

*Personal Injury Verdict Survey. Minnesota Edition* (Solon, OH: Jury Verdict Research, annual) 1 v.

Compiles plaintiff and defense verdicts and settlements from personal injury claims.

*TCJVR: Twin City Jury Verdict Reporter* (Willernie, MN (P.O. Box 334, Willernie, MN 55090-0334): Twin City Jury Verdict Reporter, Inc. 1998– ) v. 1, no.1 (First quarter 1998, Jan. 1–Mar. 31).

*TCJVR* is the only comprehensive source for personal injury verdicts in Hennepin and Ramsey counties. It attempts to provide accurate and detailed information on all personal injury verdicts in from the courts in these counties. All information is obtained from court files, and attempts are made verify all reports and to obtain additional details by contacting the trial attorneys for each case.

*Verdicts & Settlements Quarterly* (Minneapolis, MN: Minnesota Lawyer 1999– ) v. 1, issue 1 (July 1999)– .

This is a compilation of damage awards for personal injuries and a digest of personal injury cases originally reported in the *Minnesota Lawyer.*

### § 546.6. Judicial Bench Books

A bench book is a manual or handbook containing current law pertinent to the jurisdiction, rules of civil or criminal procedure, and rules of court that a judge may refer to in the course of a trial. Bench books also contain local procedures, checklists, and directory information that may be helpful in the disposition of cases. They often are compiled and published by judicial associations.

*Hennepin County Family Law Bench Book,* Sandra A. Berthene (St. Paul, MN: Mason Pub. Co. 1983) vi, 218 p., forms (loose-leaf).

*1982 Ramsey County Family Court Bench Book,* Gerald E. Rutman (St. Paul, MN: Mason Publishing Company 1982) 1 v., forms (loose-leaf).

Deals with domestic relations, civil procedure, and court rules.

*Juvenile Court, Hennepin County, Minnesota Bench Book* (Minneapolis, MN: District Court, Juvenile Division, Fourth Judicial District of Minnesota) 1 v.

Provides the juvenile code, rules of Hennepin County, adoption code, case law of Minnesota, medical treatment of minors, court services statute, and summaries.

*Benchbook for U.S. District Court Judges,* 4th ed., with March 2000 revisions ([Washington, DC]: Federal Judicial Center [2000]) 244 p. Includes bibliographical references and index.

Revisions are included and expansions have been made to keep this book current. It is prepared by experienced judges and reviewed by the bench book committee.

*Minnesota Judges Criminal Benchbook,* Minnesota State Bar Association, Continuing Legal Education (St. Paul, MN: Minnesota Continuing Legal Education 2001 ) 1 v. (various pagings).

This book covers criminal procedure beginning with legal sufficiency of investigation techniques to post-conviction remedies.

### § 546.7. Handbooks, Manuals, Etc.

Various administrative offices publish manuals or handbooks dealing with a variety of topics. The Minnesota County Attorneys Association and the Minnesota Attorney General from time to time compile procedure manuals for their employees and staff. A few examples are listed here.

*ADA Americans with Disabilities Act Compliance Manual for Minnesota: A Simplified Approach to Accessibility,* James E. Jordan, illustrated by Amy M. Jordan (Jordan Publishing 2000) 290p.

Covers the ADA and how Minnesota private and public enterprises can comply with the law.

*Americans with Disabilities Act Manual* (St. Paul, MN: Office of the Minnesota Attorney General 1992) 1 v. (various pagings).

Training manual used for a workshop to orient Minnesota attorneys to the new federal law. Designed to help the participants understand the state's legal obligations under federal law.

*Attorney General's Office Manual* (St. Paul, MN: State of Minnesota, Office of the Attorney General 1982– ) 1 v. (loose-leaf).

The "professional procedure manual" issued by the AG's office.

*Child Abuse and Neglect Procedure Manual for Hennepin County,* Sheila Regan Faulkner; a joint project of the Hennepin County Attorney's Office and the Hennepin County Community Services Department. . . . (Minneapolis, MN: Hennepin County 1978) 1 v.

Deals with the topic of child abuse and juvenile justice in Hennepin County, Minnesota. "Prepared by and for school personnel, medical

## Chapter Five. Finding Aids and Secondary Sources 185

personnel, law enforcement personnel, child protective service personnel, legal personnel." Includes bibliography.

*Civil Commitment Handbook,* Carolyn Peterson (St. Paul, MN: Minnesota County Attorneys Ass'n 2000) 1 v.
Discusses the investigation, preparation of petitions, alternatives to commitment, involuntary treatment, post-commitment procedures, discharge-related procedures, evidentiary issues, appellate process, and relationship to other courts.

*Criminal Practice Manual for Public Defenders in Minnesota,* Kevin S. Burke, Gerard W. Snell (Hennepin County, MN: Office of the Public Defender [s.l. : s.n.] 1980– ) 1 v. (loose-leaf).
A joint project of the Hennepin County Public Defenders Office and the Minnesota Public Defenders Association. Includes bibliographical references.

*Handbook for Minnesota Cities,* 8th ed. (St. Paul, MN: League of Minnesota Cities 1999) 686 p. Includes bibliographical references and index.
A very useful compendium on Minnesota municipal law written for the public officials. Contents include form and structure of the Minnesota city; elections, elected officials, and council meetings; personnel management; regulatory and development functions of cities; liability; finance, budgeting, and debt; financial reports and records management.

*Manual for Grand Jury Presentation,* Gail Baez & Lee W. Barry (St. Paul, MN: Minnesota County Attorneys Ass'n 1996) 39 p.
This brief work is designed as a guide for Minnesota county attorneys in making presentations to grand juries at both the state and federal level.

*Manual for Prosecution of Child Abuse,* 1995 update, Fred Karasov & Carol Lansing (St. Paul, MN: Minnesota County Att'ys Ass'n 1995) 1 v.
Discusses child abuse law and legislation and prosecution of such cases in Minnesota.

*Manual for Prosecution of Domestic Violence,* Julie A. Helling (St. Paul, MN: Minnesota County Attorneys Ass'n 1999) 1 v. (various pagings).
Covers trial practice as it relates to family violence and the victims of family violence in Minnesota.

*Minnesota Prosecutors Manual* (St. Paul, MN: County Attorneys' Council 1976) 1 v. (loose-leaf).
Although dated, this manual provides a detailed outline of procedures that a prosecutor should, may, or must follow in all stages of the

criminal justice process, and the time sequence for those steps taken. Provides citations of federal and state case law and state statutes.

*Minnesota Tax Handbook, 1999,* rev. ed., John P. James (Richard E. Jenis ed., Research Institute of America 1999) 192 p.

Analysis and commentary upon the Minnesota revenue statutes.

*Prosecuting the Drug-Impaired Driver* ([St. Paul, MN]: Minnesota County Attorneys Ass'n 1998) 1 v. (various pagings).

Discusses drug categorization, evaluation, and toxicology, and effective case preparation.

*Prosecution of Juvenile Delinquents* Melinda Elledge (St. Paul, MN: Minnesota County Attorneys Council 1980) 1 v.

Discusses the procedures for prosecution of juveniles in Minnesota court system. Includes bibliographical references.

*Rulemaking in Minnesota: A Guide,* Paul M. Marinac (Saint Paul, MN: Office of the Revisor of Statutes [1998]) 59 p.

This guide outlines the process of administrative procedure in Minnesota and covers the topic of delegated legislation.

### § 546.8. Statistics

The Minnesota Court Administrator as well as legal agencies and law enforcement organizations collect statistics and publish them annually or biennially. The publishing history is incomplete and confusing. Changes to the report titles as well as name changes of the office of court administrator make tracking the bibliographic history difficult. Time periods covered have not always been consecutive or complete. The Supreme Court's Office of the State Court Administrator is mandated to collect and publish statistics about the operation of the court.[387]

*Annual Report. Minnesota Courts* ([St. Paul, MN]: Supreme Court of Minnesota, Office of the Administrative Assistant, v. 1 (1964)–v. 7 (1970)) 7 v., ill.

Generated as a report to the public of the activities of the Minnesota court system. Continued by *Annual Report. Minnesota Courts* issued by Minnesota, Supreme Court, Office of the State Court Administrator.

---

387. MINN. STAT. § 480.15, subd. 5, 7, 10b. (1999).

## Chapter Five. Finding Aids and Secondary Sources 187

*Annual Report. Minnesota Courts* ([St. Paul, MN]: Supreme Court of Minnesota, Office of the State Court Administrator) v. 8 (1971)–v. 12 (1975), 5 v.
Continued by *Minnesota State Court Report* (Minnesota, Office of the State Court Administrator).

*Annual Report . . . Minnesota State Courts* (St. Paul, MN: State Court Administrator, 1997?– ) ill., 1996–1997.
Continues Minnesota, Office of the State Court Administrator, *Minnesota State Court System Annual Report.*

*(The) Minnesota Courts,* Minnesota, Office of the State Court Administrator (St. Paul, MN: State Court Administrator, Minnesota Supreme Court, [1986?]) 1 v., ill.
Covers the year 1984. Publication date uncertain.

*(The) Minnesota Courts,* Minnesota, Office of the State Court Administrator (Saint Paul: State Court Administrator, Minnesota Supreme Court, v. 1 1986).
Succeeded by *Minnesota State Court Report* (1987).

*Minnesota State Court Report* ([St. Paul, MN: Supreme Court of Minnesota] Office of the State Court Administrator 1976-77–1980) 2 v. ill.
Reports for 1978–1979 were suspended. Succeeded by Minnesota, Office of the State Court Administrator, *Minnesota Courts.*

The Minnesota Planning Criminal Justice Statistics Center[388] provides criminal and juvenile justice information, conducts research, and maintains databases for policy development. Databases can be found at <http://www.mnplan.state.mn.us/cj/index.html>.

*Criminal Justice Illustrated,* Stephen Coleman (St. Paul, MN: Criminal Justice Statistical Analysis Center, State Planning Agency 1990) iv, 44 p., charts. Includes bibliographical references.
Analyzes the impact of criminal proceedings in the Minnesota court system.

---

388. Criminal Justice Statistics Center, 658 Cedar St., Suite 300, St. Paul, MN 55155; phone 651-296-4852, fax 651-296-3698, e-mail <crimjust.center@mnplan.state.mn.us>.

*Minnesota Crime in Perspective* (1st ed. Lawrence, KS: Morgan Quitno Corporation 1994– ) v.
Contains information derived from state crime rankings, specifically for Minnesota.

*Minnesota Courts, Expediting Justice,* Minnesota, Office of the State Court Administrator ([St. Paul, MN]: State Court Administrator 1987–1994) 7 v., ill.
Succeeds *Minnesota State Court Report* (1987).

*Minnesota State Court System: . . . Annual Report,* Minnesota, Office of the State Court Administrator ([St. Paul, MN]: State Court Administrator 1996– ), v., ill.; 28 cm.
Starting with 1998, this annual report is available on the internet at <http://www.courts.state.mn.us/sca/scarpt98.pdf>.

*Minnesota State Court Report (1987)* (St. Paul, MN: Office of the State Court Administrator, Minnesota Supreme Court 1987) v., ill., 1985/1986–1987.

*Minnesota State Courts Annual Report* (St. Paul, MN: State Court Administration Office [1998]– ) ill., 1997– .
Continues Minnesota, Office of the State Court Administrator, *Annual Report . . . Minnesota State Courts.*

## § 550. LEGAL PERIODICALS[389]

§ 551. Research Aids
§ 552. Major Legal Indexes
§ 553. Other Periodical Indexes Useful to the Legal Researcher
§ 554. Minnesota Legal Periodical Indexes

Periodical literature is a resource for researching current topics. Often, discussions and descriptions of events in the legal community first appear in bar journals, law reviews, and legal newspapers.

---

389. For a comprehensive bibliography of titles, issues, and numbers of major law reviews, legal journals, and other law-related publications published in the United States see *Hein's Legal Periodical Checklist* (Buffalo, NY: William S. Hein & Co., Inc. 1991) 3 v.; Web address <http://www.wshein.com/>.

## § 551. Research Aids

*Minnesota Statutes Annotated*
Includes citations to articles in the law reviews and bar association journals that discuss a Minnesota statute.

*Shepard's Federal Law Citations in Selected Law Reviews*
Enables a researcher to determine whether a provision of the U.S. Constitution, a federal statute, a federal court opinion, or a federal court rule has been discussed in an article. Includes *Minnesota Law Review* citations.

*Shepard's Law Review Citations: A Compilation of Citations to Law Reviews and Legal Periodicals*
Enables a researcher to determine whether articles from selected law reviews have been cited in court decisions or other periodical articles. Includes citations of cases and articles that have cited *Minnesota Law Review* and *William Mitchell Law Review*.

Both Westlaw and LEXIS-NEXIS provide full-text online access to various periodicals. In the beginning, these services not only were selective as to the publications that were online, but they also were selective as to the articles. In recent years, they have added more publications[390] and have put all articles appearing in the publications online. Articles date from late 1982. Minnesota publications include *Constitutional Commentary; Hamline Journal of Public Law and Policy; Hamline Law Review; Minnesota Law Review; Journal of Law & Religion; Law & Inequality; Minnesota Journal of Global Trade;* and *William Mitchell Law Review.*

---

390. For a complete list of the titles available online see the current edition of the *Westlaw Database Directory* and the *Lexis-Nexis Directory of Online Services.*

### § 552. Major Legal Indexes

Listed below are the two national indexes to legal periodicals. Both indexes add or delete periodical titles as required.

*Index to Legal Periodicals and Books (ILP)* (H. W. Wilson Company 1908 to date).[391]

*ILP* currently indexes more than 500 law reviews, commercial legal periodicals, and bar association periodicals from English-speaking countries. Subject headings are broad. It is indexed by author, statute, and case name. CD-ROM and Web access are available and *ILP* also is accessible through Westlaw and LEXIS-NEXIS. The electronic version goes back to 1981. Publications indexed in *ILP* include: *Constitutional Commentary, William Mitchell Environmental Law Journal, William Mitchell Law Review, Minnesota Journal of Global Trade, Minnesota Law Review, Law & Inequality: A Journal of Theory and Practice, Hamline Journal of Public Law and Policy, Hamline Law Review,* and *Journal of Law and Religion.*

*Legal Resource Index (LRI)* (Information Access Corp. 1980 to date).[392]

This CD-ROM or online index covers more than 850 law reviews, commercial legal periodicals, bar association periodicals, legal newspapers, and law-related information from more than 1,000 general interest and business journals. The print edition, *Current Law Index,* excludes references to legal newspapers and the 400 general interest periodicals. *LRI* uses Library of Congress Subject Headings. It also indexes by author, title, statute, and case name. This index has been approved by the American Association of Law Libraries. CD-ROM, Web, Westlaw, and LEXIS-NEXIS access are available. Publications indexed in *LRI* include: *Bench & Bar of Minnesota, Constitutional Commentary, William Mitchell Environmental Law Journal, William Mitchell Law Review, Minnesota Journal of Global Trade, Minnesota Law Review, Hennepin Lawyer, Law & Inequality: A Journal of Theory and Practice, Hamline Journal of Public Law and Policy, Hamline Law Review,* and *Journal of Law and Religion.*

---

391. H. W. Wilson Company, 950 University Ave., Bronx, NY 10452-4297; phone 212-588-8400.
392. Information Access Corp., 11 Davis Drive, Belmont, CA 94002; phone 800-227-8431; Web address <http://www.galegroup.com/>.

## § 553. Other Periodical Indexes Useful to the Legal Researcher

*Index to Periodical Articles Related to Law: Thirty Year Cumulation 1958–1988* (Glanville Publishers 1989), 4 vols. (supplemented by 1989–1992 vol.).
Published quarterly with occasional cumulations, this unique index is arranged by subject and accompanied by an author index. It provides bibliographic information on law-related periodical articles not included in *Current Law Index, Index to Foreign Legal Periodicals, Index to Legal Periodicals, Legal Resource Index,* or *Legaltrac.* Includes a list of periodicals indexed as well as a list of other indexes covering articles related to law.

*Current Index to Legal Periodicals (CILP)* (University of Washington, Marion Gould Gallagher Library) (monthly).
This index reviews the tables of contents of more than 500 legal publications and indexes articles under 100 relevant subject headings. *CILP* is available four to six weeks before commercial legal periodical indexes.
*CILP* closes the gap existing between the present and the last issue of most standard indexes. The index is found on Westlaw at *CILP.* Minnesota legal periodicals indexed are: *Constitutional Commentary, William Mitchell Environmental Law Journal, William Mitchell Law Review, Minnesota Journal of Global Trade, Minnesota Law Review, Law & Inequality: A Journal of Theory and Practice, Hamline Journal of Public Law and Policy, Hamline Law Review,* and *Journal of Law and Religion.*

*Criminal Justice Abstracts* (Willow Tree Press, Inc. 1968 to present) (updated quarterly).
Provides comprehensive coverage of international journals, books, reports, dissertations, and unpublished papers on criminology and related disciplines. Summarizes worldwide criminal justice literature from all disciplines, particularly social sciences, law, and public administration. Available online or on CD from SilverPlatter Information, Inc.[393] One Minnesota publication is indexed, *Hamline Journal of Public Law & Policy.*

*PAIS International* (Public Affairs Information Service, Inc.).[394]
PAIS provides indexing to a full range of social sciences including law, history, political science, etc., and 1,200 journals and more than 8,000

---

393. Web address <http://www.silverplatter.com/catalog/cjab.htm>.
394. 521 West 43rd St., New York, NY 10036-4396; Web address <http://www.silverplatter.com/catalog/pais.htm>.

monographs are indexed each year. Foreign-language publications include books, periodicals, government documents, pamphlets, statistics, etc. It is available in various formats.

## § 554. Minnesota Legal Periodicals[395]

§ 554.1. Minnesota Legal Periodical Indexes
§ 554.2. Law Reviews
§ 554.3. Bar Journals
§ 554.4. Representative Special Interest Publications or Newsletters
§ 554.5. Periodicals That Have Ceased Publication
§ 554.6. Legal Newspapers

Legal periodicals published in Minnesota or for the Minnesota legal community have fluctuated throughout the years. Some became quite popular and have survived for many years, others have had short runs.

### § 554.1. Minnesota Legal Periodical Indexes

*Index to Minnesota Legal Periodicals* (St. Paul, MN: Mason Division, Butterworth Legal Publishers 1981–Dec. 1983).

Approximately one dozen Minnesota law reviews, commercial legal periodicals, and bar association periodicals were included. Only two issues were produced that provided author, title, and subject indexing as well as a table of cases.

*Minnesota Legal Periodical Index* (published as part of the County Law Library Project, Minnesota State Law Library 1984 to date).

For a list of titles indexed see <http://www.state.mn.us/courts/library/period.html>.

This index continues the *Index to Minnesota Legal Periodicals*. It is compiled by the staff of the Minnesota State Law Library and is published as part of the Bulletin, County Law Library Project (CLLP). It lists articles by subject, title, and author; lists book reviews; and has a table of cases. The cumulative editions are 1984–1987 and 1988–1994.

---

395. This list includes all substantial titles located by the authors.

## Chapter Five. Finding Aids and Secondary Sources

### § 554.2. Law Reviews

Law reviews, published by law schools, contain legal articles and book reviews written by law professors or other authorities, and notes and comments written by students. The titles below are listed alphabetically.

*Constitutional Commentary* (Minneapolis, MN: University of Minnesota Law School, v. I, no. 1 (Winter 1984) to date) (semiannual).

Indexing began: *Legal Resource Index*, 1984– . *Index to Legal Periodicals*, Summer 1984– . Westlaw: Selected coverage from 1985, full coverage from 1993. LEXIS-NEXIS from 1995.

*Criminal Justice Abstracts*

Westlaw: Selected coverage from 1987, full coverage from 1994. LEXIS-NEXIS: From 1997.

*Hamline Journal of Public Law and Policy*[396] (St. Paul, MN: Hamline University School of Law[397] v. 7, no. 1 (Spring 1986) to date) (semiannual).[398]

Indexing began: *Index to Legal Periodicals*, Fall 1989– . *Legal Resource Index*, 1988– .

*Hamline Law Review*[399] (St. Paul, MN: Hamline University School of Law v. 1978, no. 1 to date) (semiannual[400]).

Indexing: Annual index in each volume. Indexing began: *Index to Legal Periodicals*, Jan. 1982– .

*Journal of Law and Religion* (St. Paul, MN: Hamline University School of Law and Council on Religion and Law v. 1, no. 1 (Summer 1983) to date) (semiannual).[401]

Indexing began: *Legal Resource Index*, Winter 1983– . *Index to Legal Periodicals*, 1990– . Westlaw: Selected coverage from 1988, full coverage from 1993.

---

396. The *Hamline Journal of Public Law and Policy* was preceded by *Hamline Journal of Public Law* (1981–1985) that was preceded by the *Journal of Minnesota Public Law* (1980–1981).
397. Volumes 1, 2, and 4 consisted of one issue. Volume 3 had two issues.
398. Web address <http://www.hamline.edu/law/pages/journal/>.
399. Web address <http://www.hamline.edu/law/pages/lawreview/>.
400. Volumes 1–3 consisted of one issue. Volume 4 had three issues. Volume 5 began biannual publication.
401. Web address <http://www.hamline.edu/law/lawrelign/jlr/>.

*Law & Inequality: A Journal of Theory and Practice* (Minneapolis, MN: University of Minnesota Law School v. 1, no. 1 (June 1983) to date) (semiannual).

Indexing began: *Index to Legal Periodicals,* Feb. 1984– . *Legal Resource Index,* June 1983– . Westlaw: Selected coverage from 1985, full coverage from 1993. LEXIS-NEXIS: From 1993.

*Legal Resource Index,* May 1980– .

Westlaw: Selected coverage from 1983, full coverage from 1993. LEXIS-NEXIS: From 1997.

*Minnesota Intellectual Property Review* (Minneapolis, MN: University of Minnesota Law School v. 1, no. 1 (2000– ) to date).[402]

This is the newest journal from the Minnesota Law School. It is published twice yearly in electronic (HTML format) as well as in hard copy. Web address: <http://mipr.umn.edu>.

*Minnesota Journal of Global Trade* (Minneapolis, MN: University of Minnesota Law School v. 1, no. 1 (Fall 1992– )) (semiannual).[403]

"A journal dedicated to the study of international economic law and policy." Westlaw: Selected coverage from 1992, full coverage from 1994. LEXIS-NEXIS: From 1993.

*Minnesota Law Review* (Minneapolis, MN: University of Minnesota Law School v. 1, no. 1 (Jan. 1917) to date) (six issues per year).

Annual index in each volume; cumulative indexes for volumes 1–36 and volumes 37–65.

Indexing began: *Index to Legal Periodicals,* Nov. 1981– ; *Legal Resource Index,* Jan. 1980– . Westlaw: Selected coverage from 1983, full coverage from 1985. LEXIS-NEXIS: From 1982.

---

402. Web address <http://mipr.umn.edu>.
403. Web address <http://www.law.umn.edu/globaltrade/>.

## Chapter Five. Finding Aids and Secondary Sources 195

*William Mitchell Law Review* (St. Paul, MN: William Mitchell College of Law. v. 1, no. 1 (1974) to date). Index to volumes 1–4 in volume 4; Index to volumes 5–8 in volume 10 (irregular[404]).[405]
Indexing began: *Index to Legal Periodicals,* 1981– . *Legal Resource Index* Spring 1980– . Westlaw: Selected coverage from 1982, full coverage from 1993. LEXIS-NEXIS: From 1993.

### § 554.3. Bar Journals

Bar journals fulfill the function of an association newsletter and contain articles on topics of local interest. Some publications have lengthy articles of local interest such as commentary on new legislation or developments in local law. William S. Hein & Co., Inc. has a subscription service that provides microfiche editions of many titles thus saving the trouble of individual subscriptions and the use of shelf space.

*(The) Barrister* (St. Paul, MN: Ramsey County Bar Ass'n, v. 1, no. 1 1974– ).
Continues *Ramsey Barrister.*

*Bench & Bar of Minnesota—Official Publication of the Minnesota State Bar Association* (Minneapolis, MN: Minnesota State Bar Ass'n, v. I, no. 1 (Dec. 1943) to date) (eleven issues per year).[406] Web address <http://www2.mnbar.org/benchandbar/>.
Indexing began: *Legal Resource Index,* 1980– . Index to volumes 20–34 (1968–1978) in 34 *Bench & Bar of Minnesota* 37 (Aug. 1978). Index to volumes 35–40 (1978–1983) in 41 *Bench & Bar of Minnesota* 27 (Jan. 1984). Index to volume 41(1984) in 42 *Bench & Bar of Minnesota* 37 (Mar. 1985).

---

404. Volumes 1–3 consisted of one issue. Volumes 4, 5, and 9 had two issues. Volumes 6–8 had three issues. Quarterly publication began with volume 10.
405. Web address <http://www.wmitchell.edu/current/nonacademic/student_orgs/lawreview/index.html>.
406. Earlier issues of *Bench & Bar of Minnesota* were published intermittently between 1928 and 1940 as follows: unnumbered issues for October 1928, December 1928, May 1929; supplements to 14 and 15 *Minnesota Law Review* (1928–1930), five issues; volumes 1–8 (1931–40) in newspaper format (irregular). Some of the better articles appearing between 1967 and 1973 were updated and printed in *Best of Bench & Bar,* published as a joint venture of Minnesota State Bar Association and Continuing Legal Education, University of Minnesota (Gerald A. Regnier (ed.) 1974). A separate publication containing newsletter information was published under the title *Bench & Bar Interim* every other month from May 20, 1981, through November 1982. During this period *Bench & Bar of Minnesota* also was published bimonthly.

*County Law Library Program Bulletin* (St. Paul, MN: Minnesota State Law Library, first published 1980) (three times per year).
Deals with news and information about the county law library project. This title also continues the *Minnesota Index to Legal Periodicals*.

*Family Law Forum*[407] (Minneapolis, MN: Minnesota State Bar Ass'n Family Law Section 1992– ).
Publication of the Minnesota State Bar Association Family Law Section.

*(The) Hennepin Lawyer* (Minneapolis, MN: Hennepin County Bar Ass'n v. I, no. 1 (Feb. 1933) to date) (eleven issues per year).
The official publication of the Hennepin County Bar Association. Information for Hennepin County lawyers about current issues and events relating to the law and lawyers. Indexing began: *Legal Resource Index,* Sept. 1993– .

*Loquitur* (St. Paul, MN: Minnesota State Law Library v. 1, no. 1 (Oct. 1983)– ) (semiannual).
News and information about the Minnesota State Law Library activities.

*Minnesota Defense* (Minneapolis, MN: Minnesota Defense Lawyers Ass'n v. I, no. 1 (May 1980) to date) (quarterly).
This periodical deals with trial practice and civil and criminal defense issues.

*Minnesota Legal Register. Minnesota Tax Court Decisions* (Minneapolis, MN: Minnesota Legal Register. 1968 to date) (loose-leaf) (includes index).
Even-numbered issues called Tax Court Decisions; odd-numbered issues called Attorney General Opinions.

*Minnesota Trial Lawyer*[408] (St. Paul, MN: Minnesota Trial Lawyer's Ass'n v. 2, no. 5 (Aug. 1976) to date) (irregular).
Advice for lawyers regarding trial practice and assessment of damages. Preceded by Minnesota Trial Lawyer's Association, *Newsletter* v. 1–2, no. 4; 1974–Apr./May 1976.

*New Matter* (St. Paul, MN: Minnesota Intellectual Property Law Ass'n, Inc.[409] v. 1, no. 1 (Aug. 1977) to date) (six issues per year).
Available on-line at <http://www2.mnbar.org/mipla/new-matter.pdf>.

---

407. This title succeeds *Family Law Section News*.
408. Continues *MTLA Newsletter.* v. 1 (May 1974) to v. 2, no. 4 (Apr.-May 1976).
409. Formerly Minnesota Patent and Trademark Law Association, Inc.

## Chapter Five. Finding Aids and Secondary Sources

*Public Law News* (Minneapolis, MN: Minnesota State Bar Ass'n v. 1– ; 1992– ).
Published by the Public Law section of the MSBA.

### § 554.4. Representative Special Interest Publications or Newsletters

Consult individual law schools for lists of student newspapers and alumni newsletters. Many government agencies and special interest groups publish newsletters, contact the specific organization for information on current publications.

*Administrative Law Reports—Summarizing Decisions of Administrative Law Judges of the Minnesota Office of Administrative Hearings and Related Developments* (St. Paul, MN: M. Martin, v. 1, no. 1 (Sept. 1984– )) (monthly).
This is a monthly publication that summarizes opinions of administrative law judges of the Minnesota Office of Administrative Hearings.

*Americans with Disabilities Act Bulletin* (St. Paul, MN: Minnesota Dept. of Employee Relations, Equal Opportunity Division 1992).
Deals with recent developments in law and legislation as well as the legal status of the disabled and employment discrimination.

*Drinking/Driving Law Letter* (Minneapolis, MN: Chandler Pub. 1981– , v. 1, no. 1 (Jan. 15, 1982) (imprint varies); May 31, 1985– , Wilmette, IL: Callaghan & Co.).
This biweekly loose-leaf publication contains the latest information regarding law, procedure and technical issues in drunk driving cases.

*Family Law Newsletter* (St. Paul, MN: Creative Legal Publications, v. 1, no. 1– (1985– )) (twelve issues yearly).
Covers cases, law, and legislation in Minnesota regarding domestic relations, marriage, divorce, divorce settlements, equitable distribution of property, and child custody.

*Law Alumni News* (Minneapolis, MN: University of Minnesota Law School) ill. v. 35, no. 2 (fall 1985)– , semiannual.
The University of Minnesota Law School news for alumni. Varied publishing history. Continues *Minnesota Law Alumni News* v. 20, no. 2 (spring 1970)–v. 33, no. 1 (winter/spring 1983) and *University of Minnesota Law School News.* v. 1, no. 1 (Feb. 1951)–v. 20, no. 1 (winter 1970).

*Legal Advisory,* Workers' Compensation Reinsurance Association (St. Paul, MN: The Association v. 1 (1983)).

Also known as *WCRA Legal Advisory.* News and information concerning workers' comp law and legislation in Minnesota.

*MACA Monitor,* Minnesota Association for Court Administration; Minnesota Supreme Court, Office of Continuing Education for State Court Personnel (St. Paul, MN: MACA 1989– ), v., ill., port.; 28 cm. This current-awareness publication is for Minnesota court administrators.

*Metro Voice: A Metropolitan Council Publication on Twin Cities Area Issues* (St. Paul, MN: The Council, v. 1 (winter 1992) to date) monthly.

Focuses on regional planning issues for the Minneapolis and Saint Paul Metropolitan Areas. Continues *Metro Monitor.*

*Minnesota Ballot Bulletin* (St. Paul, MN: Secretary of State, Election Division v. 1, no. 1 (Jan. 1990)– ).

Covers election law and legislation, voting, ballots, etc. in Minnesota.

*Minnesota Cities*[410] (St. Paul, MN: League of Minnesota Cities 1916– , v. 61, no. 10– , Sept. 1976– ) (monthly) ill.

Focuses on issues of interest to municipal government officials, e.g., taxes, fiscal management, new and proposed legislation, public labor law, and court decisions. Continues *Minnesota Municipalities.*

*Minnesota Employment Law Letter* (Nashville, TN: Published for Felhaber, Larson, Fenlon &Vogt, P.A., by M. Lee Smith Publishers & Printers v. 1, no. 1. (Mar. 1991)) (monthly).

This monthly newsletter is sponsored by the law firm of Felhaber, Larson, Fenlon and Vogt in Minneapolis. It deals with developing employment law issues of concern to Minnesota businesses.

*Minnesota Family Law Journal* (Charlottesville, VA: Lexis Publishing, v. 1, no. 1 (Nov. 1981)– ) (bimonthly).

Deals with issues in domestic relations with various articles, case comments, and court decisions.

---

410. Formerly *Minnesota Municipalities.*

## Chapter Five. Finding Aids and Secondary Sources

*Minnesota Family Law Quarterly,* Robert E. Oliphant (St. Paul, MN: Creative Legal Communications 1986– ), 1 v. (loose-leaf).
News of court decisions affecting issues in domestic relations. Format changed in 1992 to "newsletter."

*Minnesota Government Report* (Willimie, MN: Minnesota Government Report, vol. 1, no. 1 (Jan. 3, 1984)– ) (twice-weekly newsletter on state government).
News of court decisions affecting Minnesota state government and other administrative agency activities. Also known as *The Minnesota Government Report's Court Report.*

*Minnesota's Journal of Law and Politics*[411] (Minneapolis, MN: BRJG Publishing Corp. v. 5., no. 1 (Apr. 1990) to Jan. 1997).
A "newsy" approach to popular and controversial issues in Minnesota legal and political circles. Continues *Minnesota Law Journal* and continued by *Minnesota Law & Politics.*

*Minnesota Law & Politics*[412] (Minneapolis, MN: Law and Politics, Inc., first published 1990; Dec. 1996 to date) (eight times per year).
Continues *Minnesota's Journal of Law and Politics.* Popular format focusing on law, politics, and public policy issues in Minnesota.

*Minnesota Law Journal* (Minneapolis, MN: Minnesota Law Week Pub. v. 1, no. 1 (Mar. 7, 1986)) (bi-weekly).
Focuses on law, government, and politics in Minnesota. Continued by *Minnesota Law & Politics.*

*Minnesota Municipalities*[413] (Minneapolis, MN: League of Minnesota Municipalities, 61 v. 24–28 cm. v. 1–61, no. 9; 1916–Aug. 1976).
Indexed in *Public Affairs Information Service Bulletin* vols. 36–45, 1952–60, 1 v. Continues *League of Minnesota Municipalities. Proceedings of the Annual Convention of the League of Minnesota Municipalities.*

*Minnesota Real Estate Law Journal* (Butterworth Legal Publishers-Mason Division v. 1, no. 1 (Nov./Dec. 1981) to date (eight issues per year).
Deals with real property, vendors and buyers, and the real estate business in general in Minnesota.

---

411. Previous title was *Minnesota Law Journal.* v. 1. no. 1 (Mar. 7, 1986 to 1990(?)).
412. Continues *Minnesota's Journal of Law and Politics.* Web address <http://www.lawandpolitics.com/>.
413. Continued by *Minnesota Cities.*

*Motor Carrier News* (South St. Paul, MN: Office of Motor Carrier Services, Minnesota Dept. of Transportation, v. 1, no. 1 (Fall 1993)– ) (quarterly).
Covers law and legislation in the automotive transportation and trucking businesses in Minnesota.

*MWL: Minnesota Women Lawyers* (v. 1 (1978) to date).
Organization news and information, e.g., Members on the Move, Upcoming Programs and Events. Continues *News* (Minnesota Women Lawyers, Inc.) and *MWL Newsletter* (1978).

*Notice and Hearing Bulletin* (St. Paul, MN: Minnesota Dept. of Transportation, Rail and Motor Carrier Proceedings, July 26, 1996– ).
Published weekly except when there are no material additions or modifications to the previous week's bulletin. Covers proceedings of the Minnesota Department of Transportation Rail and Motor Carrier agency. Continues *Transportation Calendar*.

*ODP Catalyst* (St. Paul, MN: Minnesota Dept. of Public Safety, Office of Drug Policy, Jan. 1990– )
The Minnesota Office of Drug Policy publishes information about law and legislation dealing with drug abuse.

*Politics in Minnesota* (St. Paul, MN: Political Communications, Inc. v. 1, no. 1, 1983– ) (22 issues per year).
Reports, analysis, and discussion of Minnesota state politics.

*Pro Bono Report* (Minnesota Justice Foundation, Mar. 1985 to date).[414]
The MJF's monthly newsletter, "focusing on public interest law and legal assistance to the poor in Minnesota."

*Sales Tax Newsletter* (Minnesota Department of Revenue, Sales and Use Tax Division, St. Paul: The Department, 1979– ) (quarterly).
Provides information regarding the Minnesota sales tax and its application. Available on the Internet at: <http://www.taxes.state.mn.us/newslett/>.

---

414. 229 19th Ave. So., Minneapolis, MN 55455.

*Small Business Notes* (St. Paul, MN: Minnesota Small Business Assistance Office, no. 1 (Nov. 1985)– ) (monthly).

"A joint venture of the Minnesota Small Business Assistance Office and the U.S. Small Business Administration" covering law and legislation regarding small businesses in Minnesota.

*State of Minnesota Bureau of Mediation Services Digest* (St. Paul, MN: Minnesota Bureau of Mediation Services 1989 to date, 12 v.) (loose-leaf) (monthly).

A monthly digest of decisions interpreting the Minnesota Public Employment Labor Relations Act and the Minnesota Labor Relations Act. Includes indexes.

*(The) Verdict: The Official Publication of the Minnesota Legal Administrators Association* (Minneapolis, MN: Minnesota Legal Administrators Ass'n (MLLA) 1983– ).

News and articles of interest to legal administrators in Minnesota.

*(The) Waste Management Act Examiner* (St. Paul, MN: Minnesota Office of Environmental Assistance, v. 1, no. 1 (Feb. 1997)– ).

Covers the law and legislation regarding refuse and refuse disposal. "Updates on the Waste Management Act Examination Process."

*William Mitchell Magazine* (St. Paul, MN: William Mitchell College of Law[415] (summer 1984– )) (quarterly).

Also known as *William Mitchell College of Law Alumni Magazine.*

### § 554.5. Periodicals That Have Ceased Publication

*(The) Advocate, A Weekly Law Journal* (Minneapolis, MN: The Advocate Co. Nov. 1888–June 1890) 2 v.

*Attorney General's Messenger* (St. Paul, MN: Office of the Attorney General, State of Minnesota Apr. 1976–July/Aug. 1978) 3 v.

An informational service prepared by the Office of the Minnesota Attorney General for County Attorneys and other public officials involved with the administration of local and state government.

---

415. 875 Summit Ave., St. Paul, MN 55105.

*Bench and Bar Interim* (Minneapolis, MN: Minnesota State Bar Ass'n, May 20, 1981 to Nov. 1982).

A newsletter designed to serve as an interim publication to *Bench & Bar*.

*Bulletin*, State of Minnesota, Department of Labor and Industry (St. Paul, MN: The Dept., Oct. 1909–[1920?]) 12 v., no. 6–no. 17.

Originally published to keep employers, government officials, and the legal community informed about workers' compensation law and legislation in Minnesota. Preceding title *Accident Bulletin*.

*Capitol Reporter* (Saint Paul, MN: Phillips Legislative Service, [v. 1]–v. 4, no. 51; Dec. 10, 1974–June 29, 1978).

Superseded by *Minnesota Government Report,* the twice-weekly newsletter on state government (Willernie, MN, v. 1– , July 3, 1978– ).

*Daily Recorder* (St. Paul, MN: Daily Recorder Co. , v. 1 (1888)– ?).

This daily (except Sundays and holidays) newspaper served the purpose of providing legal notices and advertising regarding the legal and business communities.

*Interchange: A Monthly Forum and Digest for the Criminal Justice System in Minnesota* (St. Paul, MN: Minnesota Supreme Court, Continuing Education for State Court Personnel v. 1, no. 1 (Oct. 1973)–v. 9, no. 1 (winter 1981)) ill.

Originally published to keep Minnesota court personnel informed of current issues in criminal courts and the administration of criminal justice in Minnesota.

*Law Book News, A Monthly Review of Current Legal Literature and Journal of Legal Bibliography* (West Publishing Co. 1894–1895) 2 v.

*Legal Advisory* (St. Paul, MN: Workers' Compensation Reinsurance Ass'n 1983–199?).

*Legal Record* (St. Paul, MN: West Pub. Co., v. 1, no. 1 (Mar. 1, 1880)–?).

"A monthly publication in the interests of justices of the peace, county officers, town officers. . . . "

*Legislative Bulletin,* Minnesota Association of Commerce and Industry (St. Paul, MN: Minnesota Ass'n of Commerce and Industry, v. 1 (1969, no. 1)–1969, no. 19).

## Chapter Five. Finding Aids and Secondary Sources

*Minnesota Administrative Law Journal* (St. Paul, MN: Mason Publishing Co. 1982–19??) (eight issues per year) (loose-leaf).

*Minnesota Business and Commercial Law Journal* (Butterworth Legal Publishers-Mason Division, May 1982–Sept./Oct. 1983) 1 v.

*Minnesota Continuing Legal Education* (Callaghan & Co. 1963–1964) (2v.; publication ceased with vol. 2, no. 1).

*Minnesota Environmental Compliance Update* (Madison, CT: Business & Legal Reports, Inc. Sponsored by Oppenheimer, Wolff & Donnelly v. 1 (1994)) (monthly).

*Minnesota Insurance Law Journal* (St. Paul, MN: Mason Publishing Co. 1982–19??) (eight issues per year) (loose-leaf).

*Minnesota Journal of Trial Advocacy* (St. Paul, MN: Butterworth Legal Publishers-Mason Division June 1982–May 1983) 1 vol.

*Minnesota Labor and Employment Law Journal* (St. Paul, MN: Mason Publishing Co. 1982–1984) (eight issues per year) (loose-leaf) (ceased v. 1, no. 6).

*(The) Minnesota Law Journal*, George H. Selover, ed. (Law Journal Publishing Co.)
Originally published monthly, St. Paul, MN: Frank P. Dufresne. v. 1 (May 1893)–v. 5 (Dec. 1897). 5 v. (monthly; except Nov. & Dec. 1893). Photo duplication reprint by Dennis & Co. (Buffalo, NY: 1963). Continued by *Minnesota District Court Reporter.*

*Minnesota Law Reports* (St. Paul, MN: Mason Publishing Company 1982–19??) (bi-weekly) (loose-leaf).

*Minnesota Lawyer*[416] (Minneapolis, MN: Minnesota Lawyer Newspapers, v. 1, no. 1 (1985–1992)).

*Minnesota Legal Register: Minnesota Tax Court Decisions* (Duluth, MN: Philip G. Bradley, ed. & pub., v. 1– , 1985– ) (annual) (loose-leaf), index.

---

416. Succeeded by *Minnesota Journal of Law and Politics.*

*Minnesota Legal Register: Opinions of the Minnesota Attorney General* (Duluth, MN: Philip G. Bradley, ed. & pub., v. 1, no. 1 (1968– )) (monthly) (loose-leaf). Index.
Available on microfilm and microfiche from William S. Hein & Co., Inc.

*Minnesota Regulation News* (St. Paul, MN: William Mitchell College of Law, Trustees Chair in Administrative Law, v. 1, no. 1 (Feb. 1984) to date) (irregular).

*Minnesota Tax Court Reports* (St. Paul, MN: Mason Publishing Co. 1982–1983) (four issues per year) (loose-leaf).

*Minnesota Tax Law Journal* (St. Paul, MN: Butterworth Legal Publishers-Mason Division v. 1, no. 1 (Dec. 1982) to 1989) (four issues per year) (loose-leaf).

*MSBA in Brief* (Minneapolis, MN: Minnesota State Bar Ass'n 1985–1997) (monthly).

*Newsletter—Minnesota Trial Lawyers Association* (1974–1976).
Succeeded by *Minnesota Trial Lawyer*.

*Quaere* (Minneapolis, MN: University of Minnesota Law School first published 1974(?) 1985–1992) (monthly during school year).
Student newspaper of the University of Minnesota Law School.

*Ramsey Barrister* (St. Paul, MN: Ramsey County Bar Ass'n v. 1, no. 1 (Mar. 1974) to 1991) (irregular).

*Register-Mirror* (Minneapolis, MN: Philip G. Bradley[417] v. 94 (July 1978)–v. 103 (Apr. 1988)) (weekly).
Continued the *Progress-Register* and the *Weekly Mirror*. Absorbed by *Finance & Commerce*.

*Rural Practice Law Journal, Minnesota Edition* (Butterworth Legal Publishers, Mason Division, v. I, no. 1 (Nov. 1984)–1985) (six issues per year).

---

417. P.O. Box 3253, Minneapolis, MN 55403; phone 612-332-0726.

*State Bar Advance Sheet* (St. Paul, MN: Minnesota State Bar Ass'n v.1 (1975–19??)).

*State Register* (St. Paul, MN: State of Minnesota, Dept. of Administration, Office of the State Register, v. 1, no. 1 (July 13, 1976)–v. 14, no. 52 (June 25, 1990)).
Official publication of the State of Minnesota for official notices, administrative rules, and executive orders. This is the predecessor to the *Minnesota State Register.*

*Statehouse Review a Quick Summary of the ... Session of the Minnesota Legislature* (St. Paul, MN: Minnesota Legislative Reference Research Bureau).

*William Mitchell Commentator* (St. Paul, MN: William Mitchell College of Law v. 1 (1966)–v. 7 (1972)).

*William Mitchell Environmental Law Journal* (St. Paul, MN: William Mitchell College of Law, Environmental Law Society. v. 1, no. 1 (May 1983)–v. 3 (1985)).

*Minnesota Law Reports* (St. Paul, MN: Mason Publishing Co., v. 1, no. 1, (Oct. 15,1982)–v. 2, no. 3 (1983)).

### § 554.6. Legal Newspapers

Various Minnesota statutes require that legal notices be published in a legal newspaper. To qualify as a medium for official and legal publication a newspaper must meet statutory requirements. "Qualified newspaper" means a newspaper that complies with all of the provisions of Minn. Stat. § 331A.02(8) (1999). The following terms, when found in laws referring to the publication of a public notice, shall be taken to mean a qualified newspaper: "qualified legal newspaper," "legal newspaper," "official newspaper," "newspaper," and "medium of official and legal publication."[418] A current list of all qualified legal newspapers in Minnesota is available from the secretary of state.[419]

---

418. MINN. STAT. § 331A.01 (1999).
419. Legal Newspaper Registrar, 180 State Office Building, St. Paul, MN 55155-0001. An alphabetical listing by county has been published in the *Minnesota Legislative Manual.* This last appeared in the 1979–1980 edition at page 455.

The following is a list of Minneapolis/St. Paul legal newspapers that contain legal materials exclusively.

*Finance and Commerce* (Dolan Media[420]) (Tuesday–Saturday).

The proceedings of the Minneapolis City Council and the Hennepin County Commissioners are published in the daily issues. It is the official designated newspaper of City of Minneapolis, County of Hennepin.

*Minnesota Lawyer* (Minneapolis, MN: Finance and Commerce, v. 1, no. 1 (Sept. 7, 1997– )) (weekly).

Successor to the appellate courts edition of "Finance and Commerce" Contains news for the Minnesota legal community and a digest of decisions as well as full text of recent Supreme Court, Court of Appeals, and Tax Court opinions.

*Minnesota Lawyer,*[421] *Appellate Court Edition* (Finance and Commerce v. 1, no. 1 (1997?)) (weekly).

Includes full text of opinions of the Minnesota Supreme Court and Minnesota Court of Appeals. Including published and unpublished opinions along with orders and special term opinions.

*Minnesota State Register* (St. Paul, MN: Department of Administration; Print Communications Division,[422] v. 1, no. 1 (1976– )) (weekly).

Contains index and cumulative index (*see supra* § 321). This official weekly publication of the State of Minnesota fulfills the legislative mandate set forth in Minn. Stat. § 14.46. The *State Register* contains proposed, adopted, exempt, emergency, and withdrawn rules; executive orders of the governor; appointments; proclamations; commendations; orders; official notices; state grants and loans; contracts for professional, technical, and consulting services; non-state public bids, contracts, and grants; certificates of assumed name, registration of insignia, and marks.

*Saint Paul Legal Ledger*[423] (1927 to date) (daily).

Synopses of appellate court and attorney general opinions and full-text proceedings of the St. Paul City Council are published.

---

420. 730 Second Ave. South, Suite 100, Minneapolis, MN 55402-2418; phone 612-333-4244; Web address <http://www.finance-commerce.com>.
421. Web address <http://www.minnlawyer.com>.
422. 117 University Ave., St. Paul, MN 55155-2299.
423. 640 Minnesota Building, 4th & Cedar, St. Paul, MN 55101; phone 651-222-0059; Web address <http://www.legal-ledger.com/>.

## § 560. Materials in Special Formats

§ 561. Loose-Leaf Services
§ 562. Legal Newsletters
§ 563. Microforms
§ 564. CD-ROM
§ 565. Videotapes and Audiotapes
§ 566. Computer-Assisted Research
§ 567. Internet Resources

### § 561. Loose-Leaf Services

A loose-leaf service is a form of information retrieval that combines materials from numerous sources, both primary and secondary, to provide comprehensive and current access to legal topics. Some cases and administrative rulings that are unavailable elsewhere are published in these services. Loose-leaf services usually are published for subjects, such as tax, labor law, and regulated industries, where change is rapid and legislation and administrative regulations predominate.

Many of the services provide comprehensive coverage not only of federal law but also of state law. These state laws may be either dispersed throughout a service or arranged in a separate section. Occasionally, separate volumes dealing exclusively with state law are published. An excellent source of loose-leaf services available is *Legal Looseleafs in Print*.[424] It is arranged by subject with a title and publisher index.

### § 562. Legal Newsletters

Newsletters are a means of keeping abreast of current issues, matters, affairs, and events. A source of those newsletters that are available for subscription is *Legal Newsletters in Print*.[425] Arranged by subject with a title and publisher index.

### § 563. Microforms

A microform reproduces text or drawings in sizes that cannot be read without magnification. There are four basic types of microform—microfilm, micro-opaques, microfiche, and ultrafiche. U.S. Supreme

---

424. New York, NY: InfoSources Pub. 1981– (annual).
425. New York, NY: InfoSources Pub. 1985– (annual).

Court records and briefs, legal periodicals, historical legal materials, West's National Reporter System, and the CCH Tax Library are examples of legal documents available on microform.

A variety of Minnesota materials are reproduced on microform. Readers are referred to *Guide to Microforms in Print: Author/Title*,[426] and *Guide to Microforms in Print: Subject*.[427]

### § 564. CD-ROM

Compact discs with "read-only memory" (CD-ROMs) are a data storage format used with a computer. Many legal publishers have marketed CD-ROM products in recent years. The capacity of these compact discs has increased greatly since they were introduced in 1982. Law offices facing ever increasing cost for storing large libraries have turned to CD technology not only to reduce their need for more books, but also for the ease of data retrieval. Most CD-ROM products are updated at regular intervals and are purchased by subscription. Various products are available at local law libraries. Full-text documents such as case reports, statutes, rules, and regulations are available as well as research aids, such as citators, and indexes and bibliographic materials. In the end, however, the documents found on the CD must be printed.

### § 565. Videotapes and Audiotapes

Videotape and audiotape technology provide a means for educating paralegals, law students, practicing attorneys, and the general public regarding legal issues and procedures. Students can see and hear lectures by well-known practicing attorneys, legal educators, and scholars. A bibliography of tapes available for purchase can be found in *Law Books and Serials in Print: A Multimedia Sourcebook*.[428]

### § 566. Computer-Assisted Research

Computers are used in a number of ways in the legal profession with word processing being most common. Law firms use computers for

---

426. Munich: Saur Verlag 1978– , 1 v.
427. Munich: Saur 1978– , 1 v.
428. New Providence, NJ: R.R. Bowker 2000, 3 v. (annual).

## Chapter Five. Finding Aids and Secondary Sources 209

accounting purposes and for collating, retrieving, and managing evidence in complex litigation. Courts use computers for jury management, docket control, calendar currency, and statistical reporting. Law libraries use computers as cataloging and reference tools, and for retrieval of bibliographic information on books cataloged by subscribing libraries. The best known use of computers in the legal profession is research. A number of vendors have developed databases of case reports, administrative rules, statutes, and other law-related materials such as treatises, periodicals, indexes and directories. In recent years, the two leading vendors, LEXIS-NEXIS and Westlaw, have been met with competition. Listed below are several vendors and brief descriptions of the services.

- ▶ Westlaw. Westlaw is an extensive set of databases encompassing federal and state law. Included are cases, statutes, codes, session laws, administrative rules, law reviews, treatises, forms, encyclopedia, news sources, practice materials, public records, and directories. Access is by subscription.[429]
- ▶ LEXIS-NEXIS. LEXIS-NEXIS is a wide-ranging series of federal and state legal materials including case law, statutes, codes, session laws, administrative codes, law reviews, financial, market, tax, Shepard's citations, international, public records, directories, legal reference, forms, and securities materials. Access is by subscription.[430]
- ▶ Loislaw. Loislaw.com has a Minnesota law library that contains approximately 273,000 documents of Minnesota primary law in the databases (listed below). The databases are duplications of the law received from the Minnesota courts, legislature, Office of Administrative Law, or other sources. Materials include: Minnesota Supreme Court case law from 1924 to present; Minnesota Court of Appeals from 1983 to present; court rules (state and federal); *Minnesota Statutes*; Minnesota current legislative acts; Minnesota regulations; hyperlinks to all cited state and federal case law, statutes, and administrative rules; and cite checking for cases and statutes. A subscription is required to access these materials.[431]
- ▶ Quicklaw. Quicklaw America is an editorially enhanced and comprehensive online research service offering court decisions, topical

---

429. Web address <http://www.westlaw.com/>.
430. Web address <http://www.lexis-nexis.com/>.
431. Web address <http://www.loislaw.com/>.

databases, and an up-to-date collection of statutes and regulations. The Minnesota law library has federal appellate decisions, Minnesota appellate decisions, Minnesota statutes, Minnesota court rules.[432]

▶ VersusLaw. VersusLaw has a Minnesota law library that dates from 1930. Federal materials also are included. Textual as well as field searching is possible. Access is by subscription.[433]

## § 567. Internet Sources

By now, most legal researchers are familiar with the World Wide Web. Throughout this research guide links to various websites are included. For the most part, these links refer to various websites or from a hardcopy citation to its electronic version. There also are resources which are uniquely electronic and have no counterpart in print. Many of these websites are administrative offices, government agencies, associations, and the like which have a great deal of information for the legal practitioner.

These legal resources, which once only were available in law libraries, law offices, and government agencies, now are available to nearly anyone who has the need or desire to use them. Legal research in the twenty-first century continues to change rapidly as the technology continues to develop. Nearly every professional association has information and training readily available.

Nevertheless, users have a continuing need to evaluate the reliability, accuracy, and authority of resources. For this purpose internet research guides have been published to help the legal researcher find resources and evaluate their worth. Some Minnesota resources regarding the Internet are listed below.

*New Law Office Technology to Enhance Client Services,* Minnesota State Bar Association, Continuing Legal Education (St. Paul, MN: Minnesota Continuing Legal Education 2001) 1 v. (various pagings).

Includes bibliographical references. Discusses how technology has affected the practice of law; research websites; software; network security; using Internet resources in making presentations; and developing websites for law offices.

---

432. Web address <http://www.quicklawamerica.com/>.
433. Web address <http://www.versuslaw.com/>.

## Chapter Five. Finding Aids and Secondary Sources

*Legal Research Emerges in Cyberspace,* presented by Joan S. Howland & George R. Jackson ([Minneapolis, MN]: University of Minnesota Law School [2000]) 1 v. (various pagings).

Covers computer network legal resources. Presented as the University of Minnesota, Summer Program of Continuing Legal Education (21st: 2000: Minneapolis), University of Minnesota. Law School. Includes bibliographical references.

*The Lawyer's Internet Toolbox,* prepared by Michael J. McGuire; Minnesota State Bar Association, Continuing Legal Education (St. Paul, MN: Minnesota Continuing Legal Education 2000) 1 v. (various pagings).

Deals with Internet research resources for lawyers.

*Internet Legal Research "101,"* [presented by Michael J. McGuire]; Minnesota State Bar Association, Continuing Legal Education (St. Paul, MN: Minnesota Continuing Legal Education 1999) 1 v. (various pagings).

This is a basic introduction to search engines, browser software, privacy concerns, computer networks, and future developments.

*Internet Strategies for the Paralegal in Minnesota,* by George R. Jackson & Linda Swanson (Eau Claire, WI: Institute for Paralegal Education 1998) 145 p.

Includes bibliographical references. An introduction to the World Wide Web and its use for substantive legal research.

*Your Presence on the Internet,* produced by Minnesota Institute of Legal Education (Minneapolis, MN: Minnesota Institute of Legal Education 1997) 1 v. (various pagings).

Deals with how lawyers can enhance their practice of law by creating a presence on the internet.

*Advanced Legal Research on the Internet,* Minnesota State Bar Association, Continuing Legal Education (St. Paul, MN: Minnesota Continuing Legal Education 1997) 1 v. (various pagings).

Deals with browsers; websites with a particular legal focus; search engines; using and saving what you find on the Web.

*Using the Internet for Legal Research,* Minnesota State Bar Association, Continuing Legal Education (St. Paul, MN: Minnesota Continuing Legal Education 1996) 1 v. (various pagings).

Basic information regarding the Web, home pages, retrieving information from the Internet, legal and news sources, and terminology.

*The Internet and the Practice of Law,* Minnesota State Bar Association, Continuing Legal Education (St. Paul, MN: Minnesota Continuing Legal Education 1995) 1 v. (various pagings) ill.

Deals with terminology, hardware, Internet resources, and comprehensive sites.

# CHAPTER SIX
# Institutions and Organizations

This chapter discusses the various institutions and organizations that support the Minnesota legal community.

## Chapter Contents

§ 610. Libraries
§ 620. Library School Programs
§ 630. Law Schools
§ 635. Alternative Dispute Resolution
§ 640. Bar Associations
§ 650. Legislatively and Judicially Sanctioned Agencies
§ 660. Continuing Legal Education
§ 670. Legal Assistance
§ 680. Support Personnel

## § 610. LIBRARIES

§ 611. Law Libraries
§ 612. Private Law Libraries
§ 613. Academic Law Libraries
§ 614. Government Law Libraries
§ 615. Federal Document Depository Libraries in Minnesota
§ 616. Minnesota State Document Depository Libraries
§ 617. County Law Libraries
§ 618. Non-Law Libraries
§ 619. Library Organizations

Minnesota is fortunate to have excellent information resources in the form of libraries. There are institutions of higher learning, professional schools, government libraries, and special libraries of various kinds. There is a spirt of cooperation among libraries and librarians. There has been some attempt to correlate acquisitions, provision of services, and sharing collections among the law libraries in Minnesota, but no formal agreement exists. There are informal relationships regarding lending and borrowing.

## § 611. Law Libraries

Libraries are designated as law libraries if the bulk of their collections consists of legal materials.[434] Law libraries may be divided into three categories—private law libraries, academic law libraries, and government law libraries.

## § 612. Private Law Libraries

Private law libraries generally fall into two categories: Those maintained by law firms or individual lawyers as working legal reference libraries, and those maintained by corporations for use by their legal departments. Practicing lawyers depend on a law library and occasionally several individuals or firms may establish a joint law library. Private libraries are neither listed nor described here because materials generally are not available for use by members of the public. The Minnesota Association of Law Libraries *Membership Directory* lists many of the private law firms that have professional library leadership. Cooperation and information exchange exist between public and private law libraries.

## § 613. Academic Law Libraries

§ 613.1. Hamline University School of Law Library
§ 613.2. University of Minnesota Law Library
§ 613.3. University of Saint Thomas, School of Law Library
§ 613.4. William Mitchell College of Law, Warren E. Burger Library

Probably because of their easy accessibility, extended hours, and large collections, the four law schools libraries in the state often are the first to be used by lawyers. Each collection first serves the needs of the law school faculty and students. In most instances the library collection is available for in-house use to the general public. Circulation privileges vary for each library.

---

434. Most academic and government law libraries have electronic catalogs that are accessible via the World Wide Web or through another medium.

## Chapter Six. Institutions and Organizations

*A Guide to Major Law Library Collections in the Twin Cities* ([Minneapolis, MN?]: s.n. [1994]) 281 p.

Result of an informal committee composed of representatives from each of the major law libraries in the Twin Cities. These are Hamline University Law School Library, Hennepin County Law Library, Minnesota State Law Library, Ramsey County Law Library, University of Minnesota Law School Library, and William Mitchell College of Law, Warren E. Burger Library.

### § 613.1. Hamline University School of Law Library

Library-MS-D2010, 1536 Hewitt Avenue, St. Paul, MN 55104-1237; phone 651-523-2125; Web address <http://www.hamline.edu/law/library>.

### § 613.2. University of Minnesota Law Library

229 19th Avenue South, Minneapolis, MN 55455-0401; phone 612-373-2737 (taped message), 612-373-2738; Web address <http://www.law.umn.edu/library/home.html>.

### § 613.3. University of Saint Thomas, School of Law Library

MPL 440, 1000 LaSalle Avenue, Minneapolis, MN 55403-2005; phone 651-962-4985; Web address <http://www.department.stthomas.edu/lawschool/>.

### § 613.4. William Mitchell College of Law, Warren E. Burger Library[435]

871 Summit Avenue, St. Paul, MN 55105-3030; phone 651-227-9171; Web address <http://www.wmitchell.edu/library/index.html>.

---

435. The library is named for Warren Earl Burger, 15th Chief Justice of the United States Supreme Court, who graduated with honors from what was Saint Paul College of Law, now William Mitchell College of Law, in 1931.

## § 614. Government Law Libraries

§ 614.1. Minnesota State Law Library
§ 614.2. Federal Court Libraries

Government law libraries meet the needs of court and government personnel. Collections focus on local and federal materials. Most government libraries are open to the public.

### § 614.1. Minnesota State Law Library[436]

The library opened in its present location in 1990, and celebrated its 150th anniversary on November 9, 1999. The library is under the jurisdiction of the Supreme Court and is staffed by professional librarians and library technicians. In cooperation with other agencies and libraries, the State Law Library is attempting to provide statewide access to legal information.[437] The library provides photocopying service, Westlaw research, and interlibrary loan. Fees charged are to cover costs.[438]

### § 614.2. Federal Court Libraries

§ 614.21. Eighth Circuit Library, Minneapolis
§ 614.22. Eighth Circuit Library, St. Paul

Minnesota is in the Eighth Circuit Court of Appeals, which has its seat in Saint Louis, Missouri. The federal courts in Minnesota maintain small collections for use by the judges and staff in the district courts. A larger collection for the Eighth Circuit Court of Appeals is staffed by a professional librarian. Use by the public may be arranged.

---

436. Minnesota Judicial Center, 25 Constitution Ave., St. Paul, MN 55155-6102; phone 651-296-2775; Web address <http://www.courts.state.mn.us/library/>.
437. The library publishes a newsletter, *Loquitur* (St. Paul, MN: Minnesota State Law Library, v. 1, no. 1 (Oct. 1983) to date).
438. *See also* MINNESOTA GUIDEBOOK TO STATE AGENCY SERVICES 1996–1999 (8th ed. [St. Paul]: State of Minnesota, Dept. Administration 1996) at 366 [hereinafter MINN. GUIDEBOOK].

Chapter Six. Institutions and Organizations

## § 614.21. Eighth Circuit Library, Minneapolis

United States Courthouse, Suite 1102, 300 South 4th Street, Minneapolis, MN 55415-2249; phone 612-664-5830; Web address <http://www.ca8.uscourts.gov/index.html>.

## § 614.22. Eighth Circuit Library, St. Paul

541 Federal Building, 316 North Robert Street, St. Paul, MN 55101-1461; phone 651-290-3177; Web address <http://www.ca8.uscourts.gov/index.html>.

## § 615. Federal Document Depository Libraries in Minnesota

### § 615.1. Government Publications Library[439]

Federal government documents often are valuable legal research sources. There are twenty-five libraries in Minnesota designated as Federal Depository Libraries.[440] The regional depository is the Government Publications Library at the University of Minnesota. Law libraries that also are Federal Depository Libraries are: University of Minnesota Law Library; William Mitchell College of Law Library; Hamline University School of Law Library; and Minnesota State Law Library.

## § 616. Minnesota State Document Depository Libraries[441]

Since 1974, the Legislative Reference Library (LRL) has been the Minnesota state document depository library. Minn. Stat. § 3.302 (1999) mandates that the LRL is to receive all documents[442] published by the state and any documents published privately at the direction of the state that may be of value or interest to the library.

---

439. University of Minnesota, Wilson Library, 309 19th Ave. South, Minneapolis, MN 55455-0414; phone 612-624-5073; Web address <http://govpubs.lib.umn.edu>.
440. See Appendix J for a detailed list.
441. *Directory of Minnesota Depository Libraries,* [William G. Kenz & Dan Mollner; with the assistance of Karla Eck, Marla Smith & Ginny Bakke] ([St. Peter, MN?]: MLA/GODORT 1994) 64 leaves.
442. See MINN. STAT. § 3.302(3) (1999) for a definition of "document."

Thirty-eight Minnesota libraries have been designated as state document depository libraries.[443] These libraries are tax-supported libraries and include community colleges, state universities, public libraries, University of Minnesota campus libraries, and state agency libraries. Microform copies of documents have been distributed to the depositories during the last twenty years.

Minnesota state documents are cataloged by these libraries and holdings are accessible through the library's catalog. Because many of the state depository libraries are part of the PALS (Project for Automated Library Systems) online union catalog of state universities, community colleges, state agencies, etc. access to documents is fairly easy.

In addition to access to the documents provided by the library's catalog, there are library publications designed to make the state documents more accessible:

- *Guide to Minnesota State Documents and Selected Law-Related Materials*, Marsha L. Baum & Mary Ann Nelson ([Chicago, IL]: American Association of Law Libraries [1986]) iii leaves, 31, [2] p.; Annual State Documents Bibliography Series. Occasional papers, no. 3-24, State documents bibliography no. 3-24.
- *Minnesota Resources: A Selected List of Current Minnesota State Documents,* Minnesota, Legislature, Legislative Reference Library (St. Paul, MN: Legislative Reference Library 1987– ). Current lists available online at <http://www.leg.state.mn.us/lrl/resource/mnres.htm>.
- *Minnesota State Agency Periodicals* (St. Paul, MN: Legislative Reference Library 1990– ). Current list available online at <http://www.leg.state.mn.us/lrl/mndocs/mnper.htm>.

## § 617. County Law Libraries

§ 617.1. Anoka County Law Library
§ 617.2. Dakota County Law Library
§ 617.3. Hennepin County Law Library
§ 617.4. Ramsey County Law Library
§ 617.5. Saint Louis County Law Library
§ 617.6. Scott County Law Library

---

443. For a list of Minnesota State Document Depository libraries, see Appendix M.

**Chapter Six. Institutions and Organizations** 219

§ 617.7. Stearns County Law Library
§ 617.8. Washington County Law Library

County law libraries may be freely used by the judges of the state; state officials; judges of the district, municipal county, and conciliation courts of the county; city and county officials; members of the bar; and inhabitants of the county.[444] The statute empowers the county board to provide quarters; provide for a board of trustees who govern the library by establishing bylaws and regulations; financial oversight by the county auditor; appointment of library staff; and setting of law library fees. The Minnesota State Law Library[445] is the advisory agency for these libraries. In 1980, the County Law Library Project was created to facilitate their growth and development. The project publishes a bulletin[446] and other reports of interest as well as a directory of county law libraries that includes a listing of county law library boards and contact persons.[447]

One of the first efforts of the project was to catalog all the materials held at county law libraries. This resulted in a union catalog.[448] With the advent of the online catalog, the union catalog on microfiche was discontinued.[449]

Listed below are those county law libraries with full-time library staff. Some county law libraries have part-time library staff,[450] and the

---

444. *See* MINN. STAT. § 134A.02 (1999).
445. Minnesota State Law Library, County Law Library Project, Minnesota Judicial Center, 25 Constitution Ave., St. Paul, MN 55155-6102; phone 651-297-2087.
446. *County Law Library Project Bulletin* (St. Paul, MN: County Law Library Project, Minnesota State Law Library 1984– ).
447. *Directory of County Law Libraries* (St. Paul, MN: County Law Library Project, Minnesota State Law Library 1984– ). This list also can be found at <http://www.courts.state.mn.us/library/clldir.html>.
448. *Minnesota State Law Library Union Catalog on Microfiche, 1986* [microform] 27 microfiche. Arranged in two segments: author/title (16 fiche) and subject (11 fiche).
    Union catalog of books cataloged at the State Law Library and at the county law libraries of Anoka, Hennepin, Kandiyohi, Ramsey, Saint Louis, Stearns/Benton, and Nobles counties during the period 1978–1986.
449. The holdings of the State Law Library, county law libraries, and many state agencies are available through PALS, <http://www.pals.msus.edu/webpals.home.html>.
450. County law libraries staffed by part-time library employees are Clay County (Morehead); Freeborn County (Albert Lea); Kandiyohi County (Willmar); Marshall County (Warren); Mille Lacs County (Miliaca); Mower County (Austin); Olmstead County (Rochester); and Wright County (Buffalo). County seats are in parentheses.

remainder have law clerks or other judicial personnel who maintain the libraries as needed.

### § 617.1. Anoka County Law Library

Anoka County Courthouse, 325 East Main Street, Anoka, MN 55303-2483; phone 612-422-7549.

### § 617.2. Dakota County Law Library

Judicial Center, 1560 Highway 55, Hastings, MN 55033-2343; phone 651-438-8080.

### § 617.3. Hennepin County Law Library

C2451, Government Center, Minneapolis, MN 55487-0541; phone 612-348-3023; Web address <http://www.co.hennepin.mn.us/lawlibrary/lawlib.htm>.

### § 617.4. Ramsey County Law Library

1815 Courthouse, St. Paul, MN 55102-1690; phone 651-266-8391.

### § 617.5. Saint Louis County Law Library

Courthouse—Duluth Branch, 100 North Fifth Avenue Room 515, Duluth, MN 55802-1202; phone 218-726-2611.

### § 617.6. Scott County Law Library

Scott County Government Center, 200 Fourth Street, Shakopee, MN 55379-1263.

### § 617.7. Stearns County Law Library

725 Courthouse Square, Room 105, Saint Cloud, MN 56303-4781; phone 320-656-3678; Web address <http://www.co.stearns.mn.us/departments/other/index.html#law>.

### § 617.8. Washington County Law Library

14949 62nd Street North, P.O. Box 6, Stillwater, MN 55082-0006; phone 651-430-6330; Web address <http://www.washcolaw.lib.mn.us/>.

## § 618. Non-Law Libraries

§ 618.1. James J. Hill Reference Library
§ 618.2. League of Minnesota Cities
§ 618.3. Association of Minnesota Counties
§ 618.4. Legislative Reference Library
§ 618.5. Minnesota Historical Society
§ 618.6. Metropolitan Council
§ 618.7. University of Minnesota Human Rights Library

Many useful items for the legal profession are available in public libraries, for example government documents; stock quotations; business reference materials; directories; social, political, and historical materials; and non-legal computer-assisted research services. Public and private library resources are shared statewide through the Minnesota Inter-Library Telecommunications Exchange (MINITEX), the state-funded interlibrary loan system.[451]

Metronet[452] has compiled a Minnesota Library Directory that is available online at <http://www.metronet.lib.mn.us/mnlibs/>. Although it may not be a comprehensive listing of libraries in Minnesota, it represents the best efforts to provide a useful tool for locating information about Minnesota's libraries.

Directory information regarding Minnesota libraries also can be found in the *ALA Membership Directory*[453] as well as Name Address Directory on OCLC. The ALA membership directory[454] is available online in Westlaw. Listed below are a few of the libraries with collections containing specialized legal resources.

---

451. MINITEX Office, 15 Andersen Library, University of Minnesota, 222 21st Ave. South, Minneapolis, MN 55455-0439; phone 612-376-4649 or 612-376-3926; Web address <http://kinglear.minitex.umn.edu/>.
452. Metronet is a multi-type library organization serving academic, school, public, and special libraries in the Twin Cities of Minneapolis and St. Paul, Minnesota. Web address <http://www.metronet.lib.mn.us/>.
453. AMERICAN LIBRARY ASSOCIATION, ALA MEMBERSHIP DIRECTORY (Chicago, IL: American Library Ass'n 1996– ).
454. Although the *ALA Directory* is not available at the ALA website, the site has much information available at <http://www.ala.org>.

### § 618.1. James J. Hill[455] Reference Library[456]

This special library emphasizes the growth and development of business in the north central and northwestern states. The library staff has compiled several unique and useful directories over the years.[457] Of special interest is its collection of standards published by various professional groups. Hill receives all standards issued by the American National Standards Institute and the National Fire Protection Association. Additionally, the library maintains a union list for the Twin Cities Standards-Cooperative, a group of company, public, and academic libraries that share their voluntary engineering standards with each other and the public.

### § 618.2. League of Minnesota Cities[458]

The library exists primarily for league staff, to assist them in delivering services to city members, and especially for the research department staff, who respond to 7,500 information requests annually—primarily from member cities—on issues that arise in the day-to-day running of city government. The general public may use the library with the assistance of a league staff member by arrangement only. Regular business hours are Monday through Friday from 8:30 a.m. until 5:00 p.m. Limited telephone reference is available.

The library contains a core legal library with specialized treatises pertaining to city government, zoning, etc. The library has a collection of city ordinances, internally produced memoranda, a series of "Information Memos" on topics of municipal interest (such as Conflict of Interest, Competitive Bidding, or Local Improvement Guide). Information Memos are available on the website under publications/research memos. Several of the newest memos also are available there in full-text PDF format.

---

455. James J. Hill, the builder of the Great Northern Railway, endowed the library. Personal papers and archives dealing with the Great Northern R.R. and the Hill family are housed there in addition to an extensive reference collection.
456. 80 West Fourth St., St. Paul, MN 55102-1669; phone 651-227-9531; Web address <http://www.jjhill.org>.
457. DIRECTORY OF MINNESOTA BUSINESS AND PROFESSIONAL ASSOCIATIONS 1996, 8th ed. (Patrick Clark, Laurie Dahl & Anne Johnson (eds.), St. Paul, MN: James J. Hill Reference Library 1996).
458. 145 University Ave. West, St. Paul, MN 55103-2044; phone 651-281-1200; Web address <http://www.lmnc.org>.

## Chapter Six. Institutions and Organizations

### § 618.3. Association of Minnesota Counties[459]

The Association of Minnesota Counties (AMC) is a voluntary statewide organization that assists the state's eighty-seven counties in providing effective county governance to the people of Minnesota. The association works closely with the legislative and administrative branches of government in seeing that legislation and policies favorable to counties are enacted. Additionally, the association provides educational programs, training, research, and communications for county officials.

### § 618.4. Legislative Reference Library[460]

Established in 1969, the Legislative Reference Library (LRL) provides information to members of the legislature and their staff. The library is open to the public. The library is the depository for all state documents. The definition of "state documents"[461] includes any publication issued by state offices and agencies as well as publications prepared by private entities at the state's request. *Minnesota Statutes* mandate that six copies of each state document be collected by the library[462] (*see* 226.4, *supra*).

### § 618.5. Minnesota Historical Society[463]

This library is the official custodian of the state's history and contains about 98% of the available material about Minnesota. The Archives and Manuscripts Division contains the State Archives which hold the official, non-current, and historically valuable records of the governors, other executive officers, state agencies, judicial and legislative branches of state government, and many local governments. Consequently, it is the depository for past legislative history. The society also publishes materials that aid the public in using its collections and in understanding Minnesota history including its law (*see* § 226.4 , *supra*).

---

459. 125 Charles Ave., St. Paul, MN 55103-2108; phone 651-224-3344; Web address <http://www.mncounties.org>.
460. State Office Building, St. Paul, MN 55155-1288; phone 651-296-3398; Web address <http://www.library.leg.state.mn.us/>.
461. *See* MINN. STAT. § 3.302(3) (1999).
462. *See id.* § 3.195(a).
463. History Center, 345 Kellogg Blvd West, St. Paul, MN 55102-1906; phone 651-296-1430; Web address <http://www.mnhs.org>.

### § 618.6. Metropolitan Council[464]

Started in 1967, the Metropolitan Council oversees various services for a seven county area comprised of Anoka, Carver, Dakota, Hennepin, Ramsey, Scott, and Washington Counties.

### § 618.7. University of Minnesota Human Rights Library[465]

The University of Minnesota Human Rights Center's principal goal is to help train effective human rights professionals and volunteers. In partial fulfillment of this goal the center maintains the University of Minnesota Human Rights Library which is described as being the nation's largest collection of human rights books, monographs, periodicals, and other published materials from around the world.

## § 619. Library Organizations

§ 619.1. Minnesota Association of Law Libraries (MALL)
§ 619.2. Capitol Area Library Consortium (CALCO)
§ 619.3. Special Libraries Association (SLA)
§ 619.4. American Society for Information Science (ASIS)
§ 619.5. Metropolitan Library Service Agency (MELSA)
§ 619.6. Metronet
§ 619.7. Minnesota Library Association (MLA)

Continuing the Minnesota library tradition, cooperation among law libraries is excellent. Professional exchange exists in organized associations and among the librarians within small special-interest groups that meet occasionally for mutual interchange of ideas.

---

464. *See* MINN. STAT. §§ 473.123–473.249 (1999). "A metropolitan council with jurisdiction in the metropolitan area is established as a public corporation and political subdivision of the state." Mears Park Centre, 230 East Fifth St., St. Paul, MN; phone 651-602-1000; Web address <http://www.metrocouncil.org>.
465. Human Rights Center, University of Minnesota, 229 19th Ave. South, Minneapolis, MN 55455; phone 612-625-5027; Web address <http://www1.umn.edu/humanrts/>.

## § 619.1. Minnesota Association of Law Libraries (MALL)[466]

The Minnesota Association of Law Libraries (MALL) is affiliated with the American Association of Law Libraries.[467] MALL membership includes all professionally staffed law libraries in Minnesota as well as members from North and South Dakota law libraries. The association sponsors institutes on legal research and other aspects of law librarianship. Regular meetings center around topics of current interest. Committees work on issues of professional concern and provide placement, consulting, and resource exchange programs. Publications of the association include the *MALL Newsletter*,[468] *Legal Materials for Non-Law Libraries, Union List of Legal Looseleaf Services*[469] *in the Twin City Area, Guidelines for Legal Reference Service*,[470] and a brochure describing the association.

The Downtowners is group of law librarians employed at law firms and government organizations in Minneapolis who have found common interest in their work. They meet for lunch on a monthly schedule to discuss issues and concerns and to provide in-service training.

Law libraries also participate in multi-county, multi-type library networks. These organizations encourage and develop sharing of resources among all types of libraries within a large geographic area crossing county lines. Participants agree to share resources, engage in long-range cooperative planning, and participate in development of a bibliographic database, a communications system, and document delivery.[471] Other services are based upon the needs of the participating libraries.

---

466. Care of (c/o) Minnesota State Law Library, 25 Constitution Ave., St. Paul, MN 55155-1500; Web address <http://aall.wuacc.edu/chapter/mall/backgr.htm>.
467. American Association of Law Libraries, 55 West Jackson Boulevard, Suite 940, Chicago, IL 60604-3668; phone 312-939-4764; Web address <http://www.aallnet.org>.
468. The *MALL Newsletter* is an online publication and can be found at <http://www.aallnet.org/chapter/mall/mallnews.htm>.
469. The *Union List of Looseleaf Services* can be found at <http://www.aallnet.org/chapter/mall/looseleaf/looseleaf2.htm>.
470. *See* Appendix G.
471. *See* MINN. STAT. §§ 134.001–134.46 (1999).

### § 619.2. Capitol Area Library Consortium (CALCO)[472]

Minnesota's state government libraries formed a consortium consisting of twenty-three libraries and information centers.[473] The libraries are in executive, legislative, and judicial branches of Minnesota government. The consortium maintains a bulletin board, website, etc.

### § 619.3. Special Libraries Association (SLA)[474]

Some law librarians in Minnesota and especially in the Twin Cities, are members of the Special Libraries Association. The Minnesota chapter is active in presenting various events of interest to special librarians.

### § 619.4. American Society for Information Science (ASIS)[475]

Founded in 1937, ASIS, the American Society for Information Science has as its goal the advancement of information professionals and the field of information science by providing methods of communication and continuing education and by encouraging research and development in the field of information science. There is a Minnesota chapter of ASIS.

---

472. Web address <http://www.state.mn.us./libraries/calco.html>.
473. For a list of these libraries, see Appendix O. Capitol Area Library Consortium Directory (CALCO) may be accessed at <http://www.state.mn.us/libraries/directry.pdf>.
474. 1700 18th St. N.W., Washington, DC 20009-2514; phone 202-234-4700; Web addresses <http://www.sla.org> (national organization website), <http://www.sla.org/chapter/cmn/index.html> (Minnesota chapter website), <http://www.slalegal.org> (legal division website).
475. 8720 Georgia Ave., Suite 501, Silver Spring, MD 20910-3610; phone 301-495-0100; Web address <http://www.asis.org>.

## Chapter Six. Institutions and Organizations

### § 619.5. Metropolitan Library Service Agency (MELSA)[476]

MELSA is a federation of Minneapolis/St. Paul metropolitan city and county public libraries[477] that provides all members with cooperative and cost-saving programs and services. The seven-county metropolitan Twin Cities service area accounts for more than half of the state's population.

### § 619.6. Metronet[478]

Metronet is a multi-type library organization serving academic, school, public, and special libraries in Minneapolis and St. Paul.

### § 619.7. Minnesota Library Association (MLA)[479]

The Minnesota Library Association is a non-profit corporation comprised of types of libraries and librarians, including public, academic, school, special, multi-type, institutional, and non-specified. MLA also lobbies the legislature on behalf of libraries and library networks. MLA is a chapter of the American Library Association.

## § 620. LIBRARY SCHOOL PROGRAMS

§ 621. College of Saint Catherine
§ 622. University of North Texas
§ 623. University of Wisconsin–Milwaukee

The University of Minnesota closed its library school in the 1970s; however, professional library education has not been lacking. Citizens of Minnesota have been granted resident tuition privileges with Iowa and Wisconsin, each of which maintain ALA-accredited schools of library and information science in Iowa City, Milwaukee, and

---

476. 1619 Dayton Ave., Suite 314, St. Paul, MN 55104-6206; phone 651-645-5731; Web address <http://www.melsa.lib.mn.us/>.
477. MELSA is composed of nine member library systems, including Anoka County, Carver County, Dakota County, Hennepin County, City of Minneapolis, Ramsey County, City of Saint Paul, Scott County, and Washington County, and comprises more than 100 library facilities.
478. 1619 Dayton Ave., Suite 314, St. Paul, MN 55104-6206; phone 651-646-0475; Web address <http://www.metronet.lib.mn.us/about/contact.htm>.
479. 1619 Dayton Ave., Suite 314, St. Paul, MN 55104-6206; phone 651-641-0982; Web address <http://www.lib.mankato.msus.edu:2000/>.

Madison. The mainstay of library and information science education in the Twin Cities has been the College of Saint Catherine.

### § 621. College of Saint Catherine[480]

The college offers a Master of Library and Information Science with Dominican University (River Forest, IL). It is an ALA-accredited program with a twelve-course curriculum designed to educate entry-level librarians and information specialists. A law librarianship course is offered.

### § 622. University of North Texas (UNT)[481]

UNT offers a master's program in cooperation with Saint Cloud State University. Classes are held on the Saint Cloud campus and in suburban Minneapolis. Classes began in Fall 1999. They also offer a Web-based program that will be available in Fall 2001.

### § 623. University of Wisconsin–Milwaukee (UWM)[482]

UWM sponsors a distance-education program that offers coursework each semester toward a master's degree in library and information science. The coursework is offered via the Internet or compressed video. Credits may be applied to the MLIS or school media certification. For details about this particular program see the website at <http://www.slis.uwm.edu/new98/distance_ed.htm>.

---

480. 2004 Randolph Ave., St. Paul, MN 55105-1750; phone 651-690-6802; Web address <http://www.stkate.edu/offices/academic/mlis.nsf>.
481. School of Library and Information Sciences, Information Services Building, Room 205, Post Office Box 311068, Denton, TX 76203-1068; phone 940-565-2445; Web address <http://www.unt.edu/slis/distance/mn/mn.htm>.
482. School of Library and Information Science, 2400 East Hartford Ave., Enderis Hall Room 1110, P.O. Box 413, Milwaukee, WI 53211-3159; phone 414-229-4707; Web address <http://www.slis.uwm.edu/>.

## § 630. LAW SCHOOLS

§ 631. Hamline University School of Law
§ 632. University of Minnesota Law School
§ 633. University of Saint Thomas
§ 634. William Mitchell College of Law
§ 635. Alternative Dispute Resolution

In Minnesota,[483] an applicant for admission to the bar must have graduated from a law school that is provisionally or fully approved by the American Bar Association (ABA).[484] The following law schools in Minnesota have been accredited by the ABA.

### § 631. Hamline University School of Law[485]

§ 631.1. Dispute Resolution Institute
§ 631.2. The Dred & Harriet Scott Institute for International Human Rights
§ 631.3. Annual Law, Religion, and Ethics Symposium

Hamline University School of Law was established as Midwestern School of Law in 1972 and affiliated with Hamline University, where it now is located, in June 1976. In addition to the three year J.D. program, Hamline offers a six-year B.A.-J.D. degree plan and a flexible day program for persons unable to pursue a full-time day or part-time evening law school education. Summer session classes are offered. There are summer study programs in Norway, Israel, and Italy. Hamline also offers several J.D.-master's programs with University of Saint Thomas. An LL.M. program for foreign lawyers was started in 1998. Also available is a joint degree program with the School of Public Administration leading to a Master of Arts in Public Administration and J.D.

---

483. Rules for Admission to the Bar, Rule II(A)(3) General Requirements for Admission.
484. OFFICIAL AMERICAN BAR ASSOCIATION GUIDE TO APPROVED LAW SCHOOLS, prepared by the Section of Legal Education and Admissions to the Bar in cooperation with the Office of the Consultant on Legal Education to the American Bar Association (New York: Macmillan 1998– ).
485. Dean, MS-D2005, 1536 Hewitt Ave., St. Paul, MN 55104-1237; phone 651-523-2941; Web address <http://www.hamline.edu/law>.

### § 631.1. Dispute Resolution Institute[486]

The Dispute Resolution Institute (DRI) was established in 1991 to offer high-quality dispute resolution training for law students, lawyers, and other professionals. DRI currently has several core academic programs: the Summer Institute; January term courses; an international program at the Università di Modena Law School in Italy; and an Annual Fall Symposium on Advanced Issues in Dispute Resolution. The DRI has offered a certificate program in dispute resolution since 1996. The certificate program allows law students, lawyers, and other professionals to further develop their ADR knowledge and skills in an organized, thoughtful, and scholarly way resulting in a valuable credential.

### § 631.2. The Dred & Harriet Scott Institute for International Human Rights[487]

The Dred and Harriet Scott Institute was founded to promote observance of and respect for international human rights and fundamental freedoms. The activities of the institute are marked by a special emphasis on minority rights, as defined under international human rights law, and the experience of African Americans in the United States. The institute is a project of Hamline University School of Law, and is designed to provide educational and research opportunities for law students, lawyers, judges, human rights scholars, and members of the community.

---

486. Associate Director, Hamline University School of Law, MS - D2004, 1536 Hewitt Ave., St. Paul, MN 55104-1237; phone 651-523-2897; Web address <http://www.hamline.edu/law/adr/>.
487. Hamline University School of Law, 1536 Hewitt Ave., St. Paul, MN 55104-1237; phone 651-523-2120; Web address <http://www.hamline.edu/law/scottinstitute/>.

## Chapter Six. Institutions and Organizations

### § 631.3. Annual Law, Religion, and Ethics Symposium[488]

For the past dozen years, Hamline's School of Law and the United Theological Seminary[489] has sponsored a symposium on law, religion, and ethics. The theme and focus of the symposium differs each year.

### § 632. University of Minnesota Law School[490]

§ 632.1. Institute on Criminal Justice
§ 632.2. Human Rights Center
§ 632.3. Institute on Race & Poverty

The University of Minnesota Law School was established in 1888. It is a charter member of the Association of American Law Schools. In 1978, the law school moved to a new building on the west bank of the Minneapolis campus. Admission to the law school is granted only on a full-time basis; classes are held during the day. A limited number of courses are offered during the summer. Students receive a J.D. degree after three years of study. Combined degree programs are available allowing simultaneous study toward the J.D. and another advanced degree. There is a European exchange program and joint degree programs in law, health, and life sciences.

### § 632.1. Institute on Criminal Justice[491]

The Institute on Criminal Justice is an information agency whose goal is to advise legislators, criminal justice administrators, and lawyers of current issues in the field and to influence public policy. In some instances, the institute sponsors research projects to further its programs.

---

488. Sponsored by Hamline University School of Law and the United Theological Seminary of the Twin Cities. Web address <http://www.hamline.edu/law/symposium/>.
489. United Theological Seminary of the Twin Cities, 3000 5th St. NW, New Brighton, MN 55112-2598; phone 651-633-4311; Web address <http://www.unitedseminary-mn.org>.
490. 229 19th Ave. South, Minneapolis, MN 55455-0401; phone 612-625-4300; Web address <http://www.law.umn.edu>.
491. Web address <http://www.law.umn.edu/centers/crimjust.htm>.

### § 632.2. Human Rights Center[492]

The University of Minnesota Human Rights Center was founded in December 1988. The center offers training, public education activities, and a library, and promotes research on the topic of human rights. The center attempts to keep the public aware of new developments on human rights and provides opportunities for students and other professionals to assist victims of human rights abuses.

### § 632.3. Institute on Race & Poverty[493]

The Institute on Race & Poverty (IRP) was founded in 1992. Its mission is to study the effect of race on an individual's economic condition and the effect racial discrimination has on economic conditions. The institute conducts research and studies in an attempt to influence public policy regarding the racism and economic welfare.

### § 633. University of Saint Thomas, School of Law[494]

The University of Saint Thomas School of Law provides an innovative, challenging, and practical approach to legal education. The full-time, day program will begin in Fall 2001. As yet, the UST law school has not been accredited by the American Bar Association.[495]

---

492. Web address <http://www.law.umn.edu/centers/hrcenter.htm>.
493. Web address <http://www.law.umn.edu/centers/race-pov.htm>.
494. MPL 440, 1000 LaSalle Ave., Minneapolis, MN 55403-2005; phone 651-962-4895; Web address <http://www.department.stthomas/lawschool/>.
495. STANDARDS FOR APPROVAL OF LAW SCHOOLS (compiled and distributed by the Office of the Consultant on Legal Education to the American Bar Association, Indianapolis: The Office [1999]).

## § 634. William Mitchell College of Law[496]

§ 634.1. Center for Conflict Management/Americord®
§ 634.2. Center for Health Law & Policy
§ 634.3. Center for Professional Programming

William Mitchell College of Law, which celebrated its centennial in 2000, received its present name in 1956,[497] when the Saint Paul College of Law (founded in 1900) merged with the Minneapolis-Minnesota College of Law. The college offers both day and evening instruction. Classes are held in the summer. Day students generally receive a J.D. degree after three years of study; night students after four years. William Mitchell participates in a summer "Law in London" program along with several other American law schools.

### § 634.1. Center for Conflict Management/Americord®

The Center for Conflict Management brings the benefits of alternative dispute resolution (ADR) processes to the larger community. The center provides high-quality, professional, neutral services to help disputing parties resolve their differences. Access to a wide range of services and educational experiences is made to all. The center also offers training in negotiation, mediation, arbitration, and other conflict-management skills and concepts for practicing lawyers, managers of business, government, educational, and social service organizations, and individuals. The center promotes advances in the field of conflict management through research, scholarship, and enhanced curriculum.

### § 634.2. Center for Health Law & Policy

Established in 1998, the Center for Health Law & Policy provides timely and relevant educational resources of exceptional quality in the areas of health law and policy that are accessible to all individuals in the community including law students, attorneys, health care professionals, and consumers. The center fulfills this mission through

---

496. 871 Summit Ave., St. Paul, MN 55105-3030; phone 651-290-6357; Web address <http://www.wmitchell.edu>.
497. Founded in 1900, the college of law is named for the Minnesota Supreme Court Justice William Mitchell (1832–1900) who served on the High Court from 1881–1900.

curriculum enhancement, research and publication, professional education and development, and community outreach—all conducted in an inclusive and neutral manner.

### § 634.3. Center for Professional Programming

The Center for Professional Programming provides a broad range of custom-designed educational resources, focusing on legal issues and how the law affects an individual's everyday work. Skill training is provided for judges, paralegals, law enforcement officers, religious leaders, human resources managers, clergy, social workers, teachers, engineers, judges, paralegals, attorneys, and other professionals. Through seminars, conferences, and roundtables, the center provides practical application of legal skills on contemporary legal issues.

### § 635. Alternative Dispute Resolution[498]

§ 635.1. American Arbitration Association—Minnesota Regional Office
§ 635.2. Hamline University's Dispute Resolution Institute
§ 635.3. Center for Conflict Management/Americord®

Alternative dispute resolution (ADR) is an umbrella term that includes mediation, private trials, neutral expert fact-finding, mini-trials, and arbitration. These alternative methods of settling disputes and avoiding litigation have been endorsed by the Minnesota legislature in Minn. Stat. 484.76 (1999) which directs the Minnesota Supreme Court "to establish a statewide alternative dispute resolution program for the resolution of civil cases filed with the courts. The supreme court shall adopt rules governing practice, procedure, and jurisdiction for alternative dispute resolution programs established under this section."[499]

---

498. *See* DIRECTORY OF LAW SCHOOL ALTERNATIVE DISPUTE RESOLUTION COURSES AND PROGRAMS: A DIRECTORY OF COURSES, CLINICS, PROFESSORS, KEY CONTACTS, COURSE DESCRIPTIONS AND TEACHING METHODS IN DISPUTE RESOLUTION 2d ed. (Washington, DC: Section of Dispute Resolution, American Bar Ass'n 1997).
499. *See* COMPREHENSIVE DIRECTORY MINNESOTA ALTERNATIVE DISPUTE RESOLUTION PROGRAMS (Conflict Management Center, William Mitchell College of Law (comp.), St. Paul, MN: William Mitchell College of Law 1992) 20 p.

## Chapter Six. Institutions and Organizations

### § 635.1. American Arbitration Association (AAA)[500]—Minnesota Regional Office[501]

This non-profit organization was established seventy-five years ago to promote the use of ADR to settle a wide range of disputes in many fields, for example commercial, employment, securities, medical, labor, and construction. The AAA uses a variety of methods through mediation, arbitration, fact finding, and mini-trials. The AAA has a regional office in Minneapolis.

### § 635.2. Hamline University's Dispute Resolution Institute[502]

The Dispute Resolution Institute was established in 1991 to offer high-quality dispute resolution training for law students, lawyers, and other professionals (*see* § 631.1, *supra*).

### § 635.3. Center for Conflict Management/Americord®[503]

The center provides professional neutral services to help disputing parties resolve their differences. It also offers training in negotiation, mediation, arbitration, and other conflict-management skills and concepts (*see* § 634.1, *supra*).

---

500. *See* MARTINDALE-HUBBELL INTERNATIONAL ARBITRATION AND DISPUTE RESOLUTION DIRECTORY: THE SINGLE-SOURCE REFERENCE GUIDE TO GLOBAL DISPUTE RESOLUTION (New Providence, NJ: Martindale-Hubbell 1994– ) (annual) ("[t]he single-source reference guide to dispute resolution: practitioners, organizations, areas of practice, rules; published in cooperation with the American Arbitration Association").
501. 700 Pillsbury Center, 200 South Sixth St., Minneapolis, MN 55402-1092; phone 612-332-6545; Web address <http://www.adr.org/>.
502. MS- D2004, 1536 Hewitt Ave., St. Paul, MN 55104-1237; phone 651-523-2897; Web address <http://www.hamline.edu/law/adr>.
503. William Mitchell College of Law, 871 Summit Ave., St. Paul, MN 55105-3030; phone 651-290-6357; Web address <http://www.wmitchell.edu/community/cll/americord.html>.

## § 640. BAR ASSOCIATIONS[504]

§ 641. Minnesota State Bar Association
§ 642. Hennepin County Bar Association
§ 643. Ramsey County Bar Association
§ 644. Bar Associations in Greater Minnesota
§ 645. Special Interest Bar Associations in Minnesota

### § 641. Minnesota State Bar Association[505]

The Minnesota State Bar Association (MSBA), organized in 1883, is made up of twenty-one district bar associations,[506] and its members number approximately 14,500. The official publication of the association is the *Bench & Bar of Minnesota*[507] (*see* § 554.3, *supra*). A directory of members and a list of the association's sections and committees is published annually in an issue of *Bench & Bar of Minnesota* as well as the *Minnesota Legal Directory* (*see* § 536.3, *supra*). Section and committee reports are published in the May-June issue as well as on the website. Many district bar associations issue their own newsletters.

### § 642. Hennepin County Bar Association[508]

The largest county bar association in Minnesota, the Hennepin County Bar Association (HCBA) has more than 8,200 members. Along with member services, the HCBA provides various services to the public, one of which is Tel-Law, an audiotape information service. The tape recordings contain general legal information about a variety of subjects and are from three- to six-minutes long. The tapes can be accessed by telephone at any time. The association also has a speakers bureau that provides speakers to the community at large. The Hennepin County Bar Association publishes the *Hennepin Lawyer* (*see* § 554.3, *supra*).

---

504. DIRECTORY OF MINNESOTA LEGAL ASSOCIATIONS ON THE WEB <http://www.priweb.com/mnlegalassns.htm>.
505. 600 Nicollet Mall, Suite 380, Minneapolis, MN 55402-1039; phone 612-333-1183; Web address <http://www2.mnbar.org>.
506. See Appendix N for a complete list.
507. *See* <http://www2.mnbar.org/benchandbar/>.
508. Minnesota Law Center, 600 Nicollet Mall, Suite 390, Minneapolis, MN 55402-1043; phone 612-752-6600; Web address <http://www.hcba.org>.

## § 643. Ramsey County Bar Association[509]

The Ramsey County Bar Association provides legal education to its members and the public. The association coordinates a lawyer referral service and publishes *The Barrister* (see § 554.3, *supra*).

## § 644. Bar Associations in Greater Minnesota

There are twenty-one local bar associations in Minnesota. The district bar associations do not coincide with the judicial districts. Some district associations are comprised of a single county while others are multi-county. For a map of the Minnesota State Bar Association (MSBA) districts and the officers for each, see the directory issue of the *Bench & Bar of Minnesota* published in January of each year.

## § 645. Special Interest Bar Associations in Minnesota

Numerous other legal associations exist for lawyers with special interests. Minnesota legal directories, such as the *Bench & Bar of Minnesota* annual directory issue; the *Minnesota Attorney's/Paralegal's/Secretary's Handbook* or the *Minnesota Legal Directory* includes a list of most of these associations (*see* §§ 536.2, 536.3).

- ▶ Academy of Certified Trial Lawyers of Minnesota
- ▶ American Academy of Matrimonial Lawyers, Minnesota Chapter[510]
- ▶ American Immigration Lawyers Association, Minnesota-Dakotas Chapter[511]
- ▶ Federal Bar Association, Minnesota Chapter[512]
- ▶ Hmong Bar Association
- ▶ Minnesota American Indian Bar Association[513]
- ▶ Minnesota Association of Black Lawyers[514]

---

509. First National Bank Building, 332 Minnesota St., Suite 1401, St. Paul, MN 55101-1325; phone 651-222-0846; Web address <http://www.ramseybar.org>.
510. Web address <http://www.aamlmn.com/>.
511. Web address <http://www.capriotti.com/aila/mndak>.
512. Web address <http://www.fedbar.org/>.
513. Web address <http://www.maiba.org>.
514. Web address < http://www.mabl.org/>.

- Minnesota Association of Criminal Defense Lawyers
- Minnesota County Attorneys Association[515]
- Minnesota Defense Lawyers Association[516]
- Minnesota District Judges Association
- Minnesota Intellectual Property Law Association, Inc.[517]
- Minnesota Minority Lawyers Association
- Minnesota Trial Lawyers Association[518]
- Minnesota Women Lawyers, Inc.[519]

## § 650. LEGISLATIVELY AND JUDICIALLY SANCTIONED AGENCIES

§ 650.1. Board of Pardons
§ 650.2. Board of Judicial Standards
§ 650.3. Client Security Board
§ 650.4. Commission on Judicial Selection
§ 650.5. Continuing Education for State Court Personnel
§ 650.6. Court Information Office
§ 650.7. Lawyers Professional Responsibility Board
§ 650.8. Lawyers Trust Account Board
§ 650.9. Minnesota Sentencing Guidelines Commission
§ 650.10. Office of the State Court Administrator
§ 650.11. Office of Administrative Hearings
§ 650.12. State Board of Continuing Legal Education
§ 650.13. State Board of Law Examiners
§ 650.14. State Board of Legal Certification
§ 650.15. State Board of Public Defense

---

515. Web address <http://www.safenet.org/mcaa/mcaa.html>.
516. Web address <http://www.mdla.org/>.
517. Web address <http://www.aipla.org/>.
518. Web address <http://www.atlanet.org/>.
519. Web address <http://www.mwlawyers.org/>.

## Chapter Six. Institutions and Organizations

§ 650.16. State Public Defender
§ 650.17. Tax Court
§ 650.18. Workers' Compensation Court of Appeals

More than a dozen administrative agencies are sanctioned by the legislature or the Supreme Court to create rules and policy, administer hearings, and perform other various governance activities dealing with the judiciary, the practice of law, and the administration of justice. The following section is a list of such agencies.

### § 650.1. Board of Pardons

The Board of Pardons consists of the governor, chief justice of the supreme court, and the attorney general. The board may grant pardons and reprieves and commute the sentence of any person convicted of any offense against the laws of the state in the manner and under the conditions and rules prescribed but not otherwise.[520] For procedural rules see Minn. R. 6600.0200–1110 (1998).

### § 650.2. Board of Judicial Standards

Established in 1971, this independent agency investigates charges of ethical misconduct by Minnesota judges and referees. It consists of ten members, one court of appeals judge, three trial judges, two lawyers with at least ten years experience in Minnesota, and four public members. Discipline may be censure, suspension, retirement or removal of judges, or private reprimand.[521]

### § 650.3. Client Security Board

The Client Security Board consists of five Minnesota attorneys and two non-attorneys. The board administers a fund that was established by the Minnesota Supreme Court in 1987. The fund receives money from

---

520. MINN. STAT. § 638.01 (1999).
521. *Id.* §§ 490.15–490.16; 15 MINN. STAT. 1270 (1998) Rules of the Board of Judicial Standards. *See* MINN. GUIDEBOOK, *supra* note 438, at 368.

attorney's registration fees. It is used to reimburse clients who lose money or property due to the dishonest conduct of their attorney.[522]

### § 650.4. Commission on Judicial Selection

This legislatively mandated commission makes recommendations to the governor for the appointment of judges to newly created judgeships or to vacancies caused by the resignation, death, retirement, or removal from office.[523]

### § 650.5. Continuing Education for State Court Personnel

This office is part of the Office of the State Court Administrator. This office conducts in-service training for the many levels of court personnel from bailiffs to judges.[524]

### § 650.6. Court Information Office

The Court Information Office provides a variety of information services including education-related resources to educators for use in schools. It also provides judicial information to the news media and general information about the courts to individuals and community groups in a variety of formats, including print, video, and Web based.[525]

### § 650.7. Lawyers Professional Responsibility Board[526]

This board was established by the Minnesota Supreme Court in 1971 and is funded by money received from attorney's registration fees. The board consists of thirteen lawyers, nine non-lawyers, and a chair. The

---

522. *Id.* § 481.20; CSO Rules 1.01–4.01. 15 MINN. STAT. 1228 (1998), Rules for the Client Security Board. *See* MINN. GUIDEBOOK, *supra* note 438, at 368. Web address <http://www.courts.state.mn.us/csb/csb.html>.
523. MINN. STAT. § 480B.01 (1999).
524. *See* MINN. GUIDEBOOK, *supra* note 438, at 365.
525. Web address <http://www.courts.state.mn.us/cio/infobook.htm>.
526. DIRECTORY OF LAWYER DISCIPLINARY AGENCIES, LAWYERS' FUNDS FOR CLIENT PROTECTION. FEE ARBITRATION PROGRAMS AND UNAUTHORIZED PRACTICE OF LAW COMMITTEES (Chicago: ABA Center for Professional Responsibility) (annual).

## Chapter Six. Institutions and Organizations

board's mandate is to investigate complaints of unethical conduct against any Minnesota attorney.[527]

### § 650.8. Lawyers Trust Account Board

The Lawyers Trust Account Board receives funds from lawyers' interest-bearing trust accounts and makes appropriate temporary investments of such funds pending disbursement of them. The interest is used to award grants and appropriations, many of which are for legal education of the public and for legal aid organizations.[528]

### § 650.9. Minnesota Sentencing Guidelines Commission

Created by the legislature in 1978, the commission's goal is to provide guidance in uniform sentencing throughout the state. It maintains a model for judges to follow regarding prison terms as well as when probation or local incarceration might be appropriate.[529]

### § 650.10. Office of the State Court Administrator

The administrator is appointed by the Supreme Court. The duties include the administration of the Supreme Court and other appellate courts by managing facilities, budget, human resources, planning, and research. The state court administrator also assists the judicial district court administrators for planning and management.[530]

### § 650.11. Office of Administrative Hearings

The Office of Administrative Hearings was created by 1975 Minn. Laws ch. 380, § 15.052. Its mission is ensure a process of fair, prompt, and impartial hearings where citizens have disputes with the government. OAH is an independent agency and was created in part to eliminate the appearance of impropriety in cases where the state was a party.

---

527. 15 MINN. STAT. 1170 (1998), Rules on Lawyers Professional Responsibility. Web address <http://www.courts.state.mn.us/lprb/index.html>.
528. 15 MINN. STAT. 1213 (1998), Rules of Lawyers Trust Account Board.
529. MINN. STAT. § 244.09 (1999). MINN. R. 3000.0100–0600 (1999). Web address <http://www.msgc.state.mn.us/>.
530. *See* MINN. GUIDEBOOK, *supra* note 438, at 365.

Since its creation more than twenty-five years ago, the Office presides over Workers' Compensation cases, cases coming under the state Administrative Procedure Act, hearings involving rulemaking, and licensing and personnel cases.

The OAH is led by a chief administrative law judge who is appointed by the governor and approved by the Senate. The OAH is part of the executive branch of government. The administrative law judges are experienced attorneys and are assigned cases based on their subject matter expertise.[531]

## § 650.12. State Board of Continuing Legal Education

Because all lawyers must complete forty-five hours of CLE every three years, this board approves programs that comply with the requirements set by the Minnesota Supreme Court. The board consists of three non-lawyers, one judge, and nine lawyers. Failure to complete the CLE requirement may result in suspension of an attorney's active license.[532]

## § 650.13. State Board of Law Examiners[533]

This board conducts background investigations of prospective bar candidates as well as prepares the bar examination, grades the exam, and recommends candidates to the Supreme Court for admission. The board consists of seven lawyers and two non-lawyers.[534]

---

531. MINN. STAT. 14, 176 (1999). MINN. R. 1400 et seq. (*see* § 322, *supra*). *See* MINN. GUIDEBOOK, *supra* note 438, at 18. Web address <http://www.oah.state.mn.us>.
532. 15 MINN. STAT. 1202, Rules of Minnesota Board of Continuing Legal Education. *See* MINN. GUIDEBOOK, *supra* note 438, at 368. Web address <http://mbcle.state.mn.us/>.
533. *NCBE Directory*, National Conference of Bar Examiners (Chicago: American Bar Ass'n, the Conference) (annual).
534. See the Court Rules volume of the *Minnesota Statutes*. MINN. STAT. § 481.01 (1999); 15 MINN. STAT. 1179 (1998) Rules of the Supreme Court and of the State Board of Law Examiners for Admission to the Bar. *See* MINN. GUIDEBOOK, *supra* note 438, at 366. Web address <http://www.ble.state.mn.us/>. *See also* National Conference of Bar Examiners at <http://www.ncbex.org/>.

## Chapter Six. Institutions and Organizations

### § 650.14. State Board of Legal Certification

Consisting of nine lawyers and three non-lawyers, this board certifies lawyers as specialists in particular areas of legal practice.[535]

### § 650.15. State Board of Public Defense

This board could be described as the governing board for the state public defender. It is mandated that women and minority groups be represented. It recommends to the legislature the budget for the public defenders and distribution of funding as well a various standards and procedures to be used for the operation of the agency.[536]

### § 650.16. State Public Defender

The state public defender provides representation to all indigent defendants in criminal cases for post-conviction appeals as well as parole revocation proceedings. The public defender also represents inmates in civil proceedings and prison disciplinary proceedings. The state public defender also is responsible for supervising the chief public defender in each of the ten judicial districts.[537]

### § 650.17. Tax Court[538]

*See* § 331, *supra*. For rules of procedures see Minn. R. 8610.0010–0150.

### § 650.18. Workers' Compensation Court of Appeals

*See* § 332, *supra*.[539]

---

535. 15 MINN. STAT. 1219 (1998) Plan for the Minnesota State Board of Legal Certification; 15 MINN. STAT. 1222 (1998), Internal Rules for the State Board of Legal Certification. *See* MINN. GUIDEBOOK, *supra* note 438, at 368. Web address <http://www.courts.state.mn.us/blcert/index.html>.
536. MINN. STAT. § 611.215 (1999). Web address <http://www.pubdef.state.mn.us/>.
537. MINN. STAT. § 611.26 (1999). *See also* MINN. GUIDEBOOK, *supra* note 438, at 369. Web address <http://www.pubdef.state.mn.us/>.
538. MINN. STAT. § 271.01 (1999). Web address <http://www.taxcourt.state.mn.us/>.
539. MINN STAT. § 175A, 176. MINN. R. 9800.0100–1800. *See also* MINN. GUIDEBOOK, *supra* note 438, at 371. Web address <http://www.workerscomp.state.mn.us/>.

## § 660. CONTINUING LEGAL EDUCATION (CLE)

§ 661. Advanced Legal Education
§ 662. Minnesota Continuing Legal Education
§ 663. Minnesota Institute of Legal Education
§ 664. Professional Education Systems, Inc.
§ 665. Law School Programs
§ 666. Other Organizations

Minnesota was the first state to require the practicing bar to attend post–law school education classes.[540] The CLE requirement was initiated in 1975. Each attorney is required to complete forty-five hours over a three-year period. Three hours of legal ethics are required in each reporting period as well as two hours dealing with the topic of bias. Credit may be gained by student course work or as a lecturer. The reporting date is August 30[541] (*see also* § 650.11, *supra*).

### § 661. Advanced Legal Education[542]

The Advanced Legal Education unit at Hamline ceased operation in 1991.

### § 662. Minnesota Continuing Legal Education[543]

Minnesota Continuing Legal Education is a non-profit division of the Minnesota State Bar Association that provides seminars and workshops for practicing lawyers. More than 500 seminars are presented each year on various topics for various levels of expertise. Supplementary course materials are available to the practicing bar. Videotaped copies of seminars are made available to bar members in many locations in greater Minnesota. Law students may attend at no cost, contingent upon seating, but are not entitled to receive the course materials.

---

540. The exceptions to the mandatory continuing education requirement are: Alaska, Connecticut, Hawaii, Illinois, Maine, Maryland, Massachusetts, Michigan, Nebraska, New Jersey, and South Dakota.
541. Supreme Court Rules for Continuing Legal Education, Rule 3.
542. Hamline University, School of Law, 1536 Hewitt Ave., St. Paul, MN 55104-1237.
543. A Division of the Minnesota State Bar Association, 40 North Milton St., St. Paul, MN 55104-7027; phone 651-227-8266; Web address <http://www.minncle.org>.

### § 663. Minnesota Institute of Legal Education[544]

Minnesota Institute of Legal Education (MILE) is a non-profit organization that provides continuing education for legal professionals. More than eighty seminars are offered each year. Faculty members are drawn from the practicing bar, the judiciary, and other specialists.

### § 664. Professional Education Systems, Inc.[545]

Professional Education Systems, Inc. (PESI) was founded in 1979 and provides practice-oriented seminars, workshops, self-study tapes, and in-house training for attorneys, judges, paralegals, legal assistants, and secretaries.

### § 665. Law School Programs

Law schools often conduct continuing legal education programs for their alumni. Contact the alumni office of the individual law school. For addresses, phone numbers, websites, see § 630, *supra*.

### § 666. Other Organizations

Many other law-related organizations provide continuing education for their members. Individuals may contact these organizations or access their calendars at their websites.

## § 670. LEGAL ASSISTANCE

§ 671. Public Defenders
§ 672. United States Attorney for the District of Minnesota
§ 673. County Attorneys
§ 674. Attorney General
§ 675. Legal Aid
§ 676. Law School Clinics

---

544. Suite 202, 1313 5th St. SE, Minneapolis, MN 55414-4504; phone 612-379-1128; Web address <http://www.mile.org>.
545. 200 Spring St., Post Office Box 1428, Eau Claire, WI 54702-1428; phone 800-825-7155; Web address <http://www.pesi.com/legalsem/htm>.

§ 677. Public Education and Referral Services
§ 678. Pro Bono Programs

A number of organizations or agencies provide legal assistance to indigent persons. These agencies are funded by tax dollars, gifts, grants, or other provisions. The services provided differ from agency to agency, with some providing criminal defense assistance, some providing general assistance, and some providing assistance with respect to certain limited civil matters. Each organization establishes its own eligibility requirements. Information on some of these organizations may be obtained from bar associations.

Section 480.241 of *Minnesota Statutes* institutes a $25 surcharge on specified civil filing fees to establish a legal services fund. Conciliation court actions impose a $3 surcharge. The funds are distributed to qualified legal services programs by the Legal Services Advisory Committee. This eleven-member body appointed by the Supreme Court consists of lawyers, non-lawyers, and indigence program clients.

The Minnesota State Bar Association has established a system of lawyer referral services to lower the cost of initial contact when a person is unsure of the need for a lawyer. The Hennepin County Bar Association sponsors Tel-Law, a library of tape recordings from three- to six-minutes long that contain general legal information about a variety of subjects. The tapes can be accessed by telephone at any time.[546]

The Lawyers Trust Account Board[547] was established July 1, 1983, to operate the Interest on Lawyers Trust Accounts (IOLTA) program. The nine member board consists of six attorneys and three public members appointed by the Supreme Court awards grants to programs meeting the need for legal services to the poor, law-related education, and projects for the improvement of the administration of justice (*see* § 650.7, *supra*). Alternative dispute resolution also may be available (*see* §§ 450, 635, *supra*).

---

546. In the Minneapolis/St. Paul area phone 612-752-6699.
547. *See* Rules of Lawyer Trust Account Board in Professional Rules section of the Court Rules volume of the *Minnesota Statutes*.

Chapter Six. Institutions and Organizations

## § 671. Public Defenders

§ 671.1. Federal Public Defender
§ 671.2. State Public Defender
§ 671.3. The Legal Advocacy Project (LAP)
§ 671.4. Public Defense Corporations
§ 671.5. Legal Assistance to Minnesota Prisoners (LAMP)
§ 671.6. Law Library Service to Prisoners Project

### § 671.1. Federal Public Defender[548]

Federal public defenders are appointed by the magistrate of the district court to represent indigent clients or those determined to be in need of representation. The financial standards imposed in most state courts are not the same as in the federal court system. The office consists of a chief federal public defender and a staff of six licensed attorneys.

### § 671.2. State Public Defender[549]

The Minnesota Public Defender position was created in 1965.[550] The act creating it has since been amended a number of times. The public defender represents all indigent clients in criminal cases involving appeals[551] and in parole revocation proceedings, and supervises the training of all state and district public defenders. A separate division handles civil matters in regard to prisoners. The state public defender may assist in casework when requested and may assign cases to any public defender. A majority of judges of any judicial district may establish a public defender system. There are public defenders in all judicial districts. [552]

---

548. 300 South Fourth St., Suite 107, Minneapolis, MN 55415-2282; phone 612-664-5858.
549. 331 Second Ave. South, Suite 900, Minneapolis, MN 55401-2233; phone 612-349-2565; Web address <http://www.pubdef.state.mn.us>.
550. Minn. Laws 869.
551. State Public Defender's Office, Appellate Division, 2829 University Ave. SE, Suite 600, Minneapolis, MN 55414-3230; phone 612-627-6980.
552. *See also* MINN. GUIDEBOOK, *supra* note 438, at 369.

### § 671.3. The Legal Advocacy Project[553]

A division of the State Public Defender, the Legal Advocacy Project (LAP) represents inmates in prison disciplinary hearings, parole revocations, and sex offender notification. The division is staffed by licensed attorneys.

### § 671.4. Public Defense Corporations[554]

Assisting the public defender are some organizations that do criminal court defense work. These are listed below.

- Legal Rights Center, 1611 Park Avenue S., Minneapolis, MN 55404-1611; phone 612-337-0030
- Neighborhood Justice Center, 464 South Robert Street, St. Paul, MN 55107-2236; phone 651-227-8497
- Dakota County Juvenile Office, 1068 South Robert Street, St. Paul, MN 55118-1457; phone 651-455-0472
- Leech Lake Reservation Criminal and Juvenile Defense Corp., P.O. Box 308, Cass Lake, MN 56633-0308; phone 218-939-2215
- White Earth Reservation Criminal and Juvenile Defense Corp., Box 342, Mahnomen, MN 56557-0342; phone 218-939-2215
- Indian Legal Assistance, 107 West First Street, Duluth, MN 55802-2092; phone 218-727-2881

### § 671.5. Legal Assistance to Minnesota Prisoners[555]

Legal Assistance to Minnesota Prisoners (LAMP) was established in 1972 and has its office at the University of Minnesota Law School. It is a clinical program that represents Minnesota prisoners regarding their civil legal problems. This clinic is a program offering at the three Minnesota law schools in the Twin Cities. Students handle cases under the supervision of a licensed attorney. An attempt is made to have the student lawyers handle all phases of the case, from interviewing to conclusion (*see* § 632.1, *supra*).

---

553. State Public Defender, 2829 University Ave. SE, Suite 600, Minneapolis, MN 55414-3230; phone 612-627-5416.
554. *See also* MINN. GUIDEBOOK, *supra* note 438, at 369–70.
555. 95 Law Center, University of Minnesota Law School, 229 19th Ave. South, Minneapolis, MN 55455-0401; phone 612-625-6336.

## § 671.6. Law Library Service to Prisoners Project[556]

The Law Library Service to Prisoners Project[557] is a cooperative effort with the Public Defender, the Department of Corrections, and the Minnesota State Law Library to provide law library services to prisoners. A core collection is maintained in each of the five adult correctional institutions and a professional librarian makes visits to the facilities on a regular schedule to provide legal research assistance.

## § 672. United States Attorney for the District of Minnesota[558]

The United States Attorney's Office (USAO), District of Minnesota, is located in the Federal Courthouse in downtown Minneapolis, Minnesota. The USAO is divided into three sections: criminal, civil, and community relations.

The Criminal Division, in turn is divided into three sections: economic crimes; narcotics and repeat offenders; and major federal crimes such as bank robbery, counterfeiting, immigration, and crimes from the Red Lake and Bois Forte Indian Reservations. The Civil Division represents the United States in all civil actions brought to federal or state court in Minnesota in which the federal government is a party. The Community Relations Division works with the media, witnesses, victims, law enforcement, and anti-crime prevention groups in the community.

---

556. Outreach Services Librarian, Minnesota State Law Library, 25 Constitution Ave., St. Paul, MN 55155-1500; phone 651-297-2087.
557. Each year a report is filed describing the activities of the project. LAW LIBRARY SERVICE TO PRISONERS... REPORT (St. Paul, MN: Minnesota State Law Library) (annual).
558. 600 U.S. Courthouse, 300 South Fourth St., Minneapolis, MN 55415-2200; phone 612-664-5600, 888-264-5107; Web address <http://www.usdoj.gov/usao/mn/index.htm>.

## § 673. County Attorneys[559]

The county attorney is the prosecutor and chief legal advisor to the county. Requests for opinions and advice must come from the county board or county officers and concern official matters or duties. Some of the larger counties, such as Hennepin and Ramsey, do provide assistance to the general public.

The Minnesota County Attorneys Council[560] is a service and planning agency. The council has established advisory standards for county attorneys' offices and provides educational, informational, and technical assistance.

The Minnesota County Attorneys Association provides leadership on legal and public policy issues related to the duties of county attorneys. It also provides training, education, and support to county attorneys. There are several national associations and institutes that support prosecuting attorneys.[561]

## § 674. Attorney General[562]

§ 674.1. Consumer Division
§ 674.2. Human Rights Division

From time to time, the legislature may direct the attorney general, as chief law enforcement officer, to conduct investigations into various activities. Topics of recent reports filed have been school safety; juvenile prostitution; funding legal services; criminal gangs; landfill cleanup; etc. (*see* § 545.2, *supra*). These documents are filed with the Legislative Reference Library and various state document depository libraries. Most are cataloged and accessible through PALS.[563]

---

559. Minnesota County Attorneys Association, Hamline Park Plaza, 570 Asbury St., Suite 203, St. Paul, MN 55104-1850; phone 651-641-1600; Web address <http://www.safenet.org/mcaa/mcaa.html>.
560. *See* MINN. STAT. § 388.19 (1999).
561. *See* National District Attorneys Association, 99 Canal Center Plaza, Alexandria, VA 22314-1588; phone 703-549-9222; Web address <http://www.ndaa.org/>.
562. *See also* National Association of Attorneys General, 750 First St., NE, Suite 1100, Washington, DC 20002-8012; phone 202-326-6000; Web address <http://www.naag.org/index2.html>.
563. Project for Automated Library Systems.

Of the Minnesota Attorney General's various departments and divisions, there are two that have direct impact on the citizens of the state: Consumer Division and Human Rights. The AG website is <http://www.ag.state.mn.us/>.

### § 674.1. Consumer Division[564]

This attorney general division works on behalf of Minnesota consumers. It looks after enforcement of consumer legislation, and investigates and prosecutes cases. The division also publishes brochures dealing with a variety of consumer-related issues.

### § 674.2. Human Rights Division

Although the Department of Human Rights[565] is a separate entity, this attorney general division represents it in any legal action. The division files petitions and enforces the law regarding discrimination in housing, employment, public accommodations, education, and other services.

### § 675. Legal Aid[566]

§ 675.1. Minnesota Legal Services Coalition (MLSC)
§ 675.2. Minnesota Legal Services Coalition (MLSC) State Support Center

Numerous programs exist for legal services in Minnesota. There is a broad range of services that serve various constituencies. Most of these services are prohibited from handling criminal matters by contract or funding agreement. Some civil matters that might be fee generating may not be represented by legal aid. Personal injury, accident claims, and wrongful death cases are not represented by legal aid. Both private and public funding guidelines prohibit many agencies from taking

---

564. Consumer Division, Office of the Attorney General, 1400 North Central Towers, 445 Minnesota St., St. Paul, MN 55101-2131; phone 651-296-3353, 800-657-3787; Web address <http://www.ag.state.mn.us/home/consumer/default.shtml>.
565. Minnesota Department of Human Rights, Army Corps of Engineers Centre, 190 East Fifth St., Saint Paul, MN 55101-2070; phone 651-296-5663; Web address <http://www.humanrights.state.mn.us/>.
566. THE . . . DIRECTORY OF LEGAL AID AND DEFENDER OFFICES IN THE UNITED STATES AND TERRITORIES (Washington, DC: National Legal Aid & Defender Ass'n 1981– ) (annual).

criminal cases or representing persons who are incarcerated. Criminal cases and the representation of prisoners are handled by the public defender's office (*see* § 671, *supra*). Legal aid depends greatly on volunteer attorneys and law students (*see* §§ 676, 678, *infra*). Eligibility for service depends on several factors such as residence, income requirements established according to the federal poverty guidelines, type of legal problem, and specific eligibility requirements of the Legal Services Corporation. Some of the Minnesota legal services agencies are listed below.

### § 675.1. Minnesota Legal Services Coalition (MLSC)[567]

While the MLSC's services generally only are available to individuals below a certain income level, some individuals such as the elderly and disabled are provided with legal services without regard to income. The coalition is an association of regional legal services programs that help low-income people with a broad range of civil legal matters. Each program has a number of offices located throughout the region it covers. Some special statewide projects address particular issues and are available to individuals from anywhere in Minnesota.

The coalition consists of seven regional legal services programs that generally have a number of offices within each region.

- ▶ Anishinabe Legal Services (ALS)[568] is an independent non-profit corporation that provides no-cost legal services in civil matters and community education to low-income people who live on the Leach Lake, Red Lake, and White Earth reservations, and to people aged sixty or older, regardless of income. These elder law services also include the Grand Portage and Bois Forte reservations. Priority is given to cases that involve Indian law and poverty law.
- ▶ Judicare of Anoka County, Inc.[569] is a non-profit corporation that provides free legal representation in non-criminal matters to low-income residents of Anoka County. Services are provided by

---

567. 46 East 4th St., Suite 726, St. Paul, MN 55101-1112; phone 651-228-9105; Web address <http://www.mnlegalservices.org>.
568. 411 First St. SE, P.O. Box 157, Cass Lake, MN 56633-3109; phone 218-335-2223, 800-422-1335 (clients only); Web address <http://www.mnlegalservices.org/anishinabe/index.shtml>.
569. 1201 89th Ave. NE, Suite 310, Blaine, MN 55434-3373; phone 612-783-4970; Web address <http://www.mnlegalservices.org/anoka/index.shtml>.

## Chapter Six. Institutions and Organizations

both a central staff and by private attorneys who have agreed to represent those individuals and families eligible for the Judicare program. Judicare was established through a joint effort of the Anoka County Board of Commissioners, the Anoka County Bar Association, and local community organizations. Judicare makes referrals to other agencies when needed. The agency provides senior citizens with legal advice and representation and, in some cases, does so even when their income level is above the federal poverty level. Judicare also has a speakers' bureau.

▶ Legal Aid Service of Northeastern Minnesota (LASNEM)[570] is a non-profit corporation that provides free legal advice and representation to low-income people who live in northeastern Minnesota.

▶ Legal Services of Northwest Minnesota, Inc. (LSNM)[571] is a private, non-profit corporation that provides free civil legal services to low-income and senior citizens in twenty-two counties. LSNM provides services in three offices located at Moorhead, Bemidji, and Alexandria. Generally, cases handled pertain to public assistance & disability benefits; family law; consumer issues; health law; and housing (such as tenant/landlord problems).

Some special projects include: KidsLAW, a program that addresses children's needs with community education and direct representation, where staff and attorneys inform others about children's rights and promote the rights of children to access basic necessities of life, education, protection from harm, and injustice; Focus On Fairness aims to increase public awareness to recognize, prevent, and eliminate housing discrimination by developing a series of community training opportunities and educational materials on fair housing issues; Violence Protection is a collaborative effort with local domestic violence advocacy programs to coordinate services, training, and provide a full range of civil legal assistance to victims of domestic abuse; the Elderly Law Project

---

570. Brainerd (Aitkin, Cass, and Crow Wing counties) phone 218-829-1701; Duluth (Carlton, Cook, Lake, and Southern Saint Louis counties) phone 218-726-4800; Grand Rapids (Itasca and Koochiching counties) phone 218-326-6695; Pine City (Kanabec and Pine counties) phone 320-629-7166; Virginia (Northern Saint Louis County) phone 218-749-3270.
571. Moorhead Office, 403 Center Ave., P.O. Box 714, Moorhead, MN 56560-1975, phone 218-233-8585 or 800-450-8585 (clients only), fax 218-233-8586; Bemidji Office, 215 4th St. N.W., P.O. Box 1883, Bemidji, MN 56619, phone 218-751-9201 or 800-450-9201 (clients only), fax 218-751-9217; Alexandria Office, 1114 Broadway, Alexandria, MN 56308-1471, phone 320-762-0663 or 800-450-2552 (clients only), fax 320-762-0740.

provides legal services to individuals who are more than sixty years of age with priority cases, including Medicare and health issues, advance directives, Social Security & SSI, consumer complaints, shelter, safety issues, and income maintenance.

- ▶ Mid-Minnesota Legal Assistance (MMLA)[572] provides community education programs, legal advice, and representation to low-income clients in twenty counties in central Minnesota. This large agency has offices located in Cambridge, downtown Minneapolis, North Minneapolis, Saint Cloud, South Minneapolis, and Willmar (Western Minnesota Legal Services-Willmar). A partnering agreement exists between MMLA, a non-LSC funded program, and Central Minnesota Legal Services (CMLS), an LSC-funded program, to provide legal services in virtually the same service area.

    The statewide Legal Services Advocacy Project provides legislative and administrative representation, and is part of MMLA. Some special projects include: Legal Assistance to Older Americans, Minnesota Disability Law Center, Community Legal Education Project, Housing Discrimination Law Project, Family Farm Law Project, and Legal Advocacy Project for Developmentally Disabled Persons.

- ▶ Central Minnesota Legal Services (CMLS) provides civil legal services to low-income persons in twenty counties in central Minnesota. Offices are located in downtown Minneapolis, Saint Cloud, and Willmar. Its mission is "to provide in a highly professional manner for the basic legal needs of families and children vulnerable to abuse, violence, neglect, homelessness or major economic disruptions in their lives." Clients receive legal services at no cost, unless there are court fees that cannot be waived. CMLS helps eligible clients through direct representation, brief advice, and by participating in community legal education programs.

---

572. Mid-Minnesota Legal Assistance (Downtown Minneapolis Office), Legal Aid Society of Minneapolis, Inc., 430 1st Ave. N., Suite 300, Minneapolis, MN 55401-1780, phone 612-332-1441; Mid-Minnesota Legal Assistance (Southside Office), Legal Aid Society of Minneapolis, Inc., 2929 4th Ave. S., Minneapolis, MN 55408-2460, phone 612-827-3774; Mid-Minnesota Legal Assistance (Northside Office), Legal Aid Society of Minneapolis, Inc., 2507 Fremont Ave. N., Minneapolis, MN 55411-2013, phone 612-588-2099; Mid-Minnesota Legal Assistance (St. Cloud Office), 830 W. St. Germain, Suite 300, P.O. Box 886, St. Cloud, MN 56302, phone 320-253-0121; Mid-Minnesota Legal Assistance (Willmar Office), Western Minnesota Legal Services (a division of MMLA), 620 Litchfield Ave. SW, Suite 101, Willmar, MN 56201-3246, phone 320-235-9600.

## Chapter Six. Institutions and Organizations 255

- Southern Minnesota Regional Legal Assistance (SMRLS) provides no-cost legal representation and advice to low-income residents in thirty-three counties in Southern Minnesota and to migrant farm workers throughout Minnesota and North Dakota. Special projects include: Protection from Domestic Abuse and Child Custody Program, Securing Opportunities for Self-Sufficiency While Meeting Basic Needs Program, Preservation of Affordable and Safe Housing Program, Homeless Outreach and Prevention Education Program (Project H.O.P.E.), Cambodian Law Project, Senior Law Program, Farm Law Program, Education Law Project, Teamchild Project.

The Minnesota Legal Services Coalition's statewide projects include the following.

- Farmers' Legal Action Group, Inc. (FLAG)[573] is a nonprofit law center dedicated to providing legal services to family farmers and their rural communities to help keep family farmers on the land.
- Community Legal Education Project[574] creates educational fact sheets, a newsletter, and other public education materials.
- Legal Services Advocacy Project (LSAP)[575] represents the interests of low-income Minnesotans through legislative and administrative advocacy. LSAP is a statewide division of Mid-Minnesota Legal Assistance (MMLA), a non-LSC-funded program.
- Migrant Legal Services[576] is a non-profit organization providing free legal services for migrant farm workers in Minnesota and North Dakota. Migrant Legal Services is a unit of Southern Minnesota Regional Legal Services and works together with Legal Assistance of North Dakota in the Red River Valley.

---

573. Farmers' Legal Action Group, Inc., 46 East 4th St., Suite 1301, St. Paul, MN 55101-1109; phone 651-223-5400; Web address <http://www.flaginc.org/>.
574. Community Legal Education Project, 2507 Fremont Ave. North, Minneapolis, MN 55411-2013; phone 612-588-2099.
575. Legal Services Advocacy Project, Midtown Commons, 2324 University Ave., Suite 101, St. Paul, MN 55114-1854; phone 651-222-3749; Web address <http://www.mnlegalservices.org/>.
576. Migrant Legal Services, Southern Minnesota, 700 Minnesota Building, St. Paul, MN 55101, phone 651-291-2837, 800-652-9733 (clients only); Migrant Legal Services, Red River Valley & North Dakota, 118 Broadway, Suite 305, Fargo, ND 58102-4944, phone 701-232-8872, 800-832-5575 (clients only).

▶ Minnesota Disability Law Center (MDLC)[577] is a special project of Mid-Minnesota Legal Assistance that addresses the unique legal needs of people with disabilities. MDLC has been designated as the state's protection and advocacy system for persons with disabilities in Minnesota and receives federal funds for that purpose. MDLC serves the entire state of Minnesota and provides services at no cost to individuals. Unlike most of the other Coalition Program services in the state, income guidelines do not apply to MDLC's work. The Minnesota Disability Law Center has four projects: Legal Advocacy for Persons with Developmental Disabilities in MN (DDA); The Mental Health Law Project (MHLP); Protections and Advocacy of Individual Rights (PAIR); and The Client Assistance Project (CAP).

## § 675.2. Minnesota Legal Services Coalition State Support Center[578]

The MLSC does not directly represent clients, it provides support services for legal services programs in Minnesota. MLSC provides a broad range of support services including fund raising, public education, training for staff, educational conferences, a newsletter, and a website.

## § 676. Law School Clinics

§ 676.1. Hamline University School of Law
§ 676.2. William Mitchell College of Law
§ 676.3. University of Minnesota Law School, Practical Skills Programs
§ 676.4. University Student Legal Service

The law schools in Minnesota have as part of their curricula various legal clinics designed to aid particular individuals and groups of clients. The clinics generally are staffed by law students who earn academic credit. Each of the student attorneys is supervised by a licensed staff attorney.

---

577. Minnesota Disability Law Center, Main Office, 300 Kickernick Building, 430 First Ave. North, Minneapolis, MN 55401-1780; phone 612-332-1441, (TDD) 612-332-4688, toll-free 800-292-4150.
578. 46 East 4th St., Suite 726, St. Paul, MN 55101-1112; phone 651-228-9105; Web address <http://www.mnlegalservices.org>.

## Chapter Six. Institutions and Organizations

### § 676.1. Hamline University School of Law[579]

To complete their skills education, students may choose to represent clients in one of Hamline's eight clinics, under Minnesota's student-practice rule. Supervised by clinical instructors, students handle their own caseload. These experiences help students hone their lawyering skills, including interviewing, counseling, research and analysis, mediation, trial development, and case management.

Clients are low-income individuals or groups with a need for legal advice in areas such as family law, immigration, children's rights, unemployment compensation, public policy, or legislative advocacy.

- General Practice Clinic
- Child Advocacy Clinic
- Alternative Dispute Resolution Clinic
- Education Law Clinic
- Family Law Clinic
- Business Law Clinic
- Legal Assistance for Minnesota Prisoners (LAMP) Clinic
- Student Director Clinic

### § 676.2. William Mitchell College of Law[580]

- Business Law Clinic
- Civil Advocacy Clinic
- Criminal Appeals Clinic
- Immigration Law Clinic
- Legal Assistance for Minnesota Prisoners (LAMP) Clinic
- Misdemeanor Clinic
- Law and Psychiatry Clinic (in cooperation with the University of Minnesota Medical School)

---

579. General Practice Clinic, 1536 Hewitt Ave., St. Paul, MN 55104-1237; phone 651-523-2941; Web address <http://www.hamline.edu/law>.
580. 871 Summit Ave., St. Paul, MN 55105-3030; phone 651-290-6357; Web address <http://www.wmitchell.edu>.

### § 676.3. University of Minnesota Law School,[581] Practical Skills Programs[582]

Nearly two-thirds of the law students participate in a variety of practical skills programs. The University of Minnesota is a pioneer in clinical education for lawyers. The clinic program provides an important supplement to the law school's theory-based substantive courses. Some of these programs are described below.

- Bankruptcy
- Child Advocacy
- Civil Litigation
- Criminal Appeals
- Disability
- Domestic Abuse
- Federal Prosecution
- Federal Taxation
- Housing
- Immigration
- Indian Child Welfare
- Law and Violence Against Women
- Legal Assistance to Minnesota Prisoners
- Misdemeanor Defense
- Misdemeanor Prosecution
- Public Interest Law

### § 676.4. University Student Legal Service[583]

Dating from 1976, University Student Legal Service (USLS) was founded by students at the University of Minnesota and provides legal representation and legal advice to eligible students on the Twin Cities campus. Although not part of the law school, it does function as a legal service to students. It is staffed by licensed attorneys, legal

---

581. 229 19th Ave. South, Minneapolis, MN 55455-0401; phone 612-625-4300; Web address <http://www.law.umn.edu>.
582. Web address <http://www1.umn.edu/commpub/law/practical.html>.
583. 160 West Bank Skyway, 219 19th Ave. South, Minneapolis, MN 55455; phone 612-624-1001; Web address <http://www1.umn.edu/usls>.

Chapter Six. Institutions and Organizations

assistants, and support staff. Areas of practice deal with civil matters and misdemeanor criminal offenses.

## § 677. Public Education and Referral Services[584]

Many local, county, and state bar associations offer referral services to the public. Although referral services do not provide legal advice or legal services per se, they often publish information in the form of booklets and brochures that provide basic legal information about the civil and criminal justice systems. Referral services assess whether legal services are needed. In some instances referral may be made to a social service agency or a government office. If a lawyer referral is made, often the consultation is free or for a minimal charge.

- Chrysalis Legal Assistance for Women[585] (provides assistance for women without regard to income; information sessions, brochures, and attorney referrals are available)
- Dakota County Bar Association Referral Service[586]
- Hennepin County Bar Association, Lawyer Referral Service[587] (Hennepin County only)
- Minnesota State Bar Association[588] (statewide except for Hennepin, Ramsey, Dakota, and Washington counties)
- Minnesota Women Lawyers Referral[589]
- Ramsey County Bar Association, Attorney Referral Service[590] (Ramsey County and East Metro)
- Resources and Counseling for the Arts[591] (limited legal advice is available; downloadable forms are available at the website)

---

584. *Directory of Lawyer Referral Services* ([Chicago]: American Bar Ass'n 1976– ) (annual).
585. 4432 Chicago Ave. South, Minneapolis, MN 55407-3522; phone 612-871-0118; Web address <http://www.chrysaliswomen.org/law.htm>.
586. Phone 612-431-3200.
587. 600 Nicollet Ave, Suite 390, Minneapolis, MN 55402-1043; phone 612-752-6666; fax 612-752-6601; Web address <http://www.hcba.org>.
588. 600 Nicollet Mall #380, Minneapolis, MN 55402; phone 612-333-1183, 800-882-6722, 800-292-4152 (in-state only); Web address <http://www2.mnbar.org>.
589. Minneapolis, MN; phone 612-338-3205 (statewide); Web address <http://www.mwlawyers.org/status.htm>.
590. St. Paul, MN; phone 651-224-1775; Web address <http://www.ramseybar.org>.
591. 308 Prince St., Suite 270, St. Paul, MN 55101-1437; phone 651-292-4381, 800-546-2891; Web address <http://www.rc4arts.org/>.

## § 678. Pro Bono Programs[592]

Many law firms and individual attorneys offer no-cost legal services to members of the community who qualify financially, have a particular type of legal issue, or belong to a particular client type. These programs are known as "pro bono" services and often are coordinated or otherwise administered by community organizations, professional associations, or legal services agency.

Pro bono programs[593] deal with civil matters only. The programs generally operate through an established legal services agency that recruits the services of practicing attorneys. Local, county, and state bar associations[594] generally offer such services; but legal aid societies also offer such services. Potential clients may call their local legal referral service. The American Bar Association, Division for Legal Services has compiled a state-by-state list of pro bono programs.[595]

### § 678.1. Minnesota Justice Foundation[596]

The Minnesota Justice Foundation (MJF) was founded in 1981 by University of Minnesota Law School students. The MJF was conceived in response to the cutbacks in legal services in the 1980s. Since 1983 the summer clerkship program has expanded to Hamline and William Mitchell Law schools. MJF is an independent, non-profit organization of law students and pro bono attorneys that encourages its members and the legal community to fulfill their professional obligation to serve unrepresented low-income persons. A full-time attorney executive director heads the program. Law students provide

---

592. *See* MINN. R. PROF. CONDUCT 6.1 Voluntary Pro Bono Public Service.
593. *Directory of Pro Bono Programs,* ABA Center for Pro Bono (Chicago: American Bar Ass'n, Center for Pro Bono 1996– ) (annual).
594. *See* MINNESOTA STATE BAR ASSOCIATION, LEGAL ASSISTANCE TO THE DISADVANTAGED COMMITTEE, DIRECTORY OF PRO BONO OPPORTUNITIES FOR LAWYERS (produced with support from the Minnesota State Bar Association, Minnesota State Bar Foundation, Legal Services Advisory Committee, Lawyer Trust Account Board, Minneapolis, MN: the Committee 1993).
595. Web address <http://www.abanet.org/legalserv/probono/pb-minnesota.html>.
596. MJF, Hamline Office, Room 2, Commons Level, 536 Hewitt Ave., St. Paul, MN 55104; phone 651-523-2081. MJF, U of M Office, Room 96B, Stein Plaza, 229 19th Ave. South, Minneapolis, MN 55455; phone 612-625-1584. MJF, Wm. Mitchell Office, Room 254, Legal Practice Ctr., 875 Summit Ave., St. Paul, MN 55105; phone 651-290-8658; Web address <http://www2.mnbar.org/mjf/>.

significant pro bono service by assisting volunteer attorneys, donating their time to free legal clinics, assisting with legal research and writing, and volunteering time at a public interest office. MJF and its members seek to provide quality pro bono legal services, encourage public service, shape public policy, and promote social justice. Additionally, MJF holds educational forums and career fairs.

## § 680. Support Personnel

§ 681. Legal Administrators
§ 682. Legal Secretaries
§ 683. Legal Assistants
§ 684. Law Clerks
§ 685. Court Reporters

A number of professions support the legal community. The government, courts, private law firms, and attorneys all avail themselves of services provided by paralegals, administrators, law librarians, stenographers, and others.

### § 681. Legal Administrators

§ 681.1. Association of Legal Administrators
§ 681.2. Minnesota Legal Administrators Association

The Minnesota Constitution provides for each county to have a clerk of courts.[597] This officer is appointed by a majority of the judges and serves at its pleasure. With the merger of the county courts and district courts in the early 1980s, most judicial districts replaced the clerk of court with a court administrator. The court administrator generally is professionally trained either by education or through experience.[598]

---

597. *See* MINN. CONST. art. VI, § 13.
598. *See* MINN. STAT. §§ 484.68, 485.01.

### § 681.1. Association of Legal Administrators[599]

The Association of Legal Administrators was formed in 1971 to provide support to professionals involved in the management of law firms, corporate legal departments, and government legal agencies. The association has more than 9,000 members. In 1996, the association initiated a voluntary Certified Legal Manager certification program. The ALA's published goal is to assist its members in developing their ability to manage law firms, corporate legal departments, and court systems effectively, efficiently, and economically.

### § 681.2. Minnesota Legal Administrators Association

Minnesota Legal Administrators Association has no permanent mailing address but the president's address is included in various Minnesota legal directories, such as Bench & Bar of Minnesota's annual directory issues, the *Minnesota Attorney's/Paralegal's/Secretary's Handbook*, or the *Minnesota Legal Directory*.

## § 682. Legal Secretaries

> § 682.1. National Association of Legal Secretaries (NALS) Resource Center
> § 682.2. National Association of Legal Secretaries-Twin Cities Chapter

Legal secretaries work in law firms and with individual attorneys. A number of national professional and have associated state chapters. Training and educational programs often are the focus of these organizations.

### § 682.1. National Association of Legal Secretaries (NALS) Resource Center[600]

The National Association of Legal Secretaries is dedicated to enhancing the competencies and contributions of members in the legal services profession. It accomplishes it mission and supports the public interest through continuing legal education and resource materials;

---

599. 175 E. Hawthorn Parkway, Suite 325, Vernon Hills, IL 60061-1428; phone 847-816-1212; Web address <http://www.alanet.org>.
600. 314 East 3rd St., Suite 210, Tulsa, OK 74120-2409; phone 918-582-5188, fax 918-582-5907; e-mail address <info@nals.org>; Web address <http://www.nals.org>.

## Chapter Six. Institutions and Organizations

networking opportunities at the local, state, regional, and national levels; commitment to a code of ethics and professional standards; and professional certification programs and designations.[601]

The NALS sponsors seminars and institutes, administers the ALS certificate and the Professional Legal Secretaries' (PLS) certificate program, and publishes the newsletter *Legalink*. It also has compiled a number of loose-leaf manuals and guides to forms and terminology for legal secretaries.

### § 682.2. National Association of Legal Secretaries—Twin Cities Chapter

The National Association of Legal Secretaries—Twin Cities Chapter has no permanent address but the president's address is included in various Minnesota legal directories, such as Bench & Bar of Minnesota's annual directory issue, the *Minnesota Attorney's/Paralegal's/Secretary's Handbook*, or the *Minnesota Legal Directory*.

Training for legal secretaries is available at many of the community colleges in Minnesota as well as several proprietary schools. The program titles vary somewhat and include legal receptionist, legal secretary, legal administrative assistant, legal transcriptionist, etc. Various certificates, diplomas, and Associate of Arts degrees are available. Information is available at the Minnesota State Colleges and Universities website <http://www.mnscu.edu>.

### § 683. Legal Assistants

§ 683.1. National Association of Legal Assistants
§ 683.2. American Association for Paralegal Education
§ 683.3. Minnesota Paralegal Association

### § 683.1. National Association of Legal Assistants[602]

Founded in 1975, the National Association of Legal Assistants (NALA) is the leading professional association for paralegals in the United States.

---

601. NALS Mission Statement.
602. 1516 South Boston, Suite 20, Tulsa, OK 74119-4003; phone 918-587-6828; Web address <http://www.nala.org>.

### § 683.2. American Association for Paralegal Education[603]

Established in 1981, the American Association for Paralegal Education (AAfPE) is a national organization serving paralegal education and institutions that offer paralegal education programs.

### § 683.3. Minnesota Paralegal Association[604]

The Minnesota Paralegal Association is a non-profit professional association of more than 1,100 members that provides continuing education, networking, and employment services. Chapters in Minnesota include Mankato, Rochester, Saint Cloud, Duluth, and the Twin Cities.

The use of legal assistants (sometimes called paralegals, lay assistants, or paraprofessionals) has increased greatly in recent years.[605] In 1969, the American Bar Association established a special committee to provide guidance and leadership in the training and employment of legal assistants.[606] The committee has formulated guidelines for approval of educational programs.[607]

The Minnesota Supreme Court in its rules of professional responsibility has defined what role a paralegal may take in association with a lawyer in the practice of law. *See Opinion 8. Attorneys' Guidelines for Law Office Services by Non-Lawyers.* The unauthorized practice of law is codified at Minn. Stat. § 481.02 (1999) (*see also* Rule 5.3 and Comment, Minnesota Rules of Professional Conduct).

Legal assistant programs often are two-year degree programs with curriculums consisting of general education, business, and specialized law classes. These programs prepare students to assist lawyers and administrators of law-related occupations in providing efficient legal service to the public. Not all legal assistant/paralegal programs are accredited programs. Institutions that offer paralegal education are listed in § 683.4 below, and their accreditation status is indicated.

---

603. 2965 Flowers Road South, Suite 105, Atlanta, GA 30341-5520; phone 770-452-9877; Web address <http://www.aafpe.org>.
604. 1711 West County Road B, Suite 300 North, Roseville, MN 55113-4069; phone 651-633-2778; Web address <http://www.mnparalegals.org>.
605. *See* MINNESOTA CONTINUING LEGAL EDUCATION, A MANUAL FOR MINNESOTA ATTORNEYS UTILIZING LEGAL ASSISTANTS (1981).
606. AMERICAN BAR ASSOCIATION, STANDING COMMITTEE ON LEGAL ASSISTANTS, GUIDELINES FOR THE APPROVAL OF LEGAL ASSISTANT EDUCATION PROGRAMS (Chicago: The Committee 1997).
607. Continuing education for legal assistants is offered by several entities (e.g., MCLE).

## § 683.4. Two-Year Programs

§ 683.41. Inver Hills Community College, Paralegal Program
§ 683.42. Itasca Community College
§ 683.43. North Hennepin Community College, Paralegal Program
§ 683.44. Proprietary Programs

### § 683.41. Inver Hills Community College, Paralegal Program[608]

The Inver Hills Community College paralegal program is approved by both the American Bar Association and American Association for Paralegal Education.

### § 683.42. Itasca Community College[609]

This is a sixty-four credit Associate in Applied Science degree which includes general education courses as well as specialized law-related courses. The program is not accredited by the ABA or the American Association for Paralegal Education.

### § 683.43. North Hennepin Community College, Paralegal Program[610]

The North Hennepin Community College paralegal program is approved by both the American Bar Association and the American Association for Paralegal Education.

---

608. 2500 80th St., Inver Grove Heights, MN 55076-3203; Web address <http://www.ih.cc.mn.us>.
609. 1851 East Highway 169, Grand Rapids, MN 55744; phone 218-327-4460; Web address <http://www.it.cc.mn.us>.
610. 7411 85th Ave. North, Brooklyn Park, MN 55445-2299; phone 612-424-0702; Web address <http://www.nh.cc.mn.us>.

### § 683.44. Proprietary Programs

Proprietary programs are offered by private, for-profit business schools. The programs vary widely and a certificate often is awarded upon completion of the program. The programs vary in length.

- ▶ Minnesota School of Business/Globe College, Associate in Applied Science of Paralegal Program.[611] The program is approved by the American Association for Paralegal Education.

### § 683.5. Four-Year Programs

§ 683.51. Hamline University, College of Liberal Arts, Legal Studies Department
§ 683.52. Moorhead State University, Paralegal Program, Center for Business
§ 683.53. Winona State University, Paralegal Program

### § 683.51. Hamline University, College of Liberal Arts, Legal Studies Department[612]

The Paralegal Program is approved by both the American Bar Association and the American Association for Paralegal Education.

### § 683.52. Moorhead State University, Paralegal Program, Center for Business[613]

The program is approved by both the American Bar Association and the American Association for Paralegal Education.

### § 683.53. Winona State University, Paralegal Program[614]

The program is approved by both the American Bar Association and the American Association for Paralegal Education.

The Legal Assistant Program is a four-year interdisciplinary program leading to a B.A. degree. The curriculum is composed of general

---

611. 1401 West 76th St., Richfield, MN 55423-3846; phone 612-566-7777; Web address <http://www.globecollege.com>.
612. 1536 Hewitt Ave. #223, St. Paul, MN 55104-1284; phone 651-523-2974; Web address <http://www.hamline.edu>.
613. 1104 Seventh Ave. South, Moorhead, MN 56563-0002; phone 218-236-2763; Web address <http://www.mnstate.edu/paralegal>.
614. Minne Hall, Room 212, Winona, MN 55987-3288; phone 507-457-5400; Web address <http://www.winona.msus.edu/paralegal>.

education, business administration, sociology, history, and political science as well as specialized legal courses.

## § 683.6. Post-Baccalaureate Programs

§ 683.61. Hamline University, Post-Baccalaureate Paralegal Program
§ 683.62. Minnesota Paralegal Institute, Post-Baccalaureate Certificate Program

There are two programs available in Minnesota for individuals who have completed a bachelor's degree and who wish to become legal assistants.

### § 683.61. Hamline University, Post-Baccalaureate Paralegal Program[615]

The Legal Studies Department offers a one-year post-baccalaureate program for full-time students. Students may work toward a MAPA through an articulation agreement with the Graduate School of Public Administration. The program is approved by the American Bar Association.

### § 683.62. Minnesota Paralegal Institute, Post-Baccalaureate Certificate Program[616]

Minnesota Paralegal Institute's goal is to provide high-quality education in a supportive environment for individuals who can excel in a rigorous, graduate-level, academic program and who can be employed successfully as paralegals. The program was approved by the American Bar Association in 1988.

---

615. College of Liberal Arts, Legal Studies Department, 1536 Hewitt Ave. #223, St. Paul, MN 55104-1284; phone 651-523-2974; Web address <http://www.hamline.edu/cla/academics/legalstudies/peracert.html>.
616. 12450 Wayzata Blvd., Suite 318, Hopkins, MN 55305-1928; phone 612-542-8417; Web address <http://www.mnparalegal.com>.

### § 683.7. Legal Studies

The Hamline University School of Law[617] Early Admission Program allows students who have completed three years of undergraduate education to enter law school during the senior year of a baccalaureate program. Students receive a bachelor's degree in legal studies and continue for the next two years to receive a Juris Doctor degree. Admission to the law school is not automatic, candidates must meet the law school admissions requisites.

### § 684. Law Clerks

Generally law clerks are law students. Law students are eligible for a provisional license to practice if they are enrolled in a law school clinical program and are under the supervision of a member of the bar.[618] Law clerks are employed by judges and lawyers to perform a variety of legal tasks. Judges may offer clerkships to recent law school graduates to aid in the research and writing involved with court caseloads. Notices of available clerkships often are advertised in local newspapers, at employment agencies, and at law school career service offices.

### § 685. Court Reporters

Court reporters prepare records of trials, depositions, and other legal proceedings. Reporters usually receive formal training and are certified by national organizations. Training is available at both public and

---

617. Hamline University, College of Liberal Arts, Legal Studies Department, 1536 Hewitt Ave. #223, St. Paul, MN 55104-1284; phone 651-523-2974; Web address <http://www.hamline.edu/cla/academics/legalstudies/>.
618. Rule 1 General Student Practice adopted May 24, 1982.

## Chapter Six. Institutions and Organizations

private schools. Associations provide continuing education opportunities for members, certify training programs, and represent the interests of members with licensing bureaus, legislatures, and government agencies.

- Minnesota Association of Verbatim Reporters and Captioners[619]
- National Court Reporters Association[620]
- Rasmussen College–Minnetonka[621]

---

619. Executive Director; 1821 University Ave. West, #S156, St. Paul, MN 55104-2892; phone 651-917-6240; Web address <http://www.verbatimreporters.com/index.html>.
620. 8224 Old Courthouse Road, Vienna, VA 22182-3808; phone 703-556-6272 (NCRA), 703-556-6291; Web address <http://www.ncraonline.org/>.
621. 12450 Wayzata Boulevard, Minnetonka, MN 55305-1928; phone 612-545-2000; Web address <http://www.rasmussen.edu/index.html>.

# APPENDIX A
## Constitutional Documents[622]

*Committee Reports* (St. Paul, MN: Constitutional Commission 1947–48) various pagings.
Reproduced from typewritten copy.

*Committee Reports* (St. Paul, MN: Constitutional Study Commission, Nov. 1972) 10 parts, various pagings.
Reproduced from typewritten copy.

*Constitution of Minnesota Annotated,* Harold F. Kumm. Bureau for Research in Government of the University of Minnesota. Publications, No. 3 (Minneapolis, MN: University of Minnesota 1924). 4, 1,311 p.

*Debates and Proceedings of the Constitutional Convention for the Territory of Minnesota, to Form a State Constitution Preparatory to its Admission into the Union as a State,* T. F. Andrews, Official Reporter to the Convention (St. Paul, MN: George W. Moore, Printer, Minnesotian Office) 7, xviii, [9]–624 p.
Constitutional Convention of 1857, Republican debates and proceedings. Also available on microform.

*(The) Debates and Proceedings of the Minnesota Constitutional Convention, Including the Organic Act of the Territory, with the Enabling Act of Congress, the Act of the Territorial Legislature Relative to the Convention, and the Vote of the People on the Constitution,* Reported officially by Francis H. Smith (St. Paul, MN: Earle S. Goodrich, Territorial Printer, Pioneer and Democrat Office 1857) xix, I, 685 p.
Constitutional Convention of 1857, Democratic debates and proceedings. Also available on microform.

*Final Report* (St. Paul, MN: Constitutional Study Commission Feb. 1973) 56 p.

---

622. Numerous copies of unannotated constitutions have been published, none of which are included here.

*In the Senate of the United States. . . : Mr. Douglas made the following report (to accompany bill S. 86): the Committee on Territories, to whom was referred the message of the President communicating a copy of the constitution of Minnesota, beg leave to report. In the Senate of the United States, January 26, 1858 Mr. Douglas made the following report Proposed constitution of the state of Minnesota, adopted in convention on Friday, August 28, 1857,* United States Congress, Senate. Report; 35th Cong., 1st Sess., no. 21 (Washington, DC: The Senate 1858) 56 p.

*Journal of the Constitutional Convention, of the Territory of Minnesota, Begun and Held in the City of St. Paul: Capital of Said Territory, on Monday, the Thirteenth Day of July, One Thousand Eight Hundred and Fifty-Seven* (St. Paul, MN: Earle S. Goodrich, State Printer, Pioneer and Democrat Office 1857) 209 p.

Also available on microfilm.

*Kennedy's Revision of Tentative Draft of Proposed Amendment of the Judiciary Article* (n.d.) 13 leaves.

Manuscript note; reproduced from typewritten copy.

*Message of the President of the United States, Communicating a Copy of the Constitution of Minnesota.* January 11, 1858. Referred to the Committee on Territories. Senate Executive Document No. 14, 35th Cong., 1st Sess. (Washington, DC: Government Printing Office 1858) 24 p.

*Report.* Oct. 1, 1948 (St. Paul, MN: Constitutional Commission) 120 p.

*Working Notebook.* Specially Printed for Use by Members of the Minnesota Constitutional Commission (St. Paul, MN: West Publishing Co. 1948) 180 leaves.

# APPENDIX B
## Amendments to the Minnesota Constitution Proposed to the Voters Since 1858[623]

| Year | Purpose of Amendment | (A)dopted or (R)ejected | Yes | No | Vote at Election |
|---|---|---|---|---|---|
| 1858 | To authorize $5 million railroad loan | A | 25,023 | 6,733 | Special Election |
| 1858 | To establish state government May 1, 1858 | A | 25,023 | 6,733 | Special Election |
| 1860 | To limit legislative sessions to 60 days | A | 19,785 | 442 | 34,737[P] |
| 1860 | To require popular approval of tax to pay railroad bonds; to repeal the $5 million amendment | A | 18,648 | 743 | 34,737[P] |
| 1865 | To authorize Negroes to vote | R | 12,135 | 14,651 | 36,160[G] |
| 1867 | To authorize Negroes to vote | R | 27,479 | 28,794 | 63,376[G] |
| 1867 | To subject shares in state and national banks to state taxation | R | 8,742 | 34,351 | 63,376[G] |
| 1868 | To authorize Negroes to vote | A | 39,493 | 30,121 | 71,818[P] |
| 1868 | To abolish requirement of grand jury | R | 14,763 | 30,544 | 71,818[P] |
| 1868 | To authorize sale of 500,000 acres of internal improvement lands and investment of proceeds in state or national securities | R | 19,398 | 28,729 | 71,818[P] |
| 1869 | To abolish Manomin county | A | 13,392 | 1,671 | 54,525[G] |
| 1869 | To authorize special assessments for local improvements | A | 26,636 | 2,560 | 54,525[G] |
| 1870 | To exempt holders of railroad stock from double liability | R | 7,446 | 11,210 | Legis. Election |
| 1871 | To require popular approval of changes in railroad gross earnings tax law | A | 41,814 | 9,216 | 78,172[G] |
| 1871 | To authorize state loan for asylum buildings | R | 6,724 | 40,797 | 78,172[G] |

---

623. Abbreviations: ** = Figure not available; P = Number of votes cast for president; G = Number of votes cast for governor; T = Total number of persons voting (MINNESOTA LEGISLATIVE MANUAL 2000).

| Year | Purpose of Amendment | (A)dopted or (R)ejected | Yes | No | Vote at Election |
|---|---|---|---|---|---|
| 1872 | To authorize state loan for asylum buildings | A | 29,158 | 26,881 | 90,919[P] |
| 1872 | To exempt stockholders in manufacturing or mechanical businesses from double liability | A | 23,091 | 21,794 | 90,919[P] |
| 1872 | To restrict issuance of county, town, and municipal bonds to aid railroads | A | 27,916 | 7,796 | 90,919[P] |
| 1872 | To provide for sale of internal improvement lands | A | 55,438 | 4,331 | 90,919[P] |
| 1873 | To provide for biennial sessions of the legislature | R | 14,007 | 31,729 | 77,057[G] |
| 1873 | To extend terms of representatives and senators to two and four years respectively | R | 11,675 | 24,331 | 77,057[G] |
| 1873 | To provide for state canvassing board | R | 12,116 | 25,694 | 77,057[G] |
| 1873 | To provide more effectively for the safekeeping of public funds | A | 27,143 | 5,438 | 77,057[G] |
| 1875 | To provide for an indefinite number of judges in each judicial district | A | 22,560 | 18,534 | 84,017[G] |
| 1875 | To authorize the legislature to grant women suffrage in school affairs | A | 24,340 | 19,468 | 84,017[G] |
| 1875 | To prescribe manner in which school funds could be invested | A | 28,755 | 10,517 | 84,017[G] |
| 1875 | To establish single liability for stockholders in ordinary business corporations | R | 16,349 | 25,858 | 84,017[G] |
| 1876 | To authorize governor to veto items of appropriation bills | A | 47,302 | 4,426 | 123,931[P] |
| 1876 | To establish single liability for stockholders in all corporations except banks | R | 21,721 | 22,830 | 123,931[P] |
| 1876 | To authorize district judges to sit on supreme bench when supreme court justices disqualified | A | 41,069 | 6,063 | 123,931[P] |
| 1877 | To establish biennial sessions of legislature | A | 37,995 | 20,833 | 98,614[G] |
| 1877 | To extend terms of representatives and senators to two and four years, respectively | R | 33,072 | 25,099 | 98,614[G] |
| 1877 | To provide for state canvassing board | A | 36,072 | 21,814 | 98,614[G] |

## Appendix B. Minnesota Constitutional Amendments Proposed Since 1858

| Year | Purpose of Amendment | (A)dopted or (R)ejected | Yes | No | Vote at Election |
|---|---|---|---|---|---|
| 1877 | To authorize women to vote in local option elections | R | 26,468 | 32,963 | 98,614[G] |
| 1877 | To prohibit use of state school funds to support sectarian schools | A | 36,780 | 16,667 | 98,614[G] |
| 1877 | To establish single liability for stockholders in all corporations except banks | R | 24,415 | 26,020 | 98,614[G] |
| 1877 | To authorize sale of internal improvement lands and use of proceeds to pay railroad bonds | R | 17,324 | 59,176 | 98,614[G] |
| 1879 | To restrict issuance of county, town, and municipal bonds to aid railroads | A | 54,810 | 1,700 | 99,048[G] |
| 1881 | To authorize levy of water-mains assessments on a frontage basis | A | 35,019 | 18,320 | 102,193[G] |
| 1881 | To remove time limitations from sessions of legislature | R | ** | ** | 102,193[G] |
| 1881 | To regulate compensation of legislators | R | ** | ** | 102,193[G] |
| 1881 | To prohibit special legislation on certain subjects | A | 56,491 | 8,369 | 102,193[G] |
| 1881 | To provide for sale of swamp lands and appropriation of proceeds of swamp land funds | A | 51,903 | 8,440 | 102,193[G] |
| 1883 | To make auditor's term four years, to conform to system of biennial elections | A | 74,375 | 24,359 | 130,713[G] |
| 1883 | To establish the official year and to provide for a system of biennial elections | A | 75,782 | 24,082 | 130,713[G] |
| 1883 | To make term of clerk of supreme court four instead of three years | A | 73,565 | 24,016 | 130,713[G] |
| 1883 | To make terms of justices of supreme court six instead of seven years | A | 73,565 | 24,016 | 130,713[G] |
| 1883 | To make terms of district judges six instead of seven years | A | 73,565 | 24,016 | 130,713[G] |
| 1886 | To provide for loans of state school funds to counties and school districts | A | 131,533 | 17,914 | 220,558[G] |
| 1888 | To prohibit the monopolization of the markets of food products | A | 194,932 | 13,064 | 261,632[G] |
| 1888 | To guarantee the payment of liens of workmen and material-men out of exempted property | A | 153,908 | 48,649 | 261,632[G] |
| 1888 | To extend biennial sessions of legislature to ninety days each | A | 150,003 | 52,946 | 261,632[G] |

| Year | Purpose of Amendment | (A)dopted or (R)ejected | Yes | No | Vote at Election |
|------|---------------------|--------------------------|-----|-----|------------------|
| 1890 | To provide for verdicts by five-sixths of jury in civil cases | A | 66,929 | 49,583 | 240,892[G] |
| 1892 | To extend and strengthen the prohibition against special legislation | A | 77,614 | 19,583 | 255,921[G] |
| 1892 | To authorize various gross earnings taxes and a tonnage tax on iron ore | R | 53,372 | 82,910 | 255,921[G] |
| 1894 | To authorize inheritance taxes | A | 108,322 | 41,242 | 296,249[G] |
| 1896 | To take pardoning power from governor and to confer it on a pardon board | A | 130,354 | 45,097 | 337,229[G] |
| 1896 | To prohibit aliens from voting | A | 97,980 | 52,454 | 337,229[G] |
| 1896 | To authorize home rule for cities | A | 107,086 | 58,312 | 337,229[G] |
| 1896 | To require compensation for property destroyed or damaged for public use | A | 101,188 | 56,839 | 337,229[G] |
| 1896 | To permit cities, towns and villages, as well as counties and school districts, to borrow school and university funds | A | 127,151 | 36,134 | 337,229[G] |
| 1896 | To provide flexible system for taxing large corporations | A | 163,694 | 42,922 | 337,229[G] |
| 1898 | To permit women to vote for and serve on library boards | A | 71,704 | 43,660 | 252,562[G] |
| 1898 | To make it more difficult to amend constitution | A | 69,760 | 32,881 | 252,562[G] |
| 1898 | To amend the municipal home rule section | A | 68,754 | 32,068 | 252,562[G] |
| 1898 | To provide state road and bridge fund | A | 70,043 | 38,017 | 252,562[G] |
| 1900 | To increase debt limit of municipalities borrowing permanent school funds | R | 108,681 | 30,160 | 314,181[G] |
| 1902 | To increase state road and bridge tax, and to eliminate restrictions on expenditure of fund | R | 114,969 | 23,948 | 276,071[T] |
| 1902 | To increase debt limit of municipalities borrowing permanent school funds | R | 116,766 | 20,777 | 276,071[T] |
| 1902 | To simplify the taxing provisions of the constitution | A | 124,584 | 21,251 | 276,071[T] |
| 1904 | To increase debt limit of municipalities borrowing school and university funds | A | 190,718 | 39,334 | 322,692[T] |
| 1904 | To abolish the requirement of a grand jury | A | 164,055 | 52,152 | 322,692[T] |

# Appendix B. Minnesota Constitutional Amendments Proposed Since 1858

| Year | Purpose of Amendment | (A)dopted or (R)ejected | Yes | No | Vote at Election |
|---|---|---|---|---|---|
| 1906 | To simplify the taxing provisions by a "wide open" section | A | 156,051 | 46,982 | 284,366[T] |
| 1906 | To increase state road and bridge tax, and to reduce restrictions on expenditure of funds | A | 141,870 | 49,232 | 284,366[T] |
| 1906 | To permit farmers to sell their produce without licenses | A | 190,897 | 34,094 | 284,366[T] |
| 1908 | To limit the exemption of church property from taxation to that "used for religious purposes" | R | 134,141 | 65,776 | 355,263[T] |
| 1908 | To permit unlimited state taxation for road and bridge purposes | R | 154,226 | 56,557 | 355,263[T] |
| 1908 | To authorize state hail insurance | R | 137,710 | 61,084 | 355,263[T] |
| 1908 | To authorize legislature to establish educational qualifications for county superintendents of schools | R | 169,785 | 42,114 | 355,263[T] |
| 1910 | To permit state to assume half the cost of any road or bridge project | A | 159,746 | 44,387 | 310,165[T] |
| 1910 | To repeal the requirement as to publication of treasurer's report annually in a St. Paul newspaper and also in the biennial session laws | R | 123,787 | 51,650 | 310,165[T] |
| 1910 | To authorize state hail insurance | R | 108,926 | 63,205 | 310,165[T] |
| 1910 | To authorize reapportionment of legislative representation at any time | R | 95,181 | 61,520 | 310,165[T] |
| 1910 | To authorize and require an annual state tax for reforestation work | R | 100,168 | 63,962 | 310,165[T] |
| 1910 | To authorize tax exemptions to encourage reforestation | R | 87,943 | 73,697 | 310,165[T] |
| 1912 | To authorize a one-mill state tax for roads and bridges, and to permit state to assume entire cost of any project | A | 195,724 | 51,135 | 349,678[T] |
| 1912 | To authorize state hail insurance | R | 145,173 | 60,439 | 349,678[T] |
| 1912 | To authorize investment of school and university funds in first mortgages on improved farms | R | 168,440 | 39,483 | 349,678[T] |
| 1912 | To amend the municipal home rule clause to authorize commission government and for other purposes | R | 157,086 | 41,971 | 349,678[T] |

| Year | Purpose of Amendment | (A)dopted or (R)ejected | Yes | No | Vote at Election |
|------|---------------------|---|---|---|---|
| 1912 | To authorize legislature to establish educational qualifications for county superintendents of schools | R | 167,983 | 36,584 | 349,678[T] |
| 1912 | To limit size of state senate and number of senators from any county | R | 122,457 | 77,187 | 349,678[T] |
| 1914 | To establish initiative and referendum | R | 168,004 | 41,577 | 356,906[T] |
| 1914 | To increase number of justices of supreme court, and to authorize the court to appoint its clerk | R | 127,352 | 68,886 | 356,906[T] |
| 1914 | To authorize a revolving fund for improving state school and swamp lands | R | 162,951 | 47,906 | 356,906[T] |
| 1914 | To repeal the requirement as to publication of treasurer's report annually in a St. Paul newspaper and also in the biennial session laws | R | 131,213 | 58,827 | 356,906[T] |
| 1914 | To authorize investment of school and university funds in first mortgages on improved farms | R | 159,531 | 38,145 | 356,906[T] |
| 1914 | To extend terms of probate judges to four years | R | 128,601 | 64,214 | 356,906[T] |
| 1914 | To limit size of state senate and number of senators from any county | R | 98,144 | 84,436 | 356,906[T] |
| 1914 | To authorize state bounties for reforestation | R | 108,352 | 63,782 | 356,906[T] |
| 1914 | To authorize certain public lands to be set aside as state forests | A | 178,954 | 44,033 | 356,906[T] |
| 1914 | To authorize the recall by the voters of "every public official in Minnesota, elective or appointive" | R | 139,801 | 44,961 | 356,906[T] |
| 1914 | To authorize special dog taxes and use of proceeds to compensate owners of animals injured by dogs | R | 136,671 | 59,786 | 356,906[T] |
| 1916 | To authorize a revolving fund for improving state school and swamp lands | A | 240,975 | 58,100 | 416,215[T] |
| 1916 | To authorize investment of school and university funds in first mortgages on improved farms | A | 211,529 | 56,147 | 416,215[T] |
| 1916 | To authorize the state to mine ore under public waters | R | 183,597 | 64,255 | 416,215[T] |

# Appendix B. Minnesota Constitutional Amendments Proposed Since 1858

| Year | Purpose of Amendment | (A)dopted or (R)ejected | Yes | No | Vote at Election |
|---|---|---|---|---|---|
| 1916 | To increase number of justices of supreme court, and to authorize the court to appoint its own clerk | R | 130,363 | 108,002 | 416,215[T] |
| 1916 | To authorize the governor to cut down items in appropriation bills | R | 136,700 | 83,324 | 416,215[T] |
| 1916 | To authorize condemnation of private lands for construction of private drainage ditches | R | 132,741 | 97,432 | 416,215[T] |
| 1916 | To establish initiative and referendum | R | 187,711 | 51,544 | 416,215[T] |
| 1916 | To extend terms of probate judges to four years | R | 186,847 | 72,361 | 416,215[T] |
| 1918 | To prohibit the manufacture and the sale of liquor | R | 189,614 | 173,665 | 380,604[T] |
| 1920 | To provide a state trunk highway system | A | 526,936 | 199,603 | 797,945[T] |
| 1920 | To extend terms of probate judges to four years | A | 446,959 | 171,414 | 797,945[T] |
| 1920 | To authorize state income tax and to change provisions on tax exempt property | R | 331,105 | 217,558 | 797,945[T] |
| 1922 | To establish a state rural credit system to aid agricultural development | A | 534,310 | 73,917 | 714,630[T] |
| 1922 | To tax mining of iron and other ores | A | 474,697 | 91,011 | 714,630[T] |
| 1924 | To place revenue generated by excise taxes on motor fuels in trunk highway | A | 520,769 | 197,455 | 869,151[T] |
| 1924 | To change requirements for publication of proposed amendments to city and village charters | R | 246,414 | 200,391 | 869,151[T] |
| 1924 | To establish state owned and operated public terminal grain elevators | R | 253,732 | 257,492 | 869,151[T] |
| 1924 | To authorize enactment of laws promoting forestation and reforestation of public and private lands, including irrepealable provisions for forest land tax and a yield tax on timber products | R | 428,407 | 143,977 | 869,151[T] |
| 1924 | To authorize state expenditure to prevent forest fires, including compulsory taxation, clearing and improvement of public and private wild lands | A | 460,965 | 143,518 | 869,151[T] |

| Year | Purpose of Amendment | (A)dopted or (R)ejected | Yes | No | Vote at Election |
|---|---|---|---|---|---|
| 1926 | To fix the number of justices on the state supreme court | R | 331,964 | 148,784 | 722,781[T] |
| 1926 | To authorize enactment of laws promoting forestation and reforestation of public and private lands | A | 383,003 | 127,592 | 722,781[T] |
| 1926 | To authorize the legislature to limit the liability of stockholders in corporations | R | 323,322 | 140,422 | 722,781[T] |
| 1928 | To place revenue generated by motor fuel tax ⅔ in trunk highway fund and ⅓ in bridge fund | A | 542,796 | 346,109 | 1,070,274[T] |
| 1928 | To authorize the legislature to limit the liability of stockholders in corporations | R | 506,065 | 223,725 | 1,070,274[T] |
| 1930 | To provide two elective associate supreme court justices to replace appointed court commissioners | A | 428,013 | 130,833 | 828,401[T] |
| 1930 | To authorize the legislature to exchange state public lands for federal lands | R | 378,716 | 174,231 | 828,401[T] |
| 1930 | To authorize the legislature to limit the liability of stockholders in corporations | A | 486,818 | 135,345 | 828,401[T] |
| 1932 | To authorize taxation of income, franchises and privileges of railroad companies; to authorize legislation to make taxation of national banking associations conform to federal law | R | 420,052 | 409,924 | 1,054,203[T] |
| 1932 | To authorize taxation of motor vehicles of companies paying taxes under the gross earnings taxation system | A | 537,292 | 227,634 | 1,054,203[T] |
| 1932 | To authorize the legislature to exchange state public lands for federal lands | R | 433,913 | 258,257 | 1,054,203[T] |
| 1932 | To authorize the taxation of lands acquired through rural credit system | R | 468,101 | 261,856 | 1,054,203[T] |
| 1934 | To authorize legislature to add new routes to trunk highway system | R | 509,074 | 279,877 | 1,064,332[T] |
| 1934 | To authorize taxation of lands acquired through rural credit system | R | 496,017 | 215,623 | 1,064,332[T] |

# Appendix B. Minnesota Constitutional Amendments Proposed Since 1858

| Year | Purpose of Amendment | (A)dopted or (R)ejected | Yes | No | Vote at Election |
|---|---|---|---|---|---|
| 1934 | To exempt all household goods and farm machinery and equipment from taxation | A | 630,125 | 181,126 | 1,064,332[T] |
| 1934 | To authorize the legislature to exchange state public lands for federal lands | R | 468,617 | 216,760 | 1,064,332[T] |
| 1934 | To define "academies, colleges, universities and seminaries of learning" to mean, for tax purposes, property actually used in instruction and housing of students | R | 472,374 | 247,166 | 1,064,332[T] |
| 1936 | To authorize the legislature to exchange state public lands for federal lands | R | 448,917 | 397,106 | 1,164,268[T] |
| 1936 | To exempt personal property from state tax | R | 355,588 | 543,847 | 1,164,268[T] |
| 1938 | To authorize the legislature to exchange state public lands for federal lands | A | 609,046 | 259,007 | 1,144,926[T] |
| 1938 | To change requirements for publication of proposed amendments to city and village charters | R | 488,370 | 260,152 | 1,144,926[T] |
| 1940 | To change requirements for publication of proposed amendments to city and village charters | R | 635,815 | 287,286 | 1,301,573[T] |
| 1942 | To change requirements for investment or loan of permanent school and permanent university funds | A | 415,012 | 190,563 | 818,182[T] |
| 1942 | To simplify and reduce the expense of publishing amendments to city and village charters | A | 459,868 | 144,842 | 818,182[T] |
| 1944 | To authorize state construction and operation of airports; to authorize taxes on aircraft fuel and aircraft sales | A | 737,091 | 264,149 | 1,195,297[T] |
| 1948 | To provide for 50-50 apportionment of excise tax on petroleum products | R | 534,538 | 539,224 | 1,257,804[T] |
| 1948 | To authorize submission of two or more amendments without requiring voters to vote separately on each | R | 319,667 | 621,523 | 1,257,804[T] |

| Year | Purpose of Amendment | (A)dopted or (R)ejected | Yes | No | Vote at Election |
|---|---|---|---|---|---|
| 1948 | To authorize ⅔ of the legislature to call for a constitutional convention without submitting the question to the voters | R | 294,842 | 641,013 | 1,257,804[T] |
| 1948 | To authorize the state to pay a veterans' bonus | A | 664,703 | 420,518 | 1,257,804[T] |
| 1950 | To authorize diversion of 1% of the proceeds of the occupation mining tax to the veterans' compensation fund | A | 594,092 | 290,870 | 1,067,967[T] |
| 1950 | To authorize forestry management funds by diverting certain proceeds (25%) from the public land trust fund | R | 367,013 | 465,239 | 1,067,967[T] |
| 1950 | To provide for a 50%-44%-6% apportionment of the excise tax on petroleum products | R | 420,530 | 456,346 | 1,067,967[T] |
| 1952 | To authorize a change in the investment and loan requirements governing permanent school and university funds | R | 604,384 | 500,490 | 1,460,326[T] |
| 1952 | To provide for a 60% popular majority of voters voting on the question before a new state constitution can be considered legally ratified by the electorate | R | 656,618 | 424,492 | 1,460,126[T] |
| 1952 | To clarify meaning of who shall be entitled to vote | R | 716,670 | 371,508 | 1,460,326[T] |
| 1952 | To permit legislature to extend probate jurisdiction by a ⅔ vote | R | 646,608 | 443,005 | 1,460,326[T] |
| 1952 | To provide for a 65%-10%-25% apportionment of excise tax on motor vehicles | R | 580,316 | 704,336 | 1,460,326[T] |
| 1954 | To permit legislature to extend probate jurisdiction by a ⅔ vote | A | 610,138 | 303,838 | 1,168,101[T] |
| 1954 | To authorize the legislature to limit the liability of stockholders of state banks | A | 624,611 | 290,039 | 1,168,101[T] |

# Appendix B. Minnesota Constitutional Amendments Proposed Since 1858

| Year | Purpose of Amendment | (A)dopted or (R)ejected | Yes | No | Vote at Election |
|---|---|---|---|---|---|
| 1954 | To provide for a 60% popular vote before a new state constitution can be ratified and to remove constitutional bar precluding members of the legislature from serving in a constitutional convention | A | 638,818 | 266,434 | 1,168,101[T] |
| 1954 | To permit gubernatorial appointments in case of vacancy in certain offices to run until end of term or January 1 to eliminate need for election to short terms | A | 636,237 | 282,212 | 1,168,101[T] |
| 1956 | To permit the legislature to recognize the judicial power of the state | A | 939,957 | 307,178 | 1,443,856[T] |
| 1956 | To authorize the consolidation of present trunk highway articles and sections, to increase state aid and supervision of public highways; to permit tax of motor vehicles and fuel; to apportion funds for highway purposes 62%-29%-9% to state and local highways | A | 1,060,063 | 230,707 | 1,443,856[T] |
| 1956 | To authorize the legislature to divert 50% of the occupation mining tax proceeds earmarked for education from permanent trust funds to current educational needs | A | 1,084,627 | 209,311 | 1,443,856[T] |
| 1958 | To authorize the legislature to revise and consolidate provisions relating to local government, home rule and special laws | A | 712,552 | 309,848 | 1,178,173[T] |
| 1958 | To provide for four-year terms for state constitutional officers to take effect for terms beginning in 1963 | A | 641,887 | 382,505 | 1,178,173[T] |
| 1958 | To permit members of the legislature to hold certain elective and nonelective state offices | R | 576,300 | 430,112 | 1,178,173[T] |
| 1960 | To extend the legislative session; to restrict the time during which bills can be introduced; to set qualifications for legislators running for other elective offices | R | 763,434 | 501,429 | 1,577,509[T] |

| Year | Purpose of Amendment | (A)dopted or (R)ejected | Yes | No | Vote at Election |
|------|---------------------|------|-----|-----|------|
| 1960 | To allow an extra legislative session for reapportionment if reapportionment is not complete during the regular session | R | 600,797 | 661,009 | 1,577,509$^T$ |
| 1960 | To provide for succession to the office of governor; to provide for continuity of government in emergencies caused by enemy attack | A | 974,486 | 30,245 | 1,577,509$^T$ |
| 1960 | To prescribe the place where a person moving to a new precinct within 30 days before an election may vote; eliminating obsolete provisions on the voting rights of persons of Indian blood | A | 993,186 | 302,217 | 1,577,509$^T$ |
| 1962 | To consolidate the swamp land fund and the permanent school fund; to set distribution requirements and investment restrictions | A | 828,880 | 288,490 | 1,267,502$^T$ |
| 1962 | To allow state to contract long- and short-term debts for public improvements upon approval of 3/5 of both houses of the legislature | A | 728,255 | 385,723 | 1,267,502$^T$ |
| 1962 | To remove restrictions on length of legislative sessions | A | 706,761 | 393,538 | 1,267,502$^T$ |
| 1964 | To prevent amendment of repeal of taconite tax policies for 25 years; to authorize legislature to impose limitations for not more than 25 years on taxation of copper and nickel mining | A | 1,272,590 | 204,133 | 1,586,173$^T$ |
| 1964 | To remove obsolete language from constitution | A | 1,089,798 | 254,216 | 1,586,173$^T$ |
| 1966 | To allow legislators to seek election to other offices and to provide resignation procedure for legislators | R | 575,967 | 471,427 | 1,312,288$^T$ |
| 1968 | To allow legislators to assume another elective or appointive office upon resignation from the legislature | A | 1,012,235 | 359,088 | 1,601,515$^T$ |
| 1968 | To allow legislature to present bills to governor within three days after legislature adjourns; allowing governor 14 days to sign or veto such bills | A | 1,044,418 | 316,916 | 1,601,515$^T$ |

## Appendix B. Minnesota Constitutional Amendments Proposed Since 1858   285

| Year | Purpose of Amendment | (A)dopted or (R)ejected | Yes | No | Vote at Election |
|---|---|---|---|---|---|
| 1970 | To authorize the legislature to define or limit categories of tax-exempt property | A | 969,774 | 287,858 | 1,388,525[T] |
| 1970 | To reduce voting age requirement from 21 to 19 years; to provide an age requirement of 21 years to hold public office | A | 700,449 | 585,890 | 1,388,525[T] |
| 1972 | To allow flexible legislative sessions | A | 968,088 | 603,385 | 1,773,838[T] |
| 1972 | To reorganize the state judicial system; to provide for appointment of clerks of district court; to authorize discipline and removal of judges | A | 1,012,916 | 531,831 | 1,773,838[T] |
| 1972 | To provide for the joint election of the governor and lieutenant governor; to remove the lieutenant governor as presiding officer of the senate | A | 1,064,580 | 503,342 | 1,773,838[T] |
| 1972 | To authorize bonus payment for Vietnam veterans | A | 1,131,921 | 477,473 | 1,773,838[T] |
| 1974 | To revise organization and language of constitution | A | 815,064 | 311,781 | 1,296,209[T] |
| 1974 | To ease vote requirement for amending constitution | R | 638,775 | 474,519 | 1,296,209[T] |
| 1974 | To allow legislature to determine railroad taxes | A | 741,353 | 372,158 | 1,296,209[T] |
| 1976 | To permit proceeds from increases in motor fuel taxes to be placed in the general fund; to remove restrictions on interest rate for and amount of highway bonds | R | 552,543 | 1,134,847 | 1,978,590[T] |
| 1980 | To establish a bipartisan reapportionment commission | R | 1,036,581 | 754,935 | 2,079,411[T] |
| 1980 | To require campaign spending limits for executive and legislative offices and public disclosure of campaign spending for all state candidates | A | 1,457,454 | 398,551 | 2,079,411[T] |
| 1980 | To remove restrictions on the interest rate for and the amount of highway bonds | R | 964,212 | 823,192 | 2,079,411[T] |

| Year | Purpose of Amendment | (A)dopted or (R)ejected | Yes | No | Vote at Election |
|---|---|---|---|---|---|
| 1980 | To establish initiative and referendum | R | 970,407 | 854,164 | 2,079,411[T] |
| 1980 | To remove requirement of senate approval for notaries public | R | 944,883 | 850,251 | 2,079,411[T] |
| 1982 | To allow the creation of a court of appeals | A | 1,304,127 | 385,738 | 1,834,737[T] |
| 1982 | To remove restrictions on the interest rate for and the amount of trunk highway bonds | A | 1,103,221 | 563,865 | 1,834,737[T] |
| 1982 | To permit the legislature to authorize on-track parimutuel betting on horse racing | A | 1,108,255 | 624,721 | 1,834,737[T] |
| 1982 | To provide state bonding authority for the improvement and rehabilitation of railroad facilities | A | 1,201,321 | 492,736 | 1,834,737[T] |
| 1984 | To allow public lands of the state to be exchanged for any other public land | A | 1,176,809 | 611,200 | 2,114,842[T] |
| 1984 | To remove restrictions on permanent school fund investments; establish statutory restrictions | A | 1,139,390 | 631,378 | 2,114,842[T] |
| 1988 | To establish a Minnesota Environmental and Natural Resources Trust Fund for environmental natural resources, and wildlife purposes | A | 1,645,090 | 375,752 | 2,125,119[T] |
| 1988 | To allow the use of juries of less than 12 members in civil and non-felony cases | A | 1,205,730 | 806,766 | 2,125,119[T] |
| 1988 | To permit the legislature to authorize a lottery operated by the state | A | 1,214,032 | 843,307 | 2,125,119[T] |
| 1990 | To dedicate 40% of the state lottery proceeds to the environment and natural resources trust fund until the year 2001 | A | 1,388,105 | 329,806 | 1,843,104[T] |
| 1994 | To permit off-track wagering on horse racing in a manner prescribed by law | R | 841,277 | 847,802 | 1,794,618[T] |
| 1996 | To authorize a bonus for Persian Gulf War veterans | A | 1,334,409 | 740,039 | 2,211,161[T] |

## Appendix B. Minnesota Constitutional Amendments Proposed Since 1858

| Year | Purpose of Amendment | (A)dopted or (R)ejected | Yes | No | Vote at Election |
|---|---|---|---|---|---|
| 1996 | To provide for recall of elected state officials | A | 1,833,523 | 248,778 | 2,211,161[T] |
| 1998 | To extend use of lottery for environmental trust fund | A | 1,556,895 | 460,747 | 2,105,343[T] |
| 1998 | To preserve hunting and fishing heritage | A | 1,570,720 | 462,749 | 2,105,343[T] |
| 1998 | To abolish the office of the state treasurer | A | 1,087,789 | 855,853 | 2,105,343[T] |

# APPENDIX C
# Checklist of Session Laws[624]

| Territory ||||
| --- | --- | --- | --- |
| Year | Session Number | Laws | Number of Pages |
| 1849 Sept. | 1st Leg. Assemb. | Acts, Joint Res. & Memorials | xxxvii, 107, 2, 106–213p[625] |
| 1851 Jan. | [2nd Sess.] | Sess. Laws | 53p |
| 1852 Jan. | [3rd Sess.] | Sess. Laws | 78p[626] |
| 1853 Jan. | [4th Sess.] | Sess. Laws | 89p[627] |
| 1854 Jan. | [5th Sess.] | Sess. Laws | 184p |
| 1855 Jan. | [6th Sess.] | Sess. Laws | 200p |
| 1856 Jan. | [7th Sess.] | Sess. Laws | 376p[628] |
| 1857 Jan. | [8th Sess.] | Sess. Laws | 304p |
| 1857 Apr. | Ex. Sess. | Sess. Laws | 361p |

| State ||||
| --- | --- | --- | --- |
| Year | Session Number | Laws | Number of Pages |
| 1857 Dec. | 1st Sess. | Gen. Laws | 468p[629] |
| 1857 Dec. | 1st Sess. | Spec. Laws | xii, 3–563p |
| 1859 Dec. | 2nd Sess. | Gen. Laws | l, 5–347p |
| 1859 Dec. | 2nd Sess. | Spec. Laws | I, v–viii, 3–144p |

---

624. Pagination varies in other copies. Some copies have general and special laws bound together. This publication gives the collation in the copies examined. Laws 1849 through 1859 are available on microfilm from Photo duplication Service, Library of Congress. A "+" indicates that sessions are bound together.
625. This includes "Republication of Important General Laws of Wisconsin Now in Force in the Territory of Minnesota by provision of the Organic Act" at 106–160. It also contains the U.S. Constitution and acts of Congress regarding the Northwest Territory.
626. This also is available in facsimile reprint by Statute Law Book Co. (Wash. D.C. 1906). Some copies contain Acts 1849, with Wis. Laws; Laws, 1851, *Collated Statutes* 1853, Hollinshead's Reports 1851, and Atwater's Reports 1852. Other variations may be found.
627. This also is available in facsimile reprint by Statute Law Book Co., Washington, DC (1906).
628. Variants: 376, 370–371p; 376, 370–37lp (369 unnumbered); 373, 366–369, 390p (374 unnumbered, 65 unnumbered); 376, 368–369, 390p; 379, 369–371p; 304, 297–371p.
629. This includes appendix of laws passed by 1858 but repealed by subsequent acts.

| State |||| 
|---|---|---|---|
| Year | Session Number | Laws | Number of Pages |
| 1861 Jan. | 3rd Sess. | Gen. & Spec. Laws | 448p[630] |
| 1862 Jan. | 4th Sess. | Gen. & Spec. Laws | 446p |
| 1862 Sept. | Ex. Sess. | Gen. & Spec. Laws | 6, 13–114p |
| 1863 Jan. | 5th Sess. | Gen. & Spec. Laws | 377p |
| 1864 Jan. | 6th Sess. | Gen. & Spec. Laws | 505p |
| 1865 Jan. | 7th Sess. | Gen. Laws | 248p |
| 1865 Jan. | 7th Sess. | Spec. Laws | 10, 17–282p |
| 1866 Jan. | 8th Sess. | Gen. Laws | vi, 1, 197p[631] |
| 1866 Jan. | 8th Sess. | Spec. Laws | xii, 11–301p |
| 1867 Jan. | 9th Sess. | Gen. Laws | xii, 253p |
| 1867 Jan. | 9th Sess. | Spec. Laws | 14, 419p |
| 1868 Jan. | 10th Sess. | Gen. Laws | xiv, 1, 273p |
| 1868 Jan. | 10th Sess. | Spec. Laws | xv, 500p |
| 1869 Jan. | 11th Sess. | Gen. Laws | xii, 2, 234p |
| 1869 Jan. | 11th Sess. | Spec. Laws | xv, 414p |
| 1870 Jan. | 12th Sess. | Gen. Laws | xii, 2, 295p |
| 1870 Jan. | 12th Sess. | Spec. Laws | xvi, 515p |
| 1871 Jan. | 13th Sess. | Gen. Laws | xiii, 2, 17–281p[632] |
| 1871 Jan. | 13th Sess. | Spec. Laws | xv, 17–420p |
| 1872 Jan. | 14th Sess. | Gen. Laws | xiii, 2, 17–276p |
| 1872 Jan. | 14th Sess. | Spec. Laws | xxi, 17–632p |
| 1873 Jan. | 15th Sess. | Gen. Laws | xv, 17–356p |
| 1873 Jan. | 15th Sess. | Spec. Laws | xiv, 177–448p |
| 1874 Jan. | 16th Sess. | Gen. Laws | xiii, 1, 17–400p |
| 1874 Jan. | 16th Sess. | Spec. Laws | xiii, 17–435p |
| 1875 Jan. | 17th Sess. | Gen. Laws | xiv, 17–286p |
| 1875 Jan. | 17th Sess. | Spec. Laws | xvi, 17–453p |
| 1876 Jan. | 18th Sess. | Gen. Laws | xvi, 17–239p |
| 1876 Jan. | 18th Sess. | Spec. Laws | xvi, 17–343p[633] |
| 1877 Jan. | 19th Sess. | Gen. Laws | 2, 340, 63p |

630. Treasurer's report is appended from 1861 through 1897.
631. Variant: 6, 1, 197p.
632. Some copies (in 1871 and 1872) have a table entitled "Life Insurance Companies Authorized to Transact Business in this State."
633. *See* JOHN C. SHAW & JOHN B. WEST, AN ANALYTICAL INDEX TO THE GENERAL AND SPECIAL LAWS OF THE TERRITORY AND STATE OF MINNESOTA, FROM 1849 TO 1875 (assisted by S. L. Pierce, St. Paul, MN: John B. West 1876) (121, [3], 63 p.).

## Appendix C. Checklist of Session Laws

| | State | | |
|---|---|---|---|
| Year | Session Number | Laws | Number of Pages |
| 1877 Jan. | 19th Sess. | Spec. Laws | xxiii, 17–354p |
| 1878 Jan. | 20th Sess. | Gen. Laws | 235, 64p |
| 1878 Jan. | 20th Sess. | Spec. Laws | 595p |
| 1879 Jan. | 21st Sess. | Gen. Laws | 171, 64p |
| 1879 Jan. | 21st Sess. | Spec. Laws | xxvi, 1, 517p |
| 1881 Jan. | 22nd Sess. | Gen. Laws | 279, 68p |
| 1881 Jan. | 22nd Sess. | Spec. Laws | xxviii, 1, 1024p |
| 1881 Oct. | Ex. Sess. | Gen. Laws | 116p |
| 1881 Oct. | Ex. Sess. | Spec. Laws | xvi, 273p |
| 1883 Jan. | 23rd Sess. | Gen. Laws | xvi, 278, 6, 71p[634] |
| 1883 Jan. | 23rd Sess. | Spec. Laws | xxiv, 487p |
| 1885 Jan. | 24th Sess. | Gen. Laws | xxiii, 425,1,77p |
| 1885 Jan. | 24th Sess. | Spec. Laws | xxvii, 581p |
| 1887 Jan. | 25th Sess. | Gen. Laws | xxii, 1, 456, 78p |
| 1887 Jan. | 25th Sess. | Spec. Laws | xxix, 1, 1074p |
| 1889 Jan. | 26th Sess. | Gen. Laws | xxi, 1, 602, 77, 90p |
| 1889 Jan. | 26th Sess. | Spec. Laws | xxxviii, 1, 1258p |
| 1891 Jan. | 27th Sess. | Gen. Laws | 462, 75, 81p |
| 1891 Jan. | 27th Sess. | Spec. Laws | 1138p |
| 1893 Jan. | 28th Sess. | Gen. Laws & Spec. Laws | 468, 76, 77p[635] |
| 1895 Jan. | 29th Sess. | Gen. Laws | 922, 66, 62p |
| 1897 Jan. | 30th Sess. | Gen. Laws | xi, 752, 66, 73p |
| 1899 Jan. | 31st Sess. | Gen. Laws | viii, 626, 76, 77p |
| 1901 Jan. | 32nd Sess. | Gen. Laws | v, 812, 86p |
| 1902 Feb. | Ex. Sess. | Gen. Laws | v, 250, 1p |
| 1903 Jan. | 33rd Sess. | Gen. Laws | 867, 1, 103p[636] |
| 1905 Jan. | 34th Sess. | Gen. Laws | 776p |
| 1907 Jan. | 35th Sess. | Gen. Laws | xi, 932, 144p[637] |
| 1909 Jan. | 36th Sess. | Gen. Laws | 1, 872p |
| 1911 Jan. | 37th Sess. | Gen. Laws | 732p |

634. Terms of district court are appended from 1883 to date.
635. In 1892, the voters approved an amendment to the Minnesota Constitution, art. IV, § 33 prohibiting special legislation. *See* 1893 Minn. Laws ch. 1.
636. Variant: 867, 1p.
637. Variant: XI, 932p.

| State ||||
| --- | --- | --- | --- |
| Year | Session Number | Laws | Number of Pages |
| 1916 Oct. | Spec. Sess. | Sess. Laws | + |
| 1912 June | Spec. Sess. | Gen. Laws | 68p |
| 1913 Jan. | 38th Sess. | Gen. Laws | 1115p |
| 1915 Jan. | 39th Sess. | Sess. Laws | 705p |
| 1917 Jan. | 40th Sess. | Sess. Laws | 1094p |
| 1919 Jan. | 41st Sess. | Sess. Laws | 1088p |
| 1919 Sept. | Ex. Sess. | Laws and Res. | 132p |
| 1921 Jan. | 42nd Sess. | Sess. Laws | 1318p |
| 1923 Jan. | 43rd Sess. | Sess. Laws | 1062p |
| 1925 Jan. | 44th Sess. | Sess. Laws | 1137p |
| 1927 Jan. | 45th Sess. | Sess. Laws | 1055p |
| 1929 Jan. | 46th Sess. | Sess. Laws | 1102p |
| 1931 Jan. | 47th Sess. | Sess. Laws | 1023p |
| 1933 Jan. | 48th Sess. | Sess. Laws | 1379p |
| 1933 Dec. | Ex. 48th Sess. | Laws and Res. | 171p |
| 1935 Jan. | 49th Sess. | Sess. Laws | 1266p |
| 1935 Dec. | Ex. Sess. | Laws and Res. | 231p |
| 1936 Dec. | Ex. Sess. | Sess. Laws | + |
| 1937 Jan. | 50th Sess. | Sess. Laws | 2, 5–1402p |
| 1937 May | Ex. Sess. | Laws and Res. | 238p |
| 1939 Jan. | 51st Sess. | Sess. Laws | 1671p |
| 1941 Jan. | 52nd Sess. | Sess. Laws | 1799p |
| 1943 Jan. | 53rd Sess. | Sess. Laws | 1838p |
| 1944 Mar. | Ex. Sess. | Sess. Laws | + |
| 1945 Jan. | 54th Sess. | Sess. Laws | 1837p |
| 1947 Jan. | 55th Sess. | Sess. Laws | 1449p |
| 1949 Jan. | 56th Sess. | Sess. Laws | 1664p |
| 1951 Jan. | 57th Sess. | Sess. Laws | + |
| 1951 Apr. | Ex. Sess. | Sess. Laws | 1590p |
| 1953 Jan. | 58th Sess. | Sess. Laws | 1329p |
| 1955 Jan. | 59th Sess. | Sess. Laws | + |
| 1955 Apr. | Ex. Sess. | Sess. Laws | 1762p |
| 1957 Jan. | 60th Sess. | Sess. Laws | + |
| 1957 Apr. | [60th Sess.] 1st Ex. Sess. | Sess. Laws | 2048p |
| 1958 June | [60th Sess.] 2nd Ex. Sess. | Sess. Laws | + |

## Appendix C. Checklist of Session Laws

| State |||| 
|---|---|---|---|
| Year | Session Number | Laws | Number of Pages |
| 1959 Jan. | 61st Leg. | Sess. Laws | + |
| 1959 Apr. | 61st Leg. 1st Ex. Sess. | Sess. Laws | 2141p |
| 1961 Jan. | 62nd Leg. | Sess. Laws | + |
| 1961 Apr. | 62nd Leg. 1st Ex. Sess. | Sess. Laws | 2028p |
| 1961 Dec. | 62nd Leg. 2nd Ex. Sess. | Sess. Laws | + |
| 1963 Jan. | 63rd Leg. | Sess. Laws | 1890p |
| 1965 Jan. | 64th Leg. | Sess. Laws | 2050p |
| 1966 Apr. | 64th Leg. 1st Ex. Sess. | Sess. Laws | + |
| 1967 Jan. | 65th Leg. | Sess. Laws | + |
| 1967 May | 65th Leg. 1st Ex. Sess. | Sess. Laws | 2631p |
| 1969 Jan. | 66th Leg. | Sess. Laws | 2934p |
| 1971 Jan. | 67th Leg. | Sess. Laws | + |
| 1971 May | 67th Leg. 1st Ex. Sess. | Sess. Laws | + |
| 1971 Oct. | 67th Leg. 2nd Ex. Sess. | Sess. Laws | 2808p in 3 v.[638] |
| 1973 Jan. | 68th Leg. | Sess. Laws | 2696p in 2 v.[639] |
| 1974 Jan. | 68th Leg. | Sess. Laws, ch. 1–583 | xiii,1620p. |
| 1975 Jan. | 69th Leg. | Sess. Laws, ch. 1–437 | xxix, 1789p |
| 1976 Jan. | 69th Leg. | Sess. Laws, ch. 1–348 | xiii, 1552p |
| 1977 Jan. | 70th Leg. | Sess. Laws, ch. 1–455 | xiii, 1608p |
| 1978 Jan. | 70th Leg. | Sess. Laws, ch. 465 to end | xiii, 1383p |
| 1979 Jan. | 71st Leg. | Sess. Laws | + |
| 1979 May | 71st Leg. 1st Ex. Sess. | Sess. Laws, ch. 1–340 | xiii, 1444p |
| 1980 Jan. | 71st Leg. | Sess. Laws, ch. 341 to end | xiii, 1772p |
| 1981 Jan. | 72nd Leg. | Sess. Laws | + |
| 1981 June | 72nd Leg. 1st Spec. Sess. | Sess. Laws | + |
| 1981 July | 72nd Leg. 2nd Spec. Sess. | Sess. Laws | 2814p in 2 v.[640] |

---

638. Vol. 1 ch. 1–666; vol. 2 ch. 666 to end, Ex. Sess. ch. 1–30; vol. 3 Ex. Sess. ch. 31 to end.
639. Vol. 1 ch. 1–590; vol. 2 ch. 590 to end.
640. Vol. 1 ch. 1–299; vol. 2 ch. 300–370.

| | State | | |
|---|---|---|---|
| Year | Session Number | Laws | Number of Pages |
| 1981 Dec. | 72nd Leg. 3rd Spec. Sess. | Sess. Laws, ch. 371 to end | + |
| 1982 Jan. | 72nd Leg. | Sess. Laws | + |
| 1982 Mar. | 72nd Leg. 1st Spec. Sess. | Sess. Laws | + |
| 1982 July | 72nd Leg. 2nd Spec. Sess. | Sess. Laws | + |
| 1982 Dec. | 72nd Leg. 3rd Spec. Sess. | Sess. Laws | xvi, 142, 1863p |
| 1983 Jan. | 73rd Leg. | Sess. Laws | xvi, 142, 2905p in 2 v.[641] |
| 1984 Mar. | 73rd Leg. | Sess. Laws | xvi, 2409p in 2 v.[642] |
| 1985 Jan. | 74th Leg. | Sess. Laws | xvi, 2993p in 2 v.[643] |
| 1985 June | 74th Leg. 1st Spec. Sess. | Sess. Laws | + |
| 1986 Feb. | 74th Leg. Reg. Sess. | Sess. Laws | + |
| 1986 Apr. | 74th Leg. 1st Spec. Sess. | Sess. Laws | xv, 1508p |
| 1987 Jan. | 75th Leg. Reg. Sess. | Sess. Laws | + |
| 1987 June | 75th Leg. 1st Spec. Sess. | Sess. Laws | xv, 3958p in 3 v. |
| 1988 Feb. | 75th Leg. Reg. Sess. | Sess. Laws | vii, 2241p in 2 v. |
| 1989 Jan. | 76th Leg. Reg. Sess. | Sess. Laws | xvii, 3535p in 3 v. |
| 1989 Sept. | 76th Leg. 1st Spec. Sess. | Sess. Laws | + |
| 1990 Feb. | 76th Leg. Reg. Sess. | Sess. Laws | xvii, 3124p in 2 v. |
| 1991 May | 77th Leg. Reg. Sess. | Sess. Laws | xvii, 3184p in 2 v. |
| 1992 Apr. | 77th Leg. Reg. Sess. | Sess. Laws | xvii, 2666p in 2 v. |
| 1994 May | 78th Leg. Reg. Sess. | Sess. Laws | xvii, 3003p in 2 v. |
| 1994 Aug. | 78th Leg. 1st Spec. Sess. | Sess. Laws | + |
| 1995 May | 79th Leg. Reg. Sess. | Sess. Laws | + |
| 1995 May | 79th Leg. 1st Spec. Sess. | Sess. Laws | xvi, 3777p in 3 v. |
| 1996 Apr. | 79th Leg. Reg. Sess. | Sess. Laws | xvi, 2150p in 2 v. |

641. Vol. 1 ch. 1–297; vol. 2 ch. 298 to end.
642. Vol. 1 ch. 376–584; vol. 2 ch. 585 to end.
643. Vol. 1 ch. 1–309; vol. 2 1st 1985 Spec. Sess.

# Appendix C. Checklist of Session Laws

| State |||| 
|---|---|---|---|
| Year | Session Number | Laws | Number of Pages |
| 1997 May | 80th Leg. Reg. Sess. | Sess. Laws | + |
| 1997 June | 80th Leg. 1st Spec. Sess. | Sess. Laws | xvi, 3836p in 3 v. |
| 1997 June | 80th Leg. 2nd Spec. Sess. | Sess. Laws | + |
| 1998 Sept. | 80th Leg. Reg. Sess. | Sess. Laws | xvi, 2642p in 2 v. |
| 1999 May | 81st Leg. Reg. Sess. | Sess. Laws | xvi, 3206p in 2 v. |
| 2000 May | 81st Leg. Reg. Sess. | Sess. Laws | 2745p in 2 v. |

# APPENDIX D
# Statutory Compilations, Revisions, and Codes[644]

## I. COMPILATIONS, REVISIONS, AND CODES

Following is a list of all the compilations, revisions, and codes that have been published in Minnesota. Each is described briefly by showing the reason for preparing it and its legislative effect. Entries are arranged in chronological order.

*Republication of Important General Laws of Wisconsin Now in Force in the Territory of Minnesota by Provision of the Organic Act* (St. Paul, MN: James M. Goodhue 1850), pp. 106–60.

This was printed as chapter numbers xlv through lxiii of the first volume of the session laws of the Territory of Minnesota in 1849. The index to these Wisconsin laws begins on page 203. These laws comprise the laws of Wisconsin that were in force in the territory of Minnesota and that later were incorporated into *Revised Statutes* 1851.[645]

*The Revised Statutes of the Territory of Minnesota, Passed at the Second Session of the Legislative Assembly Commencing January 1, 1851* ... (St. Paul, MN: James M. Goodhue 1851), xvi, 734 p.

According to section 12 of the 1849 congressional Organic Act establishing the Territory of Minnesota, the laws of Wisconsin at the date of the admission of Wisconsin to statehood would be in force in Minnesota "so far as the same be not incompatible with the provisions of this act, subject, nevertheless, to be altered, modified, or repealed."[646] The Wisconsin acts were scattered through nine or ten different publications, some of which were almost impossible to obtain.

In 1851, Governor Ramsey recommended[647] and a legislative joint resolution[648] authorized the compilation and revision of the laws of the

---

644. This is a revised edition of the "History of Statutory Publications in Minnesota," by Arlette M. Soderberg, which is included in the Preface of *Minnesota Statutes*.
645. This title also is available on microfilm from the Library of Congress Photoduplication Service. For a listing see A GUIDE TO THE MICROFILM COLLECTION OF EARLY STATE RECORDS (1950).
646. 9 Stat. 403, § 12 (1849).
647. MINN. COUNCIL J. 12 (Jan. 7, 1851); MINN. HOUSE J. 16 (Jan. 7, 1851).
648. MINN. COUNCIL J. 43 (Jan. 21, 1851); MINN. HOUSE J. 49 (Jan. 21, 1851).

territory. M. S. Wilkinson, with the assistance of L. A. Babcock and William Holcombe, supervised the work and inserted the marginal notes. These statutes were intended to present an entire system of laws for the Territory of Minnesota. Chapter 2, section 5, of the completed *Revised Statutes* 1851 states that this revision is to be designated as "Revised Statutes." Section 11 provides that these statutes are "entitled to be read in evidence in any court of justice, or in any other place...."

The outline and the arrangement of *Revised Statutes* 1851 follow the outline and arrangement of the 1849 *Revised Statutes of the State of Wisconsin*; the numbering system, however, is different. Some of the sections appear to be verbatim copy, others have been revised extensively. The volume represents only a compilation of the Wisconsin laws applicable in Minnesota. Other laws from *Laws of Minnesota* 1849 are appended but not incorporated into the compilation.

*Amendments to the Revised Statutes of the Territory of Minnesota, Passed at the Third Session of the Legislative Assembly, Commencing January 6, 1852* (St. Paul, MN: Owens and Moore, Printer. Minnesotian Office 1852), 45 p.[649]

This publication is arranged in the same order as *Revised Statutes* 1851 and must be used in conjunction with it.

*Collated Statutes of the Territory of Minnesota and Decisions of Supreme Court. Collated Pursuant to a Resolution of March 5, 1853* (St. Paul, MN: Joseph R. Brown 1853), 198, 96 p.[650]

This is an official listing, not in chronological order or in any other apparent logical arrangement, of both the general laws and the private acts that were in force July 1, 1853, and that had not been included in *Revised Statutes* 1851. A joint resolution of the legislature authorized these acts to be "collated, properly noted and indexed."[651]

Also included in the volume are William Hollinshead's reports of cases argued and determined in the Supreme Court of the Minnesota Territory in July term, 1851, and Isaac Atwater's reports, July term, 1852.

---

649. *Supra* note 637.
650. *Id.*
651. Authorizing the secretary of the territory to collate, and cause to be printed, certain acts, and for other purposes, J. Res. 3, 1853 Minn. [Territorial] Laws 64.

## Appendix D. Statutory Compilations, Revisions, and Codes 299

*Code of Pleadings and Practice in Civil Actions in the Courts of this State*, reported to the Legislature of Minnesota by Aaron Goodrich, one of the Commissioners appointed to review the laws (St. Paul, MN: Earle S. Goodrich, state printer, Pioneer and Democrat office 1858), 280 p.[652]

There had been much disagreement in Minnesota about whether to retain the old common law or to adopt a new statutory code of practice and pleadings such as the *Code of Procedure of the State of New York*, also known as the "Field Code," which New York adopted in 1848. The Minnesota legislature chose to adopt a code.

According to the Minnesota Code's introduction, a joint resolution was passed by the Minnesota legislature in March of 1858 directing that commissioners Aaron Goodrich, Moses Sherburne, and William Hollinshead prepare a system of pleadings and practice to be followed in the state courts, using the "Field Code" as a guide, "having reference to the brevity and legal intent of the pleadings; and that they cause the result of their labors to be printed and laid before the Legislature at the earliest day practicable." The dissents of Goodrich from many of the Minnesota Code's provisions are reported in the introduction.

A "Report of the Select Committee on the Code of Procedure," which urged the adoption of the proposed code, is published in the *Journal* of the House of Representatives for March 19, 1858, at page 558. This code somewhat conforms to the Field Code.

*The Public Statutes of the State of Minnesota (1849–1858)*, compiled by Moses Sherburne & William Hollinshead, Commissioners; published by state authority (St. Paul, MN: The Pioneer Printing Co. 1858), 14, ix–lxxi, 73–1071 p.[653]

The object of this official compilation was to republish the general laws contained in *Revised Statutes* 1851 and incorporate the laws contained in *Laws of Minnesota* for the years 1849 through 1858. An attempt was made to include only the laws in force and to omit those repealed.

Chapters 7 and 37 of *Laws of Minnesota* 1858 provided that commissioners were to prepare this compilation and that justices of the Supreme Court were to examine and approve it. Chapter 3, section 31, of *Public Statutes* (1849–1858) provided that when so approved and published, the compilation "shall be received in all places whatsoever as the laws of the state. . . ." The statutes were not enacted by the legislature.

---

652. *Supra* note 637.
653. *Id.*

*General Statutes of the State of Minnesota, Prepared by the Commissioners Appointed to Revise the Statutes of the State, by Act of the Legislature, Passed February 17, 1863* (St. Paul, MN: Press Printing Co. 1865), 895, 9 p.

Chapter 25 of *Laws of Minnesota* 1863 provided for the appointment of commissioners to revise the statutes. Their report, made at the legislative session of 1866, was referred to a select joint committee which examined the revision chapter by chapter and added such amendments as it deemed advisable. This revision then was presented to the legislature. Each chapter was enacted separately.

Bound with the revision is an "Appendix to Report of the Commissioner of Revision. Embracing the Amendments to the Same, Adopted by the Legislature" and several of the session laws of 1866 that were not included in *General Statutes*. These amendments and laws were prepared by Judge E. C. Palmer, who had been one of the Commissioners of Revision.

*The General Statutes of the State of Minnesota Revised by Commissioners Appointed Under an Act Approved February 17, 1863, and Acts Subsequent Thereto, Amended by the Legislature, and Passed at the Session of 1866. . . .* (St. Paul, MN: Davidson and Hall 1866), xi, 874 p. (other imprints published 1867, 1872).

Chapter 17 of *Laws of Minnesota* 1866 provided for the publishing of the commissioners' revision that officially was enacted into law. This compilation apparently is based upon the *Public Statutes* (1849–1858) but removes laws subsequently repealed and adds laws included in *Laws of Minnesota* for the years 1859 through 1866. Editing is attributed to E. C. Palmer. Chapter 121, section 9, of *General Statutes* 1866 states:

> [The] provisions of the General Statutes so far as they are the same as those of existing laws, shall be construed as a continuation of such laws, and not as new enactments, and references in laws not repealed to provisions of laws incorporated into the General Statutes, and repealed, shall be construed as applying to the same provisions so incorporated.

The volume contains a list of acts previously repealed, a glossary, and an index.

## Appendix D. Statutory Compilations, Revisions, and Codes

*The Statutes at Large of the State of Minnesota Comprising the General Statutes of 1866 . . . Together with All Laws of a General Nature in Force, March 7, A.D. 1873. . .* , compiled & arranged by A. H. Bissell (Chicago, IL: Callaghan and Co. 1873), 2 v.

This is an unofficial compilation of statutes. It is based upon the *General Statutes* 1866 omitting those parts that were repealed and adding new laws from *Laws of Minnesota* for the years 1867 through 1873.

The first appearance of annotations is found in this compilation. The preface states that an "endeavor has been made to cite every case to be found in our state reports bearing in any way upon the statutes." References also are given to Wisconsin decisions and to those of other states with similar statutes in which the interpretation has been different. Some changes in the numbering system were made. Curative and legalizing acts after 1857, except those of the year 1861, are included in part V.

Chapter 79, section 1, of *Laws of Minnesota* 1874 provides that *Statutes at Large* be "admissible in all the courts of law of this state, and on all occasions as prima facie evidence of such laws. . . ."

*An Analytical Index to the General and Special Laws of the Territory and State of Minnesota from 1849 to 1875,* by John C. Shaw & John B. West (St. Paul, MN: John B. West 1876), 121, [3], 63 p.

The preface sums up the purpose and value of this publication.

> An Index of the Laws of this State has long been needed; none has been before compiled; and since 1866 there has been no authorized revision of the General Laws. Parties wishing to trace any law have been obliged to hunt through some twenty-five volumes . . . and even then the result has been very unsatisfactory, owing to the fact that the several indexes have been made by different persons, after different plans, and in a hasty manner. . . . General Laws enacted prior to 1866 that have no importance and have been superseded by the revision, have been briefly referred to, while all laws enacted since are indexed in detail.

This is an index of session laws only, with general and special laws indexed separately. Special laws, especially those relating to roads, taxes, and titles to real estate, are fully indexed.

*The General Statutes of the State of Minnesota, as Amended by Subsequent Legislation, with which are Incorporated All General Laws of the State in Force at the Close of the Legislative Session of 1878*, prepared by George B. Young (St. Paul, MN: West Publishing Co. 1878), 2, xvi, 1031, 186 p. (2d ed. 1880), 2, xii, 1032, 186 p. (3d ed. 1881), 2, xii, 1032, 186 p. (4th ed. 1883), 3, xii, 1032, 186, 2, 141, 127 p.

Chapter 67 of *Laws of Minnesota* 1878 authorized George B. Young and others to compile, arrange, and put into chapters the laws in force, with appropriate headings and references to the decisions of the Supreme Court. It is based upon *General Statutes* 1866 and all session laws included in the *Statutes at Large* plus *Laws of Minnesota* for the years 1874 through 1878. The arrangement of *General Statutes* 1866 was retained, but it was necessary to renumber the sections in most chapters.

Chapter 67 of *Laws of Minnesota* 1879 provided that these "shall be competent evidence of the several acts and resolutions therein contained in all the courts of this state, without further proof or authentication," and that they are to be cited as "General Statutes 1878."

*Changes in the General Statutes of 1878 Effected by the General Laws of 1879 and 1881, Arranged with reference to Chapter and Section Amended* (St. Paul, MN: West Publishing Co. 1881), 2, 141 p.

*Changes in the General Statutes of 1878, of the State of Minnesota, Effected by the General Laws of the Extra Session of 1881, and the Regular Session of 1883. Arranged with reference to Chapter and Section Amended* (St. Paul, MN: West Publishing Co. 1883), 127 p.

Both of these volumes merely are supplements showing the new laws, the amendments, and the repealed laws of *General Statutes* 1878. The 1881 edition adds *Laws of Minnesota* for the years 1879 and 1881. The 1883 edition adds *Laws of Minnesota* from the 1881 special session and 1883 session. The section numbers of *General Statutes* 1878 were retained. The 1881 changes also are bound in the third edition, and both 1881 and 1883 changes are bound in the fourth edition of *General Statutes* 1878.

Chapter 75 of *Laws of Minnesota*, Extra Session 1881, stated that the changes in the 1881 third edition of *General Statutes* 1878 made by the laws of 1879 and 1881 "shall be and hereby is made prima facie evidence of the several acts therein contained in all the courts of this State without further proof or authentication." This third edition is to be "cited and designated as '1881 Supplement General Statutes 1878.'" There seems to be no similar act for either the second edition of 1880 or the fourth edition of 1883.

## Appendix D. Statutory Compilations, Revisions, and Codes

*The Penal Code of the State of Minnesota to Take Effect January 1, A.D. 1886, with Notes of Decisions, Furnished by the Attorney General* (St. Paul, MN: Pioneer Press Co. 1885), 297 p.

Chapter 240 of *Laws of Minnesota* 1885 authorized and directed the Secretary of State to publish the "penal code . . . in a volume by itself . . . and to omit said code from the volume of general laws of this session." The attorney general was to supervise the citation of authorities. The Minnesota Penal Code is an adaptation of the New York Penal Code of 1881.

Numerous amendments and additions were made to the Penal Code throughout the years without much regard for consistency with prior provisions. No major revision was made until the 1963 Criminal Code was adopted. The Penal Code is included in most compilations between 1885 and 1963.

*General Statutes of the State of Minnesota in Force January 1, 1889* . . . (St. Paul, MN: West Publishing Co. 1888), 2 v.

Volume I of this set merely is a reprint of *General Statutes* 1878. Volume 2, arranged by H. J. Horn, includes subsequent legislation also included in the 1881 and 1883 editions of *Changes in the General Statutes* plus the laws in *Laws of Minnesota* for the years 1885 through 1887. It follows the same chapter, title, and section subdivisions as volume 1. The statutes, according to the preface, "have been most carefully and exhaustively annotated" by Stuart Rapalje. The general index was prepared by the editorial staff of the National Reporter System.

*General Statutes of the State of Minnesota in Force January, 1891,* compiled & annotated by John F. Kelly (St. Paul, MN: 1891) (2d ed. 1891) (3d ed. 1893) 2v.

This is an unofficial compilation; it was not enacted. The compiler again changed the numbering system. References were made to the chapter and title numbers of prior statutes. This compilation also is based on the *General Statutes* 1866 and adds all subsequent session laws ending with *Laws of Minnesota* 1889.

Chapter 37, section 1 of *Laws of Minnesota* 1891 provided that this compilation "shall be competent evidence of the laws therein contained, in all courts of this state and in all proceedings, without further proof or authentication." Section 2 stated that the "same may be cited in judicial proceedings as the General Statutes, giving the section number only."[654]

*Index Digest to All the Laws of the State of Minnesota General and Special Including the Joint Resolutions and Memorials to Congress,* by John F. Kelly (St. Paul, MN: The Kelly Law Book Co. 1894), 417 p.

The preface explains the purpose and use.

> This index concentrates all the Minnesota Law, general and special, enacted by the legislature, so that crude, inconsistent and disconnected laws may be apparent and future legislation and interpretation consistent and harmonious. The law now in force is first cited and then the prior, superseded or repealed law relating to the same subject, for the reason that to know the present law, the past law should also be known.

The indexes of the session laws were incomplete and hard to use, so an index of this sort had much value. It included laws, passed from the first territorial session in 1849 through the session of 1893, arranged to show all the law in force as well as the amended, repealed, superseded, and obsolete laws. Tables were included to show the changes made in revisions and compilations so that any general law could be traced to its origin.

*The General Statutes of the State of Minnesota as Amended by Subsequent Legislation, with which are Incorporated All General Laws of the State in Force December 31, 1894* (St. Paul, MN: West Publishing Co. 1894), 2 v.

This unofficial compilation is based on *General Statutes* and adds all subsequent session laws ending with *Laws of Minnesota* 1893. It follows the chapter arrangement of *General Statutes* 1878 with a few changes and additions. Generally the titles of *General Statutes* 1866 were retained, but a consecutive numbering of sections from beginning to end was adopted. Annotations contained in volume 2 of *General Statutes* 1888 were preserved and brought up to date. This set was compiled and edited by Henry B. Wenzell, assisted by Eugene F. Lane, with annotations by Francis B. Tiffany and others. The index was prepared by the editorial staff of the National Reporter System.

These statutes were not enacted as such, but chapter 310 of *Laws of Minnesota* 1895 states that they "are hereby declared competent evidence of the several acts and resolutions therein contained in all the courts of

---

654. The year 1891 should be added to *General Statutes* to distinguish this compilation from previous ones that use the same name.

## Appendix D. Statutory Compilations, Revisions, and Codes

this state without further proof of authentication, and shall be known and cited as 'General Statutes, 1894.'"

*Revised Laws of Minnesota 1905 as Reported by the Commission Appointed under Chapter 241, Laws of 1901, to Revise and Codify the General Laws, Acting in Pursuance of Said Chapter as Modified by Chapter 157, Laws of 1903* (St. Paul, MN: West Publishing Co. 1905), xiii, 1084 p.

Chapter 241 of *Laws of Minnesota* 1901 provided for the revision and codification of the general laws. Supreme Court justices were authorized to appoint a commission of three to revise, codify, and annotate the public statutes. They also were directed to examine and compare the existing laws "together with the judicial interpretation and construction, thereof, and to propose and recommend such revision and codification thereof as shall, in their opinion, simplify, harmonize and complete said public statutes of this state." Chapter 157 of *Laws of Minnesota* 1903 further provided that all laws enacted at the extra session 1902 and the regular 1903 session, and a list of recommended repeals of special, local, and temporary laws, be included.

This is the revision of the laws that the commission presented to the legislature. It is apparently based on *General Statutes* 1894 but removes laws subsequently repealed and adds general laws from *Laws of Minnesota* 1895 through 1903.

*Report of the Statute Revision Commission to Accompany Its Draft of a Proposed Revision of the General Laws Submitted to the Legislature of Minnesota at the Session of 1905 with an Index to the Draft* (St. Paul, MN: West Publishing Co. 1905), 458 p.

A forty-page report, with the spine title "Index" explains the work and the difficulties encountered by Commissioners Daniel Fish, Thomas J. Knox, and Milton R. Tyler. It discusses the reasons behind the changes, chapter by chapter. A comprehensive index, not included in *Revised Laws* as reported by the commission, is appended on pages 41 to 458.

*Revised Laws Minnesota 1905 Enacted April 18, 1905 to Take Effect March 1, 1906,* edited & annotated by Mark B. Dunnell (St. Paul, MN: Published by the State 1906), viii, 1210, 170 p.[655]

This is a complete official revision of the Minnesota statutory law, the first since 1866, and the last until the 1940s.

The *Revised Laws of Minnesota 1905 as Reported by the Commission,* discussed above, was presented to the legislature in the form of a single

---

655. Variant: [4] 1210, 170 p.

legislative bill without annotations and subsequently was passed with amendments and approved in April 1905. Although enacted in 1905, the revision does not include session laws passed in that year; it includes only those enacted through 1903.

While the commission was authorized to codify the general laws, no attempt was made to write a new and complete code of laws. It merely is a rearrangement and restatement of previously existing statutory law.

Chapter 218 *of Laws of Minnesota* 1905 provided that Mark B. Dunnell be appointed commissioner to edit and annotate *Revised Laws* 1905. He "shall annotate the sections with references to the decisions of the supreme court relevant to the particular section, and in doing so he shall merely state in a short catch-line the general effect or purport of the decision. . . ." A new consecutive numbering system was adopted. References to session laws and to section numbers of *General Statutes* 1894 were included where applicable.

By authority of *Minnesota Statutes* § 3.C.13., in all courts and proceedings this compilation is prima facie evidence of the statutes it contains.

*Complete Index of Unrepealed General Laws of Minnesota Not Contained in Revised Laws of 1905 from the Year 1866 to and Including the Session Laws of 1903* (St. Paul: Review Publishing Co. 1906), 29 p.

The title is self-explanatory. The index is arranged alphabetically by subject. Under each heading laws are listed chronologically.

*Revised Laws of Minnesota Supplement 1909 Containing the Amendments to the Revised Laws, and Other Laws of a General and Permanent Nature, Enacted by the Legislature in 1905, 1907, and 1909 with Historical and Explanatory Notes to Prior Statutes and Full and Complete Notes of all Applicable Decisions,* compiled & annotated by Francis B. Tiffany (St. Paul, MN: West Publishing Co. 1910), xiv, 1197p.

The character of this volume is indicated by its title. It is believed to contain all laws in force, general and permanent, from *Laws of Minnesota* 1905 through 1909. It follows the chapter and section numbers of *Revised Laws* 1905.

By authority of *Minnesota Statutes* § 3.C.13., in all courts and proceedings this compilation is prima facie evidence of the statutes it contains.

*General Statutes of Minnesota 1913,* compiled & edited by Francis B. Tiffany (St. Paul, MN: West Publishing Co. 1913). xv, 2473 p.

This is an official compilation. Chapter 299 *of Laws of Minnesota* 1911 provided for the Statute Compilation Commission to provide for the "preparation, compilation, and publication" of the general statutes in force including the session laws of 1913. The arrangement and annotations of the

## Appendix D. Statutory Compilations, Revisions, and Codes

*Revised Laws* 1905 were retained as far as possible, but a new numbering system, with the *Revised Laws* 1905 section number in parentheses, was used. The compilation adds all subsequent session laws ending with *Laws of Minnesota* 1913. A table showing the allocation of session laws from 1905 through 1913 is appended.

By authority of *Minnesota Statutes* § 3.C.13., in all courts and proceedings this compilation is prima facie evidence of the statutes it contains.

*General Statutes of Minnesota Supplement 1917 Containing the Amendments to the General Statutes and Other Laws of a General and Permanent Nature, Enacted by the Legislature in 1915, 1916, and 1917,* compiled by Francis B. Tiffany (St. Paul, MN: West Publishing Co. 1918), xiv, 969 p.

The arrangement of this supplement follows the chapter and subdivision arrangement of *General Statutes* 1913 but only contains the text of the new laws from *Laws of Minnesota* 1915 through 1917 inserted in their proper order. Annotations and Key Numbers of the American Digest System are included. A table showing the allocation of the session laws is appended.

*General Statutes of Minnesota 1923,* compiled & edited by Hubert Harvey (St. Paul, MN: Review Publishing Co. 1924), [6], xxxvi, 1758 p.

Chapter 95 of *Laws of Minnesota* 1923 created the Minnesota Statutes Compilation Commission consisting of the governor, chief justice of the Supreme Court, and attorney general, and provided for a new compilation that would include historical documents and brief case annotations. The compilation is based on *Revised Laws* 1905 and *General Statutes* 1913 but includes all session laws added by other intervening compilations and adds laws from *Laws of Minnesota* 1919 through 1923. The recompilers had no powers of revision, so the work includes numerous duplications in subject matter. Appropriation acts and temporary acts were omitted, and many purely local acts, technically within the constitutional prohibition against special legislation, were reduced to notes with references to them in the index. A few curative acts also were reduced to notes, but the full text of many of them was printed. The *Complete Index of Unrepealed General Laws,* published in 1906 (described above), is reprinted in Appendix II. A table showing the allocation of the *Laws of Minnesota* from 1905 through 1909 also is appended. The Honorable George Nordlin assisted with annotations. A new numbering system was devised, but references to the section numbers in *Revised Laws* 1905 and *General Statutes* 1913 were inserted.

By authority of *Minnesota Statutes* § 3.C.13., in all courts and proceedings this compilation is prima facie evidence of the statutes it contains.

*Appendix and Addenda to the General Statutes of Minnesota 1923,* compiled and edited by Hubert Harvey & Carl L. Yaeger (St. Paul, MN: Review Publishing Co. 1926), 99 p.

The appendix contains tables of *General Statutes 1913 and of the Laws of Minnesota* from 1915 through 1923 showing the disposition of each section, whether amended, repealed, omitted, or reduced to a note.

An addendum supplies omissions from *General Statutes* 1923 and *Laws of Minnesota* from 1919 through 1923.

By authority of *Minnesota Statutes* § 3.C.13., in all courts and proceedings this compilation is prima facie evidence of the statutes it contains.

*Mason's Minnesota Statutes 1927* (St. Paul, MN: Citer-Digest Co. 1927), 2 v.

Volume 3—1940 Supplement, covers the acts passed from 1929 through 1939, 4, x, 1979 p. Volume 4—1944 Supplement, covers the acts passed from 1941 through 1943 with pocket-part supplement through Feb. 1946, 4, xii, 1192 p.

This unofficial compilation was prepared because of a demand for relief from the defects of *General Statutes* 1923. Neither the text nor the numbering system of the 1923 compilation was changed, but a new index and expanded tables were prepared, and the 1923 annotations were brought up to date.

The original compilation was based upon *General Statutes* 1923 and adds laws from *Laws of Minnesota* 1925 through 1927. Supplements prepared in 1931, 1934, 1936, and 1938 were superseded by the volume 3, 1940 supplement. A 1941 supplement was superseded by the volume 4, 1944 supplement.

The Citer-Digest Company took over the state contract authorizing the Review Publishing Company to publish the statutes. Mr. William H. Mason acted as editor in chief.

By authority of *Minnesota Statutes* § 3.C.13., in all courts and proceedings these compilations are prima facie evidence of the statutes they contain.

Supplement volumes 3 and 4 include conveyancing forms and an update to *Stalland's Minnesota Curative Acts.*

*Stalland's Minnesota Curative Acts Affecting Title to Real Estate,* edited & compiled by Knute D. Stalland of the Dakota County Bar (St. Paul, MN: Mason Publishing Co. [c. 1930]), 52 p.

A curative act is a form of retrospective legislation passed to validate legal proceedings that otherwise would be void because of defects or irregularities (*see* § 255, *supra*).

## Appendix D. Statutory Compilations, Revisions, and Codes 309

*Minnesota Statutes 1941,* edited by William B. Henderson, Duncan L. Kennedy & Jessie E. Scott (State of Minnesota [1942]), 2 v.

The Office of Revisor of Statutes was created by chapter 442 of *Laws of Minnesota* 1939 to make a topical, continuous revision of the statutes. By authority of *Minnesota Statutes* § 3.C.13., any statutory compilation certified by the revisor is prima facie evidence of the statutes contained in it in all courts and proceedings.

The annotations, notes, and index were prepared completely independently of *Mason's Minnesota Statutes* using *Revised Laws* 1905 as a basis and adding all subsequent *Laws of Minnesota* through 1941. Unnecessary sections, private and local acts, obsolete sections, duplications, and sections declared unconstitutional were deleted. A new decimal classification system allowing for expansion was adopted.

Section 645.06, subdivision 5, of *Minnesota Statutes 1982* states "*Minnesota Statutes 1941,* when published shall be prima facie evidence of the statutes therein contained, in all the courts of this state, without further proof of authentication; but shall not preclude reference to, nor control, in case of any discrepancy, any original act of the legislature."

*Minnesota Statutes 1941* was not enacted because of the many errors and omissions. Therefore, it is not an official revision.

Chapter 545 of *Laws of Minnesota* 1943 directed the revisor to "prepare a supplement to *Minnesota Statutes 1941*" correcting the errors and adding certain tables. Upon approval by the attorney general "all statutes and acts set forth in the supplement shall be prima facie evidence of the provisions therein contained without further proof or authentication." Not all of the provisions of this act were carried out. Only some of the tables were prepared, and these were printed in the *Report of the Revisor of Statutes* for 1945 (see listing below).

A table of corresponding sections of *Minnesota Statutes 1945, Revised Laws 1905,* and *Mason's Minnesota Statutes 1927* was included.

*Report of Revisor of Statutes to the Senate and House of Representatives of the State of Minnesota. Published pursuant to Laws 1939, 1941.* 79 p.

This report sets forth the general purpose and duties of the office, the policy in regard to bill drafting, and recommendations, together with an explanation and listing of the new classification system. Appendices add material on copyrights, revision procedures and notes, general rules, words and phrases, references, style, and a suggested bill relating to the interpretation of statutes.

[*Minnesota Revised Statutes 1943*] (unpublished).

The Revisor was directed by chapter 545, section 2, of *Laws of Minnesota 1943* to prepare "a revised codification of all the general laws of the state in force at the close of the 1943 session ... based in general on *Minnesota Statutes 1941* and the supplement thereto incorporating the session laws of 1943." He was to "make such changes in language and arrangement as he deems necessary to consolidate, clarify, simplify, and codify the statutes...." Section 3 of the act directed the Revisor, with the advice and assistance of the Attorney General, to prepare a bill for the enactment of the codification. The revision was enacted as the Minnesota Revised Statutes. The act was approved March 8, 1945. This act was not included in the session laws but was printed in the preface of *Minnesota Statutes 1945* and all subsequent editions through 1978. In the 1980 and later editions it is separately set out following the historical documents.

*Minnesota Revised Statutes* never was published; it can be found only in the Office of the Secretary of State.

*Report of the Revisor of Statutes to the Senate and House of Representatives of the State of Minnesota 1945. Published pursuant to Laws 1943, 1945.* 43 p.

This report contains some of the tables that the Revisor was directed by chapter 545 of *Laws of Minnesota 1943* to prepare for a supplement to *Minnesota Statutes 1941,* showing which chapters of the 1943 laws were compiled into the statutes and which structural changes were made.

*Minnesota Statutes 1945* (State of Minnesota [1946]), 2v.

This official compilation contained the Minnesota Revised Statutes of 1943, which was enacted but *not* published (as explained above) and the session laws included in *Laws of Minnesota* 1945.

Section 3.C.07., of *Minnesota Statutes* provides that the "laws contained in *Minnesota Revised Statutes* are continuations of the acts from which compiled and are not new enactments."

A table of corresponding sections of *Minnesota Statutes 1945, Revised Laws* 1905, and *Mason's Minnesota Statutes 1927* was included.

*Annotations to Minnesota Statutes ... Embracing complete legislative history of the Minnesota Statutes, full explanatory notes by the Revisor, and annotations through Volume 218 of Minnesota Reports,* edited by William B. Henderson, D. L. Kennedy & Gertrude W. Thoren (State of Minnesota 1945), 2 v. (vol. 3, 1947, 1896 p. annotations through 223 Minn.; vol. 4, 1953, 6, 10–1703 p. annotations through 237 Minn.).

Between 1939 and 1945 the revisor of statutes was directed to prepare annotations to *Minnesota Statutes.* The arrangement follows the same order as the statutes. Information is given relating to origin and history of each

## Appendix D. Statutory Compilations, Revisions, and Codes

section, to digests of Minnesota Supreme Court decisions, federal decisions relative to the statutes, opinions of the attorney general, law review articles, and references to text books and other sources of law. The annotations are based on original research. Publication of these official annotations was discontinued by chapter 466 of *Laws of Minnesota* 1957.

*Minnesota Statutes Annotated* (St. Paul, MN: West Publishing Co. [1946 to date]).

This is an unofficial compilation (*see* § 263, *supra*). Chapter 462 of *Laws of Minnesota* 1945 directed the revisor of statutes to prepare official editions of the statutes, conforming to *Minnesota Statutes 1945* and retaining the same titles, chapter, and section numbers.[656] Editions were published quadrennially from 1945 through 1965. From 1967 to date, biennial compilations have been published with intervening supplements since 1973. Each incorporates new laws and deletes repealed sections.

*Minnesota Statutes 1949* (State of Minnesota [1949]), 2v.

*Minnesota Statutes 1953* (State of Minnesota [1954]), 2 v.

*Minnesota Statutes 1957* (State of Minnesota [1958]), 2v.

This compilation contained for the first time, under Table 3, 1955–1957 Local Acts, a listing of the 1955 and 1957 acts appearing to apply to certain governmental subdivisions. The subdivisions are listed alphabetically, and include a brief statement of the nature of the act and the session law citation.

*Minnesota Statutes 1961* (State of Minnesota [1962]), 2v.

Municipal court acts of cities of the first class are included for the first time.

*Minnesota Statutes 1965* (State of Minnesota 1966), 2 v.

*Minnesota Statutes 1967* (State of Minnesota 1968), 2 v.

*Minnesota Statutes 1969* (State of Minnesota 1970) 4 v.

*Minnesota Statutes 1971* (State of Minnesota 1972) 4 v.

*Minnesota Statutes 1973 Supplement* (State of Minnesota 1973) 1280 p.

---

656. *Cf.* MINN. STAT. § 3.C.08 (1998).

*Minnesota Statutes 1974* (State of Minnesota 1975) 4 v.

*Minnesota Statutes 1975 Supplement* (State of Minnesota 1975) 958 p.

*Minnesota Statutes 1976* (State of Minnesota 1976) 4 v.

*Minnesota Statutes 1977 Supplement* (State of Minnesota 1977) 874 p.

*Minnesota Statutes 1978* (State of Minnesota 1978) 4 v.

*Minnesota Statutes 1979 Supplement* (State of Minnesota 1979) 757 p.

*Minnesota Statutes 1980* (State of Minnesota 1980) 10 v.

The revisor's office made significant editorial changes based upon a user survey and a study to determine the best format. The typography and format of statutes were improved significantly, the index was corrected and improved, a cross-reference table was added, and a systematic program of style and form redrafts of statutes was implemented. All these changes are described in full in Part III of the Preface to the 1980 edition.

*Minnesota Statutes 1981 Supplement* (State of Minnesota 1981) 1732 p.

*Minnesota Statutes 1982* (State of Minnesota 1982) 10 v.

The revisor's office continued its work to improve the utility of the statutes. Table I, the local law table, was expanded to include all local laws dating back to 1893, the method of supplementation was altered, the format of the court rules was improved, several crowded chapters and sections were recodified, and further improvements were made to the index. All of these changes are described in full in Part III of the preface of the 1982 edition.

*Minnesota Statutes 1983 Supplement* (State of Minnesota 1983).

This supplement was published in pocket-part format for the first time.

*Minnesota Statutes 1984* (State of Minnesota 1984) 10 v.

The revisor's office continued its work to improve the utility of the statutes. Table I, the local law table, was expanded to include all local laws dating back to 1849. Table V was added to list all of the administrative rules promulgated under the authority of the statutes, laws concerning St. Louis County were included for the first time, numerous chapters were recodified or renumbered, and further

## Appendix D. Statutory Compilations, Revisions, and Codes

improvements were made to the index. All of these changes are described in full in Part III of the preface of the 1984 edition.

*Minnesota Statutes 1985 Supplement* (State of Minnesota 1985).
This official compilation only supplements *Minnesota Statutes 1984.* The supplement, published in pocket-part format, identifies sections or subdivisions that were repealed and adds general laws included in Laws 1985 Including 1985 First Special Session.

*Minnesota Statutes 1986* (State of Minnesota 1986).
This edition is based on *Minnesota Statutes 1984* incorporating Laws Including 1985 First Special Session and Laws 1986 Including 1986 First Special Session. Perhaps the most comprehensive change in the statutes in many years is found in this edition. All text of the statutes is revised from gender-specific to gender-neutral language under directive of the legislature. Known as the Gender Revision of 1986, the revised text was amended and enacted by Laws 1986, chapter 444. The same act also gave the revisor ongoing authority to remove gender-specific terms from the statutes. Additionally, the 1986 statutes contained several new codifications, recodifications of existing laws, and index improvements. These changes are described in full in Part III of the 1986 edition.

*Minnesota Statutes 1987 Supplement* (State of Minnesota 1987).
This official compilation only supplements *Minnesota Statutes 1986.* The supplement, published in pocket-part format, identifies sections or subdivisions that were repealed and adds general laws included in Laws 1987 and 1987 First Special Session.

*Minnesota Statutes 1988* (State of Minnesota 1988).
This edition is based on *Minnesota Statutes 1986* incorporating Laws 1987, 1987 First Special Session, and Laws 1988. Improvements in this edition range from simple to complex rearrangement of language, recodification and renumbering, changes in terminology, and corrections to erroneous cross references. Laws passed in 1987 and 1988 assigned the revisor the tasks of producing a new index to the statutes and assigning chapter numbers to enrolled acts. These changes are described in full in Part III of the preface to the 1988 edition.

*Minnesota Statutes 1989 Supplement* (State of Minnesota 1989).
This official compilation only supplements *Minnesota Statutes 1988.* The supplement, published in pocket-part format, identifies sections or subdivisions that were repealed and adds general laws included in Laws 1989.

Because the legislature met in special session after publication of the regular supplement, a special pamphlet entitled "Minnesota Statutes Second 1989 Supplement," containing changes by repeal, amendment, or addition passed in the special session, was published later.

*Minnesota Statutes 1990* (State of Minnesota 1990).

This edition is based on *Minnesota Statutes 1988* incorporating Laws 1989, Laws 1990, and 1989 First Special Session. This edition contains extensive recodification of the water law. Additionally, selected sections relating to tax provisions were renumbered into chapter 289A and all permanent local special levies were codified. A concerted effort was made to improve chapter titles and main division headings.

*Minnesota Statutes 1991 Supplement* (State of Minnesota 1991).

This official compilation only supplements *Minnesota Statutes 1990*. The supplement, published in pocket-part format, identifies sections or subdivisions that were repealed and adds general laws included in Laws 1991.

*Minnesota Statutes 1992* (State of Minnesota 1992).

This edition is based on *Minnesota Statutes 1990* incorporating Laws 1991 and Laws 1992. This edition contains many changes in the text directed by the legislature pursuant to instructions to the revisor. The changes include rearrangement of language, recodification and renumbering, and changes in terminology. A thumb cut was added to the Court Rules volume for the rules for judicial record access. The 1992 edition also reflects a change in the manner of pagination, with each volume paged separately. The purpose of the change was to facilitate more timely composition of the set.

*Minnesota Statutes 1993 Supplement* (State of Minnesota 1993).

This official compilation only supplements *Minnesota Statutes 1992*. The supplement, published in pocket-part format, identifies sections or subdivisions that were repealed and adds general laws included in Laws 1993 and 1993 First Special Session.

*Minnesota Statutes 1994* (State of Minnesota 1994).

This edition is based on *Minnesota Statutes 1992* incorporating Laws 1993, 1993 First Special Session, Laws 1994, and 1994 First Special Session. The 1994 edition expanded the set from ten to fifteen volumes. The expansion accommodated the ever-growing bulk of the statutory text, as well as the completion of an entirely new index to the set. For the new index, the statutes were examined in much greater depth and detail than ever before and entries were made for nearly every concept in the text

## Appendix D. Statutory Compilations, Revisions, and Codes

of the statutes. In addition to the new index, the 1994 edition contained many changes in text resulting from instructions to the revisor enacted in 1993 and 1994. Section 3.C.13., listing instructions to the revisor in a footnote, was expanded in the 1994 edition to include complete citations to the session laws containing the instructions, as well as brief explanations of what each instruction directed the revisor to do. The court rule volume (volume 15 of the set) contained a new thumb-cut "Sentencing Guidelines."

*Minnesota Statutes 1995 Supplement* (State of Minnesota 1995).
This official publication only supplements *Minnesota Statutes 1994*. The supplement, published in pocket-part format, identifies sections or subdivisions that were repealed and adds general laws included in Laws 1995 and 1995 First Special Session. Sections affected by revisor's instructions were included as far a practicable.

*Minnesota Statutes 1996* (State of Minnesota 1996).
This edition is based on *Minnesota Statutes 1994* incorporating Laws 1995, 1995 First Special Session, and Laws 1996. Several sections in the education subject area were renumbered to reflect the reorganization of duties under the new Department of Children, Families, and Learning. Additional changes in the education area were implemented to reflect the reorganization of duties within the department and State Board of Education. A number of other changes stemming from instructions to the revisor also appear throughout the text. A summary of the 1995 and 1996 revisor instructions can be found in the footnote following section 3.C.13.

*Minnesota Statutes 1997 Supplement* (State of Minnesota 1997).
This official publication only supplements *Minnesota Statutes 1996*. The supplement, published in pocket-part format, identifies sections or subdivisions that were repealed and adds general laws included in Laws 1997 and 1997 First and Second Special Sessions. This edition contains recodifications of liquor and tobacco product taxation statutes. Sections affected by revisor's instructions were included as far as practicable.

*Minnesota Statutes 1998* (State of Minnesota 1998).
*Minnesota Statutes* 1998 is based on *Minnesota Statutes 1996*, incorporating Laws 1997, 1997 First, Second, and Third Special Sessions, Laws 1998, and 1998 First Special Session. This edition includes recodifications of the K–12 education code and landlord-tenant and fuel tax statutes. The lengthy editorial note following section 3.C.13., which described revisor's instructions since 1957, was removed. This information continues to be updated and is kept on file by the revisor's office. The

revisor also capitalized the names of state acts and codes throughout this edition. Additionally, some of the rules in the court rules volume have been reindexed in more detail.

*Minnesota Statutes 1999 Supplement* (State of Minnesota 1999).

This official publication only supplements *Minnesota Statutes 1998.* The supplement, published in pocket-part format, identifies sections or subdivisions that were repealed and adds general laws included in Laws 1999. Sections affected by revisor's instructions were included as far as practicable.

*Minnesota Statutes 2000* (State of Minnesota 2000).

*Minnesota Statutes 2000* was compiled, edited, published, and distributed by the state of Minnesota as required by law. It is based on *Minnesota Statutes 1998* and incorporated the Laws of 1999 and Laws of 2000. This fifteen-volume set includes the addition of a new chapter, 169A relating to driving while impaired crimes; a recodified chapter 297A dealing with sales and use tax laws; and changes to insurance tax laws recodified in chapter 297I. Keeping abreast of the latest computer technology, the data practices law in chapter 13 also was recodified.

## II. LEGAL RESEARCH CHECKLIST

Many of the texts listed in Appendix H have excellent chapters on techniques for researching the law. The following checklist is presented as one method of organizing a research problem in Minnesota law. The purpose of the checklist is to reduce the variety of Minnesota legal resources to a one-page document with space for notations. Thus, it is hoped that this checklist will provide an index-digest of the relevant Minnesota law concerning a particular issue.

Obviously, no checklist is a substitute for creative legal research. The best method remains a thorough knowledge of resources so that the initial analysis of a problem will bring the resources to mind readily.

# Appendix D. Statutory Compilations, Revisions, and Codes

| MINNESOTA LEGAL RESEARCH CHECKLIST | Researcher:<br>Purpose:<br>Date Begun:<br>Date Completed: | | KEY WORDS |
|---|---|---|---|
| ISSUE | | | |
| | | | Shepard's |
| **Secondary Sources** | | ❏ Constitution<br>❏ Minn. Stat.<br>❏ Minn. Stat. Ann.<br>❏ Minn. Laws<br>❏ Minn. Sess. Law Serv.<br>❏ Slip Laws<br>❏ Dunnel Minn. Digest<br>❏ West's Minn. Digest<br>❏ NW Digest<br>❏ Advance Sheets<br>❏ Slip Opinions | |
| ❏ Loose-leaf Services | | | |
| ❏ Treatises & Practice Books | | | |
| ❏ Periodicals & Indexes | | | |
| ❏ People (Directories) | | ❏ Minn. Rules<br>❏ State Register<br>❏ Exec. Orders<br>❏ Legislative Hx<br>❏ Briefs<br>❏ Agency Decisions<br>❏ AG Opinions<br>❏ Court Rules | Topics & Key Numbers |
| ❏ Computer-Assisted | | | |

# APPENDIX E
# Reports of the Attorney General

Listed below are the reports through 1968, which was the last report to include selected opinions.[657]

| Report Ending | | Attorney General | Pagination |
| --- | --- | --- | --- |
| 1860 | Dec. 31 | G. E. Cole | 8 p. |
| 1861 | Nov. 30 | G. E. Cole | [6 p.] |
| 1862[658] | Nov. 30 | G. E. Cole | [4 p.] |
| 1863 | Nov. 30 | G. E. Cole | 30 p. |
| 1864 | Nov. 30 | G. E. Cole | [20 p.] |
| 1865 | Dec. 5 | G. E. Cole | [20 p.] |
| 1866 | Dec. 1 | W. Colvill | 6 p. |
| 1867 | Dec. 1 | W. Colvill | 8 p. |
| 1868 | Dec. | F. R. E. Cornell | [6 p.] |
| 1869 | Nov. 30 | F. R. E. Cornell | [6 p.] |
| 1870 | Nov. 30 | F. R. E. Cornell | [4 p.] |
| 1871 | Nov. 30 | F. R. E. Cornell | [4 p.] |
| 1872 | Nov. 30 | F. R. E. Cornell | [7 p.] |
| 1873 | Nov. 30 | F. R. E. Cornell | 10 p. |
| 1874 | Nov. 30 | G. P. Wilson | 12 p. |
| 1875 | Nov. 30 | G. P. Wilson | 12 p. |
| 1876 | Nov. 30 | G. P. Wilson | 9 p. |
| 1877 | Nov. 30 | G. P. Wilson | 9 p. |
| 1878 | Nov. 30 | G. P. Wilson | 10 p. |
| 1879[659] | | | |
| 1880 | Nov. 30 | C. M. Start | [11 p.] |

---

657. Brackets around a page number signify that the copy checked was paged as part of *Minnesota Executive Documents*.
658. Beginning in 1862, many reports include summaries of offences, county attorneys' reports, statistics of prosecutions, and discussions of important opinions.
659. No record of a published report has been found.

| Report Ending | | Attorney General | Pagination |
|---|---|---|---|
| 1881–82 | Nov. 30 | W. J. Hahn | [7 p.] |
| 1883–84 | July 31 | W. J. Hahn | 28 p. |
| 1885–86 | July 31 | W. J. Hahn | 102 p. |
| 1887–88 | July 31 | M. E. Clapp | 132 p. |
| 1889–90 | July 31 | M. E. Clapp | 71 p. |
| 1891–92 | July 31 | M. E. Clapp | [64 p.] |
| 1893–94[660] | July 31 | H. W. Childs | 227 p. |
| 1895–96 | July 31 | H. W. Childs | 210 p. |
| 1897–98 | July 31 | H. W. Childs | 228 p. |
| 1899–00 | July 31 | H. W. Childs | xxxvi, 246 p. |
| 1901–02 | July 31 | W. B. Douglas | xxxvii, 213 p. |
| 1903–04 | July 31 | W. B. Douglas & W. J. Donahower | xxv, 237 p. |
| 1905–06[661] | Dec. 31 | E. T. Young | 428 p. |
| 1907–08 | Dec. 31 | E. T. Young | xxxiii, 341 p. |
| 1909–10 | Dec. 31 | G. T. Simpson | 463 p. |
| 1911–12 | Dec. 31 | L. A. Smith | 396 p. |
| 1913–14 | Dec. 31 | L. A. Smith | 416 p. |
| 1915–16 | Dec. 31 | L. A. Smith | 423 p. |
| 1917–18 | Dec. 31 | L. A. Smith & C. L. Hilton | 409 p. |
| 1919–20 | Dec. 31 | C. L. Hilton | 734 p. |
| 1921–22 | Dec. 31 | C. L. Hilton | 511 p. |
| 1923–24 | Dec. 31 | C. L. Hilton | 240 p. |
| 1925–26 | Dec. 31 | C. L. Hilton | 260 p. |
| 1927–28 | Dec. 31 | C. L. Hilton, A. F. Pratt & G. A. Youngquist | 347 p. |
| 1929–30 | Dec. 31 | H. N. Benson | 390 p. |
| 1931–32 | Dec. 31 | H. N. Benson | 343 p. |
| 1933–34 | Dec. 31 | H. H. Peterson | 1337 p. |

660. Selected opinions were included in the biennial reports between 1893–94 and 1959–60.
661. Starting with the report for 1905–06, report years correspond to calendar years.

## Appendix E. Reports of the Attorney General

| Report Ending | | Attorney General | Pagination |
|---|---|---|---|
| 1935–36 | Dec. 31 | H. H. Peterson & Wm. S. Ervine | 565 p. |
| 1937–38 | Dec. 31 | Wm. S. Ervine | 744 p. |
| 1939–40 | Dec. 31 | J. A. A. Burnquist | 488 p. |
| 1941–42 | Dec. 31 | J. A. A. Burnquist | 549 p. |
| 1943–44 | Dec. 31 | J. A. A. Burnquist | 708 p. |
| 1945–46 | Dec. 31 | J. A. A. Burnquist | 451 p. |
| 1947–48 | Dec. 31 | J. A. A. Burnquist | 416 p. |
| 1949–50 | Dec. 31 | J. A. A. Burnquist | 524 p. |
| 1951–52 | Dec. 31 | J. A. A. Burnquist | 505 p. |
| 1953–54 | Dec. 31 | J. A. A. Burnquist | 393 p. |
| 1955–56 | Dec. 31 | M. Lord | 400 p. |
| 1957–58 | Dec. 31 | M. Lord | 423 p. |
| 1959–60 | Dec. 31 | W. F. Mondale | 246 p. |
| 1961–66[662] | | | |
| 1967–68[663] | Sept. 30 | D. Head | 6 leaves |

Listed below are opinions beginning with 1969, from *Minnesota Legal Register, Attorney General Opinions Issue.*

| Volume | Issues | Dates | Attorney General | Pagination |
|---|---|---|---|---|
| 2 | 1–52 | 1/22/69–1/14/70 | D. Head | 1–189 |
| 3 | 1–53 | 1/28/70–1/20/71 | D. Head | 1–176 |
| 4 | 1–52 | 1/27/71–1/19/72 | W. Spannaus | 1–111 |
| 5 | 1–28 | 1/26/72–12/30/72 | W. Spannaus | 1–100 |
| 6 | 1–12 | 1/73–12/73 | W. Spannaus | 1–77 |
| 7 | 1–12 | 1/74–12/74 | W. Spannaus | 1–51 |
| 8 | 1–12 | 1/75–12/75 | W. Spannaus | 1–61 |
| 9 | 1–12 | 1/76–12/76 | W. Spannaus | 1–68 |
| 10 | 1–12 | 1/77–12/77 | W. Spannaus | 1–50 |

---

662. No reports were found from 1961 to 1966.
663. This was issued as part of the compilation of *Selected Opinions 1960–1968.* See § 313.21, *supra.*

| Volume | Issues | Dates | Attorney General | Pagination |
|---|---|---|---|---|
| 11 | 1–12 | 1/78–12/78 | W. Spannaus | 53 |
| 12 | 1–12 | 1/79–12/79 | W. Spannaus | 1–45 |
| 13 | 1–12 | 1/80–12/80 | W. Spannaus | 1–53 |
| 14 | 1–12 | 1/81–12/81 | W. Spannaus | 1–33 |
| 15 | 1–12 | 1/82–12/82 | W. Spannaus | 1–29 |
| 16 | 1–12 | 1/83–12/83 | H. H. Humphrey III | 1–30 |
| 17 | 1–12 | 1/84–12/84 | H. H. Humphrey III | 1–21 |
| 18 | 1 | 1/85 | H. H. Humphrey III | 1–4 |
| | 3 | 2/85 | H. H. Humphrey III | 1–4 |
| | 6 | 3/85 | H. H. Humphrey III | 1–4 |
| | 7 | 4/85 | H. H. Humphrey III | 1–4 |
| | 9 | 5/85 | H. H. Humphrey III | 1–2 |
| | 11 | 6/85 | H. H. Humphrey III | 1–2 |
| 18 | 13 | 7/85 | H. H. Humphrey III | 1–4 |
| | 15 | 8/85 | H. H. Humphrey III | 1–2 |
| | 17 | 9/85 | H. H. Humphrey III | 1–2 |
| | 19 | 10/85 | H. H. Humphrey III | 1–2 |
| | 21 | 11/85 | H. H. Humphrey III | 1–3 |
| | 23 | 12/85 | H. H. Humphrey III | 1–2 |
| 19 | 1 | 1/86 | H. H. Humphrey III | 1–4 |
| | 3 | 2/86 | H. H. Humphrey III | 5–8 |
| | 5 | 3/86 | H. H. Humphrey III | 9–12 |
| | 7 | 4/86 | H. H. Humphrey III | 13–16 |
| | 9 | 5/86 | H. H. Humphrey III | 17–18 |
| | 11 | 6/86 | H. H. Humphrey III | 19–22 |
| | 13 | 7/86 | H. H. Humphrey III | 23–24 |
| | 15 | 8/86 | H. H. Humphrey III | 25–28 |
| | 17 | 9/86 | H. H. Humphrey III | 29–32 |
| | 19 | 10/86 | H. H. Humphrey III | 33–36 |
| | 21 | 11/86 | H. H. Humphrey III | 37–38 |
| | 23 | 12/86 | H. H. Humphrey III | 39 |
| 20 | 1 | 1/87 | H. H. Humphrey III | 1–2 |
| | 3* | 2/87 | H. H. Humphrey III | 3–4 |

Appendix E. Reports of the Attorney General 323

| Volume | Issues | Dates | Attorney General | Pagination |
|---|---|---|---|---|
|  | 3* | 3/87 | H. H. Humphrey III | 5–10 |
|  | 7 | 4/87 | H. H. Humphrey III | 11–12 |
|  | 9 | 5/87 | H. H. Humphrey III | 13–16 |
|  | 11 | 6/87 | H. H. Humphrey III | 17–18 |
|  | 13 | 7/87 | H. H. Humphrey III | 19–20 |
|  | 15 | 8/87 | H. H. Humphrey III | 21–22 |
|  | 17 | 9/87 | H. H. Humphrey III | 23–24 |
|  | 19 | 10/87 | H. H. Humphrey III | 25–26 |
|  | 21 | 11/87 | H. H. Humphrey III | 27–32 |
|  | 23 | 12/87 | H. H. Humphrey III | 33–34 |
| 21 | 1 | 1/88 | H. H. Humphrey III | 1–2 |
|  | 3 | 2/88 | H. H. Humphrey III | 3–4 |
|  | 5 | 3/88 | H. H. Humphrey III | 5–6 |
|  | 7 | 4/88 | H. H. Humphrey III | 7–8 |
|  | 9 | 5/88 | H. H. Humphrey III | 9–10 |
|  | 11 | 6/88 | H. H. Humphrey III | 11–12 |
|  | 13 | 7/88 | H. H. Humphrey III | 13–18 |
|  | 15 | 8/88 | H. H. Humphrey III | 19–20* |
|  | 17 | 9/88 | H. H. Humphrey III | 16–18* |
|  | 19 | 10/88 | H. H. Humphrey III | 19–20* |
|  | 21 | 11/88 | H. H. Humphrey III | 21* |
|  | 23 | 12/88 | H. H. Humphrey III | 21–22* |
| 22 | 1 | 1/89 | H. H. Humphrey III | 1–8 |
|  | 3 | 2/89 | H. H. Humphrey III | 9 |
|  | 5 | 3/89 | H. H. Humphrey III | 10–11 |
|  |  | 4/89 | H. H. Humphrey III |  |
|  | 9 | 5/89 | H. H. Humphrey III | 12–13 |
|  | 11 | 6/89 | H. H. Humphrey III | 14–15 |
|  | 13 | 7/89 | H. H. Humphrey III | 16 |
|  | 15 | 8/89 | H. H. Humphrey III | 17–21 |
|  | 17 | 9/89 | H. H. Humphrey III | 22–23 |
|  | 19 | 10/89 | H. H. Humphrey III | 24–27 |
|  | 21 | 11/89 | H. H. Humphrey III | 28–30 |

| Volume | Issues | Dates | Attorney General | Pagination |
|---|---|---|---|---|
|  | 24 | 12/89 | H. H. Humphrey III | 31–35 |
| 23 | 1 | 1/90 | H. H. Humphrey III | 1–4 |
|  | 3 | 2/90 | H. H. Humphrey III | 5–10 |
|  | 5 | 3/90 | H. H. Humphrey III | 11 |
|  | 7 | 4/90 | H. H. Humphrey III | 12–13 |
|  | 9 | 5/90 | H. H. Humphrey III | 14 |
|  | 11 | 6/90 | H. H. Humphrey III | 15 |
|  | 13 | 7/90 | H. H. Humphrey III | 16–19 |
|  | 15* | 8/90 | H. H. Humphrey III | 20–26 |
|  | 15* | 9/90 | H. H. Humphrey III | 27 |
|  | 19 | 10/90 | H. H. Humphrey III | 28–29 |
|  | 21 | 11/90 | H. H. Humphrey III | 30–31 |
|  | 23 | 12/90 | H. H. Humphrey III | 32 |
|  | 25 | 1990 Addendum | H. H. Humphrey III | 33–36 |
| 24 | 1 | 1/91 | H. H. Humphrey III | 1 |
|  | 3 | 2/91 | H. H. Humphrey III | 2 |
|  | 5 | 3/91 | H. H. Humphrey III | 3 |
|  | 7 | 4/91 | H. H. Humphrey III | 4 |
|  | 9 | 5/91 | H. H. Humphrey III | 5–9 |
|  | 11 | 6/91 | H. H. Humphrey III | 10 |
|  | 13 | 7/91 | H. H. Humphrey III | 11–14 |
|  | 15 | 8/91 | H. H. Humphrey III | 15–18 |
|  | 17 | 9/91 | H. H. Humphrey III | 19 |
|  | 19 | 10/91 | H. H. Humphrey III | 20 |
|  | 21 | 11/91 | H. H. Humphrey III | 21–22 |
|  | 23 | 12/91 | H. H. Humphrey III | 23 |
| 25 | 1 | 1/92 | H. H. Humphrey III | 1–4 |
|  | 3 | 2/92 | H. H. Humphrey III | 5 |
|  | 5 | 3/92 | H. H. Humphrey III | 6–8 |
|  | 7 | 4/92 | H. H. Humphrey III | 9 |
|  | 9 | 5/92 | H. H. Humphrey III | 10 |
|  | 11* | 6/92 | H. H. Humphrey III | 11–14 |
|  | 15* | 7/92 | H. H. Humphrey III | 15 |

# Appendix E. Reports of the Attorney General

| Volume | Issues | Dates | Attorney General | Pagination |
|---|---|---|---|---|
| | 17 | 8/92 | H. H. Humphrey III | 16 |
| | 19 | 9/92 | H. H. Humphrey III | 17 |
| | 21* | 10/92 | H. H. Humphrey III | 18 |
| | 21* | 11/92 | H. H. Humphrey III | 19 |
| | 23 | 12/92 | H. H. Humphrey III | 20–22 |
| 26 | 1 | 1/93 | H. H. Humphrey III | 1–3 |
| | 3 | 2/93 | H. H. Humphrey III | 4 |
| | 5 | 3/93 | H. H. Humphrey III | 5–8 |
| | 7 | 4/93 | H. H. Humphrey III | 9–10 |
| | 9 | 5/93 | H. H. Humphrey III | 11–17 |
| | 11 | 6/93 | H. H. Humphrey III | 18 |
| | 13 | 7/93 | H. H. Humphrey III | 19–22 |
| | 15 | 8/93 | H. H. Humphrey III | 23 |
| | 17* | 9/93 | H. H. Humphrey III | 24–26 |
| | 17* | 10/93 | H. H. Humphrey III | 27 |
| | 21 | 11/93 | H. H. Humphrey III | 28 |
| | 23 | 12/93 | H. H. Humphrey III | 29 |
| 27 | 1 | 1/94 | H. H. Humphrey III | 1 |
| | 3 | 2/94 | H. H. Humphrey III | 2 |
| | 5 | 3/94 | H. H. Humphrey III | 3–7 |
| | 7 | 4/94 | H. H. Humphrey III | 8–12 |
| | 9 | 5/94 | H. H. Humphrey III | 13 |
| | 11 | 6/94 | H. H. Humphrey III | 14–16 |
| | 13 | 7/94 | H. H. Humphrey III | 17 |
| | 15 | 8/94 | H. H. Humphrey III | 18–22 |
| | 17 | 9/94 | H. H. Humphrey III | 23 |
| | 19 | 10/94 | H. H. Humphrey III | 24–26 |
| | 21 | 11/94 | H. H. Humphrey III | 27 |
| | 23 | 12/94 | H. H. Humphrey III | 28–31 |
| 28 | 1 | 1/95 | H. H. Humphrey III | 1–3 |
| | 3 | 2/95 | H. H. Humphrey III | 4 |
| | 5 | 3/95 | H. H. Humphrey III | 5 |
| | 7 | 4/95 | H. H. Humphrey III | 6–11 |

| Volume | Issues | Dates | Attorney General | Pagination |
|---|---|---|---|---|
| | 9 | 5/95 | H. H. Humphrey III | 12 |
| | 11 | 6/95 | H. H. Humphrey III | 13 |
| | 13 | 7/95 | H. H. Humphrey III | 14 |
| | 15 | 8/95 | H. H. Humphrey III | 15–17 |
| | 17 | 9/95 | H. H. Humphrey III | 18 |
| | 19 | 10/95 | H. H. Humphrey III | 19–24 |
| | 21 | 11/95 | H. H. Humphrey III | 25 |
| | 23 | 12/95 | H. H. Humphrey III | 26–32 |
| 29 | 1 | 1/96 | H. H. Humphrey III | 1 |
| | 3 | 2/96 | H. H. Humphrey III | 2–3 |
| | 5 | 3/96 | H. H. Humphrey III | 4 |
| | 7 | 4/96 | H. H. Humphrey III | 5 |
| | 9 | 5/96 | H. H. Humphrey III | 6 |
| | 11 | 6/96 | H. H. Humphrey III | 7 |
| | 13 | 7/96 | H. H. Humphrey III | 8–11 |
| | 15 | 8/96 | H. H. Humphrey III | 12–13 |
| | 17 | 9/96 | H. H. Humphrey III | 14 |
| | 19 | 10/96 | H. H. Humphrey III | 15 |
| | 21 | 11/96 | H. H. Humphrey III | 16 |
| | 23 | 12/96 | H. H. Humphrey III | 17 |
| | 25 | 1996 Addendum | H. H. Humphrey III | 18–21 |
| 30 | 1 | 7/97* | H. H. Humphrey III | 1–4 |
| | 3 | 8/4/97 | H. H. Humphrey III | 5–10 |
| | 4 | 8/25–27/97 | H. H. Humphrey III | 11–16 |
| | 5 | 10/14/97 | H. H. Humphrey III | 17–18 |
| | 6 | 12/18/97 | H. H. Humphrey III | 19–20 |
| 31 | 1 | 3/11/98 | H. H. Humphrey III | 1–6 |
| | 2 | 11/20/98 | H. H. Humphrey III | 7–2* |
| | 3 | 12/10/98 | H. H. Humphrey III | 9–10 |
| | 4 | 12/21/98 | H. H. Humphrey III | 11 |
| 32 | 1 | 5/11/99 | M. Hatch | 1–3 |
| | 2 | 6/28/99 | M. Hatch | 4–6 |

# Appendix E. Reports of the Attorney General

| Volume | Issues | Dates | Attorney General | Pagination |
|---|---|---|---|---|
|  | un-numbered | 8/6/99 | M. Hatch | 7–9 |
|  | 4 | 9/7/99 | M. Hatch | 10–15* |
|  | 5 | 12/1/99 | M. Hatch | 10–11* |
| 33 | 1 | 5/12/2000 | M. Hatch | 1–2 |
|  | 2 | 8/22/2000 | M. Hatch | 3–12 |
|  | 3 | 10/13/2000 | M. Hatch | 13–15 |
| 34 | 1 | 5/10/2001 | M. Hatch | 1–4 |

\* Indicates actual bibliographic evidence. Pagination may break sequence or repeat. Issue numbering may break sequence or repeat.

# APPENDIX F
# Numerical Index to the Selected Opinions of the Minnesota Attorney General 1933–1968

This index is a cross-reference table from the subject classification numbers assigned by the attorney general to the numbers assigned to the selected opinions published in the biennial reports and the 1960–1968 compilation. The classification numbers are printed exactly as published. In sections marked with one asterisk (*) references are to the boldface numbers preceding each opinion in the biennial volumes and in sections marked with two asterisks (**) references are to page numbers in the 1960–1968 compilation. This list does not indicate the dates of opinions. Because opinions only were published selectively and more than one opinion may have the same classification number, it is necessary to check the volume itself to insure that the correct opinion has been located.

## 1933–34*

| | |
|---|---|
| 2a: 696 | 29a-4: 19 |
| 6-o: 719 | 29a-5: 27 |
| 9a-21: 523 | 29a-12: 43 |
| 9c-8: 706 | 29a-17: 203 |
| 10a-3: 13, 14, 171, 262, 703 | 29a-28: 35 |
| 11b-8: 542 | 29a-29: 42 |
| 12a-1: 111, 112 | 29b-3: 207 |
| 12c-1: 227, 867 | 29b-4: 18, 34 |
| 12c-3: 868 | 29b-6: 23, 24, 38, 40 |
| 18d: 266 | 29b-7: 32, 33 |
| 21f: 776 | 29b-12: 39 |
| 27f: 165 | 29b-13: 31 |
| 28a-8: 392 | 29b-17: 774 |
| 28b-1: 369 | 29d-5: 20 |
| 28b-2: 364, 367 | 32d: 83 |
| 28b-5: 372 | 32-f: 26, 29, 36 |
| 28c-8: 394 | 32j: 41 |
| 28c-11: 365, 366 | 33a-2: 119 |

33b-1: 108
34c: 521
36: 56
37a-10: 190
38c: 193
44a: 62
44a-5: 58
44a-7: 64
44b-12: 63
44b-14: 138
44b-17: 157
45a-4: 866
45b-2: 154
50b: 460
53b: 21
53E: 16
56b: 44
58a: 70
58c: 65, 66
59a-6: 71, 133
59a-7: 159, 380
59a-12: 114
59a-15: 53
59a-16: 234
59a-21: 73
59a-22: 99
59a-25: 94, 103
59a-32: 122, 125
59a-36: 59, 87, 91
59a-40: 54
59a-41: 293
59a-49: 104, 105
59b-1: 718
59b-3: 51
59b-12: 52, 136
63a-1: 110, 151
63a-3: 507
63b-7: 147

64: 376
64L: 388
64m: 378
68d: 399
82: 766
82L: 734, 799
85a: 698
85h: 701
85i: 697, 699, 700
86a-20: 375
86a-30: 810
86a-33: 821
88a-13: 709
88a-27(f): 708
88b: 541, 767
90b: 230
90b-7: 195
90d: 872
90e: 115
92a-26: 846
92b-15: 188
93a-11: 182
93a-13: 185
93a-14: 183
93a-29: 186
93a-40: 184
93b-33: 848
98a-13: 847
98b-6: 850
98c-3: 855
103i: 639
104a: 246
104a-6: 265
104a-9: 194, 240, 257
104a-12: 236
104b-9: 256
101a-1: 269
107a-2: 22, 85, 202

## Appendix F. Index to Selected Minnesota Attorney General Opinions 331

107a-4: 211
107b: 235
107b-1: 198
107b-13: 113
107b-15: 668
121c-4: 222
122b-2: 12
122b-6: 247
124f: 243
124j: 242, 244
125a-1: 220
125a-11: 233
125a-15: 191
125a-22: 192
125a-29: 196
125a-34: 655
125a-37: 650, 654
125a-39: 212
125a-40: 237, 238
125b-5: 209
125b-9: 260
127c: 306
128e: 245
131b: 681
135a-4: 11
135b-5: 10
135b-6(b): 1
135b-6(f): 4
136d: 2
136g: 408
139f: 712
139h: 711
140a-2: 200
140a-4: 208
140a-13: 221
140b-1: 84
140b-6: 98
140c-3: 57

140f-1: 37
140f-2: 199, 206
140f-3: 201, 205
141: 272
141d: 682
144b-15: 270
144b-18: 226
144b-27: 224
148a-16: 308
148c-1: 229
154: 462, 463
159a-9: 321, 322
159a-19: 348
159b-4: 324
159b-7: 325, 341
159b-10: 347
159b-11: 323
159c-4: 360
159c-5: 362
159c-9: 361
161a-6: 239
161a-8: 312
161a-25: 320
161b: 315
161b-10: 310, 319
161b-11: 340
161b-14: 317, 354
161b-15: 318
162b: 316
166a-3: 329
166a-6: 332
166c-2: 338
168b: 353
169-L: 442
169-o: 326
169p: 327, 331
172: 359
172a: 352

172c: 350
172c-2: 349, 351
172d: 357, 358
175j: 355
175s: 356
180: 330
182: 374
183c: 393
183i: 371, 403
183j: 384
184i: 401
184n: 387
185a-5: 382, 383
185b-2: 210
186: 395
187a-1: 389
187a-4: 313
187a-9: 390
196: 522
198b-6(a): 95
202: 163
202e: 874
203a-1: 166
203s: 849
204a-5: 144
208a-1: 643
208a-3: 433
208b-1: 406
208g-12: 434
208g-14: 407
209: 436
209b: 411
209c: 418, 435
209E: 423
209g: 425
209h: 419, 439
209i: 420
209j: 702

210a-1: 430
210a-4: 426, 438
210b-6: 422
210b-9: 432
210c-1: 429, 431
210d-2: 427, 428
210d-3: 424
211a: 440
211a-3: 412
211a-7: 414, 415
211a-10: 410
211b-5: 416
211c-5: 421
211c-7: 413
211c-9: 409, 417
211d-18: 441
213a: 762
213d: 644, 645
213i: 733
214a: 17
215a-1: 713
215a-4: 728
215c-8: 752
215c-9: 730
217: 602, 621, 626
217a: 567, 620
217b-1: 614, 615
217b-2: 606, 607, 608, 611
217b-6: 612, 613
217b-7: 603
217c: 618
217d: 623, 624, 625
217f-1: 627
217f-2: 610
217f-3: 548, 619, 622
217f-4: 628
217h: 604
217i: 599

## Appendix F. Index to Selected Minnesota Attorney General Opinions

218c-1: 563, 565, 568
218c-3: 564, 566
218E: 557, 569
218f: 547
218f-1: 550
218f-3: 549, 617
218f-4: 551
218g: 555, 573, 576, 581, 586, 605, 609
218g-1: 552, 559, 584
218g-1(a): 595
218g-4: 575
218g-6: 582
218g-7: 598
218g-11: 562, 590, 592
218g-12: 8, 587, 616
218g-13: 553, 580
218h-2: 588
218h-3: 589
218i: 594
218i-2: 593
218i-3: 591
218j-1: 574
218j-7: 585
218j-9: 571, 572
218j-10: 556, 558
218j-11: 570
218j-13: 577
218j-17: 596, 597
218k: 560, 600, 601
218L: 578, 579, 583
225f-1: 443
225f-3: 445
228d: 446, 447
229a-9: 490
229a-12: 496
229d-1: 487
229d-5: 488

229d-16: 493
229e-2: 448
229f: 248, 471
229i: 467
229i-1: 452
229i-4: 461
229j-4: 480
232: 795
232a: 796
234b: 48, 128
234d: 344
238d: 500, 501
238f: 520
238g: 561
240h: 437
240k: 268
240m: 486
242a-16: 808
248b-7: 532
248b-9: 531
249a-1: 533
249a-2: 537
249a-11: 543
249a-18: 535, 811
249b-14: 538
249b-22: 546
252m: 539
260a-4: 271, 281, 282
266a-2: 274
266a-3: 275
266b-1: 273
266b-8: 278
266b-9: 276, 277
266b-21: 279
268g: 651
270: 529
270a: 47
270m: 525

273a-18: 168
273c-6: 178, 179
276g: 498
280b: 770
280h: 517
285a: 107
290j-6: 7
291b: 225
291f: 469, 470
291k: 464
291j: 465
291h: 468
292d: 9
303a-7: 714
306a-1: 284
306a-4: 286
306b-6: 287, 723
307g: 288
307i: 289
307k: 290, 291
307L: 292
308a: 285
310f: 130
311f: 167
311g: 172
311j: 755
314b: 632
314b-4: 213
314b-7: 368
314b-11: 631
315a: 187
320: 635
320a: 634
320j: 633
322a-6: 884
324d: 793
324e-1: 792
324i: 794

324n: 790
325a-14: 736
329b: 715
330a-5: 173
330c-2: 126
330c-4: 877
330c-5: 127
335b: 666, 667
335c-1: 228, 669, 670, 671, 672, 673
335d: 67
337a: 717
337a-5: 716
338: 156, 160
338a: 444
339a-2: 649
339c-1: 647
339h: 653
339i-4: 664
339-o: 656, 657, 658, 661
339-o-2: 652, 659, 660, 662
339-o-4: 663
339-o-5: 665
341h: 307
341k-1: 676
341k-2: 678
341k-5: 677
341k-10: 679
341m: 675
345d: 674
346: 297
347d: 294
347e: 295
347j: 296
355e: 86
358a-1: 511, 512, 513
358a-3: 506, 514, 515
358d-4: 516
358d-5: 504

# Appendix F. Index to Selected Minnesota Attorney General Opinions

358e-1: 510
358e-4: 508
358e-8: 502, 505
358e-9: 509
358e-10: 503
358f: 518, 519
358g: 756
365a-11: 805
368d-2: 223
370g: 883
371a-3: 729
371b-1: 720, 722, 724, 726
371b-11: 731
371b-13: 732
373b: 641
373b-5: 250, 251
373b-9: 252
373b-11: 253
373b-16: 254, 255
373b-17(d): 818
373b-17f: 249
374f: 642
377a-5: 484, 485
377a-15: 495
377b-1: 451
377b-2: 458
377b-10(d): 450
377b-10(k): 483, 499
377e: 479
379c-1: 214, 449
379c-7: 459
379c-14: 492
379e-11: 482
380a-1: 215
380b-1: 216
380b-2: 457, 474
380b-3: 472
380b-4: 455, 456

380b-8: 218
384: 3
385a-2: 764
387b-9: 134
387g-8: 137
390a-4: 259
390a-12: 258, 758
390a-16: 261, 267
396a-2: 140
396c-4: 489
396c-10: 142
396c-18: 68
396f-1: 881
396g: 139
396g-11: 143
400e: 753
404c: 454
407e: 771
407g: 780
408: 491
412a-9: 823
412a-10: 219, 783
412a-11: 781
412a-13: 782.784
412a-19: 830
412a-24: 680, 832
412a-25: 829, 840
412a-28: 773
414a-3: 791
414a-9: 798
414c-3: 845
414d-6: 786, 787
414d-8: 809
414d-10: 789
414d-15(a): 788
415a: 629
418a-12: 820
418a-14: 817, 819

418c-1: 816
419f-1: 839
419f-2: 836
421a: 232
421a-5: 822, 824, 827, 828
421a-9: 826
421a-15: 831
421c: 825
421c-13: 797
423c: 833, 834, 835, 838
424a-5: 841
425b: 785
425b-2: 812
425b-4: 837
425e-5: 842
425g: 843
429: 164
429e: 175
429h: 174
434a-4: 854
434a-5: 863, 878
434b-1: 397
434b-9: 396
434b-15: 873
434b-16: 876
434b-23: 869
436h: 870
437a-13: 858
437b-9: 879
439b-1: 871
440f: 880
441b: 853, 856
442a-4: 859
442a-5: 60
442a-8: 852
442a-11: 882
442a-18: 857
442a-21: 865

442b-5: 860, 861, 862, 864
442b-11: 875
450a-6: 25
450c-2: 263
450d: 779
450d-3: 204
450e: 264
451a-9: 314
457b-3: 298
469a-5: 100
469a-9: 129
469a-16: 135
469b: 117
469b-3: 280
469b-6: 150
469c-1: 50
470b: 385
471g: 78
472c: 373
472t: 377
474b-4: 778
474e-2: 217, 477
474g: 743
476a-1: 101
476b-1: 162
476b-14: 116
476b-16: 158
477a: 124
477a-1: 123
477b-3: 120
477b-22: 121
477b-28: 141
483d: 176
484a-2: 69
484c: 851
484e-1: 49
487a-1: 544
487b-2: 536

## Appendix F. Index to Selected Minnesota Attorney General Opinions

487c-5: 540
490a: 400
490g: 398
490L: 404
494a: 305
494a-3: 283
494b-7: 300
494b-15: 302
494b-31: 299
504b-2: 710
517L: 545
519c: 97
519e: 777
519g: 814
519i: 102, 106
520L: 775
523a-18: 527
523e: 528
531: 345
531d: 807
531h: 804
531i: 346, 801, 802, 803
531j: 806
531L: 800
533b: 28
533c: 118
535a: 705
535e: 704
605a-6: 301
605a-13: 304
605b-6: 46
605b-23: 524
614: 813
614m: 815
614r: 197
616a: 686
616a-2: 684
616a-3: 15

616a-5: 683, 687
616b-4: 691, 692, 694, 695
616b-8: 688, 689
616b-10: 693
616c-1: 685
616d-7: 534
616d-13: 690
616e-2: 30
618a-2: 763
618b: 768
618c-1: 769
622a-8: 311
622a-11: 772
622a-14: 337
622i-1: 334, 335
622i-8: 336
622i-14: 343
624a-1: 90
624a-3: 155
624a-5: 145
624a-6: 89
624c-5: 88
624c-11: 146, 148
624c-12: 92
624d-6: 152
624e-5: 153
624e-11: 149
627E: 381
631m: 478
632d-3: 466
632e-1: 475
632e-12: 473
632E-24: 476
632E-36: 630
633a-13: 727
633a-20: 497
633c-3: 721
633e: 725

639: 402
639i: 379
639j: 405
642b-3: 453
645b-8: 6
688b: 72
688m: 96
688p 93
700d-13: 180
700d-18: 759
700d-32: 747
707a-9: 189
707a-10: 55
707a-12: 328, 339
707b: 79
707b-6: 80, 81
707b-11: 751
724: 757
733: 303
768a: 309
768m: 391
770c-4: 735
770e: 741, 744, 745, 746, 748, 844
770f: 737, 749
770g: 738
770i: 739, 740, 742
771b: 342
785e: 74, 76
785e-1: 75
798f: 241

802a-10: 82, 231
817f: 77, 169
817n: 481
817q: 754
829c-1: 554
829c-6: 5
832i: 109
834a: 646
840a-1: 45
844g: 707
845: 526
845c: 530
847a-3: 636
847a-5: 637
851f: 131
851i: 132, 333
851-o: 640
876: 638
901k: 494
911j: 386
911k: 363
911q: 370
928a-8: 61
928c-11: 760
928c-12: 761
928c-13: 750
980c-28: 765
983d: 177
983e: 170, 181
983L: 161
1001d: 648

## 1935–36*

6m: 155
8b: 199
12c-4: 434
21f: 391

21j: 108, 336, 362
22: 109
27a: 72
27e: 73

# Appendix F. Index to Selected Minnesota Attorney General Opinions

29a-12: 4, 7, 32
34h: 2
44a-3: 16
44a-4: 26
44h-5: 15
53b: 165, 166
59a-22: 36
59a-23: 38
59a-32: 22
59a-38: 14
59a-51: 28, 31
59b-11: 53
63b-10: 39
64a: 217
64t: 17
68f: 1
85e: 344
86a-44: 340
86a-51: 211
88a-14: 163
88a-25: 345
92a-1: 91
92c: 10, 89
93a-2: 82, 85
93a-18: 83
93a-38: 86
93a-43: 90
93b-26: 87
103f: 117
104a-3: 119
104a-9: 118
104b-5: 116
104b-13: 137
107b-1: 100
101b-5: 114
107h-1: 99
109f: 333
121a-4: 105

121a-9: 107
121b-11: 106
122b: 244
123f: 135
124a: 111, 142
124k: 115
125a-14: 113
125a-18: 59
125a-20: 95
125a-40: 84
126b: 110
128b: 138
137g: 285
140b-3: 8
140e-5: 339
144a-4: 141
144b-9: 140
144b-15: 139
146d-2: 280
146d-4: 281
148a-6: 97
159a-9: 184
159a-17: 185
159a-23: 193
159b-14: 179
161a-16: 210
168: 175, 191
168a: 176
172a: 197
172b: 198
175a: 200
175p: 201
183h: 182
184a: 212
184n: 202, 235
185a-7: 214
187a-2: 208
187a-7: 209

193b-1: 167
196j: 147
196r-1: 146
198a-2: 29
199b-4: 148
201a-1: 311
209f: 77
211b: 76
211b-2: 74
211b-5: 75
211c-2: 79
217b-7: 306
218c-3: 305
218g: 301
218g-6: 296
218g-11: 297
218g-13: 293, 294, 299, 309
218g-14: 308
218g-15: 292, 295
218g-16: 298
218j-12: 302
218j-18: 304
218n: 303
229a-10: 227, 233, 234
229b-15: 232
229k: 222
232d: 351, 371, 372
238k: 253
240d: 78
248b-3: 268
248c-4: 267
249a-13: 272
252j: 270
254a: 273
259c-16: 300
266a-11: 145
266a-12: 47
266b-8: 143

266b-21: 144
276d: 251
290j-2: 288, 289
290j-6: 20
291e: 282
291f: 283, 284, 286, 287
300f: 347
307g: 149
307i: 150, 151, 153
307k: 154
307L: 152
314b-22: 392
324: 366
324d: 369
324e: 365
324k: 367, 368
330c-5: 52
337b-4: 236
339d-1: 327
339o-4: 326, 328
339o-6: 325
341k-9: 173
346c: 156, 159
346g: 162
347a: 160
347b: 158
347k: 161
358a-1: 258, 259, 260
358a-2: 261
358a-3: 262
358a-4: 263
358a-1: 264
358d: 255
358d-5: 254
358e-1: 256
358e-6: 266
358e-7: 257
358f: 265

# Appendix F. Index to Selected Minnesota Attorney General Opinions

365a-5: 239
369i: 240
371a-2: 12
373b-1: 120, 122
373b-9(e): 128, 130
373b-10(c): 126, 127
373b-17(A): 123
373b-17(d): 125
373b-21: 121
374: 129
377a: 226
377a-1: 224
377a-5: 237
377b-3: 250
377b-4: 229
377b-8: 243
377b-10a: 246
371b-10(d): 235, 242, 247
377b-10h: 249
378b: 238
379c-1: 225
379c-14: 245
380b-1: 230
380b-2: 228
385a-2: 88
390a-6: 133, 379
390b-2: 131
390c: 134
390c-8: 407
390c-13: 387, 410
390c-14: 132
396c-6: 56
396c-10: 58
396c-17: 60
396g-12: 55
396g-15: 241
396g-16: 57
401b-2: 6

406b: 355
406c: 44
407: 416
407i: 427
408: 353
408b: 104
408d: 349, 370
409a-11: 388
409b-8: 335
412a-9: 354, 358, 417
412a-13: 403
412a-17: 363
412a-23: 376, 393, 404
412a-24: 359
412a-27: 361
414a-9: 374
414d-12: 364
414d-17: 415
414f: 322
415m: 330
418a-11: 382
418a-12: 383, 385
418a-14: 384
418b-3: 124
421a-4: 348
421c: 390
421c-15: 375
423c: 396, 399, 402, 408
425a: 428
425b-3: 418
425b-4: 398, 421
425b-5: 394, 400, 401, 405, 409, 419
425b-7: 420, 422
425c: 397
425c-2: 406, 423, 424, 426
425c-3: 425
425c-7: 395

425c-16: 411
426a-2: 195
426b-7: 186
428f: 373
434a-7: 231
434b-2: 215
434b-13(a): 431, 432
434b-13(e): 433
434b-16: 201
434b-21: 213
434b-27: 216
439e: 435
440b: 438
440e: 439
441g: 437
442a-20: 430
450b-2: 136
450d-1: 9
456f-2: 49
469a-2: 18
469a-5: 33
469a-15: 54
469b-1: 40
469b-5: 50
469b-6: 66, 61, 69
469h-1: 41
470b: 43
470g: 206
470i: 45
471a: 23
471h: 48, 51
471m: 24
471p: 307
474b-3: 360
476b-1: 291
476b-15: 65
476c-4: 37
477a: 21

481b-2: 34
481b-7: 63
487c-5: 271
490h: 218
490j-2: 114
494a-1: 170
494b-10: 171
494b-18: 172
505: 386
519c: 62
519k: 429
519m: 196, 377, 378, 389, 412, 413, 414
519q: 352
520j: 290
521a: 317
521j-2: 313
521L-2: 324
521m: 320
521p-2: 323
521p-3: 316
521r: 314
521t-1: 315
521t-2: 312
521t-4: 321
521t-5: 319
521v: 318
556a-8: 102
602e: 25
602h: 98
611a: 220
611a-8: 103
611a-9: 221
614f: 380, 381
614s: 356
616e-2: 11
622a-17: 192
622b: 188

## Appendix F. Index to Selected Minnesota Attorney General Opinions

622i: 177
622i-1: 189
622i-5: 187
624a-4: 64
624d-3: 70
624d-11: 68
627j-1: 203
632a: 310
634c: 343
635d: 274, 275
639i: 219
645b-2: 442
645b-25: 80, 441
679b: 157, 164
688h: 27
688m: 30
700a-8: 334
700d-2: 357
700d-17: 331
700d-18: 332
707a-1: 94
707a-3: 93
707a-11: 5
707a-13: 223
707b-6: 46, 436
707h-3: 92
733d: 19, 169
768d-1: 180
768d-2: 181

768k-1: 194
768n: 178
770: 329
770g: 346
779m: 42
798d: 112
817f: 183
829b: 276
829c: 278
829c-6: 277
829e-6: 279
833c: 341
833d: 342
840a-4: 190
840b-3: 13
843k: 440
844a-2: 3
844b-8: 61
844c-5: 96
844h: 248
851: 338
851g: 168
851i: 337
901a: 350
911d: 204
911r: 205
928c-14: 71
980b-31: 81
1001c: 101, 252
1001f: 269

## 1937–38*

6h: 174
8b: 211, 221
10a: 2
10a-3: 1
18a: 135

27b: 101
29a-13: 3
29a-19: 103
29a-30: 6
34f: 62

34g-2: 12
37a-11: 120
44a: 27
44a-8: 31
47f: 93
53b: 184
58c: 35
59a-11: 32, 33, 34
59a-17: 43
59a-22: 84
59a-26: 50
59a-32: 59, 60, 64, 66, 67
59a-36: 71
59b-9: 30
59b-13: 87
61j: 41
63a: 90
63a-1: 53
63a-5: 42
63b-17: 79
64: 243
64L: 238
85f: 223
86a-53: 308
90a-2: 39
90b: 140
92a-28: 4, 183
92b-1: 400
92b-7: 285
92c: 116
93a-4: 106
93a-5: 105
93a-8: 109
93a-10: 108
93a-11: 112
93a-17: 111
93a-29: 115
93a-33: 107

93b-33: 110
103a: 139
103f: 194
103i: 138
104a-2: 136
104a-8: 142
104a-9: 181
104b-7: 143
121a-8: 134
122b: 141
122b-5: 129
124a: 117
125a-14: 118
125a-20: 125
125a-41: 153
125a-52: 144
125a-64: 113, 137, 155, 156, 157, 158
128b: 170
129: 178
140b-5: 196
140c-3: 212
140f: 126
140f-11: 44
144b-15: 160, 161
144b-18: 159
144b-27: 162
148a-8: 260
148a-14: 96
148b-5: 197
159a-3: 202
159a-5: 201
159b-2: 213
159b-10: 221
159b-11: 214
161a-20: 217
161b-1: 203
161b-11: 204, 222

## Appendix F. Index to Selected Minnesota Attorney General Opinions

161b-14: 230
166a-10: 209
169b: 218, 219
169g: 220
110f-1: 199
172c: 228, 231
172c-2: 225
172c-3: 229
172c-4: 232
172d: 226
183c: 236, 240, 241
183k: 244
183r: 246, 247
184c-1: 233
184i: 234, 279
188: 376
188c: 248, 377
188d: 375
198b-5: 47
199b-3: 268
199b..4: 269
199b-5: 164
208i: 100
211a-6: 98
213c: 396
216i-1: 422
217f: 304
217f-3: 24
218c-1: 292
218g-6: 295
218g-9: 294
218g-11: 299, 303
218g-12: 302
218g-13: 296
218j-10: 293, 297
218j-17: 300, 301
218k: 298
225L: 255

225m: 378
229d-4: 9
229k: 272
232d: 423, 424
248b-6: 283
248b-10: 284
249a-17: 369
249b-13: 286
260a-4: 166
260b: 286
266a-3: 163
266a-12: 173
266b-8: 169
266b-11: 165
266b-11: 168
266b-21: 167, 171, 190
266b-23: 172
273a-23: 132
273b: 94
273c-1: 99
277a-10: 408
280h: 278, 395
290v: 195
291f: 289
291k: 288, 291
291y: 290
293b-16: 380
300a: 307
300m: 306
306b-12: 282
307i: 175, 176, 177
314b-6: 318
314b-11: 316
314b-17: 317
314b-22: 460
320b: 319
322b: 473, 475
322d: 474

324d: 418
324e: 417
324k: 420, 421
325a-5: 419
337c-1: 360
337c-2: 362
337c-3: 361
339a-2: 341, 348, 355, 398
339a-3: 340
339a-4: 346
339a-5: 334, 356, 357
339a-6: 358
339d-1: 336, 337
339d-4: 338
339g: 335
339h: 339
339o-2: 345, 347, 349
339o-3: 342
339o-4: 351
339o-5: 344. 350, 353
339o-6: 359
339p: 152
339q: 343
339s: 354
341b: 191
341k-1: 193
345d: 363
346d: 179
347k: 182
348: 180
358e-1: 275, 276
358e-8: 277
358f: 280
371a-8: 254
371b-8: 387
371b-10: 385
373a: 150, 242
373b-1: 145

373b-5: 146
313b-6: 147
313b-10(c): 149
373h-9: 148
377a-15: 273
377b-1: 256, 257
377b-2: 119
377b-4: 259, 261
377b-8: 263
377b-10(d): 265, 267
377b-10h: 262, 264
380a-1: 258
394k: 381
394L: 382
396c-6: 81, 83
396c-9: 63
396g-7: 80, 82
396g-16: 85
408d: 425
409: 444
409a-1: 401
412a-5: 403
412a-8: 451
412a-9: 434
412a-10: 405, 410, 461
412a-19: 441
412a-23: 404, 406, 413, 445, 453
414a-9: 412
414a-13: 402, 411
418a-11: 431
418a-12: 432
418b-5: 433
418c-3: 430
419f-3: 416
421a-8: 438, 439, 447
421a-9: 435
421a-11: 436, 437
421b: 104

## Appendix F. Index to Selected Minnesota Attorney General Opinions

423c: 415
423k: 414
424a-9: 443
425b-2: 426
425b-3: 409
425c-5: 459
425c-10: 407
425c-13: 449, 452
425c-17: 448
425g: 442
425i: 454, 455
426a: 198
434a-1: 266
434a-8: 249
434a-10: 305
434b-13(a): 462
434b-13(d): 467
439a: 464
450a-15: 151
451a-22: 216
456g: 58
465: 114
469a-2: 40
469a-8: 54
469a-9: 76
469a-12: 74, 75
469c-4: 28
470b: 56
470g: 281
471m: 55, 57
476a-4: 77
476b-8: 29
476b-10: 68
477b-3: 65
477b-20: 49, 52, 61
477b-37: 51
480b: 78
484e-4: 48

494a-1: 189
498c: 25
510c-9: 192
519a: 465
519h: 26
519k: 466
519m: 224, 427
521b-2: 321
521c: 322
521g-1: 323, 324
521g-3: 331
521g-4: 328
521h-1: 330
521i-2: 329
521p-3: 326
521t-2: 327, 352
521t-5: 325
525: 393, 446, 450, 458
533i: 5
540c: 309
556a-7: 154, 366
602h: 463
602j: 127, 128
605a-7: 186
611a-6: 91
611a-8: 92
614g: 429
614h: 428
616a-5: 367, 368
616b-1: 371
616b-4: 373
616d-8: 370
616d-26: 372
618a-5: 399
622a: 205
622b: 206
622j-6: 8
624a-5: 73

624c-4: 86
624c-6: 72, 364
624c-14: 365
624c-16: 88
627c-5: 239
627h: 245
632a-16: 312
632a-22: 271
632a-24: 270
632a-25: 314
632e-2: 310
632e-14: 313
632e-33: 311
632e-36: 315
636a-15: 332
636a-17(a): 333
642a-12: 121
679a: 253
681f-3: 252
688b: 45
688c: 46
700a-3: 457
700a-8: 390, 456
700d-12: 391
700d-18: 392
700d-28: 394
700d-31: 102
700e: 389
707a-1: 122
707a-4: 11
707a-7: 124
707a-10: 123
707a-12: 7, 200
707a-15: 10
707b-2: 38

707b-10: 207, 208
733: 187
733j: 188
779a-3: 215
779n: 133
785d: 37
785e-2: 36
832: 477
832j: 476
832j-1: 478
840a-1: 13, 185
840a-5: 22, 23
840a-6: 14, 15, 16, 17, 18, 19, 20, 21, 374
844b-1: 69, 70
844f-3: 210
882e: 89
885c-1: 468, 470
885f-2: 469
885g-2: 471
885t: 472
885u: 479
911a-1: 237
911j: 235
923e: 320
928a-8: 379
928c: 397
928c-13: 388
928c-17: 386
950: 250, 251
980a-11: 383, 384
983d: 95
983L: 97
1101c: 130, 131, 274
1001d: 440

# Appendix F. Index to Selected Minnesota Attorney General Opinions

## 1939–40*

12b: 298
12b-2: 183
27g: 8
28a-3: 72
28a-8: 71
28b-2: 67, 68
28c-2: 69
28c-7: 70
33b-9: 282
36c-8: 118
44a: 120
44a-4: 139
44b-17: 119
58i: 121
59a: 224
59a-1: 293
59a-22: 142
59a-40: 226
59b-11: 222
60: 185
62c: 210, 211, 212, 215, 216
63a-2: 184
64f: 79
90a: 117
90b-2: 114
90c-5: 116
90e-3: 115
90e-5: 113
92a-16: 4
93a-18: 2
93a-30: 3
98a-12: 134
98a-28: 137
103a: 187
103f: 186
103k: 188

104a-6: 206
107a-1: 315
121a: 191
121a-4: 190
121b: 243
121b-21: 189
124j: 205
125a-64: 257
125b-18: 143
125b-27: 192
133b-1: 38
133b-7: 40
133b-45: 39
140f-6: 54
148a-3: 129
150c: 122
159a-16: 56
159b-1: 55
159b-11: 57
161a-16(b): 49
161b-10: 47
166c-2: 51
166c-5: 53
166c-9: 52
168a: 65
169: 58
169-o: 63
170f-4: 45
180d: 66
182: 84
183q: 85
183r: 81
184: 74
184i: 73
185a: 83
193a-4: 17

198b-10a: 126
203t: 7
208c: 12
208e-3: 5, 6
208g: 14
208g-1: 13
208h: 22
209: 16
209d: 17
209g: 15
209k: 9
210a: 18
210a-1: 10
210a-4: 11
210d-1: 21
210d-7: 19
211a-9: 20
213f: 287
213g: 288
215c-10: 306
216g: 345
216i: 344
211b-6: 156
218: 152
218e: 160, 161, 166
218f: 161
218g-1: 153
218g-6: 163
218g-10: 157
218g-13: 158, 159
218g-14: 155
218g-15: 154
218j-a: 162
218j-8: 165
218j-12: 164
225i-2: 218, 219
225L: 221
229i-3: 133

229k-4: 138
232d: 307, 308, 309, 110, 311
246h-8: 29
248b-3: 24, 30, 31, 33
248b-7: 275
248b-11: 12, 34, 35
260a-4: 41
266b-4: 25
266b-8: 26
270: 90. 92. 93. 97
270a-2: 91
270d-7: 104
270d-9: 94. 95
273a-23: 173
276c: 82
277e: 61
280: 289
285b: 144
300a: 151
307g: 27
310: 175
310r: 176
320a: 290
322a-2: 297
324: 305
324d: 130
337b-2: 284
337c-3: 283, 285
337d-4: 234
339c-1: 256
339d-4: 235
339e-2: 277
339g-2: 262, 263, 264, 265, 267
339i: 260. 261
339m: 258. 259
339o-2: 236, 268, 270, 271, 272, 278
339o-3: 276

## Appendix F. Index to Selected Minnesota Attorney General Opinions

339o-4: 269, 273, 274
341k: 43
341k-9: 44
346b: 28
347e: 194
358a-1: 178, 180
358d-3: 179
358f: 181, 182
370L: 23
373a-4: 209
373b-6: 196, 197
373b-9b: 200
373b-10(e): 195
373b-10(g): 198
373b-16: 201
373b-17e: 199
377a-3: 132
377a-8a: 136
377b-3: 131
387g-5: 168
390a-1: 203
390c-11: 204
396e: 170
396g-7: 171
396g-16: 172
407d: 292
408: 330
412a-9: 338
412a-10: 333, 334, 335, 336
412a-11: 303
412a-23: 340
412a-26: 294, 295, 296
414a-2: 299
414a-11: 300
414b-3: 326
414d-6: 291
418b-19: 321
418b-21: 320

419f: 343
421a-8: 319
421a-10: 110
421a-11: 328
421a-17: 324, 325
421b-5: 327
421c-28: 329
423c: 341, 342
423f: 332
423h: 339
424a-16: 301
425c-6: 302
425c-7: 304
436c: 207
437a-11: 86
442a-21: 135
442b-9: 227
450b-2: 193
469a-9: 225
472a: 87
472e: 76
472n: 80
474d-1: 331
475g: 208
476a-3: 141
477b-1: 214
477b-21: 213
480a: 169
490d: 88
505j: 323
519: 317
519a: 313
519j: 314, 316
519m: 318
520: 1
520b: 346
521a: 251
521g: 240, 242

521j-2: 255
521L-2: 254
521p: 241
521p-4: 244, 245, 246, 241, 248, 249, 250
521t-2: 252, 253
521w: 239
523a: 105
531h: 312
559a: 42
611a-1: 217
622b: 50
622i-7: 48
624d-5: 223
624d-9: 174
627f-1: 77
632a-8: 177
632e-5: 322
635e: 145, 146
639e: 89
640a: 230, 279, 280
642a-12: 128
644: 286
679k: 233
688a: 123
707a-4: 111

707a-7: 101, 109, 112
707a-12: 46
101a-15: 108
68b: 62
770g: 347, 348, 349, 350
772c-4: 106
785e-2: 124
840a-5: 36, 229
840a-6: 231, 232, 238
840a-10: 237
840b-2: 228
844f: 60
844f-3: 59
851p: 202
876: 147
882f-1: 281
885: 281, 85, 96, 98, 99, 100, 101, 102, 103
911d-17: 8
911m: 75
916b: 125
927: 64
928a-8: 140
989a-16: 121
1001a: 220
1001c-1: 266

## 1941–42*

8-B: 131
12-B-1: 185, 186, 187
16-B: 153
18-D: 296
21-A: 193
24: 293
27-G: 6
28-B-3: 63, 75, 78, 79

28-C-7: 67
33-B: 283
36: 124
36-B: 123
37-a-7: 284
37-B-6: 126
44-B-16: 136
58-M: 102

## Appendix F. Index to Selected Minnesota Attorney General Opinions

58-o: 103
59-A-1: 98
59-A-3: 121, 122
59-A-5: 188
59-A-40: 257
59-B-5: 245
59-B-10: 253
59-B-12: 252
62-B: 232, 234, 235, 238
85a: 118
85E: 119
85-I: 120
90-B: 197
90-B-8: 99
90-C-2: 31
90-F: 287
91i: 242
98a-12: 112
102: 17
103-D: 191
104-A-8: 113, 194
104-A-9: 114
101-a-10: 130
107-B-4: 127
107-B-16: 129
121-A-7: 190
121-B-7: 189
122-B-3: 196
125-A-28: 147
125-a-64: 68, 195, 217, 218, 273, 278
125-B-1: 125
127-a: 151
130-B: 328
133-b-59: 30
135-B-1: 85
140-a-7: 105
144-B-5: 18, 19

148a-19: 111
159-a-4: 35
159-a-10: 44
159-a-13: 42, 45
159-a-16: 41
159-B-b: 43
159-B-11: 34
160-C: 56
161-a-12: 32, 33
161-B-2: 50
162-B: 61
166-a: 57
168: 48
169-B: 40
170h: 46
172: 55
172-C-2: 53
172-C-3: 54
180: 59
180a: 58
183-F: 74
183-H: 73
184-D: 75, 76, 77
184-E: 65
185a-5: 81
193-a-4: 84
197-C: 294
199-B-4: 20
203-L-2: 289
208-A-3: 5
208-G: 10
108-1-3: 16
209: 1
209-H: 2
210-D-2: 7
210-D-7: 9
210-D-8: 11
211-C-13: 4

211-D-19: 14
215-C-b: 342
216-1: 304
216-1-3: 331
217-B-9: 169
217-H: 170
218-C-1: 167, 168
218-F-3: 172
218-g: 165
218-G-6: 164
218-G-13: 162, 163, 173, 175, 236
218-G-15: 166
218-J-12: 171
218-L: 161
218-R: 174
229-A-8: 142
232-d: 307, 333
234-B: 176
248-B-11: 27
249-B-16: 148
253-a-7: 86
254-D: 87
266-B-11: 22
266-B-27: 21
270-d-9: 88
277-A-11: 231
277-B-2: 139
280-D: 292
280-h: 290, 291
285-D: 47
291-F: 160
292-E: 237
293b-1: 29
293-B-14: 128
300: 93
300a: 92
300-J: 94
306-B-7: 24

307-I: 25
310: 300
311-D-8: 317
311-F: 318
311-H: 12
322-G: 146, 262
324-E: 286
325: 341
325-A: 330
331-B-1: 115, 116, 117
339-C: 270
339-G-2: 274
339-I-1: 272
339-0-2: 277
339-0-4: 264, 276
347-I: 199
358-A-5: 228
358-B-1: 220
358-B-3: 222
358-E: 219
358-E-2: 227
358-E-7: 229
358-F: 223, 224, 225, 226
369-M: 259
370: 13
373-A-2: 203
373-B-5: 204
373-B-9-a: 207
373-B-9-e: 208
373-B-10-i: 205
374-g: 282
374-J: 209
377-a-11: 37, 144
377-A-15: 145
379-C-8-c: 143
382-a: 133
382c: 244
384a: 96

# Appendix F. Index to Selected Minnesota Attorney General Opinions

387-B-1: 178
387b-10: 178
390-A-11: 210, 212
390-A-17: 150, 213
390-C-10: 215
390-C-11: 211
390-C-13: 214
396-C-3: 258
396-C-4: 180
396-C-17: 181
396-G: 183
396-G-1: 177
396g-4: 180
396-G-7: 179
396-G-10: 182
396-G-16: 184
407-H: 323
407-L: 344
409-A-1: 311
410-B: 312
412-A-10: 297, 298, 299, 301, 305
412-A-13: 303, 306
414b-4: 347
414-D-6: 308
418-A: 336
419-B: 326
421-A-17: 340, 343
421-C: 339
423-K: 345, 346
424-a-2: 325
425-c: 313, 316, 329
425-C-1: 327
425-C-3: 309
425-C-6: 324
425-C-13: 315, 320, 321, 322
425-C-15: 310
429-G: 348
434-A-6: 261

434-B-2: 64, 66
442a-23: 132
442-B-9: 134
450-B: 198
454-E: 332
469-A-1: 216
469-a-9: 243, 244
469-A-15: 254
476-B-4: 137
476-B-10: 135, 256
477-b-34: 239
484-E-1: 97
484-E-2: 255
490-d: 192
490-F: 82
498-A: 233
518: 83
519c: 178, 260
519-I: 334, 335
519M: 51, 52
521-g: 266
521-P-4: 206, 261, 268
521-T-2: 269
602-B: 107
602-J: 106, 108, 109, 110, 111, 112
614-G: 337
614-L: 338
618-A-9: 281
622-D: 38
622-I-4: 36
624-C-2: 248
624-C-5: 251
624-C-11: 246, 249
624-C-14: 250
624-D-5: 319
624-E-1: 247
627-B-1: 69
627-B-8: 71

627-L: 70
634-D: 39
639-a: 62
644-F: 285
672-B-8: 80
681-A: 349, 350
688-K: 140
700-A-3: 314
700-D-26: 15
707-A-15: 247
707-B-7: 100
733-D: 28
768-C: 60
785-E-1: 101
785-E-2: 201, 202, 240, 241
798-B: 104

802-A-16: 200
802-B: 154
829-C-1: 155, 156, 157, 158, 159
840-A-5: 263
840-a-6: 23, 264
844-C-3: 149
844-C-5: 152
847-A-3: 230
885-a-1: 200
885b: 89
885-C-2: 91
885d-1: 90
911-1: 72
916-B: 141
985-F: 26
1001-D: 275

## 1943–44*

9: 249
9A: 249
9A-10: 252
10-A: 246
18-D: 207
21-A: 340
21-D: 395, 396
27-G: 85
28-B-1: 135
29-A-18: 24
29-A-20: 23
29-B-9: 22
50: 212
53-A-18: 25
53-B: 29, 30, 31
53-D: 26
59-A: 206
59-A-3: 175

59-A-14: 12
59-A-22: 204
59-A-32: 240
62-B: 235
62-C: 237
85-A: 159, 160
85-C: 162
85-F: 163
90-B-8: 169
90-F: 269
92-A-24: 33
92-B-1: 32
93-A-33: 27
107-A-5: 181
107-A-9: 183
107-B-16: 190
107-B-19: 377
107-B-20: 362

## Appendix F. Index to Selected Minnesota Attorney General Opinions

120: 100, 174
121-B: 218
121-B-7: 82
125-A-20: 216
125-A-46: 189
125-A-64: 157, 179, 311
125-B-16: 178
125-B-20: 177
136-D: 16
144-B: 67
144-B-3: 65, 66
144-B-24: 68
148-A-9: 38
148-A-14: 36
148-A-21: 46
150-C: 41
159-A-18: 101
159-B-1: 111, 112
159-B-8: 103
161-A-11: 114, 117
161-A-25: 116, 118
166-A-7: 91, 94
166-A-8: 93
166-C: 98
166-C-6: 97, 99
168: 123, 124, 125
168-D: 126, 127, 128
169-B: 87
169-D: 92
169-E: 88
169-P: 89
172-C-2: 129, 130
180-D: 95
180-O: 96
180-J: 90
184-i: 136
193-B-1: 80
197: 250

197-B: 274, 275
198-A: 187
198-B-3: 186
198-B-6-d: 184
208-B-4: 49
208-G: 47
209-A: 51
209-D: 53
209-E: 52
210-A: 48
211-A-5: 50
211-A-8: 54
211-C-6: 58
213-D: 278
215-B-3: 294, 295
217-B-8: 194
217-C: 197
217-F-3: 202
218-F: 191
218-G-6: 196
218-G-15: 195
218-J-10: 198, 199, 201
218-J-17: 200
218-L: 192, 193
225-B-4: 81
230: 248
232-D: 392, 393, 394
234-B: 1, 2, 3, 4, 5, 6, 7, 8, 10, 11
234-D: 13, 14
248-B-2: 336
248-B-3: 335
248-B-7: 337
248-B-11: 78
249-A-3: 143
253-A: 142
254: 382
256: 141
260-A-8: 71

266-B-11: 72, 73
270-D: 154, 155, 156
270-D-12: 115
280: 283
280-G: 282
280-H: 280, 281
280-K: 279
280-O: 284, 285
285-B: 180
292-B: 15
300-D: 69
307-J: 74
310-5: 158, 164, 165
311-L: 338
322-A-2: 18
322-G: 19
324-M: 357
328-A-1: 254, 255
328-A-9: 253
331-A-1: 270
331-A-6: 271
331-A-9: 272
337-C-3: 256
339-I-1: 326
339-L: 330
339-M: 327
339-O-3: 331
341-i: 79
341-K-10: 86
345-B: 292
349-E: 75, 76
358-A-2: 232
358-A-3: 231
358-B-1: 77
358-E-9: 230, 233
365-A: 296
370-D: 176
371-A-5: 293

373-B-9-b: 219
373-B-17-c: 220
377-B-1: 188
387-B-1: 209
387-B-9: 243
387-D: 242
387-G-5: 245
390-A-17: 221
390-C-6: 222
390-C-11: 223, 224
390-C-13: 225, 226
396-C-1: 203
396-C-18: 213
396-F-3: 214
407-O: 386, 390
408: 388, 389
408-B: 397
408-C: 339
409-B-5: 350, 351
409-C-2: 398, 399
410: 277
412-A-9: 345, 346, 349
412-A-10: 341, 342, 343, 344, 347, 348
412-A-13: 352
412-A-23: 348
414-A-2: 354
414-A-9: 355, 356
414-A-11: 360
414-D-4: 358
414-D-11: 353
414-D-12: 359
416-A: 251, 276
421-A: 383
421-A-8: 384
421-C: 381
421-C-20: 185
423-C: 367

## Appendix F. Index to Selected Minnesota Attorney General Opinions

425-C: 363, 364, 375, 376
425-C-6: 366, 370
425-C-13: 365, 368, 369, 371, 372, 373, 374
425-C-14: 361
425-C-15: 374
450-E: 227, 228
450-f-3: 229
451-A-5: 121
451-A-23: 122
454-E: 273, 286
474-J-1: 387
474-J-2: 391
476-B-8: 208
476-C-1: 182
477-B-34: 236
477-B-35: 239
480-A: 210
480-B: 211
490-J-2: 139
494-B-16: 83
499: 257, 258
519D: 378
519K: 379, 380
519m: 113
521G: 301, 302, 303, 304, 309
521-J-2: 305, 306
521-O: 319
521-P-1: 298, 299
521-P-3: 307
521-P-4: 55, 308, 311, 312, 313, 314, 315, 316, 317, 318, 320, 321, 322, 323
521-R: 297
521-T-3: 300
521-V: 324
521-W: 325
556-A-8: 328, 329
596-B-6: 261

602-B: 34
602-E: 37
602-J: 40, 42, 43, 44, 45
614-R: 102
622-A-6: 105
622-I-1: 107
622-i-2: 109
622-i-4: 108
622-J-23: 106
622-K: 110
624-C-4: 244
624-C-10: 241
624-D-10: 215
632-A-16: 287, 288
632-C: 289
632-E-14: 290
632-E-19: 291
639-A: 132
639-E: 131, 133, 140
644-C: 263
644-D: 264, 265, 266
644-E: 267
644-F: 262, 268
644-G: 161
645-A-8: 17
645-B-8: 17
679-G: 334
681-A: 28
88-B: 172, 173
688-M: 185
700-D-23: 57
700-D-28: 56
705-A: 62
705-A-2: 61
705-A-6: 63, 64
707-A-4: 166, 168
707-A-8: 167
707-A-15: 170

768-K: 119, 120
785-E: 171
802-B-3: 84
817-F: 9
832: 21
832-A-9: 20
840-A-7: 332
840-A-9: 333
844-A-9: 217
844-f-3: 104
850-E: 238
851-F: 134
885-A: 152
885-A-1: 153
885-C-1: 144, 145

885-C-2: 148, 149, 150, 151
885-D-1: 146, 147
885-D-2: 153
901-M: 35
911: 137
911-J: 138
921-J: 39
980-A: 247
983-D: 60
983-H: 59
985: 260
985-A: 259
989-A-6: 70
989-B-1: 234
1001-A: 205

## 1945–46*

9-A-46: 204
28-A-2: 37
28-A-3: 38
28-B-1: 40, 41
28-B-2: 39
29-A-20: 9
36-C: 93
43-B-4: 95, 96
50-B: 101
53-A-19: 10
53-F: 7, 8
58-C: 84
58-G: 85
59-A: 119
59-A-1: 82
59-A-7: 94
59-A-22: 98, 99, 100, 108
59-A-32: 153, 154, 155
59-A-36: 168

59-A-40: 171, 175, 177, 179
59-A-51: 97
59-A-53: 125
59-B-11: 173
62-B: 151
62-C: 152
64-N: 51
64-S: 47
85-F: 36
88-A-27: 201
90-A-1: 141
92-C: 11
102: 12
104-A-10: 139
104-B-15: 138
120: 13, 14, 73
125-A-20: 120
125-A-33: 143
125-A-36: 178

## Appendix F. Index to Selected Minnesota Attorney General Opinions

125-A-64: 192
126-A: 129
126-G: 128
133-B-45: 25
133-B-51: 28
136-i: 6
144-A-1: 22
144-A-4: 17
144-B-18: 18
144-B-27: 9, 20
161-A-25: 32
166-A-10: 30
169-P: 31
172-C-2: 34
175-A: 35
182: 49
183-R: 48
198-B-6-a: 185
213-A: 42
217-B-2: 69
217-F-3: 70, 71
218-C-2: 60, 61, 62, 63
218-G: 26
218-0-13: 65
218-G-15: 57, 58, 59, 68
218-R: 64, 66
234-B: 1, 2, 3
248-B-7: 200
253-B-4: 52
254-D: 53
270: 56
280-B: 207
280-H: 208, 209, 210
290-J-10: 72
292-C: 4, 5
300: 21
310: 74
310-S: 75

339-i-1: 202
339-O-2: 203
347-i: 24
358-A: 146
358-B-1-a: 147
358-E-3: 144
358-E-9: 145
373-B-9: 130
373-B-16: 133
373-B-17-d: 132
373-B-19: 131
374-J: 105, 134
377-A-11: 110
377-B-1: 103
377-B-3: 109
379-C-4: 106
387-B-10: 12b
387-G-3: 122
390-A-2: 136
390-B-2: 135
396-C-6: 127
396-C-10: 126
396-G: 124
396-G-7: 113, 114, 117
406-B: 214
408-C: 211
409-A-1: 212
410-B: 227
412-A-10: 213
414-A-9: 217
414-A-11: 215
414-D-4: 216
414-D-6: 218
418-C-1: 219
421-A-8: 220
423-C: 222
425-C: 224, 225, 226
425-C-13: 223

434-A-1: 102
434-B-18: 46
441-B: 188, 189
442-A-6: 107
450-A-3: 137
450-F-1: 221
454-E: 206
455-C: 140
469-A-12: 172
469-A-15: 174, 176
472-J: 45
476-B-10: 92
477-B-3: 150
477-B-7: 148, 149
477-B-34: 156
480-A: 115, 116
480-G: 123
482-A: 199
484-E-4: 83
519-Q: 67
520-D: 23
521-G: 193
521-P-1: 198
521-P-4: 194, 195, 196, 197
525: 180
596-B-2: 205
605-B-35: 27
622-A-6: 33
624-A-4: 159
624-B-1: 164

624-C-6: 162, 163
624-D: 166, 167
624-D-10: 118
624-D-11: 165
624-D-19: 169, 170
627-C-7: 43
627-L: 44
639-A: 49
639-C: 50
641-K: 29
644-C: 15
644-D: 16
688-B: 86, 87
688-J: 158
688-K: 157
688-M: 181, 182, 183, 184
707-A-7: 78, 81
707-A-12: 76
707-A-15: 80, 160, 161
707-B-7: 79
707-D-4: 77
772-A-1: 91
772-E: 90
785-E-3: 88, 89
785-M: 186, 87
785-S: 142
817-N: 104
840-A-6: 190
804-C-2: 191
844-B-8: 111, 112
885-D-1: 54, 55

## 1947–48*

9-A-24: 176
12-D: 192, 195
12-E: 193, 194
19: 59

28-A-3: 41
28-A-6: 42
28-B-1: 47
28-B-2: 43, 44, 45, 46

## Appendix F. Index to Selected Minnesota Attorney General Opinions

47-F: 188
48-B-1: 149
53-A-1: 1
58-C: 87, 88, 89, 90
58-I: 92
58-0: 91
59-A-3: 99
59-A-5: 28
59-A-7: 96, 97
59-A-9: 145
59-A-32: 144
59-A-40: 160, 161
59-A-41: 95
59-A -53: 142
62-C: 140
63-A-11: 121
82: 180
85: 79
85-A: 80, 81
86-A-34: 179
90-B-3: 132
103-I: 22
104-A-6: 130
107-A-12: 104
107-B: 102
107-B-1: 98
120: 93
124-B: 123
125-A-41: 159
128-D: 16
133-B-59: 23
140-F-2: 101
145: 175
145-A: 178
145-B-1: 17, 18, 19
148-A-10: 3
159-A-3: 30
159-B-1: 34

159-B-10: 32
159-C-6: 33
166-A-10: 39
166-E-4: 31
174-B: 38
183-G: 53
183-K: 55
183-S: 40, 56
184-I: 48
199-B-4: 20
210-D-7: 14
213-H: 182
217-B-5: 73
217-F: 75, 76, 77
217-F-4: 74
218-C-3: 61, 62
218-E: 70, 71
218-G-1: 65
218-G-13: 66, 67
218-G-15: 64
218-J-1: 63
218-J-9: 72
218-R: 68, 69, 100, 162
232-D: 202, 211
234-B: 83
240-H: 181
248-A-1: 187
248-B-3: 186
270-D-12: 60
273-A-23: 15
280-G: 52
285-B: 146
310: 82, 234
310-H-1-A: 78
320-I: 177
357: 224
358-A: 114
358-A-3: 112

358-A-7: 111
358-D: 115
358-D-3: 116
358-E-1: 119
358-E-4: 120
358-E-6: 113
358-E-7: 117, 118
361-D: 7
373-B-5: 125
373-B-15: 126
373-B-17-D: 231
373-B-18-A: 124
374: 127
379-C-8-B: 105
385-B-2: 183
387-G-1: 108
387-G-7: 156
390-B-1: 128, 129
390-C-12: 131
396-C-18: 109
396-G-16: 110
406-B: 190, 191
407-H: 196
408-C: 155
414-A-9: 219
414-A-11: 198, 203, 204, 206, 207
4b4-B-12: 209
414-D-6: 199
414-D-7: 205
4b4-D-12: 200, 201
414-D-13: 208
414-D-14: 210
419-F-1: 197
421-A-5: 216
421-A-17: 220, 221, 222, : 223
421-B-5: 217, 218
425-C-13: 232, 233
430: 230, 235

431: 141
434-A-1: 2, 133
434-A-6: 139
434-B-12: 54
434-B-13-A: 51
439-H: 135
440-B: 158
460-E: 193
469-A: 138
470: 136
470-B: 137
472-I: 58
474-J-2: 225
476-B-1: 103
476-C-1: 157
477-B-34: 143
494-A: 24
510-B-9: 27
519-D: 83
519-D-1: 215
519-I: 212
519-M: 37, 213, 214
521: 171
52b-D: 167
521-P-4: 168, 169, 170, 172
540-B: 164
540-C: 163
540-J: 165
541: 122
554-E: 227, 228, 229
556-A-1: 173, 174
602-B: 8, 9, 10
602-C: 12
602-D: 11
602-E: 4
602-G: 6
602-I: 5
602-J: 13

# Appendix F. Index to Selected Minnesota Attorney General Opinions

624-C-2: 152
624-C-4: 153
624-E-5: 151
627-E: 50
627-J-3: 49
642-B-4: 106
672-B-7: 57
679-G: 21
688-A: 150
688-M: 147, 148
707-A-7: 84
707-C: 86

733: 25. 26
785-E-2: 94
817-F: 36
830-C: 226
840-C-13: 166
844-A-3: 85
844-B: 154
844-F: 35
844-G: 184, 185
847: 134
851-F: 29
870-B: 189
989-A-12: 107

## 1949–50*

6: 12
12-B-4: 145
12-D: 139
12-E: 146
21: 257
28-A-3: 60
28-A-9: 62
28-B-2: 61
37-B-3: 93
45-D: 148
58-G: 82
59-A-4: 126
59-A-8: 149
59-A-9: 43, 163
59-A-14: 88
59-A-22: 101
59-A-29: 142
59-A-32: 164
59-A-34: 196
59-A-40: 182
59-A-41: 137
59-A-49: 110

59-A-53: 105, 177
82-L: 203
85-A: 136
85-C: 140
90-B: 156
103-A: 151
104-B-8: 157
107-A-1: 108
107-B-4: 94
120: 134, 135
121-B-3: 153
121-B-4: 152
124-J: 154, 155
125-A-15: 89
125-A-17: 81
125-A-20: 180
125-A-64: 198, 199, 200
128-B: 13
133-B-8: 38
133-B-13: 31
144-B-3: 16
144-B-5: 15

144-B-17: 14
159-B-1: 45, 57
159-B-7: 49
161-A-16-b: 54
166-C: 40
166-C-3: 41
166-E-4: 50, 51, 52, 53
168: 58
170-D: 55
170-H: 56
174-A: 59
183-J: 64
193-B-24: 30
197-B: 207
216i: 230
217-B-8: 70
217-B-9: 73
217-D-8: 71
217-F-3: 74, 75
217-H: 72, 76, 77
218-G-10: 66
218-G-13: 67
218-J-4: 65
218-J-6: 68
18-J-8: 69
218-R: 103, 147
229-A-11: 114
232-d: 211, 213, 214, 215, 216, 217, 218
234-B: 86
260-A-4: 18
266-A-12: 21
266-B-11: 19, 20
268-H: 22
280-B: 204
280-M: 205
285-A: 100
285-B: 23, 24

307-B: 25
324-G: 220
324-K: 221
331-B-1: 144
339-G-2: 195
339-O-2: 197
341i: 39
347i: 29
347-K: 28
348-B: 26
353-A-3: 91
358-B-1: 130
358-D-4: 133
358-E-1: 129
358-E-7: 131, 132
365-a-12: 210
371-A-5: 209
371-B-9: 208
373-A-2: 158
373-B-9-E: 160
373-B-10: 159
373-B-16: 161
377-A: 119A
377-B-1: 113
377-B-8: 118
377-B-10: 186
371-B-10-d: 116, 117
379-C-8-c: 119
380-B-4: 115
382-B: 189
387-B-10: 176
390-A-21: 11
390-C-1: 162
396-F: 128
396-G-7: 127
406-d: 254
406-E: 83
407-K: 240

## Appendix F. Index to Selected Minnesota Attorney General Opinions

408: 245
410-B: 262
412-a-10: 251
414-A-11: 227, 228, 229, 231
414-D-4: 222
414-D-6: 224, 225
414-d-10: 226
414-d-12: 223
419-B: 260
421-a-5: 247, 248
421-a-8: 243
421-a-17: 249, 250
421-B-1: 246
421-C-4: 242
421-C-25: 241
423-C: 252, 253
423-H: 256
425-C: 259, 261
425-C-11: 258
425-C-17: 263
430: 84, 85
434-A-6: 175, 188
437-a-20: 187
440-B: 96, 97, 99, 190
441-B: 184
441-H: 191
450-A-16: 109
469-A-13: 138
469-C: 167
469-C-5: 183
471-K: 143
474-J-2: 219
476-A-5: 95
476-B-10: 104
484-E-1: 122
484-E-4: 123
505-i: 255
505-J: 212

510-B: 32
510-B-5: 33, 34
519-A: 234
519-H: 106, 107, 235
519-K: 236
519-M: 237
521-P-4: 27, 194
531: 232
531-K: 233
540: 192
541: 150
554-i: 244
596-B: 202
602: 6
602-B: 1
602-C: 2
602-E: 3, 7
602-H: 4, 5
602-J: 8
605-A-13: 181
614-R: 92, 238
622-B: 42
622-i-1: 48
622-i-2: 47
622-i-8: 47~A
624-A-6: 171
624-C-2: 169
624-C-10: 170
624-C-11: 168
624-D-3: 173
624-D-10: 172
624-D-11: 179
627-M: 63
632-a-14: 239
632-B-2: 37
642-A-5: 112
642-B-4: 111
642-B-11: 1

643-F: 178
688-C-1: 165
688-M: 98
705-A-3: 9
707-A-4: 78
707-A-7: 79, 80
707-A-12: 46
707-B-5: 117
785: 166
785-S: 147
802-C: 185
817-F: 87

817-N: 120
817-O: 44
840-A-9: 10
840-C-3: 193
844-B-7: 124, 174
851-I: 17, 201
905-B: 141
913-F: 125
983-L: 206
989-A-6: 35
989-A-24: 36
1001-B: 90
1001-H: 102

## 1951–52*

12-A: 140
12-A-3: 143
12-B: 142
12-B-1: 141
12-B-5: 144
37-B-1: 94
40-A-6: 45
43-B-4: 96
44-B-2: 97
59-A-7: 93, 95
59-A-22: 102
59-A-40: 188
59-A-53: 95, 124
61-D: 105
85-C: 147
85-F: 82, 83
103-F: 26
103-i: 27
104-A-9: 152
104-B-8: 147
107-A-1: 108
107-A-8: 109

107-B-5: 99
120: 91, 92
121-A-1: 29
121-B-7: 36
124-A: 145
124-H: 146
125-A-27: 200
125-A-33: 168
125-A-40: 106
125-A-64: 166, 202
127-B: 98
131: 24
133-B-8: 31
133-B-24-d: 33
133-B-43: 28
133-B-59: 37
140-F: 100
144-A-1: 10
144-A-4: 11
146: 30
154-B-4: 49
159-A-5: 43

## Appendix F. Index to Selected Minnesota Attorney General Opinions

159-A-17: 47
159-A-18: 48
159-B-2: 44, 46
166-C-9: 41
166-F-2: 39
166-F-3: 40
166-F-7: 40
169: 57, 58
170-F-2: 59
172-C: 62
180-d: 61
183-i: 65
183-R: 68
187-A-6: 42
187-A-9: 67, 69, 70
188-B: 132
217-B-8: 75
217-C: 179
218-J-12: 77, 78
218-K: 73
218-R: 76
225-A: 194
229-D-15: 128
232-d: 217
238-H: 210
238-i: 101, 133
260-A-5: 12
266-B-7: 15
266-B-17: 14
266-B-24: 17
268-H: 203
270-D: 164, 165, 167
276-C: 214
277-B-4: 128
285-B: 23
306-A: 21
306-B: 20
306-B-6: 18

306-B-9: 22
307-J: 19
310: 245
310-L: 81
339-C: 205
339-M: 208
339-O-2: 206, 207
341-K-9: 13
347-K: 25
358-A-3: 173
358-B-1-a: 172
358-B-2: 174
358-E-2: 175
358-E-9: 176
359-A-21: 153
365-B-12: 213
373-A-4: 148, 152
373-B-9-e: 149
373-B-11: 151
373-B-17-d: 150
317-A-11: 50, 113
377-B-1: 112
377-B-10-j: 120
377-B-10-k: 119
379-C-1-d: 111
379-C-8-c: 118
379-C-11: 114, 115, 116
387: 197
387-B-10: 134
390-A-1: 154
390-A-8: 155
390-A-12: 159
390-B-1: 156
390-C-9: 157, 158
396-C-4: 117
396-F-1: 139
396-F-3: 121
396-G: 136

396-G-6: 137
396-G-10: 138
401-B-21: 171
401-B-22: 170
412-A-9: 227
412-A-10: 227
412-A-13: 226
412-A-24: 237
414-A-2: 216
414-B-5: 219
414-D-6: 215
414-D-11: 218
419-f-1: 240
421-A-9: 232
421-A-14: 234
421-A-17: 235
421-C-4: 236
421-C-25: 233
424-A-11: 220, 221
425-C-6: 244
425-C-11: 241
425-C-13: 243
430: 129, 130
434-A-6: 189, 190
434-C-8: 191
437-A-12: 111
441-H: 182, 183
442-A-1: 104
469-A-13: 169
469-A-15: 192
470-C: 162, 163
471-M: 160
472-C: 64
474-D-1: 238
474-G-2: 239
476-A-15: 103
477-A: 180
477-A-1: 177

477-A-34: 181
480-A: 135
484-E-1: 184, 186
484-E-2: 185
490-J-2: 66, 71
495-C: 211
498-C: 24
510-C-5: 35
519-C: 224, 225
519-D: 231
519-K: 229
519-L: 230
519-M: 60
519-q: 228
521-P-4: 204
546-d: 209
554-i: 222
556-A-5: 193, 200
602: 6
602-F: 5
602-i: 7
602-J: 8, 9
622-A-6: 57
622-A-19: 51
622-i-8: 54, 55
622-i-16: 53
622-J-20: 56
632-B-2: 32
639-e: 63
639-i: 66
642-A-12: 3, 4
642-B-9: 110
645-B-16: 212
681-A: 89
700-A-3: 242
707-A: 87
707-A-1: 8
707-A-4: 85, 86

# Appendix F. Index to Selected Minnesota Attorney General Opinions

707-A-7: 88
707-A-12: 38, 90
707-A-15: 84
733-d: 34, 178
733-G: 74
772-C-5: 223
779-A-5: 161
785: 196
817-F: 52
835-A: 79. 80
844-F-3: 131
844-F-6: 50

850-i: 72
851: 195
870-J: 187
904: 199-A, 201
923-D: 2
923-P: 1
989-A-16: 123, 125
989-A-18: 122, 127
989-A-19: 126
989-A-24: 16
1001-A: 198
1001-B: 107, 199
1001-H: 103

## 1953–54*

12-B-1: 157
12-D: 109
12-E: 107, 108
16-B: 22
21-A: 174
37-A-1: 49
37-B-7: 78
44-B-17: 145
58-C: 67, 68
59-A-14: 74
59-A-29: 123
59-A-33: 122
59-a-41: 124
59-A-52: 158
59-B-11: 146
62: 130
85-a: 122
85-F: 41
90-B: 172
90-C-8: 35
90-E-6: 123
107-A-1: 81

107-B-16: 84
120: 69, 70, 71, 72, 73
121-A-4: 110
125-a-42: 136
125-B: 75
144-B-15: 15
144-B-18: 14
159-A-5: 38, 43
161-A-22: 36
161-B-5: 39, 40
166-C: 32
166-C-2: 29
166-C-5: 27, 28
166-C-8: 30
166-E-3: 33, 34
166-E-4: 27
166-F-4: 37
166-F-6: 31
172-C: 44
180-D: 45
183-R: 47
193-A-3: 24

217: 56
217-B-5: 57
217-F-1: 42
217-F-2: 59
217-H: 58
218-G-8: 54
218-J-1: 55
238-i: 134
248: 147
248-B-3: 23
249-B-23: 50
266-A-12: 19
266-B-7: 17
266-B-24: 18
268-F: 20, 21
270-A-3: 51
210-D: 124
285-C: 94, 95
292-E: 131
310-H-1-A: 61
322-G: 93
339-D-4: 149
353-a-1: 151
358-B-2: 127
358-D-5: 126
358-e-2: 125
358-e-9: 128
369-M: 150
373-B-6: 112
373-B-11: 113
373-B-15: 115
373-B-17-a: 116
373-B-17-c: 111
373-B-17-d: 114, 174
377-A-4: 88
377-A-13: 83
377-A-15: 87
377-B-10-h: 89

379-C-8-b: 85.
379-C-8-c: 86
379-C-13-d: 90
387-B-1: 97
387-G-8: 98
390-A-11: 118
390-A-16: 111
390-A-17: 119
396-C: 100, 102
396-C-1: 96
396-C-18: 105
396-G-16: 103, 104
406-B: 153
408-C: 154, 155, 156
410-B: 173
414-A-11: 160
414-D-12: 159
414-D-14: 161
418-a-1: 164
421-C: 165
421-C-4: 166
421-C-14: 167
425-C: 168, 169, 172
425-C-13: 170, 171
440-B: 77
442-A-20: 76
471-K: 120
474-C: 152
476-A: 79, 145
477-B-20: 133
477-B-26: 132
480-B: 99, 101
484-E-1: 135
505-D: 168
519-O: 162
519-q: 163
520-D: 9
521-G: 148

# Appendix F. Index to Selected Minnesota Attorney General Opinions

521-P-4: 15
602-B: 3
602-F: 6
602-i: 4, 5
602-J: 7
622-B: 42
622-i-11: 43
624-C-16: 142, 143
624-D-9: 144
624-D-11: 106
627-B-3: 46
642-A-12: 80
688-a: 140
688-K: 141
705-A-3: 8
707-A: 62
701-A-2: 66
707-A-7: 63
707-A-15: 64, 65
763-B: 1

772-A-6: 2
779-K: 16
785-3: 121
802-A-10: 53
802-A-15: 52
817-A: 82
817-F: 111
835-A: 60
840-A-3: 12
840-C-2: 10, 13
840-C-1: 11
850-i: 50
851-F: 139
870-J: 129
905-J: 137, 138
911-K: 48
989-A-6: 26
989-A-12: 92
989-A-18: 91
989-A-24: 25

## 1955–56*

4: 4
9A: 7
9A34: 6
12-D: 102
29-A-3: 10
29-A-20: 8
29-A-26: 9
53-B: 11
59-A-9: 87
59-A-32: 88, 118, 119
59-A-40: 89, 90, 91
59-A-53: 92, 93
59-B-11: 94
59-B-14: 95

63-A-11: 57
85-C: 16
90-B: 103
90-C-2: 42, 43
92-A-16: 25
92-B-11: 26
92-C: 2
103-A: 104
107-B-10: 148
120: 12, 14, 105
121-A-7: 106
125-A-20: 107
133-B-45: 31
135A8: 5

135-B-5: 3
159-A-20: 47
159-B-4: 48
166-A-3: 56
166-C: 39
166-C-3: 38
166-C-8: 46
166-e-4: 44, 50, 51
169-D: 52
172-C: 54
180-D: 55
185-B-4: 45
187-A-6: 59
193-a-3: 108
196-N: 15
201: 18
209: 19
209-G: 20
217-B-9: 84
217-F-3: 82
218-G-5: 80
218-J-10: 83
218-R: 81
229-A-7: 72
232-D: 140
234: 1
242-A-2: 142, 143
248-A-2: 32
248-B-11: 130
250: 76
252-L: 96
266-A: 27
266b-14: 28
270-D: 77, 78, 109
270-D-12: 79
271: 67, 68, 69, 70, 71
273-D-2: 97, 120
276-H: 98

217-A-4: 63
291: 73
300-M: 85
306-A: 30
311-G: 21
331-B: 121
341-F: 35
347-F: 131
349-a-2: 29
353-A-3: 129
358-f: 115
365-A-5: 134
373-B-11: 110, 111
373-b-17(f): 112
374: 135
379-C-11: 113
387-B-9: 99
396-G-1: 122
408-C: 100, 123
418-A-13: 144
418-B-6: 145
421-A-14: 146
421-C-30: 139
424-A-3: 138
425-C-10: 147
434-A-6: 116
434-B-20: 60
441-H: 111
472-F: 61
484-E-4: 62, 124
510-B: 31
519-D-1: 53
521-j-2: 132
523-E-4: 125
531: 141
602-J: 22
605-A-5: 34
616-B-11: 136

618-A-11: 131
618-B: 49
632-E-12: 86
639-K: 58
644-B: 13
688-K: 126
705: 24
705-A-2: 23
707-A-12: 40, 41
733-g: 36, 37
785-S: 127
817-a: 149
835: 17

840-B: 133
843: 152
843-K: 153
844-B-1: 101
885-A-1: 66
885-B: 64, 65
920: 2
920-C: 151
920-D: 150
989-A-7: 75
989-A-18: 74
989-A-24: 33
989-B-5: 128
1001-A: 114

## 1957–58*

10-A: 50, 143
16-C: 106
18-D: 107
21-A: 177
29a-5: 3
29a-12: 5
29a-26: 4
53a: 21
58-C: 90
59-A-22: 96, 101
59-A-25: 92
59-A -53: 100
59-B-11: 82
61-i: 81
62-C: 65
63-A-2: 87
63-A-5: 80
63-B-20: 94
64-N: 63
90-E-5: 83

92a-12: 9
120: 84, 151
121-A-8: 113
121-B: 25
124-B: 115
124-C: 124
125-A-27: 120
125-A-28: 109, 116
125-A-64: 158
125-B: 110
125-B-27: 42
140-F-2: 104
141d-7: 10
159-B-1: 48
161-A-25: 47
166-B: 41
166-D-1a: 35
166-E: 37
166-E-3: 38
166-F-3: 36

172-C-5: 53
175-A: 111
175-K: 169
180-D: 40
185-B-1: 60, 61
186-G: 62
199b-3: 33
201c: 8
211a-7: 6
218-R: 78
229-A: 67
238-i: 66
249-B-3: 75
249-B-8: 54, 55
266a-11: 11
266a-13: 14
266b-8: 12, 13
268f: 31
268h: 30
270-D: 52, 86
273-A-7: 74
277-H: 129
280-D: 76
280-G: 59
280-H: 77
285-B: 39, 118
307c: 34
307i: 16
307j: 18
307k: 17
311-A: 174
316: 56, 58
322-B: 108
328-A-1: 159
331-A-1: 162, 166, 167
331-A-4: 165
331-A-11: 168
331-B: 161, 163, 164

331-D: 51, 170, 172
338-A: 98
347d: 22
341j: 20, 23
358-A-3: 114
358-E-1: 85
358-E-6: 146
310i: 24
373-B-23: b1b
377-A-3: 127
377-A-7: 102
377-B-1: 130, 131, 132
377-B-3: 103
396-G-7: 138
396-G-9: 68
399: 117
408-C: 93, 95
421-A-4: 176
425-C-10: 105
441-H: 133
442-B-11: 128
469-A-11: 150
469-A-12: 152
469-B-1: 88
469-B-6: 136, 137
470-B: 141
471-B-1: 147
471-E: 139
471-H: 144
411-M: 142
477-A: 99
477b-28: 19
478-A: 145
484-E-4: 135, 140
494b-7: 26, 27, 28
494b-23: 29
519: 173
519-M: 43, 45

521-J-2: 157
521-P-4: 155, 156
602-H: 126
602-J: 123
605b-35: 32
622i-11: 46
624D-11: 149
624D-17: 153
632-D: 71
635-D: 72
644-B: 73
645-B-23: 160
700d-21: 7
705-A: 175
707-A-4: 91

768-R: 49
785-B: 148
802-A-10: 79
817-F: 64, 69, 134
817-o: 44
833-f: 1
840-A-1: 154
844-B-8: 89
851-F: 97, 112
851i: 15
933-p: 2
980-A-8: 57
983-G: 125
989-A-18: 70
1001-B: 119, 121, 122

## 1959–60*

12b: 130
12c-1: 104
18d: 31
21d: 91
59a-4: 68
59a-25: 70
59a-32: 11
59a-40: 1
59b-4: 9
85b: 112
90a-1: 118
102b-2: 75
103f: 23
104b-8: 21
120: 67, 125
123d: 29
123e: 30
133b-35: 52
135a-8: 2

146c: 3
159a-8: 132
159a-13: 40
161b-2: 39
161b-4: 41
166a-4: 44
166c-8: 131
169-L: 43
185b-4: 53
203e-4: 16
206: 76
210d-2: 17, 19
211d-16: 18
217b-2: 58
217f-2: 57
218g-11: 56
229a: 71
232d: 89, 90
238-i: 14

240g: 46
248b-7: 74
253b-4: 49
266b-11: 31
266b-21: 36
268-A: 1
268b: 38
270-d: 42, 129
270-K: 48
273a-16: 133
285b: 26, 28
290b: 108
291f: 60
301c-1: 34
306b-3: 61
307j: 63
307k: 64
307-L: 62
310: 96, 97
311f: 103
328a-6: 22
331a-1: 47
358b-2: 72
358e-1: 8
358e-9: 128
370-K: 20
373b-15: 32
377-A-4: 13
377b-1: 107
379c-13c: 109
387a-3: 59
396c-6: 65
396g-4: 12
396g-17: 127
410b: 98
412a-8: 101
412a-9: 77
412a-11: 102

412a-27: 95
414a-9: 85
418a: 80
418a-11: 82, 83
418b-13: 81
419f-1: 93
421a: 88
421a-4: 86
421a-13: 84
421c-4: 87
425c: 99
425c-11: 94
425c-13: 100
469a-8: 66, 69
469b-7: 115
471m: 105
472-o: 55
414e-2: 92
476a-3: 113
476a-9: 124
484e-1: 123
484e-4: 116
484f: 5, 10
487c-3: 50
521a: 73
523c: 27
531: 78, 79
618a-2: 111
624d-8: 106
644e: 15
707a-4: 6
707a-15: 117, 119, 120, 121
779k: 35
798b: 25
817d: 24
817n: 110
843-k: 45
847a-6: 122

905j: 33
928a-2: 4

928b: 51
989a-25: 54
1001h: 114, 126

## 1961–68**

5f: 299
8: 211, 301
10a: 81
18d: 63
21-f: 118
24: 97
28a-9: 312
28b-2: 310
28c-5: 304
29a-3: 291
29-A-18: 290
29a-20: 296
32: 292
47f: 277
53b: 292
59a-1: 205, 307
59a-4: 120, 121
59a-5: 89
59a-9: 2, 208
59a-15: 9, 13
59-A-22: 43, 44, 46, 51, 287
59-A-23: 18, 187
59-A-32: 1, 225, 229, 234, 236, 238
59a-35: 58, 66, 72, 103
59a-36: 36
59a-40: 29, 40, 41, 42, 51, 55, 67, 70, 122
59a-40(1): 52
59-A-46: 31
59a-54: 224
59b-4: 24
59b-11: 68, 69

59b-14: 209
61j: 60
62b: 35, 70
63b-2: 11
63b-5: 310
63b-24: 211
82-L: 137
86a: 302
90-G: 95
92b-18: 83
107b: 48
107-B-19: 129
107b-23: 173
110: 218
125a-14: 46
125a-38: 286
1 25-A-45: 275
125a-56: 20
125-A-64: 187
125-A-66: 23
125b-20: 55
125-B-22: 176
125b-35: 63
133b-1: 243
133b-48: 241
145b: 195, 199
145b-1: 196
156c: 186
157: 172, 174
159a-3: 145
159a-16: 144, 166
160-h: 168

161-A-14: 149
161a-20: 161
161b: 219
161b-4: 92, 98
161b-10: 163, 168
161b-11: 162
166-A-8: 155, 156, 157
166f: 141, 143
169: 161
169-j: 150
169-p: 158, 159, 160
169-W: 177, 178
170-i: 169, 110
172-C-5: 169
172-L: 99
180-g: 109
182: 313
183-G: 311
183n: 306, 309
183q: 307, 308
184f: 306
185a-4: 146
185a-5: 309
188b: 88
188d: 85, 86.88
199a-3: 245
201-A-2: 241
201b: 241
210d-7: 276
21ba-5: 276
213-f: 90, 94
213-i: 102
217f: 257
217f-2: 259, 266
217F-3: 258
218b: 264
218c-3: 265
218e: 259

218g-13: 256
218g-15: 256
218g-19: 260, 261, 262, 263
218r: 256
225i: 19, 26
229a: 274, 275
229a-9: 71
230: 287
232d: 111, 113
238-i: 228
240v: 193
248d: 181
266a-13: 249
266b-1: 247
266b-7: 249
266b-8: 248
266B-9: 272
266b-25: 248
268-L: 198
270-A-4: 260
270d: 77
270d-12: 79, 80
271: 77
273a-17: 221, 222
273a-20: 283
273c-6: 284
280b: 95
285a: 18, 21, 23
290L: 82
291f: 270
300m: 197
306B-13: 271
310: 106
310-H-1a: 100, 101
310-L: 105
311a: 135
335c-2: 186
339D-4: 191

# Appendix F. Index to Selected Minnesota Attorney General Opinions

339i-5: 194
339-o-2: 190, 191, 192
339-S: 188
346f: 179, 180
373b-17: 297
373b-17d: 298
373b-18: 74
377b-10j: 62
387-g-5: 30
387-g-7: 35
390b-1: 89
396-G-6: 64
396-G-17: 224
407: 115
408-G: 133
412a-9: 135
412A-18: 115
412a-24: 134
414a-2: 122
414A-10: 129
414A-11: 128
4b4c-7: 127
414d-2: 123
414d-6: 123, 127
414d-12: 122
418b-13: 114
418b-17: 113
418b-18: 114
421c-40: 116, 132, 136
424a-1: 117
425: 130
425c-11: 131
430: 210
434-A-6: 65, 215
441-H: 237, 239
442a-20: 45
469a-9: 49
469-A-12: 42, 53

469a-15: 57
469a-18: 239
469c-6: 50
469c-11: 64, 65
469c-12: 4
471e: 59
471f: 19, 44, 120, 223
471g: 55
47bj: 61
474g-2: 136
476: 22
476a: 171
476a-3: 32
476-B-2: 36, 59
416-B-10: 54
476-C-4: 30
477-A-1: 2
477b-3: 229
477B-19: 226
477-B-20: 184
477B-34: 227, 230, 232
484e-1: 202, 207
484e-4: 206
484f: 202
494a: 245
494a-1: 273
494a-4: 246
494b-7: 286
510b-3: 253
510c-5: 251
510c-10: 251
519q: 111
519t: 138
521b-1: 185
531s: 117, 119
602: 288
605a-20: 243
616b-4: 294

616b-10: 293
616b-11: 83
622-A-6: 148
622-A-14: 165
622b: 164
622i-3: 167
624a-3: 5
624a-6: 37
624c-11: 48
624d-5: 33, 34
624e-5: 11
627c-9: 315
627h: 312
632e: 269
635d: 270
635e: 268
635j: 268
641: 314
644: 96
644b: 99
644g: 104
688-K: 32, 71
707a: 9
707a-7: 14

707a-12: 6, 10
707a-15: 5, 12
733b: 250
733D: 252
733g: 249
775: 39
775a: 31
785d: 27, 28
829e-2: 242
835a: 105
840a-2: 193
844b: 102
850i: 3
851i: 73, 75
858: 316
876b: 87
983q: 278
983r: 278
989a-1: 76
989-A-8: 273
989a-25: 264
1001b: 54
1003: 280, 281, 282
1006: 107
1008: 182

# APPENDIX G
# Minnesota Guidelines for Legal Reference Service

The *Guidelines for Legal Reference Service*[664] were drafted in response to a need voiced by the reference librarians of the major law libraries in the Minneapolis/St. Paul area to offer consistent and responsible service to their non-primary patrons. The first draft was prepared by Barbara Golden[665] based upon ideas gleaned from a literature search and a survey of practices in major public law libraries throughout the United States. Revisions then were made by the committee members to reflect the local practices and needs of Twin Cities libraries. Reprinted below are the *Guidelines* as they were approved by the committee in January 1980, with two exceptions. To avoid confusion, references in the *Guidelines* to "appendix" were changed to "attachment" and one section has been revised to provide the correct references.

## GUIDELINES FOR LEGAL REFERENCE SERVICE

Approved by the Public Services Liaison Committee, Minnesota Association of Law Libraries.

### In General

1. The library staff will do its best to respond to all inquiries, from any source or for whatever reason. If we cannot supply the information requested, we will suggest other possible sources.
2. The staff is asked to use good judgment in deciding how much time and effort can be devoted to any one patron if others are waiting for assistance.
3. Try to identify the issues involved in a reference inquiry without allowing the patron to provide a detailed account of his/her problem or probing the motive of the patron.

---

664. As they appeared in the *Minnesota Legal Research Guide* (1st ed. 1985).
665. Co-author of the first edition.

4. Never give a patron the impression that "this is the law, the entire answer." For any inquiry beyond bare factual information, a warning should be provided (for same examples of warnings, *see* Attachment 1).
5. A librarian can provide legal information, but *under no circumstances* legal advice. That would be unauthorized practice of law, forbidden by Minnesota Statutes § 481.02.
6. Remember, the main reason why those not engaged in the practice of law, including librarians, should not practice law is that it would be contrary to the interests of those seeking assistance.
   a. A lawyer has better access to the facts in the case.
   b. A lawyer usually has more complete knowledge of the law.
   c. A lawyer is able to research the law at length.
   d. A lawyer understands the practical functioning of the legal system.
7. For a discussion of the differences between legal advice and legal information, see:
   a. Schanck, Peter C., "Unauthorized Practice of Law and the Legal Reference Librarian," 72 *Law Library Journal* 57 (Winter 1979).
   b. Mills, Robin K., "Reference Service vs. Legal Advice: Is It Possible to Draw the Line?" 72 *Law Library Journal* 179 (Spring 1979).

### In-House Reference

1. Reference service to patrons in the library has priority over telephone callers.
2. Assistance is provided for locating and using all library materials. Try to avoid using legal or library terminology that would be unknown or confusing to the patron. If possible, accompany the patron to the source and then demonstrate its use.
3. Patrons should not expect the library staff to do their research for them. Avoid explaining or interpreting substantive material as this may be construed as giving legal advice. Instead, attempt to provide alternative sources of information.
4. When possible, return to the patron and check on his/her progress. Often, a few uninterrupted moments of use in one source will help the person to understand the problem and better explain it. If the patron still has difficulty understanding the material, refer to legal aid or a legal referral service.

5. Few people are aware that the referral service will recommend a lawyer who will offer counsel on what is involved in the problem and how complex it may be for a relatively small fee. Point out that many problems can lead to the loss of more money than a lawyer would cost. Agency referrals also may be suggested (*see* Attachment 2).

## Telephone Reference

Law librarians disagree as to the advisability of providing legal reference service over the phone. On the one hand is the desire to provide optimum reference service, efficiently and conveniently, and on the other side is the increased danger of misunderstanding or neglecting to provide a pertinent piece of information. Caution and increased use of warnings is advised (*see* Attachment 1).

1. The patron in the library receives priority.
2. Telephone calls should be kept brief. To prevent excessive delays for waiting patrons in the library, take the necessary information and telephone number of the person calling and return the call as soon as it is possible to do so. Give the caller an approximate time span.
3. The telephone patron should not be permitted to take an excessive amount of staff time to do work which should be performed by the patron. The general rule would be to respond to any inquiry for factual information—a date, name, an address, etc., but should not extend to searching out a variety of facts from many sources, or to reading extended portions of printed materials aver the telephone.
4. Answers should be provided from written sources only. Inform the patron as to what source(s) you are using and what it says. **Do not** interpret the language or apply it to any particular case or set of facts.
5. If the question is too complicated to be handled over the telephone:
    a. Request that the patron come into the library.
        1. If possible, indicate the scope of the problem by stating what resources should be checked and approximately how much time this might take.

2. Indicate the extent of in-house reference service available (e.g., aid in using resources but no advice).
  b. Refer the patron to an attorney or another agency which may be better able to assist him or her (for referral suggestions, see Attachment 2).

# Attachment 1. Sample Warnings[666]

| Question | Warning |
|---|---|
| *In all cases* indicate currentness of the source. | This information is (dated from) (current through) . . . |
| Is there a law on . . . | To find the law, you must check statutes, cases, and administrative rulings and regulations. If you come into our library, we will be glad to show you how to use these sources, or you may want to consult an (attorney) (agency). |
| Is there a statute on . . . | We have the statutes in this library. We would be happy to show you how to use them if you come into the library. Public libraries also have the statutes. I would advise you to call them first to make sure they are available. *Or* I have checked the indexes to the (statutes) and (have not found one.) (this is all I've found.) There may be (something) (more) that I have not found. You should check further with an (agency) (attorney) or come into the library and research it more yourself. *And* You should be aware that case law may affect the interpretation of the statutes. If you come into the library, we also will be able to direct you to those. (**Never** give a patron a simple yes or no answer.) |

---

666. These are suggestions only. They are provided as examples of the types of statements recommended for complete and responsible legal reference service. Whether they would provide legal protection against liability for misinformation has not been determined.

| | |
|---|---|
| What is the statute of limitations? | In general, the statutes require that an action for _____ be brought within _____ (years) (months) of the act. However, I am not qualified to determine whether your particular situation will fall within this statute. (You will have to research the case law to determine when the statute is applied.) |
| What are the requirements for getting married in _____? | The statutes state _____ However, there may be some local procedures not reflected in the statutes. I would suggest that you call or write the county clerk to avoid any problems. |
| What form do I use? | These are sample forms used in this area of the law. It would be the unauthorized practice of law for me to advise you on which form to use, or how to adapt and complete them. |
| In *referring* to another library or agency. | We have (no) (very few) materials on this subject. The (library) (agency) can provide more resources. I would suggest that you phone first to determine what services they can provide you. |

## ATTACHMENT 2. MINNESOTA STATE LAW LIBRARY SUGGESTED REFERRALS[667]

### Sources

- Federal Information Center, phone 800-688-9889 (for help in getting the right federal agency).
- First Call for Help (Hennepin County), Community Information & Referral Service of United Way, Citizens Aid Building, 404 S. Eighth St., Minneapolis, MN 55404.
- First Call for Help (Ramsey, Dakota & Washington Counties), Community Information & Referral Center of United Way, 166 E. Fourth St., #310, St. Paul, MN 55101.
- *Minnesota Guidebook to State Agency Services,* State of Minnesota, Minnesota's Bookstore, 117 University Ave., St. Paul, MN 55155.

### Agencies/Organizations

- Public Information Policy Analysis, 651-296-6733 (provides assistance to citizens and government agencies in answering questions about Minnesota government data practices, including freedom of information and data privacy).
- Minnesota Attorney General, 651-296-6196 or 800-657-3787 (for interpretation of state laws).

### African Americans

- Minneapolis Urban League, 651-521-1099.
- St. Paul Urban League, 651-224-5771.

### Aged

- Legal Advocacy for Older Americans, 651-332-1441 (people aged 60 and older).
- Legal Services for Senior Citizens (Anoka County), 651-427-4613.
- Minnesota Age and Opportunity Center (MAO), 651-863-1000 (people aged 55 and older).

---

667. Web address <http://www.lawlibrary.state.mn.us/refer.html>; phone: 651-296-2775; fax: 651-296-6740.

- Ombudsman-Senior Services (Minneapolis), 651-673-3004 (for all senior citizens).
- Senior Advocates (St. Paul), 651-224-7301 (people aged 60 and older).

## Agriculture

- Minnesota Family Farm Law Project/Farmers' Legal Action Group, 651-223-5333 or 800-233-4534 (provides specialized legal information and services concerning agriculture and farming).

## AIDS-HIV-ARC

- Minnesota AIDS Project. 341-2060. Provides legal assistance, health assistance, transportation, case management, counseling, and other services to people with AIDS or AIDS-related complex.

## Consumers

- Hennepin County Attorney, citizen protection/economic crime, 651-348-4528.
- Minnesota Attorney General Consumer Protection, 651-296-3353 or 651-296-9663.
- Minnesota Public Interest Research Group (MPIRG), 651-627-4035.

## Crime Victims

- Battered Women's Legal Advocacy Project, St. Paul 651-223-6223 or 800-313-2666.
- Citizens' Council Victim Services (24 hrs.), 651-340-5400.
- Crime Victim Ombudsman-State of Minnesota , 651-282-6258 or 800-247-0390.
- Family Violence Network - Crisis Line (24-hour hotline), 651-770-0777.
- Sexual Assault Resource Service (Hennepin County Medical Center), 651-347-5832.

# Appendix G. Minnesota Guidelines for Legal Reference Service

## Criminal

- Criminal Defense Services, Inc., 651-215-0668 (for those who don't qualify for public defender).
- Dakota County Public Defender, 651-437-4188.
- Federal Public Defender, 651-348-1755.
- Hennepin County Public Defender, 651-348-7530.
- Legal Rights Center, 651-337-0030 (an alternative public defender program providing criminal defense attorneys for low income and disadvantaged adults and juveniles).
- Neighborhood Justice Center (NJC), 651-222-4703 (an alternative public defender program and private nonprofit organization providing criminal defense for minorities and low-income people).
- Ramsey County Public Defender, 651-215-0600.
- Scott County Public Defender, 651-454-8689.
- State Public Defender, 651-627-6980 (handles criminal defense appeals for indigent people).
- First District Office, State Office, 651-953-6070 (Public Defenders Office).

## Disabled

- Minnesota Disability Law Center, 651-334-5785 or 800-292-4150; TDD 612-332-4668 (provides specialized legal information for people with developmental and physical disabilities).
- Minnesota Mental Health Law Project, 651-332-1441 or 800-292-4150; TDD 612-332-4668.
- Parent Advocacy Coalition for Education Rights, 651-827-2968.

## Divorce

- Chrysalis-Legal Assistance for Women, 651-871-2603.
- Men's Defense Association, 651-464-7887.
- U.S. Divorce Reform, 651-890-7459.
- Women's Advocates, 651-227-8284 (crisis line) or 651-227-9966 (business line).

### Gays and Lesbians

- Lambda Justice Center, 651-379-2383 (preventive legal education, referrals and work place diversity training, for lesbian, gay, bisexual, and transsexual people).
- Gay and Lesbian Community Action Council Legal Advocacy Program, 651-822-0127 (provides legal referrals and related services).

### Human Rights

- Minnesota Civil Liberties Union (MCLU), 651-522-2423.
- Minnesota Human Rights Department, 651-296-5663.
- Minnesota Advocates for Human Rights, 651-341-3302.

### Landlord/Tenant

- Community Action HOME Line, rental housing problem: 651-933-0017; mortgage foreclosure: 651-933-9639, ext. 0 (serves suburban Hennepin County).
- Minnesota Multihousing Association Hot Line, 651-858-8222.
- Minnesota Tenants Union, 651-871-7485.
- St. Paul Tenants Union, 651-221-0501.

### Lawyers Referral

- Dakota County, 651-431-3200.
- Hennepin County Bar Association, 651-339-8777 (lawyer referral and information line).
- Minnesota Women Lawyers, 651-338-3205.
- Minnesota State Bar Association (statewide), 800-292-4152 (provides information and referrals to people not served by Hennepin, Dakota, Ramsey, and Washington counties' legal services programs).
- Ramsey County Bar Association, 651-224-1775 (attorney referral line).
- Resources and Counseling for the Arts, 651-292-4381 (referrals and information; once referred to a lawyer, the lawyer will provide up to one-half hour of free legal consultation to artists).
- Washington County Attorney Referral Service, 651-351-7132.

Appendix G. Minnesota Guidelines for Legal Reference Service 393

## Legal Assistance

- Dakota County Legal Assistance, 651-431-3200.
- Judicare of Anoka County, 651-783-4970, fax 651-783-4959 (provides free legal services to low income residents of Anoka County; civil cases only).
- Legal Aid Society of Minneapolis, 651-332-1441, main number 651-334-5970; new client number 800-292-4150; mental health number TDD, 651-332-4668 (serves Hennepin County; handles consumer, family, housing, juvenile, and public benefits law; has special programs to help Southeast Asian refugees, older Americans and people with developmental disabilities and mental illnesses).
- Legal Aid Society of Minneapolis, Northside office, 651-588-2099 (handles residents of north and northeast side of Minneapolis; legal help for low-income people; civil cases only. Consumer issues).
- Legal Aid Society of Minneapolis, Southside office, 651-827-3774 (handles residents of south side of Minneapolis; housing discrimination in the Hennepin area).
- Legal Assistance of Ramsey County, 651-222-5863, new clients, 651-222-4731, between the hours of 9:00–12:00 and 1:00–3:00 (helps low-income families in family law, housing, social security benefits, and welfare).
- Southern Minnesota Regional Legal Services, 651-440-1040 (serves low-income families in Dakota, Carver, and Scott counties).
- University of Minnesota Law School Clinic, 651-625-5515 (serves low-income people of Hennepin and Ramsey counties with civil legal problems (if a student/clerk is available)).
- Volunteer Lawyer Network, 651-339-9139 (same number for TDD) (serves low-income people of Hennepin county with civil legal problems).
- William Mitchell Law Clinic, 651-290-6351 (serves people of Hennepin and Ramsey counties with civil legal problems (if a student/clerk is available)).

## Migrants

- Migrant Legal Services. 291-2837 or 800-652-9733 (provides civil legal information and services to migrant workers).

## Municipal Law

- League of Minnesota Cities, 651-281-1200.
- Office of Citizen Service, 651-266-8989 (serves St. Paul citizens. Includes the Mayor and City Council information and complaint functions, the City Clerk's office and a communication unit).

## Native Americans

- Southern MN Regional Legal Services and East Side American Indian Outreach Office, 651-771-4455 or 800-326-1752 (serves Ramsey, Dakota, and Washington counties).
- Minnesota American Indian Bar Association, 651-282-5708 (provides legal information for Native Americans).

## Prisoners

- Legal Advocacy Project (LAP), 651-627-5416 (a division of the State Public Defender; handles prison disciplinary cases and supervisor release hearing of relocation hearing (parole revocation hearing)).
- Legal Assistance to MN Prisoners (LAMP), 651-625-6336 (a division of the State Public Defender; provides civil legal assistance to incarcerated people in Minnesota state institutions).

## Research and Writing

- Legal Research Center, 651-332-4950 (provides legal and factual research and writing to U.S. and Canadian attorneys in corporate or private practice and factual medical research).

## Southeast Asians

- United Cambodian Association of Minnesota (UCAM), 651-222-3299 or 800-326-1588 (provides legal services to Cambodians).

## Spanish-Speaking

- Centro Legal, 651-642-1890 (provides legal representation to Hispanic and low-income individuals in immigration, family, consumer, housing, employment, and government benefits law. Only serves Minneapolis and surrounding areas).

- SMRLS Oficina Legal, 651-291-0110 or 800-223-1368 (clients only) (immigration law).

## Taxes

- Federal, 800-829-1040.
- Minnesota, 651-296-3781 (Help Line).

## Special Collections in Law Libraries

### Hamline University Law Library

- English law.

### Hennepin County Law Library

- Municipal codes for cities in Hennepin County.
- State encyclopedias.
- Practice materials.

### Minnesota State Law Library

- Canadian law.
- Selected Minnesota documents.

### Ramsey County Law Library

- Municipal codes for cities in Ramsey County.

### University of Minnesota Law Library

- State administrative codes.
- Foreign and international law.
- Selected state documents from all states.

### William Mitchell College of Law Library

- U.S. Supreme Court records and briefs.

## ATTACHMENT 3. LEGAL SERVICES MEMORANDUM

O. James Werner, San Diego County Law Librarian, has composed the following memorandum to be kept at the reference desk and handed out to patrons as needed. The Public Services Liaison Committee thinks that this is a particularly clear and concise statement of the law librarian's position.

[Letterhead]

MEMORANDUM

TO:  Persons Needing Legal Services

FROM: The Librarian

SUBJECT: Legal Services and the Law Library

Some library patrons do not realize that it is unlawful for members of the Law Library staff to help patrons *interpret* legal materials they read or to *advise* them how the law might apply to their situation. That type of service would constitute the unauthorized practice of law and could subject the staff member and the Law Library to prosecution. It would also require an amount of personal service beyond what a staff of our size can provide and still carry out their other duties.

For those reasons, our staff must limit themselves to advising you which books might be helpful to you, where they are located, and how to find information in them. Please do not think our staff is being uncooperative when they suggest that you interpret the materials you read for yourself and make your own decision as to how the materials you have read applies to you. Our staff will be happy to help you find the materials you need, and to show you how to use the various legal publications.

If you need further help to solve your legal problem, you may consult [relevant legal services directory, e.g., *People's Rights and the Law: Where*

## Appendix G. Minnesota Guidelines for Legal Reference Service

*to go for Legal Help in the Twin Cities*] at our Public Services Desk. Also, listed below are additional services not included in that directory.

- ▸ *Conciliation Court: A User's Guide to Small Claims Court,* from the office of Minnesota Attorney General Mike Hatch (Rev. version., St. Paul, MN: Minnesota Attorney General's Office 1999) 11 p.; 28 cm.
- ▸ Hyser, Susan M., *A Guide to Minnesota's Conciliation Court: People's Rights and the Law* (St. Paul, MN: Minnesota Legal Services Coalition 1998) 25 p.: ill.; 28 cm. Developed by the Community Legal Education Program of Mid-Minnesota Legal Assistance and written by Susan M. Hyser.
- ▸ Greeman, James, *People's Courts: A User's Guide to Conciliation Courts in Minnesota* ([Minneapolis, MN: Minnesota Public Interest Research Group 1991) 52 p.: ill.; 21 cm.

# APPENDIX H
## Selected Legal Research Texts

This is a very selective listing of general legal research texts the authors consult when faced with a difficult legal research problem. They are personal favorites of the authors, and the list is not exhaustive by any means.

*Effective Legal Research,* Miles O. Price, Harry Bitner & Shirley Raissi Bysiewicz (4th ed. Boston: Little, Brown 1979), xix, [9], 643 p.; ill.; 24 cm.
Includes bibliographical references and index.

*Fundamentals of Legal Research,* J. Myron Jacobstein, Roy M. Mersky & Donald J. Dunn (7th ed. New York: Foundation Press 1998), xlii, 810 p.; ill.; 26 cm.
University textbook series. Includes bibliographical references and index.

*How to Find the Law,* Morris Cohen, Robert C. Berring & Kent C. Olson (9th ed. St. Paul, Minn.: West 1989), xxxiv, 716 p.; 26 cm.
American casebook series. Includes bibliographical references and indexes.

*Specialized Legal Research,* Leah F. Chanin (general editor); with contributions from Joseph James Beard et al. (New York: Aspen Law & Business 1997– ), 1 v. (loose-leaf); 26 cm.
Includes bibliographies and index.

Two continuing legal education courses have produced general legal research manuals for the legal professional.

*Legal Research for Paralegals and Research Assistants* (St. Paul, MN: Minnesota State Bar Ass'n, Continuing Legal Education 1996), 1 v. (various pagings); 30 cm.

*Legal Research for Legal Assistants* (St. Paul, MN: Minnesota State Bar Ass'n, Continuing Legal Education 1995) 1 v. (various pagings); 30 cm.

Publishers' manuals are very helpful in identifying editorial quirks and biases. Also valuable are other state legal research texts that point out the special characteristics of the published legal materials of their respective states.

# APPENDIX I
# Minnesota Supreme Court Justices 1858–1999

The 1857 Minnesota Constitution vested judicial power in a system of courts and provided for a Supreme Court that would have a chief justice and two associate justices. The Constitution also provided that the number of Supreme Court justices could be increased in number (not to exceed four) by a two-thirds vote of the legislature. The court remained a "three-judge panel" until 1881 when the legislature increased the number of associate justices from two to four.[668]

In 1929, having reached the constitutional limit as to the number of associate justices, the legislature proposed a constitutional amendment to increase the number of associate justices from four to six.[669] The amendment was presented to the electorate in 1930 and was "to make provisions for two elective associate justices of the supreme court to take the place of two court commissioners now appointed by legislative authority." The vote was 428,013 "yes" and 130,833 "no."[670]

In 1973, the Minnesota Constitution was "restructured." Article 6 section 2 was amended to allow for as many as six associate justices but not more than eight. With that allowance, the legislature amended the statute to read "the supreme court shall consist of one chief justice and eight associate justices. . . ."[671]

With the creation of an intermediate Court of Appeals in 1982, the legislature reduced the number of Supreme Court associate justices from eight to six. This reduction was accomplished by attrition, for example resignation or retirement.[672]

The members of the Minnesota Supreme Court during the past 140 years are laid out in the chart below. Chief justices are listed in italics.

---

668. 1881 Minn. Laws ch. 141, §1 (amending General Statutes 1878), v. 2, ch. 63, § 1a.
669. 1929 Minn. Laws ch. 430.
670. *1931 Legislative Manual* at 364–65.
671. 1973 Minn. Laws ch. 726, § 1.
672. 1982 Minn. Laws ch. 501, § 16.

| Justice | Appointment Date | Office Tenure | |
|---|---|---|---|
| **1858–1864** ||||
| *Lafayette Emmett* | May 24, 1858 | 1858–1865 | |
| Charles E. Flandrau | May 24, 1858 | 1857–1864 | Resigned |
| Thomas Wilson | July 6, 1864 | 1864–1865 | Appointed; replaced Atwater |
| Isaac Atwater | May 24, 1858 | 1858–1864 | Term expired |
| Samuel J. R. McMillan | July 6, 1864 | 1864–1874 | Appointed; replaced Flandrau |
| **1865** ||||
| *Lafayette Emmett* | May 24, 1858 | 1858–1865 | Term expired |
| *Thomas Wilson* | July 6, 1864 | 1865–1869 | Appointed; replaced Emmett as Chief Justice |
| John M. Berry | Jan. 10, 1865 | 1865–1887 | Elected; replaced Wilson |
| Samuel J. R. McMillan | July 6, 1864 | 1864–1874 | |
| **1866–1869** ||||
| *Thomas Wilson* | July 6, 1864 | 1865–1869 | Resigned in 1869 |
| *James Gilfillan* | July 14, 1869 | 1869–1870 | Appointed; replaced Wilson as Chief Justice |
| John M. Berry | Jan. 10, 1865 | 1865–1887 | |
| Samuel J. R. McMillan | July 6, 1864 | 1864–1874 | |
| **1870** ||||
| *James Gilfillan* | July 14, 1869 | 1869–1870 | Lost election to Ripley |
| *Christopher G. Ripley* | Jan. 7, 1870 | 1870–1874 | Defeated Gilfillan in 1869 election |
| Samuel J. R. McMillan | July 6, 1864 | 1864–1874 | |
| John M. Berry | Jan. 10, 1865 | 1865–1887 | |
| **1871–1874** ||||
| *Christopher G. Ripley* | Jan. 7, 1870 | 1870–1874 | Resigned |
| *Samuel J. R. McMillan* | Apr. 4, 1874 | 1874–1875 | Appointed; replaced Ripley as Chief Justice |

## Appendix I. Minnesota Supreme Court Justices 1858–1999

| Justice | Appointment Date | Office Tenure | |
|---|---|---|---|
| John M. Berry | Jan. 10, 1865 | 1865–1887 | |
| George B. Young | Apr. 16, 1874 | 1874–1875 | Appointed; replaced McMillan |
| **1875–1880** | | | |
| *Samuel J. R. McMillan* | Apr. 4, 1874 | 1874–1875 | Resigned Mar. 10, 1875; replaced by Gilfillan |
| *James Gilfillan* | Mar. 10, 1875 | 1875–1894 | Appointed; replaced McMillan as Chief Justice |
| John M. Berry | Jan. 10, 1865 | 1865–1887 | |
| George B. Young | Apr. 16, 1874 | 1874–1875 | Term expired |
| F. R. E. Cornell | Jan. 11, 1875 | 1875–1881 | Elected; replaced Young |
| **1881[673]** | | | |
| *James Gilfillan* | Mar. 10, 1875 | 1875–1894 | |
| John M. Berry | Jan. 10, 1865 | 1865–1887 | |
| F. R. E. Cornell | Jan. 11, 1875 | 1875–1881 | Died May 23, 1881 |
| Daniel Ashley Dickinson | June 27, 1881 | 1881–1893 | Appointed; replaced Cornell |
| Greenleaf Clark | Mar. 14, 1881 | 1881–1882 | Appointed to new seat |
| William Mitchell | Mar. 14, 1881 | 1881–1900 | Appointed to new seat |
| **1882** | | | |
| *James Gilfillan* | Mar. 10, 1875 | 1875–1894 | |
| John M. Berry | Jan. 10, 1865 | 1865–1887 | |
| Daniel Ashley Dickinson | June 27, 1881 | 1881–1893 | |
| Greenleaf Clark | Mar. 14, 1881 | 1881–1882 | Resigned |
| William Mitchell | Mar. 14, 1881 | 1881–1900 | |

---

673. In 1881 the legislature increased the number of associate justices from two to four. 1881 Minn. Laws, ch. 141, § 1.

| Justice | Appointment Date | Office Tenure | |
|---|---|---|---|
| Charles E. Vanderburgh | Jan. 12, 1882 | 1882–1894 | Elected; replaced Clark |
| **1883–1887** ||||
| *James Gilfillan* | Mar. 10, 1875 | 1875–1894 | |
| John M. Berry | Jan. 10, 1865 | 1865–1887 | Died Nov. 8, 1887; replaced by Collins |
| William Mitchell | Mar. 14, 1881 | 1881–1900 | |
| Daniel Ashley Dickinson | June 27, 1881 | 1881–1893 | |
| Charles E. Vanderburgh | Jan. 12, 1882 | 1882–1894 | |
| Loren Warren Collins | Nov. 16, 1887 | 1887–1904 | Appointed; replaced Berry |
| **1888–1893** ||||
| *James Gilfillan* | Mar. 10, 1875 | 1875–1894 | |
| William Mitchell | Mar. 14, 1881 | 1881–1900 | |
| Daniel Ashley Dickinson | June 27, 1881 | 1881–1893 | Term expired; replaced by Buck |
| Charles E. Vanderburgh | Jan. 12, 1882 | 1882–1894 | |
| Loren Warren Collins | Nov. 12, 1887 | 1887–1904 | |
| Daniel Buck | Oct. 2, 1893 | 1893–1899 | Elected; replaced Dickinson |
| **1894** ||||
| *James Gilfillan* | Mar. 10, 1875 | 1875–1894 | Died Dec. 6, 1894 |
| William Mitchell | Mar. 14, 1881 | 1881–1900 | |
| Charles E. Vanderburgh | Jan. 12, 1882 | 1882–1894 | Term expired; replaced by Canty |
| Loren Warren Collins | Nov. 12, 1887 | 1887–1904 | |
| Daniel Buck | Jan. 1, 1894 | 1894–1899 | |
| Thomas Canty | Jan. 1, 1894 | 1894–1900 | Elected; replaced Vanderburgh |

### Appendix I. Minnesota Supreme Court Justices 1858–1999

| Justice | Appointment Date | Office Tenure | |
|---|---|---|---|
| **1895** | | | |
| *Charles M. Start* | Jan. 7, 1895 | 1895–1913 | Elected; replaced Gilfillan as Chief Justice |
| William Mitchell | Mar. 14, 1881 | 1881–1900 | |
| Loren Warren Collins | Nov. 12, 1887 | 1887–1904 | |
| Daniel Buck | Jan. 1, 1894 | 1894–1899 | |
| Thomas Canty | Jan. 1, 1894 | 1894–1900 | |
| **1896–1899** | | | |
| *Charles M. Start* | Jan. 7, 1895 | 1895–1913 | |
| William Mitchell | Mar. 14, 1881 | 1881–1900 | |
| Loren Warren Collins | Nov. 12, 1887 | 1887–1904 | |
| Thomas Canty | Jan. 1, 1894 | 1894–1900 | |
| Daniel Buck | Oct. 2, 1894 | 1887–1899 | Resigned Nov. 20, 1899; replaced by C. Brown |
| Calvin L. Brown | Nov. 20, 1899 | 1900–1906 | Appointed; replaced Buck |
| **1900** | | | |
| *Charles M. Start* | Jan. 7, 1895 | 1895–1913 | |
| William Mitchell | Mar. 14, 1881 | 1881–1900 | Term expired Jan. 1, 1900; replaced by Lovely |
| Loren Warren Collins | Nov. 12, 1887 | 1887–1904 | |
| Thomas Canty | Jan. 1, 1894 | 1894–1900 | Term expired Jan. 1, 1900; replaced by Lewis |
| Calvin L. Brown | Nov. 20, 1899 | 1900–1906 | |
| John A. Lovely | Jan. 1, 1900 | 1900–1905 | Elected; replaced Mitchell |
| Charles L. Lewis | Jan. 1, 1900 | 1900–1912 | Elected; replaced Canty |

| Justice | Appointment Date | Office Tenure | |
|---|---|---|---|
| **1901–1904** ||||
| *Charles M. Start* | Jan. 7, 1895 | 1895–1913 | |
| Loren Warren Collins | Nov. 12, 1882 | 1887–1904 | Resigned Apr. 1, 1904; replaced by Douglas |
| Calvin L. Brown | Nov. 20, 1899 | 1899–1912 | |
| John A. Lovely | Jan. 1, 1900 | 1900–1905 | |
| Charles L. Lewis | Jan. 1, 1900 | 1900–1912 | |
| Wallace B. Douglas | Mar. 31, 1904 | 1904–1905 | Appointed; replaced Collins |
| **1905** ||||
| *Charles M. Start* | Jan. 7, 1895 | 1895–1913 | |
| Calvin L. Brown | Nov. 20, 1899 | 1899–1912 | |
| Charles L. Lewis | Jan. 1, 1900 | 1900–1912 | |
| John A. Lovely | Jan. 1, 1900 | 1900–1905 | Term expired; replaced by Elliot |
| Edwin A. Jaggard | Jan. 4, 1905 | 1905–1911 | Elected; replaced Douglas |
| Charles B. Elliott | Oct. 2, 1905 | 1905–1909 | Appointed; replaced Lovely |
| **1906** ||||
| *Charles M. Start* | Jan. 7, 1895 | 1895–1913 | |
| Calvin L. Brown | Nov. 20, 1899 | 1899–1912 | |
| Charles L. Lewis | Jan. 1, 1900 | 1900–1912 | |
| Edwin A. Jaggard | Jan. 4, 1905 | 1905–1911 | Elected; replaced Douglas |
| Charles B. Elliott | Oct. 2, 1905 | 1905–1909 | Appointed; replaced Lovely |
| **1907–1909** ||||
| *Charles M. Start* | Jan. 7, 1895 | 1895–1913 | |
| Calvin L. Brown | Nov. 20, 1899 | 1899–1912 | |
| Charles L. Lewis | Jan. 1, 1900 | 1900–1912 | |
| Edwin A. Jaggard | Jan. 4, 1905 | 1905–1911 | |

# Appendix I. Minnesota Supreme Court Justices 1858–1999

| Justice | Appointment Date | Office Tenure | |
|---|---|---|---|
| Charles B. Elliott | Oct. 2, 1905 | 1905–1909 | Resigned Sept. 1, 1909; replaced by O'Brien |
| Thomas B. O'Brien | Sept. 1, 1909 | 1909–1911 | Appointed; replaced Elliott |
| **1910–1911** | | | |
| *Charles M. Start* | Jan. 7, 1895 | 1895–1913 | |
| Calvin L. Brown | Nov. 20, 1899 | 1899–1912 | |
| Charles L. Lewis | Jan. 1, 1900 | 1900–1912 | |
| Edwin A. Jaggard | Jan. 4, 1905 | 1905–1911 | Died Feb. 13, 1911; replaced by Bunn |
| Thomas B. O'Brien | Sept. 1, 1909 | 1909–1911 | Term expired; replaced by Simpson |
| George L. Bunn | Feb. 18, 1911 | 1911–1918 | Appointed; replaced Jaggard |
| David E. Simpson | Jan. 3. 1911 | 1911–1912 | Elected |
| **1912** | | | |
| *Charles M. Start* | Jan. 7, 1895 | 1895–1913 | |
| Charles L. Lewis | Jan. 1, 1900 | 1900–1912 | Term expired; replaced by P. Brown |
| Calvin L. Brown | Nov. 20, 1899 | 1899–1912 | |
| George L. Bunn | Feb. 18, 1911 | 1911–1918 | |
| David F. Simpson | Jan. 3. 1911 | 1911–1912 | Resigned; replaced by Holt |
| Andrew Holt | Jan. 2, 1912 | 1912–1942 | Appointed; replaced Simpson |
| Philip E. Brown | Jan. 1913 | 1912–1915 | Elected; replaced Lewis |
| **1913** | | | |
| *Charles M. Start* | Jan. 7, 1895 | 1895–1913 | Resigned as Chief Justice, Jan. 6, 1913; replaced by C. Brown |
| *Calvin L. Brown* | Jan. 7, 1913 | 1913–1923 | Elected as Chief Justice to replace Start |
| George L. Bunn | Feb. 18, 1911 | 1911–1918 | Appointed to fill Brown's seat |

| Justice | Appointment Date | Office Tenure | |
|---|---|---|---|
| Andrew Holt | Dec. 21, 1911 | 1912–1942 | |
| Philip E. Brown | Jan. 1913 | 1912–1915 | |
| Oscar Hallam | Jan. 7, 1913 | 1913–1923 | Elected; filled Bunn's seat |
| **1914–1915** | | | |
| *Calvin L. Brown* | Jan. 7, 1913 | 1913–1923 | |
| George L. Bunn | Feb. 18, 1911 | 1911–1918 | |
| Andrew Holt | Dec. 21, 1911 | 1912–1942 | |
| Philip E. Brown | Jan. 1913 | 1912–1915 | Died Feb. 6, 1915; replaced by Schaller |
| Oscar Hallam | Jan. 7, 1913 | 1913–1923 | |
| Albert Schaller | Mar. 1, 1915 | 1915–1917 | Appointed; replaced P. Brown |
| **1916–1917** | | | |
| *Calvin L. Brown* | Jan. 7, 1913 | 1913–1923 | |
| George L. Bunn | Feb. 18, 1911 | 1911–1918 | |
| Andrew Holt | Dec. 21, 1911 | 1912–1942 | |
| Oscar Hallam | Jan. 7, 1913 | 1913–1923 | |
| Albert Schaller | Mar. 1, 1915 | 1915–1917 | Term expired; replaced by Quinn |
| James H. Quinn | Jan. 2, 1917 | 1917–1928 | Elected; replaced Schaller |
| **1918** | | | |
| *Calvin L. Brown* | Jan. 7, 1913 | 1913–1923 | |
| George L. Bunn | Feb. 18, 1911 | 1911–1918 | Died Oct. 9, 1918; replaced by Dibell |
| Andrew Holt | Dec. 21, 1911 | 1912–1942 | |
| Oscar Hallam | Jan. 7, 1913 | 1913–1923 | |
| James H. Quinn | Jan. 2, 1917 | 1917–1928 | |
| Homer B. Dibell | Oct. 12, 1918 | 1918–1934 | Appointed; replaced Bunn |

# Appendix I. Minnesota Supreme Court Justices 1858–1999

| Justice | Appointment Date | Office Tenure | |
|---|---|---|---|
| **1919–1923** | | | |
| *Calvin L. Brown* | Jan. 7, 1913 | 1913–1923 | Died Sept. 24, 1923; replaced by Wilson |
| *Samuel B. Wilson* | Sept. 29, 1923 | 1923–1933 | Appointed; replaced Brown as Chief Justice |
| Andrew Holt | Dec. 21, 1911 | 1912–1942 | |
| Oscar Hallam | Jan. 7, 1913 | 1913–1923 | Resigned May 25, 1923; replaced by Stone |
| James H. Quinn | Jan. 2, 1916 | 1917–1928 | |
| Royal A. Stone | May 25, 1923 | 1923–1942 | Appointed; replaced Hallam |
| Homer B. Dibell | Oct. 12, 1918 | 1918–1934 | |
| **1924–1928** | | | |
| *Samuel B. Wilson* | Sept. 29, 1923 | 1923–1933 | |
| Andrew Holt | Dec. 21, 1911 | 1912–1942 | |
| James H. Quinn | Jan. 2, 1916 | 1917–1928 | Resigned Jan. 1, 1928; replaced by Hilton |
| Homer B. Dibell | Oct. 14, 1918 | 1918–1934 | |
| Royal A. Stone | May 25, 1923 | 1923–1942 | |
| Clifford L. Hilton | Jan. 1, 1928 | 1928–1943 | Appointed; replaced Quinn |
| **1929** | | | |
| *Samuel B. Wilson* | Sept. 29, 1923 | 1923–1933 | |
| Andrew Holt | Dec. 21, 1911 | 1912–1942 | |
| Homer B. Dibell | Oct. 14, 1918 | 1918–1934 | |
| Royal A. Stone | May 25, 1923 | 1923–1942 | |
| Clifford L. Hilton | Jan. 1, 1928 | 1928–1943 | |
| **1930[674]** | | | |
| *Samuel B. Wilson* | Sept. 29, 1923 | 1923–1933 | |
| Andrew Holt | Dec. 21, 1911 | 1912–1942 | |
| Homer B. Dibell | Oct. 14, 1918 | 1918–1934 | |
| Royal A. Stone | May 25, 1923 | 1923–1942 | |

---

674. As permitted by article 6, section 2 of the Minnesota Constitution. The number of associate justices was increased by 1929 Minn. Laws ch. 430.

| Justice | Appointment Date | Office Tenure | |
|---|---|---|---|
| Clifford L. Hilton | Jan. 1, 1928 | 1928–1943 | |
| Ingervall M. Olsen | Nov. 20, 1930 | 1930–1936 | Appointed to fill newly created seat |
| Charles Loring | Nov. 20, 1930 | 1930–1944 | Appointed to fill newly created seat |
| **1931–1933** | | | |
| *Samuel B. Wilson* | Sept. 29, 1923 | 1923–1933 | Resigned Sept. 4, 1933; replaced by Devaney |
| *John P. Devaney* | Sept. 7, 1933 | 1933–1937 | Appointed; replaced Wilson as Chief Justice |
| Andrew Holt | Dec. 21, 1911 | 1912–1942 | |
| Homer B. Dibell | Oct. 14, 1918 | 1918–1934 | |
| Royal A. Stone | May 25, 1923 | 1923–1942 | |
| Clifford L. Hilton | Jan. 1, 1928 | 1928–1943 | |
| Ingervall M. Olsen | Nov. 20, 1930 | 1930–1936 | |
| Charles Loring | Nov. 20, 1930 | 1930–1944 | |
| **1934** | | | |
| *John P. Devaney* | Sept. 7, 1933 | 1933–1937 | |
| Andrew Holt | Dec. 21, 1911 | 1912–1942 | |
| Homer B. Dibell | Oct. 14, 1918 | 1918–1934 | Died Feb. 17, 1934; replaced by J. Olson |
| Royal A. Stone | May 25, 1923 | 1923–1942 | |
| Clifford L. Hilton | Jan. 1, 1928 | 1928–1943 | |
| Ingervall M. Olsen | Nov. 20, 1930 | 1930–1936 | |
| Charles Loring | Nov. 20, 1930 | 1930–1944 | |
| Julius J. Olson | Mar. 5, 1934 | 1934–1948 | Appointed; replaced Dibell |
| **1935–1936** | | | |
| *John P. Devaney* | Sept. 7, 1933 | 1933–1937 | |
| Andrew Holt | Dec. 21, 1911 | 1912–1942 | |
| Royal A. Stone | May 25, 1923 | 1923–1942 | |
| Clifford L. Hilton | Jan. 1, 1928 | 1927–1943 | |

# Appendix I. Minnesota Supreme Court Justices 1858–1999

| Justice | Appointment Date | Office Tenure | |
|---|---|---|---|
| Ingervall M. Olsen | Nov. 20, 1930 | 1930–1936 | Resigned Dec. 12, 1936, effective Jan. 15, 1937; replaced by Peterson |
| Charles Loring | Nov. 20, 1930 | 1930–1944 | |
| Julius J. Olson | Mar. 5, 1934 | 1934–1948 | |
| Harry H. Peterson | Dec. 15, 1936 | 1936–1950 | Appointed; replaced Olsen |
| **1937** | | | |
| *John P. Devaney* | Sept. 7, 1933 | 1933–1937 | Resigned Feb. 15, 1937; replaced by Gallagher |
| Henry M. Gallagher | Feb. 15, 1937 | 1937–1944 | Appointed; replaced Devaney as Chief Justice |
| Andrew Holt | Dec. 21, 1911 | 1912–1942 | |
| Royal A. Stone | May 25, 1923 | 1923–1942 | |
| Clifford L. Hilton | Jan. 1, 1928 | 1927–1943 | |
| Charles Loring | Nov. 20, 1930 | 1930–1944 | |
| Julius J. Olson | Mar. 5, 1934 | 1934–1948 | |
| Harry H. Peterson | Dec. 15, 1936 | 1936–1950 | |
| **1938–1942** | | | |
| *Henry M. Gallagher* | Feb. 15, 1937 | 1937–1944 | |
| Andrew Holt | Dec. 21, 1911 | 1912–1942 | Resigned Oct. 6, 1942; replaced by Streissguth |
| Royal A. Stone | May 25, 1923 | 1923–1942 | Died Sept. 12, 1942; replaced by Pirsig |
| Clifford L. Hilton | Jan. 1, 1928 | 1927–1943 | |
| Charles Loring | Nov. 20, 1930 | 1930–1944 | |
| Julius J. Olson | Mar. 5, 1934 | 1934–1948 | |
| Harry H. Peterson | Dec. 15, 1936 | 1936–1950 | |
| Maynard E. Pirsig | Oct. 6, 1942 | 1942–1942 | Appointed; replaced Stone |
| Thomas O. Streissguth | Oct. 6, 1942 | 1942–1942 | Appointed; replaced Holt |

| Justice | Appointment Date | Office Tenure | |
|---|---|---|---|
| **1943** | | | |
| *Henry M. Gallagher* | Feb. 15, 1937 | 1937–1944 | |
| Clifford L. Hilton | Jan. 1, 1928 | 1927–1943 | Retired May 1, 1943; replaced by Magney |
| Charles Loring | Nov. 20, 1930 | 1930–1944 | |
| Julius J. Olson | Mar. 5, 1934 | 1934–1948 | |
| Harry H. Peterson | Dec. 15, 1936 | 1936–1950 | |
| Luther W. Youngdahl | Jan. 4, 1943 | 1943–1946 | Elected; replaced Pirsig |
| Thomas F. Gallagher | Jan. 4, 1943 | 1943–1967 | Elected; replaced Streissguth |
| Clarence R. Magney | July 1, 1943 | 1943–1953 | Appointed; replaced Hilton |
| **1944** | | | |
| *Henry M. Gallagher* | Feb. 15, 1937 | 1937–1944 | Retired; replaced by Loring |
| *Charles Loring* | Nov. 20, 1930 | 1944–1953 | Appointed; replaced Gallagher as Chief Justice |
| Julius J. Olson | Mar. 5, 1934 | 1934–1948 | |
| Harry H. Peterson | Dec. 15, 1936 | 1936–1950 | |
| Luther W. Youngdahl | Jan. 4, 1943 | 1943–1946 | |
| Thomas F. Gallagher | Jan. 4, 1943 | 1943–1967 | |
| Clarence R. Magney | July 1, 1943 | 1943–1953 | |
| Thomas O. Streissguth | Oct. 6, 1942 | 1944–1944 | Appointed; replaced Loring who was appointed Chief Justice |
| **1945** | | | |
| *Charles Loring* | Nov. 20, 1930 | 1944–1953 | |
| Julius J. Olson | Mar. 5, 1934 | 1934–1948 | |
| Harry H. Peterson | Dec. 15, 1936 | 1936–1950 | |
| Luther W. Youngdahl | Jan. 4, 1943 | 1943–1946 | |

# Appendix I. Minnesota Supreme Court Justices 1858–1999

| Justice | Appointment Date | Office Tenure | |
|---|---|---|---|
| Thomas F. Gallagher | Jan. 4, 1943 | 1943–1967 | |
| Clarence R. Magney | July 1, 1943 | 1943–1953 | |
| Thomas O. Streissguth | Oct. 6, 1942 | 1944–1944 | Term expired; replaced by Matson |
| Leroy E. Matson | Jan. 2, 1945 | 1945–1960 | Elected; replaced Streissguth |
| **1946** | | | |
| *Charles Loring* | Nov. 20, 1930 | 1944–1953 | |
| Julius J. Olson | Mar. 5, 1934 | 1934–1948 | |
| Harry H. Peterson | Dec. 15, 1936 | 1936–1950 | |
| Thomas F. Gallagher | Jan. 4, 1943 | 1943–1967 | |
| Luther W. Youngdahl | Jan. 4, 1943 | 1943–1946 | Resigned Mar. 16, 1946; replaced by Christianson |
| Clarence R. Magney | July 1, 1943 | 1943–1953 | |
| Leroy E. Matson | Jan. 2, 1945 | 1945–1960 | |
| William C. Christianson | Mar. 26, 1946 | 1946–1946 | Appointed then resigned; replaced Youngdahl; was replaced by Gallagher |
| **1947** | | | |
| *Charles Loring* | Nov. 20, 1930 | 1944–1953 | |
| Julius J. Olson | Mar. 5, 1934 | 1934–1948 | |
| Harry H. Peterson | Dec. 15, 1936 | 1936–1950 | |
| Thomas F. Gallagher | Jan. 4, 1943 | 1943–1967 | |
| Clarence R. Magney | July 1, 1943 | 1943–1953 | |
| Leroy E. Matson | Jan. 2, 1945 | 1945–1960 | |
| Frank T. Gallagher | Jan. 6, 1947 | 1947–1963 | Elected; replaced Christianson |

| Justice | Appointment Date | Office Tenure | |
|---|---|---|---|
| **1948** ||||
| *Charles Loring* | Nov. 20, 1930 | 1944–1953 | |
| Julius J. Olson | Mar. 5, 1934 | 1934–1948 | Retired May 10, 1948; replaced by Knutson |
| Harry H. Peterson | Dec. 15, 1936 | 1936–1950 | |
| Thomas F. Gallagher | Jan. 4, 1943 | 1943–1967 | |
| Clarence R. Magney | July 1, 1943 | 1943–1953 | |
| Leroy E. Matson | Jan. 2, 1945 | 1945–1960 | |
| Frank T. Gallagher | Jan. 6, 1947 | 1947–1963 | |
| Oscar R. Knutson | May 10, 1948 | 1948–1962 | Appointed; replaced Olson |
| **1949–1950** ||||
| *Charles Loring* | Nov. 20, 1930 | 1944–1953 | |
| Harry H. Peterson | Dec. 15, 1936 | 1936–1950 | Resigned May 11, 1950 |
| Thomas F. Gallagher | Jan. 4, 1943 | 1943–1967 | |
| Clarence R. Magney | July 1, 1943 | 1943–1953 | |
| Leroy E. Matson | Jan. 2, 1945 | 1945–1960 | |
| Frank T. Gallagher | Jan. 6, 1947 | 1947–1963 | |
| Oscar R. Knutson | May 10, 1948 | 1948–1962 | |
| Theodore Christianson | May 15, 1950 | 1951–1955 | Appointed; replaced Peterson |
| **1951** ||||
| *Charles Loring* | Nov. 20, 1930 | 1944–1953 | |
| Thomas F. Gallagher | Jan. 4, 1943 | 1943–1967 | |
| Clarence R. Magney | July 1, 1943 | 1943–1953 | |
| Leroy E. Matson | Jan. 2, 1945 | 1945–1960 | |
| Frank T. Gallagher | Jan. 6, 1947 | 1947–1963 | |
| Oscar R. Knutson | May 10, 1948 | 1948–1962 | |
| Theodore Christianson | May 15, 1950 | 1950–1955 | |

# Appendix I. Minnesota Supreme Court Justices 1858–1999

| Justice | Appointment Date | Office Tenure | |
|---|---|---|---|
| **1952–1953** | | | |
| *Charles Loring* | Nov. 20, 1930 | 1944–1953 | Retired July 16, 1953; replaced by Dell |
| Thomas F. Gallagher | Jan. 4, 1943 | 1943–1967 | |
| Clarence R. Magney | July 1, 1943 | 1943–1953 | Retired Jan. 12, 1953; replaced by Dell |
| Leroy E. Matson | Jan. 2, 1945 | 1945–1960 | |
| Frank T. Gallagher | Jan. 6, 1947 | 1947–1963 | |
| Oscar R. Knutson | May 10, 1948 | 1948–1962 | |
| Theodore Christianson | May 12, 1951 | 1951–1955 | |
| Martin A. Nelson | July 16, 1953 | 1953–1972 | Appointed; replaced Dell |
| Roger L. Dell | Jan. 12, 1953 | 1953–1953 | Appointed; replaced Magney; then appointed Chief Justice to replace Loring |
| **1954–1955** | | | |
| *Roger L. Dell* | July 16, 1953 | 1953–1962 | |
| Thomas F. Gallagher | Jan. 4, 1943 | 1943–1967 | |
| Leroy E. Matson | Jan. 2, 1945 | 1945–1960 | |
| Frank T. Gallagher | Jan. 6, 1947 | 1947–1963 | |
| Oscar R. Knutson | May 10, 1948 | 1948–1962 | |
| Theodore Christianson | May 12, 1951 | 1951–1955 | Died Sept. 19, 1955; replaced by Murphy |
| Martin A. Nelson | July 16, 1953 | 1953–1972 | |
| William P. Murphy | Sept. 26, 1955 | 1955–1972 | Appointed; replaced T. Christianson |
| **1956–1960** | | | |
| *Roger L. Dell* | July 16, 1953 | 1953–1962 | |
| Thomas F. Gallagher | Jan. 4, 1943 | 1943–1967 | |
| Leroy E. Matson | Jan. 2, 1945 | 1945–1960 | Died Feb. 28, 1960; replaced by Loveinger |

| Justice | Appointment Date | Office Tenure | |
|---|---|---|---|
| Frank T. Gallagher | Jan. 6, 1947 | 1947–1963 | |
| Oscar R. Knutson | May 10, 1948 | 1948–1962 | |
| Martin A. Nelson | July 16, 1953 | 1953–1972 | |
| William P. Murphy | Sept. 26, 1955 | 1955–1972 | |
| Lee Loveinger | Apr. 4, 1960 | 1960–1961 | Appointed; replaced Matson |
| **1961** | | | |
| *Roger L. Dell* | July 16, 1953 | 1953–1962 | |
| Thomas F. Gallagher | Jan. 4, 1943 | 1943–1967 | |
| Frank T. Gallagher | Jan. 6, 1947 | 1947–1963 | |
| Oscar R. Knutson | May 10, 1948 | 1948–1962 | |
| Martin A. Nelson | July 16, 1953 | 1953–1972 | |
| William P. Murphy | Sept. 26, 1955 | 1955–1972 | |
| Lee Loveinger | Apr. 4, 1960 | 1960–1961 | Resigned Mar. 16, 1961; replaced by Otis |
| James C. Otis | Mar. 29, 1961 | 1961–1982 | Appointed; replaced Loveinger |
| **1962** | | | |
| *Roger L. Dell* | July 16, 1953 | 1953–1962 | Resigned Jan. 26, 1962; replaced by Knutson |
| *Oscar R. Knutson* | May 10, 1948 | 1948–1962 | Appointed; replaced Dell as Chief Justice |
| Thomas F. Gallagher | Jan. 4, 1943 | 1943–1967 | |
| Frank T. Gallagher | Jan. 6, 1947 | 1947–1963 | |
| Martin A. Nelson | July 16, 1953 | 1953–1972 | |
| William P. Murphy | Sept. 26, 1955 | 1955–1972 | |
| James C. Otis | Mar. 29, 1961 | 1961–1982 | |
| Walter F. Rogosheske | Feb. 1, 1962 | 1962–1980 | Appointed; replaced Knutson |
| **1963** | | | |
| *Oscar R. Knutson* | May 10, 1948 | 1962–1973 | |
| Thomas F. Gallagher | Jan. 4, 1943 | 1943–1967 | |

# Appendix I. Minnesota Supreme Court Justices 1858–1999

| Justice | Appointment Date | Office Tenure | |
|---|---|---|---|
| Frank T. Gallagher | Jan. 6, 1947 | 1947–1963 | Retired; replaced by Sheran |
| Martin A. Nelson | July 16, 1953 | 1953–1972 | |
| William P. Murphy | Sept. 26, 1955 | 1955–1972 | |
| James C. Otis | Mar. 29, 1961 | 1961–1982 | |
| Walter F. Rogosheske | Feb. 1, 1962 | 1962–1980 | |
| Robert J. Sheran | Jan. 8, 1963 | 1963–1970 | Appointed; replaced F. Gallagher |
| **1964–1967** | | | |
| *Oscar R. Knutson* | May 10, 1948 | 1962–1973 | |
| Thomas F. Gallagher | Jan. 4, 1943 | 1943–1967 | Term expired; replaced by Peterson |
| Martin A. Nelson | July 16, 1953 | 1953–1972 | |
| William P. Murphy | Sept. 26, 1955 | 1955–1972 | |
| James C. Otis | Mar. 29, 1961 | 1961–1982 | |
| Walter F. Rogosheske | Feb. 1, 1962 | 1962–1980 | |
| Robert J. Sheran | Jan. 8, 1963 | 1963–1970 | |
| C. Donald Peterson | Jan. 3, 1967 | 1967–1986 | Elected; replaced Gallagher |
| **1968–1970** | | | |
| *Oscar R. Knutson* | May 10, 1948 | 1962–1973 | |
| Martin A. Nelson | July 16, 1953 | 1953–1972 | |
| William P. Murphy | Sept. 26, 1955 | 1955–1972 | |
| James C. Otis | Mar. 29, 1961 | 1961–1982 | |
| Walter F. Rogosheske | Feb. 1, 1962 | 1962–1980 | |
| Robert J. Sheran | Jan. 8, 1963 | 1963–1970 | Resigned July 1, 1970; replaced by Kelly |
| C. Donald Peterson | Jan. 3, 1967 | 1967–1986 | |
| Fallon Kelly | July 6, 1970 | 1970–1980 | Appointed; replaced Sheran |

| Justice | Appointment Date | Office Tenure | |
|---|---|---|---|
| **1971–1972** ||||
| *Oscar R. Knutson* | May 10, 1948 | 1962–1973 | |
| Martin A. Nelson | July 16, 1953 | 1953–1972 | Resigned Jan. 3, 1972; replaced by Todd |
| William P. Murphy | Sept. 26, 1955 | 1955–1972 | Resigned May 1, 1972; replaced by MacLaughlin |
| James C. Otis | Mar. 29, 1961 | 1961–1982 | |
| Walter F. Rogosheske | Feb. 1, 1962 | 1962–1980 | |
| C. Donald Peterson | Jan. 3, 1967 | 1967–1986 | |
| Fallon Kelly | July 6, 1970 | 1970–1980 | |
| John J. Todd | Jan. 3, 1972 | 1972–1985 | Appointed; replaced Nelson |
| Harry H. MacLaughlin | May 1, 1972 | 1972–1977 | Appointed; replaced Murphy |
| **1973**[675] ||||
| *Oscar R. Knutson* | May 10, 1948 | 1962–1973 | Resigned Dec. 18, 1973; replaced by Sheran |
| *Robert J. Sheran* | Dec. 18, 1973 | 1973–1981 | Appointed; replaced Knutson as Chief Justice |
| James C. Otis | Mar. 29, 1961 | 1961–1982 | |
| Walter F. Rogosheske | Feb. 1, 1962 | 1962–1980 | |
| C. Donald Peterson | Jan. 3, 1967 | 1967–1986 | |
| Fallon Kelly | July 6, 1970 | 1970–1980 | |
| John J. Todd | Jan. 3, 1972 | 1972–1985 | |
| Harry H. MacLaughlin | May 1, 1972 | 1972–1977 | |
| Lawrence R. Yetka | June 2, 1973 | 1973–1992 | Appointed to newly created seat |

---

675. In 1973, the Minnesota Constitution (art. 6, § 2) was amended to allow as many as eight associate justices on the Supreme Court. The legislature promptly passed legislation creating two more seats on the court. 1973 Minn. Laws. ch. 726, § 1.

# Appendix I. Minnesota Supreme Court Justices 1858–1999

| Justice | Appointment Date | Office Tenure | |
|---|---|---|---|
| George M. Scott | July 3, 1973 | 1973–1982 | Appointed to newly created seat |
| **1974–1977** | | | |
| *Robert J. Sheran* | Dec. 18, 1973 | 1973–1981 | |
| James C. Otis | Mar. 29, 1961 | 1961–1982 | |
| Walter F. Rogosheske | Feb. 1, 1962 | 1962–1980 | |
| C. Donald Peterson | Jan. 3, 1967 | 1967–1986 | |
| Fallon Kelly | July 6, 1970 | 1970–1980 | |
| John J. Todd | Jan. 3, 1972 | 1972–1985 | |
| Harry H. MacLaughlin | May 1, 1972 | 1972–1977 | Resigned Sept. 29, 1977; replaced by Wahl |
| Lawrence R. Yetka | June 2, 1973 | 1973–1992 | |
| George M. Scott | June 22, 1973 | 1973–1982 | |
| Rosalie E. Wahl | Oct. 3, 1977 | 1977–1994 | Appointed; replaced MacLaughlin |
| **1978–1980** | | | |
| *Robert J. Sheran* | Dec. 18, 1973 | 1973–1981 | |
| James C. Otis | Mar. 29, 1961 | 1961–1982 | |
| Walter F. Rogosheske | Feb. 1, 1962 | 1962–1980 | Resigned Sept. 7, 1980; replaced by Simonett |
| C. Donald Peterson | Jan. 3, 1967 | 1967–1986 | |
| Fallon Kelly | July 6, 1970 | 1970–1980 | Resigned July 6, 1980; replaced by Amdahl |
| John J. Todd | Jan. 3, 1972 | 1972–1985 | |
| Lawrence R. Yetka | June 2, 1973 | 1973–1992 | |
| George M. Scott | July 3, 1973 | 1973–1982 | |
| Rosalie E. Wahl | Oct. 3, 1977 | 1977–1994 | |
| John E. Simonett | Sept. 8, 1980 | 1980–1994 | Appointed; replaced Rogosheske |
| Douglas K. Amdahl | July 7, 1980 | 1980–1981 | Appointed; replaced Kelly |

| Justice | Appointment Date | Office Tenure | |
|---|---|---|---|
| **1981** | | | |
| *Robert J. Sheran* | Dec. 18, 1973 | 1973–1981 | Resigned Dec. 18, 1981; replaced by Amdahl |
| James C. Otis | Mar. 29, 1961 | 1961–1982 | |
| C. Donald Peterson | Jan. 3, 1967 | 1967–1986 | |
| John J. Todd | Jan. 3, 1972 | 1972–1985 | |
| Lawrence R. Yetka | June 2, 1973 | 1973–1992 | |
| George M. Scott | July 3, 1973 | 1973–1982 | |
| John E. Simonett | Sept. 8, 1980 | 1980–1994 | |
| Rosalie E. Wahl | Oct. 3, 1977 | 1977–1994 | |
| Douglas K. Amdahl | July 7, 1980 | 1980–1981 | Appointed Chief Justice; replaced Sheran |
| Glenn E. Kelley | Dec. 18, 1981 | 1981–1990 | Appointed; replaced Amdahl |
| **1982**[676] | | | |
| *Douglas K. Amdahl* | Dec. 18, 1973 | 1981–1989 | |
| James C. Otis | Mar. 29, 1961 | 1961–1982 | Resigned Sept. 1, 1982; replaced by Coyne |
| C. Donald Peterson | Jan. 3, 1967 | 1967–1986 | |
| John J. Todd | Jan. 3, 1972 | 1972–1985 | |
| Lawrence R. Yetka | June 2, 1973 | 1973–1992 | |
| George M. Scott | July 3, 1973 | 1973–1987 | |
| Rosalie E. Wahl | Oct. 3, 1977 | 1977–1994 | |
| John E. Simonett | Sept. 8, 1980 | 1980–1994 | |
| Glenn E. Kelley | Dec. 18, 1981 | 1981–1990 | |
| M. Jeanne Coyne | Sept. 1, 1982 | 1982–1996 | Appointed; replaced Otis |

---

676. With the creation of the Court of Appeals in 1982, the legislature reduced the number of associate justices from eight to six. This reduction was accomplished by attrition (i.e., resignation or retirement), and was not fully accomplished until 1989. 1982 Minn. Laws ch. 501, § 16.

# Appendix I. Minnesota Supreme Court Justices 1858–1999

| Justice | Appointment Date | Office Tenure | |
|---|---|---|---|
| **1983–1985** ||||
| *Douglas K. Amdahl* | Dec. 18, 1973 | 1981–1989 | |
| C. Donald Peterson | Jan. 3, 1967 | 1967–1986 | |
| John J. Todd | Jan. 3, 1972 | 1972–1985 | Resigned. Not replaced |
| Lawrence R. Yetka | June 2, 1973 | 1973–1992 | |
| George M. Scott | July 3, 1973 | 1973–1987 | |
| Rosalie E. Wahl | Oct. 3, 1977 | 1977–1994 | |
| John E. Simonett | Sept. 8, 1980 | 1980–1994 | |
| Glenn E. Kelley | Dec. 18, 1981 | 1981–1990 | |
| M. Jeanne Coyne | Sept. 1, 1982 | 1982–1996 | |
| **1986** ||||
| *Douglas K. Amdahl* | Dec. 18, 1973 | 1981–1989 | |
| C. Donald Peterson | Jan. 3, 1967 | 1967–1986 | Resigned. Not replaced |
| Lawrence R. Yetka | June 2, 1973 | 1973–1992 | |
| George M. Scott | July 3, 1973 | 1973–1987 | |
| Rosalie E. Wahl | Oct. 3, 1977 | 1977–1994 | |
| John E. Simonett | Sept. 8, 1980 | 1980–1994 | |
| Glenn E. Kelley | Dec. 18, 1981 | 1981–1990 | |
| M. Jeanne Coyne | Sept. 1, 1982 | 1982–1996 | |
| **1987** ||||
| *Douglas K. Amdahl* | Dec. 18, 1973 | 1981–1989 | |
| Lawrence R. Yetka | June 2, 1973 | 1973–1992 | |
| George M. Scott | July 3, 1973 | 1973–1987 | Retired Nov. 15, 1987; replaced by Popovich |
| Rosalie E. Wahl | Oct. 3, 1977 | 1977–1994 | |
| John E. Simonett | Sept. 8, 1980 | 1980–1994 | |
| Glenn E. Kelley | Dec. 18, 1981 | 1981–1990 | |
| M. Jeanne Coyne | Sept. 1, 1982 | 1982–1996 | |
| Peter S. Popovich | Nov. 15, 1987 | 1987–1989 | Appointed; replaced Scott |

| Justice | Appointment Date | Office Tenure | |
|---|---|---|---|
| \multicolumn{4}{c}{1988–1989} ||||
| *Douglas K. Amdahl* | Dec. 18, 1973 | 1981–1989 | Retired Jan. 31, 1989; replaced by Popovich |
| *Peter S. Popovich* | Feb. 1, 1989 | 1989–1990 | Appointed Chief Justice Feb. 1, 1989 |
| Lawrence R. Yetka | June 2, 1973 | 1973–1992 | |
| Rosalie E. Wahl | Oct. 3, 1977 | 1977–1994 | |
| John E. Simonett | Sept. 8, 1980 | 1980–1994 | |
| Glenn E. Kelley | Dec. 18, 1981 | 1981–1990 | |
| M. Jeanne Coyne | Sept. 1, 1982 | 1982–1996 | |
| Alexander M. Keith | Feb. 1, 1989 | 1989–1990 | |
| \multicolumn{4}{c}{1990} ||||
| *Peter S. Popovich* | Feb. 1, 1989 | 1989–1990 | Resigned Nov. 30, 1990; replaced by Keith |
| *Alexander M. Keith* | Feb. 1, 1990 | 1990–1998 | |
| Lawrence R. Yetka | June 2, 1973 | 1973–1992 | |
| Rosalie E. Wahl | Oct. 3, 1977 | 1977–1994 | |
| John E. Simonett | Sept. 8, 1980 | 1980–1994 | |
| Glenn E. Kelley | Dec. 18, 1981 | 1981–1990 | Resigned Aug. 30, 1990; replaced by Gardebring |
| M. Jeanne Coyne | Sept. 1, 1982 | 1982–1996 | |
| Esther M. Tomljanovich | Sept. 1, 1990 | 1990–1998 | Appointed; replaced Popovich |
| Sandra S. Gardebring | Jan. 4, 1991 | 1991–1998 | Appointed; replaced Kelley |
| \multicolumn{4}{c}{1991–1992} ||||
| *Alexander M. Keith* | Feb. 1, 1990 | 1990–1998 | |
| Lawrence R. Yetka | June 2, 1973 | 1973–1992 | Term expired; replaced by Page |
| Rosalie E. Wahl | Oct. 3, 1977 | 1977–1994 | |
| John E. Simonett | Sept. 8, 1980 | 1980–1994 | |
| M. Jeanne Coyne | Sept. 1, 1982 | 1982–1996 | |

# Appendix I. Minnesota Supreme Court Justices 1858–1999

| Justice | Appointment Date | Office Tenure | |
|---|---|---|---|
| Esther M. Tomljanovich | Sept. 1, 1990 | 1990–1998 | |
| Sandra S. Gardebring | Jan. 4, 1991 | 1991–1998 | |
| **1993** ||||
| *Alexander M. Keith* | Feb. 1, 1990 | 1990–1998 | |
| Rosalie E. Wahl | Oct. 3, 1977 | 1977–1994 | |
| John E. Simonett | Sept. 8, 1980 | 1980–1994 | |
| M. Jeanne Coyne | Sept. 1, 1982 | 1982–1996 | |
| Esther M. Tomljanovich | Sept. 1, 1990 | 1990–1998 | |
| Sandra S. Gardebring | Jan. 4, 1991 | 1991–1998 | |
| Alan C. Page | Jan. 4, 1993 | 1993– | Elected; replaced Yetka |
| **1994** ||||
| *Alexander M. Keith* | Feb. 1, 1990 | 1990–1998 | |
| Rosalie E. Wahl | Oct. 3, 1977 | 1977–1994 | Retired Aug. 27, 1994 Replaced by Anderson |
| John E. Simonett | Sept. 8, 1980 | 1980–1994 | Retired June 30, 1994; replaced by Stringer |
| M. Jeanne Coyne | Sept. 1, 1982 | 1982–1996 | |
| Esther M. Tomljanovich | Sept. 1, 1990 | 1990–1998 | |
| Sandra S. Gardebring | Jan. 4, 1991 | 1991–1998 | |
| Alan C. Page | Jan. 4, 1993 | 1993– | |
| Paul H. Anderson | July 1, 1994 | 1994– | Appointed; replaced Wahl |
| Edward C. Stringer | Sept. 1, 1994 | 1994– | Appointed; replaced Simonett |

| Justice | Appointment Date | Office Tenure | |
|---|---|---|---|
| **1995–1996** ||||
| *Alexander M. Keith* | Feb. 1, 1989 | 1990–1998 | |
| M. Jeanne Coyne | Sept. 1, 1982 | 1982–1996 | Resigned Oct. 31, 1996; replaced by Blatz |
| Esther M. Tomljanovich | Sept. 1, 1990 | 1990–1998 | |
| Sandra S. Gardebring | Jan. 4, 1991 | 1991–1998 | |
| Alan C. Page | Jan. 4, 1993 | 1993– | |
| Paul H. Anderson | July 1, 1994 | 1994– | |
| Edward C. Stringer | Sept. 1, 1994 | 1994– | |
| Kathleen A. Blatz | Nov. 4, 1996 | 1996– | Appointed; replaced Coyne |
| **1997** ||||
| *Alexander M. Keith* | Feb. 1, 1989 | 1990–1998 | |
| Esther M. Tomljanovich | Sept. 1, 1990 | 1990–1998 | |
| Sandra S. Gardebring | Jan. 4, 1991 | 1991–1998 | |
| Alan C. Page | Jan. 4, 1993 | 1993– | |
| Paul H. Anderson | July 1, 1994 | 1994– | |
| Edward C. Stringer | Sept. 1, 1994 | 1994– | |
| Kathleen A. Blatz | Nov. 1, 1996 | 1996– | |
| **1998** ||||
| *Alexander M. Keith* | Feb. 1, 1989 | 1990–1998 | Resigned Jan. 29, 1998; replaced by Blatz |
| *Kathleen A. Blatz* | Jan. 29, 1998 | 1998– | Appointed; replaced Keith |
| Esther M. Tomljanovich | Sept. 1, 1990 | 1990–1998 | Resigned Sept. 1, 1998; replaced by Anderson |
| Sandra S. Gardebring | Jan. 4, 1991 | 1991–1998 | Resigned Sept. 7, 1998; replaced by Lancaster |
| Alan C. Page | Jan. 4, 1993 | 1993– | |
| Paul H. Anderson | July 1, 1994 | 1994– | |

# Appendix I. Minnesota Supreme Court Justices 1858–1999

| Justice | Appointment Date | Office Tenure | |
|---|---|---|---|
| Edward C. Stringer | Sept. 1, 1994 | 1994– | |
| James H. Gilbert | Jan. 29, 1998 | 1998– | Appointed; replaced Blatz |
| Russell A. Anderson | Sept. 1, 1998 | 1998– | Appointed; replaced Tomljanovich |
| Joan Ericksen Lancaster | Sept. 8, 1998 | 1998– | Appointed; replaced Gardebring |
| **1999–** | | | |
| *Kathleen A. Blatz* | Jan. 29, 1998 | 1998– | |
| Alan C. Page | Jan. 4, 1993 | 1993– | |
| Paul H. Anderson | July 1, 1994 | 1994– | |
| Edward C. Stringer | Sept. 1, 1994 | 1994– | |
| James H. Gilbert | Jan. 29, 1998 | 1998– | |
| Russell A. Anderson | Sept. 1, 1998 | 1998– | |
| Joan Ericksen Lancaster | Sept. 8, 1998 | 1998– | |

# APPENDIX J
# Federal Depository Libraries in Minnesota

The Federal Depository Library Program provides federal government information to designated libraries in each Congressional District in the country. Those libraries make the information available for use by the public at no charge. Depository libraries receive government reports, laws, regulations, legislative materials, periodicals, statistics, and directories in paper, microfiche, diskette, CD-ROM, and online. The program is administered by the U.S. Government Printing Office, and provides a unique partnership between the government and local libraries to assure that all people have access to their government's information.

Minnesota has twenty-five Federal Depository Libraries. The Regional Depository at the University of Minnesota's Government Publications Library receives all materials distributed under the program. The other depositories select materials to serve the needs of their clientele. This directory indicates the proportion of available materials which is selected by each depository. It also indicates whether materials are retained beyond the five years required by law.

The GPO Access service of the Government Printing Office program provides online access to many essential Federal databases such as the *Federal Register, Congressional Record, Commerce Business Daily,* and congressional bills. Federal Depository Libraries provide public access to this service and assistance in using it.

Some libraries list government documents in their library catalogs, but some do not. To see if specific information is available, please telephone your depository.

- Anoka County Library System, Northtown Central Library, 711 County Rd 10 NE, Blaine, MN 55434-2398; phone: (763) 717-3267, fax: (763) 717-3259; Web address: <http://www.anoka.lib.mn.us/>
- Bemidji State University, A.C. Clark Library, Government Publications, 1500 Birchmont Drive NE, Bemidji, MN 56601-2699; phone: (218) 755-3342, fax: (218) 755-2051; Web address: <http://www.bemidjistate.edu/library/>.

- Carleton College, Laurence McKinley Gould Library, One North College Street, Northfield, MN 55057-4077; phone: (507) 646-4260, fax: (507) 646-4087; Web address: <http://www.library.carleton.edu/collections/govdocs.html>.
- Dakota County Library System, Wescott Library, 1340 Wescott Road, Eagan, MN 55123-1099; phone: (651) 688-1500, fax: (651) 688-1515; Web address: <http://www.co.dakota.mn.us/library/>.
- Duluth Public Library, 520 West Superior Street, Duluth, MN 55802-1578; phone: (218) 723-3802, fax: (218) 723-3815; Web address: <http://www.duluth.lib.mn.us/Reference/Govdocs.html>.
- Gustavus Adolphus College, Folke Bernadotte Library, Government Documents, 800 West College Avenue, Saint Peter, MN 56082-1498; phone: 507-933-7569, fax: 507-933-6292; Web address: <http://www.gac.edu/oncampus/academics/Resources/Library/govdocsearch.html>.
- Hamline University, School of Law Library, MS-D2010, 1536 Hewitt Avenue, Saint Paul, MN 55104-1235; phone: (651) 523-2125, fax: (651) 523-2236; Web address: <http://www.hamline.edu/law/library/>.
- Hennepin County Library System, Southdale-Hennepin Library, 7001 York Avenue South, Edina, MN 55435-4287; phone: (952) 847-5933, fax: (952) 847-5976; Web address: <http://www.hennepin.lib.mn.us/pub/>.
- Minneapolis Public Library, Technology/Science/Government Documents Department, 300 Nicollet Mall, Minneapolis, MN 55401-1992; phone: (612) 630-6120, fax: (612) 630-6210; Web address: <http://www.mpls.lib.mn.us/techscigov.asp>.
- Minnesota State University, Mankato, Memorial Library, P.O. Box 8400, MSU Box 19, Maywood & Ellis, Mankato, MN 56002-8419; phone: (507) 389-5952, fax: (507) 389-5155; Web address: <http://www.lib.mankato.msus.edu/lib/govdoc/govhome.html>.
- Minnesota Supreme Court, Minnesota State Law Library, Minnesota Judicial Center, 25 Constitution Avenue, Saint Paul, MN 55155-6102; phone: (651) 296-2775 or (651) 297-7661, fax: (651) 296-6740, TDD: 651-282-5352; Web address: <http://www.lawlibrary.state.mn.us/govdocl.html>.

## Appendix J. Federal Depository Libraries in Minnesota

- Moorhead State University, Livingston Lord Library, Documents Department, 1104-7th Avenue South, Moorhead, MN 56563-0002; phone: (218) 236-2349, fax: (218) 299-5924; Web address: <http://www.mnstate.edu/govdocs/>.
- Ramsey County Public Library, Roseville Library, 2180 North Hamline Avenue, Roseville, MN 55113-4294; phone: (651) 628-6803, fax: (651) 628-6818; Web address: <http://www.ramsey.lib.mn.us>.
- Saint Cloud State University, James W. Miller Learning Resources Center, Documents Section, 720-4th Avenue South, Saint Cloud, MN 56301-4498; phone: (320) 255-4755, fax: (320) 255-4778; Web address: <http://lrs.stcloudstate.edu/guides/govt.html>.
- Saint John's University, Alcuin Library, Collegeville, MN 56321-2500; phone: (320) 363-2125, fax: (320) 363-2126; Web address: <http://www.csbsju.edu/library/about/services/docs/index.html>.
- Saint Olaf College, Rolvaag Memorial Library, 1510 Saint Olaf Avenue, Northfield, MN 55057-1097; phone: (507) 646-3452, fax: (507) 646-3734; Web address: <http://www.stolaf.edu/library/research/govdocs/>.
- Saint Paul Public Library, 90 West Fourth Street, Saint Paul, MN 55102; phone: 651-292-6178, fax: 651-292-6284; Web address: <http://www.stpaul.lib.mn.us/>; e-mail: <gpo@stpaul.lib.mn.us>.
- Saint Paul Public Library, Hamline-Midway, 1558 West Minnehaha Avenue, Saint Paul, MN 55104-1264; phone: (651) 632-5179, fax: (651) 642-0323; Web address: <http://www.stpaul.lib.mn.us/pages/pubpg/governme.htm>.
- Southwest State University, Library, 1501 North State Street, Marshall, MN 56258-1598; phone: (507) 537-6176; fax: (507) 537-6200; Web address: <http://199.17.208.53/govinfo/index.htm>.
- University of Minnesota, Government Publications Library, 10 Wilson Library, 309-19th Avenue South, Minneapolis, MN 55455-0414; phone: (612) 624-5073, fax: (612) 624-4836; Web address: <http://govpubs.lib.umn.edu/>; e-mail: <govref@tc.umn.edu>.

- University of Minnesota, Law Library, 229-19th Avenue South, Minneapolis, MN 55455-0401; phone: (612) 625-4309, fax: (612) 625-3478; Web address: <http://www.law.umn.edu/library/home.html>.
- University of Minnesota, Duluth, Library, 10 University Drive, Duluth, MN 55812-2495; phone: 218-726-8100, fax: 218-726-6205; Web address: <http://www.d.umn.edu/lib/collections/gov.html>.
- University of Minnesota, Morris, Rodney A. Briggs Library, Documents Department, 4th Street & College Avenue, Morris, MN 56267-2134; phone: (320) 589-6180, fax: (320) 589-6168; Web address: <http://www.mrs.umn.edu/library/govdocs.shtml>.
- University of Minnesota, Saint Paul, Magrath Library, 1984 Buford Avenue, Saint Paul, MN 55108-6034; phone: (612) 624-1212, fax: (612) 624-3793; Web address: <http://magrath.lib.umn.edu/gov/>; e-mail: <stpref@zazu.lib.umn.edu>.
- William Mitchell College of Law, Warren E. Burger Library, 871 Summit Avenue, Saint Paul, MN 55105-3030; phone: (651) 290-6424, fax: (651) 290-6318; Web address: <http://www.wmitchell.edu/library/inetres.html>.
- Winona State University, Main Library, 176 West Mark Street, Winona, MN 55987-5838; phone: (507) 457-5146, fax: (507) 457-2679; Web address: <http://www.winona.msus.edu/library/gov/>.

# APPENDIX K
## Minnesota Abbreviations

| | |
|---|---|
| Bench & B Minn | Bench and Bar |
| Bench & B Interim Minn | Bench and Bar Interim |
| Ex. Sess. | Extraordinary Session |
| 1st Sp. | First Special Session |
| Gen. St. | General Statutes |
| Gil. | Minnesota Reports (Gilfillan Edition) |
| Hamline J. Pub. L. & Pol'y | Hamline Journal of Public Law and Policy |
| Hamline L. Rev. | Hamline Law Review |
| Hennepin Law. | Hennepin Lawyer |
| HCLL | Hennepin County Law Library |
| LRL | Legislative Reference Library |
| MAG | Minnesota Attorney General |
| MCLE | Minnesota Continuing Legal Education |
| MILE | Minnesota Institute for Legal Education |
| Min. | Minnesota Reports |
| MnL | Minnesota Law Review |
| Min. R. | Minnesota Reports |
| Min. Rep | Minnesota Reports |
| Minn | Minnesota Supreme Court Reports |
| Minn. Admin. Reg. | Minnesota State Register |
| Minn. Code Agency | Minnesota Code of Agency Rules |
| Minn. Code Ann. | Minnesota Code Annotated |
| Minn. Const. | Minnesota Constitution |

| | |
|---|---|
| Minn. Cont. L. Ed. | Minnesota Continuing Legal Education |
| Minn. Cont. Legal Ed. | Minnesota Continuing Legal Education |
| Minn. Ct. Rep. | Minnesota Court Reporter |
| Minn. D.L. & I. Comp. | Minnesota Department of Labor and Industries. Compilation of Court Decisions |
| Minn. Gen. Laws | Minnesota General Laws |
| Minn. (Gil) | Minnesota Reports (Gilfillan edition) |
| Minn. J.L. & Pol. | Minnesota Journal of Law and Politics |
| Minn. Law J. | Minnesota Law Journal |
| Minn. Laws | Laws of Minnesota |
| Minn. Law J. | Minnesota Law Journal |
| Minn. L. Rev. | Minnesota Law Review |
| Minn. LR | Minnesota Law Review |
| Minn. R. | Minnesota Rules |
| Minn. R. & W.C. | Minnesota Railroad and Warehouse Commission |
| Minn. Reg. | Minnesota State Register |
| Minn. Rep | Minnesota Reports |
| Minn. Reps | Minnesota Reports |
| Minn. Sess. Law Serv. | Minnesota Session Law Service (West) |
| Minn S.B.A. | Minnesota State Bar Association |
| Minn. St. | Minnesota Statutes |
| Minn. Stat. | Minnesota Statutes |
| Minn. Stat. Ann. | Minnesota Statutes Annotated (West) |
| Minn. T. Law | Minnesota Trial Lawyer |
| Minn. Trial Law. | Minnesota Trial Lawyer |
| Minn. W.C.D. | Minnesota Workmen's Compensation Decisions |

# Appendix K. Minnesota Abbreviations

| | |
|---|---|
| Minnesota L. Rev. | Minnesota Law Review |
| ML | Minnesota Lawyer Appellate Courts Edition |
| MnAG | Minnesota Attorney General Opinions |
| MS | Minnesota Statutes |
| MSBA | Minnesota State Bar Association |
| MSA | Minnesota Statutes Annotated |
| MSL | Minnesota State Law Library |
| N.W. | North Western Reporter |
| N.W.2d | North Western Reporter, Second Series |
| Op. Atty. Gen. | Opinions of the Attorney General |
| Prof. Resp. Bd. | Lawyers Professional Responsibility Board |
| Rev. Laws | Revised Laws |
| RCP | Rules of Civil Procedure |
| RcrP | Rules of Criminal Procedure |
| Sp. Sess. | Special Session |
| WmM | William Mitchell Law Review |
| Wm. Mitchell L. Rev. | William Mitchell Law Review |

# APPENDIX L
# Directory of Local Pro Bono Programs

## STATEWIDE

Minnesota AIDS Project[677]
City: Minneapolis
Phone: 612-341-2060
Counties served: Statewide

Refugee & Asylum Project
Minnesota Advocates for Human Rights
City: Minneapolis
Phone: 612-341-3302
Counties served: Statewide

## MULTI-COUNTY

Central Minnesota Legal Services
Volunteer Attorney Program
City: Minneapolis
Phone: 612-332-8151
Counties served: Big Stone, Chippewa, Kandiyohi, Lac Qui Parle, Lincoln, Lyon, Meeker, Renville, Swift, Yellow Medicine

## ANOKA COUNTY

Judicare of Anoka County, Inc.
City: Blaine
Phone: 612-783-4970
Counties served: Anoka

---

677. DIRECTORY OF LEGAL RESOURCES FOR PEOPLE WITH AIDS & HIV (Clifton J. Cortez Jr. & Joel M. Long eds., prepared by American Bar Association, AIDS Coordination Project Washington, DC: The Project 1997).

## BLUE EARTH COUNTY

Southern Minnesota Regional Legal Services, Inc.
Private Bar Involvement Program
City: Mankato
Phone: 507-387-5588
Counties served: Blue Earth, Brown, LeSueur, Martin, McLeiod, Nicollett, Sibley, Waseca, Watonwan

## CLAY COUNTY

Legal Service of Northwest Minnesota
City: Moorhead
Phone: 218-233-8585
Counties served: Becker, Beltrami, Clay, Clearwater, Douglas, Grant, Hubbard, Lake of the Woods, Norman, Pennington, Polk, Red Lake, Stevens, Wadena

## CROW WING COUNTY

CASS-Crow Wing-Atkin
Volunteer Attorney Program
City: Baxter
Phone: 218-829-1701
Counties served: Crow Wing

## DAKOTA COUNTY

Legal Assistance of Dakota County, Ltd.
City: Apple Valley
Phone: 612-431-3200
Counties served: Dakota

## FREEBORN COUNTY

Southern Minnesota Regional Legal Services Volunteer Attorney Program
City: Albert Lea
Phone: 507-377-2831
Counties served: Freeborn

## HENNEPIN COUNTY

Chrysalis, A Center for Women
Assistance for Women (L.A.W.)
City: Minneapolis
Phone: 612-870-2425
Counties served: Metro area

Volunteer Lawyers Network
City: Minneapolis
Phone: 612-339-5500
Counties served: Hennepin

Volunteer Family Law Program
Legal Aid Society of Minneapolis
City: Minneapolis
Phone: 612-332-1441
Counties served: Hennepin

## ISANTI COUNTY

East Central Minnesota Legal Services
Volunteer Attorney Program
City: Cambridge
Phone: 612-689-2849
Counties served: Isanti

## ITASCA COUNTY

Legal Aid Service of Northeastern Minnesota
City: Grand Rapids
Phone: 218-326-6695
Counties served: Itasca, Koochiching

## NOBLES COUNTY

Southern Minnesota Regional Legal Services Private Bar Involvement Program
City: Worthington
Phone: 507-372-7368
Counties served: Cottonwood, Jackson, Murray, Nobles, Pipestone, Redwood, Rock

## OLMSTED COUNTY

Legal Assistance of Olmsted County
Volunteer Attorney Program
City: Rochester
Phone: 507-287-2036
Counties served: Olmsted

## PINE COUNTY

Legal Aid Service of Northeastern Minnesota (LASNEM)
City: Pine City
Phone: 320-629-7166
Counties served: Kanabec, Pine

## RAMSEY COUNTY

Southern Minnesota Regional Legal Services Volunteer Attorney Program
City: Saint Paul, MN 55101
Phone: 612-222-5863
Counties served: Ramsey

## SCOTT COUNTY

Southern Minnesota Regional Legal Services Volunteer Attorney Program
City: Prior Lake
Phone: 612-440-1040
Counties served: Colver, Scott

## Saint Louis County

Arrowhead Lawyers Care
Volunteer Attorney Program
City: Duluth
Phone: 218-723-4005
Counties served: Carlton, Cook, Itasca, Lake, Saint Louis

## Stearns County

Minnesota Family Farm Law Project
Saint Cloud Area Legal Services
City: Saint Cloud
Phone: 325-253-0121
Counties served: Serving twenty counties in central and southern Minnesota

Volunteer Attorney Program
City: Saint Cloud
Phone: 320-253-0138
Counties served: Benton, Mille Lac, Morrison, Sherburne, Stearns, Todd, Wright

## Washington County

Volunteer Attorney Program
Washington County
City: Stillwater
Phone: 612-351-7172
Counties served: Washington

## Winona County

Southern Minnesota Regional Legal Services, Inc.
City: Winona
Phone: 507-454-6660
Counties served: Dodge, Fillmore, Goodhue, Houston, Wabasha, Winona

# APPENDIX M
# Minnesota State Document Depository Libraries

The Legislative Reference Library is "a depository of all documents published by the state and shall receive them automatically without cost."[678] The general library of the University of Minnesota also is a depository of all books, pamphlets, maps, and other works published by or under the authority of the state of Minnesota.[679]

Since 1981, depository libraries have received microfiche copies of most documents issued by the executive, judicial, and legislative branches of Minnesota state government.

- Anoka-Ramsey Community College
- Austin Community College
- Bemidji State University
- Brainerd Community College
- Cambridge Community College
- Duluth Public Library
- Fergus Falls Community College
- Hibbing Community College
- Inver Hills Community College
- Itasca Community College
- Lakewood Community College
- Mankato State University
- Mesabi Community College
- Minneapolis Community College
- Minneapolis Public Library
- Minnesota Historical Society
- Minnesota Legislative Reference Library
- Minnesota Office of Library Development and Services
- Minnesota State University, Akita, Japan

---

678. MINN. STAT. § 3.302, subd. 3 (2000).
679. MINN. STAT. § 137.04 (2000).

- Minnesota State Law Library
- Moorhead State University
- Normandale Community College
- North Hennepin Community College
- Northland Community College
- Rainy River Community College
- Rochester Community College
- Saint Cloud State University
- Saint Paul Public Library
- Southwest State University
- University of Minnesota, Crookston
- University of Minnesota, Duluth
- University of Minnesota, Minneapolis
- University of Minnesota, Morris
- University of Minnesota, Saint Paul
- Vermilion Community College
- Willmar Community College
- Winona State University
- Worthington Community College

# APPENDIX N
## District Bar Associations

The district bar associations do not follow the lines of the judicial districts, instead they are grouped to reflect the population distribution around the state. The following is an alphabetical list of each county and its district bar association.[680]

| County | District |
| --- | --- |
| Aitkin | District 15 |
| Anoka | District 21 |
| Becker | District 7 |
| Beltrami | District 15 |
| Benton | District 7 |
| Big Stone | District 16 |
| Blue Earth | District 6 |
| Brown | District 9 |
| Carlton | District 11 |
| Carver | District 8 |
| Cass | District 15 |
| Chippewa | District 12 |
| Chisago | District 19 |
| Clay | District 7 |
| Clearwater | District 15 |
| Cook | District 11 |
| Cottonwood | District 13 |
| Crow Wing | District 15 |

---

680. <http://www2.mnbar.org/sec/bardist.htm> (last visited Jan. 24, 2002).

| County | District |
|---|---|
| Dakota | District 1 |
| Dodge | District 5 |
| Douglas | District 7 |
| Faribault | District 17 |
| Fillmore | District 10 |
| Freeborn | District 10 |
| Goodhue | District 1 |
| Grant | District 16 |
| Hennepin | District 4 |
| Houston | District 3 |
| Hubbard | District 15 |
| Isanti | District 18 |
| Itasca | District 15 |
| Jackson | District 17 |
| Kanabec | District 19 |
| Kandiyohi | District 12 |
| Kittson | District 14 |
| Koochiching | District 15 |
| Lac Qui Parle | District 12 |
| Lake | District 11 |
| Lake of the Woods | District 15 |
| LeSueur | District 8 |
| Lincoln | District 9 |
| Lyon | District 9 |
| Mahnomen | District 14 |
| Marshall | District 14 |

# Appendix N. District Bar Associations

| County | District |
|---|---|
| Martin | District 17 |
| McLeod | District 8 |
| Meeker | District 12 |
| Mille Lacs | District 7 |
| Morrison | District 7 |
| Mower | District 10 |
| Murray | District 13 |
| Nicollet | District 6 |
| Nobles | District 13 |
| Norman | District 14 |
| Northern St. Louis | Range Bar (District 20) |
| Olmsted | District 3 |
| Otter Tail | District 7 |
| Pennington | District 14 |
| Pine | District 19 |
| Pipestone | District 13 |
| Polk | District 14 |
| Pope | District 16 |
| Ramsey | District 2 |
| Red Lake | District 14 |
| Redwood | District 9 |
| Renville | District 12 |
| Rice | District 5 |
| Rock | District 13 |
| Roseau | District 14 |
| Scott | District 8 |

| County | District |
|---|---|
| Sherburne | District 18 |
| Sibley | District 8 |
| St. Louis | District 11 |
| Stearns | District 7 |
| Steele | District 5 |
| Stevens | District 16 |
| Swift | District 12 |
| Todd | District 7 |
| Traverse | District 16 |
| Wabasha | District 3 |
| Wadena | District 7 |
| Waseca | District 5 |
| Washington | District 19 |
| Watonwan | District 6 |
| Wilkin | District 16 |
| Winona | District 3 |
| Wright | District 18 |
| Yellow Medicine | District 12 |

The following lists Minnesota District Bar Associations and those counties that comprise them.

| District | County |
|---|---|
| District 1 | Dakota, Goodhue |
| District 2 | Ramsey |
| District 3 | Houston, Olmsted, Wabasha, Winona |
| District 4 | Hennepin |
| District 5 | Dodge, Rice, Steele, Waseca |

# Appendix N. District Bar Associations

| District | County |
|---|---|
| District 6 | Blue Earth, Nicollet, Watonwan |
| District 7 | Becker, Benton, Clay, Douglas, Mille Lacs, Morrison, Otter Tail, Stearns, Todd, Wadena |
| District 8 | Carver, LeSueur, McLeod, Scott, Sibley |
| District 9 | Brown, Lincoln, Lyon, Redwood |
| District 10 | Freeborn, Fillmore, Mower |
| District 11 | Carlton, Cook, Lake, St. Louis |
| District 12 | Chippewa, Kandiyohi, Lac Qui Parle, Meeker, Renville, Swift, Yellow Medicine |
| District 13 | Cottonwood, Murray, Nobles, Pipestone, Rock |
| District 14 | Kittson, Mahnomen, Marshall, Norman, Pennington, Polk, Red Lake, Roseau |
| District 15 | Aitkin, Beltrami, Cass, Clearwater, Crow Wing, Hubbard, Itasca, Koochiching, Lake of the Woods |
| District 16 | Big Stone, Grant, Pope, Stevens, Traverse, Wilkin |
| District 17 | Faribault, Martin, Jackson |
| District 18 | Isanti, Sherburne, Wright |
| District 19 | Chisago, Kanabec, Pine, Washington |
| Range Bar (District 20) | Northern St. Louis |
| District 21 | Anoka |

# APPENDIX O
# Capitol Area Library Consortium Directory

The Capitol Area Library Consortium (CALCO) website is maintained by the Minnesota Attorney General Library for the Capitol Area Library Consortium.[681] E-mail questions or comments to <karla.gedell@state.mn.us>.

**Attorney General Library**
445 Minnesota Street, Suite 1050
St. Paul, MN 55101-2109
Phone: (651) 296-8152; fax: (651) 297-4139
Web address: <http://www.ag.state.mn.us>
E-mail address: <anita.anderson@state.mn.us>
MAG (PALS), MAG (OCLC)

**Centennial Library**
300 Centennial Office Building
658 Cedar Street
St. Paul, MN 55155-1603
Phone: (651) 296-5973; fax: (651) 296-3698
Minnesota Relay Service (800) 627-3529
Web address: <http://www.library.state.mn.us>
E-mail address: <pat.loehlein@state.mn.us>, <larry.lockway@mnplan.state.mn.us>.
CNL (PALS), MAX (OCLC)

**CFL Library**
Dept. of Children, Families & Learning
1500 Highway 36 West
Roseville, MN 55113-4266
Phone: (651) 582-8719; fax: (651) 582-8898
Web address: <http://www.cfl.state.mn.us/library>
E-mail address for library requests: <cfl.library@state.mn.us>
CFL (PALS), MDE & MIL (OCLC)

---

681. <http://www.state.mn.us/libraries/calco.html> (last updated Aug. 24, 2001).

**Department of Economic Security**
Employee Resource Center
390 No. Robert Street
St. Paul, MN 55101-1897
Phone: (651) 297-3419; fax: (651) 297-4501
Web address: <http://des.state.mn.us>
E-mail address: <linda.woodstrom@state.mn.us>
DJT (PALS), DES (OCLC)

**Department of Health**
R.N. Barr Public Health Library
717 Delaware Street S.E., Box 9441
Minneapolis, MN 55440-2921
Phone: (612) 676-5090; fax: (612) 676-5385
Web address: <http://www.health.state.mn.us>
E-mail address: <library@health.state.mn.us>
MDH (PALS), MDH (OCLC)

**Department of Human Services Library**
444 Lafayette Road
St. Paul, MN 55155-3821
Phone: (651) 297-8708; fax: (651) 282-5340
E-mail address: <kate.o.nelson@state.mn.us>
DHS (PALS), DHS (OCLC)

**Department of Natural Resources Library**
500 Lafayette Road, Box 21
St. Paul, MN 55155-4021
Phone: (651) 297-4929; toll free (800) 766-6000; fax: (651) 297-4946
Web address: <http://www.dnr.state.mn.us>
E-mail address: <char.feist@dnr.state.mn.us>
DNR (PALS), MDN (OCLC)

## Appendix O. Capitol Area Library Consortium Directory

**Department of Revenue Library**
Minnesota Revenue Library
600 N. Robert Street, 4th Floor, Mail Station 2230
St. Paul, MN 55146-1176
Phone: (651) 296-3529; fax: (651) 297-2850
Web address: <http://www.taxes.state.mn.us>
E-mail address: <donna.davis@state.mn.us>
MDR (PALS), MRU (OCLC)

**FIRE/EMS/Safety Center Library**
Minnesota State Colleges and Universities (MnSCU)
1450 Energy Park Drive, Suite 100B
St. Paul, MN 55108-5265
Phone: (651) 649-5415; toll free (800) 311-3143; fax: (651) 523-7165
Web address: <http://www.firecenter.mnscu.edu>
E-mail address: <gwen.schagrin@so.mnscu.edu>
FIR (PALS), MFR (OCLC)

**Legislative Reference Library**
645 State Office Building
100 Constitution Avenue
St. Paul, MN 55155-1202
Phone: (651) 296-8338; fax: (651) 296-9731
Web address: <http://www.library.leg.state.mn.us>
E-mail address: <refdesk@library.leg.state.mn.us>
LRL (PALS), MLR (OCLC)

**Metropolitan Council Library**
Mears Park Centre Suite 500
230 East Fifth Street
St. Paul, MN 55101-1634
Phone: (651) 602-1310; fax: (651) 602-1464
Web address: <http://www.metrocouncil.org>
E-mail address: <jan.price@metc.state.mn.us>

**Minnesota Historical Society Library**
345 Kellogg Boulevard W.
St. Paul, MN 55102-1906
Phone: (651) 296-2143; fax: (651) 297-7436
Web address: <http://www.mnhs.org>
E-mail address: <reference.mnhs.org>
MHS (PALS), MHS (OCLC)

**Minnesota Housing Finance Agency**
400 Sibley Street, Suite 300
St. Paul, MN 55101-1998
Phone: (651) 296-9951; fax: (651) 296-8139
Web address: <http://www.mhfa.state.mn.us>
E-mail address: <kitty.cline@marge.mhfa.state.mn.us>

**Perpich Center for Arts Education**
Learning Resource Center
6125 Olson Memorial Highway
Golden Valley, MN 55422-4928
Phone: (763) 591-4742; fax: (763) 591-4747
Web address: <http://www.pcae.k12.mn.us>
E-mail address: <jim.marshall@pcae.k12.mn.us>
MCA (PALS), MUC (OCLC)

**Pollution Control Agency Library**
520 Lafayette Road
St. Paul, MN 55155-4194
Phone: (651) 296-7719 or 296-6623; fax: (651) 282-1537
Web address: <http://www.pca.state.mn.us/netscape.shtml>
E-mail address: <kathy.malec@pca.state.mn.us>; <helena.peskova@
   pca.state.mn.us>
PCA (PALS), MDF (OCLC)

## Appendix O. Capitol Area Library Consortium Directory

**State Law Library**
Room G25, Minnesota Judicial Center
25 Constitution Avenue
St. Paul, MN 55155-6102
Phone: (651) 296-2775; fax: (651) 296-6740
Web address: <http://www.lawlibrary.state.mn.us/>
E-mail address: <askmarvin@courts.state.mn.us>
MSL (PALS), MSL (OCLC)

For answers to Minnesota tax questions, please call one of the following numbers (*not* the library).
- Minnesota individual income tax: 800-652-9094 or 651-296-3781
- Minnesota business taxes (sales, withholding, corporate): 800-888-6231 or 651-297-4213
- Minnesota income tax forms: 800-657-3676 or 651-296-4444
- Minnesota tax information recorded messages: 800-652-9094 or 651-296-3781

**Department of Trade and Economic Development Library**
500 Metro Square
121 7th Place East
St. Paul, MN 55101-2146
Phone: (651) 296-8902 or 296-7952; toll free (800) 657-3858; fax: (651) 215-3841
Web address: <http://www.dted.state.mn.us>
E-mail address: <pat.fenton@state.mn.us>
DTE (PALS), MEG (OCLC)

**Department of Transportation Library**
Minnesota Department of Transportation
Mn/DOT Library, M.S. 155
395 John Ireland Boulevard
St. Paul, MN 55155-1899
Phone: (651) 296-2385; toll free (800) 657-3774; fax: (651) 297-2354
Web address: <http://www.dot.state.mn.us/library/>
E-mail address: <library@dot.state.mn.us>
MDT (PALS), MDT (OCLC)

**Minnesota Trade Office International Library**
1000 World Trade Center
30 East 7th Street
St. Paul, MN 55101-4942
Phone: (651) 297-4170 or (651) 297-1318; fax: (651) 296-3555
Web address: <http://www.dted.state.mn.us>
E-mail address: <liz.wade@state.mn.us>
DTE (PALS), MEG (OCLC)

**Senate Index**
110 State Capitol
St. Paul, MN 55155-0001
Phone: (651) 296-0268; fax: (651) 296-6511
Web address: <http://www.senate.leg.state.mn.us/committee/>
E-mail address: <margok@revisor.leg.state.mn.us>

# INDEX

*150 Years of Justice*, 143
*60th Anniversary: 1938–1998*, 147
A.L.R See *American Law Reports*
AALL. See American Association of Law Libraries
*AALL Universal Citation Guide*, 131
*AALS Directory of Law Teachers*, 135
academic law libraries, 213, 214
Academy of Certified Trial Lawyers of Minnesota, 237
accelerated review, 88
access tools, 148
*Accident Bulletin*, 202
Act Authorizing a State Government, 48
*Act of admission*, 6, 10, 48
Act to Establish the Territorial Government of Minnesota, 5
action by the governor, 21, 25
*Acts and Cases by Popular Names*, 60. See also popular names
*Admin. Minnesota*, 78
administrative agencies, 63, 68, 69, 86, 91, 113, 138, 141, 174, 199, 239
*Administrative Codes and Registers; State and Federal Survey*, 74
administrative courts, 63, 76
administrative hearings, 68, 70, 75, 182, 197, 238, 241. See also Office of Administrative Hearings
administrative law, 63, 75, 197, 203, 204, 209, 242
*Administrative Law Reports*, 75
Administrative Office of the U.S. Courts, 100
*Administrative Practice and Procedure*, 167, 174
Administrative Procedure Act, 69, 70, 75, 242

administrative rules, 36, 49, 68, 69, 205, 209, 312
Administrative Services Division, 89
administrators, 83, 89, 91, 92, 94, 95, 97, 99, 108, 117, 122, 143, 186–188, 198, 201, 231, 238, 240, 241, 261, 262, 264
*Advance*, 33, 37, 38, 40, 43, 71, 104, 108, 113, 125, 126, 136, 168, 205, 254, 317
ADR. See alternative dispute resolution
advanced legal education, 164, 167, 244
*Advising Minnesota Corporations & Other Business Organizations*, 165
*Advisory Committee on Civil Procedure. Report*, 155
*Advisory Committee on Judicial Growth and Enrichment*, 155
*Advisory Committee on the Minnesota Rules of Juvenile Procedure*, 155
*Advisory Task Force on the Civil Commitment System*, 155
*Advisory Task Force on the Guardian Ad Litem System*, 155
*Advisory Task Force on the Juvenile System: Final Report*, 155
*Advisory Task Force on Visitation and Child Support Enforcement*, 155
*Advocate, A Weekly Law Journal*, 201
agency decisions, 68, 75, 86, 174
*ALA Membership Directory*, 221
ALE. See advanced legal education
*Almanac of the Federal Judiciary*, 136
ALR. See *American Law Reports*
alternative dispute resolution, 83, 116, 117, 159, 213, 229, 230, 233–235, 246, 257
*ALWD Citation Manual*, 131

455

AMC. See Association of Minnesota Counties
amending the constitution, 91
amendments, 7–11, 15, 16, 20, 23, 24, 26, 29, 40–42, 47–50, 55, 57, 64, 70, 71, 74, 91,102, 113, 127, 272, 273, 276, 279, 281, 282, 284, 285, 291, 298, 300, 302, 303, 306, 307, 314, 401
American Association for Paralegal Education (AAfPE), 264
American Association of Law Libraries, 131, 190, 218, 225
*American Bench*, 136
*American Jurisprudence*, 59, 61, 150, 151, 153
*American Jurisprudence 2d Desk Book*, 61
*American Jurisprudence Legal Forms 2d*, 151, 153
*American Jurisprudence Pleading and Practice Forms Annotated*, 59, 153
American Law Institute, 54, 148–150
*American Law Reports*, 11, 59, 128, 129, 148, 154
*American Law Reports Federal*, 129
American Society for Information Science, 224, 226
*Americans with Disabilities Act Bulletin*, 197
*Americans with Disabilities Act Manual*, 184
Anishinabe Legal Services, 252
annotations, 50–52, 56, 59, 114, 129, 147–150, 152, 154, 173, 301, 304, 306–311
*Annual Expenditure Report, Fiscal Year*, 160
*Annual Report. Minnesota Courts*, 186, 187
Anoka County Law Library, 218, 220
*Antitrust Annual Report*, 160
APA. See Administrative Procedure Act
appeals, 75–77, 83, 86–88, 91, 92, 95–97, 99–102, 104–106, 108, 111, 113, 116, 119, 127, 136, 143, 144, 146, 169, 175, 182, 206, 209, 216, 239, 243, 247, 257, 258, 286, 391, 401, 420
*Appellate Rules Annotated*, 173
appendix, 297, 307–309, 316, 319, 329, 383, 399, 401, 427, 431, 435, 441, 443, 449
apportionment, 15, 16, 281, 282
arbitration, 112, 117, 233–235, 240
*Arbitration Award Summaries*, 117
ASIS. See American Society for Information Science
Association of Legal Administrators, 261, 262
Association of Minnesota Counties, 56, 221, 223
*ATLA Law Reporter*, 105
Attorney General. See Minnesota Attorney General
Attorney General opinions. See Minnesota Attorney General Opinions
Attorney General reports. See Minnesota Attorney General Reports
*Attorney General's Messenger*, 201
*Attorney General's Office Manual*, 184
attorneys, 90, 102, 112–114, 116, 119, 121, 122, 131, 138–141, 154, 161–163, 170, 173, 176, 183–186, 201, 208, 233, 234, 238, 239, 242, 245–248, 250, 252, 253, 256, 258, 260–262, 264, 391, 394
*Atwater's Reports*, 103, 289, 298
availability of opinions, 66, 67
award summaries, 117

*Bachman Legal Directory*, 136
bankruptcy, 100, 129, 136, 152, 176, 258
bar associations, 69, 113, 120, 129, 137–139, 140, 144, 149, 150, 157, 164, 166, 173, 175–177, 181, 184, 189, 190, 192, 195, 196, 210–213, 229, 232, 236, 237, 244, 246, 253, 259, 260, 264–267, 392, 394, 432, 433, 435, 443, 446

# Index

Bar Associations in Greater Minnesota, 236, 237
bar journals, 188, 192, 195
*Barrister*, 195, 204, 237
*Beginning a Judicial Tradition*, 143
*Bench & Bar Interim*, 195
*Bench & Bar of Minnesota*, 117, 122, 139, 164, 190, 195, 236, 237
*Benchbook for U.S. District Court Judges*, 184
*Best of Bench & Bar*, 195
*Between the Media and the Bar*, 117
bibliographic sources, 57, 60
bibliographies, 12, 60–62, 78, 145, 148, 151, 172, 176, 185, 188, 202, 208, 218, 399
*Bibliography of Bibliographies of Legal Material*, 60
*Bibliography of Minnesota Territorial Documents*, 78
*Biennial Report*, 67, 68, 160–163
*Biennial Report of the Attorney General of Minnesota*, 160, 161
*Biennial Report of the Attorney General to the Governor*, 68
biennium, 15, 25, 40
bills, 9, 14, 17, 20–27, 30–33, 35–41, 46, 64, 131, 132, 272, 274, 279, 283, 284, 306, 309, 310, 427
bills enacted into law that are coded, 32
bills enacted into law that are not coded, 32, 33
bills introduced during a current legislative session, 30, 31
bills introduced during prior legislative sessions, 30, 32
bills not enacted into law, 32, 33
*Biographical Sketches of Justices of the Minnesota Supreme*, 136, 144
*Black's Law Dictionary*, 134
*Blue Book*, 133. See also *Legislative Manual*
*Bluebook: A Uniform System of Citation*, 130, 131, 132
*Blue Pages*, 139

*BNA's Directory of State Administrative Codes and Registers: A State-by-State Listing*, 74
Board of Continuing Legal Education, 121, 122, 164, 238, 242
Board of Pardons, 238, 239
Board of Tax Appeals, 76
Board on Judicial Standards, 118
boards, 83, 118, 219, 276
*Book of the States*, 54, 61
*Brief Bank Index*, 108
*Briefly*, 31, 297, 301
briefs, 11, 24, 35, 42, 83, 90, 92, 103, 107–112, 116, 127, 130, 137, 138, 143–145, 151, 175, 177, 181, 182, 185, 204, 208, 209, 254, 307, 311, 315, 317, 385, 395
briefs on microfiche, 107, 108
*British and Foreign State Papers*, 3
*Bulletin*, 141, 192, 196–200, 202, 219, 226
Bureau of Mediation Services, 117, 201
*Business Guide Book to Law & Leading Attorneys*, 139
business law, 139, 174, 176, 179, 257
*Business Law Deskbook*, 174

CALCO. See Capitol Area Library Consortium
calendar number, 109
*Calendar of General Orders*, 24
calendars, 21, 24, 38, 109, 200, 209, 245, 320
Cambodian Law Project, 255
CAP. See Client Assistance Project
Capitol Area Library Consortium, 224, 226, 449
CCH. See Commerce Clearing House
CD-ROM, 67, 104, 130, 150, 190, 207, 208
Center for Conflict Management, 233–235
Center for Health Law & Policy, 233
Center for Professional Programming, 233, 234

Central Minnesota Legal Services, 254, 435, 437
changing the constitution, 6, 9
*Charters of the British Colonies in America*, 2
*Check List of Minnesota Public Documents*, 79
*Checklist*, 26, 40, 75, 145, 172, 188, 289, 316, 317
*Checklist of Legislative Journals of the States*, 26
*Child Abuse and Neglect Procedure Manual for Hennepin County*, 184
*CIS Abstracts*, 62
*CIS Index*, 62
citation forms, 130
*Citation Manual*, 130, 131
citation of legal authority, 130
citations, 11, 32, 33, 40, 42, 47, 49–51, 53–61, 68, 69, 73, 74, 102, 103, 108–110, 114, 124, 125, 127–134, 136, 148, 149, 167, 168, 172, 176, 186, 189, 209, 210, 303, 311, 315. See also Shepard's
citators, 123, 127, 128, 129, 149, 208
citators in general, 127
*Civil Commitment Handbook*, 185
*Civil Commitment in Minnesota*, 156, 165, 168
*Civil Commitment in Minnesota. Final Report*, 156
*Civil Jury Instruction Guide*, 173, 180, 181
*Civil Practice Forms*, 152, 174
civil procedure, 96, 112, 155, 159, 168, 173, 180, 183, 433
*Civil Rules Annotated*, 173
CIVJIG. See Jury Instruction Guides, Civil
CLE. See Minnesota Continuing Legal Education
*CLE Approved Courses*, 122
CLE publications, 165
clerk of the appellate courts, 91, 101, 109, 113
clerks of court, 92, 94, 105, 106, 122, 151, 261

Client Assistance Project (CAP), 256
Client Security Board, 114, 118, 121, 238–240
clinics, 234, 245, 248, 256–258, 261, 393
CMLS. See Central Minnesota Legal Services
*Collated Statutes of the Territory of Minnesota*, 1853, 103
*Collection of Treaties Between Great Britain and Other Powers*, 3
College of Saint Catherine, 227, 228
*Comments on the Restructured Constitution of 1974*, 51
Commerce Clearing House, 76, 175
commercial code, 48, 51, 64, 165, 176
Commercial Publishers of Legislative Materials, 26, 35
*Commercial Real Estate*, 152
Commission on Judicial Selection, 84, 238, 240
Commission on Uniform State Laws. See National Conference of Commissioners on Uniform State Laws
commissions, 7, 8, 15–20, 45, 46, 54, 62, 76, 79, 84, 116, 137, 156, 159, 238, 240, 241, 271, 272, 277, 285, 305–307, 432
commissions and offices that aid the legislature, 15, 18
commitment, 96, 112, 155, 156, 165, 168, 185, 263
committee books, 26, 29, 34
committee hearings, 15, 21, 22, 23, 30, 35
Committee of the Whole, 23, 24
*Committee on the Role of Judges in Pro Bono Activity. Report*, 156
Community Legal Education Project, 254, 255
compacts. See interstate compacts and agencies
compilation of statutes, 301
*Compilations of State Regulations on One Subject*, 69, 74
*Compilations of State Statutes on One Subject*, 57

## Index

compilations, revisions, codes, 45
compiled rules, 69, 71. See also *Minnesota Rules*
complaints of professional misconduct, 119. See also Lawyers Professional Responsibility Board
computer-assisted research, 207, 208, 221. See also LEXIS-NEXIS; Westlaw
conciliation courts, 86, 87, 91, 95, 97–99, 116, 159, 219, 246, 397
Conciliation Courts in Hennepin and Ramsey Counties, 98, 99
conference committees, 21, 24
*Consent Calendar*, 24
*Constitution of Minnesota*, 6, 9, 12, 48, 51, 271, 272. See also Minnesota Constitution
*Constitution of the United States*, 48, 53
constitutional amendments, 8, 9, 15, 16, 41, 42, 47, 57, 64, 91, 401
*Constitutional Change by Amendment: Recommendations*, 7
*Constitutional Commentary*, 189–191, 193
constitutional convention, 6, 7, 9, 271, 272, 282, 283
Constitutional Convention of 1857, 6, 271
constitutional documents, 6, 10, 271
constitutional officers, 63, 79, 283
constitutional reform, 6, 7
Consumer Division, 65, 250, 251. See also Minnesota Attorney General
consumers, 21, 65, 97, 139, 154, 160, 177, 178, 233, 250, 251, 253, 254, 390, 393, 394
Contents of Official Session Laws, 40, 41
contested district court trials, 106
continuing education, 88, 89, 118, 121, 122, 155, 198, 202, 226, 238, 240, 244, 245, 264, 269
continuing education for state court personnel, 89, 121, 122, 198, 202, 238, 240

continuing legal education. See Minnesota Continuing Legal Education
continuing legal education publications, 163, 164
convention, 6, 7, 9, 199, 271, 272, 282, 283
*Corporation Law and Practice*, 174
*Corpus Juris Secundum*, 50, 125, 150
corrections, 80, 116, 136, 249, 313
Council of State Governments, 54, 58, 61
county attorneys, 116, 141, 162, 184–186, 201, 238, 245, 250, 390, 392
County Court Act, 95
county courts, 87, 93–96, 113, 143, 261
county law libraries, 55, 67, 108, 110, 192, 196, 213, 215, 218–220, 395, 431. See also law libraries
County Law Library Project, 192, 196, 219
court administrators, 83, 89, 91, 94, 97, 99, 108, 117, 122, 143, 186–188, 198, 238, 240, 241, 261
*Court Consolidation Study Commission. Final Report*, 156
court decisions, 1, 36, 76, 86, 101, 103, 104, 148, 167, 174, 189, 196, 198, 199, 203, 209, 311, 432
Court Information Office, 238, 240
*Court Links*, 106
court of appeals, 75–77, 83, 86–88, 91, 92, 96, 97, 99–102, 104, 106, 111, 113, 116, 119, 136, 143, 144, 146, 182, 206, 209, 216, 239, 243, 286, 401, 420
court of appeals judges, 91, 113, 239
court of appeals jurisdiction, 91
court of appeals procedures, 91, 92
court opinions, 102, 103, 105, 106, 189, 206
court procedures, 87, 90, 93, 95
court records, 89, 95, 116, 208, 395
court reporters, 89, 102, 105, 107, 122, 129, 158, 203, 261, 268, 269, 432
court reports, 129, 133, 187, 188, 199, 204, 431
court rulemaking procedures, 112, 113

court rules, 1, 43, 51, 83, 88, 95, 100–102, 107, 112–115, 127, 128, 141, 151–153, 159, 171, 173, 180, 183, 189, 209, 210, 242, 244, 246, 312, 314–316, 317
Court System in Hennepin and Ramsey Counties, 87, 98
court unification, 83, 99
*Courtroom Handbook of Minnesota Evidence,* 174
courts of record, 118
*Creditors' Remedies,* 152
*Criminal Appeals,* 108, 169, 257, 258
*Criminal Appeals: Effective Practice and Procedure,* 169
*Criminal Code of 1963,* 46
*Criminal Courts Study Commission. Final Report,* 156
*Criminal Evidence,* 169
*Criminal Evidence: Constitutional, Statutory,* 169
*Criminal Jury Instruction Guide,* 173, 181
*Criminal Jury Trial Handbook,* 169
*Criminal Justice Abstracts,* 11, 61, 191, 193
*Criminal Law,* 152, 169, 173, 181
*Criminal Law and Procedure,* 169, 173
*Criminal Pretrial Practice,* 169
criminal procedure, 52, 99, 152, 165, 169, 172, 180, 183, 184, 433
*Criminal Procedure from Police Detention to Final Disposition,* 165
CRIMJIG. See Jury Instructions Guide, Criminal
*Cumulative Index to Local Laws,* 42
curative acts, 40, 41, 44, 47, 51, 175, 301, 307, 308
*Current Index to Legal Periodicals,* 191
*Current Law Index.* See *Legal Resource Index*
current opinions, 101, 102, 104, 106

*Daily Journals,* 27, 31, 35
*Daily Recorder,* 202

Dakota County Bar Association Referral Service, 259
Dakota County Juvenile Office, 248
Dakota County Law Library, 218, 220
Data Privacy Act, 77
*Data Privacy: Everything You Wanted to Know About the Minnesota,* 77
*Debtors' and Creditors' Rights and Remedies,* 165
*Defendant-Plaintiff Table of Cases,* 124, 125
definitions, 134, 171, 217, 223
Department of Human Services, 80, 156, 450
depository libraries, 79, 80, 213, 217, 218, 250, 427, 441
*Descriptive Word Index,* 43, 125, 126
desk manual, 166
determinate sentencing. See Minnesota Sentencing Guidelines
digests, 37, 42, 50, 54, 56–60, 67, 76, 104, 105, 114, 115, 123–126, 132, 134, 140, 150, 167, 171, 183, 201, 202, 206, 304, 307, 308, 311, 316, 317
*Directory, United States District Court,* 136
*Directory of County Law Libraries,* 219
*Directory of Law School Alternative Dispute Resolution Courses,* 234
*Directory of Lawyer Disciplinary Agencies, Lawyers' Funds,* 240
*Directory of Lawyer Referral Services,* 259
*Directory of Legal Aid and Defender Offices in the United,* 251
*Directory of Minnesota Business and Professional Associations,* 222
*Directory of Minnesota City & Village Officials,* 141
*Directory of Minnesota City Officials,* 141
*Directory of Minnesota Depository Libraries,* 217
*Directory of Minnesota Judges 1998,* 136

# Index

*Directory of Minnesota Law Firms on the Web*, 139
*Directory of Minnesota Municipal Officials*, 141
*Directory of Pro Bono Opportunities for Lawyers*, 260
*Directory of Pro Bono Programs*, 260
Disciplinary proceedings against attorneys, 119
Dispute Resolution Institute, 229, 230, 234, 235
district administrators, 89, 92, 94
district court administrators, 97, 241
district court judges, 93, 94, 100, 113, 136, 145, 181, 184
district court jurisdiction, 93
district court jury trials, 106
district court procedures, 93, 95
district courts, 83, 87, 93–100, 102, 103, 105, 106, 110, 111, 113–116, 136, 138, 144, 145, 181, 183, 184, 203, 216, 241, 247, 261, 285, 291
District Courts in Hennepin and Ramsey Counties, 98
Division of Conciliation, 116
*Divorce in Minnesota for Non-Lawyers: A Guide to the Legal System*, 178
dockets, 94, 106, 107, 110, 209
document depository, 80, 213, 217, 218, 250, 441
downtowners, 225
drafting, 10, 19–21, 131, 153, 166, 173, 176, 309
*Drafting Wills and Trust Agreements*, 166
Dred & Harriet Scott Institute, 229, 230
DRI. See Dispute Resolution Institute
*Drinking Driver in Minnesota: Criminal and Civil Issues*, 166
*Drinking/Driving Law Letter*, 197
*Dunnell Minnesota Digest*, 124, 132, 134, 150, 167
*Dunnell's Edition*, 67, 104
DWI, 139

economic security, 86, 91, 450
Education Law Project, 255
effective date, 21, 25, 43, 48, 57
Eighth Circuit Court of Appeals, 100, 111, 136, 216
Elderly Law Project, 253
electronic availability of opinions, 66, 67
*Employer's Guide to Employment Law Issues in Minnesota*, 166
*Employment in Minnesota: A Guide to Employment Practices*, 167
*Employment Law and Practice*, 174
*Enabling Act*, 5, 6, 10, 271
enactment of legislation, 13, 21
*Encyclopedia of American Law*, 151
*Encyclopedia of Associations*, 62
encyclopedias, 62, 124, 147, 150, 151, 164, 209, 395
English sovereignty, 1, 3
engrossment, 23, 30
estate planning, 166, 176, 179, 180
Ethical Practices Board, 50
ethics, 157, 229, 231, 244, 263
*Evidence*, 84, 112, 115, 128, 143, 169–171, 173–175, 209, 298, 301–304, 306–309, 327
Executive branch, 63, 69, 76, 77, 95, 142, 143, 242
Executive orders, 64, 71, 205, 206

fact-finding hearings, 106
family court, 96, 98, 183
Family Farm Law Project, 254, 390, 439
*Family Law*, 139, 140, 152, 164, 166, 171, 174, 183, 196–199, 253, 257, 393, 437
*Family Law Forum*, 196
*Family Law Newsletter*, 197
*Family Law Section News*, 196
Farm Law Program, 255
Farmers' Legal Action Group, 255, 390
federal court libraries, 216

federal courts, 50, 51, 83, 100, 101, 103, 106, 109, 111, 114, 115, 124, 129, 137, 189, 216, 247
federal courts in Minnesota, 83, 100, 103, 109, 111, 115, 216
Federal Document Depository Libraries in Minnesota. See Depository Libraries
*Federal Jury Practice and Instructions*, 116
*Federal Local Court Rules*, 115
*Federal Procedure Rules Service*, 115
federal public defenders, 247, 391
*Federal Register*, 427
*Federal Reporter* series, 106, 134
*Federal Supplement* series, 134
felonies, 99, 105, 118, 169, 286
*Felony Sentencing in Minnesota*, 169
file number, 14, 23, 25, 27, 33, 35, 39, 43, 102, 108, 109. See also Senate file; House file
*Finance and Commerce*, 113, 136, 182, 206
*Finance and Commerce Legal Directory*, 136
finding aids, 123, 125, 126
*Finding Your Way Around the Court System*, 83
*First 100 Years*, 100, 144
FLAG. See Farmers' Legal Action Group
Focus on Fairness, 253
*For the Record: 150 Years of Law and Lawyers in Minnesota*, 144
foreign jurisdiction, 1
form books, 147, 151, 153
forms, 5, 7, 16, 17, 21, 23, 32, 43–46, 58, 59, 66, 70, 97, 107, 112, 121, 127, 128, 130, 131, 137, 147, 151–154, 165–183, 185, 207, 209, 213, 259, 263, 271, 305, 308, 312, 388, 453
*Forms on Disk*, 152
Foster Care and Adoption Task Force. Final Report, 157
four-year programs, 266
freedom of information, 389

French sovereignty, 1, 2
*From Diploma to License*, 119

general laws, 25, 41, 106, 289, 297–299, 301–307, 310, 313–316, 432
*General Rules of Practice Annotated*, 173
*General Rules of Practice for the District Courts*, 99, 114
*General Statutes*, 51, 300–308, 401, 431
*Getting a Divorce: A Basic Guide to Minnesota Law*, 178
*Getting Protection From Abuse and Harassment*, 178
*Gilfillan's Reports*, 103
Globe College, 266
Government Data Practices Act, 77, 170
government law libraries, 213, 214, 216
government personnel, 81, 135, 141, 216
government publications, 60, 62, 75, 217, 427, 429
*Government Publications and Their Use*, 60
Government Publications Library, 217, 427, 429
governor, 4, 5, 15, 16, 20, 21, 25, 35, 40, 63, 64, 68, 84, 91, 119, 159–162, 206, 223, 239, 240, 242, 273, 274, 276, 279, 284, 285, 297, 307
grand jury, 84, 85, 185, 273, 276
gross misdemeanor offenses, 106
*Guide for Depository Libraries*, 79
*Guide to American Law*, 151
*Guide to Major Law Library Collections in the Twin Cities*, 215
*Guide to Microforms in Print: Author/Title*, 208
*Guide to Microforms in Print: Subject*, 208
*Guide to Minnesota Bar Admission for Law Graduates*, 119
*Guide to Minnesota State Documents and Selected*, 218

# Index

*Guide to Public Assistance Programs,* 178
*Guidebook to State Agency Services,* 18, 63, 69, 78, 83, 89, 142, 216, 389
*Guidelines for Legal Reference Service,* 225, 383
*Guidelines for Minnesota Court Facilities. Final Report,* 157
*Guidelines for the Approval of Legal Assistant,* 264

*Hamline Journal of Public Law. See Hamline Journal of Public Law and Policy*
*Hamline Journal of Public Law and Policy,* 189–191, 193, 431
*Hamline Law Review,* 171, 189–191, 193, 431
Hamline University, 108, 110, 111, 164, 167, 168, 193, 214, 215, 217, 229–231, 244, 256, 257, 266–268, 395, 428
Hamline University School of Law, 108, 110, 111, 164, 167, 168, 193, 214, 215, 217, 229–231, 256, 257, 268
Hamline University's Dispute Resolution Institute, 234, 235
*Handbook for Minnesota Cities,* 185
*Handbook to Minnesota State Government,* 141
handbooks, 73, 105, 154, 163, 164, 182, 184
hardcopy availability of opinions, 66
HCBA. *See* Hennepin County Bar Association
headnotes, 47, 48, 102–104
hearings, 15, 17, 21–23, 30, 35, 36, 68, 70, 71, 75, 86, 90, 94, 96, 100, 106, 112, 113, 170, 178, 182, 197, 200, 238, 239, 241, 242, 248, 394
*Hein's Legal Periodical Checklist,* 188
Hennepin County, 55, 67, 93, 97, 98, 110, 137–139, 183–185, 196, 206, 215, 218, 220, 227, 236, 246, 259, 389–393, 395, 428, 431, 437

Hennepin County Bar Association, 137, 139, 196, 236, 246, 259, 392
*Hennepin County Family Law Bench Book,* 183
Hennepin County Law Library, 67, 110, 215, 218, 220, 395, 431
*Hennepin Lawyer,* 105, 190, 196, 236, 431
Historical Society, 12, 18, 20, 29, 30, 32, 64, 78, 79, 95, 143, 145, 221, 223, 441, 452
historical works, 130, 143
History Center, 223
*History of Minnesota,* 1, 12
*History of the American Law Institute and the First,* 149
*History of the Bench and Bar of Minnesota,* 144
*History of the Constitution of Minnesota,* 6, 12
*History of the Office of the Attorney General,* 144
*History of the United States District Court for the District,* 144
Hmong Bar Association, 237
*Hollingshead's Reports,* 103
home rule, 42, 55, 276, 277, 283
Homeless Outreach and Prevention Education Program, 255
House file, 32, 41, 43
*House Index,* 14, 27, 31
House Information Office, 13, 143
*House Journal,* 31
House of Representatives, 4, 5, 13, 15, 16, 27, 31, 143, 299, 309, 310
housing courts, 98, 99
Housing Discrimination Law Project, 254
*How a Bill Becomes a Law,* 22
*How to File for Divorce in Minnesota: With Forms,* 178
*How to Form a Simple Corporation in Minnesota,* 178
*How to Form Your Own Minnesota Corporation,* 179
*How to Incorporate & Start a Business in Minnesota,* 179

*How to Make a Minnesota Will*, 179
*How to Shepardize, Your Guide to Legal Research Using Shepard's*, 128
*How to Start a Business in Minnesota*, 179
human rights, 57, 221, 224, 229–232, 250, 251, 392, 435
Human Rights Center, 224, 231, 232
Human Rights Division, 250, 251

ILP. See *Index to Legal Periodicals*
*Impact of Rule 114 on Civil Litigation Practice*, 158
*In Pursuit of Excellence: A History of the University*, 145
incorporation by reference, 73
*Index Digest to All the Laws of the State of Minnesota General*, 42, 304
*Index to Foreign Legal Periodicals*, 191
*Index to Legal Periodicals*, 11, 12, 61, 190, 191, 193–196
*Index to Minnesota Legal Periodicals*, 190, 192
*Index to Periodical Articles Related to Law*, 191
*Indian Affairs*, 2
Indian Legal Assistance, 248
Information Systems Office, 89
initiative. See referendum
Institute on Criminal Justice, 231
Institute on Race & Poverty, 231, 232
intent. See legislative intent
*Interchange: A Monthly Forum and Digest for the Criminal*, 202
*Interstate Compacts & Agencies*, 53
interstate compacts and agencies, 54, 162, 208.
introduction of the bill, 21, 22
Inver Hills Community College, 265, 441
IOLTA. See Lawyers Trust Account Board
IRP. See Institute on Race & Poverty
Itasca Community College, 265, 441

James J. Hill Reference Library, 79, 221, 222
JIGS. See Jury Instruction Guides
*Journal of Law and Religion*, 190, 191, 193
*Journal of Minnesota Public Law*, 193
*Journal of the House of Representatives*, 14, 27, 29, 299
*Journal of the Senate*, 14, 27, 28
journals, 11, 14, 20, 24–27, 30, 31, 33–35, 61, 64, 188–192, 195
*Judges of the United States*, 137
Judicare of Anoka County, 252, 393, 435
Judicial Advisory Service, 89
judicial bench books, 163, 183
judicial boards, 83, 118
judicial branch, 95, 138, 142, 226
judicial conference, 137
judicial directory, 137
Judicial Information System (SJIS), 89
*Judicial Profiles Desk Book*, 137
judicial websites, 83
*Judicial Yellow Book*, 137
judicially sanctioned agencies, 213, 238
judiciary, 29, 83, 106, 118, 135, 136, 144, 154–156, 163, 239, 245, 272
juries, 4, 83–85, 87, 96–98, 105, 106, 112, 115, 116, 128, 157, 163, 169, 173, 180–183, 185, 209, 273, 276, 286
jury instruction guides, 112, 115, 163, 173, 180, 181
*Jury Instruction Guides, Civil*, 173, 180, 181
*Jury Instruction Guides, Criminal*, 173, 181
jury instructions, 112, 115, 116, 128, 163, 173, 180–182
Jury Verdict Research, 105, 182
jury verdicts, 105, 163, 182, 183
justice courts, 96
justices of the peace, 5, 96, 202

# Index

juvenile court, 96, 155, 169, 183
Juvenile Court Act, 96
*Juvenile Court Handbook: A Practitioner's Guide*, 169
*Juvenile Court, Hennepin County, Minnesota Bench Book*, 183
*Juvenile Law and Practice*, 174
*Juvenile Representation Study Committee. Report*, 157
juveniles, 86, 96, 98, 155, 157, 160, 169, 174, 177, 183, 184, 186, 187, 248, 250, 391, 393

Kensington Runestone, 2
key numbers, 50, 102, 104, 125, 148, 307, 317
*KeyCite*, 129, 130
KidsLAW, 253

labor law, 164, 174, 198, 207
LAMP. See Legal Assistance to Minnesota Prisoners
*Landfill Cleanup Insurance Recovery Project: 1997 Progress Report to the Legislature*, 161
LAP. See Legal Advocacy Project
LASNEM. See Legal Aid Service of Northeastern Minnesota
*Law & Inequality: A Journal of Theory and Practice*, 190, 191, 194
*Law Alumni News*, 197
*Law and Use of Interstate Compacts*, 53
*Law Book Catalogue of the Minnesota State Library*, 109
*Law Book News*, 202
*Law Books and Serials in Print: A Multimedia Sourcebook*, 208
law clerks, 89, 220, 261, 268
*Law Finder*. See *West's Minnesota Digest 2d Law Finder*
law libraries, 2, 11, 27, 52, 55, 66, 67, 73, 74, 78, 79, 107–111, 122, 131, 145, 146, 148, 151, 165, 190, 192, 196, 208–210, 213–220, 221, 224, 225, 247, 249, 383, 384, 389, 395, 396, 428, 430, 431, 433, 442, 453

law library holdings, 107, 109
Law Library Service to Prisoners Project, 247, 249
*Law Office Systems*, 152
law reviews, 11, 61, 114, 128–130, 132, 149, 171, 188–193, 195, 209, 311, 431–433
law school clinics, 245, 256, 393
law school library, 108, 215
law school programs, 244, 245
law schools, 135, 144, 193, 197, 213, 214, 229, 231–233, 245, 248, 256, 260
*Law, Courts, and Lawyers in the Frontier Days of Minnesota*, 1, 145
*Laws of Minnesota*, 10, 26, 27, 32, 33, 40–42, 47, 48, 72, 298–311, 432
Lawyers Professional Responsibility Board, 118–120, 139, 238, 240, 433
Lawyers Trust Account Board, 238, 241, 246
*Lawyer's Almanac*, 62
League of Minnesota Cities, 55, 141, 185, 198, 221, 222, 394
Leech Lake Reservation Criminal and Juvenile Defense, 248
legal administrators, 201, 261, 262
*Legal Advisory*, 198, 202
*Legal Advocacy for Persons with Developmental Disabilities*, 256
Legal Advocacy Project (LAP), 247, 248, 394
Legal Advocacy Project for Developmentally Disabled Persons, 254
legal aid, 241, 245, 251–254, 260, 384, 393, 437, 438
Legal Aid Service of Northeastern Minnesota (LASNEM), 253, 438
legal assistance, 156, 157, 180, 200, 213, 245–248, 253–260, 390, 391, 393, 394, 397, 436, 438
Legal Assistance to Minnesota Prisoners (LAMP), 247, 248
Legal Assistance to Older Americans, 254

legal assistants, 168, 245, 259, 261, 263, 264, 266, 267, 399
*Legal Ledger*, 35, 36, 113, 206
*Legal Looseleafs in Print*, 207
*Legal Materials for Non-Law Libraries*, 225
*Legal Memoranda and Appellate Brief Bank Index*, 108
legal newsletters, 207
*Legal Newsletters in Print*, 207
legal newspapers, 39, 55, 65, 66, 76, 103, 105, 113, 147, 188, 190, 192, 205, 206
legal periodical indexes, 188, 191, 192
legal periodicals, 11, 61, 123, 147, 168, 188–196, 208
*Legal Record*, 202
legal research, 19, 58, 63, 80, 123, 128, 151, 175, 210, 211, 217, 225, 249, 261, 316, 383, 394, 399, 400
*Legal Resource Index*, 11, 12, 61, 190, 191, 193–196
Legal Rights Center, 248, 391
legal secretaries, 261–263
legal services, 97, 120, 160, 162, 163, 177–180, 246, 250–262, 264, 389, 392–394, 396, 397, 435–439
Legal Services Advisory Committee, 246, 260
Legal Services Advocacy Project, 254, 255
Legal Services of Northwest Minnesota, 178, 253
legal studies, 266–268
*Legalink*, 263
*Legaltrac*. See *Legal Resource Index*
legislation, 1, 13, 14, 17, 21, 27, 31, 33, 37–39, 42, 44, 46, 52, 55, 57, 58, 60, 64, 69, 78, 89, 95, 99, 157, 161, 165, 176, 178, 179, 185, 186, 195, 197, 198, 200–202, 207, 223, 251, 275, 276, 280, 291, 302–304, 307, 308, 418
legislative branch, 80, 143, 223, 441
*Legislative Bulletin*, 202
legislative commissions, 18

Legislative Coordinating Commission, 16
legislative district maps, 17
legislative drafting, 10
legislative history, 13, 26, 30, 33, 34, 127, 172, 223, 310
legislative intent, 26, 34 , 36, 105, 299
*Legislative Manual*, 10, 16–18, 63, 65, 69, 138, 142, 205, 273, 401
legislative members, 142
legislative offices, 13, 18, 285
legislative offices that serve the public, 13
Legislative Reference Library, 16, 18–20, 30, 32, 34, 39, 75, 79, 80, 217, 218, 221, 223, 250, 431, 441, 451
legislative research, 26, 33, 70
Legislative Research Committee, 33
legislative rules, 22
legislative sessions, 6, 8, 17, 27, 29–32, 35, 37, 38, 43, 44, 52, 142, 273, 283–285, 300, 302
legislature, 5–10, 12, 13, 15–22, 25–27, 30, 31, 33, 34, 35, 37, 38, 40–46, 53, 55, 57, 58, 60, 63, 64, 69, 70, 80, 83, 94, 95, 99, 112, 116, 117, 131, 142, 143, 148, 154, 158–163, 180, 205, 209, 218, 223, 227, 234, 239, 241, 243, 250, 269, 271, 274, 275, 277, 278, 280–286, 298–300, 304–307, 309, 313, 314, 401, 403, 418, 420
LEXIS-NEXIS, 35, 37, 40, 43, 62, 127, 130, 132, 140, 150, 153, 154, 189, 190, 193–195, 209
*Lexis-Nexis Directory of Online Services*, 189
*Lexis Publishing Law on Disc— Minnesota, Dunnell's Edition*, 104
*Liability Reports*, 105
library organizations, 213, 221, 224, 227
library school programs, 213, 227
*Limits of Municipal Power Under Home Rule*, 55
liquor liability, 172
local documents, 63, 78, 81

# Index

local government, 13, 42, 55, 69, 223, 283
local law, 42, 47, 59, 195, 208, 312
local lawmaking bodies, 53, 54
locating bills, 26, 30
Loislaw, 209
loose-leaf services, 59, 60, 70, 75, 105, 106, 207, 225, 317
*Loquitur*, 196, 216
LRI. See Legal Resource Index
LRL. See Legislative Reference Library
*LRL Checklist of Minnesota Government Publications*, 75

M.S.A. See *Minnesota Statutes Annotated*
*MACA Monitor*, 198
magistrates, 100, 136, 247
Major Legal Indexes, 188, 190
MALL. See Minnesota Association of Law Libraries
*MALL Newsletter*, 225
*Manual for Grand Jury Presentation*, 185
*Manual for Minnesota Attorneys Utilizing Legal Assistants*, 264
*Manual for Prosecution of Domestic Violence*, 185
*Manual of Model Criminal Jury Instructions*, 181
*Manual of State Agency Rules*, 72
*Martindale-Hubbell International Arbitration and Dispute*, 235
*Martindale-Hubbell Law Digest*, 124, 126
*Martindale-Hubbell Law Directory*, 58, 140
Mason Publishing Company, 183, 203
*Mason's Dunnell on Minnesota Probate Law*, 167
*Mason's Minnesota Motor Vehicle Law*, 167
*Mason's Minnesota Statutes 1927*, 32, 48, 308–310
materials in special formats, 123, 207
MCAR. See *Minnesota Code of Agency Rules*

MCLE. See Minnesota Continuing Legal Education
mediation, 89, 117, 156–158, 201, 233–235, 257
*Medical Malpractice Reform and Healthcare Costs: Final Report*, 161
MELSA. See Minnesota Library Services Agency
*Membership Directory, Minnesota American Indian Bar Association*, 140
memorial resolutions, 25
memorials to Supreme Court justices, 102
Mental Health Law Project (MHLP), 256
*Methods of Practice*, 173
Metronet, 221, 224, 227
Metropolitan Council, 57, 198, 221, 224, 451
Metropolitan Council Library, 451
Metropolitan Library Service Agency, 224, 227
MHLP. See Mental Health Law Project
microfiche, 66, 78, 80, 107–111, 195, 204, 207, 219, 427, 441
microfilm, 67, 111, 204, 207, 272, 289, 297
microforms, 207, 208, 218, 271
Mid-Minnesota Legal Assistance (MMLA), 254, 255
Midwestern School of Law, 229
Migrant Legal Services, 255, 393
MILE. See Minnesota Institute of Legal Education
MINITEX, 221
*Minnattorney.com*, 140
Minneapolis Municipal Information Library, 81
*Minnesota Administrative Law Journal*, 203
*Minnesota Administrative Practice and Procedure*, 167
*Minnesota Administrative Procedure*, 70
*Minnesota Adoption Law and Practice with Forms and Statutes*, 167

*Minnesota American Indian Bar Association, Membership Directory,* 140
*Minnesota Annotations,* 148–150
*Minnesota Annotations to the Restatement of the Law,* 150
*Minnesota Annotations to the Restatement of the Law of Property,* 150
Minnesota appellate courts, 101, 109, 124
Minnesota Association of Black Lawyers, 237
Minnesota Association of Criminal Defense Lawyers, 238
Minnesota Association of Law Libraries, 214, 224, 225, 236, 259, 383, 428
*Minnesota Association of Law Libraries Membership Directory,* 214
Minnesota Association of Verbatim Reporters and Captioners, 269
Minnesota Attorney General, 18, 19, 50, 56, 63, 65–68, 104, 108, 128, 129, 144, 154, 159–163, 168, 184, 196, 201, 204, 206, 239, 245, 250, 251, 303, 307, 309–311, 319, 321, 329, 389, 390, 397, 431, 433, 449
Minnesota Attorney General opinions, 50, 66–67, 104, 128, 159, 160, 161, 163, 204, 311, 329, 433
*Minnesota Attorney General reports,* 68, 154, 159, 319
*Minnesota Attorney's/Paralegal's/Secretary's Handbook,* 137, 237, 262
*Minnesota Ballot Bulletin,* 198
*Minnesota Blue and White Book,* 133
*Minnesota Business and Commercial Law Journal,* 203
*Minnesota Case Reports,* 105, 182
*Minnesota Cause of Action Manual,* 170
*Minnesota Citations,* 11, 55, 68, 127–130, 132, 133
*Minnesota Cities,* 51, 55, 141, 185, 198, 199, 221, 222, 394

*Minnesota Civil Commitment and Treatment Act Training Seminar,* 168
*Minnesota Civil Mediation Act,* 117
*Minnesota Civil Practice,* 152, 168
*Minnesota Civil Trialbook,* 114
*Minnesota Code of Agency Rules,* 72, 74, 431
*Minnesota Code of Agency Rules Reprint,* 72
*Minnesota Collections,* 168
*Minnesota Compiled Rules,* 69, 71
*Minnesota Condemnation Law,* 168
*Minnesota Congressmen, Legislators, and Other Elected Officials,* 145
Minnesota *Constitution,* 1, 6, 8–13, 41, 55, 57, 63, 83, 93, 95, 261, 273, 291, 401, 409, 418, 431
*Minnesota Constitutional Study Commission,* 7, 8
Minnesota Continuing Legal Education, 59, 77, 114, 121, 122, 151, 153, 158, 163–166, 172, 173, 176, 184, 195, 203, 210–213, 238, 242, 244, 245, 262, 264, 399, 431, 432
*Minnesota Corporation Law & Practice,* 168
*Minnesota Corporations Practice Manual,* 168
*Minnesota County Attorney Directory,* 141
Minnesota County Attorneys Association, 184, 238, 250
Minnesota County Attorneys Council, 186, 250
*Minnesota County Directory,* 142
Minnesota court of appeals, 86, 101, 143, 144, 146, 206, 209
Minnesota courts, 50, 83, 86, 101, 112, 114, 125, 141, 143, 144, 146, 151, 157–159, 171, 186–188, 198, 202, 206, 209, 210, 432
*Minnesota Courts, Expediting Justice,* 188
*Minnesota Crimes and Defenses,* 169
*Minnesota Crimes, Vehicles and Related Statutes,* 169

# Index

*Minnesota Criminal Gang Oversight Council*, 162
*Minnesota Criminal Jury Trial Handbook*, 169
*Minnesota Criminal Law* series, 169
*Minnesota Criminal Pretrial Practice & Procedure*, 169
*Minnesota Damages Awards: Personal Injury & Intentional Torts*, 182
*Minnesota Data Privacy Opinions Reporter*, 170
*Minnesota Defense*, 196, 238
Minnesota Defense Lawyers Association, 238
*Minnesota Digest*, 124–126, 132, 134, 150, 167
Minnesota Disability Law Center, 254, 256, 391
*Minnesota Disbarred and Currently Suspended Lawyers*, 120
*Minnesota Dissolution of Marriage*, 170
*Minnesota District Court Reporter*, 203
Minnesota District Judges Association, 115, 136, 173, 181, 238
*Minnesota Divorce & Family Lawyers & Law*, 140
*Minnesota Divorce Law*, 179, 180
*Minnesota Divorce Revolution*, 180
*Minnesota e-Direct*, 137
*Minnesota Elected Officials*, 142
*Minnesota Employment Law Letter*, 198
*Minnesota Employment Laws*, 174
*Minnesota Environmental Compliance Update*, 203
*Minnesota Environmental Law Handbook*, 170
*Minnesota Evidence Courtroom Manual*, 170
*Minnesota Evidence Trialbook*, 170
*Minnesota Evidentiary Foundations*, 171
*Minnesota Executive Documents*, 78, 319

*Minnesota Family Law Digest*, 171
*Minnesota Family Law Journal*, 198
*Minnesota Family Law Practice Manual*, 171
*Minnesota Family Law Primer*, 171
*Minnesota Family Law Quarterly*, 199
*Minnesota Gang Strike Force*, 162
*Minnesota Government Report*, 35, 199, 202
*Minnesota Government Report's Court Report*, 199
*Minnesota Guidebook to State Agency Services*, 18, 63, 69, 78, 83, 89, 142, 216, 389
Minnesota Historical Society, 12, 18, 20, 29, 30, 32, 64, 78, 95, 145, 221, 223, 441, 452
Minnesota Institute of Legal Education, 164, 172, 211, 244, 245, 431
*Minnesota Insurance Law*, 171, 203
*Minnesota Insurance Law Journal*, 203
Minnesota Intellectual Property Law Association, 238
*Minnesota Intellectual Property Review*, 194
*Minnesota Journal of Global Trade*, 189–191, 194
*Minnesota Journal of Law and Politics*, 203, 432
*Minnesota Journal of Trial Advocacy*, 203
*Minnesota Judges Criminal Benchbook*, 184
Minnesota Judicial Center, 76, 122, 146, 216, 219, 428, 453
*Minnesota Judicial Directory*, 137
*Minnesota Jury Instruction Guides, Misdemeanor*, 181
*Minnesota Jury Instruction Guides: Civil*, 115, 181
*Minnesota Jury Instruction Guides: Criminal*, 115
Minnesota Justice Foundation, 200, 260, 261

*Minnesota Labor and Employment Law Journal*, 203
Minnesota Labor Relations Act, 116, 201
*Minnesota Law & Politics*, 199
*Minnesota Law Journal*, 199, 203, 432
*Minnesota Law Reports*, 101, 203, 205
*Minnesota Law Review*, 128, 189–191, 194, 195, 431–433
*Minnesota Lawyer*, 166, 174, 182, 183, 203, 206, 433
Minnesota Legal Administrators Association, 201, 261, 262
*Minnesota Legal Directory*, 138, 140, 236, 237, 262, 263
*Minnesota Legal Forms*, 152, 153
Minnesota Legal Periodical Indexes, 188, 192
Minnesota Legal Periodicals, 191, 192
*Minnesota Legal Register*, 66, 68, 76, 196, 203, 204, 321
*Minnesota Legal Register* (Attorney General Opinions Issue), 66
Minnesota Legal Services Coalition (MLSC), 251, 252
*Minnesota Legal Systems, Probate*, 171
*Minnesota Legislative Manual.* See Legislative Manual
Minnesota Library Association, 79, 217, 224, 227
*Minnesota Library Directory*, 221
Minnesota Library Services Agency, 224, 227
*Minnesota Limitations Manual*, 171
*Minnesota Liquor Liability Law*, 172
*Minnesota Mechanics Liens Practice Manual*, 172
*Minnesota Medical Malpractice*, 172
Minnesota Minority Lawyers Association, 238
*Minnesota Misdemeanors and Moving Traffic Violations*, 172
*Minnesota Municipalities*, 198, 199
*Minnesota News Council*, 117

*Minnesota Nonprofit Corporations*, 172
*Minnesota Nonprofit Corporations: A Corporate and Tax Guide*, 172
*Minnesota No-Fault Automobile Insurance*, 172
*Minnesota Objections at Trial*, 173
Minnesota Paralegal Association, 263, 264
Minnesota Paralegal Institute, 267
*Minnesota Partnership Practice*, 173
*Minnesota Pleading*, 152, 167, 176
*Minnesota Practice*, 77, 114, 115, 125, 152, 173, 181
*Minnesota Practice Series* (West Group), 114
*Minnesota Probate*, 167, 177
*Minnesota Prosecutors Manual*, 185
*Minnesota Public Sector Labor Law*, 174
*Minnesota Real Estate*, 174, 175, 199
*Minnesota Real Estate Law Journal*, 199
*Minnesota Real Estate Law Practice Manual*, 175
*Minnesota Regulation News*, 204
*Minnesota Reporter*, 67, 101, 104, 134, 138
*Minnesota Reports*, 101–103, 109, 110, 128, 133, 134, 138, 310, 431, 432
*Minnesota Residential Real Estate*, 174
*Minnesota Resources: A Selected List of Current*, 80, 210, 218
*Minnesota Revised Laws 1905*, 32
*Minnesota Revisor's Manual with Styles and Forms*, 21, 66, 131
*Minnesota Rules*, 21, 72–77, 90, 92, 112, 114, 115, 155, 173, 175, 264, 432
*Minnesota Rules Drafting Manual*, 21
*Minnesota Rules of Court*, 114, 115
Minnesota Rules of Professional Conduct, 264
*Minnesota Rules Practice*, 173
Minnesota School of Business, 266

# Index

*Minnesota Sentencing Guidelines,* 112, 116, 238, 241
*Minnesota Session Law Service,* 40, 43, 52, 113, 142, 432
Minnesota session laws, 11, 40, 43, 52, 113, 142, 432. See also *Laws of Minnesota*
*Minnesota Standards for Title Examination,* 44, 175
*Minnesota State Agency Periodicals,* 80, 218
Minnesota State Bar Association, 113, 120, 149, 150, 164, 166, 173, 175–177, 181, 184, 195, 196, 197, 204, 210–212, 236, 237, 244, 246, 259, 260, 392, 432, 433
Minnesota state court, 93, 102, 114, 187, 188
*Minnesota State Court Report,* 187, 188
*Minnesota State Court System Annual Report,* 187
Minnesota state courts, 83, 87, 187, 188
*Minnesota State Documents,* 17, 40, 75, 78–80, 218
*Minnesota State Documents Lists,* 80
*Minnesota State Documents: A Guide for Depository Libraries,* 79
Minnesota State Law Library, 55, 73, 78, 79,107–110, 145, 146, 192, 196, 215–217, 219, 225, 249, 389, 395, 428, 433, 442, 453
*Minnesota State Law Library 150th Anniversary Event,* 146
*Minnesota State Law Library Union Catalog on Microfiche,* 1986, 219
*Minnesota State Register,* 64, 69–71, 73, 74, 76, 142, 143, 205, 206, 317, 431, 432
*Minnesota State Regulations,* 72
*Minnesota State Rules of Evidence with Objections,* 175
Minnesota statehood, 4, 5, 51, 297
*Minnesota Statutes,* 10, 11, 32–34, 38– 54, 57, 63, 67, 69, 70, 73, 76, 77, 87, 112, 114, 125, 133, 134, 142, 150, 152, 154, 162, 170, 171, 180, 189, 205, 209, 210, 223, 242, 246, 297, 306–316, 384, 432, 433
*Minnesota Statutes Annotated,* 10, 11, 32, 39, 43–45, 49–54, 67, 70, 76, 77, 112, 114, 125, 133, 134, 150, 189, 311, 432, 433
Minnesota Supreme Court, 76, 83, 86, 101, 103, 110, 112, 121, 130, 136, 138, 144, 155–158, 165, 187, 188, 198, 202, 206, 209, 233, 234, 239, 240, 242, 264, 311, 401, 428, 431
*Minnesota Supreme Court Decisions,* 101, 311
*Minnesota Tax Appeals,* 175
*Minnesota Tax Court Decisions,* 196, 203
*Minnesota Tax Court Reports,* 204
*Minnesota Tax Law Journal,* 204
*Minnesota Tax Reporter: State and Local,* 175
Minnesota territory, 4, 5, 298
Minnesota trial courts, 86, 101, 105, 109, 110
*Minnesota Trial Lawyer,* 182, 196, 204, 432
Minnesota Trial Lawyers Association, *105, 238*
*Minnesota Trial Transcript,* 108
*Minnesota Trial Transcript, Medical Index,* 108
*Minnesota Unemployment Insurance Guide,* 175
*Minnesota Uniform Commercial Code Deskbook,* 176
*Minnesota Wills & Estate Planning,* 176
Minnesota Women Lawyers, 141, 200, 238, 259, 392
*Minnesota, a Bicentennial History,* 1
*Minnesota's Journal of Law and Politics,* 199
misdemeanor violations bureaus, 99
MJF. See Minnesota Justice Foundation
MLA. See Minnesota Library Association

MLSC. See Minnesota Legal Services Coalition
MMLA. See Mid-Minnesota Legal Assistance
*Monthly Catalog of U.S. Government Publications*, 62
Moorhead State University, 266, 429, 442
*Motor Carrier News*, 200
motor vehicles, 167, 169, 176, 280, 282, 283
MSA. See *Minnesota Statutes Annotated*
MSBA. See Minnesota State Bar Association
*MSBA in Brief*, 204
MTLA. See Minnesota Trial Lawyers Association
*MTLA Newsletter*, 196
*Municipal Codes of Minnesota: A Working Bibliography*, 176
municipal courts, 87, 96, 98, 105, 113, 311
*Municipal Yellow Book*, 142
MWL. See Minnesota Women Lawyers

*N.W.2d advance sheets*, 108
National Association of Attorneys General, 250
National Association of Legal Assistants, 263
National Association of Legal Secretaries—Twin Cities Chapter, 262
National Conference of Commissioners on Uniform State Laws, 18, 19, 54, 69
National Court Reporters Association, 269
National District Attorneys Association, 250
*National Reporter Blue Book*, 133
*NCBE Directory*, 242
*Negligence and Compensation Cases Annotated*, 105
Neighborhood Justice Center, 248, 391
*New Matter*, 196

*Newsletter—Minnesota Trial Lawyers Association*, 204
newspapers, 16, 17, 19, 32, 33, 36, 39, 55, 65, 66, 76, 103, 105, 113, 147, 182, 188, 190, 192, 195, 197, 202, 203–206, 268, 277, 278
nominative, 103
non-law libraries, 213, 221, 225
North Hennepin Community College, 265, 442
*North Western Digest*, 124, 126, 132
*North Western Reporter*, 101, 102, 103, 104, 108, 109, 113, 125, 126, 128–130, 133, 134, 136, 138, 433
*North Western Reporter Citations*, 129–130
*Northwest Ordinance of 1787*, 4–6, 10, 48
Northwest Territory, 4, 289
*Northwestern Citations*, 127, 133
*Northwestern Reporter*, 101–104, 108, 109, 113, 129
*Northwestern Reporter 2d*, 101, 103, 104, 108, 109, 113
*Notice and Hearing Bulletin*, 200
*Notice of Change in the Release of Appellate Opinions*, 104
*Numerical Index to the Selected Opinions of the Minnesota*, 67, 329

OAH. See Office of Administrative Hearings
*ODP Catalyst*, 200
Office of Administrative Assistant to the Supreme Court, 89
Office of Administrative Hearings, 68, 70, 75, 182, 197, 238, 241, 242
Office of Attorney General, 160
Office of the Chief Clerk of the House, 14, 27, 29, 31, 40
Office of the Secretary of the Senate, 14, 27, 29, 40, 143
Office of the State Court Administrator, 83, 186–188, 238, 240, 241

# Index

*Official American Bar Association Guide to Approved Law Schools*, 229
*Official Directory of the Minnesota Legislature*, 143
official session laws, 40, 41. See also Laws of Minnesota; Minnesota session laws
*Opinions of the Attorney General.* See Minnesota Attorney General Opinions
*Opinions of the Lawyers Professional Responsibility*, 119
*Opinions of the Minnesota Attorney General.* See Minnesota Attorney General Opinions
*Opinions of the Minnesota State Appellate Courts Archive*, 102
Oppenheimer Wolff & Donnelly, 147
ordinances, 4–6, 10, 48, 55–57, 86, 96, 99, 127, 128, 176, 222
Organic Act, 5, 10, 48, 271, 297
Organic Act of Minnesota (1849), 10
original jurisdiction, 87, 93, 96
*OSHA Staffing: A Report to the Legislature*, 161
other sources of law, 13, 53, 311
*Overview of the Rules of Criminal Procedure*, 52

PAIR. See Protections and Advocacy of Individual Rights
*PAIS International*, 191
PALS, 19, 20, 75, 80, 218, 219, 250, 449–454
parallel citations, 102, 127, 130, 133
*Parental Cooperation Task Force. Final Report*, 157
*Periodical Indexes Useful to the Legal Researcher*, 188, 191
periodicals, 11, 19, 39, 50, 56, 60, 61, 80, 123, 128, 147, 164, 168, 188–196, 201, 208, 209, 218, 224, 317, 427
periodicals that have ceased publication, 192, 201

personal injury, 105, 139, 152, 153, 166, 182, 183, 251
*Personal Injury Valuation Handbooks*, 105
personnel who aid the Court of Appeals, 91
personnel who aid the District Court, 93, 94
personnel who aid the Supreme Court, 87, 89
PESI. See Professional Education Systems
petit jury, 84, 85
petty misdemeanor cases, 100
Phillips Legislative Service, 35, 202
*Phillips' Legislative Interim Reporter*, 35
*Pimsleur's Checklists of Basic American Legal Publications*, 4, 148
*Pirsig on Minnesota Pleading*, 152, 167, 176
*Politics in Minnesota*, 35, 36, 199, 200
popular name tables, 130, 132
popular names, 14, 49, 60, 130, 132, 133
popular works, 163, 177
practice manuals, 77, 115, 147, 163–165, 168, 171, 172, 175, 185
*Practitioner's Guide to Minnesota No-Fault Act*, 176
*Practitioner's Guide to Minnesota Personal Injury Forms*, 153
*Premise*, 67, 104
Preservation of Affordable and Safe Housing Program, 255
primary sources, 1, 150, 164, 177
prisoners, 247–249, 252, 257, 258, 394
privacy, 63, 77, 135, 170, 211, 389
privacy rights, 63, 77
private law libraries, 213, 214
private warnings, 119
pro bono programs, 246, 260, 435
*Pro Bono Report*, 200
probate, 5, 46, 86, 89, 95, 96, 98, 152, 164, 167, 171, 177, 278, 279, 282
Probate Code, 46, 167, 177
probate courts, 95

procedures for changing the Constitution, 6, 9
proclamations, 8, 10, 64, 206
professional boards, 118
Professional Education Systems, 244, 245
professional rules for attorneys and judges, 112, 114
*Progress-Register*, 204
Project H.O.P.E, 255
property, 36, 44, 96, 148, 150, 158, 174, 175, 179, 194, 196, 197, 199, 238, 240, 275–277, 279, 281, 285
proprietary programs, 265, 266
*Prosecuting the Drug-Impaired Driver*, 186
*Prosecution of Juvenile Delinquents*, 186
Protection from Domestic Abuse and Child Custody Program, 255
Protections and Advocacy of Individual Rights (PAIR), 256
public access, 63, 77, 95, 113, 120, 427
public defender, 116, 165, 185, 239, 243, 245, 247–249, 391, 394
public defense corporations, 247, 248
public education, 232, 246, 255, 256, 259
*Public Law News*, 197
published opinions, 102

*Quaere*, 204
questions of professional conduct, 119
Quicklaw, 209
*Qwest Dex White Pages*, 143

Railroad and Warehouse Commission, 76, 432
*Ramsey Barrister*, 195, 204
Ramsey County, 55, 93, 97–99, 110, 138, 147, 183, 195, 204, 215, 218, 220, 227, 236, 237, 259, 391–393, 395, 429, 438
Ramsey County Bar Association, 236, 237, 259, 392
*Ramsey County Family Court Bench Book*, 183
Ramsey County Law Library, 110, 215, 218, 220, 395
reading, 21, 23, 24, 33, 54, 385
reciprocal statutes, 53, 54
recording, 30, 105
Records and Briefs in Cases Decided by Federal Courts, 109, 111
Records and Briefs in Cases Decided by Minnesota Appellate, 109
Records and Briefs in Cases Decided by Minnesota Trial Courts, 109, 110
Records and Briefs in Cases Decided by the U.S. Supreme Court, 109, 111
referees, 94, 99, 118, 239
referendum, 53, 57, 278, 279, 286
referral service, 237, 246, 259, 260, 384, 385, 389, 392
*Register-Mirror*, 204
*Report of the Advisory Committee to Review Lawyer Discipline*, 157
*Report of the Attorney General to the Governor*, 68, 160, 161
*Report of the Attorney General, Minnesota*, 68
*Report of the Attorney General's Arson Task Force*, 161
*Report on Juror Compensation Issues*, 157
*Report on Records of the Minnesota District and County Courts*, 95
*Report on the Minnesota Court Interpreter Program Fees*, 158
*Report on the Use of Para-Judicial Personnel*, 158
*Report Pursuant to Minnesota Statutes Sections 8.08 and 8.15*, 162
*Report to the Legislature from the Task Force for Funding*, 162
*Report to the Legislature on the Status of Indian Gambling*, 162
*Report to the Minnesota Legislature Concerning Interscholastic*, 162
*Report to the Senate Committees on Environment and Natural*, 163
reports of cases, 83, 101, 298

# Index

*Reports of the Attorney General.* See *Minnesota Attorney General Reports*
Reports of the Judiciary, 154
Reports to the Supreme Court, 154, 155
research aids, 46, 47, 49, 50, 66, 67, 71, 188, 189, 208
*Residential Real Estate,* 152, 174
resolutions, 20, 21, 25, 26, 31, 32, 38, 26, 40, 42, 43, 78, 83, 116, 117, 158, 159, 213, 229, 230, 233–235, 246, 257, 297–299, 302, 304
Resources and Counseling for the Arts, 259, 392
*Restatement in the Courts,* 149
*Restatement of the Law,* 148–150
*Restatement of the Law of Conflict of Laws,* 149
*Restatement of the Law of Contracts,* 149
*Restatement of the Law: Permanent General Index,* 148
*Restatements,* 123, 147–149
*Restructured Constitution of 1974,* 6, 8, 11, 51
*Revised Laws 1905,* 32, 48, 51, 305–307, 309, 310, 433
revision, 45, 148,297,
revisions, 7, 9, 12, 45, 46, 52, 148, 155, 181, 272, 184, 297, 298, 300, 301, 303–307, 309, 310, 313, 383
Revisor of Statutes, 16, 18–21, 38, 43, 47, 62, 70, 72, 73, 131, 142, 186, 309–311
*Revisor's Manual,* 21, 66, 131
*Rulemaking in Minnesota,* 70, 186
rules after 1983, 71, 73
rules before 1970, 71
rules from 1970 to 1976, 71, 72
rules from 1976 to 1977, 71, 72
rules from 1977 to 1982, 71, 72
rules from 1982 to 1983, 71, 72
*Rules of Civil Procedure Annotated,* 173
rules of court. See court rules

*Rules of Minnesota Board of Continuing Legal Education,* 164, 242
*Rules of Public Access to Records of the Judicial Branch,* 95
*Rules of the Minnesota Board for Continuing Legal Education,* 121
*Rules of the Minnesota Supreme Court,* 121
*Rural Practice Law Journal, Minnesota Edition,* 204

S.F., 8
Saint Louis County Law Library, 218, 220
Saint Paul College of Law, 215, 233
*Saint Paul Legal Ledger,* 35, 36 113, 206
Scott County Law Library, 218, 220
*Search for Place,* 146
*Second Annual Report (1965),* 83
secondary sources, 116, 123, 147, 317
Secretary of State, 40, 63–65, 71, 99, 138, 142, 198, 205, 303, 310
Secretary of the Senate, 14, 23, 27, 29, 31, 40, 143
*Secretary's Guide,* 153
Securing Opportunities for Self-Sufficiency While Meeting Basic Needs Program, 255
selected Minnesota Attorney General reports, 159
selected opinions of the Attorney General, 160, 161, 163
selected reports to the Supreme Court, 154, 155
selected treatises and practice manuals, 163, 165
Senate, 13–25, 27–34, 40, 41, 43, 51, 64, 70, 77, 84, 119, 143, 163, 242, 272, 278, 285, 286, 309, 310, 454
Senate file, 25, 27, 32, 33
*Senate Index,* 14, 27, 31, 454
*Senate Journal,* 14, 25, 27, 31, 64
Senate Public Information, 13, 14
Senior Law Program, 255
sentencing, 51, 105, 112, 116, 137, 169, 238, 241

sentencing guidelines, 51, 112, 116, 238, 241
*Session Law Service.* See *Minnesota Session Law Service*
session laws, 4, 10, 11, 13, 20, 21, 32, 40–43, 46–48, 52, 60, 64, 127, 128, 209, 277, 278, 289, 297, 300–304, 306, 307, 310, 315
*Session Weekly,* 31
Shepard's, 11, 55, 56, 58, 60, 68, 123, 127–130, 132, 133, 149, 189, 209, 317
*Shepard's Acts and Cases by Popular Names—Federal and State,* 133
*Shepard's Citations,* 127, 128, 130, 149, 209
Shepard's Citations in General, 127
Shepard's citators, 123
*Shepard's Federal Law Citations in Selected Law Reviews,* 189
*Shepard's Law Review Citations: A Compilation of Citations,* 189
*Shepard's Lawyer's Reference Manual,* 58
*Shepard's Minnesota and Northwestern Citators Compared,* 127
*Shepard's Minnesota Citations,* 11, 55, 68, 127–130, 132, 133
*Shepard's Northwestern Citations,* 127, 133
Shepard's Online, 127, 130
*Shepard's Ordinance Law Annotations,* 56
*Shepard's Restatement of the Law Citations,* 149
SJIS. See Judicial Information System
SLA. See Special Libraries Association
slip laws, 25, 40, 317
slip opinions, 104, 317
*Small Business Notes,* 201
small claims court. See conciliation courts
SMRLS. See Southern Minnesota Regional Legal Assistance
sources of court rules, 112, 114
sources providing statutory citations, 57, 59

sources providing text or digest of laws, 57, 58
Southern Minnesota Regional Legal Assistance, 255, 395
sovereignty, 1–4
*Special Court Reporter Certification Fact Finding,* 158
special formats, 123, 207
special interest bar associations, 140, 236, 237, 394
special interest publications, 192, 197
special laws, 33, 40–43, 283, 289, 290, 301
*Special Legislation and Municipal Home Rule,* 42
*Special Legislation in Minnesota,* 42
Special Libraries Association, 224, 226
special sessions, 41, 64, 302, 313–315, 431, 433
*St. Paul Legal Ledger.* See *Saint Paul Legal Ledger*
*Stalland's Minnesota Curative Acts Affecting Title to Real,* 44, 308
*Standards for Approval of Law Schools,* 232
*State Advisory Committee Reports. Minnesota,* 159
state archives, 29, 223
*State Bar Advance Sheet,* 205
State Board of Continuing Legal Education, 121, 164, 238, 242
State Board of Law Examiners, 118, 119, 238, 242
State Board of Legal Certification, 114, 118, 120, 238, 243
State Board of Public Defense, 238, 243
State Claims Commission, 76
State Court Administrator, 83, 89, 91, 94, 117, 186–188, 238, 240, 241
state document depository libraries, 213, 217, 218, 441
state documents, 17, 19, 40, 75, 78–80, 213, 217, 218, 223, 250, 395, 441

# Index

*State Government Attorneys: An Attorney General Report*, 163
State Law Library. See Minnesota State Law Library
State librarian, 89, 90
*State of Minnesota Bureau of Mediation Services Digest*, 201
*State of Minnesota Telephone Directory*, 143
*State of Minnesota, Opinions of the Attorney General*, 68
State public defender, 239, 243, 247, 248, 391, 394
*State Register*. See *Minnesota Sate Register*
*State Yellow Book*, 143
statehood. See Minnesota statehood
*Statehouse Review*, 205
statistics, 56, 95, 164, 186, 187, 192, 319, 427
*Status Report: Joint Executive Legislative Task Force*, 163
statute of limitations, 388
*Statute Revision: Its Nature, Purpose and Method*, 45
*Statutes of the Forty-Eight States, by Subject*, 60
*Statutes—Construction—Revisions—Age of Majority of Females*, 46
statutory citations, 54, 57, 59–61, 176
Stearns County Law Library, 219, 220
*Stein on Probate*, 167, 177
*Story of the American Law Institute*, 148
*Student Lawyer: A Guide to Minnesota's Legal System*, 177
*Student Lawyer: High School Handbook of Minnesota Law*, 177
*Subject Compilations of State Laws*, 58, 61, 74
*Sullivan's Law Directory for the State of Minnesota*, 141
supplementation, 46, 49, 50, 52, 128, 137, 152, 167, 168, 170–176, 312
support personnel, 118, 122, 139, 213, 261

Supreme Court, 5, 71, 75–77, 83, 86–95, 97, 100–104, 107–115, 117–122, 129, 130, 136, 138, 144–146, 151, 154–159, 165, 182, 186–188, 198, 202, 206, 208, 209, 215, 216, 233, 234, 239–242, 244, 246, 264, 274, 275, 278–280, 298, 299, 302, 305–307, 311, 395, 401, 418, 428, 431
Supreme Court jurisdiction, 87
Supreme Court justices, 87, 88, 102, 145, 233, 274, 280, 305, 401
Supreme Court procedures, 87, 90
*Syllabi*, 35, 103

tables, 17, 21, 33, 40, 42, 43, 48, 50, 52, 59–62, 74, 104, 112, 124, 125, 130, 132–134, 137, 144, 145, 153, 162, 191, 304, 308–310
tables of cases, 56, 102, 104, 106, 109, 124–126, 130, 132, 134, 192
tape recordings, 20, 26, 30, 33, 34, 236, 246
*Task Force for Gender Fairness in the Courts. Final Report*, 158
*Task Force on Alternative Dispute Resolution. Final report*, 159
*Task Force on Financing of the Trial Courts. Final report*, 159
*Task Force on Racial Bias in the Judicial System. Final report*, 159
*Task Force on Recommendation on Conciliation Court Rules*, 159
Tax Court, 76, 86, 87, 104, 175, 182, 196, 203, 204, 206, 239, 243
*Tax Court Decisions*, 76, 196, 203
*TCIS On-line Access Pilot Project: Report to the Legislature*, 95
Teamchild Project, 255
Tel-Law, 236, 246
*Tenants' Rights in Minnesota*, 180
*Territorial Existence and Constitutional Statehood of Minnesota*, 51
treaties, 2, 3, 4
*Treaties Between the United States and the Indian Tribes*, 2

treatises, 12, 46, 60, 61, 123, 125, 132, 134, 147, 151, 163–165, 167, 168, 209, 222, 317
*Treaty of Amity, Commerce and Navigation*, 3
*Treaty of Peace and Amity*, 4
trial courts, 86, 87, 89, 91, 92, 99, 101, 105, 108–110, 114, 119, 159
trial de novo, 97
*Trial Handbook for Minnesota Lawyers*, 177
trial transcript, 107, 108
*Twin City Jury Verdict Reporter*, 183
two-year programs, 265

U.S. district court, 100, 111, 116, 136, 184
*U.S. Law Week*, 106
unauthorized practice of law, 240, 264, 384, 388, 396
unification, 83, 99
uniform acts, 19, 50, 51, 54, 69
uniform laws, 54, 58, 59
*Uniform Laws Annotated*, 59
uniform state laws, 18, 19, 53, 54, 69
*Uniform System of Citation*, 130, 131, 132
*Union List of Legal Looseleaf Services*, 225
United States Attorney for the District of Minnesota, 245, 249
*United States Code*, 115, 125, 133
*United States Code Annotated*, 115, 125, 133
*United States Code Service*, 115, 133
United States District Court, 136, 144
United States sovereignty, 1, 4
*United States Statutes at Large*, 53
*United States Supreme Court Digest*, 115
*United States Supreme Court Reports, Lawyers' edition*, 129
United Theological Seminary, 231
*Universal Citation Guide*, 131
Università di Modena Law School, 230
University Charter, 48

University of Minnesota, 2, 12, 66, 74, 79, 108, 109, 111, 145, 193–195, 197, 204, 211, 214, 215, 217, 218, 221, 224, 227, 229, 231, 232, 248, 256–258, 260, 271, 393, 395, 429, 430, 441, 442
University of Minnesota Human Rights Center, 232
University of Minnesota Human Rights Library, 221, 224
University of Minnesota Law Library, 2, 66, 74, 109, 111, 214, 215, 217, 395
University of Minnesota Law School, 108, 145, 193, 194, 197, 204, 211, 215, 229, 231, 248, 256, 258, 260, 393
University of North Texas, 227, 228
University of Saint Thomas, 214, 215, 229, 232
University Student Legal Service, 256, 258
unpublished opinions, 206
updating agency rules, 69, 74
*USOC*. See *Uniform System of Citation*
*Usury Laws in Minnesota*, 177

verdicts, 105, 163, 180, 182, 183, 201, 276
*Verdicts & Settlements*, 105, 183
*Verdicts & Settlements Quarterly*, 183
VersusLaw, 210
veto, 25, 64, 274, 284
*View from the 17th Floor: Oppenheimer Wolff & Donnelly*, 147
Violence Protection, 253

Warren E. Burger Library, 214, 215, 430
Washington County Law Library, 219, 220
*Waste Management Act Examiner*, 201
*Weekly Mirror*, 204
*Welcome to the Minnesota State Court System*, 93, 102

# Index

*Welcome to the United States Court of Appeals,* 100
welfare, 56, 178, 232, 258, 393
*West Legal Directory,* 141
Westlaw, 11, 12, 35, 38, 39, 43, 49, 50, 58, 59, 62, 67, 101, 104, 125, 129, 130, 132, 150, 153, 154, 189–191, 193–195, 209, 216, 221
*Westlaw Database Directory,* 189
*West's Encyclopedia of American Law,* 151
*West's Legal Forms,* 151, 154
*West's Minnesota Digest.* See *Minnesota Digest*
*West's Minnesota Digest 2d.* See *Minnesota Digest*
*West's Minnesota Digest 2d Law Finder,* 124, 125
*West's Minnesota Session Law Service.* See *Minnesota Session Law Service*
*West's North Western Digest.* See *North Western Digest*
*West's North Western Digest 2d.* See *North Western Digest*
*Where to Go for Legal Help in the Twin Cities,* 396–397
*Who's Who,* 135, 137, 142, 143
*Who's Who in American Law,* 135

William Mitchell College of Law, 108, 110, 111, 145, 146, 195, 201, 204, 205, 214, 215, 217, 229, 233–235, 256, 257, 395, 430
*William Mitchell College of Law: Opportunity,* 146
*William Mitchell Commentator,* 205
*William Mitchell Environmental Law Journal,* 190, 191, 205
*William Mitchell Law Review,* 128, 189–191, 195, 433
*William Mitchell Magazine,* 201
Wilson Library, 217, 429
Winona State University, 266, 430, 442
*With Satisfaction and Honor: William Mitchell College,* 146
*Words and Phrases,* 125, 130, 134, 309
Workers' Compensation Court of Appeals, 75–77, 86, 87, 239, 243
*Workers' Compensation Decisions,* 75, 77
*Workmen's Compensation Decisions Cumulative Index,* 77
writ of habeas corpus, 4, 86
writ of mandamus, 86
writ of prohibition, 86